THE PRICE OF TRUTH

Cultural Memory
in
the
Present

Mieke Bal and Hent de Vries, Editors

THE PRICE OF TRUTH

Gift, Money, and Philosophy

Marcel Hénaff

Translated by Jean-Louis Morhange
with the collaboration of Anne-Marie Feenberg-Dibon

STANFORD UNIVERSITY PRESS

STANFORD, CALIFORNIA

Stanford University Press
Stanford, California

The Price of Truth was originally published in French in 2002 under the title
Le prix de la vérité. © Éditions du Seuil, 2002.

Printed in the United States of America on acid-free, archival-quality paper

Library of Congress Cataloging-in-Publication Data
Hénaff, Marcel.
 [Prix de la vérité. English]
 The price of truth : gift, money, and philosophy / Marcel Hénaff ; translated by
Jean-Louis Morhange with the collaboration of Anne-Marie Feenberg-Dibon.
     p. cm.--(Cultural memory in the present)
 "Originally published in French as Le prix de la vérité."
 Includes bibliographical references.
 ISBN 978-0-8047-6081-2 (cloth : alk. paper)--ISBN 978-0-8047-6082-9 (pbk. :
alk. paper)
 1. Economic anthropology. 2. Gifts--Philosophy. 3. Money--Philosophy. 4.
Value--Philosophy. 5. Exchange--Philosophy. I. Morhange, Jean-Louis, 1956-
II. Feenberg-Dibon, Anne-Marie, 1943- III. Title. IV. Series: Cultural memory in
the present.
 GN449.6.H46 2010
 306.3--dc22   2010013546

Typeset by Bruce Lundquist in 11/13.5 Adobe Garamond

Contents

Acknowledgments

During the final stage of this project I benefited from the careful reading, criticism, and suggestions of several friends, such as Gérald Sfez, who brought his competence as a rigorous philosopher, and Jean-Pierre Milovanoff, who contributed his talent as a poet-reader. I would like to mention in particular the copyediting work Jean Delaite provided on the first version of the original French manuscript, as well as the exacting, generous, and always inspiring copyediting work Anny Milovanoff performed without sparing her effort in the last stages of the project. I would like to tell them once again how deeply grateful I am for their contributions. Many thanks also to Jean-Louis Morhange for his documentary research over the years and his clear-sighted observations. Finally, I would like to thank Olivier Mongin for the warm welcome he gave this book at Éditions du Seuil from the outset and for the many relevant observations he took the time to make and to discuss with me.

During the years of research required by this investigation I benefited several times from the funding provided by the Academic Senate Committee on Research of the University of California, San Diego, where I teach, and from the support provided by UCSD's Humanities Center and its then-director Frantisek Deak. I must also mention a substantial grant from the Elaine and Albert Borchard Foundation in Los Angeles. The friendly support provided by many of my colleagues at UCSD is worth mentioning as well. I have not forgotten that this research began in Paris in 1985 with a seminar I taught at the Collège International de Philosophie under the very title of this book. The final adjustments and revisions (as well as work on a different project) were facilitated by the exceptional environment of the Research Institute in the Humanities and Social Sciences— Jinbunken—of the University of Kyoto, Japan, where Shigeki Tominaga gave me a most generous welcome during the 2000–2001 academic year.

    With respect to the English version of this book, I would like to thank Hent de Vries and Emily-Jane Cohen for the warm welcome they gave me at Stanford University Press. I also owe special thanks to Jean-Louis Morhange for his patient and rigorous translation work, reinforced by the attentive copyediting provided by Philip Gunderson and Erin Malone. Let me also praise Joe Abbott's scrupulous copyediting. I am especially grateful to Anne-Marie Feenberg-Dibon, who translated the introduction, the conclusion, and Chapter 5. I would like to tell all of them once again that I am aware of the debt of gratitude I owe them.

Abbreviations

Apo.	Plato's *Apology*
AWP	Malinowski's *Argonauts of the Western Pacific*
Cra.	Plato's *Cratylus*
CW	Malamoud's *Cooking the World*
EE	Aristotle's *Eudemian Ethics*
Eum.	Aeschylus's *Eumenides*
Euth.	Plato's *Euthyphro*
G	Mauss's *The Gift*
NE	Aristotle's *Nicomachean Ethics*
Oly.	Pindar's *Olympians*
PE	Weber's *The Protestant Ethic and the Spirit of Capitalism*
Pol.	Aristotle's *Politics*
PM	Simmel's *The Philosophy of Money*
Pro.	Plato's *Protagoras*
SL	Montesquieu's *The Spirit of the Laws*
Soph.	Plato's *Sophist*
Soph. Ref.	Aristotle's *Sophistical Refutations*
Thea.	Plato's *Theaetetus*
TI	Levinas's *Totality and Infinity*

THE PRICE OF TRUTH

Overtures

Money, money, one of these days I will say something about you. In this century he who does not dare tell the truth about money is no poet.

HENRI MICHAUX, *Ecuador, a Travel Journal*

We no longer ask what things are but what they cost.

SENECA, *Ad Lucilium Epistolae Morales*

Knowledge and money have no common measure.

ARISTOTLE, *Eudemian Ethics*

I believe he is a real shaman for just that reason: he would not allow those he had cured to pay him.

QUESALID (KWAKIUTL SHAMAN), in Boas, *The Religion of the Kwakiutl Indians*

The witness that I can offer to prove the truth of my statement is, I think, a convincing one—my poverty.

SOCRATES, IN PLATO, *Apology*

Overture I
The Incorruptible Wise Man and the Value of Truth

A rumor has spread in the streets of Athens: Socrates is going to die. He has been in prison for almost a month, awaiting the execution of the sentence pronounced by the judges of the Areopagus. The wait is coming to an end. His old friend Crito, who has come for an early morning visit, lets him know that the ship that brought the sacred procession to Delos has returned. They both know that no capital execution can take place between

the departure and return of this ship, whose annual voyage honors the wish
Theseus made after his victory over the Minotaur. The ship has already
gone past Cape Sunion and will be in Pireus this very evening. According to
tradition, the next day the jailer is to offer the prisoner the cup of poison.[1]

Socrates is going to die, and his profound serenity disarms Crito,
who came to urge him to flee. Crito is determined to buy the jailers' com-
plicity. He implores Socrates:

> But look here, Socrates, it is still not too late to take my advice and escape. Your
> death means a double calamity for me. I shall not only lose a friend whom I can
> never possibly replace, but besides a great many people who don't know you and me
> very well will be sure to think that I let you down, because I could have saved you if
> I had been willing to spend the money. And what could be more contemptible than
> to get a name for thinking more of money than of your friends? (Plato *Crito* 44b–c)

Thus Socrates faces this dilemma: either flee by letting his friend bribe the
guards—in and of itself a reprehensible act of corruption—or remain and
allow people to believe that his friend was reluctant to use his wealth to
save him. Socrates counters: does his friend's honor rest on nothing more
than the opinion of the crowd (*ta polla*), the very opinion that has led to
his own condemnation? And isn't this opinion wrong? If so, why worry
about it? This honor would be very shallow indeed. Crito understands
the argument but believes it to be rhetorical. He thinks Socrates, in fact,
wishes to prevent him and his allies from falling into the hands of the syco-
phants, those professional informers who demand large sums in exchange
for their silence. He tries to reassure Socrates:

> Very well, then, don't let it distress you. I know some people who are willing to res-
> cue you from here and get you out of the country for quite a moderate sum. And
> then surely you realize how cheap those informers are to buy off; we shan't need
> much money to settle them, and I think you've got enough of my money for your-
> self already. And then even supposing that in your anxiety for my safety you feel
> that you oughtn't to spend my money, there are these foreign gentlemen staying in
> Athens who are quite willing to spend theirs. One of them, Simias of Thebes, has
> actually brought the money with him for that very purpose, and Cebes and a num-
> ber of others are quite ready to do the same. So, as I say, you mustn't let any fears
> on these grounds make you slacken your efforts to escape. (Plato *Crito* 44e–45a–b)

Here Socrates faces a subtler and more dangerous temptation. Unlike
the Sophists, he has consistently refused any form of payment for his teach-

ing. He has consistently warned against the risk of corruption inherent in money, and now he is asked to save his own life by buying his jailers and thus by breaking the law. Crito makes it clear to him that the amounts involved are not very large and that, moreover, several friends intend to contribute. For Socrates, however, the very fact that some of these friends are foreigners is a relevant detail. In his attacks on the Sophists he had always suggested that their status as noncitizens exempted them from civic responsibilities. It would thus be the height of inconsistency for his life to be spared thanks not only to money but to money paid by foreign friends. Thus Socrates patiently—and, given the circumstances, heroically—expounds on the necessity to act according to justice without giving any other consideration to such things as the reputation of friends or the care owed to his children. "Our real duty, I fancy, since the argument leads that way, is to consider one question only, the one we just raised right now. Shall we be acting rightly in paying money and showing gratitude to these people who are going to rescue me, and in escaping or arranging to escape ourselves, or shall we really be acting wrongly in doing all this?" (Plato *Crito* 48c–d).

Socrates' question is far-reaching and already has the form of what, since Kant, has been called the categorical imperative: "Is it just to . . . ?" No other consideration associated with empirical benefit—no hypothetical imperative, especially money given by friends—can counterbalance this categorical imperative, which is further developed later in the dialogue in the "prosopopoeia of the laws." Crito understands that Socrates will not give in and decides to stand by him until the very end.

It is remarkable that in the last hours Socrates has left to live, he would insist precisely on recalling a requirement that has guided his entire life: the rejection of all financial advantage. For him it constitutes the fundamental criterion of an authentic search for wisdom.[2] He had already mentioned this to his judges, according to Plato's *Apology*:

You will not easily find another one like me, gentlemen, and if you take my advice you will spare my life. I suspect, however, that before long, you will awake from your drowsing, if you doubt whether I am really the sort of person who would have been sent to this city as a gift from God (*hupo tou theou tēi polei dedosthai*) you can convince yourself by looking at it from this way. Does it seem natural that I should have neglected my own affairs and endured the humiliation of allowing my family to be neglected for all these years, while I busied myself all the time on your behalf, going like a father or an elder brother to see each of you privately, and urging you to set your thoughts on goodness? If I had got any enjoyment (*apolauon*) from it, or if [I] had been paid for my good advice (*misthon*), there would have been some explanation for my conduct, but as it is you can see for yourselves, that although my accusers unblushingly charge me with all sorts of other crimes, there is one thing that they had not had the impudence to pretend on any testimony, and that is that I have ever exacted or asked a fee from anyone. The witness that I can offer to prove the truth of my statement is, I think, a convincing one—my poverty (*egō parekhomai ton martura hōs alēthē legō, tēn penian*). (Plato *Apology* 31a–c)

Socrates is going to die. He has been unjustly condemned. As the ultimate proof of his innocence and the final guarantee of the authenticity of his teaching, which his accusers denounce as corrupting the young, he proclaims that he has never pursued any financial gain nor obtained any material advantage from his position: money has had no power over him, and his best witness is his poverty. This is the surprising message addressed to us at the origins of philosophy by "the wisest of the Greeks" and one who has remained the emblematic figure of the Wise Man in the Western tradition. We must acknowledge that between money and philosophy there has been a quarrel and a profound incompatibility from the outset. Why? Almost twenty-five centuries after Socrates the reasons for his attitude may seem obscure, yet we sense their nobility. Still, we must be careful not to misinterpret them.

Unlike other spiritual masters, such as Buddha or Jesus, Socrates does not require poverty of his disciples. He has never despised the wealth possessed by some of his friends, nor does he refuse their lavish hospitality when it is offered. He simply does not care about these things. In fact, for a Greek citizen there is nothing shameful about having a substantial income. Plato himself is a rich heir. Aristotle will emphasize the fact that for a free citizen honest wealth is a desirable component of the good life. The problem lies elsewhere. It has to do with the source of one's wealth. Wealth is good when it stems from the earth or from any form of productive work. But wealth that comes from trade and financial profit is suspect.[3] In Plato's view this is the category that applies to those who exchange knowledge for money. But why? Why can shoemakers sell shoes or farmers their fruit and grain without dishonor while philosophers or any other men of knowledge cannot ask to be paid for their teaching without disgrace? Today this distinction seems puzzling. In *Eudemian Ethics* Aristotle explains, "Knowledge and money have no common measure" (7.10). Once again we ask why this is the case. We will have to clarify the exact meaning of this very precise formulation. We will see that it involved a complex debate, which proved particularly bitter in the case of the Sophists. The figure of Socrates has taught us that the wise man can only be wise if he lacks self-interest, if he offers his knowledge for free, and, ultimately, if his way of life shows indifference to wealth.

Socrates' attitude during his last hours deserves careful consideration. What is so strange about money for it to be such a crucial concern for the wise old man as he faces death? What does money mean for philosophy? What is its power? Why does it seem to become so dangerous as soon as it involves something beyond the realm of useful goods? To buy food and clothing or to pay artisans for their work is considered necessary and thus perfectly reasonable, yet when it comes to compensating writers, artists, or scholars, not only is it difficult to set a pay scale, but the very consideration of payment has long appeared problematic. No immediate answer is available to us. Because this question involves the assessment of activities and productions of the mind, it is one of the most fundamental problems of human life and has haunted philosophical thought for centuries but without ever becoming truly explicit or focal. It is as if the foundations of this question are so obvious and well-accepted that it is unnecessary or unseemly to explicitly state them as such.

The Price of Truth

How are we to understand the phrase "the price of truth"? It ought to be enough to say that we should understand it literally. This means that we are not employing the usual metaphoric sense of the phrase, which refers to the moral cost of the effort or renunciation required to proclaim, discover, or confess the truth.

Whether the question of truth concerns self-discovery—either in a spiritual journey or through a technique of self-awareness—a search for knowledge—as in the natural or experimental sciences—or finally, an investigation to establish the facts—as in a legal procedure—it always involves an aspect of reality that is either misunderstood, difficult to grasp, or obscured by some form of resistance or refusal that needs to be overcome. In this case the "price" of truth designates the honesty or courage required to proclaim or recognize proven facts; in other words, to refuse to lie, whether it be in research, a confession, or an investigation. It is a spiritual price, a symbolic price.

Why then do we have to borrow the metaphorical phrase for this effort from the language of economics? Could there be a literal price of truth, a situation where truth could be bought and sold? We have to acknowledge that we can find no examples of this, at least not in this form. It is inconceivable that in exchange for a monetary amount one could obtain scientific results, spiritual depth, or legal certainty. At most one could secure indirect tactical benefits that would fall under the category of corruption. We should then conclude that the phrase has no literal content and is metaphorical from the outset.

The title of this volume, however, clearly signals my intention to redirect the metaphorical sense toward the literal sense. I will not ask how truth might be the object of a financial transaction. This would be meaningless. Given that philosophy has always been defined as a search for truth—a definition I will challenge later as being overly general—my purpose here is to discover in what specific ways philosophy has dealt with the question of money and venality. This very question constitutes one of the essential aspects of the conflict between Plato and the Sophists. The fact that the crisis erupts with Plato is significant. He initiates and witnesses a radical transformation of the concept of truth itself, *alētheia*. This term is usually translated as the unveiling of the hidden, the movement out (*a-*) of the hidden (*lētheia*). This notion has a long history in the ancient wisdom and legal practices of Greece. A major turning point occurs when the question of money comes to play a key role—that is, the question of monetary compensation for speech. I will outline the crucial stages of this shift by drawing on the analyses developed in Detienne's classic work *The Masters of Truth in Archaic Greece*.

Before it became an essential philosophical concept with the Pre-Socratics, the notion of truth often appeared allegorically in the oldest texts on wisdom and its practices by seers, magi, and, above all, poets. *Alētheia* is consistently associated with *mnēmosunē*—memory—which has less to do with the ability to remember than with a visionary power providing access to the past, the present, and the future. The "Plain of Alētheia," where the blessed gods and heroes reside, is such a vision. The inspired and visionary song of the poet *performs* access to the divine realm. Poetic language has its effect in producing what it states. Moreover, without it the hero cannot attain the glory granted in and by the song that brings heroic actions into the light of *alētheia*. The hero becomes what the poem says about him. The performativity of language related to *alētheia* not only concerns songs of glorification but is also evident in other domains—primarily in divination, where oracular speech accomplishes what it announces, and in law, where he who has the authority to say what is just—for instance a royal figure— makes it so by pronouncing the sentence. One could say that this effective speech is a physical reality, part of the forces of nature. As such, the language of *alētheia* has at the same time poetic, divinatory, and legal powers.

This ancient configuration unravels and changes with the emergence of the city. The *polis* takes shape when the hoplite reform institutes equality among warriors and designates a neutral place in the center of their circle for the common spoils that will be distributed by lot. This place becomes the center from which everyone must talk to everyone else. This is the origin of the public space that becomes the space of debate. Magical and effective speech that creates what it states is replaced by dialogue and contested speech. Ordeal gives way to investigation and the requirement of proof. Authoritarian discourse is replaced by the exchange of arguments. Speech loses its status as full substance, as effective power. Separated from its effects it becomes an autonomous form and instrument. Opposed to *alētheia*, which is uttered by a sacred mouth, stands the *doxa*, which is the knowledge appropriate to a given situation and accessible to everyone.

According to Detienne, Simonides of Ceos is the first poet to illustrate this change and process of "secularization." He breaks with ritual incantatory poetry and the performative conception of language. Moreover, he stresses its significance as instrument and its autonomous form by positing a split between statement and act of stating, the world and its representation, image (*eikōn*) and reality. He deposes *alētheia* in favor of *doxa*. What is more, he prosaically replaces the goddess sustaining poetic inspiration and divinatory vision, the ancient *Mnēmosunē*, with mnemonic tricks. He is even credited with the invention of the alphabet. In short, Simonides is the supreme embodiment of a technical shift that affects language and the forms of knowledge.[4] With him the old *sophos*— the seer and inspired poet—has turned into a language professional. The age of the old *alētheia* is over. Then something surprising and most interesting happens: "Simonides was the first to treat poetry as a profession; he composed poems for a fee. Pindar informs us: the sweet songs of

Terpsichorus, so gentle and lulling, are for sale. With Simonides, the Muse became greedy (*philokerdēs*) and mercenary (*ergatis*). Simonides forced his contemporaries to recognize the commercial value of his art and they in turn took their revenge by treating him as a greedy man."[5] The *alētheia* of the ancient poets is up for sale to the highest bidder. Since it is for sale, will there now be a "price of truth"?

We must not underestimate the importance of this event. According to the same logic, poets now deprive the language of truth of its ritual status, and wise men discover argumentative dialogue. Rhetoricians perceive the ambiguity of all discourse and delight in games of illusions. All of them understand that mastery of the art of speech is a craft comparable to that of so many others, including that of physicians, musicians, weavers, or architects—all of whom receive wages in exchange for their services. And this is how poets, the new speech professionals, bring *alētheia* to the marketplace and set a price for it.

At the same time, however, *alētheia* ceases to be the exclusive property of *sophoi* and poets. Along with the rise of the physicist-philosophers and the emergence of mathematics, a different conception of truth comes to prevail: the objectivity of inherent relations between the things themselves. This objectivity can be reached through cognitive discipline and can no longer be identified with disciplines of self-mastery or the spiritual asceticism that provides access to immemorial wisdom. Knowledge can be passed on through public education rather than through secret procedures of initiation. Knowledge is trivialized—or rather democratized—through educational techniques that are comparable to those of various experts.

From now on two different positions emerge regarding the question of truth: on the one hand the traditional position of the old *sophoi*, which concerned itself with the interpretation of signs or oracles and presupposed a transcendental authority such as a religious deity or metahuman power like Nature.[6] On the other hand, the hermeneutic tradition of decipherment now confronts a new and seemingly triumphant tradition in which truth is viewed as objectivity, as the foundation of an agreement between reasonable minds on obvious facts or results that are self-evident to both gods and humans. What is now at stake is less discovering truth than constituting it. Within the framework of this conception forms of knowledge emerge that are neither sacred nor initiatory, such as mathematical or physical knowledge or logical argument. This knowledge can be acquired in the same way as know-how is gained—through techniques of learning. Like any skill it is an object of negotiation between those who have it and those who wish to obtain it. From the moment philosophy becomes a profession, just like medicine, rhetoric, or architecture, those who teach it inevitably have to be paid.

This new attitude, which soon comes to dominate the Western tradition, leads to a new way of raising the question of the "price of truth." It is not that truth can now be assigned a price; rather the term *truth* now emblematically designates the realm of knowledge—philosophy and the sciences—the realm of a recognized form of competence that must be paid.

If the highest forms of knowledge turn out to belong to the profane world and to depend on professionals, then inevitably they no longer only represent spiritual power but become an instrument of mastery and even a way of earning a living, an occupation, or a source of wealth. This would all be perfectly normal if it were not for the continued persistence of the old tradition and its values, which are still assumed to govern the new conception. What is worse: the new type of philosopher (particularly the Sophist as depicted by Plato) continues to enjoy the social prestige of the "old-fashioned" wise man and takes advantage of it in order to increase the income gained from his teaching. Pandora's Box has been opened. If even philosophical knowledge is subjected to financial assessment, is there anything left that could escape the power of money and could not be traded in some way? This is probably what Plato foresees and is determined to fight. For him the fate of philosophy itself is at stake.

This remains, however, an external perspective. In fact, for Plato the danger concerns the conception of truth itself. The Sophist is—or claims to be—not only a knowledge professional; he is also someone who changes the philosophical approach to knowledge itself by giving discourse a status that breaks off the relation between speech, being, and truth. The Sophists introduce the power of *pseudos* into philosophy since they use it as a mere means of arguing, and they invent games of *logoi* in which the question of truth—the being of the thing—becomes arbitrary. Indeed, the most serious problem posed by the venality of the Sophists revolves around this fundamental philosophical question. For if the Sophists sell their knowledge, it means that, much like a merchant, they do not need to know the nature of the product. Like a merchant, they need only to convince their customers to buy the product. Neither merchant nor Sophist is concerned with the nature of the thing itself—in other words, with truth. In Platonic terms this is what is at stake in "the price of truth." This involves the realm of illusion and falsehood, not the falsehood of moral malice but ontological deceit. We have probably not yet moved beyond this debate.

Overture 2
The Priceless

Twenty centuries after Plato we still face the same question but from another perspective: does knowledge have a price? Can ideas be sold? Is a work of art to be assessed according to its market value? These same questions would have provoked Marx's sarcasms and outraged Péguy, but they hardly shock us today.[7] We find it perfectly normal not only that scholarly research, the passing down of knowledge, and the use of all types of skills are compensated but that they are also subject to market valuation.

Nevertheless, something prevents us from putting on equal footing a collection of poems and an industrial product. In the same way, we are reluctant to classify the salary of a scientist and the revenues of a stock market speculator in the same category, as if the money earned were more legitimate, nobler, "cleaner" in one case than in the other.

This is, in fact, a very old story. For a very long time writers, scholars, and artists believed that, as such, they belonged to a realm different from the commercial world. A few fairly recent statements should be evidence enough that this is the case. See, for instance, in chronological order:

Rousseau: "I felt that writing to earn my daily bread would soon snuff out my genius and destroy my talent. . . . Nothing vital, nothing great can flow from the pen that is wholly venal." (*Confessions*, 393)

Flaubert: "Why publish in these abominable times? To earn money? What a joke! As though the money were an adequate reward for one's work. As if it could be! It may be when speculation is abolished. Until then, no! . . . And thus my usefulness remains imponderable and consequently cannot be paid for . . ." (letter to George Sand, Dec. 4, 1872, in *Flaubert-Sand*, 294). "I maintain that a work of art worthy of its name and made conscientiously is invaluable, has no commercial value, and therefore has no price." (letter to George Sand, Dec. 12, 1872, in *Flaubert-Sand*)

Mallarmé: "For the author, hitting it big or glowing with a mediocre monetary return would amount to the same. Indeed, there is no colossal gain to expect from any literary production. Metallurgy is better in this respect. Beside an engineer, I would always become secondary. . . . What good is it to traffic in what, perhaps, shouldn't be sold, especially when it doesn't sell?" (*Divagations*, 225)

Leafing through the volumes of the West's grand library would yield many similar accounts. Although Plato was the first to aggressively open the debate in his quarrel with the Sophists, and even though his denunciation was orchestrated with all the power of his conceptual system, we must admit that he did not invent suspicion regarding money. This suspicion was associated with a more ancient one directed at the figure of the merchant. Both journeyed together through our history until quite recently. I will return to this later and in greater detail, but for now let me briefly outline its originality.

Imposture and Transformation

The suspicion of money is, indeed, very peculiar, as becomes obvious when we compare money with other traditional subjects of radical critique such as violence, injustice, and tyranny. These critiques denounce the horrors of war and the massacre of populations or poverty in the face of opulence; they protest against the exploitation of the weak, the arrogance of the powerful, and political attacks on freedom. These situations seem to belong to the unfortunate and often terrible side of human destiny. They generate indignation, rebellion, resistance, and struggle.

When we deal with the critique of money and the denunciation of the harm caused by venality or corruption, however, we leave the register of tragedy. Very often something subtly different comes to light: contempt. Unlike the figures of pride, cruelty, or crime, money is not epic, except when it is allied with these classical forces of evil, as for instance in Shakespeare, Balzac, or Dostoyevsky. Money, *as such*, seems to belong to the reign of lowly things, as opposed to wealth in general, which was not always identified with it and could also have a noble and enviable status.

This judgment seems to be as ancient as the civilizations in which the use of money emerged. Sophocles states this in a surprising manner:

> Money! Nothing worse
> in our lives, so current, rampant, so corrupting.
> Money—you demolish cities, root men from their homes,
> You train and twist good minds and set them on
> to the most atrocious schemes. (Sophocles *Antigone* 73)

The suspicion of money seems to stem from a kind of immunity that it enjoys. All its privileges are viewed as strange and unjustified. Money appears endowed with boundless powers of acquisition and appropriation, boundless meaning that is excessive beyond all measure; yet there is a normal and reasonable way of buying and selling, of which Aristotle provides a precise philosophical description. Outside of this balanced exchange, however, money can have a disturbing power of appropriation. Not having made something and yet being able to acquire it whenever we want, not having deserved honor and yet obtaining it by purchase, lacking all taste and yet being able to buy exceptional works of art—these are a few of the scandalous privileges that money can secure. This is akin to the arbitrary and abusive power of the tyrant or the predator, except that neither physical risk nor audacity is required, nor even the shamelessness of a bandit. Discreetly and efficiently, this power can acquire and transform everything, turning all values upside down. No one has expressed this better than Shakespeare: the noble Timon, bankrupt and abandoned after having rashly squandered his fortune for the benefit of parasitical friends, suddenly discovers a treasure and exclaims:

Thus much of this will make
Black, white; foul fair; wrong, right;
Base, noble; old, young; coward, valiant.
Ha! You gods! Why this? What this, you gods? Why, this
Will lug your priests and servants from your sides,
Pluck stout men's pillows from below their heads.
This yellow slave
Will knit and break religions: bless th'accurs'd,
Make the hoar leprosy ador'd, place thieves,
And give them title, knee and approbation
With senators on the bench. This is it
That makes the wappen'd widow wed again: . . .
Come damned earth,
Thou common whore of mankind, that puts odds
Among the rout of nations.[8]

This virulent denunciation echoes Sophocles' but introduces a new element: the power this strange tyrant has to reverse things appears neither harsh nor bloody. On the contrary, it is pleasant and flexible. It produces soft metamorphoses but no brutal changes. It triggers reversals of values but no frontal attacks. Its domination, however implacable, is not manifested by obvious signs. Whereas tyrannical power is displayed through violence, arousing anger or desire for vengeance, money operates smoothly. It presupposes or creates agreement among partners. Money allows for the acquisition of rare goods or privileges with the consent of these partners but without having to please them. Its power—as an equivalent to everything—resides in itself. As such it passes for neutral, or rather indifferent, which may make it appear cynical. In fact, it is neither sentimental nor personal, neither tender nor cruel. Money seems able to act without heeding relationships, status, or conventions.

What, then, explains its seduction? What leads persons or groups to sell what should not be sold, to succumb to the fascination of acquiring currency? One answer is money's unlimited power of *translation*. What makes money attractive is not so much the yearning to accumulate as it is the idea that it could be converted into all sorts of things depending on desire or need, occasion or urgency. A beautiful wooded estate (as, for instance, in Chekhov's *The Cherry Orchard*) may inspire pride in its owner, who may enjoy walking through it; his heirs may prefer to sell it and take advantage of the freedom afforded by the monetary instrument. Money creates a feeling of possibility and offers an unlimited number of choices because of its very indeterminacy. It is mobile, universal, and entirely malleable. This first aspect of its seduction coincides with its functionality, in which the ominous beauty of its invention lies.

The unlimited capacity to convert also gives it, however, a kind of dangerous magic. Its power to transform anything seems superhuman. It is capable of buying those very things that ought not be sold. And, according to Timon, it can provide cowards with honors, make fools look clever, give power to the mediocre, and make the rich and selfish desirable. Referring to Shakespeare's *Timon*, Marx elaborates on this motif in an equally famous early writing:

Money, then, appears as a *disruptive* force for the individual and for the social bonds, which claim to be self-subsistent *entities*. It changes fidelity into infidelity, love into hate, hate into love, virtue into vice, vice into virtue, servant into master, stupidity into intelligence and intelligence into stupidity.

Since money, as the existing and active concept of value, confounds and exchanges everything, it is the universal *confusion and transposition* of all things, the inverted world, the confusion and transposition of all natural and human qualities.[9]

This is not a mere gloss on Shakespeare: by showing that conversion is perfectly *reversible*, Marx radicalizes the motif. Money appears as a power capable of abolishing differences in a game of equivalences devoid of any rules: "universal confusion and transposition."

In short, money is an instrument capable not only of translating anything but, above all, of concealing and deceiving. This is why it has become one of the most typical figures of *imposture*, at many levels: (1) regarding value: it can make precious what is not so by setting a high price for it; (2) regarding relationships: it can give importance or respect to undeserving persons by providing them with status; (3) regarding time: it can acquire immediately what would otherwise require a very long period and great effort for acquisition. What makes this imposture possible is the power of money to act as a *substitute*. It can replace anything and hence take the place of anything. It is the ubiquitous *usurper* par excellence. This explains why it is always associated with treachery, from the figure of Judas to that of modern spies. It is the agent of universal treachery through its power of universal translation.

Money and the Technical Order

In spite of moral criticism and theological indictments, however, and in spite of denunciation by artists and writers, money, in its form as monetary instrument, has prevailed as the most powerful tool for the evaluation and exchange of goods, as the indispensable regulator of financial flow, as the means par excellence of industrial investment and compensation for work. How can we understand, then, the traditional suspicion attached to money? Isn't this really ancient history? Isn't it time to get rid of this outdated bias?

There is no simple answer. The harm done by money has not disappeared with the success of the technologies of exchange and funding that it has made possible. The essence of the problem does not appear to have changed since Aristotle. It seems sufficient to be able to distinguish between money as a legitimate and efficient economic instrument—as currency—on the one hand and as an all-powerful instrument of acquisition, control, exploitation, or corruption on the other. The distinction is not quite so easy to make, however. The technical improvements of the instrument are closely associated with its potential for immoral use. Far from controlling the excesses of its power, refined technologies of monetary circulation have provided money with new fields of action. Corruption in high finance can be remarkably professional and, as such, more profound and serious. Not only has technological change shifted ethical questions, but it has affected our cultural foundations themselves. The imaginary dimension of money associated with its old forms—coins and banknotes—is becoming rarified. Does this matter? Apparently not at all. Nevertheless, this phenomenon has consequences. While the traditional emotional framework of our judgments and evaluations is falling apart, the emerging one is still not very expressive. From the moment money loses the vivid images it once evoked, and loses, above all, its immediate tangibility, it seems endowed with a new innocence proportional to its degree of abstraction. The financier who embezzles large sums of money is guilty of a crime equal to or worse than that of the highway bandit robbing a mail coach in the age of Beaumarchais and Balzac. In the case of embezzlement, however, the imagery remains weak; the dramatic effect is practically nil, and the crime thus seems less blatant. Mandrin will go to the galleys; the crooked banker (as Saccard in Zola's novel) will only be forced to go bankrupt or in some cases be sentenced to return the sums he embezzled, if he is able to.[10] These differences are signs of a global transformation associated with the expansion of the marketplace and the increased reach of stock markets. Money has entered a new dimension. At the level of stocks and capital flows, of investments and profits, the phenomena involved are now colossal, on the scale of climatic, geological, demographic, or epidemiological phenomena.

Given this immense scale, what happens to the requirement that some goods, activities, actions, or events must remain beyond commercial assessment? Or should we accept that this assessment is capable of encompassing everything? Is it not true that artists today view the recognition of their work in terms of the galleries that give them access to the marketplace, as well as public recognition, writers in terms of the publishers who cannot continue to distribute their books without earning a modicum of profit, researchers in terms of the laboratories that fund their work, and teachers in terms of the institutions that employ them and provide them with the income necessary to their subsistence? It would be naive and dangerous to claim that the products of the mind should be exempt from the normal means of payment or from market conditions. Indeed, this is not the case in any of these professional categories.

None of these, however, would accept the claim that their primary objective is to make a profit, something the manufacturers of consumer goods freely acknowledge. The conviction persists that there remains something about the products of the mind that cannot be evaluated. How can this remainder be defined? To appeal at the outset to a kind of transcendence or a traditional belief is certainly respectable, but it is insufficient since what are needed are specific arguments. The boundaries of this transcendence have moved and shrunk along with the extension of the successive technological revolutions of the last three centuries.

Homo œconomicus

This transformation of money from immoral agent to neutral instrument is manifest in the way Adam Smith raises the question of the economic usefulness of artists, scholars, or teachers.[11] Smith establishes a strict distinction between productive agents, who produce a quantifiable profit sufficient to ensure the continuation of their own activity, and unproductive agents, who do not produce a net profit and whose livelihood depends on the former. In the latter category belong, first of all, domestic servants but also politicians, judges, the military, artists, teachers, and clergy. Their activities leave no economic trace; that is, they are not capable of funding their future activities: "The protection, security, and defence of the commonwealth, the effect of their labor this year, will not purchase its protection, security, and defence, for the year to come" (331). And he adds: "In the same class must be ranked, some both of the gravest and most important, and some of the most frivolous professions: churchmen, lawyers, physicians, men of letters of all kinds; players, buffoons, musicians, opera-singers, opera-dancers, etc." (331). Of course, Smith does not claim that all those occupations are useless or even that they do not perform work. All he means is that they do not produce the surplus necessary for their own sustenance; in fact, they do not *produce* anything: "Like the declamation of the actor, the harangue of the orator, or the tune of the musician, the work of all of them perishes in the very instant of its production" (331).

This is not the place to discuss the overly narrow character of Smith's view of productive activity, which only considers goods involved in exchanges and does not take into account the social—that is, the political, administrative, cultural, and educational—conditions that make production possible. Nevertheless, as modern economic theory develops, attention is focused on the lack of immediate economic value of intellectual and artistic activities. Of course, this reappraisal requires an entirely new effort of reflection, since it implies questioning the reason for humans to live in society. What is more, the ends of human existence itself seem to lose their immemorial self-evidence and their foundations. Adam Smith's reasoning would have been frowned on by seventeenth-century thinkers, probably including economists (who did not yet claim this title). Public discourse at the time still expressed a hierarchy of values in which the idea of "glory" unconditionally prevailed over that of interest, tracing a clear distinction between grand and vile, noble and common. One century later, Smith is able to bring to the fore the economic sterility of occupations traditionally viewed as being among the most prestigious without sparking much comment. It is clear that the time of *homo œconomicus* has come. To produce wealth, increase the nation's income, and develop the technical means of production have become worthy goals. Moreover, the economy is now identified as the source of political and military power. Finally, the goal of existence becomes defined as happiness available to all, a goal situated in terms of access to the economy and its products. Along with *homo œconomicus, homo laborans* triumphs, to cite Hannah Arendt.[12] Perhaps he has become what Nietzsche called "the last man," the happy slave, replete with the goods that he produces and consumes without any other ideal than ensuring his own comfort and tranquility.

We know, however, or we sense that there is something else that resists this shift. The marketplace may well claim to set a price on what is priceless, but we are aware that it cannot determine the value of the priceless or grasp its boundless character. We know that no commercial equation will ever express the price of life, of friendship, of love or suffering, of shared memories—or the price of truth. We know without having been taught that only a relationship of unconditional generosity can open the realm of the priceless.

The Realm of Gift-Giving

The philosophical rejection of money inaugurated by Plato and the numerous similar condemnations proclaimed in the course of our intellectual history are only expressions of this conviction. What is its source?

It is accepted that the activities and productions of the mind belong to a type of exchange different from market exchange, which anthropologists call symbolic exchange. Their purpose is not to acquire or accumulate goods but to use them to establish bonds of recognition between persons or groups; this defines the gift/countergift relationship.

The compensation of writers, artists, or scholars has long been understood as exemplifying this relationship; it differs profoundly from other forms of payment and has been designated exclusively by the term *honorarium*. Wealth thus gained belongs to a mode of compensation due to talent, in the same manner that one present is reciprocated by another present. The problematic of gift-giving, a focus of anthropology since Marcel Mauss's famous essay *The Gift*, makes it possible to clarify this history. Goods exchanged on specific occasions—such as celebrations, encounters, or weddings—do not have any economic significance or role; their purpose is to recognize, to honor, and to bring together the parties involved. They are consumed in celebrations or returned to the circuit of gift exchange. They manifest generosity and benevolence; they bring prestige and guarantee relationships but cannot be kept or invested in a self-interested way at the risk of breaking the cycle of recognition. They are entirely outside the circuit of what is useful and profitable. Some trends in modern anthropology, such as functionalist and Marxist orientations, have mistakenly tried to interpret these exchanges from a utilitarian or economic perspective. This amounts to presupposing that *homo œconomicus*, a recent product of the marketplace civilization, has always existed. In any case gift-exchange relationships seem to have the longest history. Things should be stated in a different way, however; even though they have been constantly connected (and for this reason often mistakenly identified with each other), gift exchange and market economy belong to two different histories.

The gracious relationship subsists intact in the words and gestures that constitute courtesy. They initiate, preserve, or modulate reciprocal recognition. They still endure remarkably well in everything that involves what is priceless, such as works of the mind, works of art, or expressions of talent—which are sometimes called "gifts"—but also in moral gestures such as mutual help, compliments, and renunciation. The priceless remains omnipresent. It does not constitute the past of commercial relationships, neither their archaic form nor their alternative. It represents a different tradition and meets different needs. Which ones? What makes these questions fuzzy and difficult to analyze today is the fact that in modern societies the field of rational economy tends to encompass every form of activity or exchange to such an extent that any reciprocity of goods and services that does not meet the criteria of the marketplace is assumed to be "archaic" or, worse, "irrational." If such were the case, it would be irrational to exchange greetings, to express gratitude, or to invite friends to visit—behaviors that today constitute the most common forms of ceremonial gift exchange. The realm of gift exchange and the realm of utilitarian exchange are both perfectly compatible with rationality, but they do not belong to the same category or operate within the same system. Moreover, the difference between them varies in proportion to technological growth and to the quantity of goods available. Utilitarian exchange is now so prevalent that we believe in the existence of a market for what in principle cannot have a price: works of art, rare objects, gastronomic pleasures, entertainment, leisure activities, and all forms of festive celebrations. From this perspective the entertainment industry presents a particularly interesting case. It mobilizes enormous financial resources to produce "entertainment." An extraordinary machinery of economic management—for example, investments, staff, cost-benefit analyses, and salaries—is marshaled in the service of something that is in and of itself unproductive. This is paradoxical but not a new phenomenon, as a simple example will show. When tulip production was launched in the Netherlands in the seventeenth century, speculation on tulip bulbs reached such colossal sums that in 1637 a speculator pawned his house to obtain one single bulb of a rare kind of tulip. It could be argued that what was at stake was commercial value, but, interestingly, this value did not involve useful commodities such as ores or cereals but an object destined for pure pleasure and decoration. Perhaps, then, the market for what is priceless and not useful reveals the best-kept secret behind what is prosaically useful and whose value seems obvious to all. Paradoxically, this remark could lead to two radically divergent approaches. The first could be a commentary on Georges Bataille's *The Accursed Share*. The second could involve a discussion of so-called neoclassical economic theory, which classifies as "useful" *anything* that is or can be the object of market demand, including that which cannot be sold. An extensive and rigorous literature already exists on both of these approaches. Other approaches are also possible, which I will attempt to explore and formulate.

The problem of the priceless brings us back to Plato's concern with payment for what cannot be measured in cash, starting with the teaching of philosophers. Is this still a tenable position? Does it not effect a confusion between the contents taught and the empirical means of the teaching? Medieval theology understood that what was at stake was not buying the master's speech but compensating his work. It remains to be determined whether our era is still capable of preserving this necessary distinction. This distinction does not seem relevant in the case of painting and the visual arts in general. One buys a work of art; one does not compensate an artist for his effort. And yet the question remains: how can the value of a work of art be assessed? Who decides on its price? By what mechanisms does the marketplace manage to combine critical judgments, fashion phenomena, and general economic conditions? In the end and in spite of the triumph of commercial valuation—even regarding the goods most resistant to its operation—we can no longer evade the question of the priceless. For this very reason the question arises in more radical terms for us than in traditional societies.

On reflection one finds that evaluating and measuring are very strange approaches. Why, in relationships between groups or individuals, are the offer and exchange of goods that are regarded as precious the means par excellence by which to recognize one another, to show each other esteem, and to ensure the continuity of the relationship? How can these goods represent a bond with invisible beings who are believed to be capable of deciding our destiny? What constitutes a gift from the gods? What do we owe them in return? How does the sacrificial phenomenon emerge? What do we owe each other? How does debt arise and disappear? Is there any relation between symbolic debt and a financial debt?

The history of our civilizations is filled with these implicit questions. Gift-giving, sacrifice, debt, and grace are the topics of all our narratives. We may ask if the whole of the enormous movement of the modern economy—what is now a global production machine—might not be the last and most radical way to eliminate the gods, to do away with gift-giving and debt. It may be that we produce, exchange, and consume in order to reduce our relationship to the world and to each other to the management of visible and quantifiable goods, to prevent anything from escaping the calculus of prices and control by the marketplace, so that the very concept of the priceless would finally disappear. Then nothing would remain out-side the realm of commerce. Material innocence would finally have been achieved: no more faults, sin, gift-giving, or forgiveness, nothing other than mistakes in calculations, positive or negative balance sheets, and pay-ments within agreed deadlines. This seems to be the world that is in the process of emerging in our ordinary practices of production and exchange.

These questions will trace the horizon of this book. Our starting point was the very specific issue of Socrates' moral integrity as guaranteed by his indifference to money. This question of integrity has reappeared and become increasingly important throughout intellectual history as the symptom of an entire culture. What it involves is not only the presence or absence of self-interest but the very nature of the social bond. We are deal-ing not only with economic history; as we will see, the anthropological foundations of our mode of being together are at stake in the questions of profitable exchange and generous gift-giving.

PART ONE

MERCENARY FIGURES

The Refusal of Mercenary Knowledge

Scientia donum Dei est, unde vendi non potest.

MEDIEVAL PROVERB[1]

In a series of notes written about his friend Helvétius's posthumous book, *A Treatise on Man,* Diderot, clearly annoyed by the author's theses, according to which physical sensibility and propensity to pleasure provided the ultimate explanation for everything, put forth several examples that could support the opposite position. His intention was to object to Helvétius's excessive views by presenting an indubitable case: "You can be sure that when, at age twenty, Leibniz shut himself in a room and spent thirty years in his robe, buried in the depth of geometry or in the obscurity of metaphysics, he was not thinking of gaining a position, of sleeping with a woman, or of filling an old chest with gold, anymore than he would have, had he been living his last hour."[2] This was indeed the prototypical figure of the philosopher, for whom a passionate yearning for knowledge and the search for truth superseded all other considerations and even all temptations, including those of the flesh, but even more those presented by money: "Force his door," writes Diderot, "enter his study with a pistol in your hand, and tell him, 'Your money or your discovery of *The Calculus of Fluxions*!' He will give you the key to his safe with a smile on his face. Go further: display on his table all the enticement of wealth and offer him an exchange—he will disdainfully turn his back on you" (570). The fictional tempter then makes a few more fabulous proposals that leave the philosopher completely unmoved: "You will no sooner sway him than you would sway an owl into becoming a diurnal bird or an eagle into becoming a nocturnal bird" (570). Diderot's point, of course, was to claim that some human beings are impervious by nature to the most highly sought pleasures. But what matters to me is that Diderot would have chosen a philosopher as an example for his demonstration and the financial temptation as the core of this example. He could have considered different professions: engineer, painter, musician, poet, all of which are regarded as being attached to their work rather than to any material advantage; moreover, he could have considered a religious figure recognized for his or her holiness. The figure of the philosopher, however, appeared to him to be the most obvious example of a character for whom nothing—neither pleasure nor wealth—could enter into consideration when disregard for self-interest and the incomparable value of the productions of the mind had to be established.

The philosopher occupies the position of the priceless par excellence. Diderot's choice was not a random one. He belonged to a tradition whose roots extend back to the most ancient thought (especially that of the so-called School of the Cynics). What is surprising is precisely this resistance along the centuries of the exemplary figure of the wise man, in view of the competition presented by the figure of the saint. This is at least the case within cultured circles, while the figure of Socrates has remained almost unnoticed compared to that of Jesus in the expressions of folk worship. It even seems that, independent of the transmission of a tradition, a kind of a spontaneous ascetic attitude is called for on the part of the philosopher engaging in the path of knowledge and wisdom, as if it were not possible to desire simultaneously wealth, honor, pleasure, and truth.

No better witness to this could probably be found than another of Diderot's difficult companions, Jean-Jacques Rousseau. The question of the incompatibility of money and truth arose very early on in his *Confessions.* When, after spending happy years as a child at the house of Pastor Lambercier, he was placed as an apprentice under an engraver who behaved toward him in a rough and rude manner—according to the narrator—young Jean-Jacques lost his sense of acquired virtue and, under the influence of one of his mates, started to engage in petty theft. Yet, he noted, this mostly involved food or inexpensive objects. "I have never been much tempted by money. . . . I have no particular taste for things that can be bought. I only want pleasures that are pure, whereas money poisons everything. . . .

Money has never seemed to me the precious thing it is supposed to be. Indeed, it has never even seemed to me to be much of a convenience; in itself it is good for nothing and; you must, to enjoy it, exchange it; you must buy, bargain, be often cheated, pay dearly, be poorly served."[3]

Money is the universal intermediary and the obligatory translator. This is precisely what disgraces it, since in the final analysis it only provides a semblance. What interested Jean-Jacques was the thing itself, not the means to obtain it. Money is thought of as a marvelous tool, and it is true that having it ensures a necessary independence; this is precisely why it brings with it the risk of being desired for itself. The sign obscures what it stands for. The mediation usurps the object to which it should lead. Money always interposes itself. It is the thing turned into a sign, but this sign "must in turn be transformed to be enjoyed." It must be returned to where it came from. It imposes an unnecessary detour. This involves much more than moral suspicion; what is at stake is the order of things and the truth of the world. From the outset Jean-Jacques' uneasiness came from this loss of transparency and, at an even deeper level, from the breach in the immediacy of the relationship with the world and other human beings. Losing transparency amounts to losing substance. From the beginning money has had a conflicting relationship with the yearning for truth; it is constitutively the first obstacle faced by anyone intending to confront the demand to think.

But in addition to this ontological problem a different and no less serious one is involved: money is supposed to remunerate talent (that of the writer, artist, or expert). Yet whoever writes to acquire wealth no longer has anything to say; worse, this also applies to anyone who writes for a living. The work of art or thought requires complete and unconditional lack of self-interest. "I felt that writing to earn my daily bread would soon snuff out my genius and destroy my talent. . . . No, I have always felt that the condition of author is, and only can be, distinguished and honourable in so far as it is not a profession. It is too difficult to think nobly when one is thinking only in order to live. . . . I had a profession that would support me even if my books did not sell well; and it was precisely this that made them sell."[4] This is the paradox confronted by anyone who aims to "think nobly"; what is involved is not the old dichotomy between the work of commoners and the idleness of aristocrats but the exclusion of any mercenary attitude and of every kind of financial advantage for anyone who intends to think and write. Only then, as a supplement, and outside of any yearning for appropriation or self-interested calculation, can affluence be bestowed on the thinker or artist.

What is money, then, for it to worry philosophy to this extent? Why does the suspicion of venality—and therefore corruption—emerge as soon as the philosopher enjoys an income that would be viewed as unproblematic in the case of any other profession? If this is no longer the case today, at least it was for a long time. What event, set of conditions, or reversal in what mode of thinking changed the table of values? What happened? It is difficult to answer this question without first returning to the beginning of a history that runs through the whole of our tradition. The first conflict between philosophy and money is familiar to us; it was the conflict between Socrates and the Sophists, at least as Plato constructed its narrative. It is indispensable for us to rediscover it.

1

Plato and the Sophists' Money

Those also who sell wisdom for money to whoever wishes it they call sophists just as if they were prostitutes.

XENOPHON, *Memorabilia*

SOCRATES: Wouldn't you be ashamed to hold yourself out among the Greeks as a Sophist?
HIPPOCRATES: Of course I would, Socrates, if I am to say what I really think.

PLATO, *Protagoras*

All the highly paid individuals the public calls sophists.

PLATO, *Republic*

The sophist is one who makes money from an apparent but unreal wisdom.

ARISTOTLE, *Sophistical Refutations*

For Plato the question of philosophy was inseparable from the recognition of the authentic figure of the philosopher. That is why dialogue involved a theatrical process of selection. The time had long past since "masters of truth" of various kinds (bards, poets, wizards, healers, seers, and rhetoricians) had been plentiful, yet new ones were appearing who were attempting to embody every aspect of these ancient figures at once. Of all these dubious candidates, the most dangerous, because he was the most similar and the closest in appearance to the philosopher, was the Sophist.[1] How could he be identified and exposed? Plato had a preliminary criterion of great efficacy: the Sophist was he who demanded to be compensated for his teaching. As a consequence the philosopher could first be recognized by the fact that he did not demand any wages. Following the remarkable example of Socrates, he had to display an unfailing indifference to financial profit.

Was this primarily a moral requirement, and if so, on what was it based? Indeed, what was immoral about demanding compensation for a professional activity that was recognized—and even valued—in the city? It is more plausible that, beyond any ethical aim (such as the promotion of the beauty of disinterestedness), what was at stake in the rejection of any form of compensation was the very status of philosophy and the purpose of its quest, which is truth. We must therefore ask how the presence or absence of compensation could have had an essential relation to what constituted the philosopher's approach and the very content of his knowledge. What might be the relationship between money and the question of truth? Did money have a privileged association with error, lies, and illusion, and was it in and of itself of a sophistic nature? These are the questions to which this reading of Plato should lead us; they most often remain implicit in his writings. But before we take them up, we must consider one immediately identifiable and insistent motif: the denunciation of the greed of the remunerated master.

Hippias: Vanity and Venality

Plato's first charge—and from the outset one of his most scathing—against what he presents as the mercenary character of the Sophist appears in *Hippias Major*. This is an early dialogue, the purpose of which was to attempt to define the beautiful. Hippias, whom Plato had already cast in an earlier dialogue—*Hippias Minor*—was a fairly well-known Sophist, although his renown was not comparable to that of such great figures as Gorgias, Prodicus, and Protagoras.

Nothing in this text indicates what the circumstances of Hippias's encounter with Socrates were. The latter addresses him right away with hyperbolic praise: "Here's that fine expert, Hippias! It's ages since you descended on Athens" (281a). Hippias, who has an exaggerated sense of his own importance and knowledge, explains with false modesty that his long absence from Athens has been due to the many diplomatic missions that he, rather than any other man, has been entrusted with by his city, Elis. This immediately earns him ambiguous congratulations: "Well, Hippias, this is the sort of thing a true all-around expert must expect. I say 'all-around' because not only are you capable, in the private sphere, of giving the young men who pay you their money's worth and more in terms of benefits, but also, in the public sphere, you are able to help your own city, which is only right and proper for someone who intends to gain the public's esteem and avoid its contempt" (281c). It should be said that this praise is not just ambiguous but even treacherous. Indeed, it is known that Hippias used these diplomatic missions to recruit his future students, thus mixing together, as most Sophists did, two things that the Greeks insisted on keeping clearly separate: public affairs, which were disinterested by nature, and private business, which had to do with gaining and increasing income. The city itself was founded on this distinction, which made it possible to define a "common good" that stood above rivalries and private interests.[2]

Yet not only does Hippias fail to notice Socrates' sarcasm, but he thinks that this art of playing both sides at once is precisely the superior art of the Sophists, which, according to him, places them above the ancient wise men who had been less successful in business: "What other reason can there be, Socrates, apart from their complete inability to use their wisdom for accomplishments in both spheres, the public [*ta koina*] and the private [*ta idia*]?" (281c). By ascribing to Hippias this conflation of the two spheres and presenting him as proud of doing just that, Plato is certain to incite his readers' contempt for the Sophist from Elis.

Pretending to agree wholeheartedly with Hippias, Socrates concludes that a similar kind of progress has occurred in this realm as in the technical realm since the days of Dedalus, to the extent that if the wise men of ancient times were to return, they would look foolish. This analogy with craftsmen is not innocent, since the specific enterprise of the Sophists consisted of turning knowledge into a *tekhnē*, which was exactly what made it possible for knowledge to be transmitted through mere devices. A technique can indeed be perfected. In this case the technique that the Sophists developed amounted to the art of selling their knowledge. This made them the possessors of a new kind of mastery. Their *epistēmē*, being a type of know-how, was capable of producing objects that could be obtained through exchange. Access to knowledge therefore no longer required a conversion (*periagōgē*) on the part of disciples but merely the means to re-munerate a professional for his services.

Pretending to recognize this new superiority expressed as "the ability to combine private with public business" (282b), Socrates himself cites Gorgias as an example: "Not only was he popularly regarded as the best speaker ever to have addressed the Assembly, but he also gave lectures as a private individual and met with our young men and earned and received a lot of money from our city" (282b). In the same way Prodicus was capable of filling the Council with wonder, as well as "earning an incredible amount of money from giving lectures as a private individual and meeting with our young men" (282c). This reminder of the heroic deeds of famous Sophists is apparently meant to comfort Hippias; in fact, it is a way for Socrates to tar them all with the same brush, since all of them largely mixed public and private business. Socrates implies that if Hippias views such a mixture as progress, it should be concluded that the great thinkers who lived before the Sophists were quite mediocre. "None of those men of old ever thought it right to be remunerated or to display wisdom by lec-turing [*epideixis*] to all sorts of people. That's how simple they were: they didn't realize how valuable money is" (282c).[3] Hippias does not bat an eye-lash, since all this seems indisputable to him.

All in all, the money earned has become the criterion for the value of the knowledge imparted. This is why Hippias feels put down by this re-minder of the financial success of Gorgias and Prodicus: he is necessarily superior to them since he can boast much higher earnings. "You don't re-alize how fine the situation is, Socrates: you'd be astonished if you knew how much money *I* have earned. . . . I would go as far as to suppose that *my* earnings are more than the total earnings of any other two sophists you care to mention" (282e). For Hippias this is unarguable proof. His van-ity leads him to describe the highly profitable campaigns he conducted in Sicily, which Socrates is mischievous enough to portray as raids, clever and victorious attacks perpetrated on a helpless population.

Socrates then suggests that Anaxagoras (who had been a friend of and adviser to Pericles) should be regarded as a fool because he was unable to become a rich man, and he provides Hippias with the obvious conclu-sion: "You can define the wise man by seeing who has earned the most money." No suspicion crosses Hippias's mind; he is delighted and agrees with Socrates. He feels fully justified in his claim and recognized as superior in terms of a kind of knowledge that is measured by the amount one earns. He remains completely unaware of Socrates' mockery. His ordeal is about to begin.

Didn't you often go to Sparta? Socrates asks. Isn't this city famous for its austerity and contempt for wealth? How much did you earn there? Hippias has to admit that his visit to Sparta has brought him no income; worse, he has not even been allowed to give lessons there. Socrates appears surprised: this means that either Hippias's knowledge was worthless or Sparta had no money. After both hypotheses have been ruled out, the Sophist will have to admit that money was not the proper criterion to evaluate knowledge, if only to be able to maintain his claim to real competence. Yet, before leading Hippias to this inevitable recognition, Socrates magnanimously presents him with a third hypothesis: might Sparta's laws be faulty? Hippias, lost and confused, is reluctant to cling to this explanation capable of outraging all reasonable people; he backs down and acknowledges that Sparta is a well-organized city with good laws. Yet these laws did not allow for money and education to be associated. Hippias admits that laws in general are a good thing and that the wise men who enacted Sparta's laws are right; he cannot therefore maintain that his claim to be remunerated is founded on law, since this would mean that "the Spartans are on the wrong side of the law" and "in contravention of the law" (285b); Hippias, realizing that he has backed himself into a corner, is quite prepared to agree, at the risk of contradicting himself, and he does so. Let Sparta fall, let the law perish, as long as his wages are preserved!

At this point Hippias has lost face and confidence. He knows it and becomes confused, as he will increasingly become confused about the purpose of his encounter with Socrates (defining the essence of the beautiful). Indeed, the reason he came to Athens was precisely to teach young men, in exchange for a fee, how to succeed in the public arena and how to become famous through the splendor of their speeches. After this disastrous beginning the dialogue goes on to display ever more evidence of Hippias's inability to establish just distinctions and to determine the essence of what he means to teach.

But pursuing this evidence would lead to a discussion that does not concern us here. Nor do we need to decide whether this presentation of Hippias was factually objective (it was probably excessive if not unfair).

This prologue, however, has given us a glimpse into the core of our issue: the device by which Plato, before coming to the fundamental discussion, exposes the figure of the Sophist as a figure of mercenary knowledge. It is as if the confusion of thought displayed by Hippias and his imitators has a direct relationship with this new claim, according to which the value of knowledge can be measured according to the profits it brings. This is the original sin of the Sophist, from which everything else follows: the primary reason why the Sophist's thought is false, uncertain, and above all deceitful is its mercenary character. The same suspicion can be found unchanged in Aristotle (although he is notoriously more lenient toward the Sophists), who states, "The sophist is one who makes money from an apparent but unreal wisdom" (*Soph. Ref.* 165a22–23).

To sum up, in this beginning section of *Hippias Major* Socrates' pointed remarks are aimed at three targets. First, the way the Sophists lump together two spheres that should remain separate at the risk of ruining the city: public business (*ta koina*) and private business (*ta idia*). Plato makes sure to mention that it is most often while carrying out official missions concerning the relationships between different cities that the Sophists go about recruiting their customers/students by presenting model lectures (*epideixeis*) intended to attract them, thereby turning the function of citizen into a profitable activity. Second, the Sophists' behavior threatens the very purpose of education: if the relationship between master and student is a mercenary one, then the claim to prepare young men for public life—which is to say the requirement to allow the "public good" to prevail—becomes self-contradicting. Third, and most important, setting up a system of equivalence between the amounts received and the value of the knowledge imparted effects the worst possible confusion and reduction, since it implies that knowledge can be measured in the same way as any production of a *tekhnē* available on the market. Yet in the beginning of *Hippias Major* the word that is often sufficient to disqualify the Sophist as a character devoted to mercenary activity never comes up: *merchant*. More precisely, the Sophist is presented as a "trader in spiritual things"—*psukhemporos*, a trader in words, as we would say today. This phrase will appear in the *Sophist*, in which Hippias's imitators will be defined in a precise and unexpected manner, namely from the perspective of trade. We will return to this later.

For now, we have become familiar with the typical Sophist through the figure of Hippias. His portrayal is not a flattering one. Can such a figure enable us to understand what the Sophist movement and its schools represented? This is doubtful. We must revisit this debate.

The Sophist: A New Kind of Scholar

It is now generally accepted that Plato's ironical and usually negative presentation of the Sophists does not do justice to their teaching practice or their thought. Scholarly research conducted during the past fifty years has made it possible to rectify this unflattering image, which has long been held self-evident by the philosophical tradition.[4]

The innovative character of the Sophists' approach is much more apparent today; some even regard them as modern figures. The Sophists seem to have embodied a trend of thought consistent with the profound transformations that had occurred in Greek society (particularly in Athens, where the most famous Sophists were only visitors). The Sophists unquestionably represented a new way of thinking that was more directly consistent with a new class of citizens who, following the Greek victories against the Persians and the economic growth that had marked the time of Pericles, yearned for more public recognition and saw no interest in defending the traditional values of aristocratic clans. The Sophists fit this trend and acted as interpreters of a generation that wished to ask questions in a different way than had their elders. This historical contextualization does not explain, however, the specificity of the figure of the Sophist.

What does *sophist* mean? It has been shown that the term itself was broadly used well before Plato but in a broader sense and without any derogatory connotations.[5] It denoted anyone with expertise in a moral or technical field. In preclassical Greece the term *sophistēs* was almost interchangeable with the term *sophos*. *Sophos* described a man with cautious and measured knowledge; *sophistēs* applied to an educator or transmitter of knowledge. "Probably it was assumed that a *sophistēs* would be a teacher," William Guthrie writes, but the word first applied to poets, who were primarily viewed as educators.[6] It also designated musicians, in their function as poets playing the lyre while chanting. The term later extended to prose writers: "A *sophistēs* writes or teaches because he has a special skill or knowledge to impart. His *sophia* is practical, whether in the fields of conduct and politics or in the technical arts."[7] This sense of the word was still common in Plato's time, and Plato himself used it several times in this context.[8] The

Sophists inherited this whole tradition, and it is clear that they assigned the mission of educating men—*paidein anthrōpous*, in Protagoras's own words (*Pro.* 317b)—to themselves. Werner Jaeger's *Paideia* also recognizes it as their main quality.

The emergence and success of the Sophists are inseparable from a new pedagogical ideal, which was associated with a new value system. In accordance with the Greek model the aim remained to be the best and to distinguish oneself. This distinction, however, no longer involved the warrior ideal or traditional martial virtues; what now sanctioned a young man's success was his ability to take part in the organization of the city, which is to say public life and the debates associated with it. In this new democratic society power was no longer determined by the sword but by the word. True power depended on one's ability to convince others. This high regard in which the Greeks held language and argument was probably fairly unusual in the classical world. It was evidence of a transformation that was rich with promise, since it involved a movement that assigned a high priority to the functions associated with knowledge and the mastery of formal operations—in short, everything that developed the technologies of intelligence within a culture: writing and calculation but also rhetoric, argument, literature, and, above all, philosophy.[9]

"The Sophists put their talent as teachers at the service of this new ideal of the political *aretē*: the training of statesmen, the formation of the personality of the city's future leader—such was their programme," writes Henri-Irénée Marrou. "Thus the revolution in education that has come to be known as Sophistry seems to have had a technical rather than political origin: on the basis of a mature culture, these enterprising educators developed a new technique, a form of teaching that was wider in its scope, more ambitious and more effective than any previous system."[10] The innovative character of the Sophists' teaching was above all its form, which was also the first target of Plato's criticism. Indeed, what the Sophists implicitly undermined was the relationship of initiation between master and disciple. This relationship had its roots in the timeless tradition of the *sophoi*, the wise men, seers, healers, and storytellers who educated their disciples through a long training process that involved trade secrets, meditations, and ordeals with an often ceremonial character.[11] This pedagogical model persisted, although in a highly secularized form, in Plato's view of philosophical training, that is, the Socratic training—in which a personal bond remained.

The Sophists gave up the initiatory model. They did not claim to take charge of the young men who asked for their help, since they did not aim to lead them on a spiritual journey or an inner reversal, which the Platonic *periagōgē* could be. They merely meant to pass down a competence, in the same way as any specialized craftsmen might, or anyone possessing a particular know-how (such as rhetors, grammarians, or masters of music or gymnastics). They meant to offer training in the art of argument to the public in the same way as the art of building or healing might be taught. In a quite logical and normal manner, *and like other experts*, they wanted to be remunerated for their services.[12] It so happened that Protagoras, who inaugurated this market practice, was also the first who assigned himself the term *Sophist*. He was thus asking to be recognized as an "expert," with the understanding that his expertise applied to the arts of speech and argument and consequently to any form of knowledge that involved discourse; in Socrates' words, "he has knowledge of wise things" (*ton tōn sophōn epistēmona* [*Pro.* 312c]).

It was possible for the Sophists to request fees in exchange for their lessons because prior to this they had changed the very status of their teaching. It was possible for the new generations to accept this practice without feeling any outrage because philosophy—or at least this philosophy—no longer appeared to them as a form of inner conversion but as an operational knowledge that gave access to the means of influencing others. Yearning for wisdom gave way to technical mastery and will to power.

The Question of Money

People listened to him gladly because they thought it was so nice that a man with so many ideas also had so much money.

ROBERT MUSIL, *The Man without Qualities*

Plato's hostility toward the Sophists developed within the very specific social context that I have just discussed. It is particularly worthwhile to underscore the privileged relationship that evolved between Sophists (as well as professional rhetors) and newly wealthy families. Who were the latter, and why did they resort to the services of the Sophists and other masters of eloquence? This can be explained by the transformations that arose from the various reforms conducted by Solon in the early sixth century BCE, Clisthenes in the late sixth century, and finally Pericles in the middle of the fifth century, which made it possible to discharge the debt owed by poor citizens and helped enrich a new class of artisans, traders, and mine vendors. The newly wealthy were impatient to gain access to the most prestigious offices, which involved political power.

The difficulty confronting these upstarts was that access to positions of decision and prestige was mostly determined through public debate, which was judged in terms of one's talent in convincing or even seducing the people in assembly. This talent could not be improvised, and young men from noble families were traditionally prepared for it by an entire education. Eloquence and the art of argument were the respective contributions of rhetors and philosophers. The Sophists were confident that they could provide both at the same time. This was why the newly wealthy resorted to their services. The Sophists offered access to a mastery that was beyond their clients' reach. But since the clients were too old to gain such a complex know-how, they most often transferred their ambition onto their sons. This gave rise to the association between money, knowledge, and power. The amounts spent on this education were sometimes stupendous,[13] which makes it plausible that the main element that undermined the image of the *sophistēs* was the high fees they demanded. This was what connected the Sophists (this capitalization exclusively designates those identified as such by tradition) to the figure of the merchant.

Plato was neither the first one nor the only one to criticize them on this matter. Isocrates, a great rhetor who was loath to be confused with them, vehemently denounces their fees in "Against the Sophists." After a few critical remarks about the Sophists' claim to teach wisdom and, above all, to promise happiness as a guaranteed consequence of their lessons, he immediately turns to what seems to him the most serious issue:

Now these people have become so bold that they try to persuade the young that if they study with them they will know what they need to do and through this knowledge they will become happy. And once they have established themselves as teachers and masters of such great goods, they are not ashamed to demand only three or four minas for them. If they were selling some other property for such a small fraction of its worth, they would not dispute that their reasoning is faulty. And although they value all of moral excellence and happiness so little, nevertheless they still claim to be sensible teachers of others. They say they have no need for money, disparaging wealth as "mere silver and gold," but in their desire for a little profit they almost promise to make their students immortal.[14]

This criticism may seem surprising coming from a rhetor who also requested significant fees in exchange for his lessons. But Isocrates believed that he was passing down a very precise technique and art consisting of mastering language relative to a content—the question at hand—and nothing else. He viewed the remuneration he requested as reasonable because it was proportional to the know-how that he was passing down. He did not claim to promise what was beyond the reach of a human being. His arguments against the Sophists can be summarized as follows: first, the price—three or four minae—that the Sophists assigned to their lessons was inconsistent and laughable, since it could not match the entire value of the virtue and happiness to be gained; second, the Sophists were hypocrites, since they asked for payment while speaking against wealth (this criticism was aimed at minor disciples of Socrates, such as Antisthenes and Euclid); third, "What is most ridiculous of all is that they distrust those from whom they have to get this small profit—those to whom they intend to impart their sense of justice—and they deposit the fees from their students with men whom they have never taught. They are well advised to do this in regard to their security, but it is the opposite of what they teach."[15] They did not trust those who paid them; in other words, they did not think that those whom they were educating could acquire the virtues that they were teaching; those who kept the deposits had not received the Sophists' teaching, which showed that they did not need it in order to be honest.

We should, however, carefully consider the meaning of Isocrates' remonstrations. He does not say that the Sophists should not receive remuneration but only denounces the incoherence of their discourse and attitudes. Above all, he blames them for demanding so little money in exchange for the promise of such great knowledge. By doing so, they devalue the authentic knowledge of other masters.[16] Plato situates the issue at an entirely different level: under no circumstances should philosophical knowledge be the object of financial transactions. It remains for us to understand why.

In the dialogues Socrates very often finds the opportunity to mock the hypothesis according to which paying a recognized master should be enough to reach knowledge. Plato carries this irony a long way: one must possess knowledge of intrinsically different value depending on whether one took cheap and downscale lessons or expensive and upscale ones. Here is how Socrates addresses Hermogenes in *Cratylus*, at a time when the discussion is becoming especially arduous: "Hermogenes, son of Hipponicus, there is an ancient proverb that 'fine things are very difficult' to know about, and it certainly isn't easy to get to know about names. To be sure, if I'd attended Prodicus' fifty-drachma lecture course, which he himself advertises as an exhaustive treatment of the topic, there'd be nothing to prevent you from learning the precise truth about the correctness of names straightaway. But as I've heard only the one-drachma course, I don't know the truth about it" (384b–c).

This mockery of the idea that knowledge's value could be proportional to its associated invoice recurs almost every time one of Socrates' interlocutors refers to the Sophists' teachings. Thus, when young Hermogenes says, "I'd really rather find out what you yourself have to say about the correctness of names," Socrates, remaining true to his learned ignorance, is careful not to answer but pretends to believe that others hold definite answers or should at least be assumed to do so since they are able to exchange them for large sums of money: "The most correct way is together with people who already know, but you must pay them well and show gratitude besides—these are the sophists. Your brother Callias got his reputation for wisdom in return for a lot of money. So you had better beg and implore him to teach you what he learned from Protagoras about the correctness of names, since you haven't yet come into any money of your own" (*Cra.* 391b–c). Hermogenes appears to be unaware of Socrates' irony: to acquire knowledge, one need only buy the lessons of scholars (*epistamenoi*) or else try to obtain secondhand information from those who have been able to pay for such instruction.

Experts or Merchants?

It is thus clear that Plato's criticisms of the reduction of philosophy to a technical approach and of the payment of the Sophists' teaching originate in the same impulse. He cannot question the one without denouncing the other. This is all the more so because the Sophists make sure to protect themselves from accusations of venality precisely by claiming their "professional" status and demanding to be paid their wages, as any other expert would. In fact, Plato fully recognizes this: it is as experts that they claim legitimacy and ask to be paid.[17] This is why he first attacks them on this point. His criticism amounts mostly to questioning the definition of their area of competence and, above all, their general claim to have any competence at all of the kind that can be unhesitatingly accorded to physicians, sculptors, or musicians. Even so, the only constant feature of the Sophist is that he *sells* his knowledge. He is therefore above all a merchant (in wholesale or retail, trader and shopkeeper, *emporos* and *kapēlos*; we will return to this distinction pointed out in *Protagoras* and the *Sophist*). This is Plato's main thesis regarding the profession of Sophist. The Sophist was not an expert but a merchant; what does this entail? That, *after the fashion of a merchant, he has no need to know the nature of the wares that he sells.* While the truly philosophical question (which is also the question of truth) is, "What is the thing itself?" the Sophist is only concerned with setting a price to talk about it—a price for truth.

Is the Sophist an expert? Does he really know the field of his profession? Does his knowledge even cover a field? These are the preliminary questions, and they are raised in particular in *Meno*. The eponymous character is a rich Thessalian who had been a student of Gorgias; with regard to philosophy he seems to be an enlightened amateur. His attitude toward Socrates is friendly and open. He presents the old master with this frequently debated question: Can virtue—*aretē*, excellence—be taught? Socrates replies that he unfortunately lacks the assurance of a scholar such as Gorgias. He knows nothing about it, he states, first of all because he does not even know what virtue is. He and Meno will therefore have to start with trying to define it. Is virtue a gift from nature or the result of education? Meno asks. Is it innate or acquired knowledge? This is what is addressed in the famous passage in which a young slave is questioned, and the answer given by Socrates is that knowledge is a form of recollection. The example chosen is geometry, which precisely leaves the question of *aretē* unresolved. Now, there are masters of geometry and other sciences. Meno readily agrees. If *aretē* can be taught, this means that it is a science. In this case surely there have to be such things as "masters of virtue," Meno tells Socrates, who, as a tactical matter, keeps to facts and assures Meno that he has never met any such masters. He carefully avoids answering at the level of principle: can they exist? He waits for Meno to develop an answer. Then, just at the right moment, a third man arrives, the populist politician Anytos, who hates Sophists and all other great talkers (including Socrates). Instead of asking him Meno's question—can *aretē* be taught?—Socrates starts with a series of questions about professions and trades, such as cobbler, physician, and musician; he notes that when we resort to these professionals, we recognize their competence and pay them for it; it is understood that if one of them proves to be incompetent, he should be immediately fired; are not their wages recognition and proof of competence? If payment has not been contested, then the result has to have been judged satisfactory (see *Meno* 90d). At this point Socrates ironically reverses his reasoning, folding effects back onto causes: there are people who are paid to teach *aretē*, and they are not accused of incompetence. Therefore *aretē* is indeed recognized as a science. Who are these people who make themselves out to be "masters of virtue" and are recognized as such? They are the Sophists. At this point Socrates' position could appear ambiguous to someone unfamiliar with his method. By reversing the syllogism about competence (supposedly demonstrated by the fact of payment), he gives the impression that he lacks clear-sightedness. This is, of course, a pretense. It does not take long for the counterreversal to come: if there is a payment but no transmission of *aretē*, then the Sophist really is a faker and an illusionist, or even worse, a cheat. The Sophist bases his whole strategy on identifying himself with experts, who are masters of a specific know-how, but he has no such specific know-how to pass on. He only knows a little of everything (he is a scholar in matters of "knowledge," as Protagoras acknowledges). Actually—and this is the intended lesson of this passage from *Meno*—the Sophist is ignorant but does not know he is, whereas Socrates transcends his ignorance by recognizing it as the condition of the possibility of knowledge and by constantly questioning it through his use of language. This is the end result: wages are supposed to prove the Sophist's competence, but they reveal only his ignorance. He is not a specialist, precisely because *aretē* cannot be taught in exchange for a set fee (as in the case of a cobbler, physician, or musician). In Platonic terms this means that his discourse has no object. This takes us back to the fundamental debate over being and nonbeing. The Sophist talks about what is not. He uses a power of language that makes it possible to say something without questioning the truth of the statement. The conclusion is unavoidable, clear, and cruel: the Sophist knows nothing but is unaware of it. He is paid to say nothing or rather to speak nothingness.

It now becomes possible to better understand the ultimate meaning of the Sophist's activity: if he does not know what he is teaching while being compensated for it, he is in the exact situation of the merchant who has no need to know his wares in order to sell them. This is indeed what

Plato intends to demonstrate in a passage from *Protagoras*. At the beginning of this dialogue Socrates addresses young Hippocrates, who has just come and woken him at dawn, breathless, to announce the great news: Protagoras is in town! One can go and listen to him! One can enroll in his classes! . . . Socrates calmly replies, "Tell me, Hippocrates. You're now undertaking to go to Protagoras and pay him money for your tuition. Who are you going to, and what will you become?" (*Pro.* 311b). Socrates pretends to go along, without failing to aim a few treacherous barbs at the "greed" of the great Sophist, implying that Protagoras might not want a student who is unable to pay full price. Plato makes sure to let his reader know that the first precondition of access to a Sophist's instruction is the student's ability to pay tuition. The following discussion shows that this is not merely a practical question (whether or not one can afford it) but a question of principle—compensation is only given for recognized competence. Thus, Socrates explains, one pays for the services of a physician or a sculptor. He continues: "Very well. But now we're going to Protagoras, you and I, ready to pay him money [*misthos*] in your behalf—our own money, if it suffices to persuade him, but if not we'll spend that of our friends" (311d). In short, this is going to cost a great deal! What is Protagoras's expertise? One only pays for the services of those who hold a recognized know-how. This is the only legitimate use of money. What is the precise profession of the illustrious visitor? The young man confesses that he has no idea, and Socrates resumes his questioning, putting forward the decisive point:

Well, Hippocrates, isn't the sophist a kind of merchant [*emporos*] or huckster [*kapēlos*] of wares by which the soul is fed? He seems that way to me.

But what does the soul feed on, Socrates?

On learning, surely, I said. And we must beware, my friend, that the sophist not deceive us in praising us what he sells, as merchants and hucksters do with food for the body. In fact, they don't know which among their wares are good or bad for the body, but they praise everything they sell; nor do those who buy of them know either, unless they happen to be physicians or trainers. It's the same way with these folk who tour our cities peddling knowledge to whomever desires it; they praise everything they sell, but perhaps some of them, dear friend, are ignorant whether the things they sell are good or bad for the soul. (*Pro.* 313c–e)

The decisive word has been dropped: the Sophist is a merchant (wholesaler and retailer: import-export and retail). We will soon see how the difference between the two is addressed in the *Sophist* and what the connotations of the very term *merchant* were in the Greek world. The relevant criterion is already provided by this comparison between trade and medicine and between food for the body and food for the soul. What trade is to goods meant for the body, the art of the Sophists is to goods meant for the soul. In the same way as the merchant sells various goods without knowing their nature, this other merchant, the Sophist, sells knowledge for the soul that he does not know about. Within this analogical system one term remains unstated, yet its place is indicated by symmetry—the physician who possesses authentic competence regarding the body has a counterpart, someone who has authentic knowledge regarding the soul: the philosopher, of course. The term is not mentioned, but its representative is there in person, Socrates himself. This place remains unstated, however, precisely because philosophy cannot be reduced to mere knowledge. It is not a competence because it is at the same time a questioning about all possible competence.

For Plato it is important to shatter the Sophists' claim to expertise, since it alone is the basis of their demand and right to receive wages. If the fact that they tend to turn philosophy into a technical specialty is indeed what makes it possible to put philosophy on the market, then it is crucial to refuse this identification that conceals the venal character of the operation. Then it becomes a matter of correctly reasoning from effects to causes: the Sophists are not paid because they are recognized as experts (as the argument presented in *Meno* could have led us to believe) but merely because they are clever at selling their knowledge, in the same way merchants are clever at selling their products. No text expresses this better than the *Sophist.*

The *Sophist* and the Art of Angling

The first part of the *Sophist*, whose purpose is to come to a definition of the eponymous character, continues to be famous as a demonstration of Plato's method of division. At the formal level this method does match the description Plato gives of it elsewhere.[18] It is clear, however, that this method, as it appears in the *Sophist*—and as it is applied to its object—takes a profoundly ironic and even parodic twist throughout (it seems surprising that this has so rarely been noticed).

But why should one bother to define the Sophist? Above all because most people confuse him with the philosopher; Plato knows only too well how damaging this confusion has been for Socrates. The apparent similarities between the two conceal the actual, incommensurable distance between them. Yet the Sophist is difficult to pin down: he claims every form of knowledge and competence. It is therefore important to flush him out, tear off his mask, and expose him.[19] This is why the attempt to define him is analogous to a "hunt": the dialogue's form reflects its object since the Sophist finds himself in the position of the "hunted hunter"—a hunter of rich youth who is in turn stalked by the hunter of truth. This is, indeed, why the method of the *Sophist* takes on a parodic element.

This becomes clear when, under the pretext of propaedeutic, the protagonist of the dialogue—the "Stranger," playing with panache and humor the part usually reserved for Socrates—proposes to test the method on an easy topic that might later serve as a model (*paradeigma*). He suggests finding a definition of "the angler": this topic seems simple and even arbitrary, as if chosen at random. It soon becomes apparent, however, that this is not the case. But this choice in and of itself is already enough to create a discrepancy between the trivial character of the example chosen and the supposed grandeur of the object to be defined—the Sophist. It should be noted that no actual Sophist is present or explicitly mentioned in the dialogue. The presence of a particular Sophist would have presented unique traits, probably making it impossible to identify the Sophist at the most general level, in his exemplary form.

A cascade of divisions—whose purpose is to circumscribe what the concept of angler, "the thing itself" (*peri to pragma auto*), is, rather than merely talking "about the name" (*peri to onoma*)—then begins. It is possible to apply this method to the case of the Sophist, the Stranger states. Such an application appears to be innocuous, yet it immediately becomes apparent that the choice of the example has not been random at all. It allows the Stranger to shift from the formal level (the art of defining in general) to the level of content (since the example chosen, which at first had appeared to be immaterial, now becomes the object of debate). The Stranger asks young Theaetetus if he does not recognize that "the one man belongs to the same kind as the other"; when Theaetetus expresses his surprise, the Stranger exclaims, "To me they both clearly appear to be hunters" (*Soph.* 221d). The division method first succeeds in making a new name appear under a name already given. It reveals a predicate that makes possible a match between the two: an angler is thus a hunter but a hunter of water game. Hence the question, what does the Sophist hunt? The task of dividing has to be taken up again in order to come to the proper definition.

The Stranger proposes to situate the art of hunting among the other known arts. According to accepted tradition they can be divided into two major categories: arts of production and those of acquisition, either making something or obtaining something that has already been made. Hunting evidently belongs to the second category, which can itself be subdivided between the things that are obtained through exchange and those that are caught. Hunting pertains to the latter; but catching can be further subdivided between open catching and catching through cunning. The case of hunting is now situated on a tree of divisions: it is an art of acquisition pertaining to catching through cunning. This crucial point is now established. But the task is not over. The art of hunting has been defined in terms of its form; it still remains to define it in terms of its object. What is it that is hunted? The dividing procedure resumes: the object could be either animate or inanimate; the latter set, which involved the work of divers—sponge collectors—is soon dealt with as being rare; this leaves the animate beings, which can be divided between land and aquatic animals, and the latter subdivided between flying and swimming animals. Fishing is now identified and subdivided—as hunting has been—between two different techniques (striking and hooking).[20]

We began from two separate definitions. First, the Sophist is a hunter of rich young men. Second, the angler (introduced as a trivial example) is a water hunter. The two definitions will now meet and overlap, as if by a happy coincidence.

This is the result of the first step: "So according to our account now, Theaetetus, it seems that this sort of expertise belongs to acquisition, taking possession, hunting, animal-hunting, hunting on land, human hunting, hunting by persuasion, hunting privately, and money-earning [*nomismato-pōlikē*]. It is the hunting of rich and prominent young men. And according to the way our account has turned out, it's what should be called the expertise of the sophist" (*Soph.* 223b).[21] Plato emphasizes the first point: it is possible to identify the Sophist as a hunter but one practicing a self-interested form of hunting that "is nothing more than a financial exchange under pretense of teaching." At this stage it might appear that the purpose of the demonstration (discrediting the Sophist as mercenary of knowledge) has been met. But this would amount to underestimating the Platonic requirement for specification: what kind of exchange is involved? What type of object is exchanged? This has to be specified.

The hunt for the hunter resumes. The movement leading to the second definition of the Sophist specifies the form of the exchange conducted: trade rather than barter, wholesale rather than retail, involving knowledge rather than tangible objects, which leads to this summing up: "We'll say that the expertise on the part of acquisition, exchange, selling, wholesaling, and soul-wholesaling [*psukhemporikē*], dealing in words and learning that have to do with virtue—that's sophistry in its second appearance" (*Soph.* 224c–d).

The details given about the specific form of exchange practiced by the Sophist involve significant connotations. For Plato, to say that the activity of the Sophists is indeed trade and not barter amounts, above all, to setting up a contrast between a mode of exchange that is viewed as natural (between goods of equivalent value) and another that is viewed as illegitimate and even dangerous for the city (this will become clearer in the next chapter). But the category of trade itself includes two different types: retail and wholesale. The first is tolerable to the extent that it remains limited and ensures convenient access to various goods; it effects the distribution of a production process that involves specialization and complementarity of tasks. But Plato views wholesale trade (*emporikē*) as dangerous for the city; it is an import-export trade often practiced by foreigners that mobilizes large amounts of money. From the start it has a negative connotation (this will not be the case for Aristotle, who on the contrary is suspicious of retail and resale). Plato categorizes the Sophist's activity as a form of wholesale. He goes even further by coining new words to describe this exchange as *psukhemporikē* (trade in spiritual things) or *mathēmatopōlikē* (trade in the sciences). These were surprising oxymorons that would have seemed quasi-monstrous to Greek ears at the time.

This second definition, however, seems aimed primarily at the non-Athenian Sophists (as was Hippias, of course, but also such great figures as Gorgias and Protagoras) who came to recruit followers (or rather, according to Plato, customers) in this prestigious city. They are therefore the ones in charge of wholesale "trade" or big business. But it is important for Plato not to ignore the subcontractors, so to speak, those local imitators or disciples who turn wholesale (*emporikē*) into retail (*kapēlikē*) wares. These shopkeepers/disciples have a choice between trying to remake the product or merely distributing it. Very quickly (since Plato seems to wish to increase the contempt in which subcontractors are held) this distinction leads to a third and a fourth definition: "So apparently you'll still say that sophistry falls under acquisition, exchange, and selling, either by retailing things that others make or by selling things that he makes himself. It's the retail sale of any learning that has to do with the sorts of things we mentioned" (*Soph.* 224e).

To tackle the fifth definition, Plato moves to a different field. His purpose is no longer to catch the Sophist through the *object* of his enterprise (already shown to be financial profit rather than truth) but through his *method* or rather his art of argument. This art was known as *eristic.* It was the art of disputing, and it was not specific to the Sophists.[22] Instead of directly discussing this technique, Plato returns to the question raised at the beginning about the arts of acquisition (which enables him to maintain the hypothesis about the angler as hunter). He now resumes the operation of division, mentioning once again that the arts of acquisition (as opposed to the arts of production) include combat, which can be subdivided between simple competition and fighting, and the latter between violence and controversy, which can itself be subdivided between public and private disputes. The former deals with justice and injustice; the latter deals with private discussions and is called antilogic (*antilogikon*); it can be carried on in an expert or nonexpert way. The latter precisely involves eristic, namely the art of debating (which is, after all, also the art that Socrates himself practices). But how is eristic also one of the forms of the art of acquisition? The Stranger replies with this alternative: eristic either wastes or makes money. The former is mere chatter and pure logical games (Plato's statement is apparently aimed at the "dialecticians"), whereas the latter is "its contrary . . . , which makes money from debates between individuals" (*Soph.* 225e). Who are the practitioners of this art? The answer can be guessed: "How could anyone go wrong in saying that the amazing sophist we've been after has turned up once again for the fourth time?" (225e). Once again the figure of the sophist is identified because of his pursuit of financial profit.

A final definition of the Sophist as discriminator is proposed, but this time the question of money is not mentioned, since doing so would only repeat the previous discussion: discrimination is merely an aspect of eristic. It is therefore perfectly clear that the dominant feature in all of these portrayals of the figure of the Sophist is the pursuit of financial gain. Or rather, Plato makes sure that the definition of this professional is never separated from the question of money. This insistence is so striking that it is surprising that it has been so little noticed by commentators. It also appears in its full extent—as if there could have been any doubt about it—in the final assessment, after the analysis of the Sophist as discriminator:

> But let's stop first and catch our breath, so to speak. And while we're resting let's ask ourselves, "Now, how many different appearances has the sophist presented to us?" I think we first discovered him as a hired hunter of rich young men. . . . Second, as a wholesaler [*emporos*] of learning about the soul [*peri ta tēs psukhēs mathēmata*]. . . . Third, didn't he appear as a retailer of the same things? . . . And fourth as a seller of his own learning [*autopōlēs*]? . . . The fifth way, he was an athlete in verbal combat [*agōnistikē*], distinguished by his expertise in debating. . . . The sixth appearance was disputed, but we still made a concession to him and took it that he cleanses the soul of beliefs that interfere with earning. (*Soph.* 231d–e)

This reminder appears to be purely didactic and meant to sum up the results of the dialogue and assess what has been discovered. But its purpose is more complex and subtle: to bring at the same time to the fore the character's totally scattered and slippery nature, his lack of coherence, and his dangerous versatility. This makes it possible to situate his mercenary attitude at a deeper level. The Stranger proposes to focus on a feature that appears to be dominant in the Sophist, at least with regard to the art of discourse: his being a disputer (*antilogikon*).[23] Might this constitute the uniting feature of this character? The Stranger does not let go of his prey. This dominant feature immediately turns into a source of disunity. Moreover, this makes it possible to reinforce the identification of the Sophist with the merchant, since the Sophist prides himself on his ability to dispute *on any topic* ("Doesn't it seem like a capacity that's sufficient for carrying on disputes about absolutely everything?" [*Soph.* 232e]). If he claims to be able to dispute anything, it is first because he boasts of being able to teach his students anything, from athletic techniques to mathematics, from eloquence to philosophical questions ("It doesn't seem to leave much of anything out, anyway" [*Soph.* 232e]). He can teach anything because he claims to *know everything* (this is precisely Hippias's boast).[24] The Stranger then asks Theaetetus if it is really possible for a man to know everything. Isn't this a uniquely divine power? And if so, where do the Sophists get it from? How do they make their listeners believe in it? "It's obvious that they didn't make correct objections against anyone, or didn't appear so to young people. Or if they did appear to make correct objections, but their disputing didn't make them look any wiser for it, then—just as you say—people would hardly be willing to pay them money to become their students" (*Soph.* 233b).

Then, the Stranger ironically remarks, the amounts invested by students in the acquisition of the Sophists' knowledge ought to prove that this knowledge is serious (which is also what Hippias has claimed and what Socrates has ironically pointed out to young Hippocrates). But the Stranger intends to pursue this argument further. As a game he asks Theaetetus to suppose that someone claimed he could "make and do everything," the sea and the earth and heaven and gods; this claim would be no different from the Sophist's claim to know everything. At the same time, the amount due would turn out to be as ridiculous as the claim, "If someone says he knows everything and would teach it to someone else cheaply and quickly, shouldn't we think it's a game [*paidian*]?" (*Soph.* 234a). The adverb *paidian* conveys not merely the idea of a game but of a children's game and an activity lacking any accountability. This reversal recalls Isocrates' argument implying that if the power and knowledge promised by the Sophists were so immense, then, far from being too expensive (for which they were frequently criticized), their lessons were ridiculously cheap. This is already a way of saying that something incommensurable was at stake. But the main point has to do with a different implication: the Sophist is presented as a multiple, slippery, and incoherent being—a specialist in everything, which is to say in nothing; he is no more knowledgeable about the reality of things than he is their author. This remark must remind us of the argument we noted in *Protagoras*: it is because the Sophist is not the author of what he presents that he can *only* be its *seller*, since acquiring goods in order to sell them is precisely the specialty of merchants. This parallel between Sophist and trader is developed in an entirely rigorous manner in *Protagoras*: rather than experts who know their wares, both are middlemen who merely know how to demand a price for them. The merchant has no knowledge of what he sells because he has not made it; besides, the goods he offers are so diverse that there is no way he could know them. Everything dissolves for him in the indifference of their mercenary value. The same is true of the Sophist, which is precisely why he is a "merchant of knowledge." In short, there is a true continuity between Sophist and merchant.

For Plato only the craftsman knows his product, in much the same way as the divine creator knows the universe. This is why human knowledge of the world is limited. In order to know, the philosopher has to gain divine benevolence through a particular approach; this *periagōgē* has nothing to do with the capture after the fact operated by the "merchant of knowledge," who exchanges a product for an equivalent—money—which teaches nothing about the thing itself. By applying his claim to the totality of things, the Sophist places himself in the position of the divine creator; yet *Phedon* has already taught us that the Sophist cannot even remain at the level of a village *demiourgos*, that of an ordinary craftsman—a cobbler—or a more highly valued one—a physician, sculptor, or architect—because he does not create or transform anything. He only handles words, as a mere game (*paidein*), without caring about truth, which is to say about being, the weight of which is born by words. In the same manner as the merchant of goods, the merchant of words can only sell what he has not made and does not know about. The sophist's wage has become the proof of his incompetence. QED.

Socrates, the Master without Self-Interest

Nor do I discuss for a fee and not otherwise. To rich and poor alike I offer myself as a questioner, and if anyone wishes to answer, he may then hear what I have to say.

SOCRATES, IN PLATO, *Apology*

He prided himself on his plain living, and never asked a fee from anyone.

DIOGENES LAERTIUS, *Lives of Eminent Philosophers*

When Aristophanes also attacks the Sophists and ridicules their methods and discourse in *The Clouds*, he mentions at the outset the question of their remuneration as the condition of access to their knowledge: "In there dwell men who by speaking persuade one that the heaven is a stove and that it is around us, and that we are charcoals" (*Clouds* 5.95–97). This is what old Strepsiades explains to his son Phidippides, whose debts he hopes to have a court cancel thanks to one of those brilliant pleas only the Sophists can make. "They're boasters, pale, shoeless men that you're speaking of, and among them that miserably unhappy Socrates and

Chaerephon" (5.102–4). Here is Socrates himself mistaken for a Sophist! Worse, in this comedy he alone represents them, to utmost ridicule; Strepsiades, on meeting him, lets him know straight out, "Whatever fee you set, I swear by the gods to pay you!"

Socrates was still alive when he was subjected to this defamatory accusation, and he had to endure it for a long time (*The Clouds* premiered at the Dionysias of 423 BCE, almost twenty-five years before Socrates' conviction in 399). For Plato there was a pressing need to cleanse the memory of his old master from this slanderous accusation of venality. Socrates could in no way be likened to the Sophists, precisely and foremost because his teaching was offered free of charge and without self-interest. This was the keystone of the admirable uniqueness of his relationship with his students. Not only did he charge no fees, but, moreover, he believed in the virtue of poverty; and he extolled indifference to wealth—to those who would listen to him. This attitude toward money was one of the first criteria that made it possible to distinguish a philosopher "friend of wisdom" from a Sophist "merchant of knowledge." According to Plato this is a crucial trait. What is at stake is not only a moral or social distinction but more profoundly something that is related to the very nature of philosophy: what genre of discourse does it belong to in relation to other forms of knowledge? In other words, who can receive it, under what conditions? Is it even a form of knowledge? Can it be reduced to things that are learned and thought to be known? Can it be acquired like an ordinary good? This amounts to asking, Can anybody gain access to philosophical knowledge simply by paying for it? We will later see how these questions are dealt with in *Theaetetus*.

In the *Apology* Plato attributes to his master comments specifically meant as retorts to the mockery of Aristophanes (his name is explicitly mentioned),[25] who had presented Socrates as an eccentric "physician" lost in "the clouds" and as a Sophist obsessed with payment. To counter this caricature, Plato's *Apology* shows us Socrates by calling up the testimony of those who knew him:

The fact is that there is nothing in these accusations. And if you have heard from anyone that I undertake to educate men, and make money doing it, that is false too. Once again, I think it would be a fine thing to be able to educate men, as Gorgias of Leontini does, or Prodicus of Ceos, or Hippias of Elis. For each of them, Gentlemen, can enter any given city and convince the youth—who might freely associate [*sunousia*] with any of their fellow citizens they please—to drop those associations and associate rather with them, to pay money for it, and give thanks [*kharin proseidenai*] in the bargain. (*Apo.* 19d–e)[26]

The false modesty of this passage is apparent enough, as is the cleverness of its mocking praise. What it underscores is, once again, a feature of the Sophists that relates them to merchants: they are itinerant philosophers, and, above all, they only provide knowledge for a fee. From the first pages of the *Apology*, the question of payment has a propaedeutic significance—as it does in many other situations. It is a kind of precondition to any judgment of anyone who means to teach. But instead of directly condemning the Sophists, Socrates presents himself as someone who has little ability to emulate them. By underscoring their talent in a hyperbolic manner ("I think it would be a fine thing"), he immediately introduces them through features that can only appear suspicious to Athenians and are exactly those of merchants and stateless, self-interested peddlers. The unaccountability that characterizes noncitizens is often emphasized by Plato (as in *Timaeus*).[27] Socrates, in contrast, prides himself on having never left Athens, except to go to war. This sedentary character of his life as a citizen has even remained one of the major features of his legend.[28]

But according to Socrates the most surprising aspect of the behavior of these mercenaries of knowledge is this: it is not enough for them to be paid by their students; in addition, they expect from them gratitude (*kharis*), which is normally due only to those who give liberally. This can be translated in the following terms: these masters impose a mercenary relationship, yet, unlike merchants, they want to retain the advantage of a gift-giving relationship, which is to say a relationship of reciprocity through the obligation to give generously. In other words, they expect to win on all counts, in the new game and in the old; they intend to be modern providers of set-price intellectual services while remaining mentors revered for their wisdom and honored by gifts in exchange for their lessons, in accordance with tradition. They want to take advantage of their competence as merchants and gain recognition for their prestige as wise men.[29]

At this point Socrates could conclude that he has said enough to demonstrate that he has nothing in common with such masters. But the accusation of venality is so serious for him that he still feels compelled to argue over this subject. There is yet another argument that makes any remuneration appear illegitimate to him: the complete disproportion that exists between the amount paid and the very content taught. A later passage of the work provides an example of this disproportion. Once again Socrates presents his argument in an understated tone:

As a matter of fact, there is a man here right now, a Parian, and a wise one, who, as I learn, has just come to town. For I happened to meet a person who has spent more money on Sophists than everyone else put together: Callias, son of Hipponicus. So I asked him—for he has two sons—"Callias," I said, "if your two sons were colts or calves, we could get an overseer for them and hire him, and his business would be to make them excellent in their appropriate virtue. He would be either a horse-trainer or a farmer. But as it is, since the two of them are men, whom do you intend to get as an overseer? Who has the knowledge of that virtue which belongs to a man and a citizen? Since you have sons, I'm sure you have considered this. Is there such a person," I said, "or not?"

"To be sure," he said.

"Who is he?" I said. "Where is he from, and how much does he charge to teach?"

"Evenus, Socrates," he said. "A Parian. Five minae."

And I counted Evenus fortunate indeed, if he really possesses that art and teaches it so modestly. For my own part, at any rate, I would be puffed up with vanity if I had any such knowledge. But I do not, Gentlemen. (*Apo.* 20a–c)

Several messages are intertwined in this text. Education presupposes a competence at least equal to that required for animal training. But precisely regarding the most important thing, which is not merely the acquisition of knowledge but also education in moral and political virtues, mere know-how can in no way be considered enough. What is needed are men who can teach through the example of their own virtue. What is Callias's reply? He found someone who provides this to his sons for a fee of five minae (which is to say a fairly modest amount).[30] This is entirely ironic. We return to Isocrates' argument denouncing those who not only sell their knowledge but also assign a ridiculous price to what remains priceless (this is also the Stranger's argument in the *Sophist* [234a–35b]).

Teaching for any wage—this is what I don't know how to do, Socrates states. This confession of incompetence turns into the proclamation of a high standard: my teaching has never been for sale; I don't know about it because it cannot be done and, above all, because it must not be done—it could only be a travesty of education. In short, they indict me by equating me with the Sophists, whereas I have never thought virtue could be exchanged for money, and I have remained poor; I have always given my lessons free of charge. Some call on obscure "merchants of knowledge" who claim to sell what cannot be bought. Let us at least admire the modest price they assign to what is priceless!

This argument is important in Plato's presentation of Socrates; it is also found in *Euthyphro*. This dialogue, which is part of the same set of writings as the *Apology*, presents Socrates on his way to court, where he will be informed of the accusation made against him by Meletos. There he meets one of his "disciples," Euthyphro. After a discussion of the way their respective discourses were received by Athenians, Socrates tells him, "Perhaps they think you give yourself sparingly, that you are unwilling to teach your wisdom. But I fear my own generosity [*philanthrōpia*] is such that they think I am willing to pour myself out in speech to any man—not only without pay, but glad to pay myself if only someone will listen" (*Euth.* 3d). Socrates recognizes that the first thing that makes him seem suspicious to some of his fellow citizens is the fact that he gives his knowledge *free of charge* and therefore free of reservations, be they rhetorical (unlike Euthyphro himself, who protects himself through comments that entertain his audience) or financial, since unlike the Sophists (who are his real targets, although they are not explicitly mentioned) he does not request any remuneration for his lessons. Moreover, he would be prepared to pay anyone who requested them, were it a precondition for listening to him. By carrying the joke this far, Socrates radicalizes the very idea of an essential relationship between knowledge and generous gift-giving. Better to reduplicate the gift than to exclude anyone from his right to receive what must be given to all and from which all should profit.[31] Plato's constant insistence on showing Socrates moving about in public places and talking to whoever will listen to him clearly indicates that the Socratic word, which is the very model of the philosophical word, has to be offered to anyone who wishes for it; and it has to be heard by all, even if it is not or cannot be understood by all (as explained in *Theaetetus*). This public character of Socrates' teaching should, however, be qualified. It does not mean that Socrates intends to speak in the political arena. In this same passage from the *Apology* (32a–e), he explicitly states that he has precisely chosen not to do so in order to allow everyone the freedom to enter into dialogue with him or just listen to him free of charge—so much so that he maintains that the idea that he has had disciples is based on a misunderstanding. Socrates' dialogues involve neither the initiatory relationship of the old *sophoi* nor the mercenary one of the present Sophists: "I have never been teacher to anyone. If, in speaking and tending to my own affairs, I found anyone, young or old, who wished to hear me, I never begrudged him; nor do I discuss for a fee and not otherwise. To rich and poor alike I offer myself, and if anyone wishes to answer, he may then hear what I have to say" (*Apo.* 33a–b).

This is a surprising statement, which not only shows the extent of Socrates' generosity but also reveals the secret of his freedom in relation to his audience. He not only will speak with whoever wishes to listen—and therefore anywhere and free of charge—but he is also able to identify and choose those who are capable of progressing in wisdom along with him. According to some commentators this is the main reason for Socrates' refusal to be paid for his teaching.[32] In fact, this second requirement is the flip side of the first. On the one hand Socrates publicly addresses everyone without any distinction, but on the other he only develops or allows attachments with those who have the capacity to let progress toward truth operate within them.

Theaetetus (149a–51e) shows us the extreme extent of Socrates' demands in this respect. His art, he says, is akin to that of the midwife (*maia*)—which was the occupation of his own mother; it consists of delivering souls of what they carried within; however, Socrates adds, not all are "pregnant" with wisdom or ready for it. This is why he prefers to send them to Prodicus, for instance, who is, according to him, an excellent Sophist. As for himself, he merely stimulates the wisdom that the young man carries within himself; he does not generate it: "God compels me to attend the travail of others, but has forbidden me to procreate. So that I am not in any sense a wise man; I cannot claim as the child of my own soul any discovery worth the name of wisdom. . . . But it is I, with God's help, who deliver them of this offspring" (*Thea.* 150c–d). He adds, "But at times, Theaetetus, I come across people who do not seem to me somehow to be pregnant. Then I realize that they have no need of me" (151b). This is the foundation of Socrates' relationship with his "students." He keeps or dismisses them based on the extent of a "choice" that is already inside them, which is to say whether or not an aptitude exists and fertilization has occurred within them. It is therefore important for Socrates to reserve the choice of accepting or refusing a candidate. This could indeed be one of the major reasons for his refusal to be paid, since anyone who expected remuneration would be bound to keep his student, regardless of the latter's qualities and shortcomings. The first reason for this is a legal one: Greek law only recognized contracts with immediate payment,[33] which is to say, paid at the time of agreement; in the case of lessons this meant payment in advance. In exceptional cases Sophists—such as Protagoras—who were highly confident in their prestige, left it to students to evaluate their teaching and, therefore, to pay for it later.[34]

But a more crucial consideration was also involved: whoever paid became the employer; whoever received remuneration became the employee indebted to the other. This was an odd relationship that reversed the hierarchy between master and student. In accordance with the *sunousia* tradition,[35] this relationship entailed a preeminence of the older person over the younger, the more experienced over the more ignorant, and the more worthy of public respect over the less worthy. In short, any relationship of education preserved the statutory difference between initiator and initiate. This relationship—along with the authority that could not be separated from it—was undermined if the student, by paying, became the one who made the decisions and, above all, the one on whom the master was materially dependent. Another form of the bond between partners was thus ruined, that of gift-giving and the movement of gratitude. The Sophists were quite aware of this and probably sensed the risk involved. To avoid eliminating the old hierarchy, they had devised an effective tactic: making access to their lessons difficult—even by paying for them—and making it a rare privilege, therefore gaining in addition to their wages the recognition that was reserved for those who gave generously. Socrates gains this recognition without seeking it; it is given as part of the personal and "erotic" relationship that bonds him with those who follow him. For Socrates, what makes this *sunousia* possible does not come from him but from the "god" whose voice inhabits him ("The god and me . . ." [*Thea.* 150d]; ". . . I help the God" [*Apo.* 23b–c]). This is the essential reason for which his teaching is not for sale. This is why he never demands a wage and why his task to teach in the public space, a task that he insists has been given to him by the "god," is marked by the immediate hallmarks of authenticity—his refusal of money and his poverty.

But perhaps there is an even more essential reason for the fact that Socrates will not be paid: he maintains that he does not possess any knowledge. How, then, can an absence of competence be remunerated? How can we understand this surprising modesty? Is it merely a rhetorical game? At the beginning of the *Apology*, in which this statement is found, Socrates explains that he is not, unlike his accusers, there before his judges to develop ornate sentences: "Gentlemen, you will hear the whole truth [*pasan tēn alētheian*]. . . . You will hear me speak naturally in the words which happen to occur to me. For I believe what I say to be just, and let no one expect otherwise" (*Apo.* 17b–c). He adds that he does not possess the art of the Sophists, who know everything about everything and get paid to teach. If such is their knowledge, then it is a divine one (and their wages are quite modest). My own knowledge, he states, is more limited and merely human (*anthrōpinē sophia*);[36] in short, it does not amount to much. But what is this "not much"? Everybody in Athens knows that Cherephon, an old friend of Socrates, consulted the oracle in Delphi to find out whether there was a wiser man—*sophos*[37]—than Socrates; the Pythia answered that no one was wiser. This oracle, Socrates says, puzzles him. He therefore resolves to question recognized experts: a politician, poets, and craftsmen. All of them claim general knowledge based on their limited fields; this knowledge soon proves illusory. While deeming himself downright ignorant, Socrates ironically discovers himself to be the wiser. Thus, he remarks about the politician: "Probably neither of us knows anything worthwhile; but [he] thinks he does and does not, and I do not and do not think I do. So it seems at any rate that I am wiser in this one small respect: I do not think I know what I do not" (*Apo.* 21d). This is the meaning of the oracle: Socrates is the wiser inasmuch as he knows the extent of his ignorance. At the same time, "the god" points his task out to him: to question anyone who wishes to hear him so that each can recognize how little he knows. "Due to this pursuit, I have no leisure worth mentioning either for the affairs of the city or for my own estate; I dwell in utter poverty because of my service to the God" (*Apo.* 23b–c). Wisdom constantly arising from lack of knowledge cannot be sold like the lessons of a specialist; it cannot even be taught. Socrates only has questions to share, in utter and naked openness.

In fact, the figure of Socrates is situated at the intersection of two different traditions of thought; the first, a very ancient one, is that of the *sophoi*, or masters of truth. Endowed with initiatory and ascetic wisdom that conferred an exceptional status on him, the wise man was a kind of shaman whom others consulted and whose mysterious knowledge was beyond the reach of ordinary mortals (these traits are still to be found in such figures as Empedocles, Epimenides, Pythagoras, and Parmenides).[38] Confronting this tradition, in which knowledge remained secret and was held by an elite, a different idea formed—that of knowledge established through open debate, the public exchange of information, and verification through mutual agreement. It was this "democratic" conception that the Sophists claimed and pushed in the direction of maximum malleability. Hence their opportunism: the knowledge that mattered was useful, effective, and available—and therefore negotiable. If excellence—*aretē*—could be taught, then it could also be exchanged for money.

To say that Socrates stood at the intersection of the ancient tradition and the new conception of knowledge is to recognize the position that Plato intended to defend. It consisted of preserving the *sophoi*'s requirement of spiritual experience and mental and ascetic mastery within philosophy. It also meant fully accepting the order of the city, public space, and (beyond mystagogic conceptions) the affirmation of mathematical knowledge, with its rational status. It was the same Socrates, led by his "god" and capable of entering a state of quasi-superhuman meditation, who also recognized no other place for scholarly debate than the street and public space, spoke everyman's language, and drew on ordinary common sense. The figure of the philosopher with which Plato presented us in Socrates was neither Empedocles—the inspired wise man—nor Protagoras—the realistic Sophist—but one that followed the inner guidance of his "god" while being also capable of drawing on all the resources of logical argument to deal with all kinds of questions such as virtue, the beautiful, language, being and nonbeing, righteousness, and love. Leaving everything to inspiration alone would have amounted to renouncing knowledge (the ultimate example of this being the poet, such as Ion, who declaimed without "knowing" what he was saying); conversely, renouncing inner experience would have amounted to reducing knowledge to technical mastery and an expertise that could be taught by professionals claiming negotiable services.

Between the ancient *sophos* and the new Sophist, the inspired thinker and the efficient expert, what gods communicated and what humans mastered, there was the uncertain and problematic place of the philosopher, lover of wisdom, or, in less grandiose terms, he-who-loves-knowledge. Whereas the seer—like the poet—was nothing more than the instrument of the god and spoke without "knowing," the Sophist was nothing more than an expert (or a self-proclaimed one) who did not know his wares anymore than a merchant knew his own. Philosophy, on the other hand, was guaranteed neither by divine authority as its source nor by the mastery of a technical field for its effects. It was questioning, yearning for knowledge, or what preserves within knowledge the fragile movement of desire. In this it was the uniquely human form of knowledge—*anthrōpinē sophia*—that questioned the aim, relevance, and limit of all knowledge. This yearning was not *pleonexia*—greedy and boundless—but the call and promise of a transfigured *erōs*. According to the *Symposium* it was this movement and oblatory opening that gave rise to all the beauty of the philosophical approach, this nonknowledge of knowledge that introduced the suspension of a surprise into all knowledge. This was not merely meant to refine the definition (which it actually did) but to recognize the—inconclusive—condition of aporia of any question. This was at the same time a gesture related to initiatory wisdom and knowledge aiming at a rigorous definition while confessing that the question would have to be forever taken up again. It was this questioning—this condition of uncertainty or anxiety—that was necessarily denied by mercenary teaching, since anyone who exercised it, such as the Sophist, had to reduce everything to useful knowledge and definite certainties. This was why for Plato philosophical yearning could never, at any price, enter into self-interested negotiation.

2

The Figure of the Merchant
in Western Tradition

All that relates to retail trade, and merchandise . . . is denounced and numbered among dishonorable things.

PLATO, *Laws*

The most foolish and the meanest profession of all is that of merchants, since they seek the meanest goal by the meanest methods. . . . They tell all manners of lies, perjure themselves, steal, cheat, deceive.

ERASMUS, *The Praise of Folly*

Commerce is, in its very essence, satanic. . . . For the merchant, even honesty is a financial speculation. Commerce is satanic, because it is the basest and vilest form of egoism.

BAUDELAIRE, *My Heart Laid Bare*

My opposition to the commercial spirit as the spirit of our time.

NIETZSCHE, posthumous fragments

Once Plato has used the word *merchant* in reference to the Sophists, it seems that everything has been said and that from then on there can be no doubt in the minds of his readers about the seriousness of the suspicion he has expressed. This suspicion seems to have persisted across the centuries. It is among the clichés of our intellectual history. We discover something odd in this if we try to compare it to the examples of other professions. It is well known, for instance, that the occupation of craftsman

underwent devaluation between archaic and classical Greece.[1] Respect for
know-how unquestionably remained prevalent, however (which is clear in
Plato's writings).[2] War and the calamities it brought were often denounced,
yet the dominant discourse about warriors was always that of courage or
tactical genius. In the same way, the coarseness of peasants was often ridi-
culed by intellectual culture, yet praise for the work of the land was a constant in philosophical and theological tradition.

The merchant, in contrast, remained a negative figure. He was sometimes an object of envy, but one could not admit to admiring him. When
a particular merchant appeared endowed with virtue, this seemed to be in
spite of his occupation. In addition, the craftsman who sold his own products in his shop and the trader who organized import-export transactions
were not placed in the same category. The first lived by exchanging what
he produced while the other speculated on the needs of his community—
or so it was thought. In many cases the merchant was likened to a usurer,
which constituted the most serious accusation. In fact, the merchant was
by definition one who dealt with money; money was his tool par excellence, his strength, guarantor, power, and kingdom. Money was, finally,
his ultimate territory because once wares had passed through his hands,
what remained in the end was money alone as the tangible result of all his
transactions—it was the invariant in all variations. This was precisely why
the merchant drew suspicion: he lived by manipulating this volatile and
ambiguous element—an element that was simultaneously necessary and
perverse, powerful and seductive: it could change, render equivalent, or
substitute for anything. This activity bordered on magic; thus, merchants
bore resemblance to figures of evil and sometimes even epitomized those
figures.

If, therefore, Plato and his disciples viewed the Sophist as discredited,
this was primarily inasmuch as he was a merchant and more precisely a
"merchant of knowledge," that is to say a seller of what is priceless—hence
the seriousness of the matter. It remains to determine what it was that
characterized the merchant for the mere mention of his name to be enough
to signify his infamy. This question is worth clarifying within the context
of Greece as a whole, since Plato's criticism does refer to a view that was
self-evident to the audience or readers of his dialogues. But before doing
so, it would be useful to recall what is said about this by Plato himself and
other philosophers who follow after him, particularly Aristotle.

Plato and Aristotle:
Keeping the Merchants Out of the City

The work in which Plato most explicitly expresses his ideas on this topic is probably the *Laws*, in particular book II (esp. 918–20). From the outset it is significant that this passage would immediately follow the considerations dedicated to fraud and its suppression: "After the practices of adulteration naturally follow the practices of retail trade" (918a). Given this brutal preamble associating fraud and trade as targets of the same reprobation, and also considering other equally severe writings regarding the activity of merchants, it can seem surprising to hear the Athenian in the dialogue (who is obviously Plato's spokesman) continue with these words of praise: "Retail trade in a city [*kapēleia kata polin*] is not by nature [*kata phusin*] intended to do any harm, but quite the contrary; for is not he a benefactor who reduces the inequalities and incommensurabilities of goods to equality and common measure? And this is what the power [*dunamis*] of money [*nomisma*] accomplishes, and the merchant may be said to be appointed for this purpose" (918b).

By its positive character and the form of its argument, this writing seems to foreshadow Aristotle's better-known *Nicomachean Ethics* 5.8 (although the Greek terms used to designate equality and proportion are not exactly the same in both writings). Plato's praise (entirely provisional, as the rest of the dialogue will show) can be understood based on at least two considerations. First, he is only referring to "retail trade in a city" [*kapēleia kata polin*], a form of trade markedly different from another one that Plato—unlike Aristotle and Cicero—always viewed negatively: wholesale trade [*emporia/emporikē*], which was mainly practiced in ports [*emporia*] and warehouses and mostly by foreigners.[3] In this passage trade is valued as a normal and useful activity of exchange consistent with the distribution of tasks and compensating for unequal access to resources (but not for the difference between various resources, of course). Second, he is only referring to trade "by nature" [*kata phusin*], meaning trade that does not involve any profit goal but is merely an extension of the exchange of products between producers. Plato's formulation foreshadows the theory that will be developed by Aristotle, namely that trade meets a necessity arising from the differentiation between occupations and therefore from the interdependence thus generated between humans. Plato is the first author to view this as the reason for men's existence in society (see the *Republic*). Although on the one hand he almost violently challenges the intrusion of intermediaries—these *kapēloi* whom he views as mere parasites and thieves—into exchange, on the other hand, and like Aristotle later, he has no objections to the necessity of reciprocal exchanges between producers.

This is, indeed, his idea of legitimate trade (we will later see that his conception belongs to a much older tradition spread throughout the Indo-European world). Merchant exchange is necessary. Trade should be a good thing. The difficulty comes from the fact that trade as it is actually practiced does not conform to its "nature." As a consequence Plato's praise immediately concludes with a severe restriction that cancels its benefit: "The hireling and the tavern-keeper, and many other occupations, some of them more or less seemly—all alike have this object; they seek to satisfy our needs [*khreiai*] and equalize our possessions. Let us then endeavour to see what has brought retail trade into ill-odour, and wherein lies the dishonour and unseemliness of it, in order that if not entirely, we may yet partially, cure the evil by legislation" (*Laws* 918c). The praise of trade has proved to be short-lived; negative criticism will be much more detailed.

To better show the extent of this deplorable state of things with respect to trade (and probably also to make his statement more striking through the use of a paradox), the Athenian suggests a radical solution that would make it possible for these occupations to escape discredit: an official prescription would reserve these trades for the most honest people. "Then we should know how agreeable and pleasant all these things are; and if all such occupations were managed on incorrupt principles, they would be honoured as we honour a mother or a nurse" (*Laws* 918c). What is at stake is nothing less than the reintegration of trade into the *oikos* and the restoration of its lost nature. For Plato the good trader would, in fact, be a kind of volunteer civil servant who would ensure the necessary circulation of products in exchange for a deduction required to support himself.

No sooner is this hypothesis put forward, however, than it is rejected, being immediately presented as "what I trust may never be and will not be" and even "a ridiculous thing" (*Laws* 918e), considered at best as an experiment. It is as if the practice of trade included in and of itself something so incurably contaminated that no possibility of salvation could seriously be entertained, and exposing honest people to it would be too risky: their virtue could not resist such profound evil. At this point Plato's argument may seem caught in a sort of contradiction, since on the one hand it reminds us that "by nature" trade is a good thing (its function being to bring equality and proportion to the circulation of goods) yet on the other it also appears that by its very nature trade perverts those who dedicate themselves to it.

We now face a paradoxical situation analogous to that found in other cases, such as those involving writing, *tekhnē*, power, or desire, in which the thing itself could be said to be good but could at any time be diverted from its end, bringing about dangerous effects. It is as if a second nature were added to the first, requiring the emergence of corrective means such as laws, institutions, disciplines, and methods of education. The solution to the problem is always prophylactic; it requires correcting, containing, and curing. Disease is not evidence against the affected organ but calls for a remedy, a *pharmakon*. What is the physician's responsibility within the realm of the body becomes the legislator's within the realm of the city. It is thus for him to devise a response to the detrimental effects of trade: "And the legislator ought always to be devising a remedy for evils of this nature. . . . In the first place, they must have as few retail traders as possible; and in the second place, they must assign the occupation to that class of men whose corruption will be the least injury to the state; and in the third place, they must devise some way whereby the followers of these occupations themselves will not readily fall into habits of unbridled shamelessness and meanness" (*Laws* 919b–c).

Thus, after considering reserving this occupation for people with guaranteed honesty and then deciding that this would expose them to too high a risk, the Athenian reaches this conclusion: this activity should be left to noncitizens who would be carefully kept away from the healthy population. The approach chosen is clearly preventive: restricting, isolating, and monitoring. Merchant activity is dealt with less like a treatable disease than like an epidemic that requires quarantine. This policy of exclusion has already been hinted at in an earlier passage in which three characters discuss the location of a future city. The Athenian insists that the city should be as distant as possible from the sea, which is to say from the ports where traders are dominant: "The sea is pleasant enough as a daily companion, but has indeed also a bitter and brackish quality; filling the streets with merchants and shopkeepers, and begetting in the souls of men uncertain and unfaithful ways—making the state unfriendly and unfaithful both to her own citizens and also to other nations" (*Laws* 705a).[4] In the

Greek worldview friendship [*philia*] between citizens was the very essence of the social bond.

At this point Plato proclaims the predominance of the political over the economic; it is not necessary for a city to be very prosperous, he says, since this would expose it to the temptation to sell its products abroad, introducing the poison of cash into the city as an immediate consequence. "Had there been abundance, there might have been a great return of gold and silver; which, as we may safely affirm, has the most fatal results on a State whose aim is the attainment of just and noble sentiments" (*Laws* 705b). It is clear that the language used is consistently that of disease and contagion. It is as if trade and money were, for Plato, among the worst conceivable threats against the city. He regards this risk as so great that he comes to deny all strategic value to the port (a place "infected" with merchants). His first argument is that naval warfare is not traditionally Hellenic; it has only been adopted by imitation in order to respond in kind to an enemy: "No city ought to be easily able to imitate its enemies in what is mischievous [*mimēseis ponēras mimeisthai*]" (*Laws* 705c–d), the Athenian states.[5]

His second argument is that, in case of attack by land, the existence of a port would make it easier to flee and would lead to cowardice. Plato thus declares that the victory at Salamis, won over a land army that had withdrawn aboard its ships, does not deserve admiration. Finally, naval warfare turns the foot soldier—the soldier par excellence, the hoplite meant for land warfare—into a sailor, which he is not, and makes him dependent on those—rowers and pilots—who operate ships and are not soldiers but noncitizens, either slaves or foreigners (let us remember that no military navy as such existed at the time);[6] naval warfare, therefore, subjected the outcome of battle to the participation of "all sorts of rather inferior persons" (707b). This criticism cannot be separated from a whole tradition of suspicion toward the marine world.[7] It is clear that for Plato the predominance of merchants in ports is enough to contaminate and devalue the entire space of the sea. His intransigence is total on this point.

These views can be contrasted with Aristotle's more nuanced ones. In the *Politics* (7.6) Aristotle also wonders what the ideal location of a city should be. Unlike Plato he argues for the strategic usefulness of ports: "The defenders of a country, if they are to maintain themselves against an enemy, should be easily relieved both by land and by sea" (*Pol.* 1327a20).

Aristotle recognizes the legitimacy of a defensive strategy in which Plato sees only the temptation for flight. But, more important, Aristotle accepts as normal the economic usefulness of the port: "So too people must import the things which they do not themselves produce, and export those of which they have a surplus" (*Pol.* 1327a25). In his *Rhetoric* (1.4.1360a12–17) he once again emphasizes the necessity of these commercial exchanges between cities. It is therefore clear that he has given up Plato's autarkical view. Here, as in the entire argument developed in book 1 of *Politics*, Aristotle moves away from his master's utopian views and intends to keep to attainable goals.

Aristotle, however, does not go so far as to claim that this trading activity should be left uncontrolled. He immediately reminds his readers that the purpose of a city cannot be to enrich itself. Its end is ethical rather than chrematistic, which means that it cannot be about profit. Therefore the city has to remain vigilant not to let its port develop in an excessive manner. The proper responsibility of the city is the life of its citizens, which is to say action [*praxis*] directed toward what is good rather than toward the enjoyment of goods: "Some throw their state open as a market for all comers for the sake of the revenue they bring; but a state in which such aggrandisement is illegitimate ought not to possess that kind of trading-center at all" (*Pol.* 1327a25–30).

Aristotle thus preserves the port; but does he spare the merchants? Actually, not much more than Plato does. Having merchants settle in the places of exchange does not seem anymore advisable to him than it does to Plato for two reasons: "To open one's state to foreigners, brought up in a different legal code, is detrimental to government by good laws; and so is the large population, which, they say, results from the using of the sea to dispatch and receive large numbers of traders" (*Pol.* 1327a15). What solution does he propose? One not very different from the solution advocated by the author of *Laws*: to use "appropriate laws" to keep merchants away from the space of the citizens—in short, to confine them by decree to specific neighborhoods and to prohibit them from spreading into the ordinary space of the city. Aristotle's answer—as it always is in matters of action—is, therefore, an attempt to find a middle ground; trade is needed, exchanges are necessary, but they should not become autonomous ends. Trade is a *tekhnē* and as such should remain subject to action toward an end. The trader is not the object of total indictment on Aristotle's part. He is merely the agent of a dangerous *tekhnē*. In fact, Aristotle sets up a clear distinction between two types of trade, which are not so much wholesale and retail as they are exchange and resale. Exchange trade is the type of exchange that takes place between members of the city whose activities are complementary (such as the mason and the cobbler discussed in *Nicomachean Ethics*). In their case there is indeed production of a work—*ergon*; this is also true of the work of the import merchant, who runs the risks involved in sea or land transportation. The reseller (*kapēlos*), however, produces nothing; he takes a profit by short-circuiting the networks of reciprocity.

This suspicion pervades the entire classical world, often verging on contempt, as it does in Plato. It is found unchanged in Cicero. In a passage of his *On Duties*, after mentioning the low status of fiscal agents of ports and usurers, Cicero points out wage-earning occupations (hard labor, as opposed to the work of properly trained craftsmen) to the suspicion of citizens, adding, "We must also consider mean those who buy from merchants in order to re-sell immediately, for they would make no profit without much outright lying."[8] Cicero thus brings us back to Aristotle's reseller. The retailer appears to be a speculator. He embodies the very type of activity that a free man should avoid.

The Merchant in the Indo-European System: Trifunctionality and Its Outcast

Mercator Deo placere non potest.

CLASSICAL AND MEDIEVAL SAYING[9]

We may now better understand what the accusation of venality brought by Greek thinkers against the Sophists might have meant. In the view of their contemporaries, to call them "merchants of words," as Plato does, amounted to blanketing them in a widespread suspicion regarding the very occupation of merchant. This was a serious insult in and of itself, involving an accumulation of mistrust that seems to have very ancient roots.

In fact, even though this denunciation was particularly scathing on the part of philosophers (for reasons having to do with the very nature of the statement of truth), it was not unique to them. This attitude already had a long history that was shared by most civilizations. Max Weber notes, "In early religions, even those which otherwise placed a high positive value on the possession of wealth, purely commercial enterprises were practically always the objects of adverse judgment. Nor is this attitude confined to predominantly agrarian economies under the influence of warrior nobilities. This criticism is usually found when commercial transactions are already relatively advanced, and indeed it arose in conscious protest against them."[10]

This was indeed the case in archaic Greece, according to Moses Finley: "Behind the market lies the profit motive, and if there was one thing that was taboo in Homeric exchanges it was gain in the exchange. . . . The ethics of the world of *Odysseus* prohibited the practice of trade as a vocation. The test of what was and what was not acceptable did not lie in the act of trading, but in the status of the trader and in his approach to the transaction."[11] One of the expressions of this attitude is the very negative description given of those who at the time were already the merchants par excellence: the Phoenicians. "They were the 'greedy sailors' who sailed across the seas to traffic in everything, always prepared to rape and abduct, as soon as there was something to gain."[12] In the classical tradition true wealth had to originate from cultivating the land. Finley notes, "The Greek landowners . . . demeaned trade."[13] Louis Gernet, another leading scholar of ancient Greece, made a similar assessment: "Commercial life itself is not indispensable, nor is it valued for itself. Commerce in general is viewed with a jaundiced eye; and even in the form of emporia, it reveals a deviant character. [This is because] it is often the domain of foreigners and metics."[14]

This assessment must be qualified. Wholesale trade was frowned on when performed by noncitizens; but it could be viewed as respectable when organized by the city itself seeking to secure the staples necessary to its survival. We have seen this with Aristotle; it is also found in Cicero, who writes,

Other arts require either greater good sense or else procure substantial benefit, for example medicine, architecture or teaching things that are honourable. They are honourable for those who belong to the class that they befit. Trade, if it is on a small scale, should be considered demeaning. If, however, men trade on a large and expansive scale, importing many things from all over, and distributing them to many people without misrepresentation, that is not entirely to be criticized. Indeed, if ever such men are satiated, or rather satisfied, with what they have gained, and just as they have often left the high seas for the harbour, now leave the harbour itself for land in the country. . . . However, there is no kind of gainful employment that is better, more fruitful, more pleasant and more worthy of a free man than agriculture.[15]

This text suggests that wholesale trade was practiced by citizens (since it was possible for them to purchase land) and that this practice was not viewed as shocking. But this was because in this case import-export activity took on the value of a service provided to the city and gave access to a supplement of noble wealth: wealth associated with land ownership.[16] It is therefore important to nuance the assessment. In truth (and despite Plato's anathema) everything depended on the status and purpose of the trader. If he was a noncitizen and his goal was profit as such, then the occupation of merchant was invariably regarded as disgraceful, whether it involved wholesale or retail trade.

This assessment does not, however, explain the origin of the exclusion. Nothing would be more inaccurate than to view it as unique to classical Greece and Rome. In fact it characterized the whole of the Indo-European world (which does not mean that it would not also be found outside of this sphere of civilization). Commercial activity is absent from the trifunctional Indo-European system as it has been illuminated by Georges Dumézil's widely recognized work. The place of the merchant had not been provided for because this occupation had only appeared late in history. It had broken away from the traditional exchange and subverted its forms. How so?

The best answer is probably provided by Emile Benveniste in the semantic investigation he conducts on the notion of trade in his *Indo-European Language and Society*. It is significant that Benveniste titles chapter 11 of his first volume "An Occupation without a Name: Commerce" and that the introductory summary concludes with "the difficulty of defining by specific terms an activity without a tradition in the Indo-European world."[17] Although there was an abundance of terms designating buying and selling, this did not in and of itself specify a commercial activity. Why not? Because the farmer who exchanged his products or even sold his surplus in a marketplace did not practice trade and was not a merchant, even if he exchanged it for cash. He was a producer making sure to meet his own needs: he bought and sold for himself.

By what features can a specifically commercial activity be recognized? It consists in *buying and selling for others*. "In the Indo-European world commerce is the task of a man, an agent. It constitutes a special calling. To sell one's surplus, to buy for one's own sustenance is one thing: to buy, to sell, for others, another. The merchant, the trader is an inter-mediary in the circulation of produce and of wealth."[18] If we ask who took on this activity, Benveniste remarks, we find out that it was never citizens but foreigners, often emancipated slaves—in short, people with a low social status.

Merchant activity was therefore eccentric in two respects: first, as a mediation added to ordinary and direct exchanges; second, as an activ-ity performed by people from outside the community. This eccentricity is marked in Indo-European languages by the absence of terms capable of designating trade and traders, except negatively: "There are only isolated words, peculiar to certain languages, of unclear formation, which have passed from one people to another. . . . Often we do not even know if the notion of commerce existed."[19] Thus, the Latin notion of *neg-otium* was modeled on the Greek notion of *a-skholia*—literally, privation of *skholē* or *otium* (leisure, rest, or immobility), thereby indicating occupation, worry, difficulty, and business. The entire vocabulary of trade is a product of this negative qualification. The trader is the busy man par excellence, he who does not have or does not grant himself the leisure that alone connotes high birth, noble activity, or genuine citizenship. This is still apparent in the forms found in more recent languages: *business* is the activity of he who is *busy*; the French *affaire* (business) is a substantivized form of *à-faire* (to be done).

From these observations Benveniste draws the conclusion that within the Indo-European tradition "commercial affairs as such have no special term; they cannot be positively defined. . . . The reason is that—or at least in the beginning—it was an occupation which did not correspond to any of the hallowed, traditional activities. Commercial activities are placed outside all occupations, all practices, all techniques."[20] Hence also the dif-ficulty in determining the place of the merchant in the caste system of traditional India; although there are regional variations in this system de-pending on the ethnic groups involved, in every case the merchant is situ-ated in the lower castes. His precise status is difficult to define, however, according to Louis Dumont, who notes that on "the question of the mer-chant, the normative texts are silent."[21]

These various analyses are very useful in that they restore the tem-poral depth of a phenomenon that runs across our entire history up until recent times and can be summed up as the insurmountable illegitimacy of the figure of the merchant. Even the Middle Ages, which, beginning with the "urban renaissance" of the twelfth century, provided merchants with social status and place in the forms of guilds (similar to those of craftsmen) and integrated them into communal life (so much so that they often dominated it),[22] did not modify the old Indo-European trifunctional system. The social order remained organized around the distribution of status among clergy, nobility, and peasants—*oratores*, *bellatores*, and *laboratores* (according to Georges Duby's analyses).[23] *Mercatores* remained offscreen. Little by little they would come to be included along with craftsmen in the very broad category of the Third Estate, which lumped together everyone who did not belong to the clergy or aristocracy. Their status did not achieve true recognition until relatively recently. One historian of capitalism has noted, "The organization of medieval society had not provided for the merchant. . . . A man devoted to the accumulation of gain undertook an illegitimate activity."[24]

In truth the situation of the merchant in the Middle Ages was more complex, as Jacques Le Goff shows in several books that revitalized the debate.[25] He first encourages us to avoid confusing the clerics' discourse on trade and merchants with concrete practices and attitudes, which were markedly different; he then identifies two different periods in clerical speech, before and after the advent of scholastic philosophy. Even though in the prescholastic period the clerics' discourse was traditionally negative regarding merchants[26] (let us leave aside the case of usurers, which, strictly speaking, remained separate—we will return to this later), it remains true that merchants were not so badly regarded in everyday life; this was all the more so because many shopkeepers (bakers, cobblers, tailors, joiners, drapers, blacksmiths, and goldsmiths) were merely craftsmen who sold their own products—as they had been in Plato's time. No one would have thought of contesting the usefulness of their presence in the life of the community. Merchants involved in larger-scale business (importers or exporters of raw materials, grain, textiles, wine, and oil) could also elicit respect for their services or for the accuracy and honesty of their transactions. This recalls the classical and biblical image of good wealth as a mark of divine favor. Therefore the activity of the good merchant could not be confused with that of people who practiced trades deemed illicit: jugglers, prostitutes, and, of course, usurers. Nonetheless, the good merchant was still a merchant; even if his wealth was an object of admiration or envy, his status remained lower than that of noblemen or clerics.[27]

These principles themselves underwent a remarkable evolution, however, starting with the renewal of cities from the eleventh century onward and above all with the development of scholastic thought from the thirteenth century onward. Two elements allowed for a gradual and relative legitimization of trade and therefore of the figure of the merchant. First, justification through common utility: the merchant gave access to products that were deemed indispensable but would have remained difficult to obtain or even out of reach without him. This was already true of local trade (since it was not easy to frequently move from city to city) and even more so of long-distance trade. As Le Goff reminds us, this utility constituted the central argument of a new moral theology, as in Thomas of Chobham's early-thirteenth-century *Manual of Confession*: "There would be great poverty in many countries if merchants did not bring what abounds in one place to another where these same things are lacking. They can therefore receive the price of their labor."[28] The same consideration is found in Thomas Aquinas: "If a person engages in trade with an eye to the public utility and wants things necessary to existence not to lack in the country, then money, rather than being the end of the activity, is only claimed as remuneration for labor."[29] In both of these writings the idea of public utility is immediately associated with that of *labor*; this was the second important element in the legitimization of trade. Considering trade as labor was in fact a very new attitude. But it must immediately be added that the concept of labor itself had just emerged in a remarkable way. The history of these developments is not a simple one. In classical Greek, for instance, the concept is difficult to circumscribe since cultivation of the land was a condition rather than a form of labor.[30] The craftsman's activity was one of transformation: *poiēsis*. He produced something (and in this respect his occupation was certainly less noble than those of the political speaker, scholar, or warrior; he therefore lacked leisure (*skholē*). In fact, only the slave labored. Only in Latin would this toil be translated as "labor" [*tri-palium*; French *travail*].

The idea of labor as something requiring both effort and *competence* emerged late in the classical world. It was established in Christian thought as the association of effort, merit, and way of life founded by Paul's proclamation, "The laborer deserves to be paid" (1 Tim. 5:18). It is unquestionable that from the thirteenth century onward the Church showed a notable concern *not* to ignore occupational activities at a time when craft-based production, the development of business, the increase in the number of schools, and the creation of universities were consigning warrior values to the background. "No trade was an obstacle to salvation, each had its Christian vocation, and all belonged to the *familia Christi*, which bound all good workers together."[31] A transition thus occurred from an essentially rural, illiterate, and warrior culture to an urban, craft-based, and scholarly one. At least this was the culture known to the clerics, who were also the ones who developed and disseminated a new discourse of legitimization regarding labor. Yet the merchant was not accepted without reservations. Why not?

Shady Figures: Intermediaries and Substitutes

According to Benveniste what characterizes the merchant is the fact that he buys and sells *for others* (whereas whoever buys and sells for himself remains outside the scope of this definition). The merchant was defined by his status as an intermediary and substitute. He was first of all an intermediary because he made a relationship possible between people who did not meet. This entailed several types of situations. First, producer and consumer did not necessarily belong to the same community; they could be located at great distances from one another. The merchant bought somewhere and sold elsewhere. Second, within a single community, specialization into different occupations could make it necessary to leave to the merchant the responsibility for setting the different goods into circulation. Finally, the merchant made it possible to play with time; the producer could sell one day and buy something else later, in some cases much later. In every case the merchant took on the function of a regulator who stocked various products and made them available on demand. He ensured this regulation relative to space (since producers and consumers far apart from one other could "communicate" through him) and time (since buying and selling could be deferred through him). The emergence of the figure of the merchant therefore presupposed leaving behind a purely local or domestic economy, which is to say an economy based on internal or neighborhood circulation.

By his very existence the merchant was not only the operator but in some way the witness to and emblem of a transformation of the old society. This was precisely what elicited the philosopher's suspicion. The merchant was suspected of being the cause of what he embodied: a break in the "natural" relationship with useful goods and their mode of circulation, which conferred a social dimension on the gesture of exchanging goods between partners. In other words, to exchange or trade these goods was also in some way to recognize one another. When there is a direct transaction between members of one or several societies, this recognition, which is at the heart of gift-exchange relationships and distinguishes them from other types of relationship, gets projected onto relationships of commercial exchange. Even if this exchange involves self-interest, it remains marked by an atmosphere of reciprocity.[32] In contrast, commercial relationships conducted through professionals tend to become abstract. Max Weber is well aware of this characteristic, which explains the resistance of traditional religions to this form of exchange:

It is above all the impersonal and economically rationalized (but for this very reason ethically irrational) character of purely commercial relationships that evokes the suspicion, never clearly expressed but all the more strongly felt, of ethical religions. For every purely personal relationship of man to man, of whatever sort and even including complete enslavement, may be subject to ethical requirements and ethically regulated. This is true because the structures of these relationships depend upon the individual wills of the participants, leaving room in such relationships for manifestations of the virtue of charity. But this is not the situation in the realm of economically rationalized relationships, where personal control is exercised in inverse ratio to the degree of rational differentiation of the economic structure.[33]

From the Christian point of view this depersonalization of the commercial relationship was precisely what constituted the obstacle to the practice of charity, which is to say a generous relationship of gift-giving between believers. It was also the obstacle that the Protestant ethic succeeded in overcoming (as we will see later), whereas the Catholic ethic refused to do so.[34]

But this is not all: the presence of an intermediary in the exchange of goods forced intellectuals to conceive of this exchange at a specific level and to rigorously distinguish it from the relationships constituting citizenship. Conversely, the political order or order of citizenship itself would have to be constantly distinguished from the commercial relationship, which was no longer a direct relationship between members of the community but a relationship mediated by a character (and through this person an entire profession and set of social activities) who was not, as such, directly involved in the life of the city and, even worse, had no interest in such involvement. At least this was the prevailing perception in the classical world; it was precisely what would change during the Middle Ages.

What made the situation even more tense is that the specialization of occupations made the function of merchant indispensable. Plato and Aristotle are well aware of this. This is why they do not call for eliminating trade and merchants but for keeping them away from the city. The measures advocated by Plato are quite severe, whereas those proposed by Aristotle are more tolerant. Merchants were to be kept away from the city in physical terms (outside its walls) but, above all, in terms of their status: because they were often foreigners, they could not take part in public life,[35] with some exceptions. Trade would therefore be a separate sphere of activity, forced to develop on its own according to its own criteria and traditions. Yet the merchant remained at the heart of the city. He was the indispensable mediator in the exchange of goods, since he had become the obligatory intermediary between producers and consumers; he was the operator of a system of relationships that shaped an essential aspect of common life. He was the one who ensured the fluidity of the exchanges between compartmentalized occupations, and he made products circulate within the community; he also brought the community into contact with the outside world through imported merchandise. He was, therefore, in the key position through which flows of goods, currencies, and information moved. He captured them, lived on them like a parasite, and made a fortune by placing himself at the strategic locus of their intersection. This is why Hermes, god of messengers and crossroads, was also the god of merchants—and of thieves.[36]

As a consequence this circulation gave rise to a bond different in nature from the political bond; the merchant was its operator and money its language. This is what made the merchant appear to the philosopher as a rival figure and money as a language competing with the language of truth. This is, at least, what a reading of Plato brings to light. This ancient conflict traverses our entire history.

The exchange of useful goods (not to be confused with gift-exchange relationships),[37] which could be an integral part of collective life in traditional societies where there is little differentiation between tasks, came to be separated from that life in complex societies where occupations are specialized. If public life—the political sphere—alone remained legitimate as the life of the community, by the same token the activity of exchanging goods was relegated to the private sphere, the realm of business to which citizens dedicated themselves because they had to ensure their material lives, survival, or comfort. The autonomy of the political relative to the economic sphere, which was so strongly affirmed by classical thought, found its counterpart in the gradual emergence of the autonomy of the economic relative to the political sphere. This autonomy, however, was without true legitimacy; it was the autonomy of what is excluded or relegated to subordinate status. For centuries Western society developed on the basis of this customary separation, or discrepancy, until it became obvious that economic activity had invaded the sphere of public life itself.[38] We may therefore wonder if the autonomy of the economic sphere was not primarily the consequence of its exclusion, associated with the delegitimization of the figure of the merchant. From this point of view commercial and financial activity was viewed by our tradition of thought in the same way as technical activity. At first they were viewed as distortions coming from the outside, as nonindigenous elements that disturbed an order that was understood to be natural. The disorder brought by trade, however, appeared much more serious than that generated by technical advances. On the horizon of technique, artifice—*mēkhanē* (traps, ruse, and illusion)—arose. But what arose on the horizon of commercial exchange and profit was greed, venality, deceit, and betrayal. The skill or even genius involved in the arts of fabrication was still acknowledged, whereas in most cases the art of making a profit was only viewed as an abuse of good faith and cause for the eventual ruin of the community.

.   .   .

What we have observed in the case of Greece regarding the indictment of trade and merchants was therefore not due to the specific hostility of philosophers. Neither Plato nor Aristotle invented this attitude, even if they eloquently exemplify it. It came before them from a long history that can be traced through the entire Indo-European world and until recently ran through the entire becoming of the West. In truth it was not even unique to the Indo-European world. Comparable attitudes can be observed in spheres of civilization as diverse as China, Japan, the Pacific Islands, Africa, and the Americas. Wherever merchants appeared, they aroused the same type of mistrust regarding the legitimacy of their profit and generated reactions of exclusion commensurate with this suspicion.

The philosophers of classical Greece did no more than reflect in their judgments and integrate into their thought convictions that were widespread in society; perhaps when we read their writings, we could effect the necessary subtraction and disregard such outdated "prejudices," and the debate would be over. But it is not; and perhaps it cannot be, for reasons that are not only historical. On this question, as early as its Platonic moment and in relation to sophistry, philosophy engaged with its raison d'être in a way that was not accidental but essential; it formulated its own requirement and, more important, drew a dividing line that situated the defining conditions for truth in a foundational manner. We are the heirs of this question, perhaps forever. This is why we will have to return to it. What we must note at this point is that the negative figure of the merchant faded in bourgeois Europe, particularly with the Reformation (which merely sped up this evolution but did not cause it).

Even though glory and prestige, or true social distinction, remained aristocratic privileges (until the late nineteenth century), it is clear that merchants and bankers had already been able to gain access to full social and political legitimacy in medieval Venice and the Florence of the Medici. Yet profit remained an object of suspicion. The merchant could become a philosopher or claim to be one (whether in a comical mode like Molière's Monsieur Jourdain or in a snobbish-serious mode like Musil's Arnheim); but money as such would never be the friend of truth. We must continue our inquiry.

3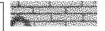

The Scandal of Profit and the
Prohibition on Appropriating Time

Sophistry is a kind of art of money-making.

ARISTOTLE, *Sophistical Refutations*

The usurer sells nothing to the borrower that belongs to him. He sells only time, which belongs to God.

THOMAS DE CHOBAM

The blame Plato heaps on the Sophists regarding the use they make of their income never implies any suspicion of dishonesty. Such a claim against their activity just does not enter into consideration. No stories suggesting so exist. Besides, not all Sophists were rich; those who probably were had a duty to participate in the sumptuary expenses of their city, as all wealthy citizens did (except when they avoided returning there, as was the case with Protagoras). Labeling them "merchants," however, was a hostile gesture on Plato's part. It was certain to bring contempt to their profession and even to them as persons. The reason for this contempt was not only that merchants took on the function of intermediaries or the fact that they were often non-Greek foreigners (or at least metics); more important, they performed the function of bankers and pawnbrokers. In short, they constituted the largest portion of the execrated profession of "usurer." Plato alludes to this in *Laws* (918d). But he does not use this as an argument against the Sophists. He does not extend the merchant metaphor, which he has used against the Sophists, to encompass the degree of infamy represented by usury. A philosophical argument supporting this metaphor would require a theory of money (as instrument of exchange and means of profit) that would make it possible to establish an analogy between money and the effects of discourse. Such a theory is not found in Plato.

Aristotle, in contrast, develops a very elaborate reflection on the nature and function of currency, the necessity of commercial exchange, and the rational yet also abusive character of profit. According to Aristotle profit involves a perversion of economic art and a transgression of the natural balance, which he calls "chrematistics," or moneymaking. It is therefore particularly interesting that he proposes—in passing—the following definition in *Sophistical Refutations*: "sophistry is a kind of art of money-making" (*Soph. Ref.* 11.171b). The term *chrematistics*, which first designated in a very general way and without derogatory connotations the art of increasing income and making money (*khrēmata*: "wealth"; "money"), ends up designating a technique whose aim is excessive profit.

It is clear that chrematistic practice has to do with a particular use of time. In lending with interest, profit is determined based on the length of time for which an amount is made available to a third party. According to Aristotle the profit thus made is associated with a disturbed form of desire—*pleonexia*, or insatiable desire. This type of analysis can help us understand what made profit suspicious within philosophical history or more generally in the system of representation that has dominated our tradition (and perhaps every tradition). What is the target of this criticism of profit? The power of money, when taken over by desire, to release itself from the reciprocity of community relationships, to turn into unreasonable accumulation, and to move past the boundaries of the city. This was a new threat at the time and perhaps the one Aristotle had in mind when he described sophistry as "a kind of art of money-making." As the art of making profit, chrematistics was undoubtedly a rational procedure, even if this profit was unjustified. Nonetheless, chrematistics was an illusion because this *tekhnē* developed in a kind of vacuum, which is to say it had no basis in production and made no reference to property. In the same way, sophistry consisted in brilliant discourse about nothing. It was a coherent and spellbinding discourse, but its object was nonexistent. This vacuum and lack of reality was made apparent in the Sophists' modus operandi by the flashy character and overly facile success of their arguments. This attracted youth and brought with it a promise of novelty. But what their teaching brought about was above all a taste for a type of discourse loaded with illusion and seduction. This is why the analogy with the merchant involved another dimension: like the merchant the Sophists came from outside, brought with them the ways of other places, filled the city with foreign air, and dared to express ideas that undermined familiar beliefs. For Plato the merchant remained an intruder and represented danger, even the risk of infection. This was the threat that money itself symbolized. As a power of seduction and disorder, of pleasure and abuse, it threatened the city, not in the spectacular and tragic way of an outburst of violence but in the insidious and hypocritical manner of a parasite and—in the words of the Athenian of *Laws*—in the way a disease emerges and spreads.

Chrematistics: Aristotle and the Critique of Profit

Unlike Plato, Aristotle understands and defines the social, economic, and political function of currency. More pragmatic than Plato, he eschews the discourse of indictment. His positions are important not only within the framework of classical thought but also because of their impact on the centuries following, especially on medieval thought (scholasticism in particular), which devotes much concern to the question of usury. This impact endured until the emergence of the first expressions of modern economic thought during the eighteenth century. Even then, it does not seem that Aristotle's heritage had been repudiated. Marx still hailed him as the first and greatest thinker on currency until the advent of political economy.

Aristotle does not display Plato's caustic wit on questions associated with money. His thought in this field is more moderate but also more precise and complete. For this very reason the questions he deals with remained relevant to us over a longer period; in many respects they are still relevant. Aristotle first sets out to define the fundamental economic functions of currency (as a measure of goods, instrument of exchange, and means of reserve), but he always relates these functions to the (distributive and corrective) forms of justice within the city.

Aristotle, however, shares with Plato a suspicion regarding the power of monetary signs to become autonomous and to start operating on their own without a referent, generating wealth that is unrelated to any product

and thus unnatural. In fact, Aristotle seems to be torn between two profoundly divergent approaches. One consists in reflecting on the technical
and political functions of currency (that is, providing equivalence between
heterogeneous goods and regulating civic relationships), and the other consists in attempting to understand how some kind of abuse has slipped into
this functioning and caused a diversion of the monetary instrument toward
operations involving purely speculative profit. In essence, these two different approaches can be respectively identified with his *Nicomachean Ethics*
and *Politics*.

It remains for us to wonder whether the questions Aristotle raises
have the same stakes as the ones Plato raises. The latter's writings on money
are mostly those against the Sophists and those aimed at defining the rules
of the future city (such as *Laws*). Aristotle does not seem very interested in
this aspect of the Sophists' behavior. The intellectual climate has changed.
Yet his writings on the question of money have had a more decisive influence than Plato's. In fact, what Aristotle raises is the whole question of the
legitimacy of lending with interest; for centuries to come it would remain
a disturbing issue for philosophers and, later, theologians. Plato questions
the venality of the Sophists and the indignity of mercenary knowledge.
Aristotle focuses on a more general issue concerning commercial exchange
as considered from the point of view of justice; more specifically, he questions the idea that the medium of exchange—*nomisma* or cash—can be
treated as a good and produced as a result of pure speculation.

But what is currency? We must briefly mention the way Aristotle discusses it in his *Nicomachean Ethics*, where he defines it as "the substitute
of need" (5.8.29).[1] This statement seems enigmatic and remains incomprehensible to us if we interpret it as designating the need of the thing as
such and view it from a modern perspective as the consumer's need. This is
not what Aristotle means: he refers to the need we have for each other because of the differentiation between occupations and their resulting complementarity. This is the question: how can an exchange be made possible
between agents who produce goods as different as shoes and houses or
medical care and grain (these are the examples given by Aristotle)? A standard is required that would allow an exact translation of these goods into
each other while at the same time establishing just relationships between
cobbler and architect or physician and farmer. This operator of proportion
between goods and hence between agents is currency. In this it is a "sub-

stitute of [the] need" we have for each other (a substitute—*hupallagma*—being at the same time a guarantor and an equivalent). Its function is not only crucial from a technical standpoint; it is also an instrument of justice and a kind of judge in and of itself.

Yet Aristotle cannot—and indeed does not—ignore the fact that money involves an activity that is not restricted to the operation of proportional equalization. But it is on the basis of this operation (the only truly legitimate one) that he attempts to describe and understand a particular movement of money that seems to be cut off from its reason for being in the exchanges of the city.

The Natural Order (I): City and Subsistence

The pages dedicated to currency in *Politics* (1.8–9) show a very different perspective than the one developed in *Nicomachean Ethics*. They do not directly discuss justice as virtue (even though this requirement has not disappeared); from the outset the framework is that of the city. It is while analyzing the constituent elements of the city that Aristotle encounters the question of the economy. For him, as for the entire Greco-Roman classical tradition, the activity of production and exchange belongs to the private realm (*oikos*), which at the time meant primarily the realm of subsistence. This realm is the responsibility of the *paterfamilias*, a perhaps improper Latin term since the Greek term was *oikonomos* or head of the household; it should be noted that the term *oikia*—family—pertains more to the place— *oikos*—of residence and existence of the group than to kinship; the latter concerns the broader level of the *genos* or clan. *Oikia* means the household, with its head, his spouse, and their children, but it also includes grandparents, slaves, and even domestic animals and real estate. It is within this space that *oikonomia* develops.

It is obvious to Aristotle that the activity of subsistence is crucial to the very existence of the city. Moreover, the interdependence between individuals in this respect constitutes the first bond of the community—from an empirical standpoint, though not from the standpoint of the city's reason for being.[2] It is important that this activity be understood and founded by philosophy, which amounts to demonstrating that *oikonomia* is necessary but only finds its meaning within the *politeia*. The city is the end (*telos*) of the family, and it logically encompasses it. "The state is by nature clearly prior to the family and to the individual, since the whole is of necessity prior to the part" (*Pol.* 1.2.1253a).

The acquisition of goods in order to feed and preserve one's *oikia* and make life pleasant is necessary; it is also entirely honorable. At this point Aristotle encounters a disturbing question: how is it that this activity turns into something that loses its respectability and even becomes reprehensible? In short, how can the process of acquiring good and honest wealth be diverted, turned into a process of unbridled accumulation of money, and become a danger for the city? Either there are two different possibilities from the outset, or the second originates from the first and is supported by an element that comes to be perverted because of a tendency found in human nature. Aristotle chooses the second hypothesis, which is what makes his analyses so complex. We will therefore have to understand what he means by legitimate wealth and grasp how in his view goods can normally be accumulated; it will then become possible to situate the pivotal point, the moment of deviance from which a perverted use of money could emerge and develop.

The Natural Order (II):
Wealth and Property

What is good wealth? Aristotle's answer is wealth that stems from the activity of the *oikonomos*—the master of the household—and proceeds from a property. Aristotle defines property (*ktēsis*) as the whole of the means of action for living. More specifically, "[A] possession [*ktēma*] is an instrument [*organon*] for maintaining life" (*Pol.* 1.1253b30). But this life as subsistence is life within the circle of the *oikos*. Property has to be defined by its position within the space under the responsibility of the *oikonomos*, who is expected to direct the instrument (*organon*) toward its goal (*telos*), to unify and direct mere living (*zēn*) toward the good life (*eu zēn*). It is therefore necessary for property to be and remain included within action and not become an autonomous instrument. Property is to the master of the household as the body is to the soul, which directs the body and assigns it its ends. Production is necessary but has to be integrated into action, which is to say into what constitutes life's goal. For Aristotle, to say that wealth is an instrument useful to life is to clearly indicate its limits, since "life is action [*praxis*] and not production [*poiēsis*]" (*Pol.* 1254a7–8). Therefore wealth still has to be considered from the standpoint of this finality. Any attitude that would turn this instrument into an end in itself would necessarily be unnatural.

The difference Aristotle establishes between action and production is known well enough to make discussion unnecessary, with the exception of its central point. An action is an activity (*ergon*) that has its own end within itself.[3] This means that it is a condition (*hexis*) or quality of the agent, such as kindness or honesty, but also thought, vision, or sensitivity. These conditions are virtually constant (even if sometimes interrupted) and therefore permanent. They are not defined by discrete results (thus vision or thought cannot be defined by separate acts). This is why Aristotle says that action has its end within itself: it cannot be divided between an act and a product different from it. In this it remains immaterial; its time is the living present, but it is a continuous present.[4] Action is not a particular way of living but the very movement of living. Because it is not defined by an external result, action finds its closure within itself. In this it is a virtue—*aretē*—or excellence. In Aristotelian terms, to have its end within itself primarily involves a physical rather than moral connotation. It designates an interruption of movement but one that is a closure (whether this applies to kindness, vision, or thought). Hence this definition: "That [movement] in which the end is present is an action."[5]

What is production, then? It is an activity of transformation that does not have its own end within itself, which means that its result is external to it and is a work (such as a house, clothes, or a song, but also the mending, study, or transportation of an object). The distinctive feature of each of these activities is their having an end point. But this end point, or result, is not assigned by the activity itself. By what is it assigned, then? By action, to which all production is subject. It is action that determines when the house should be considered finished or the medical treatment completed. The product is defined by its use relative to action. Every production implies a technique used and artifacts generated. As means—*organa*—these artifacts do not have an end in and of themselves and cannot claim autonomous existence (thus, according to Aristotle, even the slave, as a living instrument, finds his end in his master). *Organa* takes on meaning only by being integrated into action, which is the realm of ends. As a consequence what is produced by subsistence activity (such as food, objects, or financial wealth) at some point has to lose the status of being a mere product of technique in order to become a means for action. The head of the household—*oikonomos*—directs domestic production based not on technical considerations (this is the task of stewards or other executants) but on considerations pertaining to action (*praxis*), which is to say the realm of ends. The virtue of the head of the household is not instrumental skillfulness but virtue in action, which defines caution (*phronēsis*).[6] Thanks to this action conducted toward its ends, mere products become goods (*agatha*). This applies to property itself and to what constitutes its excellence: wealth (we can thus already sense the problem raised by chrematistics as the process by which the production of money becomes autonomous).

In the Greek tradition (but this was a common feature to most civilizations) wealth, as abundance and fulfillment, was perceived as a mark or even proof of divine favor. If the rich man behaved in a just, generous, loyal, and humble manner, then his wealth would be viewed as a reward for his virtue. "The judgment of antiquity about wealth was fundamentally unequivocal and uncomplicated. Wealth was necessary and it was good; it was an absolute requisite for the good life."[7] Aristotle's thought clearly remains in line with this tradition, but he intends to confer true rigor on it by presenting wealth as endowing property with excellence (*aretē*).[8] This means that acquisition attains a state of fulfillment that can be understood as follows: a family—a household or *oikos*—has to own as much as necessary to its subsistence, thus ensuring the *autarkeia* that is the condition of its freedom or *eleutheria*. The excellence of wealth therefore lies in its finite and limited character and in the fact that it precisely fulfills the needs and well-being of the *oikos*. True wealth was, then, associated with property, which is to say ownership of either a domain that one cultivated (or had others cultivate) or any other set of instruments—*organa*—of production, such as the workshop of a craftsman. It could consist of land, herds, crops, or various tools but also slaves—living tools—and, finally, money. Money was therefore a normal part of the *organa*, yet it did not have the same status as the other means since it was not a good as such but its expression (in the same way as the word is not the thing); it only translated wealth. Aristotle explains that any good can have two uses: it can be either consumed or exchanged. Money only has one: to be exchanged. This is a crucial difference, as we will see. As an organon, money has only one function: to be used in the transactions necessary for subsistence—necessary because of the diversity and complementarity of occupations; it expresses the need humans have for each other. For Aristotle wealth conforms to nature because it is in human nature to ensure one's subsistence and possess the means—property—required to this end. Any form of wealth that becomes detached from this property loses its natural character. This is precisely what happens to one of the elements of wealth—money—when it loses its specific status as organon and is dealt with as if it were a good like the others.

Nature Diverted (I):
Chrematistics and the Two Uses

Chrematistics is rigorously defined as the art of acquiring goods (*khrēmata*). Aristotle uses the notion either in a general and positive sense as the natural art of acquisition—which constitutes good chrematistics—or in the more specific and reprehensible sense of making profits through lending with interest or speculative resale. This derogatory sense is the one that tradition has preserved with regard to *chrematistics*. To some extent this constitutes a diversion of the term, inasmuch as the negative sense has ended up prevailing. Aristotle himself often participates in this reduction; we can therefore accept it. After defining the normal art of acquisition, he presents its denatured version: "There is another variety of the art of acquisition which is commonly and rightly called an art of wealth-getting [*chrematistike*], and has in fact suggested that riches and property have no limit. Being nearly connected with the preceding, it is often identified with it. But though they are not very different, neither are they the same. The kind already described is given by nature, the other is gained by experience and art" (*Pol.* 1.1257a).

If we consider chrematistics as the art of acquiring currency for itself, then it was the opposite of domestic economy, since it produced wealth that was not associated with property, which is to say with the action of an *oikonomos* or head of the household. When separated from property—it remains to be seen how this happened—wealth became denatured. As a technique it certainly had rationality; it could therefore be analyzed, but then it was nothing more than a *tekhnē* that released itself and asserted itself for its own sake. It was no longer associated with an action that assigned it its end and limit; it was in a certain way an absurd form of wealth.

Whoever used currency in this manner either removed himself from the political order (since *praxis* alone could be integrated into public activity, *praxis* alone belonged to the realm of ends) or had never belonged to it in the first place. This was the case of the merchant. He was merely an intermediary who passed on a product from one customer to another through the means of money (as we saw in Chapter 2). The merchant, however, was master of an art, that of making profits with this instrument. There was therefore a merchant *poiēsis*. Chrematistics was unquestionably a production but one that was not integrated into any action. It was an unthinkable kind of wealth because no finality could be assigned to it; or rather it was false wealth, usurping the place of property. In its form it remained a technique and therefore a rational activity, but it could not produce a good (*agathon*), which only action could. It could only produce certain goods (*khrēmata*) that were not directed toward an end. Merchant chrematistics was therefore an exchange without virtue, incapable of attaining the excellence (*aretē*) that should be the aim of every activity. Chrematistics was an art of acquisition that developed outside of what its natural locus should have been: the *oikos*. It thus cut itself off from its own nature.

It even left the circle of reciprocity, that of useful exchange associated with complementary tasks; at the same time it left the space of the city. The first area where the absence of reciprocity that characterized chrematistics activity clearly emerged was ordinary trade, in which merchants determined their own profits in transactions. The targets Aristotle aims at are not the agents who sell their own products in order to acquire those they lack (as craftsmen do in the local marketplace—since in this case there is reciprocity) but professional merchants, *kapēloi*, who practice retail trade. "Natural riches and the natural art of wealth getting . . . are part of the management of the household; whereas retail trade is the art of producing wealth, not in every way, but by exchange" (*Pol.* 1257b21–22). This is why Finley rightly proposes to translate *kapēlikē* as "trade for the sake of gain."[9] The merchant is indeed someone who buys what he has not produced and is not going to consume. He is a pure intermediary. The entire question is to determine whether he provides a service to his fellow citizens or inserts himself as a parasite between producers and consumers.

According to Aristotle the most egregious expression of this unnatural form of exchange is lending with interest, in which profit no longer even originates from a difference between a supply of currency and goods for sale but is directly and exclusively generated by the increase in value of an amount of currency through the duration of the loan. "And this term interest [*tokos*], which means the birth of money from money, is applied to the breeding of money because the offspring resembles the parent. That is why of all modes of getting wealth this is the most unnatural" (*Pol.* 1258b5). *Tokos*, which means both "child" or "offspring" and "interest," comes from a root that means "generating." The Greek language even had the phrase *tokoi tokōn* or "interest of interest," compound interest, offspring of the offspring. Modern readers might find this surprising: to say that money *generates* money could be a way of placing it under the auspices of nature. Indeed, what could be more natural than generating offspring? But for Aristotle (and his contemporaries) the ability to generate is precisely in the essence of *living beings* and not products. A product that generates something usurps a function that it does not and cannot have. This is unnatural generation. When one reads this statement, it is impossible not to recall the famous echo that Benjamin Franklin gives it while reversing its intention: "Remember that Money is of a prolific generating Nature. Money can beget Money, and its Offspring can beget more, and so on."[10] What constitutes a kind of monstrosity for Aristotle is celebrated by Franklin as the height of thrift and Puritan morality. In the meantime a shift has occurred from one universe to another. This will be the object of a different discussion (in Part Three of this book).

Marx understands the contrast between natural and speculative exchanges as stated in the *Politics* and recognizes Aristotle's merit as the first to establish a distinction between the *use value* and the *exchange value* of any good. But is this actually the difference that Aristotle establishes? Let us examine this text once again:

Of everything we possess there are two uses: both belong to the thing as such, but not in the same manner, for one is the proper, and the other the improper use of it. For example, a shoe is used for wear, and is used for exchange; both are uses of the shoe. He who gives a shoe in exchange for money or food to him who wants one, does indeed use the shoe as a shoe, but this is not its proper use, for a shoe is not made to be an object of barter. The same may be said of all possessions. (*Pol.* 1257a10–15)

The nature of the thing is defined by its utility, which is to say the purpose for which it has been produced. For Aristotle the primacy of use in situating the status of a thing is very precisely tied to its final end (*telos*).

It is clear, however, that although functional use prevails, this in no way eliminates the other use that has been clearly stated at the beginning of the paragraph: "Of everything we possess there are *two uses*: both *belong to the thing as such*, but not in the same manner" (my emphasis). Aristotle does not say that each object has two types of value—use and exchange—but indeed that it has *two uses*. In one case use—*khrēsis*—is part of the finality of the object—what it is used for; in the other case use also fulfills a finality but a different one. Which one? That of exchange, but to the extent that exchange itself is necessary (according to the explanation given in *Nicomachean Ethics*) because of the need we have of each other owing to the division and complementarity of tasks. Exchange is therefore part of the use of the thing; granted, this is a secondary use in terms of its function, but it is one that also belongs to "the thing itself": obtaining from others what one does not produce. In Aristotle's view (notwithstanding what has been said about it) what brings about the risk of denaturalization is not the exchange; on the contrary, exchange "arises at first from what is natural, from the circumstance that some have too little, others too much" (*Pol.* 1257a15–16). Thus, on the one hand, to discuss use *value* and exchange *value* in relation to Aristotle, as Marx and a few other commentators do,[11] borders on misinterpretation since exchange as one use of a thing remains a natural activity. On the other hand, it is important to understand that the second of these two uses (consuming and exchanging) can be subdivided into a good use and a bad use. In this case only the analogy with Marx's term, *exchange value*, becomes relevant. But it can be no more than an analogy since Marx's term presupposes the existence of a general marketplace of goods and values, which is not the case in the context of Aristotle's theory.[12] Aristotle associates exchange with the reciprocity of needs, whereas from the outset Marx conceives it in terms of profitable commercial operations.

Exchange becomes problematic and turns into bad chrematistics (or chrematistics period, if we keep to tradition) when its purpose is not to fill the reciprocal needs of the agents but only to accumulate profits. What makes this diversion possible is the fact that money, which belongs to the realm of legitimate wealth, has no use in consumption but only in exchange. Shoes can be either used or exchanged and so can houses and all goods produced; *money alone can only be exchanged.* This is what Aristotle wants us to understand; this argument constitutes the core of his demonstration. Money is no more than an intermediary. It is a substitute and guarantor meant to translate the value of goods—the goods one sells, as well as those one wishes to buy. As long as cash is restricted to this purpose, it remains within its "natural"—positive—function as an operator of proportion and "judge" of things. But to sell or buy with the aim of accumulation amounts to acting as if money in and of itself had a use in consumption. This amounts precisely to removing it from its exchange use, which is its only justified and suitable use. This loss of function is equivalent to a breakdown in the syllogism regarding proportional equalization between heterogeneous goods, a syllogism that defines money.[13] In the syllogism money is a middle term, a *meson* or *mesotēs* that brings two other terms (houses and shoes for instance) together and allows them to communicate. But as soon as it becomes autonomous and no longer effects this connection, the terms themselves lose the standard by which they can be measured. Chrematistics is not only a perverse accumulation of profits but also a disorder in the network of natural exchanges within the city. Through lending with interest and speculative resale, the pursuit of profit denatures money itself.

Nature Diverted (II):
Pleonexia, or the Unrestrained Desire for Money

A question arises at this point: what is it that drives men to this unreasonable pursuit of profit and the accumulation of cash? This involves a kind of enigma. How can it happen? Aristophanes observes it but does not go beyond this observation: "Anything else one can have too much of. . . . But no one ever has enough of you."[14] Why does money have this specific ability to arouse unbounded desire? Aristotle attempts to give a coherent answer to this phenomenon. He has to, given that he does not view the evil represented by the logic of profit as an event intervening from the outside but as the perversion of a potential intrinsic to the very nature of the agent (especially in the form of his yearning) and the monetary instrument.

From the moment when money no longer operates within the circle of useful reciprocal exchange and relationships of interdependence, it loses its function, which is to be the measure of need. Currency, however, remains a measuring standard. But then what does it measure? Aristotle's answer is surprising: it measures desire for money itself, which is to say money as a means of enjoyment: "As their desires are unlimited, they also desire that the means of gratifying them should be without limit" (*Pol.* 1258a). When the circle of reciprocity is broken, this natural desire for acquisition no longer has any bounds. Within the space of the *oikos*, the desire to live is a desire to live well, which is to say to achieve a life that attains its excellence or virtue (*aretē*) through the knowledge of its end and limit. But *the desire to live is in itself unlimited*: this is the seed of what threatens the agent's relationship with currency. But the agent also has to lend himself to this unlimitedness.

Within the *oikos* desire is limited by action, which means consideration of the ends sought. In chrematistic activity, in contrast, desire cut off from action regains its spontaneous unlimitedness. Chrematistics is the perverse merging of this unlimitedness of desire with a technique of acquisition lacking finality. Since reciprocity no longer exists, the spontaneous unlimitedness of desire is carried over by a vector that is also unlimited. Currency becomes the instrument and measure of this unlimitedness. It is its expression and emblem. It can be so precisely because it is a general equivalent that stands for all goods. This is why currency disconnected from property measures nothing but the desire for wealth itself. In short, what occurs is the conjunction of two kinds of unlimitedness: that of a technique, which is of a normal kind (thus, Aristotle says, there is no limit to the art of the physician or architect, in the sense that one cannot tell where the point of perfection has been reached), and that of a desire to live, which is abnormal when not integrated to the desire to live well—*eu zen*—which is to say, not subjected to the ends of the *oikos* and the city. The refusal of this subjection defines chrematistics as an art—*tekhnē*—carried by a desire disconnected from the order of ends.

The individual who is dedicated to the pursuit of financial profit can no longer be a true citizen (or has never been one, as in the case of many retailers who were either foreigners passing through the city or metics),[15] since this acquisition without reciprocity amounts to acquisition without justice. In this movement money is no longer a middle term. It presents itself as what it should not have been, the principle and end of the exchange. It becomes a good in and of itself, which is contrary to its nature as instrument. This is why commercial exchange, when directed not toward justice but toward profit alone, destabilizes the city and perverts and destroys the relationships between citizens. Money becomes an object in and of itself;

money buys money and becomes merchandise. It remains rational to the extent that it is produced by a technique, but this is rationality without justice. This is why money is capable of destroying everything that is associated with civic virtues: honor, friendship, courage, and loyalty. The practice of chrematistics threatens the city from within and breaks the political bond, which is a relationship of justice between citizens. In the just exchange money serves as intermediary between two goods; the injustice is due to the fact that, in chrematistics, money only purchases goods in order to extract resale profit from them (which Marx would condense as the shift from C-M-C to M-C-M, defining the emergence of money as capital). Money resulting from this process is not the same as it was at the beginning of the transaction: it becomes a product and a good like any other, which it should not be. This is the perversion constituted by financial profit, as expressed in technical terms according to Aristotle.

The Price of Time

Finally, the most suspicious element of the chrematistic operation in Aristotle's view comes from the fact that it assigns a price to time: by creating a profit without undertaking any production within the framework of property (namely, the set of the instruments of action), the interest paid on a loan amounts to payment for time itself. Between the amount borrowed and the amount returned the only difference is the time elapsed. The debtor returns the amount of the loan plus another amount equivalent to the duration of the loan according to a fixed rate (some percentage of the value relative to a time unit—days, months, or year). Between the two moments, the debtor himself has been able to make sufficient profit by investing the amount of the loan in his property. This profit may result from natural acquisition if the loan makes it possible to ensure his production through farming or craft production. Aristotle is aware that borrowing can have this honest effect to the benefit of the borrower. Why can he not accept that the lender be compensated? This refusal is remarkable. It points to one of the most sensitive aspects of the classic view of time.

For Aristotle the difficulty is due to the fact that currency must be impervious to time. By making it possible to postpone the purchase, currency cancels time: whoever has sold something can wait as long as he wants before purchasing a different good. This is guaranteed by the currency the seller has obtained in the exchange. He knows that the equivalence between goods as translated by currency is accepted by all. Currency must remain stable because it is the "substitute for the need" we have of each other. Currency remains a means of preserving the measure or of measuring in advance. This is why for Aristotle it remains a judge impervious to any before or after. Yet profit ruins this impartial character of money as judge. Measurement has been lost (since the value no longer remains the same after time has elapsed). Profit subjects time to its law. For Aristotle the only conceivable time is the time of *praxis* and the agent; an instrument cannot have its own time. Profit thus turns an instrument into an agent. But this agent is an impostor since it lacks a notion of its own terminus. The time of profit is an unlimited time because it is not subjected to the *telos* of the action that limits it. The desire for money is associated with an illusory time that lacks an end term. Accumulation can go on forever. In the process the citizen loses his identity. Profit becomes the ruin of the city.

The entire problem is situated in the way naturalness has been defined. According to Aristotle there are two kinds of exchanges. One of them is natural because it is required by the need we have of each other. This is the exchange necessary to subsistence. As early as the first pages of the *Politics*, Aristotle aims precisely at establishing a natural genealogy of the city— the political community or *polis*—based on the community of subsistence or *koinōnia*. The question of bad chrematistics is precisely that of a withdrawal from naturalness (as a form of exchange that applies not to useful goods but to currency itself). For the centuries that followed, this question would remain suspended. But it was the very question of artifice in general, that of an original strangeness and a displacement that had already taken place. Exchange, like technique, highlighted nature's inadequacy to itself. It remains to be determined what brings the philosopher to accept any given practice as natural. Is it the tradition to which he belongs? Is there, instead, something at a deeper level that leads him to accept this tradition? Within the operation of commercial exchange, as in the movement of technique, there is an externality, a breach of equilibrium that remains unthinkable. This breach is operated by time and is the very movement of time.

Aristotle's analyses on the phenomenon of perverse accumulation of money and interest—understood as appropriation of time—has admirable coherence and great complexity. His demonstration appears so rigorously constructed that it seems to stand beyond criticism. In fact, it would be futile to challenge him on his own ground. It is therefore best to move away from it and question the very set of presuppositions on which his theoretical construction is based. This enables us to understand that his critique of (bad) chrematistics and especially his denunciation of speculative profit have their ultimate cause in a representation of the world as a closed totality. The physical world, the order of beings, movement, the prime mover, the hierarchy of causes, and the organization of society all form a rigorously homeostatic system (this view was shared by the entire classical world and all traditional societies). Time is a movement that remains internal to this order. This is why there are no irreversible phenomena, whether in nature or in the human world. Certainly, stories and narratives are witnesses to actions that occurred within the community. But time itself is not history. Everything returns to the balance of the cosmos; the ephemeral character of the sublunar world is resorbed into the eternal stability of the divine world. Yet the chrematistic technique manifests a capacity to move away from this stable order, crack its outer wall, move across the boundaries of the city, and give rise to an unthinkable unlimitedness. For Aristotle to counter this movement with all of his conceptual means is normal and admirable (all traditional societies develop the same kind of resistance). There is no point in our judging this attitude in normative terms. Let us just note how surely Aristotle is able to identify the weak link and at the same time trace the implied outline of a possible break, a tearing away from the balanced world of gods and of men and a leap into an unlimited and irreversible time.

Theologians against Usurers

The question of time plays a crucial part in the Aristotelian indictment of profit. But medieval theology made this dimension explicit. This was not the only aspect that made usury reprehensible at the time, but it was probably the most profound because it concerned the question of the gift (to which we will return in Part II). The indictment of usury is a constant in Christian preaching, from its very beginning; it is supported both by ancient biblical texts and by injunctions in the Gospels.[16] For a long time the debate among Christians hung on the interpretation of the passage from Deuteronomy (23:19–20) which, while proscribing usury among "brothers"—in the ethnic sense—allows it when dealing with foreigners.

Christian universalism did extend the notion of brothers to the whole of humankind. In the fourth century, however, Ambrose of Milan, whose sermons in favor of the poor were famous, caused lasting confusion among theologians by taking up again the distinction from Deuteronomy but in favor of Christians alone: usury is legitimate against the enemies of the faith.[17] During the same period, however, Basil the Great, the bishop of Caesarea, does not entertain this distinction; his spiritual war against usury is consistent. He rediscovers (or is familiar with) the Aristotelian motif of the monstrous fertility of interest. Addressing the borrower, he implores, "Why bind yourself to such a prolific monster? It is said that the females of hares give birth, suckle, and conceive at the same time. The same is true of our sordid usurers, with whom money starts hatching interest and grows at the same time as soon as it has been lent. . . . This is why this form of greed draws its name, *tokos* [offspring], from the litter of evils that it generates, and so on ad infinitum. . . . Interest gives birth to interest."[18] Related to this idea of unnatural generation is the emergence of another form of denaturing that involved time. It had to do with the superimposition or mixing of acts that should instead follow one another. An acceleration occurs that is the very expression of greed. But the most serious point (one not made by Aristotle) is that debts—in reverse symmetry to profits—generate debts. This monstrous offspring devours its mother's womb (in addition to hares, vipers are also invoked by Basil in this bestiary of the sin of usury). Debt generates debt; no sooner is it born than it is already giving birth; its offspring get more and more sickly: "Animals that reproduce too early soon become sterile."[19] Time is doubly perverted by two forms of excess: too fast on the one hand and too soon on the other. This breach or exploitation of the order of time is also a motif in the sermons of Gregory of Nyssa (Basil's younger brother), who describes the passive life of the usurer: "He does not know the labor of the farmer or the worries of the shopkeeper. He always remains in the same place and fattens his monsters in his home. Everything must be produced without seeds or tilling. For a plough he has a stylus; for land, a contract; for rain, time imperceptibly increasing his crops."[20] The entire metaphor evokes images expressing the inversion and perversion of the true, most noble, and sacred production—that of the land; it ends with the appropriation of time itself, identified with rain, as what ensures the life of creatures and is for God to give. This consideration remains implicit, however. The usurer is not clearly denounced as a "thief of time," but this theme is already emerging, as it does with the anonymous fifth-century author who states, "Of all merchants, the most accursed is the usurer, for he sells something given by God."[21] On this point, however, medieval theologians are much more daring than their predecessors in the first centuries of Christianity.[22]

Let us start with one of those writings, one by a fourteenth-century lector-general of the Franciscan Order, which expresses this with crystal clarity: "Question: is a merchant entitled, in a given type of business transaction, to demand a greater payment from one who cannot settle his account immediately than from one who can? The answer argued for is no, because *in doing so he would be selling time* and would be committing usury *by selling what does not belong to him.*"[23] Thus the mere fact of selling on credit and collecting interest is enough to turn the merchant into an abusive lender—in other words, a usurer. This is obviously a radical position, since it implies an indictment of all forms of interest. What matters to us is the following argument: since the only difference between the amount lent and the amount returned is a lapse of time, what is sold is time itself. This document states that time does not belong to the merchant. To whom, then, does it belong?

The writings of Thomas de Chobham (thirteenth century) are probably the most explicit on this question: "The usurer sells his debtor nothing that belongs to him, but only the time that belongs to God [*sed tantum tempus quod dei est*]." Chobham also writes, "The usurer commits a theft [*furtum*], or usury [*usuram*], or pillage [*rapinam*], for he receives foreign goods [*rem alienam*] against the 'owner's' wishes [*invito domino*], that is to say, against God's wishes."[24] The fact that time belongs to God means at least two things. First, it is not up to human beings to produce time; in this sense time is under God's power and authority alone. Selling time is, therefore, an extremely serious sin: usury as a form of greed is listed as one of the mortal sins (meaning, liable to lead the sinner to eternal damnation in the absence of repentance and absolution prior to death). Second, God alone can *give* time; he gives it to all equitably (a more precise discussion of what giving means will be found in Part II of this book). The following writing by Guillaume of Auxerre (1160–1229) is remarkable from this point of view:

The usurer acts in contravention to universal natural law, because he sells time, which is the common possession of all creatures. Augustine says that every creature is obliged to give of itself; the sun is obliged to give of itself in order to shine;

in the same way, the earth is obliged to give all it can produce, as is the water. But nothing gives of itself in a way more in conformity with nature than time; like it or not, every thing has time. Since, therefore, the usurer sells what necessarily belongs to all creatures, he injures all creatures in general, even stones. Thus even if men remain silent in the face of usurers, the stones would cry out if they could; and this is one reason why the Church prosecutes usury. This is why it was especially against the usurers that God said: "When I take back possession of time, when time is in my hands so that no usurer can sell it, then I will judge in accord with justice."[25]

The author does not immediately say that time belongs to God, except in the end, when he states that God will take it back. Time appears as the most universal gift, offered to all creatures (and not only human beings). It is the cosmic gift par excellence. Time is therefore the principle of the generous (as opposed to profitable) and obligatory exchange, since all receive it for free. Whoever uses what he has thus received in order to draw profit from it is guilty of unforgivable abuse. It is unthinkable for the gift relationship to be transformed into a commercial relationship. A gift can only be returned, since it is above all an expression of the relationship rather than a usable good; keeping it and drawing a profit from it amounts to breaking the entire cosmic and social chain of reciprocity and turning a relationship of interdependence and recognition into one of domination and exploitation. Therefore, drawing profit from it does not merely amount to abstaining from returning what has been received (which would merely be evidence of passive selfishness) but to diverting what has been received in order to appropriate and sell it.

The principle of this argument may seem somewhat obscure to us. Its starting point is that all creatures are connected to time, which is clear to the extent that they are all mortal; the second proposition is the affirmation that time is given, first of all, because it cannot be produced by man. The document quoted above does not state at the outset from whom time has been received, but it is implicitly accepted as self-evident that it is from the Creator; this is confirmed at the end, when it is stated that God will take time back and punish the usurer. In fact, what makes this reasoning original is the fact that it presents usury above all as a break in the chain of gift-giving. The transgression is situated at this level, before any consideration of offense against God. Since all creatures benefit from this gift, its diversion offends or harms nature in its entirety. Whoever appropriates the gift without returning it thus breaks off an internal movement of circulation. This is the case for whoever commits usury. But it is true of all lending with interest. From the moment profit is present, there is temporal difference and therefore appropriation of time.

. . .

In both the Aristotelian criticism of the profit generated by money—this "chrematistics" that today we would call creation of speculative profit—and the denunciation of usury by Christian theology, the question of time is essential but in very different ways. For Aristotle what is scandalous is the creation of wealth without any natural basis, such a basis being defined by property (that is, a set of goods as instruments) associated with production or activity of transformation—*poiēsis*. This is what is missing from the "monstrous" fecundity of money—interest or *tokos*—capable of generating even though it is not a living being. Time alone seems to have contributed to this strange parturition. For Aristotle the question is not the mercenary transformation of what has been given but the breakdown of a balance and the denaturing of a well-delimited function. Time unduly appropriated appears to be pulled away from itself. *Tekhnē khrēmatistikē* itself remains a rational form of know-how, but it is cut off from any legitimate use. Instead of "measuring movement," time now literally measures a vacuum, since profit rises while no production has occurred. In the end a financial difference remains, which alone seems to turn this nothing into reality. There should be an increase in the thing itself; what emerges instead is something that should not be. The appropriation of time by profit captures temporal movement to generate artifacts that can have no place in the just city or, worse, are the seeds of its dissolution. This illuminates the meaning of the statement "Sophistry is a kind of art of money-making," for sophistry argues not about the thing but about illusions created by effects of discourse, just as chrematistics develops its profits through manipulation of currency signs, which is to say through production cut off from the ends of action.

Christian theology (that of the Founding Fathers of the Church and that of the Middle Ages) involves an entirely different hypothesis regarding time and the world. The world is everything that has been created by God and given to humanity. Time, as the opposite of eternity, defines mortal life—but life above all. As such, it constitutes the original gift. It is the obligatory framework of the existence of all beings in the world, starting with humans. It is the fundamental dimension of creation, radically beyond the power of all creatures. Time is given to them like life and existence, along with its limit, which is death. No one can attempt to appropriate time without destroying the order of things chosen by God; no one can decide its movement and its end. Yet this gesture is indeed presupposed by the operation of profit.[26] Capturing time and *making it work* to increase one's income amounts to diverting it in order to draw profit from what is, par excellence, given graciously and equally to all as the enigma of life and death.

These two different approaches (which can easily be combined) remarkably express two forms of refusal. Both of them would later be reversed, and their opposites would become two central dimensions of our modernity. What Aristotle perceives as threat of disintegration of the city is what political economy since the early eighteenth century (and even before) would consider as the very movement of emancipation of market mechanisms; this emancipation would go as far as ensuring in effect the domination of the economic over the political sphere. In short, everything that Aristotle identifies as denaturing and destructive of the city is, on the contrary, understood as the emergence of a new nature and of a new order of social life. What he diagnoses as danger is precisely what political economy regards as new opportunity. The time he views as fleeing away and falling apart in the chrematistic activity is precisely the time of history as the movement of society as a whole, which changes in proportion to its capacity to invest and produce. This endless movement, this flight into the limitless, is precisely what capitalism presupposes and confronts without seeing in it an abyss or a leap into indeterminacy. On the contrary, it is understood as promise of the new and certainty of progress.

As a result the theological arguments against usury, which is to say lending with interest, gradually faded away. This dissolution was already apparent with many Catholic theologians as early as the fifteenth century,[27] but it has above all been associated with Protestant thought. Among Christian trends Calvinism went furthest in this direction. It was also with Calvinism that the gift worldview underwent its most severe setback, opening the way to the extension of contractual exchange and to the completely instrumentalized time of investment[28]—this led to the emergence of an equation that reversed both Aristotle and traditional theology:

time is money. We will have to see how the gift worldview and its Christian form (expressed—often in an unrecognizable way—in a theology of *grace*) were and continue to be at the core of the debate on price and the priceless, albeit in less visible forms. At the same time, the entire traditional idea of *debt*, as related to unilateral gift and sacrifice (and understood as a hypothesis about time as regulated by a return to an original balance), comes to be turned upside down.

We now realize that the question of the commercial value of knowledge—which was the starting point of this inquiry, with the case of the Sophists—cannot be raised without recognizing several series of questions concerning the very idea of trade and its function in society, the legitimacy of profit, the role of money, its ordinary and speculative uses, and the power of the market. In addition, another set of questions arises. The point is not only to draw like Aristotle a contrast between legitimate exchange, which remains regulated by reciprocity between citizens, and chrematistic exchange, which destroys it, but to conceive of a relationship of exchange of an entirely different type from the commercial one. This would be the question of the gift, precisely as it would arise in theological writing on usury: what is given defines the realm of what cannot be sold. "My usefulness remains imponderable and consequently cannot be paid for," Flaubert proclaims.[29] Yet does the realm of the gift arise only from this kind of refusal? Is it nothing more than the reverse of the order of the market? Could it be that this—dominant—hypothesis makes it impossible to understand anything about the gift? An entirely different universe emerges. Our original question has opened the Pandora's Box of the world of relationships in which what is at stake is priceless, beyond any assessment. If the words and gestures of Socrates at the moment of his death are to take their full meaning, we must take up each of these questions.

PART TWO

THE WORLD OF GIFT-GIVING

The Master Who Gives and Gives Himself:
Knowledge as Priceless

Several centuries after his death, Socrates remained a legendary figure. Many narratives still extolled his wisdom and generosity. The following story, which had probably circulated long before the first century CE, is told by Seneca:

Once when many gifts were being presented to Socrates by his pupils, each one bringing according to his means, Aeschines, who was poor, said to him: "Nothing that I am able to give to you do I find worthy of you, and only in this way do I discover that I am a poor man. And so I give to you the only thing that I possess—myself. This gift, such as it is, I beg you to take in good part, and bear in mind that the others, though they gave to you much, have left more for themselves." "And how," said Socrates, "could it have been anything but a great gift—unless maybe you set small value upon yourself? And so I shall make it my care to return you to yourself a better man than when I received you."[1]

This anecdote tells it all: the relationship between master and student is a relationship of reciprocal generosity; the master's work should not be paid with money but honored with presents (this was customary); above all, this gift-giving relationship involves the giver in the thing given, so much so that the gift can be the giver himself, as in Aeschines' case; this personal relationship preserves the privileged initiatory aspect of *sunousia* in philosophical training.

Socrates lived off the gifts he received, as documented by Xenophon and Diogenes Laertius.[2] It is important to remember this because it helps us understand one specific aspect of Plato's critique of the Sophists: they not only require payment but also expect gratitude. Let me quote once again this passage from the *Apology*: "This too seems to me to be a fine thing, if someone were able to educate people . . . and the young men, who may spend time *for nothing* in the company [*suneinai*] of any fellow-citizen they wish! And they persuade them to leave the company [*sunousia*] of those people and have theirs, for a fee, *and to be grateful* [kharin] *besides*."[3]

At the time it was self-evident to any listener or reader that the attitude associated with generous reciprocity and gift-exchange relationships is gratitude (*kharis*). In buying and selling, in contrast, strict fulfillment of the commitments made was required; the relationship came to an end with the payment and reception of the product. Relationships of buying and selling were not and should not be personal. What this passage tells us is that, since the Sophists had turned into merchants, they should not have expected from their students anything other than money; they should even have thanked them because in ordinary trade the seller is indebted to his customer. Yet while the Sophists legitimized their profitable activity by presenting themselves as experts—*technitei*—they also aspired to be regarded as masters of wisdom. They pretended to believe that the money they demanded in exchange for their teaching remained within the traditional gift-exchange relationship; in short, they also aimed at the personal relationship of "erotic" *sunousia* that traditionally connected a master and a disciple—as was the case of Socrates and his followers. They intended to preserve for their own benefit the old initiatory relationship that was akin to filiation—like the relationship between adult and ephebe—and was based on the initiator's generosity and the initiate's gratitude; but they did not understand that one cannot charge for knowledge as craftsmen do for their services and merchants for their goods and at the same time aspire to the prestige, esteem, and affection traditionally awarded to the masters of wisdom who give and give themselves out of their love for truth.

Aristotle:
"Knowledge and Money Have No Common Measure"

We may wonder why Plato does not discuss this gift-giving relationship more explicitly with respect to Socratic teaching. Is it so obvious in his view that it would be unnecessary to mention? Or is our attempt to read these narratives in the light of modern anthropology an overinterpretation? In fact, many elements in these stories lend themselves to anthropological reading: while Plato seems very elusive in this respect, Aristotle, who is intent on leaving nothing unexplained (much to the Platonists' annoyance), very precisely and remarkably examines this question.

In his *Eudemian Ethics* and *Nicomachean Ethics* Aristotle wonders in the most explicit manner whether teaching—and in particular the teaching of philosophy—can be paid. At the very moment when he defines the function of money as an operator of equivalence, he precisely indicates where the level of the incommensurable is situated. According to him this operation is required in order to set a proportion between disparate goods by means of a middle term that gives numerical measure (this is what he demonstrates with respect to money in 5.8, as we will see in Chapter 9). The specific nature of each thing resists this operation, however, because a thing, as defined by Aristotle, must always be capable of preserving its uniqueness lest it be deprived of its very being. But this uniqueness is suspended by monetary operations, which are made possible by the existence of a middle term—the need humans have for each other. Remarkably, however, for Aristotle there are realms in which no equivalence, no matter how approximate or inadequate, can ever be conceived or even possible. This is the case of knowledge (*epistēmē*). He most clearly states this in *Eudemian Ethics*: "Knowledge and money have no common measure [*epistēmē gar kai khrēmata oukh heni metreitai*]."[4] This statement is echoed by the following remark from *Nicomachean Ethics*: "It is impossible that things differing so much should become commensurable."[5] According to the very definition of money as *mesotēs*—"medium-ness"—this amounts to stating that no middle term exists between the two entities. Money is radically alien to knowledge because there is nothing in knowledge that can be related to money through a common term. Therefore knowledge cannot be exchanged for a precise amount of money, whereas for a set price it is possible to secure the services of musicians, painters, rhapsodists, or any other craftsmen or artists, to the extent that their professions include an essentially technical, and therefore measurable, aspect; this is not the case for philosophical teaching.

What is the meaning of this radical heterogeneity between knowledge and money? The passage from *Eudemian Ethics* in which this proclamation is found (Book 7.10) deals with forms of friendship—*philia*—among various types of communities such as family, village, city, or any other association. *Nicomachean Ethics* 9.1 gives a similar development on the same topic. Thus Aristotle explains that in the case of friendly associations, if the reason for an agreement is utility, then the agreement is a legal one; but if the reason is gracious, then the agreement is a moral one.

It is important not to confuse the two types of relationships: in the case
of utility it is best to precisely settle the debt incurred (since a loan cannot be repaid with words or an artist compensated with admiration). In
the other case a service is reciprocated by another service in proportion
to one's means; what matters is the intention expressed on both sides. It
remains to be determined whether there are realms that can only belong
to the second category. The partners must make this assessment because
it is indeterminate, but it must be based on good faith. Aristotle gives an
example of deception on the part of a music lover—claimed to be the tyrant Denis of Syracuse—who had promised a flute player that he would
compensate him in proportion to his talent; when the artist expected to
be paid his wages, Denis let him know that he had already been generously rewarded by the pleasure the music lover had drawn from listening to him. The flutist had legitimate reason to consider himself cheated.
He was paid with esteem when he was owed wages. This esteem, which
he probably did appreciate, was useless to him if his primary need was to
secure his subsistence. As for the devious admirer, he could play on the
universally recognized fact that, beyond payment of the honorarium, the
homage given constitutes the essence of the recognition granted to the
musician's talent. Aristotle's argument concerns the following: when there
is extreme difference between the terms (which is to say when no middle
term—*meson*—is conceivable), then the only way to assess what is due is
to agree on a compensation. He then adds this surprising remark: "And so
too, it seems, should one make a return to those with whom one has studied philosophy; for their worth cannot be measured against money [*ou
pros khrēmathe' hē axia metreitai*], and they can get no honour which will
balance their services, but still it is perhaps enough, as it is with the gods
and with one's parents, to give them what one can" (*NE* 9.1.1164b2–5).
This text is clearly crucial to our inquiry.

The Gift and the Priceless

In the same chapter Aristotle addresses the case of services difficult
to assess, where the payer also sets the price. He adds that this is the way
Protagoras conducted his teaching: "He bade the learner assess the value
of knowledge, and accepted the amount so fixed" (*NE* 9.1.1164a24–26).
This is wise practice, Aristotle believes, unlike the practice of other Soph-

ists who demand payment in advance; he notes with irony, "The Sophists are perhaps compelled to do so because no one would give money for the things they *do* know" (*NE* 9.1.1164a30–32). But whether payment is made before or after does not change the fact that true philosophical teaching (and this implies that sophistic teaching is not) is by nature inestimable and therefore priceless.

At this point Aristotle is clearly referring to relationships of gift exchange. We must behave toward our masters of philosophy as we do toward the gods and our parents, he says, by compensating them to the extent that we can. What does this mean? The answer can be found in other passages from his ethical treatises or in what a shared tradition makes seem self-evident to readers. We learn that the gods are due offerings, sacrifices, and celebrations, while gratitude toward one's parents is expressed through respect, presents, and generous support.[6] Aristotle explicitly states what Plato had only hinted at and finally provides a sound argument: to establish equivalence between two elements in terms of money requires the possibility of a proportion between them—in other words the existence of a middle term. Where there is none, the only possible mode of compensation is a gift or, rather, a relationship of gift exchange. The passing down of knowledge must be considered as a present to which the beneficiary replies through the expression of gratitude conveyed by his own presents.

Flaubert still shares the same view. When he writes, "My usefulness [*mon service*] remains imponderable and consequently cannot be paid for,"[7] he very relevantly indicates the type of exchange in which writers (or, more generally, artists) are engaged with the community to which they belong and with the audience that reads or receives their works. While it is true that artists do work and that accomplishing their work demands effort or toil, the effort remains their own business. Their labor cannot be measured: the value of the work is not assessed by the time it took to produce it. To say that it is a *service* (a notion that includes at the same time the ideas of dedication and of obligation) is to say that it is a *gift*. This gift generates the countergift of recognition, which can be expressed through material gratifications granted to the artist. They testify to the esteem granted to the work, but they do not aim to enter the work into a regime of equivalence. The artist, according to Flaubert (like the philosopher, according to Plato), communicates something that remains priceless. What is returned to him belongs to the same category. The artist is the person through whom a work of art is given to the community as something that belongs to no one and must be given to all. What is honored is this gift, which is equally precious to all—this is at least the conviction that tradition has passed down to us. It is also why all services are compensated with *honoraria*.

To attempt to include the work of art or knowledge into commercial exchanges therefore involves a specific difficulty, no matter what market mechanisms may be used to set the scales and to make contracts possible. This is why this type of work or activity still belongs to a different form of exchange that relates back to the model of gift/countergift. What is this model? Is it just another form of exchange, or is it an exchange of a radically different nature? Is the term *exchange* even appropriate in this case? These questions await answers, but one thing is already certain: the question of the value of a thing, no matter what it may be, cannot be raised without the intervention of a global system of evaluation. This system transcends the economic field; it is often called symbolic—a concept in need of a precise definition. It constantly contradicts the market, even as the market never stops subjecting symbolic assessment to its own operation of equivalence, to the point of constituting a denial of Aristotle's proclamation: between knowledge and money there is indeed a common measure, as there is between money and all sorts of goods. Does the modern economy require this universal equivalence? Should we assume that all noncommercial modes of assessment and all relationships of gift exchange will eventually disappear? But what is the nature of these relationships? Can they deal with situations that cannot be dealt with through mere equivalence? In what cases and between what partners is it mandatory to give? According to what procedures? Regarding what goods? Are relationships of gift exchange an alternative to commercial relationships? Can they even be defined as exchanges of goods? It may be that they cannot and that these goods are only involved as mediators for something of a very different kind. To answer these questions, anthropological knowledge must take over from philosophical knowledge. This shift of field may force us to displace the very questions with which we have been dealing.

4

The Enigma of Ceremonial Gift Exchange

When Aristotle attempts to compensate what is inestimable, such as the passing down of knowledge, he refers to relationships of gift exchange. All the considerations found in *Nicomachean Ethics* on *philia*—friendship or generous benevolence—also refer to this relationship. The old vocabulary of gift exchange is omnipresent in these writings. The gesture of giving was already strongly internalized at the time, however (as it would later be in Seneca's treatise *De beneficiis* [*Of Benefits*]), in comparison with the language found in Homer, which was still highly ceremonial. The roots of the *philia* worldview probably lie in the ancient ritual forms that make it possible to grasp the fundamental logic of reciprocity. Reciprocity thus proves to be not merely benevolent exchange but a paradoxical relationship of challenge and trust, freedom and constraint, based on the mediation of goods considered as precious.

We can credit Marcel Mauss with identifying the essential features of ceremonial gift exchange in his 1924 essay *The Gift*. Mauss was not the first to describe gift exchange practices, but he was the first to identify them as a *problem*; he showed that ritually codified, generous reciprocity constituted the dominant fact in relationships between groups within traditional societies and formed the very cement of the social bond. Returning to these questions may enable us to understand the background behind Plato's intransigence toward the Sophists, as well as Aristotle's explanation of the impossibility to financially remunerate philosophical teaching.

To understand under what requirements the notion of the priceless has developed since time immemorial, we must again take up the analysis of the forms of ceremonial gift exchange, reconstitute "the atmosphere of the gift" (to use Mauss's words), and examine sacrificial offering, which constitutes its corollary *in certain cases*. This inquiry will shed light on that which prophetic religions and universalizing ethics have designated as *pure gift-giving*, which is to say unilateral and sovereign giving whose most elaborate theological expression is the concept of *grace*. We will see that it is a relationship between a transcendent granting source and an addressee that can only receive or, in other words, that can offer only gratitude in return—a radically dissymmetric relationship that has precisely defined truth as revelation. The very ancient *alētheia* model of the Pre-Socratic *sophoi* may have endured longer than has been assumed, merely undergoing a transformation. It is still present every time truth seems to be categorically given through the gesture of a revelation "from above" rather than elaborated through the uncertain back-and-forth of dialogue. As for this gift, which precedes any human gift, it appears that two alternative conceptions have developed: a theological worldview that accounts for it as divine favor, and a specifically philosophical approach that considers it to be a gift from no one and the very grace of the world; the latter could be called the thought of being.

But for now we must set aside this question. We will begin by examining how the entire world of the priceless opens up in the wake of ceremonial gift exchange: what is precious is what was given and received in a relationship of reciprocal recognition. The widening gap between the properly ritual forms of gift exchange and its moralized forms will have to be assessed, however (and this consideration will run throughout this book); the former are decisive moments of the collective life of traditional societies, which is to say the ones in which the essence of social relationships and statutory positions is determined by kinship systems;[1] the latter appear in political societies, in which a sovereign authority emerges that takes over and absorbs these kinship systems; this was the case of classical Greek society—in which Socrates lived. It is even more true and has reached an extreme degree in contemporary societies where relationships of gift exchange seem primarily to involve individuals.

The transformation of the system of gift exchange implied by the difference between these two models entails a transformation of what constitutes truth because this internalization goes along with the formation of a single giver, whether visible or invisible. If the social bond is no longer defined by interpersonal relationships and by a network of gift exchange between groups and individuals, then it becomes indirect. We are then connected to each other by a common love that envelops us, such as the *philia* that Zeus grants to all or, according to an entirely different model, "tenderness"—such as biblical *hesed*—on the part of the one God, heavenly grace—*hén*—spreading through the hearts of men. A vertical gift replaces the complex movements of horizontal gift exchange, which only survive within interpersonal relationships. The more that the economic invades the social realm, relegating relationships of gift exchange to private circumstances, the more a new realm opens up for unilateral giving. If no response is possible—because any response to such an incommensurable gift would be inadequate—then social relationships become more openly available for commercial exchange. As gift-giving is internalized and becomes private business, the marketplace can extend into the realm of the relationship from *socius* to *socius*, and inestimable goods are assigned commercial value. Although in very different terms, this brings to mind the horizon of Max Weber's question on the paradoxes of grace and capitalism.

Problems and Misunderstandings

What is giving? The accepted answer addresses the moral form of giving: help provided to others and the imperative of compassion and sharing. But this leaves the enigma of *ceremonial gift exchange* unexplained. In this type of giving, as described in ethnographic investigations, the specifically social dimension of the generous gesture prevails. Is this in any way part of ordinary experience in modern societies? For instance, when we receive a service or present, we recognize that we are engaged in a symbolic relationship of reciprocity.[2] It is symbolic because it precludes all numerical assessment, and its value can only be set in an analogical or simulated manner. In the same way, our response to these gestures can only be symbolic and take on the form of a service or present expressing our wish to reply, even if in commercial terms what is returned is not proportional to what was received. In short, the gift/countergift relationship remains part of our reality even though it no longer takes the rigorous ritual forms it has in traditional societies. It marks privileged moments in relationships of friendship or love; it is at the core of public and private celebrations; it is what everyone recognizes and practices through reciprocal invitations; it can appear everywhere generous challenge is expected.

What significance should be granted to these gestures? Do they have any relation at all to gestures of moral generosity? It may be that they do not. Their connections to ancient ceremonies, their traditional aspect, and their obscure origin long led sociologists to leave these questions to specialists of folklore, along with the determination of the genealogy of forms of courtesy. Classical writings have taught us, however, that practices of gift exchange were not only associated with private behavior or reducible to official good manners but constituted foundational moments of relationships between groups. This is strikingly demonstrated by traditional societies still in existence. Yet, precisely because of the significance of the goods exchanged, it long appeared self-evident that this exchange could only amount to barter. This seemed to establish its economic nature, albeit a rudimentary and clumsy one with little rationality. In contrast, some authors stress the purely generous dimension of these gestures, viewing them as expressions of spectacular prodigality or merely of moral altruism worthy of admiration. In fact, neither economic explanation nor moral interpretation is relevant, but it is significant that these two views are mutually exclusive. Ceremonial gift exchange is neither profitable exchange nor mere gesture of benevolent offering. What is it, then? What is its enigma?

The Nature of Ceremonial Gift Exchange Is Not Economic

The reduction of gift exchange rituals to economic operations is most often performed by simply lumping the two together when describing "primitive exchanges." Adam Smith, presenting a genealogy of the "inclination to trafficking" inherent to the human race in a well-known passage from book 1, chapter 2 of *The Wealth of Nations*, casually mixes up all sorts of exchanges involving services, words, gifts, and useful goods. There is nothing surprising about this: every eighteenth-century author does the same. What is more surprising is to find similar views in authors such as Max Weber and Karl Polanyi. In his *General Economic History* Weber designates traditional exchanges between African tribal chiefs or medieval princes as "gift trade," apparently unaware of the self-contradictory character of the phrase; however, when referring to documents such as the Tell-el-Amarna tables (1400 BCE), he is struck by their description of gifts without counterpart—except for the counterpart that consists of an attitude of allegiance toward givers on the part of beneficiaries. These gifts were practiced between Middle Eastern princes, particularly the pharaoh and those indebted to him. Those practices were thus strange and unreliable: "Numerous breaches of faith and trust which occurred in this connection gradually led to the imposition of mutual considerations so that a genuine trade on an accurate quantitative basis grew out of the gift trade."[3] Weber, therefore, believes that this constituted a movement toward increased rationality. Regarding the origin of currency, he writes, "The function of money as a general medium of exchange originated in foreign trade. Its source is in some cases a regular commerce by gifts outside the group. . . . A state of peace between two peoples presupposed continual gifts between their rulers; this is really a quasi-commercial exchange between the chieftains, out of which chieftain trade as such develops."[4] We will see that this is not the case and that it precisely constitutes the confusion we must avoid at all costs. Many similar examples could be given. Mauss himself, who must be credited for clarifying this question, often relies on an inadequate vocabulary in viewing these exchanges as "the market as it existed before the institution of traders,"[5] even though his entire analysis shows something different and he is led to a radical questioning of the prejudices of *homo œconomicus*.

Karl Polanyi, among economic historians one of the most sensitive to anthropological research, notes that the *kula ring*, the circuit of gift exchange in the Trobriand Island described by Malinowski, is "one of the most elaborate trading transactions known to man" and adds this categorical statement: "We describe it as trade though no profit is involved, either in money or in kind . . . , and the whole proceedings are entirely regulated by etiquette and magic. Still, it is trade."[6] Polanyi explains that although *kula* exchanges belong to the realm of gift exchange and their motivation is the prestige drawn from this ostentatious generosity, the global effect of these movements of goods over long distances amounts to a considerable circulation of wealth: "Nevertheless, the result is a stupendous organizational achievement in the economic field."[7] Polanyi's thesis is a subtle one: he recognizes that what is involved is the exchange of gifts, yet this movement of exchange is endowed with an economic significance that goes beyond it and must be recognized. There may indeed be unintended but nevertheless real economic effects. Polanyi, however, does not see that even from this point of view doubts should arise: this wealth mostly consists of ceremonial necklaces and bracelets; the time required by their manufacture and used for their circulation does not make it possible to describe this as economic success. If success does occur, it is situated on an entirely different level, which is, in fact, correctly identified by Malinowski as having an exclusively social nature: the development of a powerful network of interpersonal bonds.

Thus even Weber and Polanyi, who are among the authors most critical of economist prejudices, still rely on the model of trade when describing or explaining ceremonial gift exchange. This is all the more true of authors less demanding and attentive to data regarding traditional societies.

Thanks to new ethnographic research on ritual gift-exchange practices, doubt arose at the beginning of the twentieth century regarding their interpretation as a form of barter. First came the major investigations conducted by Franz Boas and his team, among whom was his indigenous guide George Hunt, of populations of the American Northwest,[8] their social organization, narratives, and activities of ceremonial exchange, the most spectacular of which was *potlatch*. Yet Boas, concerned with conferring economic rationality to activities that appeared devoid of it, for the benefit of federal administrators—or even his colleagues—adds to his fruitful investigations commentaries that amount to comforting the old prejudices.[9] The decisive turn no doubt came in 1922 with the publication of Malinowski's *Argonauts of the Western Pacific*, which presents the surprising practices of gift exchange that fill most of the social life of coastal Melanesian populations from the Trobriand Islands. Unlike Boas, Malinowski presents a very elaborate reflection on the original character of these ritual exchanges; above all, he clearly takes a stand against economist prejudices: "The word 'trade' is used in current Ethnography and economic literature in so many different implications that a whole lot of misleading, preconceived ideas have to be brushed aside in order to grasp the facts correctly." He adds, "We have to realise clearly that the *Kula* contradicts in almost every point the above definition of 'savage trade.'"[10] In addition, Malinowski's analyses show that an ordinary form of trade—called *gimwali*—coexists with the *kula* and also takes on highly elaborate forms, yet these barter operations are profoundly different from gift exchanges (we will return to this because it is precisely what Polanyi fails to consider).

In reopening this question that had mainly been examined by Boas and Malinowski, Mauss reformulates the problem of ceremonial gift exchange in its most general dimension and in a profoundly new manner.

He views it not merely as one of the major dimensions of social life but as its very essence. Mauss opens his investigation within a context that was difficult in two respects. First, a general and very old prejudice regarding so-called primitive people was widespread even among the most open minds (Mauss himself sometimes talks of "primitive peoples"). Second, there was universal resistance to regarding gift-exchange practices outside the framework of economic exchanges of goods, whether they involved barter or money. Mauss, who did so much to reject this reduction, sometimes gives in to the temptation to resort to the language of trade, profit, or contract. True, his hesitations remain a minor failing considering the importance of the breakthrough he achieved in such an unfavorable context. It was Mauss who showed that practices of ceremonial gift exchange dominate the life of traditional societies, including premodern Western societies (but the advent of modernity does not imply the disappearance of relationships of gift exchange). In spite of this for Mauss, as for most anthropologists, the question of gift exchange seems inseparable from that of trade and profitable economic exchange, even when the two are perceived as polar opposites. It is indeed important not to confuse these two questions, but, as we will see, it is just as important not to place them along the same line of evolution. Gift exchange is neither the ancestor of trade (since both exist at the same time) nor an alternative to trade (since they do not fulfill the same function). The two practices are entirely compatible. C. A. Gregory seems to clearly understand this, as shown by his attempt to contrast various modes of circulation of goods depending on different types of societies.[11] Among these societies he draws a particular distinction between those based on kinship and those based on economic interest. In both cases he draws another distinction between commodities and goods associated with prestige. The former are alienable, whereas the latter are not. The former aim at maximizing profit, the latter at maximizing the number of debtors. At this point we can no longer accept Gregory's interpretations. It is clear that he constructs a kind of model for two types of economies, as if the system of gift exchange aimed at a personalized distribution of goods and brought about a type of debt associated with the inalienable character of the goods involved. This is a kind of reworking of Boas's explanations (in that Boas wrongly interprets what he so accurately describes) or of Polanyi's "trade" interpretation. In short, Gregory, like those authors, cannot help interpreting the practices of gift exchange as an original version of economic relationships, which is a sure way to miss their specificity.[12] Like them he is fascinated by the fact that *goods* are involved. Here lies the misunderstanding: gift and trade relationships are seen as two modes of exchange of goods, the difference between them being that unlike the latter the former are not motivated by self-interest. Some goods are freely given, whereas others are exchanged for profit. This view seems reasonable but is, in fact, completely misleading.[13] As we will see, the aim of ceremonial gift exchange is public reciprocal recognition mediated by goods that are given. Ceremonial exchanges do not impede useful exchanges; they can show indifference to utility, but they do not attempt to reject utility.[14] There is therefore an ordinary economy embedded within the social order (which Polanyi clearly understands); this social order can be dominated by ceremonial gift-exchange relationships as defining the priorities of the group as a whole, as well as the positions of authority. The two activities coexist but do so within two significantly different realms, different in both function and importance. We will have to determine what these realms are.[15]

Ceremonial Gift-Giving Is Not a Moral Gesture

Many authors have taken a polar opposite stand to the economist interpretation of ceremonial gift exchange. This oppositional stand consists of taking as a starting point modern gift-giving and its different forms, whether at the individual level of gift-giving or the institutional level of humanitarian assistance, and of going back from this starting point to ritual forms as if the same questions were involved. This line of reasoning then returns to our modernity and shows how an entire system of generous assistance and noble gestures, which originated long ago, has compensated for the ruthless mode of operation of the marketplace. Although not entirely wrong, this genealogy distorts reality because it projects the moral aim of modern gift-giving onto ceremonial gift exchange. It must be emphasized that the practice of ceremonial gift exchange is no more a gesture of assistance or charity than it is an alternative to commercial relationships. In this case, the term *gift-giving* is probably inappropriate (Mauss recognizes this at the end of *The Gift*).[16] It would be more appropriate to speak of sumptuary offerings. What matters is not giving per se but the launching or continuing of a procedure of reciprocal recognition (in the sense of *recognizing one another*) expressed through precious goods and services. Although the gift is addressed to an individual, what matters is not the individual as such but what he or she represents. This has nothing to do with a generous act that implies an attitude of moral renouncement on the part of the giver.[17]

The debate regarding gift-giving runs a constant risk of returning to this old prejudice unless a clear distinction is drawn between private forms of generosity (whether moral or religious) and the ceremonial practice of gift exchange. This distinction does not amount to a dividing line between past and present or archaism and modernity. Ceremonial gift exchanges are still present within Western-type societies in the form of reciprocal dinner invitations, marriage or birthday presents, the celebration of achievements, and so on. These practices are very different from gestures of gratification such as anonymous donations to charities, time spent helping victims, or other admirable gestures that eschew all public promotion. The latter are gestures that involve decisions made by the donors alone. No custom accepted by all, no social expectation places pressure on those who choose to give for the purpose of giving or of helping others. In addition donors (especially when they remain anonymous) do not expect that their gesture will ensure a strengthening of the social bond within a community; they aim at ensuring the well-being or relief of people who are often unknown to them.

The case of ceremonial gift exchange is entirely different. Not only *must it be known*, but if it is not, it misses its goal, which is precisely to bring about reciprocal and public recognition in order to create or reinforce the social bond. This form of exchange can be characterized by the requirement that givers, recipients, things given, and time and circumstances of the gesture be identified. In other words this form of exchange involves neither personal virtue nor individual kindness, neither spiritual accomplishment nor pure and anonymous generosity, but foremost the bringing about of a solemn recognition of the other according to rules passed down by tradition. It is a social form of giving whose effect must be social. It cannot be assessed based on criteria applicable to moral giving. This does not imply that private gestures of offering have nothing in common with gift exchange, unlike what I have said regarding commercial relationships. There is indeed a common denominator: the generous gesture. This is probably what explains the usual confusion between these two gestures, which nevertheless have different functions and generate different effects. In this difference lies what is at stake in all of the questions I have raised from the beginning of this book. To answer them requires returning to the question of ceremonial gift exchange and trying to shed light on the enigma of this practice, which may seem so remote to us in some of its ritualized aspects.

The Problem of Ceremonial Gift Exchange: What Mauss Teaches Us

Mauss was far from being the first to show interest in ceremonial gift-exchange practices. Some field researchers—in particular Boas, Swanton, Thurnwald, Best, and Malinowski—had already done so as early as the late nineteenth century and first decades of the twentieth. But despite the quality of their investigations and the accuracy of their views, none of them had attempted to generalize the problem. Mauss takes the risk of doing so, based on his reading of their work. Better yet, he performs a comparative analysis identifying the universal character of the ceremonial gift-exchange phenomenon in space (American Northwest, Melanesia, Polynesia, and Andaman Islands), as well as in time, more specifically in the past of the so-called historical societies (Scandinavians, Celts, and, above all, Romans, Germanic peoples, and Indians). Finally, and most important for us, he emphasizes the unity of the various gestures of gift exchange and shows that they do not constitute a marginal phenomenon but one of the fundamental aspects of life in traditional societies and a practice that still survives in less-visible forms within modern societies.[18]

Thus, based on a rich ethnographic literature developed by a number of field researchers, Mauss is able to identify an essential social question where others only saw sets of "archaic" customs—hence the enduring importance of *The Gift*. It must be acknowledged, however, that in spite of his analyses the "enigma" of ceremonial gift exchange remains unsolved. Unquestionably, research on this topic has reached a dead end, yet this quasi failure has been highly instructive. We will see that it does not imply any theoretical failing but, instead, indicates a boundary that every one of us constantly confronts and that maps the blind spot of every culture. In many respects we still face the blind spot of Mauss's thought, yet what he teaches us remains: our inability to explain *why* phenomena are what they are does not prevent us from developing approaches to understanding *how* they operate. It is well known that in the social sciences a well-conducted description almost amounts to a well-stated answer.

"Total Social Fact" Revisited

Mauss became convinced that ritual gift exchange is not merely a spectacular and ultimately secondary aspect of the social life of traditional societies but, on the contrary, the central fact of their mode of being. His thinking took this direction on his reading the results of a number of investigations, the most significant of which was Malinowski's work on the *kula* circle of the Trobriand Islands and Boas's writings on the *potlatch* of coastal populations of the American Northwest. Coining a phrase that has remained famous, Mauss calls this ceremonial exchange a "total social fact." This is not a mere phrase; it is a major concept whose importance has often been emphasized, and rightly so. Nevertheless, it is crucial to avoid using it without consideration, at the risk of misstating the entire question of the relationship between sumptuary exchange and useful exchange. To understand what is at stake, we must return to some of the elements discussed in *The Gift*, starting with *kula* and *potlatch*, since these indigenous terms have become genuine concepts within anthropological literature, thanks largely to Mauss.

"It would be difficult to come across a custom of gift-through-exchange more clear-cut, complete, and consciously performed, and, moreover, better understood by the observer recording it than the one Malinowski found among the Trobriand people."[19] In this Melanesian archipelago the movement of exchange called *kula* represents a dominant aspect of the life of coastal populations. Malinowski's description of it in *Argonauts of the Western Pacific* is still recognized as a classic of ethnographic literature. The essential aspect of these exchanges of gifts involves two categories of precious goods (called *waygu'a*): on the one hand, bracelets (*mwali*), regarded as feminine and worn by men, move only from West to East; on the other, necklaces (*soulava*), regarded as masculine and reserved to women, move in the opposite direction, from East to West (according to a Trobriand myth, *mwali* and *soulava* are attracted to each other like male and female). Each expedition is carefully prepared and involves building or renovating boats; gathering the goods to be exchanged; and performing incantations and magic involving the trip, partners, and precious objects. The departure is a solemn occasion, as is the greeting received at each stop. *Kula* offering ceremonies are announced by horn calls and start with a kind of competitive exhibition presenting various *waygu'a* (stone axes, whalebone spoons, and so forth); these are *vaga*, or "opening gifts," meant to entice potential partners; anyone accepting these gifts must immediately reply through a *yotile*, or "clinching gift," by which he is bound. Then comes the most important exchange, that of bracelets and necklaces. When the exchange is over, after festivities lasting several days, departure is another solemn occasion involving appropriate words and presents. The flotilla then takes off toward a different island. The entire cycle can stretch over two or three months. On their return home the "argonauts" share the *waygu'a* in proportion to the statuses of group members and to the part each played in preparing the expedition (which clearly shows that it involves the whole community).

This surprising *kula* circuit has several salient features. The exchanges have a glorious and festive character; it is essential for the participants to display their generosity and to behave in a noble fashion by giving their most beautiful *waygu'a*. This sets a rigorous distinction between *kula* exchange and another important type of exchange, *gimwali*, or useful exchange, which can be practiced concurrently with *kula* but with different partners, and which often involves fierce barter. As for *kula* exchange, it remains above all *a way to ensure reciprocal recognition and gain prestige*. This is why *kula* giving has an obligatory character. One cannot fail to reply without breaching the rules. What is at stake is not debt but challenge. Finally, every *waygu'a* has a unique character: its provenance, former owners, and history are known, and its high value is a function of the entire memory that it embodies; thus, an entire network of personal bonds is woven between the partners. A variety of interwoven interpersonal networks symbolized by these precious goods thus develops throughout archipelago communities.

This dimension of challenge, obligation to reply, and engagement of the partners in the thing given is also found by Mauss to be present in another exemplary case of gift exchange described by Boas: the *potlatch* of coastal populations of the American Northwest. This Chinook term designates a ceremony in which a chief gives a celebration in the name of his clan (or "house") in order to honor another chief whom he treats at the same time as a partner worthy of the highest respect and as a rival. By giving the most precious goods (such as emblazoned copper pieces, woven blankets, furs, sometimes slaves, and of course sumptuary foods), a chief can publicly gain the prestige associated with this sumptuary wealth and, above all, can force the partner intent on keeping his rank to reply at a proper time with presents at least equal in value and most often of higher value. This rivalry can be exacerbated to an extreme degree.

In certain kinds of *potlatch* one must expend all that one has, keeping nothing back. It is a competition to see who is the richest and also the most wildly extravagant. Everything is based upon the principles of antagonism and rivalry. . . . In a certain number of cases, it is not even a question of giving and returning gifts, but of destroying, so as not to give the slightest hint of desiring your gift to be reciprocated. . . . Houses and thousands of blankets [are burnt]. The most valuable coppers are broken and thrown into the water, in order to put down and to "flatten" one's rival.[20]

In an exacerbated manner, everything becomes a matter of rank, prestige, and honor. Should such gestures still be called "gift-giving"? We will see that Mauss doubts it. Within the margin of this doubt may lie the most important clue that could lead us to a different hypothesis regarding the meaning of these rituals and the nature of the "enigma of gift exchange."

Mauss's questions regarding Kwakiutl *potlatch* and Trobriand *kula* are the following: in these two cases, as in every traditional society known to us, why are relationships between groups or individuals dominated by gift-exchange rituals? Who must give what goods to whom, in what circumstances, and for what purpose? More precisely, why are giving, receiving, and returning *obligatory* gestures? By asking these types of questions, Mauss brings to light an entire continent of anthropology. ("This embraces an enormous complex of facts.")[21] What he highlights are not mere forms of courtesy or attitudes of reciprocal generosity, which is to say admirable though supposedly marginal expressions of social life, but practices through which the social bond as such is constituted and expressed in a fundamental way. But what makes this a "total social fact"?

The Gift shows Mauss's first use of this notion as a central concept. How should it be understood? Mauss makes various uses of it; at least three different ones can be identified. First, ceremonial gift exchange is *total* in that it simultaneously includes every dimension of social life or, more precisely, every institution in which these dimensions are expressed: religion, law, public authority, kinship, economy, art, and morals (these categories are, of course, stated in a typically Western way). In this first aspect the practice of gift exchange has a transversal and integrating character. It calls for a form of analysis that preserves this simultaneity and avoids promoting one of its aspects as being the reason for the others; the very object of this inquiry requires a cross-disciplinary approach.[22]

But this totality also has a second meaning: in these exchanges society acts as such, as undivided reality, even though it does so through individual figures such as chiefs of clans or lineages.[23] Mauss thus writes of the Kwakiutl, "There is total service in the sense that it is indeed the whole clan that contracts on behalf of all, for all that it possesses and for all that it does, through the person of its chief" (*G* 6). This recalls the highly Durkheimian idea of society as autonomous being intensely experiencing and expressing its unity on privileged occasions such as festivals, mourning, and states of war. But Mauss goes beyond this idea: what is at stake is not merely exalted unanimism but a bonding dynamic between all individual members of the group and all of its statutory layers and subgroups (men and women, chiefs and ordinary members, clans and moieties [*G* 33]); one could add between humans and things, natural and supernatural beings, the living and the dead, humans and spirits. In other words, what is at stake is not merely functional reality but a symbolic whole that integrates functions, values, and representations.

Finally, in a third meaning, this totality designates the universal character of the gift-exchange relationship. Ritual gift exchange is certainly more important in institutional terms in traditional societies, but its existence can be verified in every society. This hypothesis makes it possible to generalize the paradigm. Mauss only indirectly alludes to this topic but his indications in the last pages of *The Gift* are unequivocal. The question of gift exchange is not merely "archaic"; it also arises in modern societies and should be raised regarding them (it remains to understand—and we will try to do so—why it no longer emerges with the same self-evident social character). In conclusion, this total character of gift exchange seems to involve every institutional aspect of a society, to involve this society as a whole, and to exist in every society.

Sociologists and anthropologists immediately perceived the theoretical and methodological stakes of the concept of the "total social fact": theoretical, in that it presupposes that social practices have an undivided character; methodological, in that it simultaneously resorts to all disciplines and calls for them to converge. From this point of view the set of questions integrated by Mauss regarding the forms of ritual gift exchange has also been applied to many different fields. Even so, misunderstandings and misinterpretations have developed, of which at least two should be mentioned.

First, to speak of "total social fact" does not mean that this type of phenomenon exclusively defines an entire society, even if it concerns this society as a whole: *total* does not mean "totalizing." Mauss thus carefully keeps from claiming that among the Trobriand or Kwakiutl "everything is gift exchange." What he claims is that gift exchange integrates every aspect of social life. There is a crucial difference between these two claims, which invites us to reject inaccurate phrases such as "gift-exchange societies" as opposed to "market societies." Making such statements amounts to claiming that the exchange of goods is performed through the circulation of gifts in some societies and through trade in others; this distinguishes two different types of cultures: those in which everything is given and those in which everything is sold. This meaningless distinction is not supported by any empirical data; these two phenomena do not belong to the same realm; they coexist under different institutional forms; one is not the alternative to the other. This is what we will have to explain.

The second type of misunderstanding is perhaps more subtle because it is associated with the descriptive categories available to us. Mauss himself sometimes falls into this trap, for instance when, in order to express the multiplicity of the social character of gift exchange, he describes it as being at the same time economic, religious, legal, political, and aesthetic. He sometimes mentions the inadequacy of these categories. The economic is the most problematic: if gift exchange is not economic in nature, then how does it integrate the economic dimension? It is tempting to claim that gift exchange is the foundation of the economy, in the same way as it has been claimed that "archaic" money is the source and the secret of commercial money. This is also a mistake. As essential as ritual gift exchange is, it is not the foundation of everything else (in the sense of a principle in reason). Yet if it accounts for the possibility and establishment of the social bond, then every other dimension—economy included—must have a decisive relationship to it.

Finally, there is another question that Mauss does not raise because the idea of evolution is self-evident to him: why has *ceremonial* gift exchange come close to disappearing in modern societies? Gift-exchange practices remain frequent, but they always have a private character; what is the meaning of this charitable gift-giving? What is its social function, assuming that it has one and that it is significant? We will have to raise these questions again, but let us first return to the analyses presented in *The Gift.*

The Three Gestures and the Paradox of Obligation

Mauss's original contribution is not so much to claim that gift-exchange practices are universally found in traditional societies as it is to show that the gesture of giving cannot be separated from the obligations to accept the gift and (most often at some later point) to reply with another gift. There is nothing simple about this giving-receiving-reciprocating operation. It is not an amicable circulation, a game to be played in turns (even if alternation is essential). This approach provides a first reason for Mauss's readers to be surprised: instead of asking, "What is giving? Why is giving obligatory?" Mauss asks, "What is giving back?" or rather, "What is reciprocating?" In traditional societies the question that matters is the following: "*What is the rule that compels the gift received to be obligatorily reciprocated?*" (*G* 1).[24] He could—and even should—ask why in certain circumstances *giving* is required. He does not justify the priority he chose but merely observes its existence: "The most important among these spiritual mechanisms is clearly one that obliges a person to reciprocate the present that has been received" (7). This approach to the obligation to give based on a priority assigned to the reciprocating gesture is probably legitimate but it is also evidence of a central—and yet unnoticed—difficulty presented by Mauss's approach. If we are able to identify this difficulty, we might reach the core of the enigma.

This difficulty can be explained as follows: in contemporary societies where moral giving predominates, what is constantly encouraged and seems to stand out as self-evident is the requirement to give. This self-evident character is probably excessive, and it points out the precise location of our blind spot. The gesture of giving seems available to anyone raised with the idea that helping others is admirable as a noble gesture or charitable act. Nothing is expected in return. This is why the obligation to reciprocate is not presented as an imperative; on the contrary, it becomes less constraining to the extent that the gift is unilateral (the poor are not expected to reciprocate the gift they have received). Mauss presupposes that the requirement to reciprocate, so pressing in traditional societies but so strange to us, makes it possible to understand the system of gift exchange not as a subjective and generous choice but as a specifically social phenomenon and a ritual practice instituting a relationship. What matters is this relationship rather than the moral accomplishment of the partners. This constraining aspect of reciprocity has probably become impenetrable for us, which is why Mauss expects that an inquiry into the imperative to reciprocate might shed light on the *social requirement to give*. It will remain to be determined whether this regressive approach has reached its objective.

Mauss first asks this question in its most general form: why do giving, receiving, and reciprocating belong to the mode of obligation? How can there be "services, apparently free and disinterested but nevertheless constrained and self-interested"? (*G* 3). He answers by providing observations such as the following (which applies to the Maori but can be widely generalized): "To refuse to give, to fail to invite, just as to refuse to accept, is tantamount to declaring war; it is to reject the bond of alliance and commonality" (13). Perhaps. But this constraint hardly seems tolerable when applied to gifts as we know them in our own societies (on the occasion of celebrations or birthdays, or in support of a cause). It is therefore this obligatory aspect that distinguishes ceremonial gift exchange from other forms of gift-giving. Once again, we expect an explanation of the obligation not only to return the gift but also to *give* in the first place. Mauss does not provide such an explanation directly. He answers by presenting an example involving the famous case of the Maori *hau*. The pages dedicated to it in *The Gift* have generated a succession of quasi-Byzantine—and still enduring—debates. It is important for us to understand what is at stake in this passage because Mauss's answer is provided in it.

His starting point is a speech by a Maori wise man from New Zealand, as reported in 1909 by Elsdon Best. This wise man, called Tamati Ranaipiri, wanted to explain to Best the obligatory character of the movement of what is given and returned between bird hunters, the forest genies who own these birds, and the priests who help capture the birds through the use of a magical object. In order to be understood, Ranaipiri gave the example of the circulation of gifts between three partners: a valuable object (*taonga*) is offered by A to B, who gives it to C, who later gives a gift to B in return. Because of a force called *hau* that inhabits their relationship, B then considers himself obligated to give A the object he received from C; it should be noted that *this object is not the one A gave B.* This is the essence of Ranaipiri's words as transcribed by Best and quoted by Mauss. But what is the precise nature of this *hau?* Mauss views it as a spiritual principle that the natives consider to be present in the thing given as its soul or force, which according to Mauss comes from the giver himself: "What imposes obligation in the present received and exchanged, is the fact that the thing received is not inactive. Even when it has been abandoned by the giver, it still possesses something of him. . . . This is because the *taonga* is animated by the *hau* of its forest, its native heath and soil. . . . It is the *hau* that wishes to return to its birthplace, to the sanctuary of the forest and the clan, and to the owner" (*G* 11–12). According to Mauss this Maori narrative calls for two considerations. First, it clearly highlights the very fact of the obligation to reciprocate the gift. Second, it should be emphasized that what the recipient is given is not merely a good but something of *the person of the giver*: "To accept something from somebody is to accept some part of his spiritual essence. To retain that thing would be dangerous and mortal, not only because it would be against [the] law and morality, but also because that thing coming from a person not only morally, but physically and spiritually, . . . exert[s] a magical or religious hold over you" (12). This is the force that inhabits the *hau* and obligates the recipient to reciprocate the gift.

This analysis sparked a well-known critique by Lévi-Strauss, who deplores Mauss's apparent endorsement of the native explanation instead of realizing that the power of the *hau* is only the figurative and unconscious form that expresses the requirement to give, receive, and reciprocate, in short the entire movement of the gift-exchange relationship.[25] Without dealing in detail with the debate generated by this critique, let me merely highlight a construction that is clearer than has been claimed.

Let me first say that Lévi-Strauss is right to emphasize (in a very Maussian way) the logic of reciprocity, since this is indeed the point that Ranaipiri wanted to explain, but Mauss very accurately perceives something that Lévi-Strauss ignores: any good entering the movement of gift exchange is understood as being *part of the very being of the giver.* The giver is satisfied when he has in turn received a gift that replies to his—not from just anybody but from the specific recipient of his own gift. After giving something of himself, he must receive something of the other. It is this "spirit of the gift," rather than the object itself, that constitutes the *hau*. Ranaipiri clearly stated that B, after giving C the gift he received from A, must return to A the gift he later received from C. This amounts to stating that the gesture of recognition must return to its initiator—the gesture itself but not the thing given, since *at no time did Ranaipiri say that the object originally given by A must return to him*; most of the misinterpretations with respect to this question are based on this mistaken assumption.[26] Let us once again read the crucial passage from the Maori wise man as transcribed by Best:

I will speak to you about the *hau*. . . . Let us suppose that you possess a certain article (*taonga*) and that you give me this article. . . . I give this article to a third person who, after a certain lapse of time, decides to give me something as payment in return (*utu*). He makes a present to me of something (*taonga*). Now this *taonga* that he gives me is the spirit (*hau*) of the *taonga* that I had received from you and that I had given to him. The *taonga* that I received for these *taonga* (which came from you) must be returned to you. . . . I must give them to you because they are a *hau* of the *taonga* that you gave me.[27]

Mauss rightly comments: it is "the *hau* [that] wants to return to the place of its birth," not the object given. This operation and its three agents can be schematized as follows:

$$A \Longrightarrow B \Longrightarrow C$$
$$A \Longleftarrow B \Longleftarrow C$$

The logic involved is quite clear. It is very similar to that of the so-called *generalized* or postponed exchange in kinship systems; what Ranaipiri wanted to explain was, indeed, this indirect and complex exchange.[28] He meant to show that reciprocity runs along the entire chain of giving and that the initial gift is not lost on the way. This gift necessarily calls for reciprocation and cannot be forgotten because it is accompanied by its spirit, the "spirit of the gift," its *hau*, which watches over its return. The reason why the reply must come through these intermediaries is that a failure to reply would amount to a breaking of the bond and the threat of a conflict. The *hau* perfectly translates this requirement to reciprocate through a sequence of postponed offerings. The case of restricted or direct exchange, however, would show the simple movement schematized below, a much more obvious one that would probably not have led the Maori wise man to provide his apologue:

$$A \Longrightarrow B$$
$$A \Longleftarrow B$$

Sahlins, who reexamines the entire question,[29] points out a very interesting fact: in different contexts, what the Maori call *hau* designates a *surplus* or advantage. This makes it easier to understand why B is obligated to give C's gift to A. The gift is, above all, what institutes a social bond between the partners in the exchange; the advantage gained by B and then by C is "spiritual" in nature. By his initial gift, A creates this increase in symbolic value. This generous contagion that he initiates must return to him in the form of a countergift because he, too, must give or reciprocate gifts to others. A makes it possible for B to give to C (this is what constitutes *hau*, advantage, or new bond), which is why C's reciprocating gift to B must be given to A and to *no other*. B could use C's countergift to open a different line of relationships advantageous to him, but doing so would amount to ignoring his obligation to reply to A. The advantage must return to he who generated it *within the sequence under consideration*. Each line of gift exchange is personal because it is always a mutual relationship; the network formed by these mutual relationships constitutes the whole of the social bond. This is the invisible hand of the gift-exchange relationship. The Maori notion of *hau* has no other meaning.

This logic of the *hau* is certainly remarkable. Yet it leaves us somehow disappointed, not for the reason it disappointed Lévi-Strauss but because it once again brings to the fore the obligation to reciprocate without shedding light on the mysterious obligation to give in the first place.

The Giver in the Thing Given

Mauss is not wrong, however, to emphasize the magical force included in the thing given. That such a force inhabits the original gift is, indeed, a native belief—in the same way that myths are. It remains to be determined why it is one of the most widespread beliefs in ceremonial gift-exchange practices. In the past few decades anthropology has tended to neglect this issue, probably wrongly so, because of a reaction against the fascination with magical phenomena that had been widespread in early-twentieth-century research (thus, in his preface to Malinowski's *Argonauts of the Western Pacific* James Frazer is so obsessed with the protection and incantation rituals that govern *kula* exchange that he almost fails to notice the importance of cycles of gift exchange). Why are these magical rituals associated with gestures of giving? Because, as Mauss once again so accurately perceives, *the giver places his own person at risk in what he gives*, and he gives in it a part of himself: "The thing received is not inactive. Even when it has been abandoned by the giver, it still possesses something of him. Through it the giver has a hold over the beneficiary. . . . To make a gift of something to someone is to make a present of some part of oneself. . . . To accept something from somebody is to accept some part of his spiritual essence" (*G* 11–12). Later Mauss reiterates that "by giving one is giving *oneself*, and if one gives *oneself*, it is because one 'owes' *oneself*—one's person and one's goods—to others" (46). The implication of the giver in the thing given is not a metaphor: it involves a transfer of soul and of substantial presence. It translates the fact that the bond between giver and recipient is personal, exclusive, and intense. The community is the global fabric of these unique and local relationships. For instance, what the *hau* means is that circuits of exchange are specific: you must reciprocate a gift to the person from which you received one before you can give to someone else in order to receive something. For the global balance to be preserved, each local circuit must abide by the order of exchanges. The giver himself circulates in the circulating object, which is a pledge and substitute of himself; this part of himself resides in others, which involves risk (hence the importance of protection rituals), but it also provides him with power: protected by its own magic, the precious object makes it possible to intervene in the partner's space. Moreover, as in the case of the *hau*, the spirit of the thing given takes charge of reciprocal relationships and watches over the reciprocation of the gift. In this case magic supports the imperative of trust. The entire network of gift exchange consists in the fact that everyone must place something of himself at risk *outside of his own place* and receive something from others *within his own space*. This gesture, of course, involves a shared risk; moreover, it constitutes the extension of the self into the core of the other—or of the other into the core of the self. Everyone is at the center of a web woven by these multiple bonds. This generates a kind of reciprocal ubiquity that overcomes the paradox of the whole and its parts, the one and the many, here and there, local and global.[30] This is what can be called the social bond. A crucial question remains: why does it take on this precise form, through the mediation of the thing given? Mauss does not provide an answer, so we will have to try to do so.

The foremost question that arises is, What is the thing that is given? What is offered in the gesture of giving? The answers usually provided have to do with objects, the countable goods with which we have become familiar through commercial exchange. From the outset Mauss points out a much richer and more complex approach: "What they exchange is not solely property and wealth, movable and immovable goods, and things economically useful. In particular, such exchanges are acts of politeness: banquets, rituals, military services, women, children, dances, festivals, and fairs, in which economic transaction is only one element, and in which the passing on of wealth is only one feature of a much more general and enduring contract" (*G* 5).

We must once again disregard this inadequate terminology borrowed from European law (especially the term *contract*, which in its exact sense is—as we will see—the very opposite of the gift-exchange relationship). In fact, it is not enough to say that what is at stake is not "things economically useful"; it must be recognized that they rarely are. The things involved are associated with prestige and decorum, even in the case of food (although nourishing, it is primarily offered as *rich food*, sumptuary and appropriate for festivals rather than for ordinary and utilitarian consumption). Mauss's list lumps together every aspect of the exchange without considering at this point the functions and the very different statuses of these elements (for instance, matrimonial alliances belong to a different order than military pacts). Mauss is remarkably aware, however, that ceremonial gift exchange involves all kinds of material, as well as nonmaterial, offerings. This is also what defines this exchange as *total social fact*. But *total* should be understood in an even broader sense given that the exchange does not only involve the human world. The atmosphere of the gift extends to the surrounding universe, pervades nature in its entirety, and includes the relationships between humans, animals, and spirits, understood as relationships of alliance. Taking up at greater depth the inquiry regarding the Kwakiutl, a later researcher understands and states this in terms that would have delighted Mauss:

The obligation to reciprocate in exchanges is not in response to specific powers in the objects but to a cosmological conception that postulates an eternal circulation of forms of being. The obligations to give and the obligations to repay are obligations to participate in this vital circulation. . . . Kwakiutl chiefs participate in exchanges as incarnates of ancestral and supernatural beings. For them, therefore, the total system of circulation encompassed a universe of men, of ancestral spirits, of supernatural beings, and through the properties that circulated, of animal and vegetable forms of life.[31]

Ceremonial gift exchange as social fact would not be total if it were not also cosmic. This is not a uniquely Kwakiutl worldview; it was shared by the old *sophoi* of preclassical Greece and is brilliantly expressed by "Anaximander's fragment" as reciprocity between natural elements, planets, and living and nonliving beings; it is also found in many theological Christian writings from the first centuries CE and the Middle Ages; it is present as parody in Rabelais' famous "Praise of debt" given by Panurge in chapter 2 of *The Third Book*.[32] The total character of the exchange makes the universe itself a partner in the alliance.

The Enigma of Ceremonial Gift Exchange: Giving, Challenging, and Binding

The reason why Mauss accounts for ceremonial gift exchange from the standpoint of the requirement to reciprocate the gift is probably that, as we have seen, this obligation is the most enigmatic for us. Contrary to what Lévi-Strauss thinks, the reason that Mauss accepts the native interpretation is not that he does not grasp the immediate unity of the three gestures—in fact he is well aware of it—but the difficulty he encounters in finding a general explanation for the very gesture of giving; he thus confesses to his perplexity regarding *kula* exchanges: "Unfortunately our knowledge of the legal rule that governs these transactions is defective" (*G* 26). This is the question that we must ask: before the reciprocating gesture occurs, what makes the gesture of giving necessary in the first place? Why give, and why is giving an obligation? At times Mauss senses that the problem has to do with the use of the very term *gift*. Its altruistic connotation remains such an integral part of the word that it makes it difficult for us to see that the primary purpose of ceremonial gift exchange is not to fulfill the recipient—in terms of goods he could enjoy—but to honor him and express the esteem in which he is held. Perhaps it would be best to give up the use of the word *gift*, which Mauss considers doing, and to use the phrase "sumptuary offering" instead.

At this point Mauss's analyses show the lack of a more radical reflection on the practice of ceremonial gift exchange as the privileged expression among humans of the encounter between groups of strangers; this lack of reflection is shared by a large part of more recent research. Even so, in the very last pages of *The Gift* Mauss senses what seems to be at the core of the issue: "Over a considerable period of time and in a considerable number of societies, men approached one another in a curious frame of mind, one of fear and exaggerated hostility, and of generosity that was likewise exaggerated, but such traits only appear insane to our eyes. . . . There is no middle way: one trusts completely, or one mistrusts completely; one lays down one's arms and gives up magic, or one gives everything" (*G* 81). It may be that the obligation to give is entirely contained in this paradoxical characteristic of human beings: at the same time all radically alien to each other and radically the same. Thus arises this questioning: who is this other—individual or group—that looks like us? Who is he, in this other space that is like our own? How can he be different from us who know quite well who we are? How can other humans seem so close to us and yet not be some of us? Should they be deterred from entering our space and expelled by force? Should they be welcomed instead? How can we express our desire for an encounter or an alliance? How can we be sure that they will accept the encounter or the alliance and will not later change their minds? How can we create a lasting bond?

These are the questions implicit in gift exchange; they are neither economic nor moral, and they involve neither utility nor charity. They primarily concern the need to be recognized rather than the requirement to be grateful. This seems to be at the core of the enigma of ceremonial gift exchange.[33]

The Symbolic Gesture

Nobody ever saw a dog make a fair and deliberate exchange of one bone for another with another dog.

ADAM SMITH, *An Inquiry into the Nature and Causes of the Wealth of Nations*

In his classical work on the circulation of *moka* offerings in the Mount Hagen region of New Guinea, Andrew Strathern writes that in the village of his informant—an old man who had witnessed the arrival of the first white men, representatives of the Australian administration—the question was raised as to whether the strange creature that had come and visited them was a human being or one of those pale cannibalistic monsters mentioned in the legends. They presented him with pigs, and in return he offered them precious shells. This was when the natives decided that they were indeed dealing with a genuine man like themselves.[34]

This is an exemplary tale in that it invites us to radically raise the ethological question of the recognition between humans and to confront the forms of relationships and encounters found in our species with those observed in various types of animal societies. These relationships include many different aspects. In each species they take on such predictable forms that they have been considered as rituals. They are associated with colors, smells, sounds, visual forms, and attitudes. The most useful ethological information in this respect is, of course, that which pertains to groups of apes, particularly gorillas and chimpanzees.[35] Modes of approach, recognition, and acceptance are subtle and highly complex. Observers are unsure whether all of these should be considered genetically programmed. There is something akin to "traditions" specific to certain groups; however, the main modes remain stable within a species, and the forms they take only show a limited range of variation. The recognition process includes at least two different aspects, which often constitute a two-phase sequence: first, recognition as identification of the other as being of one's own kind or not, a moment of adequate perception found in every living species; second, and by far the more important, recognition as acceptance and gesture of "respect" or even allegiance. It is also found in all mammal species and is, of course, most highly developed among primates. This acceptance is performed through an entire sequence of visual behaviors whose expression is relatively consistent.

On the contrary, human groups stand out because they display a considerable range of variation in these processes. It is as if the inventiveness in the modes of approach and contact were proportional to the degree of autonomy that characterizes living beings. These stabilized variations passed on from generation to generation are part of what is called culture. An invariant stands out among these variations, however: the very fact that recognition of the other (in its second step, as recognition granted to a partner) occurs through the reciprocal giving of objects considered important; this is what is called presents. Something of oneself—a good of one's own—is presented and given to the other. The precious character granted to the object expresses the fact that it is a personal possession that stands for part of oneself; it is something that one holds dear and to which one assigns value; giving it involves a risk. It is at the same time a pledge and a substitute of the giver. The recipient understands that the giver is requesting a reply of the same kind. This is why the process of encounter and exchange has two features that are meant to emphasize its importance. First, the presentation gesture is not performed in a trivial or neutral manner but is invested with great emotional charge; the occasion is solemn and associated with ambiguous feelings. There is always a concern that the gift might not be accepted or might be considered insufficient. But the wish to bond and the pleasure involved in being with partners one has chosen must also be expressed—hence the *festive* and consummatory aspect of the event. Goods are offered along with courteous words, deferential gestures, and sometimes dances, music, or delicacies. Second, all of this follows well-established protocols that amount to conventions and are meant to eliminate the risks associated with awkward improvisation, which would also give an impression of carelessness. It is this *formal* character that confers a kind of solemnity to the gestures of giving and their acceptance (in *kula*, for instance, exchanges are announced with horn blows, and everything follows set stages in an atmosphere of seriousness and mutual respect—which does not preclude festivities). Because of all this, the gift is said to be *ceremonial* according to Malinowski's definition: "I shall call an action ceremonial if it is: (1) public; (2) carried on under observance of definite formalities; (3) if it has sociological, religious or magical import, and carries with it obligations."[36]

Human recognition of the other, whether person or group, always takes place through the gesture by which one holds out a *mediating object* to the other, presenting the other with something that one is giving as a part of oneself and venturing into alien space. This gesture states the following: first, we recognize you as fellow humans; second, we accept you as possible partners; finally—once relationships have been established—we wish to remain bonded with you in the future.

It can be said that this is the very gesture of symbolism, if we accept, as etymology shows, that a symbol is a physical element that stands for a pact; *sum-bolon* literally means what is placed together. In certain ancient (Greek and Roman) forms of reciprocal commitments a piece of pottery or metal was broken in two, and each partner kept one half as proof and pledge of the agreement: because each half fit the other, it could vouch for the agreement at any time and often long afterward. In this the symbol belongs to the realm of the alliance and of relationships of reciprocity; this does not mean that symbolism is necessarily social in nature but that the formation of symbolism always presupposes a system of differentiated elements related to each other according to a convention of exchange.[37]

If the gift is indeed this unique—this specifically human—procedure of recognition, then it is essential for the gestures of the partners in the pact—the *sumballontes*—to alternate. The things offered by one side are a necessary reply to those offered by the other; the *sum-bolon* consists of the set made up by the giver, the thing given, the recipient, and the reply by which the recipient gives in turn. Symbolism is constituted by this triple implication and double movement, be they immediate (as in opening gifts) or extending through time (as in already confirmed alliances). Gift exchange cannot be reduced to an expression of amicable sociality. It is the procedure that publicly institutes the gesture by which every human or group honors another, the procedure that initiates or replays the founding act of the alliance.[38]

It is remarkable that in encounters and processes of approach between two human groups, bodily expressions, no matter how friendly, are not enough to establish recognition—in the sense of acceptance—but that an additional element is required: a physical element, a pledge of good faith, given as substitute for the group that offers an association: the thing given. No such procedure is found in any primate group. At most, chimpanzees will share the flesh of an animal killed in a collective hunt, but they never show procedures of the approach of one group by another through the offering of an object that would then be kept as testimony to the agreement and to which the partner would reply, immediately or later on, by giving a different object. Acts of sharing among primates (such as holding out a piece of food to the other) do not in and of themselves qualify as gift-exchange relationships.[39] *Ceremonial gift exchange is not the sharing of a good*; it is not an expression of altruism (a phenomenon that can be observed in all primates) or the mere taking up of a position within the group, nor is it the mere giving of one's possessions, whether out of benevolence or with ulterior motives. It is the granting of a pledge that commits the giver as substitute of himself and that stands for the conclusion of a pact. The aim of this gift—this risky offering—is not to increase the partner's possessions or to provide him with assistance. We must once again reject the economist prejudice that always focuses on the consumable good and ignores the act of challenging the other, as well as the moral prejudice that promotes the act of helping and misunderstands agonistic generosity.

It is tempting to view this pledge as a mediation (and, indeed, it is one) that embodies the opposition between subject and object—where the subject asserts himself in the thing presented. This interpretation appears coherent, but it is only relevant within the logic of the contract (the purpose of which is to separate subjective from objective elements). When applied to the alliance and to the relationship of gift exchange, it distorts the issue because what makes it possible for a thing to become pledge and substitute is that *it is an extension of the very being of the giver who gives himself through it*; it is a part of him that is mobile but not distinct from him. This is what Mauss emphasizes when he uses the phrase "a tie between souls" (*G* 12); he also sees this in the *hau* principle, and he has it in mind when he uses the term *intermingling*.[40]

Whereas in other species recognition and bonding between individuals or groups are effected through smells, colors, visual forms, sounds, gestures, sequences of postures, and global attitudes, including trust and sometimes allegiance, among humans they are achieved by presenting the other with an object that stands as part of oneself, testifies to the agreement, and guarantees it. This object is associated with words, deferential and benevolent expressions, and conventional attitudes. This is the ceremonial (which is to say public) offering that is called *giving*, which means first and foremost to solemnly and reciprocally recognize, accept, and honor each other and, above all, to engage in an alliance through the mediation of what is given to the other. For this recognition, accepting, and bonding to continue or develop, a constant renewal of gift exchanges (as on ritually marked occasions) is required, the most crucial of which is the matrimonial alliance.

The reason for the initial obligation to give is now coming to light, as is the obligation to accept and reciprocate the gift. Ceremonial gift exchanges manifest a fundamental structure of reciprocity as a condition for all social life in the human species. We can now say, as Mauss does, that we have reached the "bedrock." Yet at this point we must assess the extreme complexity of the gesture and relationship of gift exchange. What ensures that the gift will be accepted? What is implied by the relationship with another human being, another animal endowed with language? What does it mean to recognize someone? What is the status of the thing given, and what defines its significance for the partners? What is the nature of the bond generated by this gesture? What does denial of recognition or misunderstanding in the exchange entail?

Generosity and Challenge

These questions likely imply the following: how can we understand the aspects of challenge and generosity involved in gift exchange? Mauss senses this: "There is no middle way: one trusts completely, or one mistrusts completely; one lays down one's arms and gives up magic, or one gives everything." This challenge includes two aspects: the first is simply inciting the partner to reply. It is a solution to the following problem: how can one make a request that does not take the form of a request? The challenge forces the partner to reply without one having to request it. The very structure of the challenge rooted in the relationship between two equally autonomous living beings, however, remains to be understood. The second aspect is the following: what is given must be significant or must be considered precious in order to make the challenge forceful enough and to *obligate* the partner. In this case the excessive character of the gift involves a power of anticipation. It makes it possible to throw the arch of a bridge toward a still invisible shore and to ensure that the same move taken from the other side will bring the bridge to completion. Without this challenge—this unreasonable gesture—the distance between the two positions alien to each other remains insurmountable; the approach itself is inconceivable since one of the protagonists would have to give in to the other. The challenge of the gift provokes and invokes at the same time. It provokes precisely by remaining intractable. It calls for trust, and it reassures the partner by giving everything: giving oneself in the pledge offered, in the thing given.

Ceremonial generosity is not moral (or it is only so as a supplement); it is the proof that while venturing into the alien space, one is prepared to establish an alliance. Groups and individuals alike are aware that the greatest temptation is to stay among one's own and to find well-being at home. At the same time, the greatest satisfaction lies in being recognized by others. There is pleasure to be found in bonding with others and in experiencing what lies elsewhere. There is also the danger of being rejected or attacked. Gift-giving solves this dilemma. As challenge it makes it possible to risk making a move toward the other while obligating the other to risk making a move in return. It is a gamble on the possibility of going outside oneself while imposing reciprocity.

This concept of challenge makes it possible to understand several aspects of the gift-exchange relationship. The most important element we should consider is that *generosity must be ostentatious*. As Boas and Malinowski keep reminding us, the gesture of giving is glorious, and it brings prestige, yet the nature of the honor derived remains enigmatic. Should it be understood as denial of physical goods (according to the highly Hegelian interpretation put forth by Claude Lefort)?[41] Leaving aside certain cases of exacerbated *potlatch* described by Boas (and which emerged later), what matters is not to destroy goods but, on the contrary, to provide ample proof of wealth that expresses the very being of the giver and his group. Exhibiting and offering goods and displaying prodigality does not amount to claiming that all this is nothing; on the contrary, it takes it for granted that this gesture will be highly valued. But it is clear that the first goal is to honor the recipient and to show him the highest possible—even excessive—consideration and that the honor of the giver lies in this. To achieve this purpose, it is important for the act of giving to be known and seen by all and to be spectacular if possible. This makes it easier to understand that what is at stake is not charitable generosity but public liberality. To offer this challenge and uphold it in front of all is what brings prestige and glory in the *relationship of recognition* (which is clearly something entirely different from the struggle for recognition as Hegel presents it).[42]

Challenge is not primarily rivalry for a coveted object; it is a call and even a provocation for a reply. There is indeed rivalry, but it is of a sort similar to that of a game or athletic competition rather than of envy; if this rivalry becomes exacerbated, this is due to the emergence of an additional element that destabilizes the interplay of the challenge and the alternating between equal partners. But why call it a game? More precisely, it belongs to the category of games based on a *principle of alternation*;[43] these are games played by two partners who take turns replying to the other (as in chess, card games, and many ball games). These games are structured like duels or tournaments. As Huizinga shows, they are based on a kind of spontaneous convention that is also an ethic: "to each his turn"; to play twice in a row is cheating.[44] Each player must play in his or her turn because every challenge must be met by a reply. Failure to reply equals losing, or rather, it constitutes a reply by default but a reply nevertheless. With his usual insight Mauss does not fail to note this gamelike aspect of gift-exchange rituals in populations from the Northwest Coast of North America: "On this subject it would be necessary to study gambling, which even in French society is not considered to be a contract, but a situation in which honour is committed and where goods are handed over that, after all, one could refuse to hand over. Gambling is a form of *potlatch* and of the gift system."[45] Among the Tlingit and the Haida, a kind of equivalence even operates between game, *potlatch*, and warfare. One can win or lose everything (wife and children included). The game phenomenon always involves challenge as a call to the other, a venture into the unknown, and a means of seducing strangers. *Seducere* literally means drawing others toward oneself and bringing them in from elsewhere. But this wager that requests and even forces a reply from the other (which means that the challenge has crossed over to the invisible shore and reached him) calls for the reply or return move that is so obvious in the practice of games.

Roberte Hamayon, studying populations of Siberian hunters and especially their shamanistic practices, clearly shows that games are associated with ceremonial gift exchange and the system of alliance. The major seasonal rituals of preparation for hunting take the form of games; they constitute a kind of symbolic hunt directed and mimicked through dances performed by the shaman using various animal masks. Moreover, this symbolic hunt is understood as a matrimonial union between the hunter-husband and the hunted animal; the shaman mimics the rutting male trying to seduce his animal spouse. The entire ritual revolves around the alliance motif that, in addition to union with the animal, also includes union with forest spirits and with other animals. All these interactions are viewed as relationships between partners who at the same time respect, provoke, and attract each other, and who take pleasure in their exchanges, which is why "spirits enjoy games." "As in the model provided by the shaman and his animal spouse, the human community views itself as forming a pair with its environment."[46] This feeling of a kind of equal partnership is very powerful; it finds its most intense expression in games, as relationships of challenge and reply, offering and returning, enjoyment and obligation.

It may be that *potlatch* already constitutes a break with this model; how can we explain the transformation effected from playful to exacerbated or even violent rivalry? Roberte Hamayon shows in *La chasse à l'âme* that the world of alliance was replaced by the world of filiation; when hunters become herders, the ancestors who handed down the herd supersede the forest spirits who give the opportunity to capture prey. Hierarchical verticality replaces horizontal relationships between equal partners. This is probably one of the key elements that determines the emergence of a more hierarchical and authoritarian world. We will soon see that this is related to unequal gift-giving and domination, to the importance taken on by the goods that constitute the group's "treasure," and finally to sacrifice.[47]

Free Obligation

The fact that human groups are led to encounter and conduct alliances with each other can be considered a phenomenon common to many species. The fact that these encounters and alliances are performed through the mediation of ceremoniously exchanged goods is already more specific and even radically original. This would still leave us within the realm of necessity, however, if it were not for the existence of an important factor of uncertainty: the group can hasten or delay the encounter; it can give it significance or fail to do so by modulating the importance of the gifts; it can give excessive offerings; or it can refuse the exchange. In short, in the human species there is a decisive intervention of an element of choice and free will that inseparably associates necessity and freedom in the gesture of giving. What is at stake is the recognition of others, not in the purely natural sense of being able to identify them and view them as fellow members of the species but in the sense of granting them respect and acknowledging their worth, their importance, and ultimately the fact that their existence is equal to ours, although *elsewhere and in a different way*. The encounter is required by nature, but in the case of humans it is neither programmed nor programmable. All of us know that we are facing beings endowed with free will and that we must confront the same autonomy and freedom that we experience in ourselves, along with the same claim to be recognized. This ethical dimension is part of the ethology of human societies.

Nothing shows this better than the well-known procedures called opening gifts; these are gifts groups give one another when they first come into contact. What is at stake for each partner is at the same time demonstrating goodwill and avoiding showing pettiness in the offering—which would amount to lack of consideration—as well as excessive prodigality—which would amount to arrogance. What matters is displaying the wish for a partnership and doing so while respecting a certain balance. Moreover, this exchange sets a distinction between those who give in the first place and those who receive and will later reciprocate the gift. It is clear that those who give first are in the advantageous position of having the initiative while the others are in the passive position of recipients, hence the importance of the reply. What matters is not so much giving back as it is *giving in one's turn, not restituting but taking back the initiative in gift-giving*; this amounts to a claim to autonomy and freedom. This is why the term *returning* can be misleading: it focuses on the good instead of the gesture, which leads to missing the purpose of ceremonial gift exchange and above all to interpreting it as a relationship of debt when it is actually a relationship of respect and challenge. One does not "return" a gift in the way one pays back a loan but in the way one replies to a move. In its temporal sequence the back-and-forth movement of gift/countergift alternates generous challenge and equal reply. The initial gift does not generate a debt but sends out a call; it creates a requirement to reply. Gift exchange is a ceremonial duel in which autonomous beings who wish to associate without relinquishing their freedom confront each other. This is why a failed encounter can degenerate into conflict. To give is at the same time to give up what is being given and to prevail through what has been given; it is at the same time offering and challenge, game and pact, agreement always on the verge of disagreement, peace at the edge of a potential conflict. The background of the relationship remains agonistic; consensus is not a given but a horizon.

This is the condition for mutual recognition between beings endowed with an equal capacity to choose and decide, in short to conduct or not to conduct an alliance. To establish a community is to become a society of *com-munia*—shared gifts (*munia*). Gift exchange resolves the tension that exists between the necessary character of the encounter—required by nature—and the unpredictability of the response—required by freedom. This vantage point makes it possible to understand the *ritual forms* associated with these encounters as an efficient way of coding attitudes to preclude the risk that would be generated by excessive arbitrariness and to neutralize variations in private feelings or in short-lived emotions. Rites thus operate as fixed rules that make it possible to recognize the will of the group independent of the various subjective states of its members. In the exact same way, we still ensure civil and respectful contact with each other through conventional salutations and all kinds of established forms of politeness, regardless of our personal feelings. In communities of beings endowed with autonomy and freedom, rituals provide a cultural analogon of something that in other species belongs to the realm of natural constraint. They function as conventions by ensuring the stability of the forms of exchange so that they are recognizable and so that in every circumstance everyone will know what must be done and what these forms mean. This makes it easier to understand the paradox of ceremonial gift exchange—so accurately identified by Mauss—as being at the same time obligated and free. An exclusively constrained gift is a purely natural phenomenon (in the same way as the need to feed or reproduce) and, as such, teaches us nothing about the constitution of the social realm. This is why, as obligatory as ceremonial gift exchange may be for a group, it still remains a choice. Gift exchange is a free obligation because it is an obligation that involves free beings. Rituals—by defining the appropriate attitudes, moments, and presents according to circumstances, actors in the exchange, or other features—give the form of common law to the freedom of the partners. We also know that rituals are always constituted in a local and circumstantial manner, by selecting in the environment and the set of human gestures a certain number of elements that provide enough semantic content and differential features to form a code. This precisely defines symbolism.[48]

Should we view as a contradiction the fact that gift-giving, the very gesture of generosity or gratuity, is also obligatory? There is, in fact, no such contradiction; or if there is, it is only in the view of those who confuse gift-giving as private moral gesture with ceremonial gift exchange[49] and who also primarily consider gift-giving in relation to the thing given and reduce it to an isolated act of offering.[50] Yet in ceremonial exchanges giving is not generous offering; it does not mean giving a thing as a good but presenting it as a pledge in order to express reciprocity and initiate or continue cycles of exchange. This misinterpretation shows a fetishistic attitude that views the good offered as object of enjoyment for its recipient instead of as a testimony—a symbol—of alliance for the partners. From this point of view the idea of a gift that is so generous that it remains unknown by its recipient is truly absurd, since the purpose of ceremonial gift exchange is not to be morally sublime through saintly offering but to recognize one another through the back-and-forth circulation of presents, to publicly express this recognition according to rules of deference, and to provide proof of it following conventional forms. The end of the gift is neither the thing given (which captures the attention of economists) nor even the gesture of giving (which fascinates moralists) but the creation or renewal of an alliance. Ceremonial gift exchange is a relationship: a public act without which there is no community; from the perspective of ceremonial gift exchange, to wish for a gift that remains unknown is to wish for the death of reciprocal recognition.

Matrimonial Alliance: Lévi-Strauss's Analysis

What has been the most consistent, sure, and complete traditional expression of the requirement for reciprocal recognition—as yearning and as necessity? Undoubtedly, it has been the institution of matrimonial alliance. Mauss senses—but does not emphasize—that marriage between partners in gift exchange constitutes one of the most important elements in their exchanges.[51] It is, in fact, a founding element, but a precise demonstration remained to be provided. This is provided by Claude Lévi-Strauss in *The Elementary Structures of Kinship*. This work is the richest and most ambitious continuation of Mauss's *The Gift* (and I find it surprising that so few commentators have noticed this).[52] Matrimonial alliance is a founding element because exogamic alliance is what accounts for the prohibition of incest. It distinguishes human from animal societies and confirms the fact that the specific character of human societies is symbolic reciprocity.

In his approach to kinship systems in traditional societies Lévi-Strauss notes the following facts: (1) the universal character of the prohibition of incest; (2) the enigma of the preference for marriage between crossed cousins and of the quasi-universal prohibition of marriage between parallel cousins; (3) the frequent occurrence of exogamic moieties; (4) the importance of the gifts that the husband's group must offer to the wife's group on the occasion of matrimonial unions. How can these facts be understood? Is there a connection among them, in spite of their great apparent heterogeneity? The originality of Lévi-Strauss's hypotheses is to show that they involve a single problem associated with the reciprocity requirement.

When Lévi-Strauss began his research, the analysis of kinship phenomena was mostly focused on questions of filiation (whether matri-, patri-, bi-lineal, or undifferentiated); he noticed that the facts hardest to interpret (such as those mentioned above) were most often ignored or explained away through hypothetical genealogies that assume the existence of ancient institutions whose reason for being was lost. This does not explain why these institutions would have emerged in the past, what would have later caused them to disappear, or why their effects are still observed in the present. Lévi-Strauss wonders if the reason for this phenomenon could be a still-relevant one and, therefore, a logical rather than genealogical reason. This leads him to consider kinship from the point of view of alliance rather than filiation and thus to favor a structural over a genetic approach, hence this question: what determines the choice of spouses in the union between a man and a woman? Why are certain choices prohibited while others are favored? Could there be a consistent association between negative prescriptions and favored choices? The first and most universal of all prohibitions is that against incest. What is prohibited is not so much the sexual act itself as the institutional union of a father and his daughter or of a brother and his sister. As Lévi-Strauss shows, this prohibition cannot be explained by biological instinct or psychological repulsion. It is a social proscription, and its reason for being is social. What is this reason? It is clearly shown by its consequence: the women that a group prohibits to itself as spouses are available for another group that behaves in the same way, hence the emergence of alliance through matrimonial union.

This entails several consequences at the same time. The first and most general, associated with the universal character of the prohibition, means that human procreation is not left to nature but is taken charge of by the group. Nature prescribes sexual union but requires nothing more; society determines which spouses are allowed and which are proscribed; in this sense this is indicative of a shift from nature to culture. The second consideration, however, is probably the more important: this prohibition is not so much a negative rule precluding certain choices as it is a positive rule guaranteeing that other choices must be made and thus ensuring the existence of relationships of reciprocity between groups: "Like exogamy, which is its widened social expression, the prohibition of incest is a rule of reciprocity. The woman whom one does not take, and whom one may not take, is, for that very reason, offered up. To whom is she offered? Sometimes to a group defined by institutions, and sometimes to an indeterminate and ever-open collectivity limited only by the exclusion of near relatives, such as in our own societies."[53] Note this remark made by Lévi-Strauss near the end of the book: "It is the supreme rule of the gift."[54] Matrimonial alliance is the highest and most decisive form of the relationship of recognition between groups that reciprocal ceremonial gift exchange constitutes. Because the wives are essential to the group's existence, the group's very being is at stake in the recognition ensured by matrimonial alliance. This is why Lévi-Strauss explicitly refers to Mauss and *The Gift* to account for this practice of reciprocity that is by far the most institutionalized in traditional societies; he and Mauss always have this type of reciprocity in mind when they speak of *exchange*.

There are important theoretical consequences to be drawn from those analyses in order to understand other enigmatic aspects of kinship systems. The moieties system, wherever it occurs, seems ruled by the reciprocity principle; moreover, the favored union between crossed cousins and the generally prohibited union between parallel cousins become intelligible. Unlike parallel cousins, crossed cousins always belong to different lineages, which explains why reciprocity is possible between them; most traditional cultures have drawn the conclusion that union between crossed cousins should be prescribed.

The reciprocity requirement that is at the core of exogamic alliance and constitutes the essential reason for the prohibition of incest is also found in an entire set of practices, like the prohibition of eating game caught by oneself or, sometimes, of eating one's own domestic animals: this constitutes a kind of social incest.[55] What is at stake is always ensuring that one receives from the other what one has at home so that the movement of recognition will never be interrupted, since it is this gesture of recognition that constantly binds together beings that are by nature autonomous and tempted to withdraw into their local niche. Matrimonial alliance institutes this recognition and perpetuates it on a long-term basis by indexing it on the reproduction of life—of which women are the necessary mediators—and binding it to the succession of generations.

Strangers and the Gift of Oneself:
Affirming and Overcoming Otherness

It should not be surprising that one of the essential features of the gift-exchange relationship is the implication of the giver in the thing given, since the primary purpose of this relationship is to institute *reciprocal recognition*. What matters is not the thing given, as such, but the relationship created through it: "Goods reinforcing ties."[56] The value of the object matters but only to the extent that it is a symbolic value: a value that testifies to the importance of the relationship and therefore to the wish to honor the recipient. From this point of view a kind of circle is observed: the object offered is chosen because of its exceptional (or at least specific) qualities that situate it outside of ordinary uses in everyday life: jewels, blazons, precious fabric or ornaments, or rare and rich food and drinks meant for festive consumption. But some relatively common objects become precious by the very fact that they are offered and serve as pledges. *The good offered is the mediator of the recognition granted*, which is why it is important for the value of the good to be viewed as capable of honoring the recipient. But the fact that the object offered has mediated this recognition adds to its value. This explains a law noted by many observers: any good or object involved in a gift gains in value through the fact of its circulation. According to Mauss, "The emblazoned copper objects of the American Northwest and the mats of Samoa increase in value at each *potlatch* and in each exchange" (*G* 101). The same is true of Trobriand *waygu'a* according to Malinowski and of ancient Greek *agalmata* passed on from one giver to another, such as the tripod of the Seven Wise Men, a precious thing that had to be the reward of the best among them, as noted by Gernet: "Most often the initial recipient is Thales, who then yields it to someone whom he knows to be wiser. The second gives the prize to a third, and so on, until the object is in the hands of the seventh Sage; it then goes back to Thales, who consecrates it to Apollo."[57] The transfer of an object from one giver to another conferred on it a specific individuality and enriched it with a history, that of its transfer from one prestigious recipient to another. Final consecration to Apollo amounted to granting this object a value so great that it could only be expressed by offering the object to a god; but from this time on the object became part of the "treasure" of the community, in the *xoana* category—*sacra* in

Latin—that of things that were kept and not exchanged. We will soon return to this issue.

Gift-exchange relationships create a personal bond between partners; by hypothesis those who engage in this kind of relationship are allies and become close. If a stranger is involved in the exchange and the gifts are accepted by both parties, then he is no longer a stranger. The immediate effect of the gift-exchange relationship is to engage the participants in a circle of closeness. It brings the stranger close and turns him into a friend. No stranger can therefore be present in the circle of gift exchange. The stranger can be defined as someone with whom no exchange has yet taken place or who has refused the exchange. Until the exchange has occurred and reciprocal recognition has been granted, the stranger remains a virtual enemy or at least someone who must be treated with suspicion.

Moses Finley rightly underscores in Homer's world this complex relationship with strangers, wavering between fear and the most generous hospitality.[58] This relationship is placed under the sign of the most powerful of all gods, Zeus, and more precisely Zeus Xenios, or Zeus the Hospitable; but in Greek the phrase has a double meaning since *xenios* means both "host" and "stranger." The theme of the narratives developed around the figure of Zeus Xenios is precisely the requirement to welcome the stranger as a guest, whoever he or she may be, in order to bring to an end the permanent state of struggle and threat that was then prevalent among humans. The invention of the duty of hospitality is attributed to the sovereign god. The obligation to respect and welcome all strangers, even the most wretched, originates from his example: "Zeus is the God of guests who cares for the downcast stranger," the *Odyssey* proclaims (9.270–71). From this point of view the Christian attitude is not an innovation but a generalization of a recommendation that could be traced throughout the classical era, as well as in many other civilizations.

Once these relationships of hospitality are initiated, a new situation of reciprocal obligation emerges. They can be reinforced by matrimonial alliances, and they remain the basis of bonds meant to endure through time, even for very distant clans—hence the necessity to know and recite genealogies in order to keep from forgetting who were the "hereditary guests" against whom one should never fight. A famous scene from the *Iliad* testifies to this sacred hospitality. As Diomedes and Glaucus prepare to fight in single combat, the former asks the latter, "Who are you, my fine friend?—another born to die?" Glaucus replies by describing the heroic deeds of his grandfather Bellerophon:

When he heard that, Diomedes' spirit lifted. . . . "Splendid—you are my friend, my guest from the days of our grandfathers long ago! Noble Œneus hosted your brave Bellerophon once, he held him there in his halls, twenty whole days, and they gave each other handsome gifts of friendship. . . . So now I am your host and friend in the heart of Argos, you are mine in Lycia when I visit in your country. Come, let us keep clear of each other's spears. . . . But let's trade armor. The men must know our claim: we are sworn friends from our fathers' days till now!'" (*Iliad* 6.142–277)

Finley comments on this dialogue as follows: "Guest-friendship was a very serious institution, the alternative to marriage in forging bonds between rulers; and there could have been no more dramatic test of its value in holding the network of relationships together than just such a critical moment. Guest-friend and guest-friendship were far more than sentimental terms of human affection. In the world of Odysseus they were technical names for very concrete relationships, as formal and evocative of rights and duties as marriage."[59] Finley is right to note that this relationship was not primarily an emotional one; it involved a constraining ceremonial system. It could certainly be expressed in emotional terms (through joyful demonstrations, an attitude of reciprocal trust, and the pleasure of being together), but this was not what mattered. For individuals (or groups) exposed to the risk of the unknown, whether in the land where they were going or in the figure of the stranger who came to their own land, what was at stake was to establish and preserve a general procedure of peaceful encounter. It was therefore important to set up in the surrounding lands a network of faithful allies with long-term obligations: "The stranger who had a *xenos* in a foreign land— and every other community was foreign soil—had an effective substitute for kinsmen, a protector, representative, and ally. He had a refuge if he were forced to flee his home, a storehouse on which to draw when compelled to travel, and a source of men and arms if drawn into battle."[60]

Benveniste's sociophilological analysis confirms this signification in the case of Rome: "*hostis* is one who repays my gift by a counter-gift";[61] the verb *hostire* means to provide a mutual service. *Hostis* does not designate a stranger but a guest or, more precisely, someone who lives under the same law. "This recognition of rights implies a certain relation of reciprocity and supposes an agreement or compact. Not all non-Roman[s] are called *hostis*."[62] *Hostis* is one who belongs to the same community of language, customs, obligations, and beliefs. How did the word take on its meaning of hostility? "The classical meaning 'enemy' must have developed when reciprocal relations between clans were succeeded by exclusive relations of *civitas* to *civitas*."[63] This means that when gift-exchange relationships— and, above all, exogamic alliance between clans—no longer determined social statuses, when a larger and more abstract entity—the city—included *individuals* as such in society, the *hostis*—a member of a different *civitas*— became at the same time someone with whom there could be no statutory relationship of reciprocity and with whom matrimonial alliance was un- likely. He became a stranger, therefore, which meant a potential enemy. Benveniste's explanation convincingly meets the conclusions reached by contemporary anthropology.

The relationship of alliance is created through hospitality and the exchange of presents. The gift-exchange relationship possesses the surpris- ing power of instituting a bond more powerful than the emotions associ- ated with it. Reciprocal obligation is such that shirking it is considered completely dishonorable. It is remarkable that the same testimonies cor- roborate each other in very distant times and geographical areas, from Homer's world to the world of native people from the American North- west, from the Katchin of Burma to the Bororo of Brazil and from the Tro- briand of the western Pacific to the Bambara of Mali. The fact of giving could not create this privileged and constraining relationship everywhere it is found if it were not the specifically human gesture of reciprocal recog- nition and the only way to establish enduring bonds.

In this the ceremonial gift-exchange relationship also shows its lim- its: it is indeed a means of ensuring that one can live among one's own, even when meeting strangers, in the way certain groups mentioned by Lévi-Strauss turn all their allies into kin rather than admitting that they are aliens with very different customs.[64] Ceremonial gift exchange possesses the prodigious ability of making close that which is distant, of domesti- cating it, and of familiarizing it; but at the same time it makes recogni- tion of the stranger *as stranger* almost impossible. The choice seems to be between absorbing and excluding. Ignoring the difference between friend and stranger will precisely be one of the functions of the market. For the seller anyone with enough money to pay the set price is a legitimate part- ner; whether he or she is known or not makes no difference in principle in the selling and buying relationship.

The encounter with the stranger makes the tenuous border between recognition and rejection obvious. Either the offer is made and accepted and peace ensues, or no offer is made and the other remains a threat, which can mean the continuation of a state of hostility and the possibility of war. But the exchange of gifts does not in and of itself guarantee peace until it has been tested by time, which is to say until a routine has been established, or more profoundly until long-term procedures of engagement have been instituted. On the occasion of the first contact, for instance, the stranger may not be satisfied with the goods offered, or he may be offended by a detail in the forms of exchange. It takes time for the other to stop being a stranger. It mainly takes frequency and stability of the gestures and of the occasions of renewing the exchange; this seems to be the precise purpose of seasonal celebrations and rituals but, above all, of cycles of matrimonial alliances. When local communities find themselves more and more exposed to the risk posed by alien groups, when invasions and migrations make contacts frequent, then more general procedures of reciprocal recognition must be invented: we will see how the realm of grace, the order of the law, and the development of the marketplace have constituted—and continue to constitute—answers given to these difficulties. We will finally see that in the encounter with the stranger, outside of all cultural or legal guarantees, the only possible answer is ethical. But before coming to these considerations, we must reflect on a remarkable limit that the practice of ceremonial gift exchange imposes on itself.

Sacra: Goods That Cannot Be Exchanged

Recent anthropological research has brought to the fore a major problem with respect to the phenomenon of gift exchange, that of the things that are not exchanged but carefully kept within the group. From the outset they belong to a different realm.

We must therefore ask, what are these things that cannot be exchanged? Where are they kept? What is their meaning for the group? Do they have a symmetrical relationship with the things that are involved in gift exchanges, or do they belong to an entirely different sphere? In the Western tradition these things excluded from the circuit of exchange are relatively well known to us: they are the *xoana* of ancient Greece or the *sacra* of Rome. In *The Gift* Mauss notes the existence of these objects that are considered precious not because they are involved in ceremonial exchange but precisely because they are excluded from it:

> It would seem that among the Kwakiutl there were two kinds of copper objects: the more important ones that do not go out of the family and that can only be broken to be recast, and certain others that circulate intact, that are of less value, and that seem to serve as satellites for the first kind. The possession of this secondary kind of copper object doubtless corresponds among the Kwakiutl to that of the titles of nobility and second-order ranks with whom they travel, passing from chief to chief, from family to family, between the generations and the sexes. It appears that the great titles and the great copper objects at the very least remain unchanged within the clans and tribes. Moreover, it might be difficult for it to be otherwise. (*G* 134n245)

Mauss leaves us with this enigmatic conclusion. He has already tackled this question a few pages before: "Among the Kwakiutl a certain number of objects, although they appear at the *potlatch*, cannot be disposed of. In reality these pieces of 'property' are *sacra* that a family divests itself of only with great reluctance, and sometimes never" (*G* 43). This seems self-evident to Mauss precisely because he is familiar with the meaning of the *sacra*, which for the Romans were the precious goods representing the treasure of the community, kept either in each *domus* or in the city's temples. They constituted the symbols of its being, origin, spirit, and permanence through time.

Mauss discusses these Roman and Kwakiutl sacra in passing, without further questioning what their role may have been in relation to the goods that circulate in ceremonial exchanges. Until recently anthropologists were no more inquisitive than he was. In 1992, however, Annette Weiner, in her book on inalienable goods and the gesture of keeping while giving, shed new light on Mauss's remarks and drew remarkable consequences from it.[65] Having worked in Polynesia and in the Trobriand Islands, Weiner had the opportunity to reexamine—seven decades after Malinowski—the question of the circuits of gift exchange such as the *kula* circle. But rather than merely complement existing research on reciprocity, Weiner focuses on an element that Malinowski reported but did not study as such: besides the precious goods that participate in the circuit of offerings and counter-offerings, other goods that are perhaps even more precious are kept at home and cannot be "given," not out of a lack of generosity but because these—more beautiful or more rare—goods perform another essential function: to symbolize the group's identity, greatness, status, and rank. According to Weiner, they are "inalienable possessions" that cannot be given away to others (even if the giving of a good in *kula* cannot be compared to the sale of a good in a commercial contract).[66] In short, they are in some way the symbolic treasure of the group, its memorial and emblem, and the testimony to its being. Mauss is right to relate them to Roman *sacra*, which have a similar definition.

The existence of inalienable goods, which has been found to be as universal as that of gift exchange, raises difficult questions for anthropologists and historians. It is easy to see how reciprocal exchange between humans generates or reinforces the social bond (through alliances, marriages, and celebrations) or threatens it when the exchange breaks down (through vengeance or war). But what of those goods that are excluded from the circuits of reciprocal offerings? What bond can be generated by their conservation within the bounds of the community? To answer these questions we must return to fieldwork. What do various cultures have to teach us about these precious goods (assuming that these testimonies can be compared to each other)? In one way or another they all tell us that these goods are presents given by the ancestors or by the gods that protect the community. Summarizing the information provided by Boas on the American Northwest, Mauss concludes, "All these things are always, and in every tribe, spiritual in origin and of a spiritual nature" (*G* 44). We thus see that besides the system of reciprocal exchanges between humans a different system is constituted that involves humans in their relationship with the deities. Whereas the former system, symmetrical and horizontal, ensures social life in the present and only concerns relationships between humans, the latter, asymmetrical and vertical, seems designed to confront the permanence of the community through time (in this sense *sacra* also include traditions, narratives, and memory); even beyond this permanence, what is at stake is establishing a bond with the deities to which the group owes its existence and identity and on which its fate depends.

Does this mean that these goods that cannot be exchanged hold the secret of the movement of the goods that are exchanged? According to Godelier's hypothesis this is the "enigma of gift exchange." Godelier's is an important thesis: for ritual gift exchange to be more than a dual bond between partners and to involve the entire society, "there must be in what is given *something more* than a gift of oneself to the other. . . . It must contain something more, something which seems to *all* members of society to be indispensable to their existence and which must *circulate among them* in order that each and all may go on living."[67] This is the requirement: what is at stake is the very condition of the preservation and reproduction of society as a whole. Gift exchange alone does not ensure it. It can only do so through its relation to the *sacra*: "The precious objects which circulate in gift-exchanges can do so only because they are substitutes twice over: substitutes for sacred objects and substitutes for human beings."[68]

This is an attractive interpretive model; however, it is not satisfactory for several reasons. The primary reason is that it insists on presenting the movement of gifts and countergifts as a transfer of goods. It is true that precious goods are used to transport the giver, but this model ignores their essential feature: they constitute acts of reciprocal recognition of which the goods are only the witnesses and pledges. This shift of emphasis to the things themselves is manifest in Godelier's analogy, according to which the *sacra* are akin to the immobile referent constituted by the gold or currency reserves held by banks that—just like Aristotle's *primum movens*—make external commercial movements possible through the use of another substitute: money. There is a paradox in claiming to explain the movement of gifts through a financial metaphor; moreover, this interpretation completely undervalues the relationship between partners. Not only is this relationship presented as nothing more than the support for the movement of goods, but this movement itself is presented as originating in the *sacra*. The specifically *reciprocal* gift between partners, which is to say their gesture of recognition, is erased. There is another fundamental reason to question this model. It has to do with the status of the *sacra* and of the spirits or deities by which they were given: for Godelier, using a phrase found often in his writings, they are "phantasmic doubles" that dominate human beings.[69] This recalls the very old tradition of the rationalist critique of religion going back from Fontenelle and d'Holbach to Feuerbach and Marx. It presupposes that humankind is fearful and submissive and still lacks the instruments of criticism. The anthropology of gift exchange offers a different interpretation: spirits and deities are conceived of and named as the addressers of this inaugural, constant, and infinite gift of which humans know that they are the addressees.

Things can thus be viewed as follows: before the movement of exchanges of goods between humans through gifts and countergifts, a first gift came from the ancestors or the gods; the latter is symbolized by the *sacra*, and humans reply to it through offerings, words of gratitude, prayers, and in certain cases sacrifices.[70] What are these gifts? Narratives, prayers, and rituals help provide an answer: these gifts are life, the natural world, and other human beings but also the civilized arts—everything as it is, including the ambiguous gifts of death and disease, adversity and destruction. Because of their importance and of their preexistence, all these gifts remain an enigma. This is what generates the attitudes and symbolisms we usually designate as religious phenomena. The discrepancy, however, between the first gift and the difficult reply given by humans is probably not uniformly perceived. In some cases the relationship appears equal and based on alliance, remaining within the world of the reply; in others, it appears based on dependence and filiation: the world of debt emerges along with the practice of sacrifice. This may be where the decisive reason for this disparity will be found.

How can we understand the relationship between these gifts received from the deities and the gifts that humans exchange with each other? What is involved in both cases is the granting of recognition. The *sacra* proclaim the recognition of the group by the deities and testify to the reciprocal bond between gods and humans. They are the symbol of the pact, the "ark of the covenant," a stable alliance meant to endure through time and to bind generations to each other, while gift exchange between humans creates bonds within the present; the latter are therefore not substitutes for the former, which makes the bank-reserve metaphor irrelevant. Furthermore, the alliance to which the precious goods kept within the group are a testament expresses this requirement: reciprocity must bond together not only humans and gods or humans with each other but all living beings, every element, and the totality of the world: this is the first gift, from which the concept of grace most likely arises.

·   ·   ·

At the close of this first anthropological inquiry, one conclusion must be drawn: not only is ceremonial gift exchange neither economic nor moral in nature, but its function is also not to stand against either of these realms. Although ceremonial gift exchange is not a self-interested exchange of goods, it is not meant to demonstrate indifference to useful things; to think so is to interpret it based on the preoccupations of modern economy or, rather, on a critique of this economy. To assign this function of resistance to gift exchange amounts to a profound misunderstanding. Ceremonial gift exchange is neither economic nor antieconomic. This is why there is no *gift economy* (even if gifts may in some cases be valuable enough to have an effect on economic activity proper).[71]

Ceremonial gift exchange is not a relationship between humans mediated by things (this defines the economy) but a relationship between humans mediated by symbols, which may be physical goods (because they are considered precious) but also persons (as in matrimonial alliance), gestures, words, dances, music, celebrations, songs, or feasts. In this relationship the good offered is not considered something to be consumed but is presented as a mark of respect, as an expression of the desire to honor the existence and status of the other, and finally as testimony to an alliance. It is in this sense that the thing offered has no price in the marketplace of useful goods. In this it necessarily contrasts with these goods and appears to be their opposite. It is not, however, an alternative to the marketplace and commercial exchange. For instance, in the Trobriand Islands *kula* exchange ensures the recognition of the partners through challenge, greatness, and glory; at the same time, *gimwali* exchange conducts fierce negotiations of ordinary goods but with different partners. The sphere of public recognition—ensured through ceremonial gift exchange—relativizes and prevails on the sphere of subsistence ensured by the production and exchange of consumer goods. The two spheres are different and must be so; their functions are radically alien to each other.

Ceremonial gift exchange is the dominant form of public recognition between groups and individuals—depending on their statuses—in societies without a central state. It is a total social fact because it involves the entire society and society as a whole (even if it does not constitute everything in this society): it is not a marginal or private phenomenon but an institutional one. It may seem surprising that it no longer has this global function in political societies in which public statuses are defined by law, under which all citizens have equal rights. For those of us who live in such societies, this is the framework of formal recognition and publicly granted respect. It is a contractual recognition that does not presuppose mutual attachment other than a common belonging to the same city or motherland. This leaves space for reciprocal attachment through interpersonal gift exchange transferred to private realms: family bonds ("family" takes over as "kinship" fades away), bonds of friendship, or any local form of community or association; these attachments are often taken charge of by religious beliefs or charismatic figures. In fact, gift-exchange relationships remain essential in the realm of civilities: courteous phrases and gestures;[72] relationships of friendship, love, or solidarity; and all traditional forms of celebration, such as religious festivals, marriages, birthdays, invitations, and awards. These gift-exchange relationships can maintain a certain solemnity or take on ritual forms (that is, codified forms whose symbolism is known and whose effect is predictable); however, they do not amount to a total social phenomenon because they do not define society as a whole. They apparently do no more than create or preserve bonds between local groups or persons. If necessary, political society could do without them and rely only on civic bonds defined by law or on bonds based on self-interest generated by commercial exchange, but the price to pay for this is a symbolic deficit that constitutes the major problem of modern democracies. Since political societies are societies in which tasks are distributed, it is also necessary for useful exchanges of goods to be regulated by the market and subjected to a fairness principle. In summary, modern societies rely on the law for ensuring mutual public recognition, on the market for organizing subsistence, and on private gift relationships for generating a social bond. But without this social bond, without this founding relationship and mutual recognition in which everyone ventures something that is part of oneself into the space of the other, no community can exist.

Let us return to Socrates: he graciously offered his teaching because he himself had received the wisdom of the god that inhabited and inspired him. What had been given to him he could not have sold or measured in any way; in return he accepted gifts for his subsistence. To give is the gesture through which one recognizes the other; this is what makes it a generous offering. One does not give in order to reject utility and interest, yet by giving one necessarily places oneself above or outside of that realm. This makes it easier for us to understand Socrates' attitude. He had no objection to the activities of those who provided for their subsistence through wages, since any expertise deserved compensation. What he denied the Sophists was this expertise, for philosophy does not allow it. Philosophy is not a form of knowledge but a quest for wisdom; what moves us toward it does not come from us. It is not something that can be owned or traded. Socrates' relationship to his students and to all those who came to listen to him belonged to the realm of reciprocal recognition and the *agon* of dialogue: the word put forward is a constant challenge that calls for a reply; thought opens up, is formed and exposed in this back-and-forth movement, this uncertainty, and this conflict to which answers bring appeasement and which new questions reopen. At the same time as this agonistic exchange, Socrates' withdrawal, the suspense he preserved, and the absences that drew him back from conversation were signs that this wisdom was not a good he claimed as his own but something that came from the "god." The exchange involved something that could not be exchanged because it had been given in the first place. The presents students brought Socrates expressed the fact that this, above all, was what they honored in the master.

But what does it mean to honor the gods? And why are there invisible beings? Are they "imaginary doubles," to use a debatable phrase, invented by humans imposing masters on themselves and creating their own subjugation? Are they not instead the necessary figures of the givers to which humans could *reply*—reply to the challenge of the gift that precedes and encompasses them? What generates the figures of the deities is not fear or submission (let us give up this rationalist myth) but the need to designate and recognize beings to which a reply can be given that is worthy of the goods received. It is the need for the addressee to name the addresser. It remains for us to understand why in certain societies and for a certain time sacrifice was the preferred form of this reply and of this relationship.

5

The Age of Sacrifice

This is the conclusion, which is also the noblest and truest of all sayings,—that for the good man to offer sacrifice to the Gods, and hold converse with them by means of prayers and offerings and every kind of service, is the noblest and best of all things, and also the most conducive to a happy life.

PLATO, *Laws*

"To sacrifice is not to kill but to relinquish and to give": Bataille's statement in *Theory of Religion* demonstrates a profound anthropological insight.[1] The same cannot be said, however, of the subsequent analyses, where he states, for instance, "Sacrifice is the antithesis of production, which is accomplished with a view to the future; it is consumption that is concerned only with the moment."[2] Although an attractive philosophical consideration, this does not provide a definition of sacrifice as a ritual practice. Ironically, this approach confirms the hegemony of that from which it wishes to free itself, the modern economy. Defining sacrifice as the radical negation of the order of industrial production and the world of useful objects shows a double misunderstanding.

The first is chronological: if we are to take Bataille's statement seriously, ritual sacrifice (which disappeared in the West almost two thousand years ago) would be the challenge par excellence to capitalist production. This seems unlikely; even though extravagant consumption or even wasteful spending does occur, nothing about it can be attributed to sacrifice. The second mistake is epistemological, since assuming that the internal purpose of sacrifice is to negate what is sacrificed amounts to making the sacrificed thing the focus of analysis while ignoring the other protagonists or operational elements, such as the sacrificer, the beneficiary, and the circumstances—not to mention the belief systems associated with a particular ritual.

I agree that the sacrificed or given thing is withdrawn from the realm of the useful and profitable, but to claim that sacrifice only exists to repudiate the useful is to risk misunderstanding its specificity. The same mistake has been made about gift exchange, as I have noted. No less than modern ones, savage civilizations greatly value useful things for entirely comparable reasons. Neither gift exchange nor sacrifice is opposed to utility. To be sure, both appear to have an antiutilitarian purpose given that when goods are offered or sacrificed, something other than utility is intended. This perspective is an illusion and is only obvious from the point of view of *homo œconomicus*. In no way does it define sacrifice (assuming that the term has real conceptual relevance, which is arguable).

Accounts of ceremonial gift exchange tell us that some things are priceless and that some goods are intended for reciprocal exchange as a form of recognition rather than for profitable exchange. However, outside those movements of agonistic exchange, which are essential to establishing social relations in traditional societies, there are goods that are not part of the circuit of reciprocal benefits but always remain within the group. We know the reason for this: these precious things are supposed to be given by the gods, spirits, or ancestors, depending on tradition and culture.[3] Besides the exchange of gifts between humans, there is clearly another exchange—this one with invisible beings that are considered more powerful than humans. Of course, it seems paradoxical and even presumptuous to wish to establish relations of reciprocal exchange with beings that do not belong to the world of our perception and experience. And yet, remarkably, all societies have presupposed the existence of such beings and have tried to establish forms of communication with them in complex ways: offerings, invocations, prayers, rituals of possession, and divination. Sacrificial ritual is one such form. We should wonder, of course, whether we are justified in so casually using the same term and whether the phenomenon can be considered universal, no matter how widespread.

Before returning to such critical questions, we need to consider from the perspective of sociological analysis one of the difficulties inherent in this type of activity. In the case of gift exchanges between groups or individuals we deal with observable partners, social actors whose status is known and whose gestures can be described even if the underlying representations of those gestures remain difficult to define. In sacrifice the addressees remain invisible. A follower of Durkheim would say that there is a good reason for this: the partners only exist in the representations developed by the group. The methodological requirement turns into a skeptical decision. This is necessary even though it may displease the faithful of some religions. We will therefore consider "sacrifice" or any other form of relation with the "invisibles" as a social phenomenon associated with representations that are themselves social.

Before we proceed with these analyses, we must ask an essential question: what might the relationship be between sacrifice and the question of the priceless? One answer—probably closely associated with a particular tradition—might be that sacrifice, or what common sense understands as such, is a gesture of renunciation accomplished in the name of values or principles that remain beyond considerations of profit and self-interest. In short, it would be valued as an unconditional gesture pertaining to true gift-giving. For instance, we speak of "dying for one's country" or of mothers or fathers "sacrificing themselves for their children." Many such examples could be given. These phrases are so widespread that they seem to refer to universal experiences. As such they would be quite useful in our search to understand sacrifice and its relationship to what is boundless and priceless. Nonetheless, this path could mislead us or rather lead us to accept as a reference point a powerful but limited Western tradition based on the Greco-Roman heritage, biblical texts, and Christianity. The idea of renunciation in the sacrificial phenomenon, although relevant in some respects, is not the only or even the most interesting aspect. The main objection to seeing it as the central meaning of sacrifice is that the idea prevailed in traditions where the ritual itself had disappeared. It seems important to understand sacrifice as we have tried to understand ceremonial gift exchange, by focusing on the specificity and diversity of its traditional forms. It is in the context of these forms that the question of the priceless can be raised once again. This question must be discussed because sacrifice may have a crucial relation with the practice of ceremonial gift exchange. If it is a relationship of gift exchange with the deities, then it involves in a fundamental way a particular use of goods and a particular conception of what is precious. This is probably why the term *sacrifice* has generated so many metaphors related to value or even to the everyday economy ("the sacrifices required of wage-earners"). Even though the term has been misused, the question of sacrifice cannot be dismissed. But it is even riskier to think that we can understand such widespread sacrificial metaphors by seeking within ourselves—which most often means within our own cultural heritage—a conception that would be universally applicable.

We will turn, therefore, to anthropological inquiry to see what we can learn about ritual practices identified as "sacrifices." Can this one term encompass these practices in spite of their considerable diversity? Are there specific social conditions that make it possible to understand their emergence? Is there really a relation between these practices and the idea of renunciation? Is sacrifice, above all, a gift to the gods? How is it connected to gifts given to humans? How do the gods respond, or, rather, how are they assumed to respond? Could sacrifice possibly be an attempt to respond to an earlier divine gift that never ceases to call for a human response? Perhaps this asymmetrical relationship is what has led to the emergence of the notion of *debt*, already noted in the context of the *sacra*, which interrupts gift-exchange relationships between humans and establishes the predominance of divine favor. Along with the notion of debt the notion of *grace* also emerges, finally making sacrificial offering superfluous and opening up a fundamental rift between heaven and earth: God gives everything, including what humans give to God and to each other. If humans can no longer respond to God's giving, even by giving to other humans, if gift-giving is no longer their business, the only remaining alternative is to be good at business. Once again, the modern figure for finitude emerges: *homo laborans*, himself inseparable from *homo œconomicus*. If sacrifice has lost its ritual function, the moral act of renunciation remains, which for the individual in quest of salvation will have to make up for the gifts that are no longer given.

It is important, therefore, to understand under what conditions ceremonial sacrifice emerged; this would in turn enable us to understand why it disappeared. To acknowledge this disappearance is to admit that there was an "age of sacrifice" and to situate ourselves within the movement of history, in an "afterward" that is inseparable from the question I have raised. Something ontological has happened, and it remains irrevocably lost—probably because, by entailing death, sacrifice opens up an irreversible temporality.

Critical Preliminaries

The concept of sacrifice, which for a long time appeared to be self-evident, seems very vague today. Its Latin etymology (in the case of the languages in which it applies) may be misleading. The Latin word *sacer* has no relation to what we mean by *sacrifice* today. It refers to any being banished or excluded from the community for a crime or pollution; hence, at first *sacer-facere* did not mean making an offering to the gods or immolating a victim. According to Benveniste the later meaning is only a derivation.[4] Hubert and Mauss also note, "It would be difficult to find a word in Sanskrit or Greek that would correspond to the Latin *sacer*."[5]

It is, in fact, rare in most cultures to find an equivalent term for *sacrifice*. Hebrew, for instance, has no specific term.[6] As for the Greek *thusia*, it refers to an offering to the gods and is associated with combustion; this explains why the main derivations of the verb *thuein* are related to smoke and perfumes (*thuoeis*: fragrant).[7] Clearly, there is no trace of *sacer* in this. Generally speaking, Benveniste explains, Indo-European languages have no terms derived from a single root or even a common lexical family to designate "sacrifice."[8] An identical difficulty is found in most African languages. Nevertheless, there is a whole set of comparable practices that correspond to the term *sacrifice* in languages derived from Latin. This is significant, but it reinforces the need to develop precise criteria to identify the phenomenon.

The question arises of whether the concept of sacrifice itself—and, more precisely, that of ritual sacrifice—encompasses well-defined and well-observed specific realities. If it does, we should also ask whether sacrifice has a universal character or whether it only emerges—or emerged—as a ritual phenomenon in certain societies (or types of societies), which then need to be specified. Finally, when dealing with societies that practice sacrifice, criteria need to be established that can correctly define the phenomenon beyond its cultural and linguistic variations.

These uncertainties are useful in that they will require additional rigor and lucidity in an analytical field often dominated by funereal and bloody pathos. We owe some of the most incisive critiques to two authors who have written a great deal about the subject: Marcel Detienne, the Hellenist, or rather the anthropologist of ancient Greece, and Luc de Heusch, the ethnologist specializing in Africa, particularly the Bantu groups. In the introductory chapter to a collective volume,[9] Detienne considers the well-known example of the sacrifice of the child Dionysos and notes how inattention to the narrative's details soon led to a vulgarized version in which the young god is torn apart and eaten raw by the Titans. In fact, the texts tell us something fundamentally different: the body or the pieces are boiled and roasted before being consumed. The superimposition of two cooking methods points to a specific problem.[10] Before proposing theories about the ultimate meaning of Greek sacrifice, it would be of interest to identify the complex relations between the ritual and (1) a meat and vegetarian diet, (2) the role of fire in the contrast between the raw and the cooked, and the roasted and the boiled, and (3) culinary activities in general as key forms of transformation. A whole set of relations to the world of animals and plants also becomes apparent, along with relations to two major trends of religious dissidence: Orphism, which aspires to radical vegetarianism and searches for "escape by the high road" on the side of the gods, and Dionysian cults, which search for an exit "via the low road, on the side of bestiality."[11] These considerations indicate the type of investigation on which a more general reflection on sacrifice must be based.

Detienne suggests that the time has come to distance ourselves from the tradition that flourished in the nineteenth century with Robertson Smith and James Frazer, is still present in Durkheim's totemic theory of sacrifice, and continues with Ernest Cassirer's philosophy of symbolic forms. This tradition gives a sociological and philosophical gloss to what is, in essence, a tragic and Christian view of sacrifice (a criticism Detienne reinforces in a note dedicated to René Girard). While Hubert and Mauss deserve credit for attempting most rigorously to renew the theoretical analysis of sacrifice through the careful investigation of ritual procedures, even they adhere to the primacy of the Vedic-biblical model.[12] Detienne's conclusion is severe: "The notion of sacrifice is indeed a category of the thought of yesterday, conceived of as arbitrarily as totemism—decried earlier by Lévi-Strauss."[13] Does this criticism go too far? Or should we acknowledge, along with Hubert and Mauss, the existence of practices that can be identified as "sacrifice," despite the extreme diversity of terminology and cultural modalities?[14]

It is important to understand that sacrifice cannot be separated from a whole system of thought that develops around and is mobilized in certain sets of figures, categories, and values: for example, the triple relation gods-humans-animals, and oppositions such as cultivated/uncultivated, raw/cooked, vegetarian/meat-eating, and wild space/domesticated space.

Sacrifice is fascinating because it can serve as the symbolic operator that organizes the entire social and cultural life of a group. This requires an investigation that does not omit any detail, no matter how odd it may seem. This is the price of an interpretation that will lead to new ideas; these ideas will not come from theoretical grids through which only a priori notions filter.

Luc de Heusch returns to this question in the introduction to his work on sacrificial practices in many African societies. Like Detienne he is surprised that there has been no work comparable to that of Hubert and Mauss proposing a new methodological approach, even though a great deal of ethnographic data have been accumulated, especially on oral cultures. These are the very data lacking in Hubert and Mauss's analyses, which are too exclusively focused on Vedic and Semitic rituals.

Hubert and Mauss adopt the categories of the *sacred* and *profane* as elaborated by Durkheim as if they were self-evident. According to Heusch these notions are not applicable to African rituals, with their scarcely marked and varying places of worship. The analysis of sacrificial practices must start by eschewing a powerful Christian and Indo-European ethnocentrism; when speaking of the *sacred, pollution,* or *fault,* "one must not be misled by words which have a precise meaning only in particular symbolic contexts."[15] For instance, Evans-Prichard, who notes and underscores certain debatable hypotheses in Hubert and Mauss's work, also gives in to the ethnocentric temptation in his classic work on Nuer religion by resorting to the term *sin* to designate everything that involves transgression.[16] Heusch comments: "This desperate attempt to fit Nuer thinking into Judeo-Christian theology is completely without foundation."[17] In a rigorous lexical discussion he shows that Nuer sacrifice is not designed to obtain purification but to provide *compensation.* It does not have to do with pollution but with debt. Unlike the Vedic model, this type of sacrifice does not require entering sacred spaces, nor does it try to establish communication with the deities. On the contrary, it aims to keep them at a distance or even to increase this distance. Heusch makes it clear how risky or even erroneous it is to project one cultural notion onto another. This becomes even more obvious in ceremonies surrounding the ritual death of a king, often represented by that of an animal, for instance among the Swazi of Rwanda. Nothing is further from the reality of these rituals than the sociopolitical explanation of a kind of sacred lynching or the mystical reading that makes the king into a substitute for a dying god. In fact, it is clear that these rituals are associated with major seasonal cycles, for example, the shift between dry and rainy season. The royal figure occupies a key position in the articulation between the social order and cosmic forces, which explains his status as both asocial and metasocial, protective and dangerous, while his real or figurative death fulfills the need for renewed energy at the point where society and cosmos meet.

To conclude these critical preliminaries, contemporary anthropology, in returning to the question of sacrifice, seems determined to rigorously abide by several methodological requirements, including the following: (1) to refuse to make one particular tradition the reference point and therefore the interpretive model for other cultures; (2) to understand ritual practices as elements of a system of thought associated with other sets of symbols and representations, rather than to restrict them to the single category of "the religious"; and (3) to give most careful attention to ritual details, including the following: the choice of animal and the modes of immolation; the status of the performer; the choice of places, authorized participants, and appropriate times; the invocations pronounced, the sequences of gestures performed, and the instruments used; and the organization of space. An entire system of thought is expressed in the symbolic arrangements associated with concrete modalities.

One question needs to be raised before all others: can sacrifice (defined as practices corresponding to certain legitimate criteria) be found in every society? Answering this question might be the decisive step in our investigation; let us attempt to do so.

Nonsacrificial and Sacrificial Societies

The unsubstantiated claim that the practice of sacrifice is universal has been made frequently and by many authors. We know, however, that it was not found in Paleolithic societies.[18] Generally speaking, it is also unknown in hunter-gatherer societies and in nonherding societies that practice a limited form of horticulture—such as slash-and-burn itinerant farming—supplemented by hunting and gathering.[19] Hunter-gatherer societies are now very rare, but a number of groups showing combined or intermediary forms of hunting, gathering, and horticulture still exist. One expert categorically asserts, "The ethnological data are quite clear: large regions of Oceania as well as America never had sacrificial practices. Those are Australia;

New-Guinea; Melanesia; Alaska; almost all of Canada; the entire western United States; the Amazonian lowlands; the Pampas and Patagonia as far as Tierra del Fuego."[20] The areas of the hunter-gatherers of Siberia and Africa (or what is left of them) should be added to the list. This absence of sacrifice is remarkable; what is more, it prompts pertinent questions about the conditions under which sacrifice itself first appeared. Indeed, if we accept, at least for now, that sacrifice is characterized by the immolation of a living being, usually an animal, and that such an animal must be domestic (often along with cultivated plants), then we may be reaching the core of the issue.

Hunter-Gatherers and the Alliance

In hunter-gatherer societies the relation to the animal world is what could be called a relation of *equality* or (better yet) of mutual gift exchange. Animals are considered partners with which one must get along. The art of hunting or fishing is not a mere technique of capture. It is a form of negotiation—the working out of a pact—with the animals that are meant to be trapped or killed. Most often they are considered spirits or related to spirits. Myths (in North America or Siberia for instance) present them as forming societies modeled on human ones in terms of kinship systems, leadership, and thought patterns. It is a mirror-world or, rather, a different world seen as similar. Of course, the forms of alliance vary, depending on the kinship systems, but the model of the *alliance* remains. For instance, among the aborigines of Australia "the structures of kinship reach out to all living men, to all his fellow creatures, and to the rivers, the rocks and the trees."[21]

Roberte Hamayon gives a striking example of this in her research on the hunting societies of Siberia. She proposes to "analyze the relations of the hunter to nature in terms of matrimonial alliance systems, that is to find the father-in-law in the spirit of the forest and the wife in the game."[22] The narratives suggest that this model applies even to the shaman himself, whose activities are seen as a hunt. "So what is at stake here is to find in him a son-in-law who has a supernatural father-in-law and who is a symbolic game hunter, that is to say, a hunter of souls. This assimilation of the son-in-law with the hunter and the shaman suggests a unified conception of all forms of alliance: (1) among humans within a society; (2) between humans and nature; (3) between humans and the supernatural realm."[23] This hypothesis becomes even more interesting when we consider that a different model based on relations of filiation predominates among populations that moved from hunting to livestock farming. To check her hypothesis, Hamayon very carefully examines kinship systems; this enables her to pinpoint the specific terms in which the hunter is seen as the son-in-law while the shaman is seen to become the symbolic hunter and son-in-law. Moreover, "to say that the logic of alliances inspires the hunt means placing it in a universe of rules, and points to the existence of a system of hunting that is analogous to the matrimonial system. The former legitimizes the hunter in catching the game just as the latter legitimizes the son-in-law in catching a wife."[24]

The gift relationship between spirits and humans thus belongs to the specific framework of matrimonial relationships and can apply beyond the cultural area studied by Hamayon. This makes the hunt, in the same way as ceremonial gift exchange itself, "a total social phenomenon."

The model of the relationship between hunters and animals is not always strictly matrimonial, but the general relations of alliance are unquestionably those of gift exchanges.[25] Therefore it is always important to treat hunted animals with respect: they are asked to let themselves be caught willingly; they are thanked for their collaboration and are asked for forgiveness for the harm done to them. To that effect there are compensatory offerings; they are not really intended to be equivalent goods, which would be difficult and obviously absurd, but rather they constitute signs of respect, including fresh-water sprinklings, offerings of portions of game, fruit, feathers, shells, and many other goods depending on the culture; prayers and incantations accompany them.

For instance, among the Indians of the North American plains the buffalo hunt was closely associated with rites aimed at obtaining the collaboration of the animals and making sure that their spirits would not seek vengeance for their death and consumption by humans.[26] The same thing happens with salmon fishing on the northwestern Pacific coast of America. The salmon people are asked to come near, to willingly offer themselves as food, and to let other salmon know that they can expect to find a beautiful destiny among the fishing people.

Boas quoted the invocation addressed by a Kwakiutl to the first fished salmon: "Welcome, Swimmer! I thank you, because I am still alive at this season when you come back to our good place; for the reason why you come is that we play together with my fishing tackle, Swimmer. Now, go home and tell your friends that you had good luck on account of your coming here and that they shall come with their wealth bringer, that I may get some of your wealth, Swimmer; and also take away my sickness, friend, supernatural one, Swimmer!"[27]

Among the Zuñi the following words are attributed to the deer that has been hunted and ritually eaten: "I have been to my people and given them my flesh for food; they were happy and their hearts were good; they sang the song, my song, over me; I will again return to them."[28] The hunter or fisherman will treat the captured animal as a guest; he can nevertheless kill and eat it because the animal took on material form as an offering to humans. Its spirit, however, remains intact and rejoins the invisible world. In this way all violence is erased in the end (although sacrifice will precisely have to come to terms with it). Generally speaking, the entire ethnographic literature about hunter-gatherers gives evidence of privileged relations with the animal world, relations that are marked by respect and ruled by rites and prayers. The animal world is not viewed as merely natural but as supernatural from the outset, manifesting the visible and permanent presence of spirits. Those rites and prayers associated with these relationships constitute the core of what we call the religion of the hunter-gatherers. Offerings play a modest role. None of this, however, involves anything resembling sacrifice.[29] How can this be explained? We have already mentioned a very definite clue: wherever sacrifice is found, the immolated offering is a domestic animal or a cultivated plant—in short, life produced by humans. Wild animals are not "appropriate for sacrifice." The implications of this decisive fact require explanation.

For hunter-gatherers life is always a gift, never having been produced in the first instance. For them the nature/culture relation does not apply to the domestication of plants and animals. Animals belong to the side of nature and of what is granted. Thus, they supposedly remain in the sphere of the spirit-world—that is, the supernatural world. Or rather, they are its embodiments. Relations are on an equal footing and consist of mutual service. The human/animal difference lies between two complementary poles. In the case of the Americans, Testart notes, "This disjunction is the foundation of their mutual relationship: humans show respect for the spirits (in their animal form) and the spirits (still in their animal form) offer themselves to humans. The animal form is the sign of the otherness with which humans enter into exchanges."[30]

Thus, hunting and fishing, as well as the sharing and eating of the catch, are practices always surrounded by rituals. The rites are aimed at obtaining the benevolence of the hunted and killed animal on the one hand and receiving the gift of the divine powers in a reasonable manner on the other. All life, all subsistence, is offered, and this gift has to be recognized. Humans do not give themselves gods as "imaginary doubles." Doing so would deprive them of their own humanity. Instead, *they invent spirits or gods in order not to lose their humanity*. In other words, it is essential for them to place giving figures in the granted world to whom they can respond for what has been given. These givers expect something back, a response that is appropriate to the continuous and, in a sense, unlimited gift that is given to humans. Whatever the quality of the hunting techniques or the talent of the hunters, the fact remains that subsistence is taken from the surrounding world. One could say that the spirits are there to embody this given, to be its living figures, to integrate all nature and all subsistence activities into an *alliance* with humans—and finally to force the latter to observe limits in the use they make of other beings.

In the world of hunter-gatherers the divine world is in a way always visible. Instead of gods it involves spirits or genies. It is an enchanted rather than a divine world—nature is coupled with the supernatural and embedded in it. The two realms are not in opposition to one another. Spirits are present and not just in animal species; they are present in all beings, in all places—spirits of the river, the forest, the mountain, thunder, this or that tree, animal, place, or house. This is exactly the type of world that Lévi-Strauss investigates in *Introduction to a Science of Mythology*. He probably intentionally omitted from his corpus stories from groups with urban and state forms such as the Incas, Mayas, and Aztecs. Among hunter-gatherers, creation stories never recount sacrificial performances, and there are no immolation rites intended to regenerate the universe (as among the Aztecs).[31] The universe of the hunter-gatherers is a given world, available from the outset, and myths provide this world's inventories. They relate the ordering of the world and tell of the experiences of humans; they describe the world's spaces (earth, the underworld, the sky, and the heavens), its living diversity (multiple animal and plant species), and its periodicity (seasons).

The natural world *is* the divine world. What makes the world human, however (the social order, kinship relations, the cooking of food, the weaving of clothing, the making of tools, in short every technical activity), was given by spirits or the founding heroes. This cultivated world is always at the border of the natural world, modulating it, listing its contents, and sometimes inverting it. It is the natural world but modified and emphasized, a world where spirits are embodied in the animals that are seen and hunted, the plants that are gathered, and the places that are inhabited or passed through. There is no radical break between the two worlds. A kind of reciprocity and continuity develops between the two. The world is a gift, and humans must make sure to receive it with moderation, by, for example, avoiding abuses in hunting or gathering. Myths constantly highlight the virtues of moderation and show the regrettable consequences of excess. The alliance also constitutes an equilibrium, as well as a form of justice. It is mutual respect.

It should be possible, therefore, to define the world of hunter-gatherers through a set of fairly constant characteristics, in spite of considerable local variations among regions of the world, forms of subsistence, tools, and kinship systems:

- The nature/culture relation appears more as a relation of reciprocity than of domination. This is particularly true of the relationship with animals, including those that are of no interest as food.
- The natural/supernatural relation is also less a break than a continuity; it is the given world, hence observable and visible, that in certain aspects acquires supernatural value and comes to embody spirits. In other words, the perceived world is always also a world of symbols. The functional world—ordered and classified—is the same as the supernatural world, which is magical and valued. It can be said that this is precisely the world of the "savage mind."

All in all, the natural world encompasses the whole weight of "the divine." In spite of all accidents and catastrophes, it is a reliable world because of its periodicity. Narratives say so, and rites guarantee it. This stability is considered the most desirable state. This is why societies of hunter-gatherers as a whole are homeostatic societies. They seem to aim at maintaining all types of equilibrium. Their technologies are technologies of adaptation, not of rupture. They also aim at transforming but through limited forms (catching rather than producing, collaborating rather than dominating). Their demography remains within a threshold beyond which a change in "political" organization might be triggered. For reasons of subsistence—having to do with hunting or gathering territories—groups are split when they reach a certain number. The organization of authority in and through chiefs remains subject to strict constraints of reciprocity and time limits: one only becomes chief for a limited period, on condition of showering relatives and allies with presents and taking risks in combat. Just as the spirits remain partners, so do the chiefs remain subject to the imperative of mutual generosity toward the members of their group.

As for other groups, they must either enter into alliance or confront through war any attempt at domination or intrusion, as research into Amazonian societies has shown.[32] In most societies responsibility for natural/supernatural relations is assumed by the shaman, the true "master of alliance": he is the one who intervenes whenever the link between the visible and invisible comes into play, namely in celebrations, hunts, illness, and divination. In the case of Siberia (but the analysis itself has general validity), Hamayon writes:

The very principle of shamanism requires the ontological otherness of the life-giving supernatural, because it needs to treat it as a partner. This principle places the human and the supernatural in a dualistic relationship based on exchange. It conceives in a realistic manner of supernatural beings animating the natural beings upon which humans depend for life. . . . This conception of a "natural" supernatural as partner contrasts with that of the supernatural as transcendental and ideal. The attitude of reciprocity, which requires an equal footing, contrasts with the submission and worship owed to the gods.[33]

This is why these societies are not societies indebted to the "gods." This is probably also why they are not sacrificial societies.

Agropastoral Societies and Sacrifice

There can be no doubt that the sharpest and most dramatic shift of gear in our ancestors' progress along the path of human evolution was the invention of agriculture ten thousand years ago. The shift from an essentially mobile hunting and gathering existence to an essentially sedentary agricultural economy shattered a lifestyle that had first emerged at least three million years earlier, and was responsible for creating the basics of humanity in the way they are. The invention of agriculture was, without exaggeration, the most significant event in the history of mankind.

RICHARD E. LEAKEY, *Origins*

It may be possible to discover the emergence of—or shift toward—sacrifice in a population that practices an intermediary way of life: the mountain dwellers of Southeast Asia, who practice itinerant slash-and-burn cultivation.[34] Those societies also have a whole world of spirits. But the latter are more distant; relationships are not egalitarian but hierarchical; there is always a debt owed to the spirits. This shows a break between humans and the natural world. How is this different from the American or Siberian case? The answer could be that we are dealing with horticulturists and herders who only hunt occasionally. Their main resource is the domestic animal; first is the buffalo, which is bred primarily for sacrifice and consumed on that occasion; then come pigs, goats, and chickens, which provide the ordinary supply of meat. Along with the production of this plant and animal world a very different nature/culture division settles in. The spirits go over to the side of humans against the wild animals they help hunt. They no longer manifest themselves in the guise of animals but become invisible. The animal becomes the being that is dominated and used. Finally, the spirits stand above all beings; they become spiritualized and receive the buffalo as sacrifice. A different universe emerges.

What has happened? Probably something analogous to the phenomenon found by Roberte Hamayon in Siberian societies when hunters become herders. Then, she explains, what matters is to pass on the herd and ensure the collaboration of those who assembled it, meaning the ancestors, and this requires getting along with their souls. In the relationship with the invisible, ancestors take over the role of the spirits that, until then, had secured the alliance with nature. The egalitarian and familiar relations of alliance with the spirits of the forest are now succeeded by relations of worship and submission to the founders of the ethnic group.

"Then the conception of the supernatural as bestower of subsistence is overturned, and its status as the equal Other (the spirit of the game who is treated as partner) becomes that of the superior Same (that is, the ancestors from whom herds and pasture are inherited and, above them, the founder of the ethnic group). At the same time, the world order is overturned and shifts from a horizontal to a vertical organization."[35] The playful ritual in which the shaman danced with the spirits under the animal mask is replaced by strict rites for the management of livestock. Even the landscape has changed; there is no longer open nature awaiting the visit of the hunter or shaman but rather a space that has been cut up (into pastures) and tiered (ancestors are housed on high ground from which they can dominate and keep an eye on the living). "The supernatural becomes vertical and relationships with it become hierarchical; humankind no longer treats it as a partner; humans feel that their commitment to it is no longer based on exchange on an equal footing but on a relationship of dependency."[36] In short, what occurs is the disappearance of relationships of *alliance* in favor of relationships of filiation in which inheritance, ancestry, and thus the identity conferred by lineage are privileged. The relationship to nature, to time, and to other groups—everything changes. Gifts no longer come from nature but from the ancestors; the gift of the herd is in the hands of the heirs. And when only the sons inherit, takers of wives prevail over givers. The entire kinship system changes. We are truly entering a world of hierarchy and debt, which is precisely the world of sacrifice:

The possession of herds modifies the compensation owed to the supernatural in return for the subsistence that it grants: domestic animals are offered in the place of the person who breeds them. Popular wisdom [now] shuns "the voluntary death" glorified by the hunter and proclaims respect for old age, while sacrifice invades shamanistic practices. The order of acts punctuating relationships with the supernatural is inverted: whereas the hunter who had nothing was the one who took first, the herder who inherits the herd hastens to sacrifice a few heads to encourage the ancestors to give the remaining stock better rain or better grass; in other words, he invests.[37]

Incidentally, this is the polar opposite of Bataille's statement cited earlier: "Sacrifice is the antithesis of production which is done with a view to the future." Instead of merely taking what the spirits give—as in hunting—breeding implies ensuring and controlling the endless reproduction of what has been taken. This is a new power that comes at a price and involves a risk.

At this point we need to return to a decisive element that I mentioned briefly before: in all civilizations that have practiced or are still practicing sacrifice, the immolated animal is never a wild animal, except in some rare and very specific cases, but a *domestic animal*: a sheep, goat, steer, chicken, buffalo, horse, pig, or more rarely a dog. "Wild animals are excluded from normal sacrifice."[38] "Game is not sacrificial meat."[39] This has proven to be the case everywhere.[40] There are several explanations for this. The first and most plausible has to do with the fact that sacrifice is an offering, and like any other gift it consists of yielding as a pledge *something of one's own*, something assimilated to the body or goods of the sacrificer or the group offering the victim. Hence the apparently consistent hypothesis that the first sacrifices were human beings before animals were substituted for them. This genealogy has not been proven; it is even improbable. Quite possibly, the two types of victim, human and animal, may have coexisted. While it has been confirmed that in many civilizations human sacrifice was replaced by animal sacrifice, this was not so much due to a "softening of mores" as to a new conception of mastery over life, as we will soon see.[41]

It is now easier to understand the absence of sacrifice among hunter-gatherers: one cannot sacrifice that which one does not own and which does not come from oneself. A wild animal will not suffice because it is already a gift of the gods or the spirits. One part of it can be offered in return, but that is all. To be "appropriate for sacrifice," something must have been the object of human care, produced rather than given at the outset. It is as if the sacrifice had to be taken from the human world as such and had to be closest to life's principle: the life of a dependent being, typically a domestic animal or anything produced by humans such as cultivated plants or sometimes, albeit rarely, precious manufactured objects. This feature is remarkably universal and therefore constitutes an important lead for researchers. A sacrificial fact can be recognized every time this relationship of proximity, belonging, and even dependency between sacrificer and sacrificed is observed.

In the world of pastoralists and farmers, through the production of plants and domestic animals, life is both reproduced and controlled by humans who seem to be aware that they have captured part of the divine realm.[42] To be sure, pastoral and agricultural activities are very different; the former remain relatively nomadic, whereas the latter are sedentary or itinerant and can mix planting and breeding. What has been captured is the very power to reproduce life, the capacity to increase the quantity of available living beings.[43] The function of sacrifice seems to be to make the gods accept this power by showing them a symbolic renunciation: a living being produced by humans is offered to them as a sacrifice.

Why does this need to be made clear to the deities? Because even when humans produce life, they cannot be sure that domestic animals will be fertile or that they will remain healthy, or that plants will grow, or that the weather will be favorable, and so forth. The ultimate power to give remains within the province of the spirits or the deities. This still does not explain, however, *why immolation is necessary*. We might imagine, as is sometimes the case, that the offered animal be merely put aside, reserved, preserved, and made unavailable for ordinary consumption. In the case of plants it might have been enough to stick to rites of beginnings, which acknowledge the deities explicitly enough. How can sacrificial destruction be understood?

The following could be a preliminary answer: sacrifice would be the process through which humans, by immolating a living being, restore to the gods the ultimate control over nature and, above all, over life, part of which humans had appropriated. *By doing so, they ensure that their own power remains within the system of reciprocity.* When much has been taken, much must be returned. Sacrifice restores a relationship of gift exchange that seemed weakened or even threatened with extinction. Thus, it is always at the very moment when humans are developing their technical capacities and reducing their dependence on the natural world that they symbolically limit this acquired power through the practice of sacrifice. This limit involves what is not up to them to decide: the weather, the rebirth of life, the fertility of plants and animals, the time granted before death, accidental events, and the desires or will of others.

In short, pastoralists and agriculturalists constitute a more invasive world that includes domestic animals and cultivated plants. A break between domestic and wild animals thus occurs, along with a break between the human and nonhuman world—that is, the friendly, proximate world and the hostile, outside world. In the universe of the hunter-gatherers the animal is always other but possibly an ally; a wild animal is associated with the spirits, or rather is itself a spirit. In the world of pastoralists and agriculturalists the animal world splits in two. One side becomes familiar, friendly, and part of the human world; the other side is a world that remains wild and in some instances no longer represents the deities (note that there are many intermediate situations, depending on the natural environment and culture). The wild world is understood as inhuman and dangerous and tends to embody the enemy; for the Greeks, for instance, the hunt was a form of war.[44] There is no doubt that the dividing line has moved, or, rather, a new line of separation emerges between humans and gods, humans and animals, cultivated world and wild world.[45] For the Greeks what defined wild animals was their *excess*: they ate voraciously, chaotically, and above all they devoured each other. In short, theirs was a world "without justice." Their uncontrolled consumption did not secure a share for the gods. The wild world was posited as the negative of the human world and thus also of sacrifice. Not to secure a share for the gods meant not to acknowledge an orderly world; it also meant failure to acknowledge the source of life, and ingratitude. Sacrifice is thus foremost the gesture of countergiving. In contrast with wild animals, the steer is a restrained and level-headed animal that has been integrated into the human universe; it is the most humanized and hence the best of animals. This is why the Greeks also viewed it as the appropriate animal for sacrifice par excellence.

There remained, however, some nostalgia for the wild world—that lost world where the gods were close and where intact nature was directly available to humans.

The "Golden Age" described by Hesiod was, indeed, the time before the invention of agricultural tools and the domestication of animals.[46] The cult of Dionysus could also be understood as the demand for the way of life and values of the lost wild world.[47] In the world of the hunter-gatherers the "gods" had remained partners on the side of nature; now they were superior but on the side of culture. This was a considerable reversal. The gods became invisible and inaccessible by the same movement that eliminated them from the surrounding world. The need for sacrifice emerged when the gods became distant.

At this point we can draw a first conclusion: the sacrificial phenomenon is not universal because it only appears in a certain type of society, where the domestication of plants and animals establishes a new relationship to living beings and, more generally, where the domination of humans over the natural world has been established. It is therefore possible and even necessary to focus our hypothesis on the break brought about by this upheaval. Defining the problem that sacrifice is supposed to solve thus requires—and, for now, only requires—an understanding of the relationship of humans to spirits or deities on the one hand and to the natural world on the other. We have identified a global change in equilibrium— a shift in the relation between what is given and what is returned—and therefore a new demand for compensation, which sacrifice seems intended to meet. This has allowed us to locate the emergence of the phenomenon. It does not really allow us to understand one of its most specific characteristics, the immolation of the offering, nor the surprising diversity of its forms, nor its relatively rapid disappearance as a ritual in sedentary agricultural societies. Answering these questions, which are no less empirical than the preceding and involve processes no less symbolic, will make it possible for our investigation to proceed.

Elements and Functions of Sacrifice

One of the main sources of confusion in this debate is the temptation on the part of many authors (including anthropologists) to assume the existence of sacrifice or something similar in two types of situations: (1) wherever blood is spilled or death triumphs (wars, revenge, public executions, murders, road carnage, suicides, or bull fights) or (2) whenever there are acts of courageous selflessness or extreme renunciation to the point of endangering or offering one's own life.

The first case is ascribed to classic ritual forms that include the bloody immolation of a living being; the second is supposed to be the internalized expression of the ritual, and its ultimate truth is assumed to lie in its intention. It remains to be seen whether there is a link between such different forms. Given the extent, however, to which commonplace phrases appear to legitimize the indeterminate use of the concept of sacrifice, for most people this does not seem to be of great concern. Selecting various elements of the ritual seems to be enough to fuel unquestioned analogies.

It is quite possible that such analogies may sometimes be legitimate; still, the entire chain of equivalences and substitutions would need to be established. To do so would require to begin with what seems crucial: that the sacrificial phenomenon emerges under certain conditions in a certain type of society. We would then have to determine whether these analogical forms have a comparable logic even though the ritual forms have disappeared. What has taken charge of whatever task sacrifice was once supposed to accomplish? This differential is probably the place where an answer can be found or at least suggested because the enigma is great indeed. The first step is to identify these ritual forms, or at least some of their essential aspects, before asking whether the purposes of sacrifice can be clarified.

Elements: Three Essential Protagonists of the Sacrifice

To effect this critical distancing was precisely what Hubert and Mauss intended in 1899 when they published their long essay "Sacrifice: Its Nature and Function."[48] The theses developed in that essay had a considerable impact on anthropological research until it became clear that the proposed model had overly generalized the Vedic and biblical cases. Notwithstanding all the reservations and objections, the fact remains that this study represents a considerable methodological advance by approaching the question of sacrifice with a description of its constitutive elements rather than by starting with the issue of its meaning. The two authors understand that however new and fruitful Robertson Smith's or James Frazer's approaches were, they were undermined by a number of unverifiable hypotheses and unwarranted generalizations. It is necessary to return to facts and first learn to organize observations: "We shall not adopt any of the classifications usually employed."[49] From the outset they proclaim that they will limit themselves to two questions on which reliable documentation is available: Brahmanic and biblical sacrifice. Even with this limitation, their approach remains exemplary in that it proposes to establish a few criteria on which all specialists could agree. The first series concerns the protagonists of the sacrifice, the second the procedures of the ritual—its spaces, instruments, and its beginning and end.

For the moment let us consider the elements of the first series. Every sacrifice includes at least three protagonists: (1) a sacrificer; (2) a sacrificed being; and (3) a deity to whom the sacrifice is offered. In many cases the figure of a priest or officiator is also involved. These elements seem obvious, and one could ask what heuristic objective would be served by emphasizing them. Nevertheless, if we recognize that there is no sacrifice when one of these terms is missing, we can anticipate the type of problem that will be encountered by theories that are based on extrapolation from the idea of sacrifice or a purely metaphorical use of the term. Let us first return, however, to the essential aspects of the three elements brought out by Hubert and Mauss's analysis and confront them with different data from those they selected.

ONE OR MORE SACRIFICERS   *"We give the name 'sacrificer' to the subject to whom the benefits of sacrifice thus accrue, or who undergoes its effect.* This subject is sometimes an individual, sometimes a collectivity."[50] What is important in this definition is that it presents the sacrificial act as a human initiative and as a dialogical relationship with a beneficiary; the selfless act is only performed for the sake of an expected response. The term *benefits* should be understood in the broad sense, even if the intended result is a material benefit. The real-world purpose of the ritual must be acknowledged. The sacrifice is accomplished in order to maintain or change a situation or, more generally, the order of things.

Hubert and Mauss are careful to give the sacrificer a sufficiently indeterminate status, as individual or group, in order to be relevant beyond the Indian case alone. They are well aware, however, and remind us that in Vedic thought the "beneficiary" of the sacrifice is the individual, specifically the head of the family and his relatives, and not the community. He is the sacrificer whom the texts call *yajamana*, the master. Herrenschmidt explains that he is the master because without him the sacrifice could not take place, for at least two reasons.[51] First, he is the bearer of sacrificial *desire*; the gods do not desire, and it is the responsibility of humans to preserve the order of the world by sacrificing (the later discussion of Vedic sacrifice will more specifically deal with this desire). Second, the sacrificer is the one who pays the performer of the sacrifice on whom the success of the ritual depends; this payment—*daksina*—creates a strong symbolic connection that ensures the preeminence of the sacrificer and guarantees his autonomy.[52] Herrenschmidt insists that "the emphasis should not be on the priest or the officiator but on the sacrificer, not on the deity but on the sacrifice as an effective act. As a result, the victim and its destruction would lose some of the importance they are given."[53] It should be possible to use Herrenschmidt's approach to understand many other sacrificial practices and hence very diverse cultures; this approach can be summed up in two questions: Who wants the sacrifice? What can it accomplish? In other words, what are those initiating the rite *requesting*, and how do they think the request can be fulfilled? In the absence of such a request, whether explicit or not, the death of a living being or any other form of destruction is in no way a sacrifice. This approach would eliminate a number of gratuitous hypotheses: to eliminate, negate, and destroy is not to sacrifice. The sacrifice presupposes an addresser, a thing addressed to the god or spirit, and an addressee. As with gift exchange, there is a triadic relationship (*to sacrifice* is a trivalent verb); the three terms are immediately articulated according to a law.[54]

THE OFFERING OR THING SACRIFICED   "The thing consecrated serves as an intermediary between the sacrificer . . . and the divinity to whom the sacrifice is usually addressed."[55] It is not enough to note that the sacrifice is an offering to a god. Indeed, unlike many other offerings, this one is of a particular type: it is *destroyed*. What should it be called? "The object thus destroyed is the victim. It is clearly for oblations of this kind that the name sacrifice must be reserved."⁵⁶ On the one hand this definition makes it possible to exclude all sorts of offerings or libations and even certain communal meals that have been incorrectly considered sacrifices. On the other hand it makes it possible to include sacrifices that tend to be ignored by dramatic views of sacrifice: plant offerings. They too are destroyed and/or partially consumed by the officiators. There are even sacrifices that only include such offerings. Two questions then arise: (1) Why does sacrifice involve only living beings, plants and especially animals? (2) What is the purpose of immolation when consecration might be enough?

What is sacrificed is not merely a precious good but, more important, something that must have a price for the sacrificer and for the deity in the agropastoral context. Almost universally, this requirement tends to favor the choice of a living being as the victim, which normally means an animal with a major status in the breeding system where the sacrifice takes place.⁵⁷ Even if plants, or very occasionally objects, may also be "sacrificed," the shedding of blood seems to have exceptional significance. Everywhere, blood is the equivalent of life itself, and life represents the highest value.⁵⁸ Hubert and Mauss do not say much more. We will need to go further.

THE DEITY   Strangely enough, Hubert and Mauss say almost nothing about the deity for whom the sacrifice is intended, except at the end, where they analyze the transition from sacrifice *to* the god to the sacrifice *of* the god. Such discretion would be paradoxical if it were not also the recognition of the self-evident and universally accepted fact that the intended recipient is one or more deities.

This raises a number of questions that have most often been ignored: what is meant by "deities"? They are often cautiously referred to as "higher entities"; sometimes they are called, in an undifferentiated way, genies, spirits, or ancestors. Such vagueness in the language used is more than troublesome; it is regrettable. It is also probably very difficult to avoid, however, since the names used vary so much among cultures. Nevertheless, it is generally accepted to speak of spirits or genies in hunter-gatherer societies (most often including societies that practice itinerant horticulture but primarily rely on hunting and gathering). What criterion of classification should be adopted? Names come to mind: very generic ones such as forest spirit, water spirit, and spirit of the bison, the jaguar, or genie of such and such place. In highly differentiated pastoral or agropastoral societies, however, complex pantheons with a great diversity of names and functions often develop. Ethnographers or historians then speak of gods and goddesses—as, for instance, in India, Greece, Rome, among the Germans, Celts, Dogon, Bambara, and many others. But this dualistic distinction is still an oversimplification. Various types may coexist. Michel Cartry gives us a good example in his research on the sacrificial rites of the Gourmantché of Burkina Faso. The difficulty lies in accurately identifying the addressees of the rite. What emerges is a complex system of invisible beings: genies of the bush, anxious creatures concerned with births; ancestors helped by funerary rituals in passing from the status of dangerous dead to that of protectors of the group; and finally *buli*, deities with mythological status but without specific names. The latter become more specific as they are identified with places and people whose guests they are.[59]

Generally, the thorniest question concerns the use of the term *ancestors*. The relation to ancestors is presupposed to be a permanent feature of all traditional societies. This is an oversimplification. While the *cult* of ancestors is obviously present in Asia and Africa, it is nonexistent in western America and the Amazon.[60] Relationships with ancestors, as a value and as a cult marked by debt, do seem to be associated with the pastoral and agricultural phenomenon, something Roberte Hamayon notices among the Buriat of Siberia. Within this particular schema of ancestors a diversity of strata exists: the recently deceased often remain dangerous, whereas the most ancient ones merge into a nebulous mass of reassuring protectors.[61]

A more general question requires our consideration, however: how does the emergence of sacrifice change the addressees themselves? We have seen under what conditions sacrificial societies emerged. In comparison with the world of spirits in nonsacrificial societies, the world of the deities to whom sacrifice is addressed acquires a position of power and domination; it may just as well be a protective position but at a cost precisely assessed by the sacrifice. Consequently, the latter implies and confirms a hierarchical order between the divine and the human world. Unquestionably the sacrificial world is not egalitarian; sacrifice itself originates from a debt relative to an excess that needs to be offset; it testifies to a request to the deity that is just as excessive. This point, too, will require further development.

This brief reminder of the presence of the three protagonists required to identify sacrifice provides a minimal but effective critical grid. It will lead to excluding from the category certain practices, such as prestige killings, as, for instance, those observed in certain potlatches among the Kwakiutl or the killing of warriors, wives, or horses at funerals of sacred kings in West Africa.[62] In the same way, public executions in the West, even when surrounded by impressive ceremonials, the killing of the bull at the bull fight, ritual cannibalism, or self-mutilation among certain hunter-gatherers are in no way sacrifices. In short, when there is no sacrificer addressing a divinity through the immolation of an offering, any claim to identify a sacrificial act is futile, no matter what convoluted analogies may be involved. *This ternary structure (addresser, thing addressed to the god or spirit, and addressee) of the sacrificial relation is essential to its raison d'être.* The definition should therefore exclude all forms that show apparent similarities, or else there is the risk of finding sacrifice everywhere blood is shed or loss is incurred. The concept would then lose all relevance.

Functions: Four Good Reasons to Sacrifice

Is it possible to identify reasons for sacrifice without leaving the descriptive mode? This would be the best method because it would allow us to dispense with purely hypothetical theories. According to the Maussian model it is enough to be guided by the ritual elements, in short, to take them seriously by relating them to other practices that are already understood. At least four good reasons to sacrifice emerge: to give, communicate, separate, and achieve. These are not the only ones; however, on the basis of these four important and well-known functions, we might be able to state more general hypotheses.

TO GIVE   According to Hubert and Mauss, "It is certain that usually, and to some extent, sacrifices were gifts conferring on the devotee rights over his god."[63] The advantage of an approach emphasizing this fundamental dimension of the offering is to allow the integration of a variety of rituals most often considered as particular forms of sacrifice: they were designated as propitiatory, expiatory, communal, or thanksgiving sacrifices. In every case what is involved is first of all an offering, or rather a gift, to the deity. Hubert and Mauss's thought here needs to be extended. Sacrifice should be viewed as being primarily the ceremonial gift addressed to the gods. This is confirmed by the commonplace phrase, "offering a sacrifice."

The following questions arise: how is reciprocity ensured? How can one make sure that those invisible beings will respond to the received gift? To answer would perhaps amount to finally understanding the meaning of the *necessity of the immolation,* that is, the destruction of the offering. Could it be that this very act is what confers "rights over the god"?

If ceremonial gift-giving is foremost an act and ritual of reciprocal acknowledgment between groups and individuals, if it is the procedure by which something precious of one's own is given as a *pledge* in an act that both defies and seduces, offers trust, and calls for a response, then it probably constitutes the first and fundamental gesture of sacrifice. This gesture, however, presents a particular difficulty because the addressees remain invisible and do not belong to the ordinary world of our perception. How will they react to the offering? Or rather, how can the gesture be constructed so that the offering will be accepted? And, above all, how can it be ensured that the response will occur? Rituals are elaborated to meet those requirements.

Let us first consider the last question: how to ensure that the divine partner will respond? How to make sure that he will give in return and honor the gesture addressed to him with a countergift? What kind of challenge is inherent in sacrifice? It lies in the fact of creating the *irreversible* through the *destruction* of the thing offered. More precisely, when it involves a living being, it proclaims the impossibility of the gift being withdrawn. "The sacrificial destruction has precisely as its goal that the gift must necessarily be returned."[64]

The death of the victim proves to the divine addressee the unlimited confidence placed in him and calls for a response worthy of the risk incurred. This element of challenge in the sacrificial gesture is homologous to the one we observed in the gift-exchange relationship. The challenge here, however, is proportional to the fact that the addressee is invisible and does not belong to the society of humans; faced with the difficulty of gathering signs of a possible response, the reply has to be rendered inevitable. From this point of view, even more than with ceremonial gift exchanges, the sacrifice amounts to a gamble and even borders on blackmail: how could it be possible not to respond *favorably* to an act that is so risky, so final?

Nevertheless, this dramatic dimension does not exhaust the paradox of the gift challenge laid before the supernatural power. There is also a rarely noticed logical, or rather topological, dimension that plays on re-lations of inverted symmetry between the human world and the divine world, the here and the hereafter. Herrenschmidt states this as follows: "To destroy the victim is the only way to have it go from the visible to the in-visible, to send it *ad patres*, and to make it circulate."[65] He is referring to an analysis by Paul Mus explaining that to place offerings in broken vases in this world is to ensure that they will be received in unbroken ones in the other world. Sacrifice recognizes, consecrates, and transgresses a boundary: the world that lies on the other side of death is the exact opposite of this world, its reversed double. This principle of inversion goes together with the principle of reciprocity that is at the core of the logic of the forbidden: what we deny to ourselves is by that very gesture offered to someone else. This positive requirement is what underlies the prohibition of incest and in many societies stipulates that the hunter cannot eat his own catch. It also governs certain so-called totemic prohibitions. Thus the share reserved for the gods in the sacrifice is not only what is given up but also what guar-antees in return the share promised to humans. The immolation turns the visible into the invisible and ensures that the reverse movement will occur and a response will be given. A ruse? Perhaps. A logical marvel? Probably.

In this way another demand can be met by the very performance of the *ritual*, which aims at several effects at the same time: the fixed and often meticulous and mandatory procedures ensure that the appropriate *means* are taken to address the divinity. Whether certain details are rather arbitrary is not a problem: they may appear as the result of a choice made by the deity itself. Detailed analyses, however, show that the organization of the materials in the ritual is more often coherent than arbitrary. More-over, as in the case of ceremonial gift exchange, these fixed procedures breaking with ordinary gestures induce a solemn feeling and become an ac-cepted convention between humans and gods. To recall Malinowski's defi-nition, a ceremonial act has the following characteristics: it is public and observes definite formalities; it has religious and sociological import; and, finally, it carries with it obligations.[66]

In this particular case, however, gift exchange is no longer the mere act of mutual recognition specific to encounters between human groups. Those encounters are ruled by alternation and parity, qualities that also dominate relations between humans and spirits in the world of hunter-gatherers. Something has changed here: "The god needs to be fed," as the Vedic and Roman traditions have it.[67] Keeping in mind some slight differences, the same could be said of Aztec sacrifice.[68] Humans first owe something to the god that the latter does not have to return. Only later, following the challenge of reciprocity from the sacrificer, does the request become possible. What humans give is, in fact, a giving back; they are already indebted when the sacrificial offering begins. Vedic thought produced a classic doctrine on this point (which I will discuss in the next chapter). It appears in various and generally more modest forms in other traditions. What is this debt? Probably the *debt of life* associated with the mastery of domestic animals and cultivated plants—in short, the power acquired over the natural world. It is as if the underlying logic were as follows: much has been given; too much has been taken; the time has come for restitution, to give munificently in return so that the god will give again. Hence the irreversible gift of immolation, which binds the deity to the sacrificer and, moreover, ensures reversibility with the invisible world. The sacrificial gift presupposes debt and thus the inequality of partners. At this point the enigma may lie less in the response performed by sacrifice than in the very conception of an excess to be offset with respect to life.

TO COMMUNICATE   Another good reason to sacrifice now becomes clear: to establish communication with the divine world. This point illustrates the break with the world of spirits that had resulted from mastery over life. We have seen that the world of hunter-gatherers is characterized by alliance between partners who remain relatively equal. Relations are based on reciprocal service where communication is part of the alliance. The new command over nature, however, breaks this ancient pact. Spirits are no longer familiar. The natural world no longer speaks. The nearby and terrestrial tribe of the spirits is replaced by the celestial and remote society of the gods. The omnipresent circulation of the former is succeeded by the distant withdrawal of the latter. The animal world in which both the natural and the supernatural were united is replaced by a divided animal world in which the familiar and reassuring world of domestic animals now faces the alien and most often hostile world of wild animals. Sacrifice presents a solution to this communication breakdown. To offer the remote gods a life taken from the familiar and controlled animal world, which is now part of the human world, expresses a message of deference. A new pact becomes possible. Sacrifice replaces the alliance between equals. It confirms the new division and attempts to overcome the separation that has emerged.[69] But the spirit of alliance is no longer there. The relation is asymmetrical. Sacrifice recognizes this hierarchy at the moment when it becomes an instrument of communication between the two worlds. It intervenes as a way of connecting with the gods that have fled and become ethereal and invisible. To designate them as such is to recognize the existence of a rift between the old and the new world. From now on the gods can no longer be on the side of the wild world; they have become the gods of the transformed world. Within the framework of the sacrificial rite, the communion meal (when there is one) is probably the moment of greatest proximity; it amounts to acceding to the gods' table or bringing them to humanity's table. Having made sure that the gods have received their share, humans can once again claim their own share through the animal that they sacrifice and eat together with the gods.

TO SEPARATE   Communication needs to be instituted because the gods have become more remote. For the same reason, it has become risky to get too close to them. Now that the deities have become invisible—as opposed to spirits embodied by animals, winds, places, plants, water, and many other natural elements—it becomes important not to venture too far or without guarantee in this *terra incognita*.

Since sacrifice propels the sacrificer (and often the officiator, too) into the divine world, multiple precautions must be taken to avoid too brutal an intrusion and, above all, to give the entrance the necessary legitimacy. The opposition of the *sacred* and the *profane*, should we want to recast the Durkheimian categories, makes sense with respect to this requirement. It is not the affirmation of an ontological difference between two worlds. Given the condition of symbolic efficacy, the opposition becomes obvious as a significant division. Now the entrance and purification rites in Vedic sacrifice that seem so important to Hubert and Mauss can be understood. The opposition, however, cannot be generalized, for in numerous other cases such preparatory or purification rites are practically nonexistent. The opposite procedure may even occur, where the function of sacrifice is not to have the sacrificer enter the divine space but, on the contrary, to effect the movement of deities away from human space. Heusch mentions this when speaking of sacrificial practices of the Nuer and other African cases; Cartry mentions similar attitudes among the Gourmantché.[70] The

Greek case is similar: entrance into the ritual remains rather informal, and sacrifice aims at reactualizing the separation between humans and gods as much as reestablishing communication between them. In every case, whether it is to include or exclude, to bring together or alienate, sacrifice remains a procedure that regulates relations between humans and supernatural powers. It establishes or negotiates the *right distance*—conjunction and disjunction, as Heusch summarized—neither too close (imprudence is usually punished) nor too far (which would amount to a drift toward negligence or forgetting) but in the middle, between trust and respect, faith and anxiety—in short, just as in ceremonial gift exchange.

TO REALIZE   Like any ritual, the sacrifice is a mechanism that aims at obtaining results. The sequence of gestures constitutes the steps of a programmed action. Very precisely, it is a procedure. Even when associated with words (invocations, incantations, prayers provided for a particular ceremony) sacrifice is not discursive by nature. Nor is it theatrical, even if it may appear so from the outside. To be sure, sacrifice takes the form of a fully visible gesture, but it is not *mimēsis* (one of the signs that sacrifice no longer operates for the faithful is precisely that it has become mere spectacle). Sacrifice produces what it shows; it is an operative mechanism. As a symbolic process sacrifice does not want to signify but to do. Symbolism organizes elements and makes them act upon one another. It comprises neither a reflexive level nor separate levels of signifier and signified. By mobilizing material elements, the purpose of symbolism is not to say something but to create relationships, set into place, articulate, distribute, and transform. This is why there is symbolism only when it is effective.[71] What results does sacrificial action seek? To obtain what has been described above: to ensure that the gods will accept the offerings and respond to them, to render communication with them possible, to establish the proper distance from them, and to preserve or restore the order of things.

The reasons for sacrifice are internal to the system of beliefs prevailing where sacrifices take place; they are functions presupposed by the ritual. One might say that this does not reveal the ultimate and objective meaning of sacrifice itself. Nevertheless, by connecting those functions with the cultural conditions for the emergence of the sacrificial phenomenon, a hint of more profound reasons begins to appear. Sacrifice is a symbolic mechanism that aims at taking charge of the global mutation of human societies caused by the domestication of plants and animals, the emergence of sedentary farming, and in some cases the emergence of a central "political" authority. This is not merely a social mutation but an upheaval in the representation of the environment and in the very idea of the world considered as the totality of visible and invisible beings.[72]

In the hunter-gatherers' world all relations with the natural world are structured as relations of reciprocity: life is already granted and remains granted; therefore sacrifice is unnecessary. The other animals are the deities. The divine world is immediately embodied in the natural and especially the animal world—or rather it is that world. Relations with animals/spirits are relations of gift/countergift—in short, relations of alliance. On the contrary, the agropastoral world establishes a distinct boundary between nature and society. Humans depend on their techniques and intervention in the living world for their subsistence. The interplay of constant exchanges with wild nature no longer exists, or barely exists. It is as if society itself were gaining new importance as the place where transformations occur. Hence the emergence of pantheons more concerned with regulating relationships between humans than with ruling over the elements of the environment. The whole problem now centers on the difficulties of reciprocity with less accessible deities. Understandably, in this world constructed by humans the gods now appear at a greater distance. They are no longer identified with the beings that are sources of subsistence (animals hunted, fruits or plants gathered), but they remain present on the wider horizon: the order of the world, the cycle of seasons, and the organization of the city.

Thus a renewed coherence (already noted in the American and Siberian cases) emerges between, on the one hand, the world of alliance and sharing with the spirits and, on the other hand, the world of sacrifice, where separation and hierarchy predominate. At the same time it becomes necessary to both recognize and negate this distance between two worlds, which is expressed in the opposition between the cultivated world and the wild. Human power over nature is reduced and atoned for in sacrificial rituals that simultaneously express this power, compensate for it, and try to preserve it. In this system spirits or gods are placed in a new symbolic position: domination. They are no longer partners but masters who belong to a superior and powerful world. Whatever humans enjoy, know, or do belongs to them. This opens up the world of debt, which now becomes original reality. The debt expresses and confirms this dependency and ultimately attempts to explain it. The logic of the unequal gift sets in between gods and humans but also among humans themselves: the giver becomes a creditor and the receiver a debtor. The debt is conceived as an inaugural indebtedness to ancestors and spirits, and it invades the framework of ceremonial exchanges.

The gods tend to become invisible, representations and ideas. How can humans reach them and involve them in their affairs? How can the gods be obligated to help? Sacrifice is the operation by which they are acknowledged, maintained, and retained. The gods have entered the "cultivated" world; they no longer speak through the moving figures of animals and natural elements but through those of a sedentary pantheon that takes charge of society and supports the activity of transforming the world. Sacrifice establishes the gods and places them in a distant position of superiority as it renders communication with them possible and allocates them a position of reciprocity. The sacrificial process institutes a cosmic order on the basis of a new ecological situation. Through sacrifice, humans acknowledge that the world they produce still comes from the gods; therefore, the sacrificed thing must be taken from the product of their technical activities, or from anything that embodies their power, above all the overly dangerous and gratifying power they have gained over life.

Sacrifice as Technogony

Because sacrifice emerges at the brink of these cultural and technical changes by responding to the newly created situation, it translates, confirms, and celebrates the emerging new world transformed by human know-how while regulating relations between humans and spirits or gods. Sacrifice becomes operative as a ritual because all its operations aim at reinforcing the very act of achieving, transforming, and mastering. Indeed, before the domestication of plants and animals, the world is the source of subsistence available to meet needs and desires. Techniques, which vary by culture, are already important: braiding, pottery, weaving, culinary arts (roasting, boiling, and smoking), and the manufacture of fishing and hunting instruments. The hunter-gatherers' world is rich in techniques whose significance is recounted in numerous myths of invention.

With the domestication of plants and animals, however, another threshold is reached. Life itself has been mastered. This power is reflected back on all technical achievements because the way of life is changing:

generally speaking, it becomes sedentary among farming populations and hence completely dependent on human know-how. From now on the subsistence given by deities no longer consists in animals or plants present in nature but in the growth of cultivated plants, the health of domesticated animals, the regularity of seasons, and the fertility of the soil. The gods must give to humans what humans took from them. The gods must change and support the new situation. Indeed, they perform this transformation everywhere. They must sustain a universe mastered by human know-how. The world itself must change. The origin of the world or of the things offered in the world must always also be the origin of technics. Every cosmogony now has become a technogony. From now on the world begins as a world dominated by the arts of civilization and containing domestic animals. The old world is dismissed as a figure of chaos and savagery, or identified with neighbors claimed to be "inferior," before returning idealized as the "Golden Age" in narratives of origin. Sacrifice founds and consecrates the new order and presents it as having existed forever. The sacrificial fire is presented as primordial (at least in a universe in a key of fire). In certain cosmogonies (as in the Veda) the world begins as a sacrifice. Sacrifice does not center on the figure of the immolated victim but on the process of ordering the world, from the most local to the most global; its purpose is to preserve or reestablish this order. Regulation of social crisis is only one aspect; in other words, every social crisis is a cosmic crisis.

From this point of view sacrificial rituals most clearly exemplify the phenomenon of symbolism as an operative process. At the risk of inviting misinterpretation, it could be said that sacrifice is a technology (that is, a mechanism of production and mastery of causality within the environment) and even a highly complex one. Of course, it is only valid within the framework of representations and beliefs that is associated with it. Because it is a technology, sacrifice gives way to a different technology when the latter turns out to be more appropriate, effective, and reliable, in other words verifiable outside of local symbolisms. Since sacrifice emerges at the same time as the new mastery over nature resulting from the domestication of plants and animals and the acquisition of the "arts of civilization" (metallurgy, textile, and pottery) and makes up for this mastery by affirming its link to the divine world and framing it as the symbolic management of causality, it is understandable that sacrifice will also be the first ritual form to decline when the technical field becomes autonomous. Sacrifice simultaneously expresses, assumes, confirms, and absorbs the debt. According to the same logic, sacrifice will be erased by the very mastery it aimed at controlling and containing. Before turning to the reasons for that erasure, let us examine two exemplary cases of sacrifice as technogony: Greek and Vedic sacrifice.

Raw and Cooked Worlds: Greece and India

It is possible to read the main episodes of Ulysses' wanderings as organized around the following question: what is the truly human world for which we are made and to which we must return after losing it? Where is it located? According to Vidal-Naquet the island of the anthropophagi Cyclops, the island where the goddess Calypso offers immortality to the hero, the island where Circe draws Ulysses toward bestiality, and the lands of the Lotophagi and the Lestrygons all share a common feature that signals an anomaly, that is, the absence of sacrificial practices.[73] They also share a complementary feature: the inhabitants of those strange countries do not eat bread. The return to Ithaca represents the return to the properly human life of farming, with livestock and grain, which are also offerings suitable for the gods. According to Homer and his contemporaries this is the true and right cosmos, as opposed to the illusionary regions traveled by Ulysses: "Sacrifice is a double criterion in the *Odyssey*: of humanity, between humans and nonhumans; and of social and moral values, between human beings."[74] Perhaps it is even more: the guarantee of an ordered world confronting chaos, a finished world confronting an uncultured world, a real world confronting a world of illusion and seduction, and a properly human world in-between animals and gods. It is remarkable that, like India, Greece conceived of this opposition as that between the raw and the cooked.

Prometheus and the Cuisine of Sacrifice

Ancient Greek society practiced sacrifice, even during the age of the philosophers and sophists.[75] This may seem surprising to those who still consider that the emergence of analytical thought and mathematics in Greece constituted a secularizing process that seems inconsistent with religious practices considered "archaic." Historians, however, note that these practices remained unproblematic at the very time when new forms of knowledge were being developed. For instance, at the beginning of the *Re-*

public Cephalus, one of Socrates' interlocutors, was said "to carry a crown on his head because he just made a sacrifice in the court" (*Republic* 328c).

It might be quite fruitful to understand the function of sacrifice in such a society, not because we would once again expect ancient Greece to provide a better interpretive model but merely because this will shed light on two contrasting and concurrent aspects of the Greek heritage. What should be generalized is not this particular case but the questions that it raises.

Jean-Pierre Vernant has given us a classic work on the representation of sacrifice in ancient Greece.[76] I use the term *representation* here because Vernant's study does not deal with ritual practices themselves but with their elaboration in Hesiod's work, primarily in the *Theogony* but also in *The Works and Days*. Vernant starts by noting that tradition attributes the invention of sacrifice to Prometheus; it is therefore important to understand this assertion in the context of the legendary deeds of this Titan.

Vernant first remarks that the establishment of sacrificial practices is presented as a consequence of the distance that has emerged between humans and gods. They have become two distinct races, in contrast with the Golden Age when they lived together and shared the same feasts. This separation is interpreted as a consequence of the rebellion of Prometheus, thief of fire and master of technics. Second, Vernant notes that hard work (*ponos*) will from then on define the human condition and constitute its fate. Hard work is associated with the production of two essential elements of human food: meat and bread.

The sacrificial ritual instituted by Prometheus consists of offering the gods a steer, retaining for humans the most nourishing part (muscle and organs) unappetizingly wrapped, while Zeus is offered long bones wrapped in an appealing layer of white fat. What looks like a trick is, in fact, the acknowledgment that humans remain "bellies" forced to feed themselves. Long bones, however, reputed to be rot-proof, are burned along with herbs and spices and go up in smoke toward the gods, for whom such "food" is appropriate because it confirms their immortal nature. Humans are doomed to toil on the land while the gods, in their Olympus, do not know labor and suffering.

Sacrifice is therefore a ritual that stages and confirms the separation between gods and humans. It does so by reaffirming the order of things: the places of the gods, humans, and animals: "The distance separating mortals from immortals is begun in sacrifice and perpetuated by sacrifice. On the line separating the different portions taken from the victim is projected the boundary between the immutable youth of the Olympians, masters of heaven, and this ephemeral form of existence that men on earth must assume to become who they are."[77] By making the sacrifice into a feast eaten in honor of the gods, however, humans symbolically rejoin their company. Sacrifice draws them closer together at the very moment when it confirms and stages the distance between them.

This explains the ambiguous situation of humans illustrated by the story of Prometheus's ruse in the division of parts in the sacrifice, hence also the latent conflict (*eris*) that has developed between humans and gods. Sacrifice addresses this conflict, simulates it, and resolves it through the operation of the division into two worlds, the divine and the human. Human life is defined by mortality, constantly evidenced by the necessity of food production. The steer, the preferred animal offered as sacrifice, is at the intersection of two major food elements, meat and wheat, since not only can it be eaten, but it also makes plowing possible—the process through which wheat can be grown. Thus it symbolizes properly human life: food and labor. Hesiod's writing presupposes "as an evidence tacitly inscribed in the structure of the myth of symmetrical position, the complementary status between the cereal *bios* and the sacrificial victim. In the context of a meat diet the sacrificial ritual takes on the same role as cereal crops in a vegetable diet."[78]

Several points remain unclear in Vernant's stimulating argument. First of all, the symmetry he establishes between sacrifice of the steer and the growing of grain raises an obvious problem: the symmetry should concern the *raising* of beef and the *growing* of grain. Otherwise, the argument amounts to claiming that the function of sacrifice is to produce meat. To be sure, we compensate for the ellipsis in the argument by saying that it is through the sacrifice that meat consumption, which is essential for life, enters into the system of relations between humans and gods.[79] One could also ask why the process of separating from the gods and getting closer to them is not centered on wheat, an even more common symbol of the human condition among the ancient Greeks: "Bread belongs only to man. It is a sign and guarantor of civilized life, separating humanity from the animals as well as from the gods."[80] The fact that the sacrificial process is centered on the steer, therefore, means that it does not only consist in introducing meat into the cultural space. It consists in *taking life* and making immolation into an effective act with a highly symbolic charge. Hesiod, however, remains discreet on this point, along with many other authors (including his modern commentator). What interests Greek thought in sacrifice is the task to be performed more than the debt to be discharged.

Sacrifice shows that properly human life—that of farming and herding, craft, and communities ruled by law—brings humans closer to the divine world. Sacrifice confirms that divine life has gone over to the side of culture and that the new order of things is reorganized by human activity and no longer merely granted in the natural world. This is why sacrifice affirms the preeminence of the cooked over the raw, the city over the country, the written over the oral, and the law over custom.

India: Cooking Prajâpati

No civilization has given sacrifice such a central place in its representation of the world as ancient India.[81] In the cosmogony of classical Hinduism and especially in Brahmanism, its most orthodox branch, sacrifice does not appear as a ritual emerging at some point in the story of origins but is immediately present at the birth of the world. It is this birth itself. The world is formed as sacrifice, according to Madeleine Biardeau, who quotes an essential passage in one of the most ancient Vedic hymns: "When the gods returned the sacrifice with Man [Purusa, the cosmic giant] as the sacrificial material, Spring served as ritual butter, Summer as kindling, and Fall as the offering. On the sacred bedding they sprinkled Man, that is, the sacrifice born at the origins. Through him the gods accomplished the sacrifice, as did the Saints and the Seers. . . . The gods sacrificed the sacrifice through sacrifice. Those were the first institutions."[82]

The being that is everything, Purusa, is both space and time, the visible and invisible, all beings: animals, plants, and humans. He is the cosmos. "The cosmos is produced by sacrifice; sacrifice is the principle of everything."[83] Sacrifice is not something that arises after some incident in order to correct, expiate, or celebrate. It is not an event but a state. Ontologically, the world is sacrifice. So much so, according to Biardeau, that even if sacrifice is primarily addressed to the gods, it is not merely a cult devoted to them but has a far broader and more profound aim. Its task is to confirm the order of the world, support it, and sometimes restore it. It is a cosmic operation. This explains the importance of the ritual. Sacrificial procedure is homologous with the functioning of the universe. Ritual repeats the way in which the world came into being and according to which it continues to live: "The sacrificial mechanism is indeed most important; it is the universal regulator in a totality where no being can lay claim to a life that is independent from the whole."[84]

So what, then, is the role of the gods? What accounts for their superiority over the *asuras*—the demons—that are often more cunning and efficient? The answer is that the gods possess the right knowledge of sacrifice. The gods acquired their immortality through sacrifice, and sacrifice preserves their power. This is why they need sacrifice, but they themselves cannot accomplish it—feeding the gods is from then on the responsibility of humans. This responsibility is essential for at least two reasons. First, humans are desiring beings, desiring because they are mortal. They alone have tasks to perform and things to bring into being. According to Sylvain Lévi, such was at the beginning the situation of Prajâpati (another Purusa figure in later texts): "Only one feeling drives Prajâpati to create: the desire for offspring, the need to multiply."[85] Malamoud cites this sentence from Manu: "Not a single act here (below) appears ever to be done by a man free from desire; for whatever (man) does, it is the result of the impulse of desire."[86] Sacrifice is a case in point; therefore, the central character of the sacrifice is he who offers it: the sacrificer.

The second reason is that giving is a properly human task; the gods can no longer give because from the moment when they have gone beyond desire, they have become the only addressees of the offerings. At first, however, gift exchange was what distinguished them from demons, who made the offerings in their own mouths. The gods became gods by the gifts they gave each other. The act of going out of oneself and of recognition provided by gift exchange made the difference. To give to the gods and to the Brahmans who carry out the sacrificial operation has now become a human responsibility. From the start the gods have exhausted desire and gift exchange and have thus gone beyond time. Since then, sacrifice feeds the gods who preserve the world with its order, life, rhythms, and justice. This includes both the natural and the social world, heaven and earth, gods and humans: "The order that allows everything to exist and where everyone has a role to play is *dharma*: a fundamental concept, inseparable from sacrifice, as the one cannot exist without the other. The cosmic drama is thus played out on earth in a world of sacrifice."[87]

The Vedic conception of sacrifice, mentioned briefly here, is surprising to us, accustomed as we are to the idea of sacrifice as renunciation. What is this sacrifice that is at the same time the beginning of the world, the order of beings, food for the gods, balance of energies, and life and justice of the community? What exactly is it if it signifies all reality? It is tempting to say that such a broad object integrates too much and risks losing any specificity; the concept might cease to be relevant. One wonders if this kind of omnivalence is not a true product of Brahman speculation eager to formulate and celebrate in every way an activity that constitutes the justification for the masters of the ritual. Such suspicion, however, even if it were legitimate, would not obviate the need for a more in-depth study of the major impact of sacrificial activity, as shown by Charles Malamoud's analyses in *Cooking the World.* What does Vedic sacrifice do? It operates the permanent transformation of the raw into the cooked world—in other words, of the unfinished into the finished world and the limited into the deified world. This transformation is told by the narrative of the formation of the universe. After having produced multiple creatures, Prajâpati remained scattered in them. He asked the gods to reconstitute him. Agni, the fire god, was charged with the task but only accepted it on condition that he become part of Prajâpati; while the latter was on fire, the gods gave him an offering of bricks that penetrated his body as they cooked. When the building was finished, his body had become whole again. This is how the world is made, through cooking and sacrifice. In the Veda this primordial model dominates the idea of transformation or any other activity. Everything pertaining to the gods is cooked or connotes cooking. For instance, even raw milk is considered cooked as Agni's sperm. This is also why the Brahman is the cook par excellence. Finally, the cremation of the dead completes the process: the deceased is the sacrificer and becomes himself the ultimate offering. In fact, all life lived according to the rituals is but a perpetual cooking. To quote the Veda, man is "born into a world that is made [by himself]."[88] Everything that is transformed is a sacrifice, a movement toward the cooked and the divine.

But why does the cooked prevail over the raw? Why do the gods prefer it? To answer this question, Malamoud presents numerous texts that report various beliefs. What inspires these narratives? Perhaps the necessity not only to preserve a distance from the savage world but to guarantee its exclusion. Why? One indirect way to answer would be to examine the figure of the Indian ascetic and all that it implies. The ascetic returns "to the forest" or the desert, to the empty and savage world. As Malamoud explains, he abandons the cooked world and all forms of cooking, in other words the true world, the deified world.[89] He extinguishes the fires of sacrifice and goes away naked toward the wilderness. The fires, however, have now been internalized; his meditation and his destitution become spiritual cooking.

This fascination with the flip side of the cooked world, the savage world—or the world not subject to sacrificial intervention—is also fascination with the world that existed before transformation became necessary. The writings that describe this world bear a surprising resemblance to Greek writings about the Golden Age: animals living harmoniously with humans, trees offering fruit, and grains that grow on their own. This is strikingly similar—albeit in an idealized form—to the ancient hunter-gatherers' world, where food was readily available and the gods were connected to humans by relationships of alliance. This otherworld, however, idealized as ancient paradise, is the most repressed element in narratives and rituals. As in Greece, the sacrificial practice in ancient India consists first and foremost in affirming the superiority of the cooked over the raw, farming over hunting, and the domestic over the wild. The true world is an ordered world; the narratives relating its birth present it as the product of the divine craftsman (the Greek *dēmiourgos*) or as being formed by the cooking that is also the inaugural sacrifice (Prajâpati's rebirth). In Greece the space of the wilderness with its animals becomes the absolute opposite of the city. India imagined a compromise. The space outside the community becomes an alternative for the ascetic, a condition that everyone is free to choose. In both cases sacrifice signifies and establishes the break with the ancient world. It fully expresses the world that is being transformed and that must be transformed. It is the world of order and of the law. It is the ritual form of every transformation par excellence. Sacrifice consecrates this transformation and its supremacy. This is why it can be called a technogony.

Can we, however, generalize what seems so clearly established in the Greek and Indian cases? Not every universe is in a key of fire. Can we speak of technogony in the case of a simple expiatory sacrifice involving the immolation of a chicken at the edge of a Dogon village? This would obviously be excessive. The totality of the rites needs to be considered, for the sacrificial birth of the world opens up a space of intervention where multiple forms of sacrifice can take place, even the most discreet ones. It is thus possible to speak of symbolic mastery and even, at the risk of a misunderstanding, of technology through symbolic means.

This is probably true of all rituals, because they have to be effective, but all the more so of sacrificial rituals, for several reasons. The first and most general is due to the conditions of emergence of the sacrificial phenomenon. As we have seen, this emergence is always associated with the upheavals in representations and ways of life caused by the domestication of plants and animals. The sacrificial phenomenon is thus associated with a power over life that represents the highest level of demiurgy and encroaches on the divine realm.

Hence the following paradox: through the immolation of an animal or occasionally a plant, the same sacrifice that aims at compensating for the excess of power obtained over nature also constitutes a procedure that consecrates and locks in this power. The humblest expiatory sacrifice itself aims to restore a disrupted order, because the rite as such is operative and because sacrifice, through its power to produce the irreversible, is the most reliable way to ensure the hoped-for effect. The emergence of sacrifice is inseparable from an increased control over the living world and the affirmation of cultural means over nature. With the same gesture sacrifice aims at sanctioning this power while preserving relations with the deities. Sacrifice does not merely express this aim; as a procedure it accomplishes it.

This explains the intense emotional atmosphere of sacrificial rituals. To be sure, emotional intensity varies depending on the required solemnity or the occasion, culture, and the type of victim; one reacts differently to the immolation of a chicken from that of a buffalo—or even a human. This symbolic mastery needs to be all the more rigorous and meticulous because it acts with or on invisible forces that belong to the realm of divine power. To infringe on cosmic forces or the domain of the gods cannot be done without fear and trembling. The rigor of the ritual is perceived as guaranteeing, if at all possible, that no errors will be made. Sacrificial emotion cannot be separated from this anxiety. Sacrifice assumes this anguish and transcends it through immolation to guarantee that limits have been acknowledged and that life irrevocably remains a gift from the gods.

Why Sacrifice Faded Away

In some interpretations sacrificial rites are seen as regulating social relations, as ritual responses to a crisis,[90] but this function is rather rare. Their center of gravity lies elsewhere. Sacrifice is a ritual directed at the *cosmos* rather than the *socius*. It is located within the relationships of balance between nature and culture. Its purpose is to perform their proper—and yet difficult—articulation. More precisely, sacrifice makes it possible to adjust those relations within societies that have begun an active process of transforming nature and controlling other living beings. Sacrifice is a total symbolic phenomenon because it simultaneously operates at several levels and affects several different realms. It aims to restore the balance and relationship between the transformed world and the granted world; it returns what has been taken from the natural world, but it also confirms this transformative power by identifying it with the establishment of forms of recognition of the granted world. Sacrifice acknowledges the gift of the civilized arts that the deity bestowed on humans. It returns the benefits of civilization to the deity in order to preserve them. To sacrifice is to compensate for this demiurgic power and sometimes to atone for it. This amounts to limiting and restraining it but also to preserving and celebrating it. Sacrifice proclaims, simulates, repeats, establishes (or reestablishes) the order of the world or institutes or restores the proper functioning of things at a more local level. The social order is only one essential component of it. Sacrifice integrates the cosmic and the social order; it states the fact of their disjunction and the necessity of their conjunction. It is always paradoxical. It cannot be reduced to any particular level or referent but integrates them all. Regardless of the orientation of the ritual this is always the essence of sacrifice: offering, request, expiation, commitment, or pure celebration associated with seasonal cycles.

It does not make much sense to refer to sacrifice as an act of radical scope or transgression, as dramatized in later accounts of a few upsetting cases (human sacrifices, the sacrifice of the king or the god); they cannot serve as references. They should be taken into account but must first be contextualized. Often we see only the bloody spectacle rather than a set of strict and meticulous interventions associated with representations of the visible and invisible world, the "cost" of which can, of course, be deplored as in the case of human sacrifices. Sacrifice needs to be considered without any sacrificial pathos. We should give up our fascination with the question of immolation and the victim and instead try to understand how sacrifice is a conceptual operator that simultaneously mobilizes the totality of the elements of a culture at many different levels.

There is also little sense in casually projecting the concept of sacrifice onto contemporary social situations. Just as we no longer live in societies characterized by specifically ceremonial gift exchange (the level of human relationships is a different issue), it is obvious that we no longer live in societies characterized by ritual sacrifice, considering our technical means, knowledge, and economic system. There is no *direct* relation between the question of sacrifice and modern economy. To describe this economy in terms of "invisible sacrifice" or "unstated sacrifice" amounts to playing on words or claiming that the moral sense of renunciation and expiation carried over in the Christian tradition must serve as a reference. In modern societies the sacrificial model is gone. The general conditions for sacrificial ritual no longer exist, since they were determined by the emergence of pastoral and agricultural activities. Those rituals represented a global response on the part of humans endowed with new powers confronting their situation within nature, the granted world, and the transcendence of that which can only be received: the surrounding world, earlier life, and the community of one's upbringing. Sacrifice articulates the granted and the transformed, the received and the produced world. It expresses all this at the same time, and it does so effectively. Sacrifice is not a discourse but, like all rituals, a performance; like all symbolism it is operative. It brings about what it expresses. Sacrifice was a prodigious mechanism for taking charge of relations between the visible and the invisible world.

If, however, the model of sacrifice no longer exists, the problem it posed historically has not been solved and needs to be reformulated as follows: if the emergence of the sacrificial phenomenon was associated with the emergence of technical mastery over the world, and foremost over life, then we might assume that the extension of this mastery should have brought about a parallel increase of sacrificial practices; however, the opposite has happened. Why?

One answer could be that the more nature/culture regulation is performed by positive knowledge and powerful technical means, the more autonomous it becomes, which necessarily involves a different field of action and thought. Ritual regulation then fades away. Its obsolescence comes

the more autonomous
it becomes

along with a call or demand to internalize the relation to the divine. A religion of compassion and an ethic of relationships develop at the same time that the hold over the cosmos tightens. In short, even as gift exchange remains the essential form of interpersonal mutual recognition, *ceremonial* gift exchange is no longer practiced as a major institution organizing public relationships between groups. Similarly, *ritual* sacrifice can no longer assume a function of global regulation in a world defined according to different parameters and based on different resources. Because symbolic mastery through ritual means is no longer possible, gift-giving becomes the moral question of generosity—including its unconditional form—and the only element of sacrifice that remains is the ethical element of renunciation. It is important to understand that this gift-giving and this sacrifice, both reduced to spiritual schemas, no longer have any direct relation to either ceremonial gift exchange or ritual sacrifice. The internalization of the gesture signals first of all the loss of its social function.

The inconsistent way in which the term *sacrifice* is used in the field of economic practices refers to a trivialized meaning of sacrifice as renunciation, deprivation, and effort, as a basis for interpreting social attitudes that involve these virtues. This is perfectly acceptable since this meaning is recognized by a whole tradition. Using this trivial meaning, however, to introduce the entire world of ritual sacrifice, as if the two involved the same question, gives rise to a fallacious equivalence. For even if ritual sacrifice does imply renunciation—giving something of oneself—and in some cases a kind of festive consummation, it is, above all, a symbolic mechanism that simultaneously operates on multiple levels (offerings to the deities, relations with them, compensatory gestures, affirming or restoring the order of the world). None of this exists in the moral idea of sacrifice or in the analogical use of the term in political economy.

Vigilance remains necessary regarding the use of the term, especially when the word alone serves as an alibi (or catchall phrase) to permute contents that are not comparable. What is at stake is thus not to track down hidden forms of sacrifice "under the rags of modernity" or to produce a wealth of meanings by flushing out archaisms lurking under the surface of the present; rather, it is to determine how these multiple functions that were once performed by sacrificial rituals (indeed, we moderns need to use the past tense) are fulfilled today. Clearly, most of those functions have now been assumed by rational knowledge and transformative techniques. This is what has most often generated the strongest resistance to such knowledge and techniques within old cultures; this is also what feeds nostalgia within advanced industrial societies. These regrets are based on the retrospective illusion of a world where the symbolic management of things was more poetic. Ritual in itself is no more poetic than rational organization. It is merely more exotic for those who observe it from the outside and from afar. This might be another way of understanding the "disenchantment of the world." Nevertheless, the shift to knowledge and technics has not in any way eliminated the question that sacrifice meant to answer: what about the power we recognize having over the world? What are its limits? What remains for us to understand is symbolism within the world of technical power.

. . .

If it is true that sacrifice is, above all, an offering, then it constitutes the relation of ceremonial gift exchange of humans vis-à-vis the gods. Very precisely, within this relation sacrifice is the moment defined as the obligation to reciprocate. Gift-giving no longer answers a challenge but takes charge of a debt—a paradoxical debt, since it proceeds not from an excessive gift from the gods but from an excessive human mastery over this gift, over life, the quantity of accessible goods, and the power to transform.

This obligation has disappeared, along with the act of giving thanks that was inseparable from it. This is what modernity has not addressed, probably because it no longer entertains the very idea of compensation. Perhaps we feel that we have finally dealt with the debt successfully. The human world grants itself a right of unbounded intervention on nature. And yet, in the same movement of social transformation, social status within political society is no longer determined by ceremonial relationships of reciprocal gift exchange. It is as if after the age of rituals came the age of ideals: the age of sacrifice as renunciation and of gift-giving as a gesture of moral generosity. This transformation, which is presented as internalization, also inaugurates the moment of the sublime divine gift.

The movement of science and technology cannot absorb the fact and representation of the original granting: the world itself, time, life, and being in its totality. This remains the fundamental enigma that monotheistic worldviews have been intent on addressing and have tended to appropriate. There is a constant, overflowing, and infinite gift; hence the appeal to a giver who can take responsibility for it. This giver has sometimes been assigned a personal name: God. At other times it has been designated as the anonymous gesture of what is given: being.

This unilateral gift, this unexplained favor, has been called *grace*. Is it the consecration of the debt or its erasure? Those are the questions that now require answers.

6

The Logic of Debt

Let us once again remember the last days of Socrates. During his trial he reminded his judges that he had refused any financial remuneration for his teaching, and he proudly proclaimed that his poverty was the best testimony to his integrity. We know that a short time later, while in prison, he categorically rejected his friend Crito's proposal to escape by bribing his guards. Socrates did not wish to buy his freedom any more than he had accepted the sale of his teaching. Socrates asked for nothing and owed nothing. He was a man without debt because he was indifferent to wealth and even to the ordinary conveniences of life. He was a free man through a strange kind of freedom based on detachment from what he gave and received. Among men he was entirely unattached ("Modern, too modern!" Nietzsche would have said). At the last moment, however, after taking the hemlock, his limbs already cold, he turned toward his old friend and said, "Crito, we ought to offer a cock to Asclepius. Pay my debt, and don't forget."[1] These were his last words, according to Plato. Until his final moments, Socrates, who owed nothing to anyone, recognized his debt to the gods. It was a very specific debt, since Asclepius (Aesculapius for the Romans) was considered to be in charge of the crossing to Hades. It is remarkable that Socrates, who had been sentenced to death as a result in part of his supposed impiety, would have insisted at the moment of his death on providing the share due to the gods. Faithfulness to these rituals may seem surprising on the part of a thinker who had shifted the center of gravity of philosophy from "physical" issues to questions concerning moral requirements. Could this pious gesture be viewed as meant to contradict his accusers? But this suspicion would assume on his part a dependence on public opinion, which he had always dismissed. In fact, whereas great sacrificial rituals had almost disappeared from fourth-century Greece, minor domestic sacrifices were still actively practiced, involving all kinds of thanksgivings or requests to the gods. Were these remnants of earlier traditions that resisted the process of secularization? Perhaps. But, once again, in all his irony, how could Socrates have given in to mere superstitions?

We should take the last concern of the wise man seriously—this rooster to be sacrificed and this debt to be settled. Socrates was well aware that men could settle debts owed each other by giving or paying (the Sophists had precisely attempted to settle the debt of knowledge through financial means). Debt toward the gods could not be so easily erased; their gift was too great and their enigma too deep, and sacrifice expressed this in many ways. As we have seen, in the time when humans were affirming their mastery over nature and life through farming and herding (Hesiod constantly expressed amazement regarding this power), they also recognized that this share "stolen" from the gods had to be returned to them, that it was important to keep the gods on one's side while distancing oneself from them, and that the gods were the many names of the first gift to which no countergift could reply. This opened a debt that could never be paid back because it could not be assessed and because it involved the totality of beings. This is no longer the mere challenge of ceremonial reciprocity, the essentially agonistic relationship between one living being and another in which each gift and each blow is returned in kind. It is the enigmatic requirement for every loss to be compensated. A life destroyed calls for restitution according to the strict rules of vindicatory justice. What is this global equilibrium that every group destabilized by murder or hit by epidemic or natural catastrophe is so insistent on regaining? One of the main roles of vindicatory justice was to meet this homeostatic requirement through ritual forms. On a different level it was also one of the main roles of sacrifice in agropastoral societies.

But why use the past tense? Because we have to. There was an age of ritual sacrifice, and it seems forever behind us; the fires of the altars are spent, and the knives of the sacrificers have been put away. Sacrificial technogony has given way to functional technologies. For us ritual sacrifice belongs to an ancient past (too often conjured up with grandiose theatricality). But a question arises: what happened to the debt? Did it disappear along with the ritual conditions of its expression? Did it completely turn into moral debt, entirely sublimated into a feeling of guilt? Or, more empirically, was it displaced to the realm of commercial goods and converted into merely financial debt? If so, the knowledge of the Sophists, object of mastery and available to anyone with the means to pay for it, would have prevailed over Socrates' divinely related wisdom. Today's counterpart of ever-open symbolic debt would be finite and quantifiable debt, capable of being defined by contract and debited from an account. This is the new set of questions in our investigation.

Gift, Debt, and Sacrifice
The Ambiguous Lessons of Etymology

Among ceremonial gift exchange, the system of sacrifice, and the system of grace (as we will see), the debt phenomenon seems to serve as a common denominator. Many commentators recognize it in the obligation to reciprocate generated by a gift. It is also found at the core of sacrifice and thus is predominant in Veda sacrificial doctrine, as well as in the Christian doctrine of salvation. It is present in African and Asian religions. Debt could thus be viewed as constituting a unifying concept that makes possible the relation, through a single approach, of very diverse facts observed in very different cultures. If this is the case, we should celebrate the power of Nietzsche's intuition, which identifies the feeling of debt as the root of the moral and religious sentiment from which duty, guilt, and bad conscience originate: "The sense of guilt toward the divinity has continued to grow for several thousands of years, and always in the same proportion as the concept and sense of god has grown and risen into the heights."[2] According to Nietzsche, Christianity raised that religious experience of debt to its highest point, to the point of merging with it. This is why, he adds, the first purpose of atheism is to free oneself from this feeling of guilt: "The prospect that the complete and definitive victory of atheism might redeem mankind entirely from this feeling of indebtedness toward its origin, its *causa prima*, cannot be dismissed. Atheism and a kind of *second innocence* belong together."[3]

Nietzsche's questions are certainly very acute regarding Judeo-Christian monotheism, but can they simply be extended to other forms of expression of obligation and debt found in other cultures? It is doubtful. Thus in Vedic thought "debt preexists duty,"[4] Malamoud writes. He adds that in Sanskrit no connections can be established between these two terms, since the word for debt—*rná*—has no known etymology. In addition, the very concept of debt, as explicit as it may be in some religious systems and in spite of very striking immediate similarities, can refer to profoundly different models. In short, we will see that it is not possible to manipulate the concept of debt without the greatest care or without always mentioning the context in which it is used.

Nevertheless, there is something shared among all forms of obligation, and an underlying model emerges whose insistent presence across the most diverse societies suggests that it is a major cultural invariant. It could be defined as a homeostatic requirement: when equilibrium is lost, it must be restored. A gift calls for another gift in return, in the same way that a murder must be punished or compensated; if a wife is received by a group, another wife must be given by another group, either immediately or later; the transgression of a prohibition calls for reparation. What is the meaning of this universal requirement of equilibrium restoration? What model is at work? Finally, what happens when the model itself is undermined, which is to say when the very concept of equilibrium is transformed, as in modern societies? Raising these questions and attempting to answer them can shed light on the issue from which our investigation began. What is at stake is, indeed, the framework of representations within which the various modes of symbolism and the very notion of value develop. We must therefore take up once again the effort toward a definition.

The coherence of the debt-duty-fault-guilt sequence underlined by Nietzsche is clear to his German readers: *Schuld* means both "debt" and "fault," and *schuldig* means both "to be guilty" and "to owe." The verb *sollen* (to be obligated) derives from the common root *skal* (found in the English verb *shall*). Should we assume that this sequence is shared by all Indo-European languages? Benveniste shows that culturally and linguistically things are not so simple.[5] In French the relationship between the noun *devoir* (duty) and the verb *devoir* (to owe) seems obvious. It is assumed that the derivation is from the verb indicating debt (*debere aliquid alicui*) to the moral notion. But in Latin (and, as a consequence, in most Romance languages) there is no counterpart of the Germanic sequence. In Latin, debt is designated in technical and legal terms as *aes alienum*. As for *debere*, it derives from *de-habeo*: to possess (*habere*) something that was taken (*de-*) from someone. This means that one owns something that is owed to someone else, either by status or by commitment but not by *loan*. Thus things are owed that have not been *borrowed*, such as taxes, dowry, hospitality, or presents on the occasion of a celebration. On the contrary, debt proper, which constitutes someone as debtor relative to a creditor, is defined as borrowing goods (in currency or in kind) and having to return them.

Two very different lexical fields seem to coexist in Latin with respect to obligation: one in the sense of reciprocity (within the realm of gift/ countergift) and the other in the sense of returning a thing or amount borrowed (within the realm of contract). In the first case failing to reciprocate runs the risk of breaking a bond or losing face, and the sanction incurred is a social one. In the second case the lack of reciprocity amounts to failing to meet a legal commitment, risking criminal sanctions that can be severe; this involves the world of property rights or commercial exchange.

The first obligation is symbolic; the second is legal. Nietzsche tends to confuse the two realms. As for Benveniste, he establishes this distinction but does not mention what is at stake. The existence of this difference seems to suggest that the "debt-duty" genealogy is not relevant. This, however, would be too hasty a conclusion. Can it be claimed that true debt is only found on the side of legal obligation and of the relationship between lender and borrower? We must once again acknowledge how difficult it is to establish a genealogy. We know that in the Indo-European world the vocabulary of trade and contract is more recent than the vocabulary of gift exchange and that the figure of the merchant (as a distinct profession) emerged later within the system of exchanges.[6] We also know that lending with interest was not accepted until very late in the Germanic world (far from being primary, the sequence identified by Nietzsche goes back to the early Middle Ages at the earliest).[7] These observations make it possible to understand the extent to which the language of business and profitable exchange draws from the preexisting language of gift exchange. This fact is not lost on Mauss, and it is probably what sometimes leads him to mistakenly presuppose the existence of a gift exchange–trade genealogy. But the reverse effect is no less important. As the terms pertaining to the contractual were becoming dominant, their use came to influence the language of noncommercial reciprocity (generating inadequate phrases such as "bride price" or "archaic money").[8]

This suggests that the term *debt* should not be considered as belonging primarily to the realm of commercial exchange or even defined primarily relative to contract (the case of India, which we will soon consider, should provide a convincing argument). A symbolic debt exists that is larger and deeper than any financial debt. Moreover, the latter can also take on a symbolic dimension as loss of status on the part of the debtor, which is what fascinates Nietzsche. Today the most interesting phenomenon is the reverse movement: a purely financial debt is substituted for symbolic debt. An offense, damage, or even involuntary homicide can be compensated by an amount of money to be negotiated between judge and lawyers on both sides, and then settled like any ordinary invoice. In our societies this is occurring at the same time that gift-exchange relationships are being marginalized by commercial relationships, and the multiplication of consumer goods tends to subsume the very feeling of a debt. This could bring us to the end of our questioning if it were not necessary to clarify other questions first.

Debt of Reply, Debt of Dependence, and Debt of Gratitude

It is important to raise this doubt: does the gift-giving relationship really entail a relationship of debt? Does the receiving of a gift place the recipient in the particular state designated as that of debtor? If the relevant reference is the definition of debtor in commercial relationships and in lending with interest, the answer should be "no." But in terms of statutory obligation, it seems unquestionable that the receiving of a gift creates a "debt" in the sense of an obligation to reciprocate—not to return what was given (as in the case of a loan) but to give in one's turn. To reciprocate is to reply to and meet the challenge thrown by the giver. The chapter on gift exchange (see Chapter 4 above) established this point. We saw how gift-giving generally secures a social advantage for the giver, but this merely means that the giver plays in his turn; he challenges his partner. *Debt*—if the term is to be used at all—only exists in the sense that the ball is on the other side. Gift-giving generally ensures this position in the most ordinary situations, as in the case of a group that gives a wife (a situation in which, in principle, every group is placed at some point) or in any occasion of gift exchange. If an advantage does emerge, it is within a constantly shifting situation that is subject to reversal: today's giver will be tomorrow's recipient.

The circle of exchange endlessly creates and erases debt in the same way as it creates and erases inequality. Hence this question: is this truly a situation of debt? A potentially erasable and endlessly erased debt is not experienced as a debt but precisely as the moment when, after receiving recognition, one must recognize the other. The permanence and diversity of exchanges seems precisely meant to avoid the emergence of a situation of debt and therefore of inequality.[9]

In fact, three different types of situation can be observed: the first involves reply, the second dependence, and the third gratitude.

DEBT OF REPLY   In the first type debt constantly changes sides. It is as if debt itself were being exchanged, in turn affirmed and cancelled, or rather it is as if one were at the same time indebted to one person and creditor to another. As a result no primary debt, event-debt, or infinite debt can exist. It might be said that there is no situation of debt in any strict sense or at least in any strong sense. There is a relationship of alternating that characterizes every situation of playful or agonistic exchange. It could be called *debt of reply*. Should this obligation to reciprocate, inherent to the gift/countergift relationship, still be understood in terms of "debt"? Many anthropologists think so or, at least, behave as if they do, as suggested by the very language they use in their descriptions. Yet even if relationships of ritual gift exchange imply by their nature the obligation to reciprocate the gift, we must be aware that this "debt" is of a particular kind. The requirement to reciprocate is agonistic and symbolic rather than economic and legal. What is at stake is not the setting of an equivalence or compensation regarding goods. What matters is not—is never—determining whether A received from B as much as A gave B. To think in these terms would amount to bringing the interplay of replies to an end. The gift-exchange relationship does not aim at concluding but at endlessly starting anew[10] and at sustaining the movement of giving and returning according to a temporal rhythm that can be either assessed by each participant (who must act neither too soon nor too late) or defined by social conventions. What matters most is not the thing exchanged (although it does have some importance and a precise status) but what it makes possible, namely the bond between participants. To reply to a gift is, above all, to proclaim (by respecting the nature of each offering and by giving appropriate goods) that one wishes to maintain or reinforce the relationship, not that one wishes to be released from a debt (when the latter occurs, it is precisely the sign that the interplay of gift exchange has become artificial). This should not even be called debt but obligation to reply. In fact, egalitarian gift exchange does not entail debt; or, rather, it only does so in the form of compensation for an offense and in vindicatory justice (as we will see), where the ceremonial reciprocity of blows is the counterpart of the reciprocity of gift exchange.

The world of gift-giving, however, is itself not homogeneous; there is on one side the egalitarian gift exchange found in societies with a low degree of centralization and on the other the nonegalitarian form of gift-giving found in societies divided by rank or caste. This brings us back to the previously raised question of cultural territories of asymmetrical gift and sacrifice. We saw that in the hunter-gatherers' world in which the relationship with nature is a relationship of exchange and alliance, and sometimes osmosis, the divine world—the world of the "spirits"—primarily takes on the form of animals and more generally of natural beings engaged in constant dialogue with human beings. These spirits exist in the same places as humans and are embodied in natural events. No clear relationship of debt exists between humans and spirits. In fact, humans and animals "do each other mutual favors." A kind of equality exists, or rather a game of reply between human and animal world, as well as between natural and supernatural world.[11]

DEBT OF DEPENDENCE   We must, therefore, consider two different types of situations; in one case *debt* (if one insists on using the word) arises and is cancelled in the rotation of exchanges—or replies—whereas in the other case debt tends to accumulate to the benefit of some and the detriment of others, creating dependence. In a strict sense the concept of debt only applies to the latter case to the extent that every gift and countergift becomes the act of placing participants in or out of debt. Debt absorbs gift exchange. The giver becomes a creditor, the recipient a debtor. The Katchin from Burma studied by Edmund Leach and the Mong Gar from central Vietnam studied by Georges Condominas are classic examples.[12] Condominas shows how one becomes a "powerful person"—a *kuang*—by being capable of placing an entire population in debt through festivals in which large amounts of rice are offered and, above all, buffalos are sacrificed, consumed, and shared in an exacting manner—specific portions being assigned to specific guests—so that debtors can be identified.[13]

In circumstances where obligation is imperative, debtors unable to reciprocate become slaves by default (this can even apply to sons whose fathers die without settling their debts).

In these cases it is appropriate to speak of giver superiority over recipients. The definitive point is to understand what situation turns the gift-giving gesture from a call for a reply that would reverse the participants' positions (according to an alternation principle) into something that places the recipient in a situation of enduring inferiority (according to a domination or dependence principle). The answer is probably to be found in the very process of emergence of ritual sacrifice or, more explicitly, in the cultural transformation associated with the development of sociotechnical mastery over the environment, as command of the living world, of energies, and finally of one's own kind. Against the accepted thesis my claim is that *giving does not generate debt, but debt transforms giving.* Gift-giving does not create hierarchy but merely confirms and perpetuates it where it already prevails. Reciprocal recognition then turns into recognition of unequal statutory positions.

DEBT OF GRATITUDE   In addition to those two forms of symbolic debt—debt associated with the obligation to reciprocate and debt expressed in an attitude of dependence—a third form probably exists, which appears paradoxical in the sense that it does not imply or generate a requirement of reciprocity or a submissive posture. In this third form the giver rejoices in the receiver's happiness, while the receiver experiences no burden or pressure. This defines the relationship of love, no matter what its particular form may be. It generates nothing beyond the joy of receiving and the wish to give thanks. This debt is indeed a *reply*, but it is one that involves no constraint. Let us call it the *debt of gratitude.* The term itself—which derives from *gratia*—identifies the realm in which this debt is situated: grace or *kharis* in Greek, which means, above all, joy and charm (as we will see below). The child who delights in the gift he or she has received and in which he or she senses the love that the gift expresses and the beloved who feels fulfilled and overwhelmed by love itself experience an excess that situates the relationship beyond any expectation of reply or subjection. This feeling is one of openness and bliss. In this sense the expression of gratitude is indifferent to all expectations of symmetry or equivalence. It is a blooming, a supplement—just like language when it becomes song in lyrical celebration (whether slow as in the elegy or lightning-fast as in the haiku), in hymns to the deity, or in mystical prayer. The debt of gratitude thus lies at the outer limit of debt. It indicates a festive relationship that remains within the realm of desire—the intense desire to express the joy that is experienced. If it is a reply, it is outside agonistic duality, as if the giver receives while giving, as if the source of the gesture preexisted both of them and originated from an earlier overabundance, a generosity of life obscurely felt to be the very truth of life itself. It is as if the gift were from no one, from before any attribution of divine names.

It remains that the unilateral character of this gesture contains the seed of a threat: the giver risks being overcome by the *hubris* of his or her superior position, thus turning the privilege to be able to give without a need for reciprocation into a relationship of domination. This perversion of the relationship of grace can then lead to the most insidious form of debt, in which the beneficiary becomes guilty for receiving the gift. This threat and potential perversion will have to be examined in the moral or religious but also social and political experience of grace (see Chapter 7 below). Unilateral giving can bring us back to a situation of dependence, to a statutory inequality between givers and receivers. A dividing line appears between a situation in which debt (whether of reply or of gratitude) is easy to carry, and a situation in which debt is a burden capable of mortgaging the future.

Grasping the importance of the difference between these two types of processes might enable us to present relevant hypotheses on modern societies, which, like hunter-gatherer societies (but for opposite reasons), are also nonsacrificial societies (unless the term *sacrifice* is given such a broad and vague extension that it loses all conceptual pertinence) and tend to do away with symbolic debt by increasingly viewing money as the universal vehicle for extinguishing debt. Grasping the difference between sacrificial and modern societies necessarily involves a historical dimension: these nonsacrificial modern societies (such as European societies for more than two thousand years) are heirs to an ancient cultural past in which sacrifice was at the core of religious systems. This brings us back to our previous question: why did the sacrificial model fade away? And what happened to the symbolic debt that was associated with it? How can we assess what we regard as priceless? To provide an answer, it may be crucial to understand a kind of extreme example of the debt model: the Veda.

Debt without Fault: Vedic Thought

The category of debt seems omnipresent in ancient Indian writings, as Vedic specialists highlight.[14] Charles Malamoud notes that, what is even more remarkable, the term designating debt—*rná*—has no known etymology; the same is true of the term designating interest-bearing lending—*kúsida*. While debt explains a large variety of behaviors, debt itself cannot be explained by something else:

In Sanskrit therefore, the notion of debt is primary and autonomous, and does not allow a further analysis.

Now it so happens that the Brahmanas present a theory of debt as constitutive of human nature that is in a way an image, on the level of religious speculation, of the names for debt on the linguistic level. Just as the words *rná* and *kúsida* have no etymology, strictly speaking, so man's congenital debt, while it explains everything, is not itself explained by anything, and has no origin.[15]

What is the nature of this founding debt? According to the *Brahmana* it consists of three aspects (which in principle concern the Brahmin but also apply to any human being wishing to be twice born): debt of study toward sacred writings, debt of sacrifice toward the gods, and debt of procreation toward the ancestors. These specific debts can be erased by fulfilling the required tasks. As summarized by a Brahmanic writing, "He is free from debt who has a son, who offers sacrifices, and who leads the life of a brahmin student" (*CW* 96). Without taking up the debate about whether the possibility of being released from the debt is restricted to the Brahmin alone—those twice born—or whether this task can by extension be taken on by all humans, and without considering writings relative to a fourth kind of debt—hospitality—let me underline a remark made by Malamoud regarding this concept of debt: "Nothing in these texts hearkens back to the original fall—neither crime, nor oversight, nor contract—in fact, no event explains or even precedes the debtor situation in which he who comes into the world finds himself immediately ensnared. There is no mythology of the process by which one becomes a debtor" (*CW* 99).

This debt does not stem from anything; it is a founding element. This is probably why it implies no guilt; it is not the loss of an earlier state of perfection or an evil that follows an original state of innocence. It does not arise as in the biblical narrative (in the Christian reading) as a consequence of the first man's sin; therefore, it does not belong to the realm of events but to the realm of being. There is no world before debt or resulting from debt. To be born is to be indebted. This is not fault or accident. It is the order of things. Since no one has been offended, no one has to forgive or to be forgiven. Although indebtedness does not entail guilt, it does entail dependence (or at least incompleteness), hence the need for sacrifice (but then the reason for the original debt hypothesis still remains to be understood).

Brahmanic speculation involves an element that constitutes a remarkable effort to account for the congenital and universal character of debt: its relationship to death. According to the *Satapatha-Brahmana,* "As soon as a man is born, he is born in person as a debt owing to death. When he makes a sacrifice, he is buying back his person from death" (*CW* 100). The entire debt is owed to Yama, the god of death. In this sense, Malamoud explains, the other gods are mere substitutes of this ultimate creditor to whom in the end every sacrifice is addressed. One might think that debt should be cancelled by death itself, since through death Yama would collect his due. But dying by natural causes is not enough. What is required is to die well, which means to die according to a ritual that ensures one's place in the otherworld. The function of sacrifice is precisely to effect this transaction: "One of the ways of describing sacrifice is to represent it as a journey that takes the sacrificer to heaven and then brings him back to earth. During his ascension, the sacrificer reserves a place in heaven that he will occupy for good after his death. In dying, he will return the principal of his debt to Yama" (*CW* 100).

If sacrifice were merely understood as a kind of currency in the exchanges between mortals and the creditor deity, this speculation might seem trivial. In fact, sacrifice operates at a deeper level regarding debt. Debt does not call for redemption. Canonical writings state that debt can be extinguished through the study of the revealed word, procreation, and sacrifice, which means that it is up to man to "make a world for himself"—in other words, to institute an order, set a process of becoming, and know the relationships between things. It could be claimed (at least based on authoritative work in the field) that debt in the Brahmanic world is identified with the fact of human finitude: it is a debt of incompleteness because the world in which humans live has to be transformed and elaborated in order to become a truly human world. Humans are born unfinished in an unfinished world, and the means required to make it a human world are the following tasks associated with the three forms of debt: (1) study of the writings that tell the order of the world and the story of the gods, shed light on origins, define actions, and prescribe rituals; (2) procreation, which—in this traditional conception—means procreation of a son supposed to take on the father's burden in his turn (*CW* 102–5); and (3) sacrifice completes this process of elaboration of the world because it is the operation of transformation par excellence.

Vindicatory Justice and Arbitrational Justice

The question of debt can have extremely different implications, depending on whether the model applied is ontological (as in the Brahmanic tradition) or event-based (as in the Christian tradition). There is, however, another realm where debt plays an essential part, blurring the difference between these two models: vengeance. It is indeed remarkable that vengeance would take very similar forms in very different civilizations. This presents us with an object particularly suitable to comparative work. But in this case, as well, it is important to avoid hasty equivalences.

Vengeance as Justice

The feud is a political institution, being an approved and regulated mode of behavior between communities within a tribe.

EDWARD E. EVANS-PRITCHARD, *The Nuer*

The renewal of reflection on vengeance has developed in proportion to the renewal of research on the question of ceremonial gift exchange—all the more so because *these two questions are closely associated*. In the same way that ceremonial gift exchange has to be understood without measuring it by the yardstick of commercial exchange, the question of vengeance in traditional societies must be taken up without measuring it against the norms of modern law as it developed in the West or elsewhere. In truth, prejudices regarding the system of vengeance have not just emerged. They are found everywhere that state power maintains a monopoly on the exercise of criminal justice and in particular the sanction of murder. These prejudices generally consist of presenting vengeance as a savage, uncontrollable, and blind form of violence that would pit individual passions against the law of the community. This may be the case within political societies where vengeance is no longer coded (since it is considered illegitimate in principle). In this brutal form vengeance is therefore a lately arisen phenomenon. But the case is entirely different in societies without a central state, in which vengeance contrarily constitutes an extremely elaborate and controlled form of the regulation of violence. This is the important point: in traditional societies, far from being an outburst of pure violence, ceremonial vengeance is a way to rigorously restrict violence. It is indeed a sophisticated exercise of justice.

What is vengeance? To attempt to provide an answer amounts to asking why vengeance sets into motion a highly rigorous logic of debt. What, then, is the meaning of the shift from vindicatory system to legal system? How does this shift affect the global representation of society as a system in equilibrium? What is the relationship between a debt of blood and a debt of life? What is the relationship between a debt of life and symbolic debt, and thus debt in general, every form of debt, including financial debt—which is the most common one nowadays? Better than any other phenomenon, ritual vengeance enables us to understand how something is owed that is priceless, something that requires one to risk one's life, something that never leaves the loss of a life uncompensated.

Many observers note that vengeance in traditional societies is not a blind form of action but, on the contrary, a rigorously coded form of justice, yet they do not sufficiently realize the extent to which it constitutes a genuine system for regulating violence. Behind the diversity of forms and procedures a comparable logic can be identified in very dissimilar cultures. Raymond Verdier and his collaborators can be credited with bringing attention to the schemas of the *vindicatory system*. Let me mention only the most important results for our pursuit of a deeper understanding of the question of debt.

From the outset Verdier's definition breaks with accepted clichés: "Vengeance is a relationship of bilateral exchange resulting from the reversing of the offense and the permutation of the positions of offender and offended. Since an offense generates a counter-offense, the initial relationship is reversed: the offended becomes offender and vice-versa."[16] This definition immediately brings to mind the gift/countergift relationship. As we will see, the logic involved, and often the participants themselves, are the same in both cases. Vengeance is, above all, an instance of reciprocity—in the precise sense this term has in anthropology. Before returning to this essential perspective, we need to situate vengeance within the typology of forms of sanction of offenses.

Verdier shows that vengeance must be understood primarily within the system of relationships between a group (no matter how it is delimited) and its outside. Vengeance then appears as an intermediate level between *penalties*, which concern the internal operation of the group, and *war*, which involves the community as a whole against an enemy group.

Penalties apply to transgressions committed within the group. In this case the offense is dealt with as a matter that must remain within the boundaries of the group. Punishing the culprit prevents the transgression from threatening the group's life and unity. The culprit can be permanently or temporarily excluded, put to death, or subjected to sanctions and rituals of expiation or reintegration into the group. This involves a relationship between group and individual in which the community acts upon itself.

Vengeance presents the reverse situation: the group stands behind one of its members against another group. Vengeance expresses a relationship between inside and outside. The offense is perceived as collective, and it pits the entire community against the offender. There is solidarity against the opponent. This does not involve the logic of penalty but the logic of reply and action in return. Moreover, vengeance presupposes an obligation to reciprocate that is as imperative as the obligation to provide a counter-gift. The feeling associated with this obligation is called *honor*. But *within the group vengeance cannot even be considered*: "The duty of vengeance outside the group is the counterpart of the prohibition of vengeance inside. Duty and prohibition express the two sides of solidarity—external and internal. One cannot exert vengeance upon those one is precisely duty-bound to avenge. . . . Lest it break up, the group has no choice but to prohibit vengeance within itself."[17] In other words, this kind of vengeance is never left to individual initiative; it is public and collective, just like the offenses to which it replies. It can only be performed through procedures recognized by the groups involved.

There is also a third type of relationship, represented by *war*. It does not conform to the reciprocity system. At least in principle, whereas vengeance is subjected to a strict ritual meant to restrict compensation and reestablish normal relationships as soon as possible, war opens the way to the extermination of the enemy. In fact, especially in the case of societies without a central state, "no boundary can be drawn between war and blood feud";[18] however, the purpose of war is to destroy the other group, whereas vengeance concerns an individual, even if his community stands by him and defends him. Negotiation specific to vengeance concerns the type of offense committed (murder, abduction, insult, or betrayal) and the statuses of the offender and offended. It follows precise procedures depending on these parameters, and, as we will see, the status of the protagonists plays an essential part. On the other hand, and even if its starting point may be blood feud, war is a global confrontation between two groups without re-ciprocal obligations: "Situated half-way between a relationship of identity and one of absolute difference, the vindicatory relationship is essentially an adversarial relationship that binds partners who recognize each other as being both identical and different. Whereas the hostile group must be de-nied or even annihilated in order to affirm one's own supremacy, the oppo-nent group is in a situation of reciprocal confrontation with one's group."[19]

War, therefore, means absence of reciprocity, the refusal to preserve it or the impossibility of doing so. Warring groups are, in effect, telling one another: between us there can be no gift/countergift or vengeance accord-ing to rules, which is to say that there can be no justice but only confron-tation between strangers in which everything can be taken from the enemy without any condition other than winning. Yet even this is not pure vio-lence because war itself is subject to a code.[20] It is precisely nonreciprocity.

An essential aspect of vengeance involves what Verdier calls *social distance.* This means that an offense is only viewed in relation to the sta-tus of the offended: age, gender, and, above all, rank within the group, which generally means position in the kinship system. Each type of of-fense (homicide, words or gestures of contempt, disobedience, blows) en-tails specific types of replies and vindicatory procedures that depend on the status of the offended. The relationship between participants is that of *partners.* In this, vengeance is symmetrical to gift-exchange relationships. This is clearly apparent in procedures of compensation, which follow the same channels as gift exchanges and, above all, as matrimonial alliance.[21] In both cases what is at stake is *life* through its substitutes. In the same way as the goods offered by the group that requests a wife to the group that gives one represent the value of a future wife and are its pledge or stand for this value (traditionally—and awkwardly—these goods used to be called "the

price of the bride"), the goods offered in compensation for the loss of a life
by homicide (whether intentional or accidental) are the pledges of a life to
be restituted: "In both cases, the aim is not to buy a life but to give goods
that symbolize life in exchange for another life."[22] According to Verdier the
existence of this homology between the "price of blood" and "the price of
the bride" is present in many cultures. This is confirmed by the fact that
compensation for homicide very often consists of the granting of a wife. It
is therefore clear that antagonistic relationships specific to vengeance (unlike relationships of hostility specific to a state of war) remain contained
within the sphere of reciprocity, which is the sphere of partners in alliance
and gift exchange. In the same way as a countergift must reply to a gift,
a counteroffense must reply to an offense. Why is it the case? Why must
there be compensation? In every case it seems to be a response to the requirement that lost equilibrium be restored. It is this loss that is viewed as
disorder, not the reverse. This probably constitutes the major enigma of
the debt phenomenon.

Political Societies:
Central Power and Arbitrational Justice

In his discussion of the Indian epic *Mahabharata*, Charles Malamoud
notes a kind of paradox: vengeance is always present yet is not coded and
does not constitute a procedure of justice. This epic can be summarized
as the story of the offenses inflicted by one group—the Kaurava—on another—the Pandava—and the vengeance by which the latter are obligated
to reply. According to Malamoud the tradition from which this requirement derives is illustrated by sayings or principles stated as follows in the
Pañcatantra: "When a man has repaid with evil the evil done him when he
was in distress, by one man who mocked him in hard times, it is, I think,
as if he were born again" (*CW* 156). In Brahmanic thought reciprocating
action is an essential aspect of the debt that everyone has to pay. The idea
is that the universe is regulated, and balance must be restored: "These
are not mere instances of doing away with one's enemy; they are nothing
other than acts of vengeance, of committing an act of violence that is [the]
equivalent of—and, when possible, of the same order as—the violence one
has suffered" (*CW* 157). It might be expected that vengeance would have
constituted a central aspect of cosmic and social *dharma*, yet its place in

it was "a non-existent or, at least, indeterminate one. The desire for vengeance is omnipresent and [is] one of the motors for humans (and divine) activity; but, taken in isolation, vengeance is neither a thing of value, nor an institution, not even a socially regulated practice" (*CW* 159). The very notion of vengeance is not specific in Vedic tradition; it is expressed by the phrases "reaction" or "compensation" (*pratikara, pratikriya*) or the ideas of hatred or murderous intentions (*vairita, jighamsa*). How can we understand the omnipresence of vengeance in the *Mahabharata*? Why does it have no autonomous status in a world otherwise concerned with ritual and codification? Malamoud's answer is illuminating: vengeance has no status because it should not occur. It is evidence of an anomaly. It only emerges when those in charge of worldly power, the kings—*ksatriyia*—are no longer capable of performing their task or are prevented from performing it (if only because they adopt ascetic renouncement). "Revenge is taken and one's people are avenged not as a means to obeying a positive ideal of honour and solidarity, but due to the absence of any king who might impede or punish the crime" (*CW* 160). The function of the king is to preserve the proper order of the world, cosmic as well as social *dharma*, mainly by exercising punishment. "It is a bond of consubstantiality that obtains between *dharma*, the king and punishment" (*CW* 161). Malamoud cites various texts from the Laws of Manu like the following: "It is for the sake of the king that (in the beginning) the creator produced his son punishment (*danda*), which is nothing other than *dharma*" (*CW* 161).

Punishment includes no intent to humiliate or cause suffering or even to educate or deter. What is at stake is a physical law of return to equilibrium and the cosmic necessity to restore order. As a consequence this function must be closely related to Brahmanic sacrifice, since sacrifice is action par excellence and the ultimate—the most complete and intense—operation of regulation of the universe. *Sacrifice is the precise opposite of vengeance*; the victim is the alter ego of the sacrificer; various procedures are observed to ensure that the victim (animal or plant) will not experience its ritual death as murder—which could bring retaliation on the part of its own kind—but as offering to the deities. In a static system such as this one vengeance is always what can occur when order is not recognized or is actually disturbed. Vengeance, along with the wish to hurt and passion to crush one's opponent, emerges when the king's task is no longer fulfilled. It is no more than a perverse consequence of this disorder, and therefore it does not come under a traditional vindicatory system (which is a procedure of justice, as we have seen). It is evidence that the recognized form of justice, ensured by central authority, no longer works.

After considering the vindicatory system, this detour through India opens a path toward an answer. Vengeance, as it is usually understood, is not what comes before the advent of law or the legal system but the consequence of a malfunctioning of that system. The situation should therefore be presented as follows: in societies without a central state the exercise of justice takes the form of the vindicatory system (gift-exchange relationships and bonds of honor). In societies in which a central power has emerged, the exercise of justice takes the form of public arbitration. The latter applies not only to what are commonly called state-controlled societies but also to those societies in which public authority is no longer based on statutory positions in the kinship system.[23] In its personal and psychological expression vengeance is a secondary and reactive form and is evidence that the system of regulation is undergoing a transformation because it is contested or destabilized—as a result of a break with tradition—for reasons that may be either internal (for instance the crossing of a demographic threshold or the reaching of a new technological level) or external (such as administrative colonization or onset of a new religious or legal system).[24]

But how does the emergence of central authority express a tendency to substitute arbitrational justice for justice based on the vindicatory system (which, as we have seen, cannot be identified with vengeance in the ordinary sense)? The vindicatory system as procedure of justice operates in societies without a central state, which is to say societies in which forms of authority and organization are defined by positions within the kinship system (or any other statutory-type system) and therefore by positions in the interplay of gift and countergift. The kinship system and the gift/countergift system are often one and the same, as in the case of the prominent status of the givers of wives. These models of societies (which show a considerable range of variation) are dominated by relationships of matrimonial alliance that are also relationships of alliance in general. It is between these groups of partners that wives and presents are exchanged and that justice takes the form of the vindicatory system.

The specificity of systems with central power (which can be called "political" systems in reference to the Greek model) is that they institute an authority situated above the kinship system (and therefore above the network of matrimonial exchange), as well as above the authority generated by gift/countergift relationships (as observed in *kula* exchange in the Trobriand or agonistic gift exchange between *Big Men* from New Guinea).[25] If these forms of reciprocity lose their relevance in a political-type society, then the vindicatory system that is their judicial side becomes obsolete or ceases to be operational. The management of offenses and of their compensations then becomes the task of this central authority, instituted in the position of arbiter above the clans or other statutory groups; this task confers its main legitimacy on this authority. Contrary to endlessly repeated statements, the function of central authority is not so much to monopolize violence as it is to ensure that adversarial relationships (specific to groups of allies constituted of partners/adversaries) will move outside the community. In short, it is to ensure and take charge of a new dividing line between inside and outside. The trinomial—constituted by (1) solidarity with one's own group, (2) alliance or antagonism with the partner group, and (3) war or peace with the enemy group—is then reduced to a binomial: solidarity inside and antagonism or hostility outside. Level 2 has disappeared or rather it has merged with level 3.[26] It is now clear why the vindicatory system cannot be preserved: it would turn fellow-citizens belonging to different clans into potential enemies. Solidarity extends to every member of the groups that make up political society. *It is this replacement of ceremonial vengeance by arbitrational justice that opens the possibility of private vengeance.* But then vengeance is no longer the application of justice. It becomes the pursuit of personal compensation. It no longer constitutes a complete and instituted procedure. It releases individual violence instead of expressing the action of the group vis-à-vis another group.[27] It becomes the greatest threat within the community. It is clear, however, that if an offense inflicted on an individual is not compensated, then a debt remains unpaid—unless a different entity takes responsibility for it and is only defined by doing so. What is this entity? It is precisely the power that places itself at the center. Can it do so? This is what we will have to consider.

The same reason explains why war becomes the prerogative of central power. It is not a cynical appropriation of activities that until then were distributed differently. The instauration of arbitrational justice inside the group and of a relationship of global distance toward the outside is an inevitable consequence of the emergence of a metaclan authority and of the displacement of the boundary between inside and outside. The genealogy of this authority remains to be determined; this would be the object of a different inquiry. The following chart can now be presented:

I. Societies Without a Central State

	Reference Group	*Allied Group*	*External Group*
Relationship	solidarity	antagonism	hostility
Sanction	penalty	vengeance	war

II. Political Societies

	Reference Community	*Alien Community*
Relationship	solidarity	antagonism/hostility or neutrality
Sanction	arbitration justice	war

This convincingly explains why in the case of political societies, in which vengeance is no longer legitimate as a compensation system between groups, it can become a matter to be dealt with between individuals or families still connected by relationships of matrimonial alliance and obligations of generous or vindicatory reciprocity but in a minor rather than major mode.

As a good example of the emergence of arbitrational justice along with the emergence of a society that belongs to the "political" type, let us examine the legal system of the Gamo from Ethiopia (a population of about five hundred thousand living in the southeast of the country). This system constitutes a particularly clear case of affirmation of a mode of arbitrational justice. It is an interesting example for several reasons. It involves a population of sedentary farmers living on fertile land and enjoying developed individual property rights.[28] From an institutional point of view this population is distributed into autonomous communities or territories—*déré*—each comprising from five thousand to thirty thousand people and ruled by an assembly—*guta*—of representatives of villages (or areas, since settlement is spread out). No function of a chief emerges. The kinship system is underemphasized since it defines none of the official functions of Gamo organization. It is therefore not surprising that the application of justice would be defined by an arbitration system that radically opposes the practice of vengeance, hence the considerable interest presented by a different element that provides a foundation for public life: the existence of a corpus of rules—*woga*—considered sacred. Any transgression requires a reaction on the part of the community. Culprits (and plaintiffs) are subjected to the arbitration of a mediator—*saga*—who negotiates and imposes sanction and compensation. In other cases, especially those involving serious offenses such as insults or murders, the dispute is brought before the assembly. One of its strictest rulings can be banishment from the community, in other words exile (but there are also procedures for reintegration). Finally, "At every step in this process, relationships between murderer and victim's kin are short-circuited by the group, until reconciliation occurs. The injured party is the body of the political group; as such it judges, sanctions, and reconciles. There is no place for vengeance."[29]

This brief reminder of the Gamo case calls for several remarks. It involves an institutional system that transcends kinship, but this does not entail the presence of a form of centralized state. This subordination of kinship is enough, however, to impose an arbitrational justice system and to reject vindicatory justice; thus, it seems to be the necessary and sufficient condition for the emergence of arbitrational justice. It is also interesting that this case involves a strictly sedentary agricultural society with a strong relationship to the land (including individual property rights) in which there is emphasis on one's belonging to a territory (unlike what is observed in seminomadic horticultural societies). This also demonstrates the extent to which such a society differs from pastoral societies in which agriculture only plays a supporting role and the central relationship is not with the land but with the herd. In pastoral societies the kinship system preserves its preeminence as a public institution, and vindicatory justice remains dominant, even if it is associated with mediator figures. This is precisely the case of the Nuer from southern Sudan studied by Evans-Pritchard in his classic work. The Nuer are essentially cattle herders. Their entire economic, social, cultural, and religious life is organized around this activity, which entails a degree of nomadism associated with the movement of cattle and the seasons (watering places). In addition to beef, which is mostly consumed on festive and sacrificial occasions, rudimentary horticulture provides subsistence. But the Nuer store very little; they value movement, and for basic sustenance they rely on the milk (or even the blood) of their cattle. Evans-Pritchard concludes his description of this economy as follows: "Such a life nurtures the qualities of the shepherd—courage, love of fighting, and contempt of hunger and hardship—rather than the industrious character of the peasant."[30] This is the opposite of what is observed in the Gamo case. It is therefore not surprising that the entire Nuer system of justice would fit the classical model of vindicatory reply, although a role of arbiter or mediator is recognized in such figures as "leopard-skin chiefs," who exercise ritual authority.[31]

Gamo society is based on oral tradition. It is thus difficult to reconstruct the genesis of its political organization and legal procedures. Coherent hypotheses can be made, however, by comparing that society to others with more extensive records in terms of archaeological data and written documents. From this point of view archaic Greece provides very useful information about the process by which societies without a central state or at least clan organizations with chiefdoms are transformed into "political" societies and about the changes in conceptions and forms of justice that accompany that transformation. This history is relatively well known:[32] kinship bonds were erased within the circle of warriors, who were equals united by relationships of brotherhood. A common space was constituted in the middle of the circle—*meson*. What was placed there (such as the spoils of war) became collective property, and every word uttered had to concern the entire group. In short, this was the birth of public space, which would increasingly be affirmed as the very space of the city and of its laws. Laws had to be in written form, known by all, and the same for all. Aeschylus's *Oresteia* testifies to this metamorphosis, staging the crisis caused by the shift from vindicatory justice to arbitrational justice: the old form of justice still appears very powerful and legitimate through the figures of the Furies, goddesses of vengeance. Athena must treat them with care and preserve their place within the new system in which an elected court is now in charge of deliberating on the proofs of the acts at hand rather than enforcing clan rules of honor or making decisions based on oaths: "Try him fairly, and give judgment on the facts," the Chorus tells the goddess (Aeschylus *Eum.* 432–33). From the new point of view of the city, the clans' vindicatory justice has become injustice, nothing more than vengeance ignoring the law.

What separates vindicatory justice from arbitrational justice, then, is not merely the difference between violence and absence of law on one side and rule of law and reasonable mediations on the other. This would be a false alternative. In both cases there is a rigorous, complex, and balanced procedure of justice consistent with one type of social organization. Brutal vengeance only emerges when the conditions of operation of kinship systems have been disturbed and are no longer understood (for instance, as a result of a shift to sedentary agriculture, of urbanization, or of colonization by a different civilization) or when arbitrational justice, well-accepted at first, fails because of the collapse of central authority (this is the theme of the *Mahabharata*) or of the emergence of dictatorial power—as in modern societies.

Although both cases involve a procedure of justice, they do not involve the same relationship with debt. Vindicatory debt belongs to the logic of gift-exchange relationships; it is a debt of reply and a debt of honor. Reply is mandatory, as are the gestures of ceremonial gift exchange—offering, receiving, and reciprocating a gift. Debt is erased by the fulfillment of the procedure. Just like the obligation to reciprocate, vindicatory debt is constraining but limited. It is an unending back-and-forth movement in which something is sent out and returned. It is a return to equilibrium through this very movement.

The purpose of arbitrational justice is also to restore a lost equilibrium. But a different figure emerges: that of the mediator, arbiter, or judge. Instead of the kinship group, with its close personal bonds, behind him stands the community as a whole and as a global entity in charge of assessing, deciding, and sanctioning. This figure is not yet necessarily the state (there is no Gamo state, for instance), but it is already an abstract authority figure, that of the judge, administrator of the debt. The same genesis will also make him administrator of grace. In this shift debt has been transformed. Such a transformation can be observed everywhere mastery prevails over life, the transformed over the savage world, and the cooked over the raw (for cultures in a key of fire). This is the world of sacrifice. The sacrificial gesture is the answer given to this new form of debt; it is also its consecration. But the same logic will bring it to an end, since this is the very world in which cities develop, state institutions prevail, knowledge and techniques multiply, wealth grows, and exchanges and markets proliferate. Debt is settled through an accounting procedure. Or at least this is what is assumed. But before coming to this question we must continue our inquiry.

Debt and Order of the World
Equilibrium and Reserve: The Debt of Life

An enigma still remains regarding every kind of debt. It has to do with the odd requirement that equilibrium be restored and the global amount preserved. How does this create a debt to be fulfilled? It is as if in traditional societies (in many ways this representation survives their disappearance) there were a model of a reserve of life and stock of energy that could not be depleted or threatened without calling for the reserve to be restored. It is probably this logic that Verdier refers to as "life-capital."[33] This is not a very fortunate choice of phrase in that it tends to bring to mind the modern financial system. Verdier, however, immediately qualifies his statement: "If there is indeed a debt to be paid, then neither payment nor debt should be understood in a commercial sense."[34] But what does the phrase mean, then? "This life-capital, this set of persons and goods, forces and values, beliefs and rituals on which the unity and cohesion of the group are founded, is represented by two symbols: *blood,* symbol of union and continuity of lineage and generations, and *honor,* symbol of identity and difference that makes it possible at the same time to recognize the other and to demand that he respect you."[35] To use Mauss's phrase, it should even be said that the connection between these two aspects constitutes a total social phenomenon. Life, indeed, means biological life, the fact of being alive, but it also means life as cultural and spiritual existence of the group and its members, the fact of being recognized as such by others. This is the essence of the gift/countergift relationship. In the same way that spilled blood must be compensated, scorned honor must be "washed with blood." In both cases what must be fought for is life in all its forms. Life as biological fact remains outside human power. This makes life infinitely precious. Life as social existence can only be real if it is constantly shared and mutually valued. It is this life that must be preserved in its integrity, at this dual level (which Aristotle calls living—*zēn*—and good living—*eu zēn*). Any breach calls for action in return, for compensation procedure. This is the *debt of life.*

This phrase, familiar to many anthropologists,[36] accurately sums up the central question of the vindicatory system: what is at stake is not punishment meant to redeem individuals but corrective action whose purpose is to restore equilibrium in the order of things. Ceremonial vengeance does not have a psychological or moral character. It is a social and cosmic obligation, like gift exchange. Ceremonial vengeance has so little to do with psychology that it can be triggered by involuntary offenses. What matters is not intention but facts: objective breach against the reserve of life and the order of things. This reserve and order inherited by the group are a gift from the spirits, the ancestors, or the gods. This is what makes it possible for the community to exist and for each of its members to participate in it. Debt is generated when this equilibrium is breached and must be restored. This debt implies no guilt. Vengeance can only become a subjective gesture of hatred and revenge if it no longer comes under the vindicatory system. This can occur only if the vindicatory system has already been eliminated and even delegitimized by a different system. This new system is precisely the one being invented and instituted in arbitrational justice systems and, in a more radical way, in the legal forms of state organizations.

The various expressions of debt that we have examined all tell us the following: debt has a relationship to the order of the world. It is evidence of a lack to be filled, an insufficiency to be corrected. More precisely, it is the task of restoring the disturbed order. In ancient India, Brahmanic sacrifice was the operation par excellence of this restoration. This function of sacrifice is also observed in many other civilizations.

Nevertheless, it is remarkable that, in a very large number of sacrificial cultures, recognition of a disorder—whether individual (illness, breach of a prohibition), social (war, power crises, conflicts between groups), or natural (epidemics, climate disturbances, various natural disasters)—is translated in terms of debt. In a more radical way human existence itself can be experienced as loss to be compensated, as failure, or as an unfortunate adventure in and of itself. Debt is identified with existence itself without any implication that a fault was committed. This means that humanity, confronted with this constitutive insufficiency or fundamental lack, is assigned a *task* vis-à-vis the deities. This task is taken up by rituals, first among which is sacrifice. Conversely, the subjective view of debt is contemporaneous with the internalization of disorder—guilt as event—and also generally coincides with the fading away of sacrificial rituals. But as long as the idea of debt remains within the framework of sacrifice, or at least of ceremonial gift exchange, its representation remains free of all subjective assumption. Debt is thus above all the manifestation of a state of imbalance; it is the expression of a disorder to be corrected rather than of a harm to be redeemed.

What is being lost or disturbed? One possible answer is suggested by the fact that preservation of the order of things always involves an attitude of reciprocity. It is as if this order primarily has to do with a mutual recognition of the elements (as we will see in the case of Anaximander). This conception of order as deferential reciprocity and cosmic civility remains clearly identifiable in the oldest theogonies of the Indo-European traditions. These theogonies first present a model of equilibrium of forces in the form of dramatic narratives; figures are then staged that embody these forces. The conflicts or harmonious interactions between these figures are always meant to celebrate the advantage brought by respecting the order of the world. A second model associated with the first presents the world as a reservoir of energies, the use of which is limited and defined: these energies are subject to outburst and overflow. It thus becomes important to be able to articulate human world and divine world so that these excesses can be controlled. As we have seen, this is one of the major functions of sacrifice: to return to the gods what was taken from them; to pay for the additional lives generated by immolating other lives; to preserve the separation between the two worlds, as well as the just communication between them. There is debt every time this equilibrium is upset. Any social ill (political disruption, epidemic, or failure against the enemy) appears as a sign of this cosmic disturbance and gives rise to the necessity to offer the gods a fitting compensation.

This is the world of debt of dependence (as opposed to debt of reply). It is the symmetrical converse of ceremonial gift exchange, and it seems associated with the advent of sacrifice, which is to say the emergence of agropastoral societies. This new control over life and this breach of the equilibrium of life call for compensation. Representation of debt can take on different forms. Let us focus on three: (1) constitutive debt of the Veda. The previous world is erased; the world begins with debt because it is said to begin with sacrifice, which brings it into being as an ordered world and designates it as object of a task to be performed; (2) event-based debt of the Christian tradition (in its reading of biblical scripture). The event is represented as a fall, a fault due to human pride. This calls for the logic of redemption; (3) cosmic debt conceived of as imbalance between the elements, generated by a disagreement between men and gods. This debt is neither original in the way of a state of things nor arisen in the way of a fault; it is the movement away from equilibrium. It probably represents the most common of all the forms of cosmogonies and systems of thought found across widely different agropastoral civilizations: from Europe to the Americas and from Sub-Saharan Africa to Asia. This was certainly the case of ancient Greece.

Anaximander: Cosmic Debt

This perspective makes it possible to understand the famous fragment by Anaximander as reported by Simplicius: "Anaximander . . . said that the beginning and origin and element of existing things is *apeiron*. . . . It is neither water nor any other of the so-called elements, but some infinite nature, which is different from them, and from which all the heavens and the worlds within them come into being. And into that from which existing things come-to-be they also pass away according to necessity; for they suffer punishment and pay retribution to one another for their wrong-doing, in accordance with the ordinance of Time."[37]

Many commentaries have been given of this writing.[38] Without discussing them here, it seems necessary to highlight, prior to any interpretation, a few elements of anthropology and history of science. As for the scientific context,[39] it is known that in the mid-sixth century BCE Anaximander proposed that the original element is not water (as Thales had claimed shortly before, in the early sixth century) but *apeiron*, which means the unlimited (sometimes translated as "the infinite"), whereas in the late sixth century Anaximenes claims it is air. Aristotle rightly says (*Physics* 204b24ff.) that Anaximander's solution is meant to preclude the obvious objection of having to explain the origin of water and air themselves.

The second important aspect of Anaximander's conception is his view of the cosmos based on an organic model:[40] starting from the unlimited, the world grows like a living being starting from a seed. The unlimited is thus the power of virtuality, in the manner of a germ. In this conception the world is subject to change in the forms of generation, growth, destruction, and regeneration. This is the order of time (*tou khronou taxis*), with its laws and prescriptions. All living beings must recognize these laws; otherwise, they will disrupt not only the spatial order of the arrangement of things but, more gravely, their temporal order of succession. Any breach must be corrected or compensated. A kind of civility of elements exists, that of giving and returning: *I recognize your place and your share of time.*

You should do the same with me. Anaximander expresses this cosmic requirement that affects all beings in the language of reciprocity and debt: "Into that from which existing things come-to-be they also pass away according to necessity; for they suffer punishment (*dikē*) and pay retribution (*tisis*) for their wrongdoing, in accordance with the ordinance of Time."

In the language of the sixth century, *dikē* is not yet the exercise of the law in Solon's sense;[41] it is still, and above all, a personal reply given to an offense. *Tisis* belongs to the language of reciprocity and ritual vengeance. It designates giving in return, as well as compensatory punishment.[42] This fragment seems to apply to the cosmos, viewed as growth and requirement for respect of a temporal order whose moments are akin to characters tempted to usurp their positions but forced to reject the temptation and to mend their excesses. In this they are permanently indebted to each other.[43]

Anaximander's language is that of ceremonial reciprocity, not only in the gift/countergift sense but also in the sense of *vindicatory justice* as right of reply modeled on the circuits of gift exchange. We know that this relationship always involves a certain management of time: action in return, whether it is punishment or compensation, normally follows a ritually set calendar (a specific number of days after the offense was committed, according to specific modalities, under the responsibility of a specific figure of justice statutorily designated). At this point we must be even more precise. Vindicatory justice puts into play the two major forms of relationships that characterize societies without a central state: *alliance* on the horizontal or synchronic plane of gift exchange or reply to offenses; *filiation* on the vertical or diachronic axis of debt, which is passed down to the next generation if it is not paid back. But at an even deeper level there is an imperative of alternation between generations. In restricted exchange (A gives to B and B returns a gift to A) time plays a minimal part. In generalized exchange, however (A gives to B who gives to C who gives to D, etc., who returns a gift to A), a large number of partners are involved and therefore a more developed and open network of bonds. As in the case of matrimonial alliance, the countergift can be given by the next generation. But it is important to respect the right that each generation has over time (if too old a man takes too young a wife, an abuse occurs that triggers a disturbance). All beings must accept the order of time—*tou khronou taxis*—and their share of time. They must give way and alternate without overextending their turn. This is also probably the crucial lesson of the tale of Oedipus. What is the Sphinx's question? It is the question of the succession of the ages of life and of generations. Of what is Oedipus guilty? According to Vernant he is guilty of usurping an inappropriate position in time:

The story of Oedipus concerns his return to his place of origin, his reintegration into the lineage in which he is both a legitimate son and an accursed child. This return takes place, in the manner of a boomerang, not at the right time, in the correct conditions of a rightful succession that respects the regular order of generations, but in all the violence of over-identification: Oedipus does not come duly in his turn to take the place that his father has vacated and left to him; instead, he takes that place through parricide and maternal incest. He goes back too far and now finds himself, as a husband, in the belly that nurtured him as a son, and from which he should never have emerged.[44]

The prohibition of incest entails the preservation of a distance not only between siblings or cousins (at the level of alliance) but also between generations (in the order of filiation). Oedipus's incest reverses the order of time. This is the tragic mistake, since this order is inflexible and the bonds formed in time are situated on an irreversible line. This is expressed by the figure of Moira, a deity that the gods themselves cannot sway. One cannot go back in time: each moment must accept its place and give way as a way was given to it. All moments are thus connected by a form of reciprocity operated by succession: leaving one's place by giving it. Moira becomes a braid of mutual recognitions. To make up for an injustice is to restore the bond of gift exchange at the level of alliance, as well as in the line of filiation.

Anaximander thus shows us that, for him and his contemporaries, the supreme form of bond is that of reciprocal obligation, whether positive, as in gift exchange, or negative, as in vindicatory reply. This schema makes it possible for him to conceptualize the bond among beings in the world and among moments in time. By combining the organic model of growth with the anthropological model of ritual exchange, we may gain access to the essence of "Anaximander's saying." We may, and even must, therefore say that what is at stake in this fragment is, indeed, debt—not moral debt associated with guilt but debt of reply, agonistic debt generated by the failure to fulfill the obligation of reciprocity. This obligation is so imperative to the order of things that the ancient Greek worldview—like the worldview of traditional cultures known to us—presupposes the existence of this obligation not only among humans but also among all living beings and even among natural elements.[45] This is an expression of the model of ceremonial gift exchange. Vindicatory justice belongs to the same circuits and mobilizes the same agents. This writing by Anaximander translates this interlocking, the rhythm and sparring of alternating blows that characterizes every game and every conflict: the *agōn* found in every form of reciprocity.

Rabelais: Panurge and His Praise of Debt

Rabelais implicitly but perfectly perceives this symmetry between debt and gift when he has Panurge, one of his most famous characters, give a speech "in praise of debt."[46] This speech has remained a classic. This hyperbolic—and above all paradoxical—praise of debt is given by a character deliberately presented as excessive and expert in sophistic arguments: Pan-urge, *pan-ourgos*, literally means good-for-everything (and thus probably good-for-nothing), very clever and crafty: an original Sophist figure in the Renaissance. But what is it that is paradoxical about his presentation, and what can this strange praise teach us about the question of debt?

We should first note that this "praise of debt" comes after an orgy of expenses. Panurge deals with his wealth like a lord who is not just a spendthrift but is downright extravagant. In a matter of weeks he squanders the immense fortune Pantagruel granted him. But he does not do so haphazardly. He squanders it on festivals, feasts, and all kinds of pleasures, including those enjoyed with young ladies. The form taken by this squandering is significant: it does not consist of losses incurred by gambling or through risky commercial or financial investment, even less through gifts to the poor or to friends in need. It consists of festive squandering. It would seem that Panurge burns up his wealth like a carefree lord, providing an exemplary case of aristocratic expense, an indisputable model of the sumptuary consumption required to ensure one's rank. It would be tempting to say that, after receiving in abundance, Panurge is capable of giving with great liberality. It would seem that he has brilliantly fulfilled the obligation to give. Yet he has done nothing of the sort. This is what we must understand.

After the question "How did he spend his wealth?" the following question should be asked: "With whom did he spend it?" The only answer provided is that "he spent it on myriad joyous little banquets and feasts open to all comers, especially good companions, young girls, and cute wenches [*galantes*]."[47] In fact, the community is not partying; Panurge is.

The other participants remain anonymous. They are the instruments of his squandering rather than the addressees of any specific and motivated gift. Panurge behaves like a reckless spender. The others collaborate in this consumption as sidekicks rather than companions. This is not the logic of the gift, whether in its ceremonial form or in its internalized and subsequent form associated with the virtue of generosity.

Ceremonial gift exchange teaches us that giving is the specifically human way of opening or preserving a relationship with another individual or group. The giving of a gift calls for the reply of the other (and thus challenges him or her); the only possible reply is a countergift. This amounts to accepting entrance into a privileged relationship that is at the same time constraining and free, imperative and playful, involving obligation and pleasure. But giving must be recognized as such because its goal is to create and preserve a bond. One of the privileged forms of this gift-exchange relationship, or rather its most complete expression, is matrimonial alliance. It so happens that Panurge is looking for a wife. His entire quest can be summed up in this question: should I get married? Every episode in *The Third Book* is organized around this question and the answers given in turn by seers, scholars, judges, and madmen. In fact, as long as Panurge expects a response based on principle to this general question, he cannot escape the confines of language and its rhetorical and even sophistic practice. The question should be, whom can I love? With what woman can I consider living? With what group should I form an alliance? By keeping to an abstract question focused on himself, Panurge is able to rush into feasts and banquets that prevent him from having to confront the urgency of a unique encounter and the limitations of the real world. Language and its games spare him the trouble of confronting the resistance of facts, the triviality of life, and the need to take into account the existence of others. He could throw his feasts and parties as an opportunity to meet his future wife and then party again to celebrate their union. But Panurge precisely remains outside of all social obligations. What he is doing is living it up rather than preparing for his wedding. He does not give generously in order to strengthen or give rise to a community or to generate a social bond. True, he gives without expecting anything in return—which could be a gracious gesture—but he does so above all for his own enjoyment or, rather, to spare himself any obligation. His relationship to others is unilateral and his partying is a bachelor's celebration. He expects no gift in return and wishes to create no commitment or reciprocal recognition. In a way he foreshadows the libertine of the Enlightenment, in particular of the kind found in Sade's works: great spender and squanderer in every way.

But beyond the relationship of ceremonial gift exchange there is private giving, the noble gesture of so-called moral giving, and the virtue of generosity. This is the munificence of which Aristotle speaks, which expresses *philia*. It reinforces or broadens the circle of friends and preserves good feelings between members of the city. The ability to give graciously and generously is essential to the cohesion of the community. But Aristotle reminds us that this form of giving is a subtle skill; what matters is to be generous without being irresponsible, which is to say without being extravagant (*NE* 1121a–b). Extravagant givers do not give in order to strengthen *philia* but out of vanity or to gain love in a demagogic way—or out of mere carelessness or immaturity. This seems to be the case of Panurge. In addition, this kind of relationship remains asymmetrical. Panurge's expenses cannot be situated from the standpoint of ceremonial gift exchange or from that of moral giving. His parties are not meant to strengthen social cohesion (marriage would be its keystone) or friendship (his "good companions" have no real existence in the book and vanish as soon as they are mentioned).

It could be argued that Panurge still acts like a great lord. He could save stingily, gamble for small stakes, and try to increase his wealth in order to play it safe and protect his assets. Instead, he goes on a mad pursuit of bankruptcy, and he does find it. He is a prodigious squanderer. He loses everything with panache, and he is not afraid to go back to his benefactor, without embarrassment or remorse, and ask him to restore his assets. Is this not a remarkable show of daring? Panurge's innocent and thus unassailable nerve shows style. This interpretation would seem self-evident, yet it does not bear up under scrutiny because Panurge talks too much. His excess of words and arguments matches his scarcity of convictions. He tries to convince Pantagruel of the legitimacy of his expenses through a praise of debt that is paradoxical in two different ways: first, regarding the definition of his own behavior; second, because of a sophistic misappropriation of the concept of debt.

To gain credibility, Panurge should praise generosity and extravagant feasting; he should praise giving. It would be logical for him to demonstrate that great liberality is the best way to create lasting friendship and to bring a community together. This would also be the best possible praise of

Pantagruel's initial munificence toward him. He should also praise friend-ship: the friendship Pantagruel grants him and to which he should tes-tify. This would be logical and noble—too much so, perhaps. Precisely, Panurge—as Rabelais constructs the character in his writing—does not engage in ordinary logic, especially not in the logic of reciprocity. He will only attain it at the end of his quest. Pantagruel, easygoing master that he is, does not worry about it. He leaves it to future experience and setbacks and to the effect of time. Meanwhile, Panurge does not care about being thought of as a social being or a valued member of the community. In fact, he is a "spoiled child" (in the sense Baudelaire gives the phrase). In this he is akin to a parasite, always taking and never giving back. He does not re-ciprocate the gift he received, but he enlists the help of others to pursue his carefree squandering. Then he has to go back to his benefactor and ask him for the means to resume his bachelor's partying.

It should not seem surprising, therefore, that Panurge would speak in praise of debt in order to obtain renewed credit, after misappropriating the gift he received (mistaking liberality for squandering). He thus exposes himself as a Sophist. This praise is placed at the beginning of *The Third Book* in the form of a heap of paradoxes that serve as opening gate to the rest of the quest because this reversing of the signs affecting social relation-ships (and above all marriage) is the precondition for all those that are to come. This first set of sophisms is the introduction to all the others.

What is the specious argument of this praise? It develops in two steps. The first consists of transferring all the virtues of giving to debt. These vir-tues are at the same time individual and cosmic; they are individual in the sense that debt is said to generate extremely strong reciprocal bonds ("Do you always owe something to someone? By him will God be continually implored to give you a good, long, and happy life" [3.3.267]). Every debt is a relationship and even an excess of relationship, since the creditor has no choice but to hope that the debtor will pay him back. This is an ironic and pathetic relationship in that the lender is forced to bond with the bor-rower against his own will.

In a second step this demonstration enables Panurge to extend this hypothesis to the entire universe by considering "debts to be a sort of con-necting link between Heaven and earth, a unique interrelationship of the human race" (3.3.268). He thus presents two sides of the world of debt: macrocosm and microcosm (this is a commonplace of the Renaissance;

Rabelais adds to it a humorous twist). Without debt celestial bodies would no longer relate to each other and abide by their course and their interlocking. Why not? Because "the one will not repute himself obliged to the other" (3.3.269). The human body itself would then lose its unity and harmony: deprived of their obligation of reciprocal dependence, its organs would wage war against each other.

We know the nature of this goodwill that the elements show to each other: it is a relationship of gift exchange rather than a relationship of debt. Panurge's entire argument is a comical and fraudulent transfer of features from the one to the other. Since classical times, this cosmic bond between elements and planets has been the topic of a number of doxographies,[48] with the difference that the connecting force in these is not debt but *philia* or love. Beyond the character of Panurge we can sense the jubilation Rabelais experiences as he pushes his reversing turnstile all the way to these absurd consequences. His irony reaches its climax in the other aspect of Panurge's sophism, which consists of claiming that the debtor is in a favorable position, triumphant while the unfortunate creditor has no choice but to wait for the uncertain repayment of his loan and to try and please the debtor so that the latter will be kind enough to return what he owes. It is true that there are situations in which the creditor is a victim of the debtor, especially if other resources are available to the latter (as when the debtor is the prince and can hold the creditor at his mercy). Yet except for these rare cases it is the creditor that prevails. This is true of all societies in which legal sanctions exist against negligent or insolvent debtors. There were societies in which failure to repay a debt could force the debtor to become the creditor's slave. In most cases the creditor can call on the justice system to have the police intervene and seize the debtor's property. History shows endless examples of this most typical configuration.

But what matters to us in this case is not history. The intention of Rabelais' character in his sophistic reversal of the logic of gift exchange is not to send a message, not even a parodic one. His absurd praise is only the first step in a quest that will take him through delusions and language games and will eventually lead him to acceptance of the world and of what makes it livable: the true generosity of relationships. If debt appears to be the absurd reversal of gift-giving, it may be that, conversely, gift-giving can deliver us from debt. This is undoubtedly the secret of Pantagruel's wisdom: "Owe nothing . . . save love and mutual affection" (3.5.273). This form of wisdom will be the end of Panurge's initiatory quest and the lesson he will draw from his mistakes and disappointments.

But it may be that Pantagruel's prescription has become a utopia. The argumentative exuberance of this *Praise of Debt* already shows the conviction that money ties and unties relationships between human beings in an incomparably efficient manner, that in the end everything can be settled by the magic of currency signs, and that life itself is granted *on credit*. But Panurge will come to learn at his own expense the weight of words and the price of time; this will be the end point of his education. This is probably the explicit lesson of *The Third Book*: debt should not be a game and, above all, should not be confused with its opposite, which is gift exchange. Time is inflexible and must be reckoned with. But the mere fact that this praise would have been conceivable and would have been written during the Renaissance, even in parodic form, shows that by then the ancient *Moira* had already lost some of its intransigence.

Modern Debt and Time

It may, indeed, be possible to live with debt and to pay it back by borrowing again. But doing so implies a transformation in the representation of time. One takes on debt in order to invest; this is the temporality of capital. It no longer requires the restoring of an equilibrium (which it still does in Rabelais). It is defined by endless preemption over the future. This type of equilibrium can only be maintained through the speed of its own movement. No reciprocity of moments or agents remains to be fulfilled; no principle stating "to each his own turn" needs to be accepted that would bond generations with each other. Oedipus's temptation to go back in time no longer even exists. We know how to speed up time, and we can indefinitely project ourselves through time without having to wait for it to pass. A debt of reciprocity presupposed a stable universe and a global balance to be preserved, which was why all the accounts had to be settled; but a debt of investment presupposes a universe in constant movement. What is required is no longer to turn backward in order to return what was given but to endlessly produce in order to move forward. Toward what *telos*? Nobody knows: this is the modern Moira.

At the core of the vindicatory system was the question of the necessary compensation for every offense and every failing, and in the end the certainty provided in every culture by any number of testimonies that be-hind every other debt was the *debt of life*. The question we need to address is, therefore, What happens to this debt of life when the form of political society prevails? The fading away of the vindicatory system does not do away with the debt created by offenses, especially in the case of murder. What does it mean for sovereign authority alone to be allowed to judge and punish and to have to do so in abidance with norms recognized and ac-cepted by all? It probably means that *the State takes charge of the debt*[49] and that doing so constitutes one of the essential signs of the function of sov-ereignty. This responsibility is coextensive to the monopoly on sanction. This brings us back to the royal function in the Brahmanic system, but this system is not an isolated case: in spite of significant variations the system is also found everywhere a central form of sovereignty, even a modest one, asserts itself. This function clearly lies at the foundation of medieval Euro-pean monarchies, with their figure of the "king of justice."[50] What matters to us is this transfer of the *debt of life* to the sovereign institution, because it associates in an essential manner recognition of this function with politi-cal power itself.[51] This is, of course, the regalian origin of the right of grace.

By the same logic sovereign power also claims a monopoly on the minting of currency, in other words on generating collective debt indexed on public treasure and covered by it. Is there a connection between debt of life and financial debt? Could the latter have the power to release us from the former? This might be the central question. It may be that, in the same way that the function of transformation performed by sacrifice is now as-sumed by purely technological forms of knowledge and know-how, every form of debt now tends to be managed by financial procedures of credit and debit. This would imply a world without constitutive debt or original guilt: a world that is—and is no more than—the object of a task to be per-formed. This would provide an accurate description of the modern world of technoscience and capitalism. If debt has no ultimate reason, then the only thing required is for it to be settled. These two possibilities are logical end points on a horizon from which radical evil and guilt are categorically excluded. The Indo-European world (and the Greek world to the highest degree) sees error where Semites see guilt. The two do not involve the same debt or the same universe. By mixing them, European culture has created a surprising result in which two worlds are juxtaposed and intertwined: on one side the innocent world of science, the world of being, exposed to disturbances caused by error and violence; on the other a world threatened by the possibility of evil, marked by guilt, and only appeased by the gesture of forgiveness.

This investigation of symbolic debt in its traditional forms—such as the obligation to reciprocate a gift or the compensation required for an offense or the breach of a prohibition—has led us to a certain number of considerations, the most important of which is the remarkable affirmation observed in every society of a general principle of equilibrium. This principle requires that a substitute must be provided for what was lost (whether life or precious good) or injured (honor, or a right over a particular person or thing). Finally, wherever debt emerges, so does a requirement for justice, in a great variety of forms; terminology concerning equity in the relationships between groups or individuals is observed in every known society. There are certainly considerable differences in procedures and in conceptualization. Yet the same type of requirement of a return to equilibrium emerges everywhere.

These are precisely the three levels at which modernity has brought about a considerable transformation.

First, the model of equilibrium as presupposing a stable and fixed set of elements aiming at homeostasis has been radically undermined. Equilibrium is now viewed as a property of movement in that it can only be found through a constant projection into the future that is generated by the dynamics of credit and financial debt. Credit is less and less secured by available assets and increasingly granted on the basis of assurances, projects, and expectations that time alone can verify; in short, what is wagered is time itself.

Second, substitutes (animals or precious goods substituted for humans), which played such a crucial part in ritual debt, have themselves been replaced by a universal substitute: money. Its power is extraordinary: money is an agent or an instrument that effects general equivalence in specifically financial and commercial transactions, but it is also the means used to provide the compensations that traditionally belonged to the symbolic realm (whether they compensate suffering, the loss of a life, or an offense). Money tends to take on every symbolism, but it does so by forcing every activity and assessment to enter into the framework of the marketplace.

Finally, modernity has imposed the generalization of arbitrational justice, which formally consists of substituting contractual relationships between citizens for relationships of reciprocity between allies. It therefore amounts to neutralizing relationships of obligation based on kinship bonds and alliances in order to impose obligations that are identical for all and defined based on the acceptance of common rules and public statuses in a community of formally equal individuals.

. . .

Cosmic debt was associated with a world that witnessed the emergence and development of what has been called "the arts of civilization" (pottery, weaving, metallurgy, and, above all, the domestication of plants and animals) and the recognition of the enigma of a first gift, which had to be reciprocated to supernatural entities at a time when the powers newly gained by humans encroached on the powers of the deities. Sacrifice was the privileged procedure of recognition and management of this debt. Along with sacrifice this debt itself now seems to be disappearing. Our science and our technological power are developing without making us feel that we are encroaching on what belongs to the gods. As for the gods, this indifference signals their disappearance. If symbolic debt no longer exists, or tends to fade away, knowledge itself does not need to be related to any divine giver. Its development and transmission have become a skill that can be acquired and mastered like every other.

The "god" that inspired Socrates died in the *Cogito*. From the now autonomous realm of thought it becomes possible to reach back to the God who gave not thought but the very existence of thinking beings. This in no way undermines the immanence of the rules of reason. From this point on, a different history opens up. The value of knowledge is no longer defined by its origins in an invisible world but by its internal norms of rationality, its verifiable effects on the world around us, and, finally—as an inevitable and simple consequence already drawn by the Sophists—its availability in the marketplace of knowledge. At least, this is the surprising claim that we now encounter everywhere. Debt tends to be entirely secularized, which is to say subject to accounting; it has become a technical issue. To set a price in a marketplace amounts to affirming a world under control, a strictly human and functional world. For every loss, insult, or favor, compensation exists, transforming symbolic debt into financial debt. Individuals responsible for damages or offenses (or their insurance companies) pay a financial amount, sometimes considerable, and the debt is erased[52]—until the very possibility of evil has been forgotten and what prevails is the arrogance of a settlement without remains (at the cost of exacerbating guilt without cause). Knowledge is monetized in the same way as it is produced, through reproducible methods and procedures. This was the Sophists' dream. It seems to have come true: at the same time as debt was being transformed, gift-giving was also undergoing transformation. To understand this, we must examine the emergence and development of the issue of *grace*. Its paradoxes may bring us back to a question that never ceases to arise anew: *what is* appears to be *given*, even though nothing is owed to anyone except for the enigmatic requirement that obligates everyone to give in return, or to give one*self,* with grace, beyond any form of debt.

7

The Paradoxes of Grace

In the decisive moments of his existence Socrates consulted his inner oracle, the god—*o théos*—that inspired his words and attitudes. Socrates never claimed to know the truth. The truth could not be mastered or appropriated. What made philosophical discourse possible lay far beyond what was being discussed. As *Theaetetus* teaches us, Socrates' only purpose was for his listener to recognize knowledge that was already given and present in himself. Dialogue, like the relationship between the master and those in search of wisdom, arose within the space of this gift. This is why there was no place for calculable compensation in that relationship. Before any exchange can occur between humans, something has been received that makes exchange possible. Whether this earlier gift was attributed to spirits, deities, or nature—*phusis*—matters little: relationships between humans have never taken place without reference to this entity that precedes them.

Is it within this relationship that the space of debt can open up and the ritual of sacrifice arise? We saw that there was an age of sacrifice that emerged under precise conditions and disappeared along with them. It disappeared as ritual. But what had made it possible remained: constantly renewed debt as a result of excessive mastery. It can be said that at this point the time of grace opened up. Could grace be a different form of relation to this first gift, which sacrifice recognized and to which it was meant to reply? Perhaps. But what could the common element be between the *kharis* of ancient Greece, the *kharis* of Paul's Christianity, Seneca's *gratia*, and Augustine's *gratia*, and between all of those and the *hén* of biblical writings? Probably the following: grace is the expression of a favor that

is not only entirely undeserved by its recipient but above all impossible
to reciprocate. In other words grace functions in the same way as unilateral giving. This affirmation of unilateral giving entails the disappearance
of ceremonial gift exchange. The emergence of the concept of grace coincides with a crisis of the social bond and provides it with a solution. We
saw that the ceremonial reciprocal bond cannot be separated from societies
in which the central public institution is the kinship system. Matrimonial
alliance constitutes the highest form of gift-exchange relationship and recognition between groups. Along with the advent of the city-state (as in the
case of ancient Greece), clan bond was devalued for the benefit of a bond
that operated across clans: the civic bond. But how could it bind every
citizen together? If their bond was no longer secured by a network of reciprocity between lineages or by ceremonial alliances (between partners in
gift exchange or hereditary allies), then it had to be secured in a new way.
What was this way? How did the city bind its "children" to itself? How did
Greek culture respond to this situation? How could a *philia* be conceived
of that was no longer based on "blood ties" alone but on a specifically civic
association? We will have to answer these questions.

A very different case is presented by Israel, where monotheistic belief emerged in very ancient times. From the outset this belief affirmed the
asymmetry of the unilateral gift. This in no way erased the clan-based organization of society. But, in this case also, the advent of central political authority, along with monarchy, weakened traditional reciprocity. Similarly,
when Seneca was writing *De beneficiis*, the question of the social bond was
being raised in a political society dominated by the figure of the emperor,
in which the tension between the expectations of ordinary people and the
selfishness of the rich was exacerbated, and traditional religion was undergoing a serious crisis. If the highly personalized reciprocal bond provided
by the gift/countergift relationship is no longer institutionally secured,
then a gift must be collectively granted to all and recognized by everyone. There
must be a favor "from above" akin to the unconditional favor that parents
show for their children—a favor that binds its recipients, preexists them,
envelops them, and holds them together even though they themselves cannot provide more than a partial reply. The emergence of the realm of grace
always seems to be a replacement for weakened ceremonial gift exchange. It
provides a new foundation for the social bond, through a single giver that
brings scattered recipients together. A *global* bond between this single giver

and the multiple recipients of political societies comes to be substituted for the network of *local* relationships of gift exchange that are associated with traditional societies. The realm of grace implies either a monotheistic theological model (or its premise) or a political model associated with the emergence of a central authority that transcends kinship relationships; the two models are often intermingled. This vertical-relationship schema seems remarkably consistent across a diversity of cultural and religious situations. But this is precisely the point: it cannot be reduced to a religious or political question alone. It is a question of the symbolic refoundation of the community. It constitutes another side of the question of the social bond in relation to a gift that has become unilateral. What is at stake is the source of the authority of discourse that derives from a favor from "above." Finally, it is also another version of the question of the price of truth. How so? In the sense that truth is conceived of as that which originates from a previous and purely generous gift, either from God or from nature. At this point an odd paradox can emerge: this gift is viewed as so absolute and unconditional that its recipient is not capable of reciprocating it. Any possible countergift would be trivial. The only thing left for the recipient is to express gratitude to and unreserved trust in the giver—in other words, faith. This is a radical conception of grace that cuts off the realm of the gift from that of ordinary exchanges, which are left entirely to the forces of interest and the marketplace. This radical view of grace enables a world without grace, aura, or tangible mediations—the "disenchanted world" described by Weber. Gaining an understanding of this world from the starting point of the crisis of gift exchange should clarify the issue.

Preliminary Questions

The first question that arises regarding the notion of grace as it developed in the Western tradition, first through Greek and Latin as *kharis* and *gratia*, is the following: how could equivalence emerge between the idea of gift and that of beauty, charm, and effortlessness? The phrase "gracious gesture" can designate a generous action just as well as the bodily expression of an attractive person. It is as if what we consider to be beautiful was above all something given—that is, something we have not created and is not the fruit of our labor or activities. Does the joy that beauty provides us relate it to a gift? Or should we say that beauty can only be given, even in the thing we have created (thus, in the work of art, creation—*poiēsis*—would be no more than the occasion for this gift)?

First, what are the connotations of *kharis*? One of the oldest recorded meanings of the verb *kharein* is "to rejoice"; the old word *khara* meant joy.[1] *Kharis* designates, above all, the pleasure provided by something and then the charm or beauty of this thing (object or action). Later, by extension, *kharis* also comes to mean "pleasure [as basis for making a decision]" and ends up indicating favor, kind deed, or gift. As a consequence, *kharis* can mean gratitude. If we examine the entire set of these connotations, we see that *kharis* indicates either a state of the subject (such as joy or pleasure), an attribute of the object (such as charm or beauty), a generous gesture (kind deed), or a resulting attitude (gratefulness). *Kharis* seems to cover every aspect of this field in a circular manner, but one of these aspects is dominant: "in Homer, the term most often has the concrete meaning of 'kind deed' or 'mark of favor.' It specifically applies to gifts or services provided to others to make them happy or please them."[2] What is involved is indeed the granting of a favor, which is very different from reciprocal gift-giving, *dosis*, calling for countergift, *antidosis*. If *kharis* is a gift, then it is a unilateral one, generous but that obligates the recipient in terms of gratitude rather than of countergifts.

The meaning resulting from this semantic shift, which affected *kharis* late in the development of the Greek language, is, on the contrary, the first meaning of the Latin word *gratia*. From the outset the adjective *gratus* indicates the state of gratitude of the beneficiary of a kind deed. Or rather, as Benveniste notes, its meaning is ambivalent, being both active and passive: *gratus* is either one who greets or one who is greeted.[3] *Gratia* first means service or kind deed without a counterpart. This attitude, involving either gratitude or gift-giving, is explicitly expressed by an entire set of verb phrases such as *gratias agere* (giving thanks), *gratiam debere* (owing recognition), *gratiam referre* (doing a favor), and *gratiam inire* (causing a good deed).[4] This idea of generous favor is even stronger in the phrase *gratiam acere* (pardoning). Christian literature did not need to do more than confirm this evolution, and it did so profusely. This is, in short, the oldest semantic field of *gratia*. How did this Latin "favor" end up merging with the idea of "charm" specific to the Greek language? Through a clearly attested cultural contamination, which already seemed well-established in Cicero's time and even more so in Seneca's.[5]

This set of etymological data so carefully established by scholars has a surprising feature, however: it shows no attempt to connect it to the semantic field of gift-giving, so closely related (although different in its roots). Moussy briefly mentions *donum* as one possible synonym of *gratia*. Benveniste explicitly deals with gift-giving but without reference to *gratia* or *kharis*. Why? I can offer the following hypothesis: the importance gained by the notion of "grace" was proportional to the fading away of the notion of "gift-giving" (Latin *donum*; Greek *dōron* or *dosis*). Or rather—as Benveniste clearly indicated—the language of gift-giving was taken up and absorbed by the language of exchange in general and commercial exchange in particular; it ended up largely assimilated into the language of contractual law. The language of grace, on the contrary, has remained intact in the expression of the idea of favor and charm; even regarding business, it still designates a negation of profit, in other words what is free [*gratuit* in French]. It is as if these semantic evolutions provided the outline of a broader history: on the one hand, the fading away of ceremonial gift exchange along with the growth of profitable exchanges (even though the two do not belong to the same order), and on the other hand, the reinforcing of unilateral gift-giving as pure favor, as human or divine generosity—in other words, grace. By understanding the full scope of the thought centered on the concept of grace, perhaps we can also understand the extent of its influence in the crisis of gift exchange.[6] In this case we now have a better sense of what was only outlined above: on one side a spiritualizing of gift-giving and on the other an expanding of utilitarian exchanges. It is as if one side made up for the other, as though a purely generous divine gift had to be granted to all and kept growing as gift-exchange relationships between humans kept weakening.

Kharis and *Polis*: Grace Among the Greeks

An entire model of gift-giving as favor developed around the Greek notion of *kharis*. The Christian concept of *kharis* derived from this heritage, combined with the Hebraic tradition. This was a surprising development, since the presuppositions found in these two traditions remained profoundly different, even divergent, in spite of the common denominator provided by the idea of favor—generosity without counterpart. It was an unlikely merging: paradoxical—uncompleted and impossible to complete—and as such loaded with tension, which has forced an unending re-flection on this question.

What was the original specificity of the Greek *kharis*? This question can be answered by again taking up the results of the etymological investigation presented above but more precisely. Homer's writings present various situations defined as *kharis*, or rather expressed by two verbs, *kharizesthai* and *khairein*.[7] The former designates the act of handing out hospitality presents or rewards. This active aspect seems paradoxical for a middle-voice verb (the middle voice generally expresses a neutral process); it takes on the same meaning as a more directly active phrase, *kharin pherein* (to do a favor): "*Kharizesthai* always seemed associated with a subject designating the agent that showed generosity in one form or another by providing gifts or services."[8] It is this purely generous favor that brings satisfaction to the beneficiary; this is also why the adjective *gracious—kharieis*—is an attribute of the thing given or of the gesture of the giver: "It therefore seems obvious that the common function of all of these terms was to designate the action by which an external addressee benefited from the *kharis* created by a subject and carried by an object."[9] The language associated with the beneficiary can be interpreted through this active pole, this purely generous movement of favor: to give thanks, *khairein*, which can also mean to celebrate, and finally to rejoice (hence *khara*: joy, as mentioned above). This persistence of the notion of divine favor is reinforced in writings from the classical era, such as those of Pindar: "To set a god as the cause over all things" (*Pythians* 5.25); this is the source of "marvels" (*thaumata*) and, through Kharis, of all the gifts enjoyed by humans: "Beauty [*kharis*], who creates all sweet delights [*ta meilikha*] for men" (*Oly.* 1.30).

The lexical field of gift-giving and favor is therefore the precursor of the conception of *kharis* as charm and this "grace" can also characterize bodies, words, or things, in the form of charm, delighting whoever encounters them. *Kharis* therefore circulates between object and subject. This idea of beauty (which only emerges late in the Latin word *gratia*) dominates the entire Greek concept of *kharis*. Beauty as favor is what is granted to the gaze—or the ears—of others; every form of beauty is a generous gift. What is remarkable about this notion of *kharis* is its capacity to express at the same time a property of beings (their power of seduction, going as far as *kharisma*), the effect of this charm on others, the state of pleasure of those who experience it, and the gratitude they feel for receiving this favor. This is the "state of grace."

These etymological data contribute to our understanding of the original type of gift-giving relationship implied by *kharis* (and *gratia*): for no reason other than generosity, a giver fulfills a beneficiary without expecting the recipient to reciprocate the gift but only to rejoice in it (which amounts to accepting it with gratitude). This is a very different situation from the relationship of reciprocal recognition through ceremonial gift exchange. It is a different form of giving: unilateral gift-giving. It can be assumed from the outset that it does not have the same function and does not involve the same type of agents. We also sense its ambivalence, with on the one side the splendor of the generous gesture that brings about the beneficiary's happiness and fulfillment, and on the other the humble and grateful attitude observed in those who receive without being able to reciprocate (so much so that they become debtors and experience the dissatisfaction caused by dependence toward the givers, who occupy a dominant position). This negative connotation is normally not conveyed by *kharis* or *gratia*; however, it appears in a particular type of context, which we will have to identify (justifying the phrase "the paradoxes of grace").

Regarding the Greek case—in which *kharis* always appears associated with the idea of beauty or, more precisely, of charm and seduction—it remains for us to understand how these notions could constitute an essential dimension of public life and define the forms of relationships that bonded men in the city. There was indeed a specific relationship between politics and grace.[10] It was most apparent in the notion of *persuasion—peithō*—but also, in an even more crucial and subtle manner, in a certain conception of public space.

The relationship between *peithō* and *kharis* is clearly apparent in Aeschylus's *The Eumenides*, when Athena decides to intervene in the succession of murders that led Orestes to kill his mother in order to avenge his father (in which the tragedy expresses the difficult shift from vindicatory justice, no longer understood, to arbitrational justice, which prevails in the city). Appearing before the court, Athena struggles to appease the Furies, deities of vengeance, until Peitho enables her to captivate them through the charm of her speech. She then addresses Orestes: ". . . if/Holy Persuasion bids your heart respect my words/And welcome soothing eloquence, then stay with us!" (Aeschylus *Eum.* 884–86). At the end Athena recognizes how the Furies' attitude has been transformed:

Holy Persuasion too I bless,
Who softly strove with harsh denial
Till Zeus the Pleader came to trial
And crowned Persuasion with success. (Aeschylus *Eum.* 971–74)

It is worth noting that in mythical narratives the black Furies are represented as the symmetrical reverse of the white Charites, as if they were the two sides of the same ambivalent power.

But what was the meaning of this shift of charm's efficacy toward Peitho, goddess of persuasion? It meant that a change had occurred in the very status of speech. Instead of holding in and of itself the power to perform what it stated by the very fact of stating it, as did oracular speech or the poet's chant,[11] in short instead of deriving its strength from a divine power that made it operative within the framework of a ritual procedure, speech was now endowed with a different kind of magic that had to do with the art of convincing through seductive discourse, appealing words, and reasonable arguments. The Furies' performative power thus shifted to their doubles, the Charites. Even Athena, who had been associated in the oldest versions of myths with craft or warrior functions, became, as a protector of the city, a figure of gentleness and restraint that inspired respect; her charm was inseparable from her appearance—the beauty of her regular features—and the authority emanating from her entire being. Kharis and Peitho merged in her. The one could not be found without the other. This persuasive speech[12] was also par excellence what political speech had to be, because with the advent of democracy the old power to decide based on the authority of the sovereign's position alone came to an end. Between equal citizens—*isoi*—the only thing that could win the approval of the assembly was convincing discourse based on arguments.

But there is more. It can be said that the city itself became a source of *kharis* through the conception of public space that it presupposed. The birth of this space manifested a favor, according to a generalization of the significance of the schema. To understand it, we must return to the practice of ceremonial gift exchange. It takes place between recognized partners, whether individuals or groups. Transactions are always bilateral. Transactions between groups take place in front of everyone and in a festive manner, which makes them explicitly public: the purpose of the ritual is to create or reinforce bonds. But in Greece (as was established as far back as Homer's writings), an original procedure existed by which presents or booty gained in war were placed in the center—*meson*—of the group gathered; from this moment these goods became common property. From this central location what was established was no longer a relationship of bilateral gift exchange but the community itself, symbolized by the center; thus, after Achilles is offended by Agamemnon, he refuses the private compensation offered to him by the Achaean king; he wants the compensation to be placed "in the center." This shows that the *meson* acted as operator of the gift given to every citizen by the community; what was placed in the middle was given to each by all. The act of public recognition that constituted the purpose of ceremonial gift exchange was thus transferred to the city. The *meson*, the focal point of public space located at the core of the *agora* from which persuasive speech was exercised, was also the locus through which the city expressed its relationship to the citizens—hence the importance of monuments and, above all, of their beauty. The set of constructions formed by the temples, stadiums, theaters, statues, in short everything that stood "in the middle," was also what was given to all and was so given through the charm of its forms, proportions, and by being offered to the gaze of all. Public space was the space of visibility endowed with grace. Reflecting on the Greek model, Hannah Arendt views this visibility of the works as consubstantial to them, in the same way as the city can only be what it is by becoming a visible work:

[The products of art] can fulfill their own being, which is appearance, only in a world which is common to all. . . . Generally speaking, culture indicates that the public realm . . . offers its place of display to those things whose essence it is to appear and to be beautiful. . . . Seen against the background of political experience and of activities which, if left to themselves, come and go without leaving any trace in the world, beauty is the very manifestation of imperishability. . . . Without the beauty, that is, the radiant glory in which potential immortality is made manifest in the human world, all human life would be futile and no greatness could endure. The common element connecting art and politics is that they both are phenomena of the public world.[13]

The city's *kharis* was, therefore, at the same time the requirement of democratic speech expected to convince and seduce, and public space in the sense of what was given to each citizen in the name of all. This space was available for political debate, collective celebrations (religious festivals, seasonal processions, athletic competitions, or theater performances) and, above all, for the visual enjoyment of all (even a tyrant such as Pisistrates offered to Athens the temple of Athena Parthenos, rather than leaving a mausoleum dedicated to his own glory like the *basilei* of ancient times).[14]

This public form of charm was one of the essential dimensions of what united the citizens in the veneration of a beauty that transcended them all and was offered to all. Three elements emerged at the same time: the idea of a collective gift, making it possible to conceptualize the unity of the city as such; the birth of a civic bond, making up for the fading away of ceremonial gift exchange; and the requirement of individual gift-giving, left to the initiative of each person—in short, the emergence of specifically moral gift-giving. It is this type of generous gift-giving that Aristotle analyzes and encourages in the *Nicomachean Ethics*. To say that it was moral gift-giving amounts to saying that it had become a virtue (liberality, munificence) and that it was no longer primarily a gesture of reciprocal recognition (with the likely exception of encounters and festivals) but had become a gesture of mutual assistance (which is profoundly alien to ceremonial gift exchange). The citizen was granted recognition of status by the city itself, from the *meson* from which shared goods originated; the first of these goods was the law—*nomos*—recognized by all and identical for all (thus Plutarch, reflecting several centuries later on the emergence of the *polis*, summarizes his view as follows: *logou kai nomou metabolē*—transformation through speech and law).

But another element was also present. This complex phenomenon of emergence of the city through a gradual reduction of the role played by clans—*genē*—through the affirmation of shared public space, and through the recognition of written law as imposing the same obligations on all, gives rise to the following questions: what was it that bonded fellow citizens to each other? Was the *kharis* of public space sufficient to accomplish this? How could men form a society? Plato's answer in the *Republic* amounts to the following argument: the city originates from the fact of the diversity of needs;[15] this diversity generates the diversity of occupations and entails reciprocal interdependence, leading men to live together. This association (*koinōnia*) or commonality of interests constitutes the empirical reason for the existence of the city (*polis*). Aristotle takes up the same genesis in the *Politics*. But does this empirical condition of the city constitute its reason

for being, its *telos*? Plato suggests that keeping to this satisfaction of complementary needs would lead to a "community of pigs" (*Republic* 372d). In
Protagoras he answers through the myth of Prometheus, telling how, after
fire was given to human beings, techniques and know-how were granted to
them without making it possible for them to constitute a *polis* because divergent interests generated violent rivalries. Zeus, the sovereign god (as opposed
to the protective deities associated with specific trades), then intervened and
enabled humans to attain *philia*, reciprocal love, by granting them respect or
restraint (*aidōs*) and justice (*dikē*)—the political virtue (*aretē politikē*) from
which all benefit in an equal manner. This narrative says it all:[16] needs—and
the trades associated with them—are not sufficient to unite human beings;
for this to occur there must be a divine gift, an emotional bond that circulates among them and yet originates from a single source.

It matters little that this genesis of society is pure fiction from the
standpoint of anthropological knowledge; when Greek thinkers reflected
on the fact, which had become strange to them, that beings as attached to
their autonomy and resistant to all forms of submission as humans were
still managed to live together, they could give only one answer: it had
taken a divine gift—*philia*—from the sovereign god. I propose the following interpretation: the shift from clan-based to political society calls for
the need to replace the reciprocal bond from partner to partner by a collective bond that brings together the multiplicity of the members into a single
entity. It can be said that this transformation already shows the emergence
of a new idea of grace as an infinitely generous but unilateral gesture. It
can also be said that the idea of such a gift becomes necessary in proportion to the degree of division of society. The gift becomes so great that no
reply seems adequate, which opens the possibility of limitless debt. Yet to
be determined is whether this is how Greek *kharis* met Christian grace and
what discrepancies this involved; this meeting could only have occurred
through another encounter—with the biblical heritage.

Biblical Grace: The Favor of the Almighty

It is generally accepted that the Hebrew counterpart of the Greek
kharis and the Latin *gratia* is *hén* (this is at least the term used in the Sep-
tanticus). *Hén*, which designates the gift—or rather the generous gesture—
from the only God, does not really seem to match the *kharis* of the city. *Hén*

designates two different aspects of the same reality; first, it expresses the benevolent gesture of a high-ranking figure toward a lower-ranking one; second, it can also refer to the content of this favor, from which the idea of charm or even beauty can emerge and later be applied in a more general manner to persons or things. Whereas Greek grace concerns above all the visible world and from it goes back to the gesture, biblical grace pertains to the gesture and can then be extended to the visible world. This conception of a favor granted by the powerful to the weak (one of the connotations of *hén* is to bend down or to lower one's eyes in a compassionate gaze) was shared by all the cultures and religions of the ancient Middle East.[17] In biblical writings the representation of God as generous giver is a constant that structures three of the essential aspects of the Hebrew religion: the election, the covenant, and the law. Let us examine the first two terms.

The election—*bakhár*—is the initial gift, the inaugural and sovereign gesture by which Yahweh chose his people among many others.[18] This mysterious election is confirmed by every one of God's initiatives: Abraham's calling, the Exodus, the gift of the earth, the founding of the kingdom. The election is stated by Yahweh in these words: "You shall be my own possession among all peoples" (Exodus 19:5); and "Lo, a people dwelling alone, and not reckoning itself among the nations" (Numbers 23:8). In fact, the theme of the election mostly developed in the age of the prophets and then had a retrospective effect on the oldest writings and their later versions. The conception involves two deeply held convictions. First, God has a plan regarding "his people," a final purpose that no temporary desertion or sin on the part of the elect can impede. Yahweh will remain true to his choice no matter what happens. The second conviction is that God always has the initiative. Nothing can happen that he has not decided. Thus, he chooses the kings, the prophets, and the priests; he chooses those whom he rewards or punishes. When men forget this truth, Yahweh creates an event that will bring them back to it. In short, the election at the same time expresses the enigma of a divine choice that can in no way be explained by the merit of the elect—why this people rather than another?—and affirms the consistent and unconditional character of God's gift. The beneficiary's reply can only be based on the certainty that the gift received can never be reciprocated. The correct and only possible response is to recognize this impossibility. The impossibility of a reciprocal gift amounts to acceptance of God's favor, which is to say *hén* or grace. The elect are united not primarily by the bonds they establish with each other but by the common bond that brings them all together in the recognition of the same giver, the God that chose them as his people. All other bonds exist only through this single bond granted from above.

This is the requirement expressed by the covenant—*berith*—a term that normally designates all sorts of pacts between individuals or groups, such as agreements of mutual assistance or peace agreements. But the privileged meaning of *berith* is that of a pact of vassalage between a powerful protector and an individual or group placing him-, her-, or itself under his protection and dependence. This type of pact was ritually concluded through a sacrifice in which the victim (typically a calf) was cut in two; the partners then walked between the two halves and committed to the pact through an oath. A tree was then planted or a stone raised as a memorial meant to mark the event.

As far back as the earliest documents, biblical writings place this covenant at the core of the proclamation of a single god.[19] It is quite clear that the model of reference was the pact of vassalage; however, the covenant had one remarkable feature: the commitment was presented as being primarily an initiative of the overlord himself. This presentation showed striking daring. It seems that no other example of a covenant between a god and a people can be found; "this motif does appear to be specific to the religion of Israel."[20] For this small population of herders, resistant to the practices and ways of life of the urbanized populations that surrounded it, this was a way to give itself a purely religious monarchy, a king that would also be the only and invisible god. This meant that no human authority could intervene between this god and his people. From the outset this precluded the possibility of any other overlord for the "children of Israel": "By placing themselves under the authority of a god through the covenant, they took themselves out of the authority of earthly rulers, whether kings, pharaohs, or minor monarchs of Canaan's city-states. They proclaimed their complete independence and at the same time they reinforced their union, since their rules and laws . . . were sanctioned by the divine ruler and thus took on the role of the overlord's commands in pacts of vassalage."[21]

This was an extreme example of the spiritual radicalism that characterizes desert or steppe populations. The covenant expressed the privilege of election for a poor and nomadic people most often dominated by its neighbors. *Berith* proclaimed the following: by choosing his people, the only god had himself proposed the pact that united them to each other. The offer had not been requested but had come from above: "You have seen what I did to the Egyptians, and how I bore you on eagles' wings and brought you to myself. Now, therefore, if you will obey my voice and keep my covenant, you shall be my own possession among all peoples; for all the earth is mine, and you shall be a kingdom of priests, a holy nation" (Exodus 19:4–6). This entirely original structure of the covenant (within the context of the pacts of vassalage) makes it possible to understand the equally unique character of grace, divine favor, or *hén.*

Favor—as a privileged relationship—is expressed in writings by several motifs, all of which involve the gesture of unconditional generosity. The primary motif is that these writings proclaim Yahweh's unfailing fidelity toward his people, calling for a reply on the part of the elect. The offer comes before the requirement for a counterpart. This point also shows originality compared to pacts of vassalage, in which the vassal's fidelity had to be sworn first. Israel's reply was a commitment to worship no entity other than its god (hence the strict proscription of all idolatry). Yahweh can punish and impose ordeals, but forgiveness always prevails in the end. Forgiveness can find its highest expression in the language of tenderness and loyalty between lovers—*hesed.* Besides the expression of forgiveness, these terms refer to the language of engagement to wed and reveal another remarkable and unique aspect of the covenant between this people and its god, since *berith* also designates the matrimonial alliance. Furthermore, the very bond of vassalage is presented as a love relationship. Yet, in this case, too, love is a gesture of pure divine generosity that can in no way be explained by the merit of the loved one.

This rigorously unconditional, transcendent, and inexplicable character of Yahweh's favor in biblical writings, this radical character of God's gift, constitutes a unique case from the standpoint of historians of religions. The entire Christian conception of grace, starting with Paul's preaching, received and developed this heritage. But it did so precisely by adding to it all the echoes of the Greek *kharis.* Paul wrote in Greek, and what he translated as *kharis* was indeed the *hén* of biblical writings, yet these two worlds were at first profoundly different.

The visible world and public space could not have had a comparable importance in the biblical world and in the Greek world. In the latter, relationship to beauty remained subjected to the relationship defined by *justice*. Greek justice still belonged to the realm of proportion, balance, and measure. The justice of the prophets of Israel was of another kind altogether. It confronted the radical character of evil. This radical character seems to have been alien to Greek thought (the Socratic thesis that "no one does evil on purpose" was the most accomplished expression of this conception). Greek classical tradition was somehow incapable of regarding violence, injustice, horror, arbitrariness, cruelty, humiliation, and abjection as forms of intrinsic evil, except by turning them into fictional figures; there was a world of *mimēsis* the production of which knew no bounds in principle. The worst could be found under the innocent cover of a narrative. But this probably had to do with the fact that, in the Greek experience and because of the very requirement of moderation imposed by *kharis*, nothing could come close to the realm of the unbearable, not even the cruel scenes found in the *Iliad*. There was nothing comparable to the excesses of celebrations and massacres, orgies and tortures displayed by some of the civilizations the Greeks called "barbarians." Greek *kharis* made these excesses inconceivable. By doing so, it made their actual emergence in history unthinkable. In fact, it was unable to confront them.

Nevertheless, out of this history something did reach the classical world during certain periods of the Roman Empire. It is as if the Romans, who meant to be the heirs to Greek culture, had not been able to implement in practice the very model of *kharis*. The perversion of imperial power went as far as to produce instances of arbitrariness and violence that classical thought could not confront, except by placing them in the category of scandal or delirium. *Kharis* could not respond to this more radical and terrifying form of violence, whereas biblical and evangelical thought never ceased questioning it and provided a reflection on evil and a doctrine of grace capable of matching it. This is why within this thought grace did not become primarily beauty and charm but remained the gesture of giving understood as unconditional obligation, ethical relationship, and, in the end, beyond giving, the possibility of forgiveness.[22] This was no longer ceremonial gift exchange; it was the unilateral generosity of the giver. We must understand this transformation; it seems to have been at work in all the cultures of the classical world. A reading of Seneca's *De beneficiis* should help us grasp it.

Seneca and the Ethics of Unconditional Giving

Seneca's treatise *De beneficiis* has been rightly celebrated as one of the earliest philosophical syntheses on the question of giving.[23] This assessment seems well-founded, and it is surprising that a work that examined the necessity and beauty of giving with such energy and rigor would have escaped the intellectual curiosity of Marcel Mauss and other anthropologists, at least until recently. But what is the kind of giving that Seneca discusses? It is the generous and purely oblatory form of giving that every person can practice toward friends and relatives or toward strangers. This is, indeed, moral giving, but it no longer encompasses ceremonial gift exchange. The latter was no longer understood at the time and had even become an object of radical suspicion. Seneca's writing is indicative of a decisive shift. It does not merely develop a new moral view originating in Stoicism; it reveals a profound shift in the entire system of social relationships. *De beneficiis* testifies to a crisis in the communal bond and means to provide a solution to this crisis. In this it belongs to a new intellectual configuration that aims to reconsider relationships to others based on a new universalist requirement.

What is Seneca's message? The practice of giving gifts or benefits (*beneficia*) "constitutes the chief bond of human society" (*De beneficiis* 1.4). "What then is a benefit? It is the act of a well-wisher who bestows joy and derives joy from the bestowal of it, and is inclined to do what he does from the prompting of his own will" (1.6). Seneca's main theses can be summarized as follows: (1) giving is beautiful in and of itself; (2) giving without expecting any reciprocation is the very essence of giving; (3) giving defines the essential element of our relationship to others and constitutes the core of the moral relationship.

This undoubtedly constitutes an in-depth reflection on the practice of giving as ethical gesture and on mutual generosity as the foundation of the social bond. The second point needs to be reexamined, however, since the type of giving Seneca discusses has, in fact, very little to do with the type studied by Mauss and by all those who conducted research on the practices of ceremonial exchange observed in traditional societies. Yet it cannot be claimed that ritual gift exchange had disappeared by the time Seneca's treatise was published (it is assumed to have been written between 60 and 65 CE). This was even a time when everything in public and private life involved giving and reciprocating gifts. In fact it was the golden age of *euergetism*, the practice by which the wealthiest citizens were obligated to provide their city with public monuments (temples and theaters, for example), useful public works (aqueducts, thermal baths, paved roads), or shows, festivals, and feasts.[24]

But did this constitute reciprocal gift exchange? Obviously, it did not. It constituted, instead, a new kind of giving that can be called unilateral. Those who view Seneca as a precursor of Mauss have misread him. As we will see, Seneca's treatise marks a turning point: the rejection of ritual gift exchange. It must even be said that Seneca initiated a major misunderstanding of gift-giving that endures to this day. Seneca's position never ceases to surprise us: no one in the classical world brings the praise of giving as far or understands the necessity of giving as accurately as he did, yet no other writing better testifies to the extent to which the logic of traditional gift exchange had faded away. This clarification on Seneca should enable us to understand what is at play between purely ceremonial gift exchanges and purely commercial relationships, from a logical and sometimes a chronological standpoint. It is clear that Seneca is a great moralist but a bad anthropologist; his writing is a milestone on the road to modern individualism more than it is a testimony on the ancient gift/countergift relationship. His conception of pure giving, in fact, involves unilateral giving; this would have a more significant impact than is usually assumed on the emergence within the "pagan" world of a conception of grace close to Christian preaching—especially Paul's—which was becoming influential at the time. Let us therefore return to Seneca's positions.

Toward Pure Giving: Expecting No Reciprocation

Giving, Seneca writes, "is something that is desirable in itself" (*De beneficiis* 4.10). But why is it so? Seneca does not provide a demonstration but only a proclamation. It is enough for him to invoke a commonly accepted intuition: "The fruit [of bestowing benefits] is at once enjoyed by the noble mind" (1.1); "To seek, not the fruit of benefits, but the mere doing of them, . . . this is the mark of a soul that is truly great and good" (1.1). In fact, Seneca is implicitly referring to the entire tradition of sumptuary generosity as a specifically noble virtue internalized in the form of a general quality of generosity of spirit and magnanimity (the very virtue

Aristotle celebrates in his *Nicomachean Ethics*). This kind of generosity is incompatible with any expectation of advantage or reward. Seneca castigates the very idea of reciprocating a gift: "It is virtue to give benefits that have no surety of being returned" (1.1). He who gives in order to receive has not given (*qui beneficium ut reciperet dedit, non dedit*). But even more than the expectation of reciprocation, Seneca denounces the idea of deriving a profit from a generous gesture: "Let us make our benefits, not investments, but gifts. The man who, when he gives, has any thought of repayment deserves to be deceived" (*demus beneficia, non feneremus. Dignus est decipi, qui de recipiendo cogitavit, cum daret*) (1.1). "To regard a benefit as an amount advanced is putting it out at shameful interest" (*turpis feneratio est beneficium expensum ferre*) (1.2). This is a serious attack, considering the extent of the contempt in which classical civilization held usurers.[25] But it presupposes that the idea of gift exchange as challenge, requirement of reply, and generous rivalry had lost all relevance in contemporary awareness.

Seneca is thus forced to explain that a generous deed is not a loan or an investment: "In benefits the book-keeping is simple—so much is paid out; if anything comes back, there is no loss; if he does not return it, it is not lost. I made the gift for the sake of giving" (*Ego illud dedi, ut darem*) (1.2). This distinction between generous obligation and the kind of obligation associated with financial debt is essential for Seneca; he insists on it throughout the text. His antiutilitarianism (shared by the entire Stoic tradition) seems very clear in this. It must be noted, however, that already in Seneca's time the type of giving discussed in *De beneficiis* is no longer ceremonial gift-giving but an internalized form of giving. It is giving of a moral nature, to be assessed by the criterion of intention. This specifically refers, by contrast, to a world in which the idea of profitable exchange—commercial exchange—prevailed in people's minds over the idea of generous exchange. The requirement of purity in intention is proportional to the risk that self-interested considerations might be involved in giving. In other words, the fact that Seneca denounces this risk means that a confusion has already taken place in his mind and in the minds of his contemporaries: they did not understand that countergifts are not and have never been profits from or rewards for the initial gift but are only gifts in return that preserve reciprocity and provide public confirmation of the bond established. The fact that Seneca questions the reciprocation of a gift and understands it as a possibility of profit shows that the very idea of gift-giving as total social phenomenon had disappeared. This helps explain why the theory regarding "giving for the sake of giving" emerged precisely at the time when this misunderstanding began.

Seneca's position is thus testimony to the crisis of traditional reciprocity. Seneca intends to preserve giving (since he is well aware that without a relationship based on giving there can be no social bond). But he can only preserve it by moving it away from its traditional form—which is to say its ritual form—which he presents as the opposite of what it has always been. The concept of pure giving developed based on this misinterpretation or at least misunderstanding; this is still the case today.

Critique of the Myth of the Three Graces, and the Priority Given to Intention

In this context of suspicion regarding rituals Seneca comes to celebrate unreciprocated giving as the gesture of giving for the sake of giving. It is defined as joy for the giver: a moral and purely internalized form of joy. This joy results from doing good for its own sake and from giving because giving is beautiful. But how could it be known that giving was beautiful, if not for the tradition of gift-giving that had developed in an age when giving entailed reciprocating, which is to say that it instituted and nourished the social bond? This was an odd situation: giving had kept all its power in spite of the fact that the reciprocity requirement had been abandoned. It is as if the "noble gesture"—so essential to ceremonial gift-giving—had lost none of its appeal and value as a bond within a world in which the ability to reciprocate was no longer guaranteed, as if this gesture was now sufficient to preserve what the circle of exchanges used to provide: the certainty and renewed experience of forming a community.

Seneca's writing shows clear evidence that ceremonial gift exchange had become a distant practice: he denounces the classic symbolic benefits of the practice of gift-giving: prestige, glory, and honor. These advantages were now viewed as aspects of social vanity; in traditional societies, on the contrary, they were a subtle manner of acquiring a form of power entirely based on the ability to give (and thus to be recognized) and an efficient way of regulating force, and, above all, violence. But with the advent of political society and the affirmation of moral individualism (which had already been clearly established by the Sophists, Socrates, and the Stoics) an entirely different balance was being set up; a different world now prevailed, with different regulations—precisely those that can be designated as ethics.

Seneca's analysis goes even further. He not only asks that the giver express no concern for any paying off or recovering of his gift, but, above all, he wants purity of heart in the gesture of giving. Seneca entirely shifts the question of giving toward the side of *intention*. As a preliminary to this moralization of the gesture of giving, he calls on the myth of the Three Graces. His writing has been viewed as a laudatory analysis of ceremonial gift-giving, foreshadowing contemporary anthropological research. In fact, the opposite is true.

Seneca cites this myth as early as the first pages of his treatise, after an introduction dealing with ingratitude and meant to show that ingratitude is not a valid argument against the obligation to give. This resort to myth is odd; could it be a device in the vein of Plato, meant to fill in a gap between the ancient tradition of reciprocity and the new moral requirement of unreciprocated giving?[26] This would be an appealing argument, but nothing in the writing supports it. It is, indeed, ironic that, just after explaining that giving is noble in and of itself (a point to which he will return again and again), Seneca reminds his readers of a story that shows that giving is, on the contrary, a circle of exchanges, a cycle in which giving, receiving, and reciprocating cannot be separated. What is his purpose? Let us read him:

Why the Graces are three in number and why they are sisters, why they have their hands interlocked, and why they are smiling and youthful and virginal, and are clad in loose and transparent garb. Some would have it appear that there is one for bestowing a benefit, another for receiving it, and a third for returning it; others hold that there are three classes of benefactors—those who earn benefits, those who return them, those who receive and return them at the same time. But of the two explanations do you accept as true whichever you like; yet what profit is there in such knowledge? Why do the sisters hand in hand dance in a ring which returns upon itself? For the reason that a benefit passing in its course from hand to hand returns nevertheless to the giver; the beauty of the whole is destroyed if the course is anywhere broken, and it has most beauty if it is continuous and maintains an uninterrupted succession. (*De beneficiis* 1.3)

The first thing worth noticing is that this interpretation of the figures of the Three Graces as symbolizing the three fundamental gestures of the gift-exchange relationship is not consistent with tradition. The three Charites were supposed to personify strength, freshness, and youth. They even had specific names: Aglaea, Thalia, and Euphrosyne. As Seneca notes, these names were recognized by Hesiod. Traditionally, their trinity was never supposed to symbolize the three gestures or moments of the gift-exchange relationship. Seneca recalls this gloss without endorsing it; he attributes it to the Greek philosopher Chrysippus. This interpretation, which significantly changes the content of the allegory, is instructive.

By recalling this myth, Seneca seems to suggest that it is necessary to go back to ceremonial gift exchange. Does he want to prepare his readers to grasp the beauty of the triple movement of generous exchange? Not in the least: it soon becomes clear that he has only provided this reminder in order to immediately deny its relevance: the entire story is mere fable, he writes. From the outset he apologizes to the reader for this digression ("If you will permit me to digress upon questions that are foreign to the subject . . ." [1.3]). Seneca only allows himself this reminder of the myth as a concession and a means to better emphasize the fact that he is going to break with these beliefs. After describing the Graces' gestures and mentioning two versions of their traditional interpretation, he addresses the reader: "Of the two explanations do you accept as true whichever you like; yet what profit is there in such knowledge?" But, above all, at the end of this reexamination of the fable and its variants (or rather, according to Seneca, of the elements the whims of poets have added to it), he proposes to discard all of these glosses and to leave the realm of fiction and poetic arbitrariness. His tone verges on exasperation: "But for fear that I shall be guilty of the fault that I am criticizing, I shall abandon all these questions, which are so remote that they do not even touch the subject" (1.4). No more poets and fabulists! Enough with the Three Graces! The philosopher will deal with the thing itself: "What we need is a discussion of benefits" (*de beneficiis dicendum est et ordinanda res*) (1.4). The return to myth has brought no results: the triple gesture is a mere remnant, useless for reflection. With this writing Seneca certainly does not prove to be Mauss's unrecognized precursor. On the contrary, his treatise is highly representative of the shift that had occurred from the practice of gift exchange as total social fact to the practice of giving as individual moral requirement.

After this critique of the myth, however, Seneca shows the worth of his view of specifically moral giving. This generous form of giving could be called unconditional; its first characteristic is purity of intention. This applies to the gesture of giving, as well as to that of receiving. To give truly is to give with spontaneity, generosity, and joy. This primacy of intention is associated with a relativizing of the thing given and of its content: "There is a great difference between the matter of a benefit and the benefit itself; and so it is neither gold nor silver nor any of the gift[s] which are held to be most valuable that constitutes a benefit, but merely the goodwill of him who bestows it" (1.5). It is clear that the strictly moral character of the gesture of giving leads Seneca to view the movement of reciprocity with suspicion. Not that he objects to reciprocity; on the contrary, to reciprocate a gift amounts to giving in one's turn. But Seneca places the giver's initiative in an absolute position. He does so because nothing—outside of constraining ritual mechanisms—can guarantee a reciprocating gesture in a society in which rituals appear external and artificial. It is necessary to give and to give ceaselessly. Why? Because, if reciprocating is not guaranteed, then gift-giving disappears, along with the bond that unites human beings. Thus the only certainty is the giving subject. The other party is never ensured. It is up to the subject himself to create otherness. This is the sign of a new suspicion regarding the community. It is also the beginning of a long history whose narrative has not come to an end: a situation in which the other is no longer self-evident, no longer the immediate given of collective existence presupposed by the triple movement of ceremonial gift exchange. In the procedures of reciprocal gift offerings the other is there from the outset; he is radically other and at the same time present and challenged to reply. From now on the only certainty will be the individual who thinks, feels, and acts. The other will have to be deduced from the ego. At least this was the certainty in the process of being established.

The fact that in the relationship to the other the position of the giving subject had become primary from a logical, ethical, and sociological standpoint marks a turning point in the system of representations governing the bond between humans. This also concerns their bond to the divine world. In short, this ethical transformation of the way giving is viewed opened the way within the Roman world to an original conception of grace that could allow for surprising intersections with the conception then emerging in Christian preaching. This is apparent in Seneca's description of the gift from the gods.

Unilateral Giving as Giving without Return:
The Example of the Gods

It is clear that, according to Seneca, for giving to exist, a generous gesture must be regarded as unilateral. If the mere expectation of a reply is enough to contaminate this gesture by exposing it to the suspicion of being an object of calculation, then it is clear that giving no longer has anything to do with the trilogy symbolized in ancient times by the Three Graces: giving, receiving, and reciprocating. In short, ethical and unconditional giving, which appears to us supremely generous, beautiful, and noble, also—and perhaps above all—means that the social logic of reciprocity is no longer understood. Seneca's contemporaries could no longer see that the triple movement of gift-giving has nothing to do with any calculation or seeking of profit—and is even their complete opposite—but is, above all, a "circle," a general movement not of mere benevolence but of recognition (in the sense of the act of recognizing each other). There is a significant difference, however: these gestures, with their forms, times, and style, and these presents, with their choice and importance, are not decided by individuals but are set by rules or customs. The decisive element is not the partners' states of mind but the fact that a tradition and its rituals require public gestures of respect and institute bonds, alliances, and commitments. Those bonds, alliances, and commitments then call for states of mind and emotions. The bond is strong because it is preserved by unquestioned rituals and by recognized social attitudes. Emotions follow (as with Homer's hereditary host). With Seneca the affirmation of the individual had already reached a degree such that the accepted forms of reciprocity could only be viewed through the practices of exchange that now prevailed: those of trade. Instead of being understood as a gesture recognizing and honoring the giver, the gift in return was now suspected of being expected by the giver as profit, exposing a false generosity.

The *euergetism* phenomenon cannot be regarded as a valid objection in this respect. This practice, which I have already mentioned, consisted of the obligation for the wealthiest citizens to provide gifts to their city: "Euergetism means private liberality for public benefit," Paul Veyne writes.[27] In a way, by making these gifts quasi mandatory the city placed itself in the position of partner, thus performing an operation of distributive justice. ("Every class of the population benefited from gifts. . . . These gifts had substantial quantitative importance.")[28] What givers gained in return was prestige, public recognition, and, above all, power.

This was certainly a ritualized form of giving. But it was no longer gift exchange in the form of giving-receiving-reciprocating. It was the gift of a patron or protector, the *unilateral* form of giving to which no one can reply. Others can compete with it through equal or greater generosity, but rather than to reciprocate the original gift through a countergift, their purpose would then be to provide the city with a more sumptuous present. This is indeed a unilateral gift, the gift from above in its absolute form, which provides the model for Seneca's ethics. This is the kind of giving that *De beneficiis* means to spiritualize, moralize, and even radicalize: unilateral giving, but freed from its ostentatious element, from the social vanity that accompanied it, and from the advantages of public recognition called for by euergetism. In a way Seneca asks that everyone practice euergetism toward everyone else and, on this limited scale, give with generosity and joy, with no expectation of return, and, above all, with discretion. Moral requirement involves no social effect.

Seneca's position on this point could thus be summarized as follows: to give is to give unilaterally—in this, euergetism provides the formal structure of giving—but to give truly is to give without even expecting recognition; to this extent ethical giving, which is the genuine form of giving, leads outside of the social order of evaluations and reaches a more elusive and sublime level, a level through which humans can resemble the gods. Humans become capable of giving like the gods, without any calculation or concern for the gratitude of others. The gods give humans the permanent example of purely generous giving: "Not even the immortal gods are deterred from showing lavish and unnecessary kindness to those who are sacrilegious and indifferent to them. For they follow their own nature, and in their universal bounty include even those who are ill interpreters of their gifts" (*De beneficiis* 1.1).

Pure giving, Seneca explicitly states, is, above all, a divine privilege: "God bestows upon us very many and very great benefits, with no thought of any return, since he has no need of having anything bestowed, nor are we capable of bestowing anything on him" (4.9). In addition to the shift from plural to singular—from the gods to God—that gives this writing a kind of monotheistic flavor, a very new conception of the deity is worth noting: not only does it no longer need to be "fed" by sacrifice (a ritual Seneca does not even mention), but it remains out of the reach of men's gifts ("All the greatest benefits are incapable of being repaid" [3.14]). The divine gift is absolutely unilateral. It is unconditional favor, and it cannot be reciprocated. Thus, within the moral discourse of the so-called pagan world, a conception was beginning to develop that was perfectly analogous to the conception articulated at the same time but from very different premises in Christian preaching, especially Paul's. This prepared what would later become the implicit and essential thesis of the Reformation: only God can give; he alone gives, and he has no need for men's gifts.

Roman Grace and Christian Grace

The facts that the system of gift-giving has become an ethics and that this transformation is associated with a new distribution of signs and a new status of appearances mean that the old symbolic mechanism no longer functions; it is turning into a semiotic system in which the visible is split from the invisible and matter from intention. Whereas ritual is an operational symbolism that implies immediate engagement on the part of the participants, ethics is an attitude that presupposes distance and requires that a choice be made by the subject; it effects a distinction within the heritage of the ritual between the forms that have been passed on and the internalized purpose, which is claimed to constitute the truth of these forms. From then on, belief can no longer be separated from this ethical representation.

Seneca's thought—in other words Stoicism at its highest point—testifies in the clearest manner to the fading away of ceremonial gift exchange; public gestures of generosity were more and more perceived as vain ostentations. They were no longer capable of generating a social bond since they were meant to preclude any reply on the part of the beneficiaries; hence the new requirement to purify unilateral giving from any spectacular manifestation. What resulted was precisely moral giving as pure giving guaranteed by intention alone. Even before the Christian age—or at the same time—Seneca exemplifies the disjunction between heart and works. But he preserves the urgent requirement to give so that, beyond mere justice, friendship—Aristotle's *philia*—will bloom, without which the social bond cannot endure. This moral answer is not without nobility. It takes note of the end of an era and of the necessity of a new requirement for a community to exist. Is it sufficient? Probably not. A much more complete and powerful symbolic system was needed. It was Christianity's genius to be capable of providing it: a single god who envelops every human being with unconditional love without any distinction of status, gender, or nation, who becomes one of them, dies for them, and opens his kingdom to them. No philosophical school was in a position to compete with such a powerful narrative and symbolism (this is what Nietzsche finds so appalling).

As for the Roman religion, let us recall that during the whole of the first century BCE, which is to say the time when the empire was being established, it was undergoing a serious crisis: failure to maintain the temples and to renew sacerdotal functions, manipulation of divining practices by political leaders, multiplication of marginal and charismatic religious movements in reaction to the formalism of rituals. The restoration of rituals conducted by Augustus did not change the essence of the problem.[29]

At the same time, but in an entirely different context, the preachings of Jesus faced a comparable crisis; they developed in a society dominated by a situation of acute conflict between several political and religious trends (pro-Roman supporters of Herod, legalist Pharisees, tolerant Sadducees, purist Qumrânians, Samaritans, Essenians). The answer Jesus provided to this hopeless deadlock, this fragmented society, was the requirement of unconditional charity. Only this requirement could provide a way out and make a different community possible: "To the question, who should give, to whom, and what? Jesus answered: Who? Everyone. To whom? To all. What? Everything. . . . In this sense of overabundant generosity, in his refusal to limit or stop the gift, there was something akin to *potlatch* in the attitude of Jesus and his disciples."[30] (It should be added that in this *potlatch* the giver competed with himself.)

Paul's entire preaching articulates this message with incomparable speculative resources that come from both Hebrew tradition (mostly Pharisee) and Greek tradition. Like Jesus he calls for unconditional giving, but this giving only takes on meaning by taking part in the gift of Christ, the envoy of God who is also God himself. In anthropological terms this could be called a perfect gift in that the present offered is the very person of the giver. Yet this is not the ceremonial gift exchange of reciprocal recognition but the operation of grace in the Hebrew sense of favor—*hén*—as well as in the Greek sense of *kharis* as good deed (which is only one of the aspects of *kharis*). The believer's gift is, above all, the gift of oneself through faith, the gesture of absolute trust. Only faith can open the space of charity. The gift of oneself, as well as any gift given to one's neighbor, can only have meaning, or rather is only possible, because of the gift that has been received, the divine gift that is Christ himself. This is the meaning of the proclamation that will become one of the major references of Augustine and of the Reformation: "We hold that a person is justified by faith apart from the works prescribed by the law" (Romans 3:28). These "works" have traditionally been viewed as the acts of dedication or support prescribed by the books of precepts. For Paul the gesture of giving ("the good work") is itself only possible as a gift from God. Not only is this gift free of charge and without reciprocation, but it involves no exclusivity: it is not reserved to an ethnic group—a chosen people—but offered to humankind as a whole. For Paul the universal character of salvation in Christ is, above all, the universality of God's gift. This is Christian *kharis*, which in a way radicalizes the *gratia* of the Latin Stoics, especially Seneca, for whom every man, *even a slave*, is addresser and addressee of the gift. Yet Seneca remains within the framework of Roman society. Paul, however, proclaims that every human being—whether Jewish or pagan, man or woman, rich or poor, free or slave—is chosen: "For there is no distinction. . . . [All] are now justified by his grace as a gift, through the redemption that is in Christ Jesus" (Romans 3:23–24).

The universal character of God's gift thus clearly appeared as the only possibility for emergence of a community out of the multiplicity of nations, statuses, and conditions, starting with gender and class differences. It took an equal and unconditional gift, offered to all, to make humankind thinkable as such: infinite grace.[31] How did the splendor of this generosity come to be diluted and disfigured into an increasingly abstruse doctrine of the arbitrariness of God's favor that would culminate in a casuistic of predestination? This would be a question for theologians. Following Max Weber, it remains for sociologists—and historians—to ask how, through an unexpected sequence of effects, this doctrine, radicalized by Luther and above all by Calvin, strangely came to match the "spirit of capitalism" (at least at the time of its emergence) and how this constituted a new dimension of the crisis of the gift-giving relationship.

Grace, Gift, and Capitalism

Weber's study *The Protestant Ethic and the Spirit of Capitalism* is probably his most often—and sometimes most bitterly—discussed work. The reason is simple: the relation Weber establishes between a religious movement and an economic process has been and still is fascinating in as far as he is able to connect two worlds that a priori seem far removed from each other. Weber is credited with a stroke of genius that supposedly opened new perspectives and left a lasting mark on the debate between cultural and religious history on the one hand and economic history on the other. This perception is inaccurate. Although it is true that the methodological rigor of Weber's analyses and the wealth of his documentation are remarkable, the fact remains that by the end of the nineteenth century his approach was already widespread in German sociology.[32]

No matter how stimulating Weber's study may be, it leaves unresolved a problem that might seem purely theological: how are we to consider the concept of grace that is at the core of the debate? To be sure, the word *grace* appears often in the text but only as a notion put forward by Reformation theologians. It is well known that the schism between Catholics and Protestants focused on the question of *predestination*, which was a radical version of the doctrine of grace. It is essential to understand that the doctrine of grace itself was the theological version of the concept of gift-giving. We must thus reexamine Weber's study and show how it comes close to these questions without being able to ask them. Perhaps the realm of gift-giving, which has been highlighted by contemporary anthropology since Mauss, can yield another approach to the disagreement between Protestants and Catholics and help formulate a different hypothesis regarding the so-called antieconomic attitude of the latter. In the final analysis the crucial point of divergence between the two dominant faiths of the Christian West was probably the question of the gift. How did this divergence lead to different economic fates? How does it concern any society confronted with capitalist logic? This is what we must try to determine.

The Protestant Ethic and the Question of Grace: Weber and Troeltsch

Soon after the publication of *The Protestant Ethic and the Spirit of Capitalism* a kind of vulgate emerged, according to which the Reformation encouraged, or even generated, the dynamic of capitalism, even though Weber states over and over again that this is absolutely not what he intends to demonstrate.[33] He even proposes the opposite hypothesis: it was the level of economic development of certain regions that promoted the

Reformation, which presupposes the existence of ancient circumstances "in which religious affiliation is not a cause of the economic conditions, but to a certain extent appears to be a *result* of them."[34] He adds, "There arises this historical question: why were the districts of highest economic development [in Germany] at the same time particularly favourable to a revolution in the Church?" (*PE* 36).[35] After this simple reminder, which refers to other research, Weber intends to bring out the original association that developed between these two phenomena. This association seems ironic to him, since the Reformation tended to increase rather than reduce religious domination over the individual. This appears paradoxical in as far as economic development—especially in its capitalist form— tends to destroy old beliefs and to liberate the individual from submission to religious institutions. If a privileged link did develop between Protestant Reformation and emerging capitalism, according to Weber it took place at the level of religious behavior—precisely as an ethic. It occurred as a de facto conjunction rather than as a deliberate project. In the first case Weber speaks of "elective affinities" or correlations between two specific aspects, "forms of religious belief and practical ethics" (*PE* 91). Second, this conjunction eluded the very people who were its agents. The Reformers passionately proclaimed the urgency for each believer to ensure his salvation: "We cannot well maintain that the pursuit of worldly goods, conceived as an end in itself, was to any of them of positive ethical value" (*PE* 89).

They were not even tempted by a program of moral reformation. The latter was only a consequence of religious choices: "We shall thus have to admit that the cultural consequences of the Reformation were to a great extent, perhaps in the particular aspects with which we are dealing predominantly, unforeseen and even unwished-for results of the labours of reformers. They were often far removed from or even in contradiction to all that they themselves thought to attain" (*PE* 90). Weber emphasizes the indirect character of this association: the causal relationship was not between faith and economic phenomena but between ethic and spirit. Ernst Troeltsch confirms this approach: "What [influence Protestantism] has here effected, it has effected indirectly and involuntarily, by doing away with old restrictions, and favouring the developments which we have already characterized in detail. . . . The important political and economic results of Calvinism were produced against its will."[36]

We need this reminder in order to be able to conceptualize the association between Protestantism and capitalism without presupposing simplistic causal relationships. In *The Protestant Ethic and the Spirit of Capitalism* Weber does not claim to define what he means by capitalism (he does so elsewhere) but only its *spirit*. He writes the term *Geist* in parentheses (at least in the 1905 version) probably to underscore its problematic and especially non-Hegelian character. He may also want to acknowledge his debt to Sombart, who was the first to use this phrase. What is this *spirit* about? It cannot be defined, as some have claimed, by the desire to acquire, the *auri sacra fames*. This desire is as old as the earliest civilizations and has been associated with the most diverse occupations.

According to Weber what distinguishes the spirit of capitalism is the rational domination of this impulse. This means that what matters is not acquisition, as such, but the seeking of profitability, the effort to invest through the development of exchanges, the defining of transactions and accounting in monetary terms, the use of freely provided labor, the mobilizing of knowledge and techniques toward maximizing return on investment, and the strengthening of property rights. In short, the capitalist phenomenon asserts itself at every level of social and economic activity—industrial, financial, commercial, administrative, technical, scientific, and legal.

Alone, however, these forms of rationalization are insufficient to account for the surprising dynamics of capitalism. Also needed is an invisible element, an attitude, an *ethos*, or a will that goes beyond the traditional framework of companies, even very efficient ones. "The question of the motive forces in the expansion of modern capitalism is not in the first instance a question of the origin of the capital sums which were available for capitalistic uses, but, above all, the spirit of capitalism. Where it appears and is able to work itself out, it produces its own capital and monetary supplies as the means to its ends, but the reverse is not true" (*PE* 68–69). This does not require adventurers, greedy speculators, or even outstanding financiers, Weber explains: "On the contrary, they were men who had grown up in the hard school of life, both calculating and daring at the same time, above all temperate and reliable, shrewd and completely devoted to their business, with strictly bourgeois opinions and principles" (69).

It is precisely on this point—dedication to duty—that the spirit of capitalism met the Protestant ethic.[37] Weber refuses to assume that the one produced the other. He confines himself to showing their remarkable conjunction. It showed up differently in Luther and Calvin. It also presented nuances in other Protestant trends (Pietists, Baptists, Methodists, and Quakers), but in every case the model was quite clear. Weber deserves immense credit for making it so obvious. He thus highlights the original equivalency established by Luther's use of the term *Beruf* between the notions of calling and of occupation. To be sure, Weber is aware that a large part of medieval theology had already begun to revalorize work.[38] There was more, however, to *Beruf:* the believer's occupation became his task par excellence—his calling—assigned to him by God for the duration of his life on earth. "This new meaning of the word corresponds to a new idea; it is the product of the Reformation" (*PE* 80).[39] Weber notes this paradox: far from causing a secularization of religious values, this transformation led to the penetration of religion in everyday life. This religious legitimization was what provided "a most favourable foundation for the conception of labour as an end in itself, as a calling which is necessary to capitalism" (*PE* 63).

This is the point Weber emphasizes, but there is another, possibly more decisive, one that he mentions only in passing. It can be summarized as follows: accomplishing professional tasks was more important than performing charitable works; it even replaced them. Luther went as far as to assume that the division of labor in and of itself fulfilled one's obligations to others (*PE* 81). In this way, according to Weber, Luther somewhat naively foreshadowed Adam Smith. Not so naively, actually, for what was being questioned (which Weber does not mention) was the whole question of the charitable attitude as the primary condition of the social bond. And yet this view was essential, not only to the Gospel or Pauline preaching but also to the Stoic tradition of good deeds—for example, Seneca and Marcus Aurelius. To be sure, Luther meant to do away with the practice of charity as "good deeds" guaranteeing salvation. It is easy to understand how Luther's challenging of this practice was consistent with a theological notion of faith as an act of unconditional trust in God's word. What was at stake in the rupture created by the Reformation, however, was clearly more than a religious revalorizing of one's occupation as calling. More fundamentally perhaps, it devalued the generous gesture that claimed to be essential to salvation, and in the end it presented this gesture as an economically irrational act. This needs to be emphasized: what was involved in the turning point created by the Reformation was more than the explicit affirmation of a shift in doctrine regarding faith; it was the implicit statement of a different hypothesis regarding the nature of the social bond. If this bond was assumed to be generated by the complementary nature of tasks instead of the reciprocity of gift-giving, then the transformation Weber discusses was an even more radical one. This is what Calvin's thought testifies to in a hyperbolic manner.

Calvin's thought rests entirely on his fundamental dogma: the doctrine of *predestination.* This was not a new doctrine. It had already been explicitly stated in the fourth century and the fifth by St. Augustine (whom Reformers and, later, Jansenists claimed to follow); it consisted of an unconditional affirmation of divine freedom confronting sinful humankind.[40] The first manifestation of this freedom was God's sovereign and final decision to save some—the chosen—and to condemn the rest. Despite its rigor Augustine's interpretation of this decision was relatively nuanced; but Calvin's interpretation was radical. For him the abyss between God and creature was insurmountable. Divine grace was granted or denied regardless of what man did. God determined his choice on the basis of his glory and majesty alone; this phrase, with its strikingly absolutist connotation, is consistently found in Calvin's writings. Moreover, no one could be ensured of being elected. No intermediary, whether preacher, church, or sacraments, could be of any help in the recognition of eternal salvation; God himself could not change his own eternal decree by which Christ died only for the elect. So a question arises: why do good if one's fate is already a foregone conclusion? Calvin's answer was that whether we are saved or not, it behooves us to act righteously *in order to honor God's majesty.* Weber recalls this statement without inquiring further into its genealogy. But why did the very ancient doctrine of divine grace—the *hén* of biblical scripture, the *kharis* of Paul's preaching, the *gratia* of Augustine—become this strange form of divine arbitrariness in determining salvation and damnation? In short, why did what had always been understood as the gesture of giving become the final act of judgment of a distant God? Hence this paradox: the concept of grace, whose purpose had always been to make the only and transcendent God closer to humans, became precisely what would set him forever out of their reach. This is the crucial stake of which Weber does not seem to be aware.

Regardless of the genealogy of the doctrine of predestination, we may wonder what its connection to the "spirit of capitalism" was. According to Weber, however, this connection was a real and deep one. Indeed, both the individual and the collective attitudes generated by this belief, as well as the entire set of religious and moral practices associated with it, caused one of the most considerable cultural and social changes in the history of the West, owing to the fact that this ethic—and especially its Calvinist version—turned out to be a perfect match for this "spirit of capitalism."

The first and most global consequence was what Weber calls "the disenchantment of the world" (*PE* 105), a phrase that has remained famous but has often been misunderstood.[41] Its first meaning is a refusal of any sacramental mediation, of any "magical" means of attaining salvation, and of any sensual or emotional religious expression (sometimes including religious music). Grace could not be sought; this left only the proclamation of God's transcendence and precluded from faith any form of idolatrous or superstitious attitude. Generally speaking, Weber designates as "magical" or "enchanted" (*verzaubert*) any world organized by rituals, which means lacking rationality. This view is no longer accepted by contemporary anthropology, which, on the contrary, regards symbolism as conceptually quite fertile. We can sense how this opens one possible way to a critique of Weber's views.

This "disenchantment" cannot be separated from another consequence: the affirmation of radical *individualism*. In the question of election every believer faced God alone. Since there was no conceivable intermediary, the question of salvation became strictly personal. Weber sees this as "one of the roots of this pessimistic individualism, without illusions, which today still manifests itself in the national character and the institutions of peoples that have a Puritan past" (*PE* 105). Troeltsch comes to the same conclusion: "This form of Christianity [Calvinism] produces a fundamental individualism of the most interiorized and harshest kind."[42] We will have to return to the transformations of the social bond generated by this individualism.

As for the enhanced status of occupations, it followed the same logic we observed in Luther's writings. There was a notable difference, however. For Luther work took on the function that "good deeds" used to perform. Calvin brought a more radical break between the order of grace and the world below, making it possible to live on both levels in completely separate ways. Since the individual could in no way affect his or her election, the only thing left was to dedicate oneself to earthly tasks, to one's occupation-calling as the only means available for the sinner to honor God's majesty.

But this was precisely how Christians could get closer to the certainty of salvation, at least if they had been truly saved. At this point effect turned back into cause, and the exemplary accomplishment of one's tasks became a sign that one had been chosen. This work discipline that drove Calvinists was what Weber calls "rational asceticism" (*PE* 119) or "asceticism in the world" (120), as opposed to asceticism outside the world, which characterized traditional monasticism.[43] Just as monks sought mastery of the body and desires by observing exacting rules applied at every moment of the day, so, too, did Puritans aim toward complete self-mastery in the rigorous and methodical exercise of their occupation. This is why—*unintentionally, and even without being aware of it*—the Protestant ethic turned out to be remarkably consistent with the spirit of capitalism in at least one of its central facets, since this spirit involved more than the requirement of methodical and honest work.

As in Luther's case, however, it seems that Weber does not closely consider a crucial point mentioned above, that is, the way in which the Calvinist ethic tends to dismiss the traditional social bond without being able to institute a different one of comparable strength. Weber does note a number of features, such as suspicion toward others (*PE* 106), the solitude of the subject cut off from any intermediary, and pessimism without illusions, all resulting in "this tremendous tension to which the Calvinist was doomed by an inexorable fate, admitting of no mitigation" (117). We must, then, ask this question: how could there be a community under those circumstances? What was the foundation of Calvinist sociality?

Nevertheless—and this is a crucial point—a *community* of believers did exist.[44] But what made it possible was the desire on everyone's part to testify by one's disciplined behavior to a life based on the hope (but not the certainty) of election. And yet, as Weber admits, this behavior in no way amounted to personal attention and affection toward others. On the contrary, "any personal relation of person to person which is purely based on sentiment—and thus devoid of rationality—can easily be suspected of idolatry of the flesh" (*PE* 224n30).[45] In summarizing the entire set of attitudes shown by denominations of the Calvinist faith, Weber asserts that "the English, Dutch and American Puritans were characterized by the exact opposite of the joy of living, a fact which is indeed, as we shall see, most important for our present study" (41).

Having reached this point, Weber interrupts the course of his analysis.

While he does provide a remarkable description of the effects of this overly harsh and even inhuman ethic, he does not say, or does not sufficiently say, what he thinks should constitute a real communal bond or what a more fully human or loving ethic would be. In many passages of his book he seems to grant that Catholicism embodies this ethic (although he disapproves of Catholicism's conservative aspects). Thus, in contrast to the inner solitude of the Calvinist, he speaks of the "Catholic, *authentically human*, to-and-fro between sin, repentance, and absolution, followed once again by sin" (*PE* 117, my emphasis). This remains rather allusive and needs to be elaborated. Troeltsch extends the question to the field of aesthetics: "Catholicism is, in fact, more at home with sensuousness, in the widest sense of the word, than Protestantism. And, accordingly, Catholicism entered into a much deeper and more vigorous union with Renaissance art than Protestantism did."[46]

This level of the expression of sensitivity and of the communal bond is probably the locus of one of the major social effects of the break between the Reformation and the Church of Rome. It is also the level where the difference between Catholic "traditionalism" and Protestant "modernity" can be located. If for Protestants God's grace was manifested in one's acceptance of one's occupation-calling (*Beruf*), then from that point forward the social bond had to be the result of this activity. This was certainly a powerful bond but a more objective and neutral one, a primarily functional bond, which ideally should be free of emotions. Even though Weber does not raise the question in these terms, he is right in considering this an extraordinary revolution. An older type of bond thus came to be disqualified. It remains to be determined what this bond was. Did the Catholic tradition remain faithful to it, and for what reasons? And what were the consequences for economic activity?

Giving and the Religious Ethic of Fraternity

One aspect of the "disenchantment of the world," while only indirectly discussed in *The Protestant Ethic*, is given more emphasis in other writings: the disappearance of what Weber calls "the religious ethic of fraternity." The loss of this ethic can be described as "disenchantment of the community." Reexamining this theme should make it possible to define a crucial issue of which Weber has an inkling but which lies beyond the horizon of his problematic.

Weber proposes the concept of fraternity within the framework of his research on religions concerned with salvation as deliverance (*Erlösung*).[47] What is the meaning of this term? Weber refers to prophetic or ascetic movements that emerge from within established religions such as Hinduism, Judaism, Christianity, and Islam. These movements generally include (1) an attempt to internalize beliefs and thus a devaluation of rituals and "magical" practices meant to attain salvation; (2) a search for a spiritual method making it possible to regularly obtain inner goods (such as spiritual peace, clear-headedness, and moral strength), asceticism being one possible but not necessary variant of this search; and (3) an attempt to sublimate one's relationships with others into a universal love that makes every human being worthy of the believer's attention and love.

The last point is relevant for us. This love requires on the one hand the repression of kinship relationships (cutting oneself off from family and clan, as Jesus demanded, for instance); on the other hand, it establishes a community in which relationships between members are modeled on the forms of "natural kinship" (*Sippe*). This is what Weber calls "a religious ethic of brotherliness."[48] What this ethic primarily entails is reciprocity in giving gifts and providing services, material assistance in ensuring subsistence, and mutual support in suffering. The effects of this ethic on social life are significant. They can cause a softening of hierarchical relationships: the powerful owe help and protection to the weak. On an economic level the ethic of fraternity prohibits interest-bearing loans and encourages voluntary assistance and the sharing of wealth. Finally, on a more general level this ethic turns all relationships with others into *personal* relationships and shuns rational scrutiny of situations in favor of an emotional attitude of solidarity.

Weber explains that it is precisely from the starting point of this communal experience of fraternity and *personal* reciprocity, at first restricted to a "neighborhood grouping," that a leap toward universal love can occur, toward the imperative of an oblatory and generous bond with *anyone*, whether stranger, foreigner, or even enemy. According to Weber, this offer of love for the other without any distinction is what Baudelaire defined as the "holy prostitution of the soul"[49] so characteristic of Christian love.

A moment arrived when this religious ethic of fraternity ran into deep conflict with the very movement of economic development. This movement set up a rationality that had to put aside personal involvement in the exchange of goods, define the cost of every productive activity, obtain interest for the productive investment of capital, and avoid bargaining and deal with set prices in order for transactions to be efficient. The Protestant ethic happened to meet these requirements, although this was not its direct aim, while the Catholic tradition remained attached to "the religious ethic of fraternity," as Weber suggests on several occasions.

This gives us a clearer picture. Nevertheless, something enigmatic remains: the role of the concept of grace and the doctrine of predestination in the disagreement between Protestants and Catholics. Weber does take this doctrine very seriously but only in as far as it was, in Protestantism, the source of a radical break between the realm of faith and that of "asceticism in the world." He is not interested in its genealogy. As we have seen, the doctrine of predestination was a radicalization of the doctrine of grace, which was the theological version of the concept of gift-giving, at least in its Christian formulation. We need to reexamine the main elements of this significant question in order to clarify the genealogy of this *religious ethic of fraternity* and to understand its flip side: the profitable relationship that dominates commercial activity.

Weber is not particularly interested in the sociology of gift exchange.[50] Today, however, in the wake of Mauss, the literature on ritual reciprocal gift exchanges is one of the most reliable and fascinating in modern anthropology. Determining in what way the *religious ethic of fraternity* discussed by Weber was indeed a crucial instantiation of the gift-exchange phenomenon should therefore illuminate the set of issues raised by the process of "disenchantment of the world."

It has often been said and shown that a critical approach to the concept of gift-giving requires that ceremonial gift exchange not be assessed by the criterion of moral giving. On the contrary, a correct analysis of the specificity of ceremonial gift exchange can make it possible to understand the nature of moral giving. We must recall that no matter how institutional and public the practice of reciprocal gift exchange may be, the relationship established between partners is, above all, a *personal* one. It is so in two ways. First, to give is to give something of oneself, or, more precisely, it is *to give oneself* in the thing offered. Second, the exchange most often takes place between statutory partners (between brothers-in-law, between members of a clan and their chief, among chiefs) or between chosen partners (as in the Trobriand *kula* circle). Let me add that this ceremonial and bilateral form of gift exchange is specific to traditional societies in which social organization is identified with the kinship system. The question that now arises, and that will bring us back to the question of grace, is the following: what happens when traditional societies come to be included within larger institutional entities—such as empires—or are themselves transformed into political societies? Most often, practices of reciprocity are preserved and remain relatively unaffected by the emergence of a central administration. The image of a powerful external authority, however, can have a decisive impact on the idea of an asymmetrical gift, whether unequal (in which the subordinate cannot really reciprocate) or unilateral (in which only the superior can give).

At this point, based on the results obtained in the previous chapters, a global reexamination of the question of gift-giving becomes possible. We have considered three different types of gift-giving relationships: (1) the system of ceremonial reciprocal gift exchange found in traditional societies, the main purpose of which is recognition of the partners and the development of a network of communal bonds; (2) unilateral giving on the part of a deity, ruler, or city, various versions of which are provided by the Greek *kharis* and the Biblical *hēn*; this is what is called grace—a favor generously granted regardless of the merit of the recipient; and (3) individual giving of a moral type, which is based on a free decision on the part of the giver and may or may not be reciprocated but involves, above all, generosity and compassion; this is the gesture that Aristotle considers a virtue and that Seneca advocates for all to practice. This is probably the level at which what Weber calls "the religious ethic of fraternity" can be situated.

What is at stake in every case is the form of the social bond. When—as in the Greek case—a shift occurred from a clan-based society to a political society, which is to say from a traditional system based on a tight network of gift exchange to a system organized around a center (the *meson* of public space), it coincided with a crisis of ceremonial gift exchange and ritual reciprocity from which vindicatory justice could not be separated; classical tragedy (especially the *Oresteia*) testifies to this crisis. A requirement then emerged to invent for the new community—the *polis*—a bond whose power could match that of the bond ceremonial gift exchange used to provide. The answer was found in the dual movement of divine *kharis* and individual *philia*. The community as a whole had to be engaged in a relationship that ensured its unity, just as presents and acts of assistance between individuals also manifested this grace.

This practice of generous gestures and this ethic of giving remained reciprocal (Aristotle's morality testifies to this) because what was at stake was the preservation of the network of attachments. Now, *reciprocity* itself underwent a crisis; it could no longer be understood, as shown by *De beneficiis*, in which reciprocity was suspected of aiming at gaining an advantage—*do ut des*. This gave rise to the requirement of pure giving without any expectation of reciprocation. The reason why ceremonial gift exchange was no longer understood was that, within the framework of political society, it had lost its institutional function of public recognition (as the means of access to rank, the reason for matrimonial alliance, and the foundation of vindicatory justice). If gift exchange no longer had meaning for Seneca, and if giving still appeared to him to be the only source of the bond between humans, then the only form of giving that remained conceivable was unilateral and generous giving emulating the gift from the gods. Without unconditional generosity the social bond dissolved. In short, after the crisis of ceremonial gift exchange associated with the emergence of the city, Seneca provides an exemplary expression of the crisis of reciprocal giving associated with the dislocation of the city.

Each of these crises testifies to a specific stage in a process of internalizing of the gift-giving relationship, an increasingly radical movement toward purity of intent and unconditional generosity. It can be said that Luther's dissidence, and later Calvin's, instantiated this type of crisis. What was now being questioned was generous giving—giving without reciprocation—between humans. But a new and unknown threshold had been crossed: only God could give, and no human gift could add anything to his gift, which had to be received with an attitude of absolute trust: faith. As for the rest, what mattered was to keep to what constituted one's *calling* as human being: ordinary life in one's occupation. The "religious ethic of fraternity" was thus dismissed and the protestant ethic found itself in objective adequacy with the spirit of capitalism, which thrived from the moment when and in every place where the practice of gift exchange faded away. By bringing the entire realm of gift-giving to the side of God, the doctrine of predestination left the field of social relationships to regulation by work and business.

The gift-giving relationship and the personal bond it implied were now experienced as burdensome because a more profound movement was emerging. It was as if, beyond theological requirements, the Reformers' thought was ruled by the logic of a deep transformation that mostly affected Europe's urban world of commerce. It is precisely within these classes that a type of rationality that until then had only concerned clerics prevailed at the very level of everyday life.[51] It is also within these classes that commercial exchange, ruled by contract, prevailed over relationships of service, mutual assistance, or gift exchange, even when involving small-scale operations. It could be said that the legitimate denunciation of the abuse to which "good deeds" were subjected made it possible to delegitimize the relationship of charity at a time when it was important to promote the neutral and rational model of the contract—a model required to enable the type of exchange needed by capitalism. A disciple of Hegel would view this as a prodigious ruse of history. A disciple of Weber would feel obligated to extend or even go beyond Weber's analyses or at least to complement them. For instance, the following question must be asked: what happened in southern Europe during the same period? As early as the first pages of *The Protestant Ethic*, Weber raises the question of the backwardness of Roman Catholic regions in terms of economic development, yet he also often notes that Catholics were able to preserve a social bond more human and more deeply rooted in friendship than the bond that Protestants instituted. Was it because they had remained more closely associated with communities of farmers and craftsmen, despite the growth of great cities based on trade? Or was there a reason based on doctrine? In short, and in order to support the very thesis proposed by Weber, we need to examine the Catholic ethic and the spirit of noncapitalism.

Catholic Ethic, Grace, and the Economy

It is surprising that, in spite of Weber's remarks on the resistance of Catholic populations to the process of capitalist development, no serious attempt was made to interpret this inertia. It was observed but not explained. Weber does raise this question, reminding a contradictor of the importance of taking into account the effect of cultural conditions on economic history: "Why did the Catholic Church not develop these combinations and a type of training similarly oriented toward capitalism?"[52] A detailed answer would be welcome. It seems that Weber finds it sufficient to understand the general schema of the Catholic case as the converse of ascetic Protestantism. This is a coherent view, but it would be more interesting for someone to conduct an investigation on the other side.[53]

It so happens that the elements of this study can now be found in Bartolomé Clavero's *Antidora: Antropología católica de la economía moderna.*[54] What makes Clavero's investigation especially interesting, in spite of its limitations, is that, thanks to its method, documentation, and hypotheses, it convincingly provides the element missing from Weber's and Troeltsch's analyses. The two German sociologists make it possible to understand the deep connection between Protestantism and emerging capitalism. Clavero makes crystal clear the relationship between the Catholic doctrine and a conception of the economy that resisted the very emergence of capitalism. And yet presenting things in these terms still implies a retrospective approach, as if the rise of capitalism had been either resisted or applauded by one or the other, whereas no one at the time identified it or even recognized it as a global process. Catholics were no more aware that they were resisting capitalism than Calvinists were aware that they were promoting it. By placing himself as much as possible at the level of the agents of bygone eras, Clavero shows that things were experienced and understood in ways entirely different from what they appear to be in retrospect.

With respect to the Catholic world it is usually considered sufficient to mention the central role supposedly played by the condemnation of profit, identified with usury, in hampering banking and trade. This point is well established.[55] But how can we account for the fact that Luther's preaching included no less strict a condemnation? Clearly, this generalization is insufficient. Actually, the prohibition of usury was only the negative side of the essentially positive injunction of generous reciprocity. Clavero discovers a name for it, which is recurrent in theological treatises and manuals on morality during the Renaissance: *antidora,* a term taken from the Greek that literally means "countergift." In short, usury (a term whose extension included every kind of profit) was condemned, above all, because it infringed on the requirement of charity and the obligation to reciprocate. Things were more complex, however, as we will see. This injunction implied an entire mode of thinking associated with notions of love and justice, the natural and the artificial, intent and formalism, symmetrical and proportional equality, and the family and the state.

Before returning to these issues, let me make a preliminary comment on Clavero's analyses. In advancing his hypothesis the author could be expected to make an attempt to find out more about generous reciprocity, either in earlier Western thought or more generally in what anthropology since Mauss has brought to light about the gift-exchange relationship in traditional societies. Clavero does not raise these questions. He even appears to preclude them, to the extent that his methodological concern to rely solely on documents from the period in question (the sixteenth and seventeenth centuries in Spain) aims to avoid the risk of projecting alien concepts onto a specific past. This choice unquestionably enhances the credibility of his demonstration, since it produces convincing results without outside recourse. It also weakens its scope, however, since it ignores the entire philosophical tradition (exemplified by Aristotle and Seneca), as well as the entire theological tradition (that of the Church Fathers and medieval theologians) regarding the condemnation of profit and the promotion of free generosity. Most significant, it fails to situate this "Catholic anthropology" within the very general framework of a problematic of gift-giving that has been observed in every traditional culture. Finally, although his argument shows how the rejection of profit was formulated, it does not explain why the Catholic world tended to resist the emergence of economic practices that so well suited the Protestant ethic. Clarifying this difference constitutes a most demanding theoretical task.

The main aspects of Clavero's demonstration focus on a set of issues that can be summarized as follows: the priority given to generous and charitable relationships over contractual and legal ones, to proportional and distributive equality over strict commutative equality, and to family order and the order of relationships among friends over public and administrative authorities. These three types of priorities can be observed in theological treatises, as well as in exchange practices. Their ubiquity implies a whole range of important consequences regarding legal statements, debates about the legitimacy of business dealings, and finally the preeminence of the order of grace over everything that could be thought of as "the economy."

Let us consider first of all the generous relationship. In the discourse of Catholic theologians the social relationship was understood to be defined by charity. Charity amounted to benevolence, friendship, wishing the good of others, and providing them with assistance and support. This relationship was presented as the only "natural" and spontaneous one. It was natural because it arose from the order of the world chosen by God.

In the same way, God's relationship toward humanity was characterized by pure generosity devoid of calculation. There was a community among human beings only because the same type of bond that God had established with them also existed between them. "It is with the same charity that we honor God and our neighbors," Vitoria, a Spanish theologian, writes at the beginning of the seventeenth century (Clavero 49). From this alone did the illicit character of *usury* follow. Usury designated every form of profit in lending. One contemporary of Vitoria claimed, "There is no doubt that accepting usury for money exchanged is in itself unjust" (Clavero 51). Usury was identified with profit of every kind. At stake in this refusal was nothing less than God's command: "the Lord says, grant each other loans without expecting anything in return" (Clavero 51). *This did not, however, prevent the beneficiary from returning more than he had been given, not for the lender's profit but as a token of gratitude.* The surplus in restitution was in turn a sign of generosity. Vitoria and so many other theologians of his time state the issue in these surprising terms: lenders, in fact, give a kind of gift, and recipients who return it with a surplus merely reciprocate and honor the gift they have received. "Obtaining something through friendship does not constitute usury," another theologian proclaims (Clavero 100). This is indeed the operation performed by Catholic thought, translating loans into gifts and interests received into counter-gifts: *antidora*. The economic transaction did take place, but it was understood or at least presented as a gesture of generous reciprocity. This means that it remained within the realm of the personal relationship, within the logic of a "warm" social bond.[56]

The reasoning of these theologians who gave priority to the requirement of charity and the gift-giving relationship thus ended up recoding profitable activities in terms of this logic. It is easy to surmise what the "modern" problem is: disconnecting economic activity from this gift-exchange relationship, which remained personal and fraught with intense sociality, dependency, and emotions. This was precisely the disconnecting that was achieved by the Lutheran doctrine of occupation as calling (*Beruf*) and by the Calvinist concept of asceticism in the world. Thus the major challenge faced by Catholic doctrine was not only to devalue business in favor of charitable relationships but also to present business activities as a version of these generous relationships. This moral theology of exchange required that every form of commercial exchange be translated in terms of reciprocal gift. The agents of financial exchanges were running the risk of merely playing on words and hypocritically presenting money-lending as a gift and repayment with interest as reciprocation of the gift. It is precisely to ward off this risk of abuse that the question of *intention* was introduced: the generous relationship had to be primarily an inner disposition; otherwise, the gift-giving relationship could conceal "mental usury."[57] Intention made all the difference between lucrative and oblatory gestures. The power of intention, therefore, made it possible to constantly return commercial exchange to the order of charity: to loan as if one were giving, to pay back as if one were giving back liberally. Intention operated the legitimate translation of the commercial relationship into a gift-giving relationship.

This is why the order of charity was radically different from the legal relationship, from the order of *justice* ruled by the category of the *contract*: "The law of friendship (*jus amicitiae*) precedes and prevails over the Law itself" (Clavero 49). What is the purpose of friendship? It is to make friends, as Aristotle had already stated. This is another way of saying that the exchange of goods had no other purpose than to preserve or strengthen the social bond. This was not the purpose of the order of *justice*. Its aim was to preserve the formal equilibrium of relationships. Justice defined what should be done according to convention, not to nature. It ensured that no one was wronged but nothing more. It did not imply feelings of gratitude on the part of the partners involved. Thus it could guarantee that the merchant would be compensated for his efforts and his work. But these earnings had no value in terms of charity. The legal relation did not engage partners *personally*. It did not generate a social bond. It strictly ensured abidance and punished those who failed to meet commitments. Thus it functioned in a privatory rather than positive mode. It distributed, restricted, protected, constrained, prevented, punished, confirmed, and concluded. It did not create a bond between two individuals.

The most constant and relevant expression of the legal relationship is probably the contract. In business it sets prices, financial interests, and the temporal limits of commitments. It is constraining; that is, in the end the obligations it establishes—such as guaranteed profits—are imposed under threat of sanctions. It does not directly require good intentions or the expression of benevolence, even if such feelings can be associated with it or promote it. This is why the contract is the clearest expression of the order of justice. It would be excessive, however, to reduce the idea of justice to this form alone. There were indeed two types of justice. The first, which was strictly contractual and egalitarian, was called *commutative*. The other, more flexible and considered superior, and which remained compatible with the order of charity, was *distributive* or *proportional* justice. These were, of course, Aristotelian categories taken up by Thomas Aquinas in the Middle Ages.[58]

Commutative justice presupposed or instituted formal equality between partners. It ignored differences in status or resources, and it took into account only the thing exchanged. In this respect it was abstract and impersonal. This is why it was suitable for contracts, which also involve objects and tend to ignore the uniqueness of the persons contracting. Distributive justice stood higher because it was more precise and remained compatible with the order of charity. It was proportional in that it took into account the status of agents, such as the differences between husbands and wives, parents and children, masters and servants, lords and peasants. In these theologians' view this meant that it was based on the "natural" order of the world.

This conception of a natural order of things meant, above all, that society was nothing more than the association of families. Aristotle, who establishes the primary and spontaneous character of the family, nevertheless considers that the order of the city, which presupposes the family, is different from and superior to it.[59] This idea still persisted in scholastic thought. Within Catholic theology, however, the family had to a large extent prevailed as the ultimate social authority. "The family prevailed and with it charity, a dimension that has priority over justice. There existed a certain autonomy of the family that was superior to the civil, political or social order, just as there existed a religion that determined this autonomy by capturing it" (Clavero 189–90). Relationships within the Christian community were expressed in the language of the family—father, brother, sister, mother—and presupposed its natural character. This was not new, but it was reinforced by the erosion of the civil order. This was also why an economy that claimed to be "natural" was supposed to concern exclusively the family, the household, very literally the *oikos*—hence *oikonomia*. Clavero writes: "There is no general economy, but there are particular economies for each household" (144). On this point Clavero's analysis must be complemented by the knowledge developed in contemporary anthropology: the family in question was a very large set of relatives by blood or alliance, what was then called relations, the Roman or medieval *familia*, bound together by reciprocal obligations of service and mutual assistance (Weber would readily accept that this is the framework within which what he calls "the religious ethic of fraternity" could bloom).

These conceptions and practices entailed certain consequences and implications that we can now clearly identify. First, this world of the *antidora* precluded the possibility of an economy in the modern sense of the word. There was a de facto economy (as production and exchange) but *without economic aim*. Clavero should be reminded that this had been the case in the entire classical world, as well as in all traditional civilizations. Economic aim—in the modern sense of the word—presupposes the rationality of investments aiming to make profits in order to further increase the ability to invest. In contrast, in the traditional attitude the purpose of profit was to increase one's well-being and prestige. From this point of view Catholic culture was essentially faithful to immemorial practices of reciprocity between allies and to aristocratic values of sumptuary liberality. Weber is right to claim that it was impervious to capitalist rationality.

The second consequence was that the primacy of the relationship of charity over the legal order resulted in a lack of the legal formulation required to regulate contractual exchanges. It was precisely in this respect that Protestantism took the turn toward modernity by allowing the business world to enact precise rules regarding commercial and financial transactions. The rational economy could not function without these conventions, which set prices, obligations, and deadlines. But then what of the world of the *antidora*? "What developed was indeed a relationship of grace. Banking activities could leave no room for economic forecast or legal responsibility. . . . The legal system did not offer enough protection; judges were incapable of providing it." Indeed, "banks could not even rely on a specific legal process" (Clavero 170, 150). What was there instead? According to Clavero there was a society of patronage and constituencies, in which relationships based on gift-giving and on the providing of services entailed the personal commitment of the partners to each other. These were relationships between protectors and protected; they did not constitute a marginal dimension but an entire cosmos, with heavenly protectors on one side (saints with various attributions) and earthly protectors on the other (relatives or friends in positions of power). These analyses would need to be extended to show how a certain classical form of *corruption* was nothing more than the perverse intersection between the traditional logic of gift exchange and the logic of modern business; corruption marked the locus where the two clashed and became confused and incompatible. There is something remarkable in this: whereas in the Protestant context the term *grace* invariably referred to the doctrine of predestination, in the Catholic context it implied, above all, the idea of charitable gesture but also of personal favor and almost clanlike solidarity.

What conclusions can we draw from this investigation? There is no doubt that confronting the results of Clavero's research with those obtained by Weber and Troeltsch makes it possible to grasp the distance that separates the two traditions of Western Christianity (the case of the orthodox tradition remains to be examined). It is generally accepted that Catholic theology and preaching remained faithful to the concepts of charity and generous giving, that this led to a more personal and active sociality than in the Protestant world, and that the latter proved to be more modern and efficient. But this does not explain why the divergence developed within the Christian tradition. The fact that the Protestant ethic turned out to be in concordance with the business world and emergent capitalism (Weber does not make any further claims), whereas the Catholic ethic seems to have resisted them, does not explain why the Reformation spread primarily in northern Europe or why Latin countries remained more faithful to Rome. The reason usually given is the contrast between an urban and progressive North on the one side and an agricultural and traditionalist South on the other. There would thus be a contrast between the individualistic spirit of the cities and the ancient solidarity of the countryside. But then, what about northern Italy, where early capitalism first emerged? What about the great commercial centers of France and southern Germany, which remained Catholic? Conversely, how can Luther's success among the most impoverished farmers be explained? Additional parameters need to be taken into account, such as the fact that the Protestant Reformation spread almost exclusively in the areas that were not subject to the tradition of Roman law.[60] Other, probably less familiar, elements would need to be brought out to demonstrate that the divergence between Protestantism and Catholicism originated less in doctrinal differences than in a dividing line between two different models of formation of the social bond, the anthropological roots of which remain to be unearthed. The first of these models is primarily based on interdependence and the logic of needs; the second is based on the recognition of statuses and on personal commitment, in which it remains close to the traditional forms of community and thus less modern.

. . .

In his analysis of the Protestant ethic (especially that of Calvinism and the sects derived from it) Weber emphasizes the importance of the doctrine of predestination in the ascetic behavior of the believers, as well as the rational economic consequences of this ethic. He is aware that the doctrine of predestination is a central element of the theology of grace. But (along with many others) he fails to realize that the thought centered around the concept of grace is, above all, a doctrine of unilateral giving and must be situated as such within the tradition of ceremonial gift exchange in general, of which it constitutes a major transformation.

From a sociological point of view the question of grace can therefore be considered as enfolding three tightly interwoven elements. The first is the fact that this worldview has always emerged as a response to the upheaval in traditional social relationships that occurred when the organization of the group shifted from the multilateral reciprocity of kinship to a model of central authority that defined every group or individual in relation to this authority, uniting them all through a single gift from above. This shift resulted in the emergence of a debt or obligation that had to be honored or fulfilled in the same way by every member of the group (one of the instituted forms of this reply has been taxation).

The second crucial aspect of the question of grace is the process of affirmation of the authority of truthfulness associated with the figure of the one and only giver. This authority was the source of the law. It could be the authority of the city (as in Greece) or of the deity recognized as being exclusive (as in biblical writing). The only entity able to give was also the only one able to know. This structure of exclusive knowledge was manifested by the privileges that the State granted to itself—or was granted— or by those of the Church, which assigned itself guardianship of God's favor, as in the "administration of grace" discussed by Weber (in reference, among other things, to the abuses committed by the Church of Rome and denounced by the Reformation).

Third, the thought centered on the concept of grace as it came to be radicalized in Luther's and Calvin's preaching amounted to making the gesture of the one and only giver so absolute that any human reply would be deemed futile or arrogant. No reciprocation could be made to God. He did not need humans. His gesture was too boundless.[61] Human generosity—charitable work—thus lost its legitimacy. This transcendent character of the one and only gift traced a radical dividing line and opened an impassable gap between God's gift and any possible human reply. It instituted an admirable—or a terrifying—divine transcendence. This was Pascal's view. There could only be absolute trust—faith—in the giver. It was this clear-cut and uncompromising dualism that established on one side the grace/faith binomial and on the other the contract/profit pair and that legitimized the absence of communication between them. The extreme degree of separation between these two realms led to a purely spiritual faith that loomed above, without organizing it, a secular life subject to its own rules. The management of human activities became autonomous. Profitable exchange could prosper without any interference from the gift-giving relationship.

We must now return to the beginning of our inquiry: what happened to the Greek *kharis*, which blended charm and generosity? To the Latin *ratia*, which fulfilled and forgave? To biblical grace—*hén*—which was favor and tenderness? To *kharis* according to Paul, which constituted the core of Christ's message ("Love is the fulfilling of the law" [Romans 13:10])? The theological history of grace is the history of a disgrace. It is as if giving itself—the gesture of honoring and fulfilling—had lost, in the view of the authorized experts in matters of divinity, the only quality that made it a grace: unconditional generosity, the splendor of a gift that expects no reply, and, for the recipient of this grace, the joy of receiving when nothing was expected. But can the addressee remain careless when he or she is aware that he or she owes everything? Relationships of grace can probably not constitute the source of the framework of public life—that is, of the political institutions that formally guarantee the citizens' mutual recognition as subjects of law—nor can relationships of grace intervene in the realm of useful exchange without running the risk of perverting it (this was the profound requirement of the Protestant ethic). The order of justice is indispensable in those realms as constituting the order of equity—better yet, of liberty. In this arrangement the objective mediation provided by money plays a decisive role. This role is what we must now examine.

PART THREE

JUSTICE IN EXCHANGES AND THE SPACE OF TRADE

The Emergence of the Marketplace

Enough, therefore, of your banning philosophers from possessing money: no one has condemned wisdom to poverty.

SENECA, *On the Happy Life*

To one who works, wages are not reckoned as a gift but as something due.

PAUL, EPISTLE TO THE ROMANS

The intellectual concept under which the empirical concept of money falls is therefore the concept of a thing that, in the circulation of possession (*permutatio publica*), determines the *price* of all other things (goods), among which even the sciences belong, insofar as they would not otherwise be taught to others.

KANT, *The Metaphysics of Morals*

As for writers, their prize is to be found in the esteem of their peers and in the cash registers of booksellers.

BAUDELAIRE, "The Respectable Drama and Novel"

We are the heirs to a strange history. As far as cultural activities, the production of works of art, the transmission of knowledge, and scholarly research are concerned, for a long time it was as if the very idea of remuneration was regarded as suspicious or even in certain cases as intolerable. This history seems to be coming to an end before our eyes; it is even already over, at least in the West, or in the industrialized world.

Was this a regrettable yet unavoidable evolution? Didn't the traditional suspicion toward money have deep and respectable roots in the conviction that certain activities or goods could not participate in the circuit of profitable exchange without being threatened in their very essence? Isn't money to this day the major figure of corruption, just as it was ten or twenty-five centuries ago? Today its triumph is more serene and even more glorious, but is this merely because our old misgivings have now vanished? Or have we become more cynical? Yet again, has money's technical efficiency erased its immoral effects?

The starting point of this inquiry was the refusal observed among philosophers (and no less so among writers and artists) to envision their activity within the framework of profitable exchange. We tried to understand this refusal as a claim to a very ancient relationship of reciprocity, as the affirmation of the priceless character of the transmission of wisdom or of the circulation of works of art or intellect—the remuneration of which could only be provided within the framework of the recognition of talent. It was as if the only possible relationship between wise men, scholars, and artists, on one side, and those who requested their competence or productions, on the other, had been one of reciprocal gift-giving rather than commercial exchange.

We discussed this resistance and assessed this attitude without addressing the—nowadays unavoidable—issue of the existence of the *marketplace*. To speak of the marketplace in singular form already presupposes that it is no longer a particular activity that would have its place as one among others within the whole of the social realm. The marketplace has become a global dimension of society. It constitutes a "total social phenomenon," to use the phrase coined by Mauss to designate gift-exchange relationships; it is not restricted to the activity of exchange but involves and transforms every aspect of social life.

This is why raising the question of money can no longer be done by repeating the old formulations. The contrast or tension between merchants and artists is no longer between two different statutory types. It merely illustrates the diversity of occupations within a society largely defined by its economic activity, itself dominated by the financial programs and the banks that steer and control the various sectors of production and exchange.

Hence the current situation: nothing—whether scientific research, cultural activities, artistic creation, teachers' and researchers' salaries, or writers' remuneration—can now escape commercial evaluation. In each case the question of market value is raised in a specific manner. This in no way guarantees the objective character of this evaluation. But it is a field of evaluation from which no one can now be released. Besides, we are accustomed to this situation, and we readily accept it. And yet this mode of thinking is the most alien that can be conceived to every known tradition. Accepting it has required forcing, or even assaulting, the most ancient and venerable conceptions concerning the status of the works of the mind. It took a powerful process to set up in our civilization for this worldview to become familiar to us. This process began with the idea that certain activities that had seemed impossible to quantify (because they were too closely associated with the human body, too engaged in a relationship with others) could be bought and sold as if they had been mere consumer goods: work, services, land, knowledge, artworks, and money itself—this is what Polanyi analyzes in *The Great Transformation*.

Artists, philosophers, or scientists can no longer conceive of their activity outside of the market economy. Most of them are quite comfortable with this and would not accept, in the name of an immemorial suspicion on money and profit, to be treated any differently from those engaged in other professional fields. Something of the spirit of gift-giving may survive in their relationship to a public (since on both sides the idea of a grace received and reciprocated still remains), yet what matters most is that within the market society remuneration must be provided in currency, even if it is acknowledged that this remuneration is far from proportional to authentic talent and recognized merit.

What is the source of this consensus on the recognition of the market economy and on the monetary evaluation of activities that were long considered to stand outside of this space? Is it surrender to the fait accompli? Or is it a realization—at least an implicit realization—that money is not necessarily the evil instrument and universal poison denounced by Plato, despised by Rousseau, deconstructed by Marx, and still recently castigated by Flaubert and Péguy.

The classical age accepted the existence of a distinction between legitimate wealth (which could be normally expressed in currency) and money as object of insatiable desire. Modernity operates a different distinction (clearly found in the French language) between money as currency—that is, as financial instrument (means of payment, reserve instrument, expression of prices)—and money as instrument of power and corruption. A shift has therefore occurred in proportion to the affirmation of the market economy. In this shift the technical aspect of currency has been defined with ever-increasing precision and evermore readily accepted, until it came to constitute the object of a complex science. In a way, the relationship to money has been dedramatized.

This is, in fact, a very different history, a long history, in a way parallel to the one we have been tracing. We now need to establish a different genealogy that will bring to light not only the technical abilities of currency but also, and above all, its role as one of the decisive instruments of justice and liberty—so much so that it constitutes a source of anxiety for a tradition of thought in which the conviction that money remains *by its very nature* linked to greed, imposture, deception, or corruption remains very deeply rooted. What happens if this conviction is breached, if truth is no longer at stake in this, contrary to Plato's belief?

To provide an answer, we must reexamine the philosophical definition of money—its relationship to measurement, its homology with language, its means of expressing the order of the world or even of constituting it. I do not propose to present a history of the economy or even to trace the emergence of modern currency, although this history cannot be ignored, and I will constantly refer to it. My focus, however, will be on the elements of this history that raise questions specific to philosophy as the discipline whose purpose is to question the nature of truth but that initially viewed itself as being incompatible with any profitable activity.

Ceremonial Money and Commercial Money

Today the symbolic issue of money seems diluted into a technical analysis of the monetary phenomenon. No one questions the fact that money constitutes a remarkable and indispensable instrument for the evaluation and exchange of goods. There is no denying that it is the most elaborate instrument of economic activity, especially within today's complex and all-powerful financial investment networks. This is not the place for a presentation of these operations, even though we will have to take them into account.

What matters for us is this observation: nowadays no one finds it surprising that scholars, artists, writers, or philosophers are paid. There is no doubt that the gift/countergift model that underlay the conception that Plato, Aristotle, and medieval thinkers had of the transmission of knowledge—and especially of wisdom—no longer constitutes the background of the modern conception on this question. Yet even if its ceremonial forms are highly variable and hardly constraining, this model retains a strong presence in interpersonal relationships—whether they involve friendship, love, festive occasions, or charitable assistance. In the professional world, however, payment for work or production seems entirely determined by the rules of the marketplace (although this does not preclude a symbolic evaluation of the social relationships associated with this work in terms of prestige, esteem, preferential status, or other forms of public valuation).

It would be tempting to say that this transformation very precisely followed that of money, at least if we are to trust the claims made by many economic historians or even the analyses presented by many ethnologists, which proclaim in unison that a gradual shift occurred from a form of primitive money to the more complex forms constituted by commercial money. This primitive money is claimed to have constituted an awkward preparation for the sophisticated procedures effected by commercial money. This would explain why, as this evolution developed, the forms of commercial exchange came, quite predictably, to replace those of ceremonial exchange. Thus, to return to the problem with which we started, it was normal that wage-earning philosophers came to take the place of the wise men who lived on the gifts they received.

Is this explanation acceptable? Clearly, it is not. This genealogy is inaccurate. It is no more than a legend too often used, even by the best authors, as an introduction to the history of economy and money. To clarify things, we must return to the essential difference between what has sometimes been called "savage money" ("ceremonial money" would be a better term) and commercial money. This raises the entire issue of money as instrument; only by going beyond the old clichés and ancient anathemas can the value of the priceless be considered in a new light.

Misunderstandings Regarding "Savage Money"

The introductions to works dealing with the history of money still frequently present the origins of money as going back to the seashells, cowries, pearl necklaces, cut quartz, and other precious objects used by traditional societies in ceremonial exchanges (matrimonial alliances, compensation in cases of murder, offerings to ancestors, or any other form of gift exchange). The objects in these exchanges are thus designated as "archaic" or "primitive" money. Researchers with a less-evolutionist bent call them "savage" money. Mauss was tempted by the beautiful medieval German phrase "reputation" currency, but he did not adopt it. As will become clearer in the continuation of this inquiry, however, a simple and conceptually rigorous term is available: "ceremonial money."

It has been well-established that these forms of money involve units of value and that in the traditions under consideration their quantification is subject to a form of evaluation that is often very strict. It must be stated unequivocally that comparison with commercial money can be taken no further. If the word *money* is understood only in terms of its commercial use, it must be recognized that the so-called savage money is, in fact, not money at all but what should be called a *unit of reciprocal offering*. It is remarkable that (leaving aside certain exceptions that would need to be examined within their specific contexts) these units are reserved for strictly ceremonial situations and that their use in ordinary exchanges would be viewed as the expression of a lack of respect or even, in certain cases, as a serious transgression.

We must therefore recognize that when so many ethnographers speak of "money," they do so in a metaphorical manner, sometimes knowingly, other times out of mere convenience and because of the obvious lack of an adequate terminology. This approximation becomes more apparent when we compare two different types of units of reciprocal offerings. For example, on the one hand units constituted by cattle (frequently found in the Bantu civilizations of Africa) are rarely designated as money by observers, even though cattle have the same function as other units. On the other hand, observers designate seashells, metal pieces, pearls, and gems as "archaic money," probably because they can recognize in these the degree of ease of handling that characterizes the units of exchange with which they are familiar in their own culture.[1] And yet both cases demonstrate the use of a standard measurement and quantification. This operation is more obvious when it involves small objects; however, our criterion should be the function of these units, and this function is the same in both cases.

Mauss and "Archaic Money"

Marcel Mauss deserves credit for being one of the first to sense the importance of the role played in ceremonial exchanges by certain objects that function as units of circulation and should be recognized as having the characteristics of a form of money. In a text from 1914—a presentation to the *Institut français d'anthropologie*—he proposes a reflection on the "origins of the notion of currency."[2] Today this text may seem quite modest, considering the large number of studies that have since been conducted on this topic. We must remember, however, that Mauss was opening what was at the time a new direction (which he would broaden with his 1924 essay *The Gift*) and that his statements may even have appeared overly bold to an audience that probably considered that speaking of money outside commercial economies and beyond Western societies was not pertinent.[3]

Mauss meant to mitigate the cultural arrogance of his audience by show-ing that although "primitive societies" do not possess our contemporary forms of money, they do have forms of exchange standards that are already interesting and that constitute steps in an evolution that leads to modern money. These two aspects of Mauss's argument make it both an original and an ambiguous one. As we will see, his position is still held today by many anthropologists.

Let us first briefly return to this text. Mauss notes from the outset that he is referring to money as a "notion," since money is not merely a physical object but belongs to the social and institutional order and since, according to Mauss, it presupposes a form of faith. Its efficiency is pro-portional to the degree of social commitment it generates. This is a purely Durkheimian assessment already familiar to sociologists but not to econ-omists. Mauss adds that this notion is precisely observed in the societies considered the least "evolved." According to him this makes it possible to identify "the most primitive, simple, and basic form . . . of the notion of money" ("Origines" 106). Mauss discusses an example provided by an eth-nographic investigation of the Ewehé from Togo, comparing them to other societies in which seashells, gems, crystals of quartz, or objects made of gold or other metals were used as units of exchange. Mauss draws several conclusions. First, there is indeed a form of money in "archaic societies." He bases this on the following claim: "No matter how money is defined, while it is a standard of value, it is also a use value that is not fungible but permanent, transmissible, and capable of being the object of transactions and uses without being degraded. It can be a means to obtain fungible and transitory values, pleasures, and services" (110–11). Mauss is apparently lumping together consumer goods with goods involved in ceremonial ex-change—so much so that he writes: "Very early on and in the most primi-tive societies, talismans probably had the role of objects equally desired by all and whose possession conferred upon their owner a form of power that could easily become purchasing power" (111). Yet one paragraph below, in reference to an inquiry on the Palau Islands, he notes, "At first, money was not used to obtain consumer goods but luxuries and authority over men. In our view, the purchasing power of primitive money is above all the pres-tige conferred by the talisman upon its owner, who uses it to exert power over others" (111). We can see that Mauss wavers between presenting this "archaic" money as the ancestor of modern money and situating it within an entirely different type of relationship that is purely symbolic and involves reciprocal recognition and prestige.

It could therefore be expected that these confusions would be cleared up a decade later in *The Gift*. Mauss dedicates a long footnote to this question, titled, "A Note of Principle Concerning the Use of the Notion of Money" (*G* 100n29–102). In it he once again questions the economists' perspective that restricts the use of the terms *money* or *value* to units that are depersonalized (that is, cut off from individual relationships) and secured (on the authority of the state): "In my view, one only defines in this way a second type of money—our own" (*G* 100). Mauss, however, distances himself from the position he took in 1914: "It is true that these precious objects differ from what we are accustomed to conceive as instruments of discharging debts. First, in addition to their economic value, they have also a somewhat magic value" (*G* 100). This primitive money would thus be at the same time economic and symbolic. Strangely, Mauss refers the term *value* to its economic use (a restriction he just challenged a few lines above); he admits that symbolic values "are unstable, and lack that character of being a standard of measure. For example, their price rises or falls with the number and size of the transactions in which they have been used" (*G* 101). He seems more aware of the specific character of the precious objects used as "archaic money," but he does not set a strict dividing line between them and modern money. He could not do so without giving up the evolutionist hypothesis: for him the former form of money remains the ancestor of the latter. There lies the entire problem, since Mauss very explicitly presents this evolution as involving three stages: (1) choice of materials (metals, stones, and seashells) that have the advantage of not being destroyed by use; (2) use of these objects as instruments of reference and numeration; and (3) separation of these instruments from their context of interindividual exchanges in order for them to become objective and neutral references of evaluation equivalent to any kind of goods. Mauss thus describes a gradual transition from one form to the other. His purpose is to preserve two apparently contradictory claims: first, primitive money involves forms of exchange that do not pertain to modern economy but to relationships of ceremonial exchange;[4] second, primitive money carries the germ of the modern economy and foreshadows modern rationality.

Because Mauss is intent on presenting primitive money as the origin of commercial money, he does not allow himself to view it as belonging to a different realm, even though the entire purpose of the demonstration he develops in *The Gift* is to show the specificity of gift/countergift relationships and their profound and even radical difference with commercial relationships. From this point of view the ambiguity that is present in "Origines" has not really been cleared up. It is also found in other passages of *The Gift* in which the evolutionist view is still apparent.[5] We saw above, in the chapter on gift exchange, how indispensable it is to keep a distinction between ceremonial gift exchange and commercial exchange, in spite of the inevitable transfers of terminology that have occurred from one domain to the other.

We must still credit Mauss for his attempt. His main purpose is to make the advocates of the ordinary view of *homo œconomicus* aware that a different type of exchange exists and that it also involves highly sophisticated forms of *units of circulation*. It is precisely on this point that some of Mauss's remarks are very promising. He notes that the precious goods that serve as "primitive money" testify to a general ability shared by both the world of gift exchange and the world of commerce, which consists of *dividing*, *counting*, and *measuring*:

From two standpoints, these precious objects have the same function as money in our societies and consequently deserve at least to be placed in the same category. They have purchasing power, and this power has a figure set on it. For such and such an American copper object, a payment of so many blankets is due, to such and such *waygu'a* correspond so many baskets of yams. The idea of number is present, even if that number is fixed in a different way from the authority of the state, and varies during the succession of *kula* and potlatches. Moreover, this purchasing power does indeed discharge debts. Even if it is recognized only between individuals, clans, and certain tribes, or only between associates, it is none the less public, official, and fixed. (*G* 101)[6]

An Example of Ceremonial Money: The Are'are from the Solomon Islands

It is at the level of this identity of operation that a formal (but not chronological) continuity can be observed between the two types of money (at least if this designation can be accepted in both cases). But this does not change the fact that they have a radically different status. This is probably why so many anthropologists still use terms such as "archaic money"

or, more recently, "savage money," even though they are aware of the difference between ceremonial money—which consists of units of reciprocal
offering—on one side, and modern money, on the other. A good example is provided by a remarkable study published by Daniel de Coppet.[7]
An anthropologist, de Coppet presents the uses of certain units of ritual
exchange—"armfuls of pearls"—in a Melanesian population, the Are'are
from the Solomon Islands.

From the outset we learn that the pearls from seashells used in operations of exchange are the objects of precise calculations, the unit of which
is the armful—that is, the distance from right thumb to left when the arms
are extended in a straight line. This is not merely a technical unit; it is associated with the very gesture of opening one's arms (hence its definition as
"opening of the thing"). Above all, however, it serves as a unit of reference
and standard of evaluation of the height of a tree, the width of a house, the
size of a garden, or the area of a fishing zone, all of which stand in contrast
to the incommensurable character of the sky, the sea, or the forest.[8]

This basic unit is itself subdivided into twenty-four shorter ones constituted by the first two phalanxes of the thumb. In addition, these units
have names that are associated with parts of the body from thumb to ster-
num. Armfuls of pearls and their subdivisions are consistently involved in
offerings to the ancestors and in exchanges of gifts between villages or lineages and between men and women. De Coppet explains this remarkable
omnipresence: "In a society without established hierarchy, which systematically attempts to limit the content of power, and in which individual
mobility from one group to another is increased by the particular mechanisms of land tenure and of an undifferentiated kinship system, every
personal event matters and has its place within a meaningful sequence.
Everything is accounted for; everything is paid for; everything is translated
into money. Events thus rarely get out of hand. Social interplay always
seems to preserve the most exacting control."[9] This is a crucial observation. It is as if the counterpart of the fluidity of social organization and of
the lack of a strong central system were the presence of a tight network of
exchanges based on the divisibility of things and activities. This is probably
sociologic data that can be generalized in a useful manner to help grasp the
coherence of any network-based society. Lest the statement "Everything
is paid for; everything is translated into money" be understood in a commercial sense, however, which would obviously be a misunderstanding,

it should be qualified: everything is paid for in *symbolic* money. This is a ritual form of accounting; no matter how precise and rigorous it may be, it is not an accounting of costs and financial prices—all the more so because procedures of exchange and gift-giving involve numerical operations without self-interest but with numerical values that are specific to Are'are culture. These values involve the numbers one, four, and eight (the last number expresses a whole or completion). This sequence can be followed by a binomial involving the numbers nine and seven. Thus, in the case of a murder, which generates complex compensation procedures, we observe that the movement of exchange of pearl currency is precisely superimposed on the rules of matrimonial exchange;[10] it is even a kind of variant of these rules. To reestablish dialogue, a murderer from group A must give "money" for a victim from group B; this "money" is shared by B's blood relations as it would be in a marriage. Murderer A is considered by his kin as a great man, a "taker of the living"; B's relations then demand a corpse as compensation for the death they have suffered. Murderer A is then supposed to kill one of his sisters and bring her corpse to B's relations (who either eat it or abandon it); B's relations then find themselves "takers of a woman" and are thus indebted to A, as they would be in a marriage. They return to A the armfuls of pearls received as compensation for the murder. This could conclude the procedure. But B's relations remain indebted and must give an additional offering in pearl currency; this offering is called "new giving" and it constitutes the beginning of a resolution sequence. More modest "seven" offerings meant for the ancestors are then given by A's group and then by B's group. But the decisive offering is the "nine"; it is considerable and even larger than the offering provided for a marriage:

The best definition of "nine" is eight plus one, which cannot be ignored considering the symbolic value of "eight" in Are'are culture. "Nine" comes as a surplus in an exchange that had just reached equilibrium. The fact that this surplus is always the price to pay in order for peace to be restored, that it is also the only occasion in which people are obligated to help their "great man" gather this amount, and that its public and solemn presentation constitutes the only ceremony of allegiance to the "great man" implies the existence of a multiplicity of relationships, at a psychological as well as political level.[11]

This ceremony is an occasion for each of the groups to proclaim the name of its people and its lands in front of the other. De Coppet shows that the same formal schema of exchanges and compensations can also be observed on different occasions—following the ritual execution of a widow or adultery on the part of a husband. Exchanges of pearl currency are part of a process in which the relationships between the two groups are variations of matrimonial exchanges. The taking and returning of a wife, of a life, or of pearl currencies are gestures that are always associated with each other. Pearl currency itself is always a means of evaluating the gifts to be offered, of reopening dialogue, and of measuring debts and therefore lives and deaths. As de Coppet also explains, it makes it possible to divide social life and to define gestures of reciprocity, in short to create discontinuity—in the same way as an armful measures cultural space (garden, house, or fishing zone)—and thus to generate a regulation that no other authority would ensure.[12] At no time does de Coppet's description mention any use of pearl currencies in exchanges for ordinary consumer goods. Their use remains a ritual one.

The Accounting of Gift Exchange

It is clear that the use of ceremonial money as described by de Coppet involves nothing resembling commercial relationships. From the exchange of "money" that is always given or returned to the exchange of debts in terms of lives, everything remains within a system of symbolic reciprocity. As we saw regarding vengeance in traditional societies, the circuits of compensation for murder or any other offense are precisely the same as the circuits of gift exchange and matrimonial exchange.

Mauss, therefore, accurately grasps the general question this involves: the introduction of an element of quantification in gift-exchange relationships. These measurements are in fact always present in the symmetrical interplay or auction of agonistic gift exchange. Comparing very often amounts to counting, but as we will see, this still does not amount to trading or using commercial money. Ceremonial money is thus no more than the creating of units of reciprocal offering (to use an expression already presented above). These units facilitate evaluation and make it possible to refine the relations between what is received and what is returned. But these units involved in relationships of gift exchange are still not forms of monetary currency. They are nothing more than quantified gift exchange relationships. The precious objects exchanged retain a primarily symbolic value. The contrast often established between gift-exchange relationships, said only to involve quality, and commercial relationships, said to involve quantity, is based on a naive assumption. Gifts can be numerated and quantified and still remain gifts.

Recalling Mauss's analyses, we can state that ceremonial money has the following features: (a) it consists of either discrete units or divisible goods that can be enumerated; (b) it consists of nonfungible goods; (c) it involves units (measurements) of value; and (d) within a particular society it has a public, conventional, and fixed character. Therefore, it would be irrelevant to ask where "savage money" stops and commercial money begins, since this would already amount to presupposing that the one is the continuation of the other. This is not the case. Two different orders or heterogeneous realms are involved. But this heterogeneity is difficult to recognize, since both cases involve exchanges, as well as some of the same formal processes, and since the atmosphere of gift exchange can even spread to or be associated with commercial exchanges.[13] But the types of logic at play are entirely different.

This difficulty of making the necessary distinction is apparent even in authors such as Rospabé, who, in *La dette de vie*, insistently and rightly emphasizes the profound difference that separates the world of gift exchange from the world of utilitarian exchange. The goal of Rospabé's book, which is very well supported in terms of ethnologic data—something for which an economist deserves credit—is to counter the typically Western and utilitarian view of traditional exchanges—that is, gift-exchange relationships. Contemporary anthropology cannot but approve this clarification, with which it has been familiar since Mauss's *The Gift*. The subtitle chosen by Rospabé, however, *Aux origines de la monnaie* [The origins of money], is problematic. A qualification such as "savage money" would have solved the problem. But it is clear that the author's intention is to discover the buried root, the concealed origin of commercial money in relationships of ritual gift exchange and in the use of so-called savage money. It seems important to avoid following this path—although I recognize the value of the analysis of gift-exchange relationships presented in Rospabé's book. In his preface to that work Caillé writes of the goods or objects used as "savage money" that "they make it possible to pay off a debt but not to purchase anything. What is it that they pay for if they do not make it possible to buy? . . . In other words, what is money's ultimate and primary signified?"[14] We can immediately reply that there is no answer to this question. If it is true that the two types of money belong to two heterogeneous realms, then there is no primary signified that would account for both. Before coming to this statement, Caillé writes that the difference between the two forms is such that "it would probably be best to avoid the term money when designating goods with archaic value."[15] Indeed, in this case it is contradictory to assume that these goods might shed light on the nature of commercial money. In the same way, Rospabé very accurately shows that the well-known "payment for the bride" is no such thing and has nothing to do with a purchase. Anthropologists have been saying this for quite a long time,[16] but this reminder is always welcome, given the inadequacy of the phrase. This so-called payment is nothing more than one of the most widespread and important forms of gift/countergift relationships. As a consequence the "money" used on this occasion has nothing to do with commercial money.[17] Rospabé rightly notes that this money has value as *substitute for the life* represented by the future bride, provided that this life is understood not just as a biological fact but as the life of the community. The same can be said of the other goods exchanged during the matrimonial alliance. This "money" and these goods constitute the pledge that another bride will at some point be returned to the giver group. This is true of what has been called, after Lévi-Strauss, generalized exchange (that is, postponed exchange) as opposed to limited exchange (which is direct)—one bride is given for another. But, contrary to Rospabé's assumption, the value of ceremonial money (and of other goods given as compensation) as substitute for life in no way means that every kind of money, including commercial money, ultimately has the same status. If commercial money were to take on this value, then it would stop functioning as commercial money. Commercial money inaugurates or implies a form of logic entirely different from the logic of gift-exchange relationships. Ceremonial money is neither the archaic form nor the origin nor the ultimate signified of commercial money. Claiming that it is amounts to presupposing that gift-exchange relationships evolve toward commercial relationships by a kind of natural process. The genealogical shortcut according to which the one is presupposed to be not the ancestor but the core of the other risks bringing us back to this prejudice. The same suspicion can be expressed regarding the phrases "primitive money," "archaic money," and even "proto-currency,"[18] since any formulation that connotes mere anteriority inevitably implies this generating continuity along the same line of evolution. The exchange of ceremonial money is one aspect of gift-exchange relationships between groups. The difficulties of interpretation derive mainly from the ambiguous use that has been made of a term designed for commercial exchange.

Characteristics of Commercial Money

Where and when does commercial money emerge? A provisional (and insufficient) answer can be provided: it emerges wherever the emergence of the figure of the merchant is observed, that is, the figure of an intermediary who buys and sells in order not to consume but to facilitate transactions over goods between third parties.[19] For commercial money to exist, the unit of exchange must be cut off from any purely symbolic value and specified as a means of acquisition independent from the partners' status. In short, this unit—currency—must be nothing more than a sign of its general exchange value (even in the case of precious metal currencies).

Let us consider commercial money with respect to several criteria relevant to ceremonial money.

As for the *partners* involved in a transaction, their status is indifferent or at least neutral. Whether the client is a prince or a peasant, a relative or a stranger, the price of the loaf of bread is the same. Buyer and seller do not engage as such in a relationship of reciprocal recognition through the things involved in the transaction—although a symbolic effect can often be superimposed over it when buyer and seller know and appreciate each other. Even if sympathy develops between the partners and enhances the transaction, the relationship of exchange is not defined by this emotion. Anyone with the required amount of money has *the right* to purchase what is for sale. Access to the transaction is not secured by the status of the buyer but by the fact that he or she has the financial means required. From this point of view, and unlike in ceremonial gift exchange, the seller cannot be personally engaged in the thing sold, which does not stand as pledge and substitute for his or her being. In principle the relationship to the object is neutral and devoid of emotional involvement. This is also why, at the level of the operation, the relationship between the parties is impersonal, even if the transaction presupposes mutual trust.

As for the *object* of the transaction, it must be said that its *value* is nothing more than its price in currency units. The very high particular value that an object may have for one person (whether it is an old piece of furniture, a souvenir, or an inexpensive piece of jewelry) or for a group (as in the case of an object associated with shared memory, such as a monument to the dead, a flag, or a sport trophy) does not change the fact that its market value may be low or nonexistent. Market value is defined by the rules of the marketplace and is expressed in a monetary amount.

As for the *space of circulation* of commercial money, it is virtually boundless. It can of course be empirically restricted to a national territory, but (except for some specific situations) an amount of currency can be exchanged for another of equal value. Money as instrument (even in its most physical form such as coins or bills) has no individuality; it is only an amount capable of operating a transaction. It therefore has the same value in every point of the territory in which it is recognized, and it can be exchanged in foreign territories, according to agreed-upon scales.

Finally, as for the *object of exchange* of commercial money, it seems that it can be anything—not only consumer goods but also services and even activities or goods—such as political speeches, ideas for narratives, or sexual intimacy—that do not in principle belong to the realm of the sellable. In other words commercial money is so flexible, plastic, and broadly applicable that nothing seems capable in principle of escaping its evaluation—this is precisely what makes it appear threatening; we will see that its only conceivable limit is ethical.

The major difference between ceremonial and commercial money, however, probably involves *measurement*, which is in both cases inseparable from the question of *value*. We saw that in the case of ceremonial money (as Mauss was among the first to underscore) operations such as measuring, counting, and quantifying are quite common. The example analyzed by de Coppet is illuminating in this respect: "pearl currencies" are based on units of measurement such as the armful or its subdivisions into thumbs; offerings are subject to rigorous accounting; the times when procedures take place can be numerically defined. There is no doubt that a capacity to divide, calculate, and measure can be observed everywhere. Are these operations therefore comparable to those involving commercial money? Clearly they are not. Even if the cognitive processes are the same, the function of the exchange is entirely different. The purpose of symbolic exchange is the social relationship through the mediation of goods or gestures, whereas the purpose of commercial exchange is the acquisition of goods or services independent from the social relationship. What matters in the latter case is the fact that money precisely measures the good involved; it is not the personal pledge of one partner toward another. When gold objects serve as *units of measurement* in symbolic exchange, what matters is not just the required number of units but also their beauty, history, and size, as well as the identity of those who give and receive them (such as the precious objects involved in *kula* exchange in the Trobriand or the armfuls of currency of the Are'are). In commercial exchange—in which precious metals are indeed measuring units rather than rare objects—what matters is only their weight as equivalent to a precise quantity of exchangeable goods. Furthermore, they are given the neutral form of the ingot. From this point of view what matters is their precise quantity, measured with the greatest precision. The first commercial currencies in history were indeed defined by quantity alone: grains or bars of precious metal whose weight was constantly checked. The minting of coins, sometimes by private entities, more often by public institutions, emerged later. Its function was mainly to secure profits and control and, above all, to proclaim sovereignty.[20]

The term *money* can thus be used with rigor only in situations of commercial exchange, in which money is viewed as a general equivalent to all sorts of goods or services. The term *general equivalent* must be understood in a strict sense: its application is general, which is to say that (1) it does not depend on the relationships between partners (with respect to kin or social status), and (2) it can encompass an indeterminate variety of goods—such as food, everyday or luxury objects, work, artworks, services, competence, and so forth—and of situations—everyday or festive, important or ordinary, private or public, and so forth. In short, these characteristics are in every respect the polar opposite of those that define situations of ceremonial exchange. It is important for this distinction to be clearly established before we can examine how the two procedures sometimes intersect and become associated or articulated together without becoming one and the same.

Areas of Intersection between the Two Types of Exchange

It is stated in some works of economic anthropology that certain societies operate through gift exchange and others through profitable exchange. This is an unfortunate formulation. The two forms of exchange are not exclusive of each other. They do not even formally compete with each other: their finalities are not comparable. The importance that ceremonial exchanges take on in traditional societies does not entail that commercial exchanges do not exist or are unimportant. As we saw in Chapter 4, the main purpose of ceremonial exchanges is to create, preserve, or restore bonds of recognition between groups or individuals. Those exchanges do not have any directly utilitarian function, and they often even constitute a negation of such a function. As for the volume of commercial exchanges, it depends largely on the degree of autarky of the populations involved. As soon as needs appear to be complementary, profitable barter emerges, often along with exchanges mediated by some easily transportable equivalent.

Malinowski thus identified in the Trobriand trade that runs parallel to the circuit of gift exchange: "Voyaging to far-off countries, endowed with natural resources unknown in their own home, the Kula sailors return each time richly laden with these, the spoils of their enterprise."[21] This parallel barter activity is called *gimwali*: "The main characteristic of this form of exchange is found in the element of mutual advantage: each side acquires what is needed, and gives away a less useful article. Also we find here the equivalence between the articles adjusted during the transaction by haggling or bargaining" (*AWP* 189). This type of exchange, however, is itself not simple or reducible to a single kind. A *kula* visitor cannot practice *gimwali* with his partner in ceremonial exchanges but only with different village members—*gimwali* partners with whom negotiations can be fierce (*AWP* 362). But outside of these occasions for barter associated with the *kula ring*, a constant trade exists in all these islands between coastal and inland populations; the former provide fish and the latter farm products. There are thus standard equivalences between the amounts and types of products offered on both sides—such as a given amount of a particular fish for a given amount of yams. A different form of trade is also performed by groups of craftsmen who exchange wooden dishes, combs, baskets, and armbands for various products that they lack—such as coconuts and seashells. These people are peddlers with low status and are treated with some contempt, which brings us back to the type of suspicion regarding the figure of the merchant that we identified in entirely different civilizations (see Chapter 2). As Malinowski constantly emphasizes, *kula* exchange is performed with panache, with a generosity that is meant to challenge and honor the other. The prestige of the partners is always at stake. Utilitarian exchange, however, is performed in an entirely different mode and with different partners. It is associated with the trivial part of life, devoid of nobility, involving the ordinary demands of subsistence. It can be summarized by three features: "absence of ceremonial, absence of magic, absence of special partnership" (*AWP* 190). In these exchanges one can be greedy, unpleasant, or calculating, without losing face. Strict equivalence is sought, and there is no expectation of any personal obligation between the partners, especially if the operation takes place far away and on an occasional basis.

The difference between gift-exchange relationships and barter relationships may, therefore, seem clear, but things are not so simple or clearcut, as Malinowski admits. In a society such as that of the Trobriand the circuits of gift exchange and the institutions associated with them are so important and pervade the whole of social life to such a degree that every activity is influenced by them. There is thus a category of barter so closely resembling gift-exchange relationships that Malinoswski calls it ceremonial. And yet it is barter, since its purpose is to exchange useful products through precise and agreed-upon equivalences. But it goes beyond *gimwali* trade in that this form of barter takes place between official partners who cannot withdraw from it once the procedure has been initiated. Evaluations and exchanges are based on reciprocal trust and preclude any negotiation. In short, even if this kind of barter has nothing to do with *kula* exchange—in which prestige and generous challenge are at play—it is still the form of profitable exchange that "honorable people" practice. Malinowski therefore notes that it is difficult to speak of pure and simple barter or trade "because, although there exist forms of barter pure and simple, there are so many transitions and gradations between that and simple gift, that it is impossible to draw any fixed line between trade on the one hand, and exchange of gifts on the other" (*AWP* 176).

Another convincing example of the hybrid character of certain exchanges is provided by the way in which salt bars circulate among the Baruya of New Guinea. According to Godelier the status of these bars changes completely, depending on whether they are involved in internal circulation or in exchanges outside of the group.[22] These bars (which weigh four to six pounds) consist of potassium extracted from a plant ("salt cane") in conditions set by a precise ritual. They are distributed and consumed on the occasion of certain ceremonies, such as initiation. But they are also exported to neighboring tribes and exchanged for various types of goods—tools, bows and arrows, feathers from birds of paradise, cowries, seashells, bark capes, and the like. The expected amounts of each of these products are known by the partners and are strictly abided by. Two main criteria can be identified that make it possible to establish the role of general equivalent thus played by salt: (1) "it serves to measure the exchange value of other commodities since it is exchanged for them at stable rates which constitute their 'price'"; and (2) it remains a neutral instrument of relation: "When the Baruya *sell* their salt, they do not feel *personally bound* to the people with whom they have exchanged it for tools or capes."[23]

It can therefore be observed that, from one type of circuit to another, the same good can shift from the status of unit of ritual offering to that of means of payment, but it is remarkable that these two types of logic remain separate. Among the Baruya the difference between the two types involves the distinction between inside and outside: ritual use within the community and commercial use outside. In other cases the operation may consist of turning a unit of currency into a precious object: in Europe and the Middle East minted silver coins that are legal tender are sometimes used as elements of necklaces or sown onto clothes. There is another, more culturally complex, process by which traditional civilizations forced to use commercial money tend to replace ceremonial offerings of precious goods with monetary amounts deemed equivalent. This is not a neutral process: although the value may remain the same in principle, the symbolic effect is radically changed. It is not the same thing to give or receive on the occasion of a marriage a wad of banknotes or a herd of cattle (the former is now a common occurrence among the herding peoples of Africa). In addition, the ability to purchase in the ordinary marketplace the goods involved in ceremonial exchange makes their commercial value increasingly familiar; this familiarity lessens their aura and threatens their symbolic efficacy (thus there is in the Trobriand a factory—managed by a white man—of *dewayagu'a*, the necklaces and bracelets involved in *kula*; this tends to devalue these goods and to affect ceremonial exchanges). These interferences between the two realms can give rise to very complex situations. In certain cases precious goods whose market value is known are capable of rivaling modern money. Conversely, modern money can serve as substitute for these precious goods. This generates a considerable variety of effects: in some cases the blending between different modes occurs casually and without really affecting traditions; in other cases it triggers a collapse of the existing symbolic arrangements and a destructuring of the old social life.[24]

Although it must be recalled that ceremonial exchange and commercial exchange have a radically different nature and purpose, it remains the case that the first commercial money very often emerged through the use of materials identical to those that served for ceremonial exchanges. There are obvious reasons for this: to be accepted, money must be recognized as precious. Its power of equivalence must be readable in its very material and must therefore go beyond a purely local precious character—such as that of relics from the ancestors or ornaments that are not used by neighboring peoples. But the fact that the materials used were often the same does not entail that the units of ceremonial offering constitute, in logical or genealogical terms, the origin of commercial money. On this point there has been and there is still an abundance of misunderstanding. Whatever ambiguities may be associated with units of measurement and with the precious materials of which they are made, the agents involved know quite well whether the purpose of the exchange is to honor the other party or merely to sell or purchase a good.

This clarification about the difference between ceremonial and commercial money matters to us for several reasons. First, it once again brings to light the complete difference between the logic of gift-exchange relationships and that of self-interested exchanges. The fact that so many of the best economists and historians of the economy have confused the two (as shown by their attempts at establishing the genealogy of modern money) says a lot about the power of prejudice. Yet understanding and keeping this distinction is a decisive theoretical requirement if we are to account for traditional forms of gift exchange and to grasp the facts of reciprocity that can be observed in every society, independent of the period or culture considered.

The case of money illuminates the debate on the two forms of exchange because it introduces questions of the use of a standard, of measurement, and of quantification. As Mauss understood, comparing, counting, and measuring are operations entirely compatible with the units involved in traditional offerings; therefore, they are not what stands in contrast to gift/countergift relationships. Measurements or numbers alone do not introduce the domination of commercial exchange and its currency. It is true, however, that as soon as this type of exchange prevails and spreads out, these operations take on an entirely new dimension. But is this really the core of the constant contrast between the world of gift exchange and that of the marketplace? This is far from certain; it is even unlikely. The problem does not lie in commercial goods but in social relationships. The difference that must be recognized between ceremonial and commercial money brings us back to the essential difference between the logic of ritual gift exchange, whose aim is reciprocal recognition—the goods exchanged having value as symbols of a bond with others rather than as goods to be consumed—and the logic of commercial exchange, whose aim is the acquisition of goods for themselves—without the personal bond entering into play as such. There is no logical or chronological continuity between these two worlds. They constitute parallel sequences; but so many apparent analogies exist between them, and so many terms have been borrowed from one to designate the other, that they have often been confused or one has been mistaken for a modality of the other.

This confusion can also have a different source that could almost be said to be legitimate: complementarities can develop between the two sequences. Goods can be—and often are—purchased to be offered as gifts. Conversely, goods that were first received as gifts can later be sold (this is common in modern societies but remains rare or even inconceivable in traditional ones). Moreover, it is still quite customary today for gestures of giving to occur in the course of purely commercial transactions—such as meals during which negotiations are conducted, presents offered as marks of esteem, ceremonies with greetings, libations, and compliments. These ceremonies and the expenses they occasion aim at expressing consideration toward commercial partners and the desire to seduce them. But this above all is certain: although commercial exchange does create a legal relationship of partnership, it does not *as such* create a social bond. The gestures of giving associated with the transaction aim at creating or preserving this bond, which expresses the pleasure of being together and, for this reason, turns out to be beneficial to business.[25] This does not constitute a condition of commercial exchange, but it often makes it possible to open, pursue, and, above all, favorably conclude a negotiation. Beyond this it fosters a wish to preserve a long-term partnership (the question of corruption, which transforms gift-giving into a means of gaining undue advantage, is an entirely different one).

. . .

It cannot be claimed that the reason why commercial exchange is today perceived as legitimate is that it has taken over the role of ritual exchange, nor can it be claimed that commercial money has been substituted for ceremonial money. There is no such thing as an evolution that would have effected a shift from one world to the other with a few intermediate difficulties. The two worlds have always coexisted. We now better understand this: the rituals through which the requirements of reciprocal recognition are expressed cannot merge with the procedures of exchange of consumer goods. Although modern money and the marketplace have conferred incomparable power on the utilitarian order, they have not eliminated the realm of gift exchange. The requirement of reciprocal recognition remains just as fundamental in our modernity. We will see that it has found new modalities of expression, just as ritual gift exchange remains omnipresent, although it takes on forms that are less socially visible.

But if commercial money is in no way the continuation or successor of ceremonial money, why did it prevail so completely? How can it be an essential operator of equitable exchanges? Why are we no longer surprised that the Sophists charged money for their teaching? Have we lost the sense of the priceless and accepted that everything can be bought and sold? Or are we confronting a general order that it would be absurd to denounce because it has become inseparable from the political societies in which we live? This association between money and political order was already expressed in the classical age by the first currencies bearing the effigy of the prince or of the god who protected the city. Minted currency constitutes an implicit contract. Everything for which a coin can be exchanged is guaranteed by public authority. Every good has a recognized and accepted price, as does every kind of work, even this inestimable thing that is the teaching of philosophers—who welcome their wages, just like any other mortal. It remains to determine what money is, in their view, for such a power to be recognized in it.

Money:
Equivalence, Justice, and Liberty

We have reached another decisive turning point in our reflection. We must now ask why the phenomenon of commercial money emerged in so many civilizations. How can we explain the formation of a system of general equivalents in the exchange of goods? It can be assumed that this formation is not accidental. It is always associated with a global transformation of the societies considered. But what is the nature of this transformation? It is not a shift from ceremonial to commercial exchange; we have seen that this is a false genealogy. It is well-established, however, that the emergence of minted money is associated with the coexistence of two phenomena. The first has to do with social organization and is defined as the emergence of forms of organization of a "political" type—that is, authorities that transcend kinship systems. The second is associated with the differentiation of tasks or occupations, which by generating a complementarity of productions entails the exchange of goods; such exchanges no longer take into consideration relationships of alliance (whether matrimonial or of other kinds), even if they do not ignore those relationships. The circuits of exchange involving useful goods (as opposed to precious ceremonial goods) become all the more autonomous because relationships of recognition between political entities no longer take the form of the gift-exchange relationships found in traditional societies. This transformation is at the same time political, economic, and symbolic. It makes possible the emergence of money—without making it inevitable, as shown by the examples of ancient Egypt and the Inca Empire.

All sorts of legends and proverbs show that the irruption of money as a form constitutes a profound break in the conception of exchange, bringing about practices and representations capable of threatening very ancient ways of life and relationships.[1] As we have seen, Plato constantly expresses the greatest distrust toward this instrument. He—very briefly—acknowledges its efficacy, but immediately stresses the dangers it involves. Thus his *Laws* presents a kind of utopian anticommercial society liberated from the very use of money.

By contrast, Aristotle, in his attempt to analyze the rationality of currency, gives himself the means to examine the essential relationship between political society and commercial exchange. This is an essential relationship in that the use of currency is an integral part of the exercise of justice. Aristotle's purpose is to proclaim the functional and ethical necessity of money in the organization of the city, defined as a community in which two elements prevail at the same time: a sovereign, metaclan authority and an activity of exchange of goods arising from the differentiation of tasks and the diversity of needs.

Our starting question will thus be the following: is it possible to preserve Plato's rejection of any intervention of money into the philosophical relationship? Is it even possible, by extending Aristotle's reflection on currency, to preserve his axiom "Between knowledge and money there is no common measure" (*EE* 7.10.1243b)? Other questions also arise: What is it that can be measured, according to Aristotle? What can the measurement provided by money be applied to? What is its range of intervention? Do philosophers have a justification for opposing it? In this field, as in others of the same type, can the gift-exchange relationship be preserved—in its institutional form—without generating a kind of injustice? It may well be that, in political societies, the monetary measurement of goods is one of the essential conditions of equity and thus of democracy. This entails that money itself is not conceivable outside of the political order of justice. Furthermore, and contrary to a legend kept alive by philosophers and poets, the history of the affirmation of the monetary instrument has been associated with the conquest of liberty from ancient statutory dependencies. Georg Simmel is among those who understand this in the most lucid manner. We must return to his approach in order to attempt to grasp what he leaves out of the scope of his analysis: the question of gift-giving in modern political societies.

Aristotle: Money and Justice in Exchange

Because of my line of argument, I have reversed the usual order of presentation of Aristotle's theory of money. In Chapter 3 I analyzed the critique of profit that he elaborates in his *Politics*, while briefly recalling the foundations of his conception of money as they are presented in *Nicomachean Ethics* 5.8. We must now more closely examine these texts in the hope of clarifying the meaning of his statement in *Eudemian Ethics* on the incommensurability between knowledge and money.

Aristotle's main thesis on money is well known and can be summarized with a simple statement: "Money has come to serve as representative of demand" (*NE* 1133a.28–29). This definition may seem enigmatic to our modern minds used to viewing money as measurement of the market value of goods. To grasp the implications of Aristotle's definition (what do "representative" and "demand" mean?) we will have to free ourselves from a few presuppositions.

From the Old Reciprocity to Equalization through Currency

What are these presuppositions? They involve everything political economy has taught us for more than two centuries. For now it will be best to leave these results aside and to reexamine some of Aristotle's writing in view of what we have learned from Mauss and the anthropology of gift exchange, whose relevance seems obvious if we read anew the passage from *Nicomachean Ethics* 5.8 in which Aristotle's famous definition of currency is found. This passage follows several chapters dedicated to the question of justice, its definition, and its forms. Aristotle sets out to demonstrate the difference between distributive justice—which takes merit (*kata axian*) into account and operates according to proportion (*analogia*)—and corrective justice—which aims at strict equality or, more precisely, at balancing gain and loss in exchanges. This is the framework in which exchanges through sale and purchase are situated:

Some hold that reciprocity (*to antipeponthos*) is just without qualification. This was the claim of the Pythagoreans, since they defined, without qualification, what is just as reciprocity with another. Reciprocity, however, fits neither distributive (*to dianemētikon dikaion*) nor rectificatory justice (*to diorthōtikon*) (though people do take even the justice of Rhadamanthus to be a conception of rectificatory justice:

'If a person should suffer what he did, right justice would be done"), since often they conflict. For example, if a person in authority strikes someone, he should not be struck in return, but if someone has wounded an official, he should not only be struck in return, but receive an additional punishment. Again, voluntariness and involuntariness make a great difference.

When people associate with one another for the purpose of exchange (*allaktikai*), however, this kind of justice—reciprocity in accordance with proportion (*analogia*), not equality (*isotēta*) is what binds them together, since a city is kept together by proportional reciprocation (*antipoein*). For people seek to return either evil for evil—otherwise they feel like slaves—or good for good—otherwise no exchange takes place, and it is exchange (*metadosis*) that holds them together. This is why they erect a temple of the Graces in a conspicuous place, so that benefits might be repaid. This is the special characteristic of grace, because one ought both to perform a return service to someone who has been gracious, and another time to make the first move by being gracious oneself. (*NE* 1133a)

These last lines are very important. They retrospectively clarify the first part of the excerpt. What Aristotle defines is clearly what anthropology has taught us to recognize as the gift/countergift relationship. In other words the entire debate presented by Aristotle in this passage has to do with whether justice can still be understood within the framework of this relationship or whether it must be defined by a new element (which he will introduce at the beginning of the next paragraph). This model of gift exchange, confirmed by the reference to the Graces, seems to have been ignored by every commentator (most of whom are not familiar with Mauss's writings or with other investigations on ceremonial gift exchange).[2] Thus, in their very scholarly commentary on this chapter, Gauthier and Jolif acknowledge their puzzlement. It seems to them that this reciprocity introduces a different category of justice in addition to the two categories already stated. This category is indeed vindicatory justice (which I have analyzed in Chapter 6); Gauthier and Jolif are not aware of this, which is why they take the side of Seneca in viewing Aristotle's allusion to the Graces as nonsense.

Let us return to Aristotle. By questioning simple reciprocity and through it the Pythagoreans' position, these first lines amount to a claim that the gift-exchange relationship (of which talion law is a corollary applied to the settling of offenses) is not capable of defining relationships of justice in the city (see Chapter 6 above). Without reciprocity, however—recognition of the other and generosity aiming at creating or preserving relationships—there can be no true bond between human beings. Aristotle recalls this because he understands how important the gift-exchange relationship is in generating the social bond: it consists not only of doing favors but also of taking the initiative to give. According to Aristotle, however, these gestures of reciprocity are not sufficient to define justice. Does this mean that ancient societies were unjust? One could think so, in view of the example of the exchange of blows with an official: strict reciprocity does not take the character's status into account. It could be replied that there is no traditional society in which this kind of "justice" would be accepted; on the contrary, in these societies statuses are even more important than in other societies. But, just as relationships of ceremonial exchange seem artificial and obscure when they have lost their institutional efficacy, the vindicatory system—a highly coded form of justice associated with gift exchange relationships—becomes nothing more than uncontrollable vengeance once an arbitrational system of justice has been instituted.

Aristotle's analysis testifies to the transformation that had occurred in Greek society since the emergence of the city. Relationships between clans (*genē*) had been replaced with an order that deemphasized kinship relationships and ethnic entities in favor of an organization based on citizenship and law. The old system of allegiances and reciprocal offerings was precisely the one modern anthropology has observed in every traditional society. The function of ceremonial gift exchange is to establish very strong bonds between partners and to ensure public recognition between groups or individuals according to rules associated with specific statuses. This function is undermined by the emergence of societies of a political type in which public recognition is equally offered to all by law. At the level of reciprocal relationships gift-giving becomes a private gesture, which is how it soon also becomes a moral gesture. The obligation to give or reciprocate may remain constraining, but it is nevertheless largely left to individual initiative. At the level of personal interactions the gesture of giving continues to be the major source for formation of the social bond. But it is no longer what statutorily defines the relationships between the citizens and public authority, or the relationships between cities.

This is precisely the boundary that Aristotle encounters in his questioning of traditional reciprocity. The case of the Pythagoreans is interesting because although they advocate the old model, they do so by retranslating and renovating it through a complex numerical symbolism.[3] This adaptation is made possible by the fact that the very use of the term *reciprocal* (*antipeponthos*) gained general acceptance through mathematics, more specifically through geometry.[4] But in Greek the history of the term is associated with the definition of social relationships. It designates what one receives or is subjected to in return, such as services, rewards, honors, wrongdoings, or punishments. The verb *paskhein*, the participle form of which is *peponthos*, designated the experience of emotion rather than action; *antipaskhein* designates this experience in relation to someone else. The most relevant meaning is probably that of subjecting (someone) to (something good or bad) in return.[5] This is precisely the reciprocity associated with ritual obligations involving goods, words, and gestures, in which what is at stake is always recognition of the partner. This is indeed the gift/countergift world, which includes every aspect of positive and negative reciprocity. Understanding this world has already made it possible for us to account for Anaximander's statement.[6] This is also the world the Pythagoreans claim to account for.

From the outset Aristotle dismisses this old reciprocity, which is no longer compatible with the order of the city. Political relationships are no longer based on reciprocal allegiance from one leader or one group to another, as in Homer; they are based on public responsibility through acceptance of a common law that only recognizes citizens and not clans, kin, or allies. By affirming its transcendence over individuals, the political community—the *polis*—also transforms relationships of reciprocity into private relationships, whereas traditional reciprocal relationships were collective, as well as individual, which is to say that they predated the distinction between public and private. By attributing to the Pythagoreans an attachment to the old reciprocity, Aristotle aims to move into a new world. Although this reciprocity is important in interpersonal relationships, within the framework of the city it has become as obsolete as speculations on the existence of a specific number supposed to define justice.

Having done away with the old form of reciprocity, Aristotle can now present the new one. From the point of view I intend to bring to light, the following excerpt effects a surprising displacement:

It is a diagonal conjunction (*suzeuxis*) that produces proportionate reciprocation (*antidosis*). Let A represent a builder, B a shoemaker, C a house, and D a shoe. The builder must get from the shoemaker the product (*ergon*) of his labor, and must hand over his own in return. If, first, proportionate equality is established, and then reciprocation takes place, the result we mentioned will follow. If not, there is no equality, and the bargain falls through, since there is no reason why what one produces should not be more valuable than what the other produces, and the products must therefore be equated.

This is the case with the other crafts as well. For they would have been ruined if what the passive party received were not the same in quantity and quality as what the active party produced. (*NE* 1133a)

Immediately noticeable is Aristotle's use of a new term to designate reciprocity: *antidosis* instead of *antipeponthos*. The term *antidosis* also derives from the language of gift exchange; it literally designates the counter-gift that replied to *dosis*. Why doesn't Aristotle keep the word *antipeponthos*? It seems that he means to distinguish *antidosis* from the latter term, which he has used to describe the concept as both folk understanding (justice by reply, one blow for another) and debatable geometric speculation on the Pythagoreans' part. Although *antidosis* does originate from the language of gift exchange, it has taken on the more general meaning of action in return or reciprocal exchange of useful goods. It is clear that Aristotle is now referring to this acquired use (an example of the kind of transfer from the language of gift exchange to the language of commerce—or vice versa—that we encountered in the previous chapter).

This terminological shift from one paragraph to another also reveals a misunderstanding on reciprocity that should arouse the vigilance of anthropologists. Aristotle's argument consists of opposing a folk understanding of reciprocity presented as overly simplistic to a more elaborate and just form meant to be proportional, namely the reciprocity effected by money in the exchange of useful goods. Therein lies the problem: Aristotle does not realize that from one paragraph to the next he has moved to an entirely different field and that the two realms involved are not comparable. In the first case what he describes is the relationship of reciprocal recognition effected by gift exchange and vindicatory justice. This relationship has nothing to do with the exchange of useful goods that coexists with the former and generally involves barter, although certain goods such as salt, grain, and metals sometimes play the role of units of measurement. What should be compared to the exchange made possible by the monetary instrument are these ancient forms of useful exchange. This confusion that Aristotle and, later on, Seneca make between different realms is already present in Plato. It will characterize the entire Western intellectual tradition and will remain unnoticeable because the same authors also promote moral giving and virtues associated with generosity. In fact this movement and transformation are already at work in Greek tragedy since Aeschylus in the form of the replacement of the old *dikē* of the *genē*—clan-based justice—by the arbitrational justice provided by the city and the authority of the law that equally applies to all (see Chapter 6 above). At times Aristotle still senses how the old relationship of gift exchange can be the stronger, as in the case of the Charites: according to him, without the generosity they symbolize, no bond can exist between men. In addition, unlike Plato he understands how vindicatory justice deserves credit for affirming the victim's rights.[7] Nevertheless, he shares the dominant view of his time and subscribes to the new conception of justice called arbitrational justice, which demands adherence to common law. This is the level at which he should situate his reply to vindicatory reciprocity and to the Pythagoreans. Instead, he replies by giving the example of the exchange—*antidosis*—of goods as governed by the use of money. By doing so he shifts from one sphere of justice to another and confuses the issue. The following chart may help to clarify:

	I. *GENOS*	II. *POLIS*
A. *Forms of organization and social bond*	Reciprocal bonds through ceremonial gift exchanges	Civic bond based on common law
B. *Public forms of justice*	Vindicatory justice between groups	Arbitrational justice defined by law
C. *Subsistence I: Production*	Limited differentiation between tasks	Extensive differentiation between occupations
D. *Subsistence II: Useful exchanges*	Barter or exchanges using calibrating goods	Commercial exchanges using minted currency

Aristotle shifts from column I A and B to column II D, whereas he should develop his argument by shifting from I D to II D. In short, he presupposes that commercial exchange is what has taken over from ceremonial gift exchange.

The confusion Aristotle makes is not his alone. It indicates a presupposition that views history as progress and will never cease to separate an age deemed archaic from a present that alone is worthy of a new organization of life in common—the city—and of a rational legal order. By presenting the form of justice specific to commercial exchange—even if this exchange is primarily between citizen-producers, as we will soon see—as the favored alternative to the old vindicatory justice, Aristotle effects an undue shift. But the interesting point is precisely the fact that he is not aware of it (nor is anyone at the time or any of his commentators later). This probably means that *in the city ruled by law, the exchange of useful goods is no longer a mere matter of subsistence but has become a fundamental aspect of justice and, more precisely, of equitable relationships between citizens*. This is the seed of what will be the problem of modern societies in which political life can no longer be separated from economic life. This is one of the major questions that we will have to consider later in this book.

We can now return to the passage quoted above, which constitutes the introduction to a definition of money. Aristotle proceeds through several steps. He starts by asking if it is possible to exchange entirely heterogeneous goods in an equitable manner and how these goods can be made equivalent (the term he uses is *equalized*). Aristotle is aware—as shown by a point he makes later—that this question is constantly raised and solved in relationships of barter (we could add that ethnographic literature provides abundant evidence of the great precision shown by indigenous evaluations). Aristotle's intention is not to claim that the operation of equivalence only emerges along with money but to present a formal model of this equivalence and then to show how the invention of money is its most rigorous expression.

What is this formal model? Aristotle describes it as "diagonal arrangement" according to the following schema:

This means that A needs good *d* produced by B while B needs good *c* produced by A. What the schema represents is not the operation itself but the result to be achieved. Aristotle wonders how a relationship can be established between goods as disparate as houses and shoes and thus how a fair compensation can be assigned to each producer for his work. This diagonal—that is, proportional—arrangement is only possible if a proportional adjustment has first been made; otherwise, the members of a community cannot have common interests.

Koinōnia: Community of Interest and Reciprocal Need

What is this condition that preexists the diagonal arrangement? The next passage provides the answer:

> It is not two doctors who associate for interest (*koinōnia*), but rather a doctor and a farmer, and in general, people who are different and unequal, and must be made equal. This is why everything that is exchanged must be in some way commensurable. This is where money comes in; it functions as a kind of mean (*meson*), since it is a measure of everything, including, therefore, excess and deficiency. It can tell us, for example, how many shoes are equal to a house or some food. Then, as builder is to shoemaker, so must the number of shoes be to a house. For without this, there can be no exchange and no association; and it will not come about unless the products are in some sense equal. (*NE* 1133a)

This "association for interest"—*koinōnia*—defines the condition of emergence of the city, which would not exist without the initial fact that we depend on one another owing to the differentiation and complementarity of occupations. Aristotle presupposes that this genealogy is known. He discusses it more explicitly in the *Politics*. This association for interest is an effective but not an ultimate cause, since the foundation of the *polis* as such is its *telos*: to live together in a just manner. Plato already states in the *Republic* that the city originates from the reciprocity of needs.[8] Aristotle confirms Plato's analysis: humans are by nature social animals and for this reason they organize life according to a convention and they distribute differentiated tasks. Reciprocal dependence is an integral part of this very sociality. Thus the need humans have for a good cannot be separated from the need they have for each other—that is, from the need for those who produce other goods. Therefore, to make it possible for different goods to be exchanged, equivalence has to be established between them. But through this operation the agents involved in the exchange—the producers of these goods—are also "equalized." The association of interests—and therefore the city—will only exist if every agent is guaranteed not just to be able to obtain what he does not produce himself but also to be able to find it in equitable proportion ("in quantity and quality") relative to what he or she offers. The technical aspects of the question cannot be separated from its ethical aspects. The measuring operation must be just in the mathematical, as well as in the legal, sense.

This is what money makes possible, as Aristotle claims in the continuation of this passage:

Everything, then, must be measured by some one standard, as we said before. This standard is in fact demand, which holds everything together; for if people needed nothing, or needed things to different degrees, either there would be no exchange or it would not be the same as it now is. But by social convention money has come to serve as a representative (*hupallagma*) of demand (*khreia*). And this is why money is called *nomisma*, because it exists not by nature but by convention (*nomos*), and it is in our power to change its value and to render it worthless. (*NE* 1133a)

In the modern view the objects of our need are the goods that are assumed to be capable of making individual existence possible. These needs concern individual subsistence and the requirements of a decent social life. In contrast, for Aristotle, needs are not needs for things but the needs humans have for each other in order to obtain the goods necessary for living. It is tempting to think that Aristotle understands needs as being social from the outset. In this he would be radically modern. But should we really hail him as a precursor? We must reexamine this question, since it is the notion of need that allows Aristotle to define money, and it is money that makes justice in exchange possible.

When Aristotle states that money is the representative of need, he specifies that this developed by convention (*kata sunthēkēn*). The relation between money and need is not inherent but occurred at a particular time. It is worth noting that this definition of money follows considerations of what makes it possible for goods to be exchanged between individuals who produce very dissimilar things—things as dissimilar as shoes and houses. How can this dissimilarity be reduced? His answer is that "everything, then, must be measured by some one standard. . . . This standard is in fact demand, which holds everything together" (*NE* 1133a). To say that need is a standard for goods seems obscure to us today.

What was the nature of the relation between need and measurement? When we read Aristotle's statement on the necessity of a common measure, we expect him to propose a calculable reference, a quantifiable one (in the way political economy discusses amounts of working time invested). He does no such thing. He proposes as standard the need humans have for each other. A common measure is not only a calculable amount that can be used as standard but is, above all, a common element or term of reference. Aristotle asks what is shared among the men who make goods circulate among them? His answer is that preceding those goods themselves is the fact that humans do not produce everything and thus need one another; this is what we usually designate as the complementarity of tasks. Need is not a standard in and of itself. It is an invariant in exchanges, since it makes these exchanges possible at the same time that it makes them necessary. Because it is the only common element between all exchanges, it is what makes these exchanges commensurable, since the goods themselves—such as shoes and houses, to use Aristotle's examples—have nothing in common.

Need is therefore at the same time the demand for various goods and the fact that human beings cannot live without others who produce them. This is how need expresses reciprocal dependence and assigns a value to goods: it sets their price and their exchange value in proportion to this dependence. Two dimensions are therefore always involved at the same time: dependence and demand. Money expresses this dual reality by representing both the need for a thing and the need for other human beings. In this sense it can be said that this need is social.

At this point the impression can arise—and rightly so—that Aristotle's reasoning is circular: there is a missing link. Aristotle clearly states the nature of reciprocal need and of the complementarity of occupations. He also describes the operation by which a proportion is set between different goods. But he does not say what made it possible to determine how many shoes a house is worth. Money translates this quantity, but it presupposes that the assessment itself has already taken place. Yet this assessment is not described. It is presupposed as being self-evident. This certainty will be questioned by political economy in the form of the famous question of value for classic theory. For Smith and Ricardo this value will be work; for Marx it will be working time.

Civic Exchange or Commercial Exchange?

What is the status of the partners in the exchange discussed by Aristotle in this text? Most commentators regard it as self-evident that these partners are merchants or behave as if they were. This point may seem secondary, but it is actually essential. *In fact the partners discussed in* Nicomachean Ethics *are citizens who conduct exchanges with each other as such and without intermediaries.* Aristotle speaks of the equality to be established between shoemaker and builder or between farmer and physician. At no point in his analyses does he mention the mediation provided by the merchant. In his scheme of exchange there is no third party that would intervene as a professional.

We know that in the Greek world, and in the classical world in general, the figure of the merchant was viewed as profoundly illegitimate (see Chapter 3). This was the reason—although not the only reason— why the equality that was sought had to be established between members of the community on the basis of their own activities and productions. Money, as Aristotle means to define it, does not have a primarily commercial meaning. Money is a sign and a pledge: a sign of the need humans have for each other, which it translates, and *for which it is substituted,* and a pledge of this very operation, in that it will remain available in the future for identical operations.

In fact, in this text Aristotle keeps to a purely political definition of money. His purpose is to understand money within the framework of a theory of justice. He means to establish its most general reason for being without considering any illegitimate uses. It is precisely because he defines money within the framework of civic justice that the exchanges he considers are understood as being direct exchanges between citizens. Money is thus not only a legitimate but also a necessary thing, first because it has a technical function—to represent goods and to guarantee future exchanges—but, above all, because it expresses an operation of just equivalence, that is, establishing equality between disparate goods. The reason Aristotle never mentions merchants is precisely that their presence is not compatible with his definition of money. It is as if for him shoemakers conducted direct exchanges with builders and farmers with physicians. Exchanges of goods therefore constitute not commerce but the necessary exchange that results from the complementarity of tasks within the framework of the city, as well as the operation by which equivalence is established between the heterogeneous products of these activities. Money, understood as contributing to the implementation of justice, is an operator of proportional equality—that is, of the commensurability of goods between citizens. It translates and regulates civic reciprocity, which is at the same time interdependence and recognition. Introducing merchants into this operation would be not only inappropriate in law but also useless in fact, since in Aristotle's time merchants were often unnecessary—crafts-men and farmers still frequently sold their own products directly, without intermediaries—but, above all, because, as we saw above, most profes-sional merchants were noncitizens.

The way Aristotle analyzes the phenomenon of exchange of goods clearly shows that for him the *polis* constitutes the framework and the boundaries of the marketplace.[9] But this community of citizens presup-poses as its empirical condition *koinōnia* or association of interests. At this level reciprocity in the sense of interdependence emerges. This reciprocity of needs is ruled by justice, of which money is an instrument. This does not amount to a marketplace in the modern sense, but the fact that this notion is not recognized does not mean that a mechanism comparable to a marketplace did not exist at the time in the form of local and international networks, the interplay of supply and demand, the movement of prices, and financial investments.[10] The idea that the marketplace can constitute an autonomous order remains unthinkable. When faced with evidence of its emergence (such as chrematistics), philosophers have legitimate reasons to find it alarming. For Aristotle, as for all of his contemporaries, exchanges are conducted from person to person based on need.[11] To recognize the ex-istence of a marketplace with its own laws would amount to accepting that, in the realm of action, beyond exchanges between agents there are causalities and mechanisms that have to do with the things themselves and that escape the knowledge and, above all, the will of the agents. Aristotle is aware of this possibility, but it seems unacceptable to him because for him true action is voluntary action. Understood within the framework of a theory of justice, money must remain an instrument in the hands of the citizens. Like language money is a form of expression. It makes relations possible. This status does not imply any negative connotation. From this perspective Aristotle's view parts with that of Plato, who from the outset regards money with suspicion, before—very summarily—examining the reason why it exists.

Many authors, Marx being the most prominent of them, inaccu-rately view Aristotle as a precursor of political economy in the sense this concept has taken on since the eighteenth century. In fact, Aristotle's con-ception remains strictly that of the classical city. He does not stray in any way from the conceptual horizon of traditional societies. He does sense a dynamic that will later be recognized as that of political economy, as the beginning of a movement that capitalism will later make explicit. But economic activity, as Aristotle understands it, remains defined by a field of production and consumption whose only purpose is to ensure the subsistence of the "household"—*oikos*—and the balance of the city's accounts. This involves physical activities necessary to public and private well-being, not a virtually boundless movement of production and exchange aiming at increasing power. Wealth cannot be a goal in and of itself without immediately becoming perverse and perverting. It primarily has an instrumental function relative to the essential ends of life. It takes on enviable statutory value when it originates from an estimable source. It can never be viewed as being in and of itself an instrument of power; it is only the auxiliary of politics. It is a condition of life, not its end. It ensures living, the purpose of which is good living. It organizes the association of interests whose aim is civic community.

Two important conclusions should be drawn from this examination. First, far from heralding the advent of political economy, Aristotle posits a hierarchy that is incompatible with any conception implying the hegemony of the economy over politics. Such a conception is alien to him, as it is to all of his contemporaries. He merely states that in a society with differentiated occupations the complementarity of needs makes commercial exchange necessary. Money is the instrument that makes it possible for this exchange to be just—that is, proportional. Aristotle elaborates a *theory of justice* meant for a society in which products must be exchanged and which possesses the most precise instrument for measuring the value of these products. When the emergence of a break in this equilibrium becomes manifest in the search for pure profit—*chrematistic*—then Aristotle criticizes money's bivalency (that is, its intrinsic potential for legitimate and illegitimate uses).

The second conclusion to be drawn from the analysis of this passage from *Nicomachean Ethics* is that Aristotle implicitly dismisses the old form of justice associated with gift-exchange relationships. Like the great tragic authors, he cannot view this form of justice as anything other than a primitive and obsolete form—such as the reciprocity of the talion—even though, better than Plato, he recognizes the right of the offended to reciprocate. Like every classical Greek thinker, Aristotle takes the side of the new *dikē* on which the *polis* is founded. What is this new *dikē*? It is, above all, the arbitration of public law, known by all and equal for all. But it is also the fact that in the city, which is characterized by the differentiation of occupations and the complementarity of needs, the exchange of the goods necessary to subsistence has become an essential dimension of relationships of justice. This is a new phenomenon. Aristotle provides an answer to the question, What should the form of justice be in the city that produces and exchanges goods? How is currency the proper instrument of justice? Therein lies the modernity of his view as opposed to that of Plato, which precludes these very questions. But the shift from Plato's conception of money to Aristotle's also shows us that gift-exchange relationships have lost their institutional status (but not their privilege of generating the social bond between individuals—*philia*). Aristotle is able to articulate this shift and to perceive a less glorious and personal version of the social bond that is the unquestionable fact of the new city: the bond generated by the interdependence of needs ("This standard is in fact demand, which holds everything together" [*NE* 1133a]), which only becomes specifically political if it is subjected to the norm of justice.

Aristotle did not invent political economy, but he was probably the first to conceive of the economy according to the order of politics. This requirement remains intact for us today, even though the terms of the debate have become more complex. By positing money as the necessary instrument in the exercise of justice—a gesture that makes it possible to consider the association of interests within the space of the political community—Aristotle shows that money as instrument (as opposed to the bad use of this instrument in speculation) should not be viewed with distrust by philosophers. *Nicomachean Ethics* thus shows that the ancient suspicion against money is not or is no longer justified. This clarifies his apparently enigmatic statement that "between knowledge and money there is no common measure," which should be understood not as a denunciation of money's claim to appropriate knowledge but merely as the observation that the operation of proportional equivalence—such as that between houses and shoes—is not possible in this case because knowledge cannot be divided into discrete amounts. No units of knowledge exist that could be isolated and subjected to exchanges. This is true of all knowledge (Aristotle does speak of *epistēmē*), but it is even more true of philosophy because of its lack of self-interest. Philosophy is the art of being surprised. More so than any other type of knowledge, it cannot be related to any kind of advantage. This is why it is indivisible as an activity and as a form of knowledge and also why it remains priceless and can only be transmitted in a gift-giving relationship ("as with our parents or with the gods"). For Aristotle, philosophers can and must claim this exception while at the same time recognizing the necessity of the monetary instrument in governing the exchanges within the city according to the requirement of justice.

This position involves several paradoxes: Aristotle recognizes that without the gift-exchange relationship no community is possible, yet he dismisses the old vindicatory justice that presupposes this relationship and is its corollary; but he returns to this relationship when he must assess what is inestimable. He identifies and foreshadows all the problems and contradictions that political society will never cease to confront. They are still with us today. Modernity started very early.

The Universal Translator
and the New Roads to Autonomy

Money is freedom in the form of coins.

FYODOR DOSTOYEVSKY, *The House of the Dead*

If we accept that, as currency, money is primarily an instrument no less legitimate than any other, then it remains for us to wonder what its powers are and, above all, whether, beyond the function Aristotle recognizes in it as the operator of just equivalence, it possesses other, more dynamic properties or virtues.

Money as Joker, or the Truly General Equivalent

Money as currency has sometimes been technically defined as the *general equivalent*; this distinguishes it from signs proper, since every sign is part of a set of various and specific signs; there is no truly general sign. Money is the expression not of particular things as such, but only of their exchange value. As general equivalent it is capable of neutralizing every particularity. This is actually its main virtue; this is why it exists. The activity that made its acquisition possible remains indiscernible. Whether a given amount is earned through the activity of a baker, a professor of philosophy, a musician, a farmer, a banker, a laboratory researcher, or any other (including illicit ones), currency carries no trace of its origin or mode of acquisition.

Conversely, this money can be exchanged for an unlimited variety of goods or services: food, travel, clothes, payment of bills, books, entertainment, education, speculative investments, charitable donations, restaurant meals, pleasures of various kinds, or anything else that one may wish to obtain.

Money is thus capable of effecting this translation in both directions: it can be the equivalent of any activity and any good, and it can acquire any of them. Money's status as universal translator in exchange is the source of its undeniable power of seduction. It makes life flexible and fluid. It makes the world available. What we are discussing is, indeed, money as cash. This is the source of its power and appeal—its availability rather than its amount (many misunderstandings have been based on this point). What fascinates the possessor of an amount of money—even a modest one—is, above all, the sense of the possibilities it carries. Money virtually opens an unlimited number of choices—that is, of access to goods, pleasures, encounters, professional activities, or adventures. Very few of these will actually be realized, but this is irrelevant since what matters is the openness inherent to cash, from which a sense of freedom arises. No one expresses this idea better than Balzac in *Père Goriot*:

> The instant money comes sliding down into a student's pocket, it is as if some fantastic column sprouts up inside him, and on which he now securely rests. He walks more briskly than before, he feels as if he has a fulcrum on which he can lever anything; his glance is open, direct, his movements are quick; he may have been beaten, yesterday, when he was humble, timid, but tomorrow he'll triumph over the Prime Minister himself. Incredible things start to happen inside him: he hungers for everything, and is capable of everything, he feels impulses, desires over which he has no control whatever, he becomes perpetually cheerful, generous, expansive. In a word, he who a moment before was a bird that could not fly has suddenly recovered his wings. The penniless student snatches at a scrap of pleasure like a dog stealing a bone in the face of thousands of dangers, he splits it open, he sucks out the marrow, and then he goes off running, but the young man who can feel a few fugitive pieces of gold slipping and sliding in his pocket can savor his pleasures, itemizing them, delighting in them; he's walking on air, he no longer even understands the word "poverty." Paris quite simply belongs to him, lock, stock, and barrel. (77)

Rastignac, the character described in this passage, is not actually rich; he only possesses a small amount of money sent to him by his family. But this is enough for the exhilaration of possibilities to arise in him.

What little he has opens for him the sense of the whole because what he has is cash, and through this general equivalent an indeterminate variety of goods, actions, and events is promised or even guaranteed to him. An immense amount of wealth that would be frozen—for legal or other reasons—would not generate this feeling. If money were to lose this power of equivalence, it would immediately cease to fascinate—as is observed in the case of depreciated or inconvertible currencies.

Money—as cash—is what Michel Serres calls the joker or blank element: "Money is the general equivalent, . . . the joker, it has all values, it has all meanings, having none. . . . Money is indeterminate, it is everything, a kind of general equivalent, it is nothing, a kind of blank meaning. . . . Money is bereft of meaning, it has all the meanings. It is blank and polysemous."[12] But money is not a joker like any other, precisely because it is the most powerful of all. It is the universal substitute. This does not mean that money is as good as the thing itself. As Croesus learned, gold—into which he wanted everything to be transformed—does not replace water when thirst must be quenched or bread when hunger must be satisfied. But in a world based on exchanges, money can make anything accessible—or so it is believed. Because money has no value in and of itself, it can take on any value. It is a promise. It is a magical being endowed with every possibility. Is this its most deceptive mask or the expression of an authentic form of freedom?

Simmel: Monetary Exchange and the Process of Emancipation

The seminal passage from *Nicomachean Ethics* on the function of money could have gone some way toward ending the old suspicion of money. In fact, Aristotle himself still shares this suspicion, for reasons having to do with the bad kind of chrematistics, which he explains in the *Politics*. However remarkable the monetary instrument may be, in Aristotle's view it remains capable of generating perverse effects—the very effects that philosophers have never ceased to warn us against. We now better understand why they did so. This view is not restricted to a narrow intellectual tradition. An entire civilization shared and disseminated this suspicion regarding the way the relationship to wealth—its production, circulation, appropriation, and market value—undermine the free character with which what is given, the world, and knowledge itself, was originally endowed. This is what Plato never ceases to emphasize through the teaching of Socrates. Rousseau and Marx are the last great figures of this resistance, which grew stronger at the time—between the seventeenth century and the nineteenth—when a new kind of thinkers—economists—were beginning to consider money and the production of wealth as a phenomenon comparable to natural phenomena—as an autonomous world subject to objective laws. Marx's economic writings can be viewed as an extraordinary attempt to extend criticism into the very core of the enemy. In a way this kind of attack has always been one of the "natural" tasks of philosophers.

This reminder makes it possible to better appreciate how surprising the publication in 1900 of Georg Simmel's *Philosophie des Geldes* [*The Philosophy of Money*] must have been. Simmel dispassionately explains the nature and potential of the monetary instrument. He highlights its role as instrument and dimension of modern liberty.[13] His entire demonstration is based on individual experience, even though its purpose is to show that this experience is situated within objective social conditions of which the development of the monetary economy is a part. The tone and language certainly seem highly influenced by the psychological concerns prevalent in European philosophy at the threshold of the twentieth century, as expressed in specific national trends—in this case those of Germany. Nonetheless, this book includes analyses that are highly original and unexpected from the perspective of the philosophical tradition. How can we grasp this conception of liberty in which money is credited with a decisive power of emancipation? Its presentation is complex and often tortuous. Three sets of questions can be identified, however. The first involves money's instrumental qualities; the second, liberation from personal social dependencies; the third, the new possibilities of action offered to individuals by the monetary economy.

From the outset Simmel situates his reflection within the framework of societies with monetary economies, which as a consequence develop through rational production and exchange. He thus recognizes that money has technical qualities that amount to forms of boundless plasticity. The first quality he attributes to money is *divisibility*, its capacity to represent as specific amounts every nuance of the market value of the products exchanged. It should even be said that it is money's divisibility that leads to refined or exacting evaluation of products. It is at this point that precision in measurement—that is, monetary evaluation—reaches a critical threshold where quantitative and qualitative aspects merge. Money thus allows for objectivity in exchange; in other words, it makes equitable exchange possible: "Only money—because it is nothing but the representation of the value of *other* objects, and because there is almost no limit to its divisibility and accretion—provides the technical possibility for the exact equivalence of exchange values."[14]

An additional quality of money is its *usability*, meaning that when sellers receive money for the things they sell, they are then able to buy things in their turn; but they can do so at a later point, and they can buy any kind of good they wish for or need. In other words, money represents what one might need at any time, precisely because it remains available to be exchanged for anything that is needed (in fact, Aristotle had already identified this quality). Money makes it possible to make the appropriate choice and to acquire the product or service required at any time and in any place. Because money represents a pure quantum of value, it attains an incomparable universality of action. This makes it able to "set free a maximum of the latent value that lies in the form that we give to the contents of life" (*PM* 293). By making precise choices possible, it gives access once again to the uniqueness of things. In short, according to Simmel the general equivalent that is always viewed as the power of undifferentiation is, above all, power available for what has not yet been expressed and means of valuation of what has remained outside the circuits of evaluations and transactions. The most general equivalent ensures access to the most specific goods.

The Instrument of Liberty

The general character of equivalence is therefore not merely a theoretical representation of value; it provides unlimited plasticity to the economic action of the subject. This is how money is associated with the affirmation of individual liberty. Simmel shows that the advent of the monetary economy has historically accompanied or made possible a break with specifically personal social dependencies. It has also ensured autonomy from specific places and from the things themselves, which was impossible before its emergence.

These dependencies range from the most constraining and intolerable (slavery and serfdom) to the most common and best accepted (work for wages). Simmel addresses the issue in the following terms: productive activity generates rights over its products in terms of subsistence and way of life. The counterparts of the rights of some agents are the obligations of others, defining precise forms of autonomy and degrees of reciprocal liberty (ethnographic data could have provided Simmel with a great variety of examples; he does not use them). But this is only true in principle. In fact, everything depends on the extent to which the social relationship encompasses the person in the product: "Naturally, every obligation is generally resolved through the personal actions of the subject, but it makes a great deal of difference as to whether the rights of the person entitled to some service extend directly to the person under obligation himself or simply to the product of the latter's labour or, finally, to the product in itself—regardless of whether the person under obligation acquired the product through his own labour or not" (*PM* 284).

This defines three levels of dependence. The first is extreme; the second is more flexible; the third is very open. Simmel only briefly alludes to them, so let us try to examine them more precisely. *Slavery* represents the first possibility. In the service provided by the slave—whether hard work or domestic work—the obligation is entirely personal, in several ways. Most important, the very person of the slave is property of the master in the same way as a piece of furniture or a domestic animal (which is how Aristotle defines him, with a sort of scholarly neutrality that seems shocking today). The service expected from the slave extends as far as the master deems it useful, consistent with the amount of energy the slave can reasonably provide. Within this framework there are no limits to the service that can be required. In principle the slave owes his entire activity—his energy and everything he produces—to his master. Therefore, he cannot separate himself from what he produces or consider that what he owes is embodied in his production as an objective element beyond which a space of autonomy remains for him. From the outset his work and his productions are emanations of his person as instrument and good belonging to someone else. This total lack of self-belonging is manifested by the fact that the slave cannot sell anything, since his very person has been purchased. What he makes or transforms is not his. His condition is the sum total—without remainder—of his person, his work, and his productions as goods appropriated by a master. The true constraint of slavery does not so much lie in the obligation to obey—as burdensome as it may be—as it does in the impossibility for a slave to exchange his work and productions for any equivalent that would enable him to place *his very being* outside the circuit of mere things.[15]

How is the question of *serfdom* different? It must be recognized that in this case also the person of the serf and his activity are under personal dependence to the lord. Bondage to the land leaves little freedom of movement, and the abuses associated with this dependence—such as the authoritarian imposition of charges, surveillance, and punishments—are often as severe as those suffered by slaves. There is, however, a significant difference: the person of the serf is not, as such, property of a master, and the services required are limited and defined in terms of durations and amounts. When the products required have been provided and the duties performed, then the serf can enjoy relative autonomy, the limit of which is primarily material and due to lack of means. Two elements are important in this respect: first, the serf's obligations are defined by a percentage and thus by a quantum; second, he owns a few goods—no matter how modest—which he can consume and, above all, exchange as he wishes. This defines a first margin of liberty. It could even be said that liberty itself slips in through this margin. This can be observed in the development of the monetary economy in Europe starting with the urban renaissance of the eleventh and twelfth centuries, when lords tended to impose fees payable in cash. This equivalence foreshadowed a far-reaching shift: the service owed by serfs could be replaced by taxation. This is indeed what happened. But the precondition is that the work provided by the serf cannot be identified with a service associated with his very person (as it is in slavery). The serf owes something outside of himself, but he does not owe his own person. This differentiation, made possible by serfdom, is also what made the disappearance of serfdom possible. But the crucial precondition is that the serf must be able to exchange the products of his work, that is, to acquire not just products of equal value, but a good—money—capable of opening to him the space of equivalence of every possible good. This was so true and so well-understood that in certain cases serfs and even sharecroppers were forbidden from selling their own products because this would have opened for them a sure path toward emancipation.

This freedom of exchange specifically characterizes the situation of *free farmers* and *independent craftsmen*. This does not mean that their products are created for the purposes of exchange. In small, traditional communities exchanges remain very limited. What matters is the fact that they are possible, because it means that products are now separate from their producers and recognized as such in their use (that is, in the consuming, sharing, and handling of them). This distance between producers and their products is greatest when the latter can be put into relations of equivalence with others and exchanged for cash, which already presupposes an abstract representation of their value, since even if evaluation is local, its operation has a general character. Being able to *exchange* (rather than merely produce and consume as slaves do) proves that the person of the producer is not or is no longer part of someone else's body. Being able to buy and sell presupposes the existence of property rights and even of a recognized status as owner. The very possibility of exchange matters more than the volume of the transactions involved. To this possibility, money provides a new dimension: cash constitutes a guarantee offered by the community. Minted currency amounts to credit publicly granted to any user; this defines its "liberating power," a very accurate term. Every coin (or bill) embodies a contract between issuing power and user. It represents a reciprocal commitment, an implicit convention.[16] This manifests the very order of the law and is the opposite of personal dependence. Whoever possesses cash is by right a member of the community of citizens who produce and exchange goods within the political space in which the currency is legal tender.

This leads to the emergence of a new sphere in which, at a different level, the means of liberation can become an instrument of oppression; but this is a different history, which Simmel considers to be well known. In his view it is preferable to assess the space of liberty opened by the use of money. This can be most readily done in the case of wage labor. *Payment through wages* undoubtedly constitutes a decisive form of emancipation for those—such as laborers, seasonal workers, company employees, and civil servants—who are not independent workers—as opposed to farmers, craftsmen, and artists. Payment through wages completes the break with the personal relationship between employer and employee. These very terms indicate that the worker is no longer involved in a relationship with a master or a lord. Two conditions are thus required to preclude any risk of returning to a situation of personal dependence: (1) labor—as a type of task and as time invested in production—must be considered as a quantum of assessable activity; (2) this quantification must be fully translated into a monetary equivalent.

The first operation completes the situating of labor activity within an objective sphere of evaluation in which reasoning is conducted in terms of energy expended and competence demonstrated rather than of personal service to anyone. The second makes it obvious that the skill involved can be compared to others and that its possessor can view it as a way of making a living wherever there is demand for it on the market. Of course, if supply is insufficient in the labor market, conflicts can develop, forming the long history of wage labor's struggle to attain a higher level of recognition. It is still the case, however, that as part of a first stage or initial condition of a new socioeconomic order, wage-earning created a situation of maximum distance between the person of the worker and that of the employer, as shown by the profound transformation undergone by the legal conception of labor. According to the oldest tradition, whoever worked for someone else fulfilled a rental contract. In a way workers rented themselves for a specific duration (this type of contract endured into the twentieth century in servants' engagements). This rental contract had precise definition in the forms of Roman law.[17] The distinction between persons and their activity remained hazy. "However, as soon as the labour contract emerges as the purchase of labour as a commodity—and this is the final result of the money economy—we are dealing with the offer of a completely objective work activity" (*PM* 335). As for employers, they purchase this labor commodity in order to produce goods meant for the marketplace—that is, for unknown consumers with whom their only connection is the mediation provided by money. For workers the mediation of money is the guarantee of incipient autonomy: "He no longer feels subordinate as a person, but rather contributes only an exactly prescribed amount of work—prescribed on the basis of its monetary equivalent—which leaves the person as such all the more free, the more objective, impersonal and technical work and its regulation become" (*PM* 335). Ironically, this release from alienation consists of a shift from an organic to a mechanical model. And yet there is no irony in claiming that this is a step toward greater autonomy for workers and an even greater step toward the affirmation of their uniqueness (which should not be confused with the claims of individualism). Simmel sums up this shift with a clear-cut statement: "In the process of differentiation between the person and his achievement, money supports the independence of the person" (*PM* 342).

At the same time, the independence gained with respect to persons is also achieved with respect to things. The development of the monetary economy brings about a profound transformation of the very idea of property. Without entering the immense debate about the origin and modalities of the various types of property from a legal point of view, we can keep to Simmel's definition: "Property is nothing but a sum total of rights over the object" (*PM* 306). Or, "Property is the socially guaranteed potentiality for the exclusive enjoyment of an object" (*PM* 309). These two definitions are meant to be classical and are stated in terms of objects. But they are intended to highlight the profound way money changes this relationship with objects:

> This concept of property is enhanced, as it were, if it is realized in terms of money. For if someone owns money he is assured by the constitution of the community not only of the possession of money, but thereby of the possession of many other things as well. If the ownership of an object means only the possibility of some specific use of that object that the nature of this object permits, then the possession of money implies the possibility of the enjoyment of an indefinite number of objects. (*PM* 309)

It is this indetermination that ensures the maximum openness in action and gives this sense of possibilities I identified above as one of the major emotions associated with the possession of money. From this point of view, and as compared to traditional ownership of physical goods (land, house, furniture, or even precious objects), money provides its possessors with incomparable mobility. The entire history of money could be understood as a movement toward evermore fluid forms of expression (from coins to bills, checks, credit cards, and electronic payments) and as an expansion of the means of autonomy available to the subject: "Everywhere the immovability of property—whether connected with the collectivity or with inheritance—testifies to the obstacle whose removal would permit a corresponding progress in differentiation and personal freedom. Money, as the most mobile of all goods, represents the pinnacle of this tendency" (*PM* 354). This is a new field offered to will, Simmel claims: the will is essentially constrained by the nature of the outside world in which it intervenes. It must adjust to the uniqueness of objects and situations. But from the moment it deals instead with their monetary equivalent, this difficulty vanishes: "[Money] adjusts with equal ease to every form and every purpose that the will wishes to imprint it with" (*PM* 325).

It is clear that at this level Simmel's purpose is not to analyze the social and often abusive use of the monetary instrument. He does not ask who possesses it or accumulates it—how, and at whose expense—or in what way these questions are related to money's ambiguous nature. He only considers its constitution and its formal effects on the social relationship prior to any bifurcation of its effects. This systematic elision surprised or even upset many readers. There is no doubt that Simmel does not sufficiently analyze the situations of conflict associated with the possession of money and its financial manipulation. What he fails to do is to take into account the perverse effects entailed by the very qualities of money. This would be a different debate. Still, Simmel is able to show in an original manner that through this instrument a new figure of liberty is taking shape, with three main modalities: objectivity, substitutability, and fluidity.

Objectivity is associated with the depersonalization of work relationships—with the fact that it is labor itself that is recognized as such by wages. Liberty thus conquers the ancient dependences that used to absorb the body of the laborer into that of the master. According to Marx the evaluation of labor as quantum is what made exploitation in the capitalist mode possible; but for Simmel it is, above all, what allowed labor to break away from the model of serfdom and later from the paternalistic model of the guilds. More generally, this "objectification" is also what opens a movement toward justice, toward the defining of norms recognized by all.

Substitutability is money's ability to express all sorts of needs and situations for the subject who uses it. Simmel's analysis goes far beyond the powers of equivalence and representation generally recognized in money. Money does not merely represent the possibility of acquiring any good at any time and in any place. The substitution it effects is even more complete with respect to the subject. Money can act for the subject and without him in situations where it is important that the subject's person not be directly involved. This is true of taxation, for instance (which replaced duties and services in kind), but it can also apply to compensation for a wrong that has harmed the community: the amount paid as a fine meets the public requirement for justice. In neither of these cases does the subject have to be present in person in the process. This does not necessarily satisfy the moral requirement, which is entitled to appeal to a different authority—such as conscience—but it makes it possible to clearly separate the objective order of justice from the subjective order of ethical attitudes. By representing the subject, money releases him or her from the confusion between these two orders.

Fluidity involves, first of all, money's speed of circulation but also its plasticity, its ability to adjust to all sorts of complex and unpredictable requirements. While the monetary economy contributes to the elimination of personal dependences, it also multiplies objective dependences. But money's indeterminate character enables it to act on each of those dependences, not by purchasing privileges but by providing means of action: "Money . . . is the representative of abstract group forces, the relationship of individual persons to others simply duplicates the relationship that they have to objects as a result of money" (*PM* 301).

What Simmel means is that monetary circulation has become one of the fundamental conditions of communication and action in modern societies. Beginning with the industrial revolution, its expansion has not been primarily an effect of capitalist logic alone; it has been the condition of a socialization that would have been impossible without this instrument. Simmel's argument is the following: "The more people develop relationships with one another, the more abstract and generally acceptable must be their medium of exchange; conversely, if such a medium exists, then it permits agreements over otherwise inaccessible distances, an inclusion of the most diverse persons in the same project" (*PM* 347). Money makes this integration possible—not by some kind of transindividual virtue but because it functions as operator of a convention accepted at every level of economic life. In this it is the de facto expression of a social contract between economic agents. This is not merely the effect of some "invisible hand," which is to say that it does not result from an objective and spontaneous convergence of individual interests capable of generating the public good. It is the formal process of an implicit consensus, a constant agreement on the value of goods and on the possibility of having access to them.

These are a few (though not all) of the perspectives opened by Simmel's reflection. His essay is not intended to be an economic analysis of currency or—as has been claimed—a psychological interpretation of the role of money but a cultural analysis of the phenomenon of exchange, of which money constitutes the most accomplished instrument. Simmel's originality as philosopher and sociologist lies in his setting aside moral or even political standpoints and restricting himself to the standpoint of the cultural and social potentialities of the instrument. In this he was breaking with an entire tradition of suspicion that had never been contradicted since Plato. It is true that since the seventeenth century economists had begun to consider currency in purely functional terms and that they admired its powers. But they were interested primarily in objective mechanisms, and their goal was to understand the economic sphere as analogue of the physical world. Simmel situates money within the whole of social life and attempts to understand how this instrument of exchange presupposes and generates a radical transformation of the relationships between humans. This transformation is neither a tragedy nor a panacea. In it he sees one of the essential aspects of a process that involves both the subject's conquest of autonomy and the constitution of an objective world that can function as the framework for the exercise of justice. He also views it as permanent testimony to an implicit and general agreement between social agents about the value of goods and the modalities of their circulation.

This kind of analysis was necessary in order to go beyond the ritual condemnation of money that philosophers usually engage in out of something akin to statutory obligation. Monetary exchange must, in fact, be examined in the same way as other phenomena with bivalent status. At least two examples can be mentioned, which are often associated with money and also involve perverse effects: technics and language. These two fields provide useful elements of contrast, since no condemnation of technics has ever involved denouncing the activities of craftsmen or engineers. Plato himself constantly refers to professional trades as models of authentic competence and opposes them to what he views as the amateurism of the Sophists. Language has also been the object of various forms of art and knowledge, from grammar to rhetoric, philology, and modern linguistics. The complex functioning of language and the multiple instruments it provides have been analyzed without ever giving rise to considerations that the practices of lying, flattery, or chatter—or of other forms of abuse of speech—cast into doubt the necessity of verbal communication or the production of discourse. Only commercial exchange and the use of currency have occasioned this radical mistrust—hence the criticism of which philosophy, more than any other discipline, has been the accredited mouthpiece. We now better understand why: the stakes involved are different. The purpose of philosophy is to state not only the nature of things but also their value. When value is involved, when what is most precious is at stake, the ancient tradition of gift-giving always tends to push aside the self-interested approach. Simmel extends his effort at rehabilitation to the farthest reaches. Too far, some will say. An examination into the nature of the bond that connects the agents of commercial exchange does give reason for suspicion.

Contract and Social Bond

Money makes it possible to establish just equivalences when what is involved is useful exchange, when the aim is the acquisition or selling of a good rather than the recognition of a partner. The exchange presupposes a procedure of reciprocal commitment that must be precise and effective. This procedure is the contract—the exact opposite of ceremonial gift exchange in its forms and implications. This is the very reason why the contract provides a guarantee of justice and autonomy. Does the bond it creates between parties constitute a social bond? An examination of the temporality it entails makes it possible to assess the extent of its effects: every contract is a commitment in time, with the dual effect of binding time in advance and suspending it. Before coming to a description of its characteristics, let us consider the surprising use Mauss makes of it with respect to the exchange of ceremonial goods.

The term *contract* is recurrent in *The Gift* when Mauss is describing commitments between partners ("exchanges and contracts take place in the form of presents" [3]; "we shall describe the phenomena of exchange and contract in those societies" [4]; "there is total service in the sense that it is indeed the whole clan that contracts on behalf of all" [6]; "this system of contractual gifts in Samoa" [8]). Mauss also considers sacrifice as a contractual relationship with a deity ("A start can be made on formulating a theory and history of contract sacrifice" [17]). Before showing why the concept of the contract is an inappropriate choice in the case of ceremonial gift exchange, we need to understand what leads Mauss to use the term. At least two reasons can be considered. The first is a general one: Mauss resorts to a broad sense of this notion meant to designate any mode of commitment between different partners. He could just as well speak of a pact (which he sometimes does). *Contract*, then, designates a form of mutual commitment between parties.

But there is another, more decisive, reason: gift-exchange practices entail a constraint that can only be compared to the constraint exercised by contracts. Mauss's interest in the question of gift exchange arose precisely while he was working on the origins of the contract and certain archaic forms of law (in the Roman, Scandinavian, and Hindu cases). At the same time, Georges Davy, another sociologist and a former student of Mauss, developed an interest in these questions and published in 1922 a book on the topic, *La foi jurée*, which almost exclusively consists of a study on the *potlatch* of the Kwakiutl, Tlingit, and Haida. In this book ceremonial gift exchange is immediately situated or rather preinterpreted within a legal framework familiar to European culture. At first Mauss seems to adopt this approach, since integrating gift exchange to the paradigm of the contract enables him to recognize in it the two major criteria of the social fact according to Durkheim: being from the outset both coercive and collective. Several reticent allusions Mauss makes to Davy, however (in *The Gift* and elsewhere), show his unease. Besides the fact that Davy situates *potlatch* within an evolution that leads to the modern contract, what most disturbs Mauss is the fact that the agonistic character of *potlatch* makes it incompatible with the very concept of contract. More precisely, for Mauss the contractual character involves only the obligatory aspect of gift exchange. But gift exchange is neither a variety of contract nor its ancestor; it is a specific phenomenon and even a "total social fact." In one passage from *The Gift* the discrepancy between the status of gift exchange and that of the contract is clearly indicated with respect to the phenomenon of gambling, "which even in French society is not considered to be a contract, but a situation in which honour is committed and where goods are handed over that, after all, one could refuse to hand over."[18] Even though Mauss does use the term *contract*, his intention is not to subject ceremonial gift exchange to the criteria of modern legal practices—which Davy does, following an evolutionist schema—but to make it possible to understand one of its aspects: obligation. His entire study clearly aims at bringing to light the irreducible originality of gift exchange.

It is now possible for us to adopt the reverse approach and to briefly indicate the main features of the contract that profoundly distinguish it from gift exchange. Since my purpose is to highlight its contrast with ceremonial exchange, I will restrict my consideration to the contract of sale and purchase, which can be described as follows: (1) it presupposes a *negotiation* between partners meant to obtain the maximum mutual advantage possible; this negotiation may be easy or fierce or even hostile, with each partner defending his own interest; (2) even if the contract is established between persons—generally two,[19] whether natural persons (that is, individuals) or artificial persons (legal entities such as corporations)—it is not personal in nature; it commits persons not as particular subjects but as subjects of law; the contract, therefore, has an *impersonal form*; if someone buys from or sells to a friend, this friendship may be mentioned but must not be part of the grounds of the contract (one cannot commit to remain friends or define love relationships by contract);[20] (3) in contractual exchange the goods exchanged are exhaustively defined and described; the transaction involves these goods and not others; *the object of the contract is therefore strictly limited*, even if the sequence remains open; (4) by hypothesis the goods involved in a contractual procedure of sale are *alienable* goods—persons, honors, or public offices, for instance, cannot be sold by contract without it being immoral and against the law; (5) the obligation contracted by the partners is public and legally defined; failure to meet the commitment is subject to *legal sanction* (such as fines, imprisonment, or loss of rights); (6) finally—and this is a crucial point— the specific character of the contract is that it is *limited in time*; it applies over a delimited period and becomes null and void beyond it.

It is clear that each of these points is in profound contradiction with the logic of ceremonial gift exchange. The contract of sale is a procedure whose purpose is not to seek recognition by the partner but to conduct a clear, effective, and measurable exchange. This is why the monetary instrument is so suitable to it. This is also why it is important for the contract to remain distinct from gift-exchange relationships. The Protestant ethic was able to draw this boundary by radically separating the world of gift-giving—the realm of grace—which is left to God, from the world of business, which belongs to men and is the object of "asceticism in the world." Conversely, we saw how the Catholic ethic allowed a contamination between these two different types of logic. This is the type of question Mauss anticipates near the end of *The Gift*:

It is precisely the Romans and Greeks, who, perhaps, following upon the Semites of the north and west, invented the distinction between personal and real law [i.e., law applicable to things], separated sale from gift and exchange, isolated the moral obligation and contract, and in particular, conceived the difference that exists between rites, laws, and interests. It was they who, after a veritable, great, and admirable revolution, went beyond all the outmoded morality, and this economy of the gift. It was too dependent on chance, was overexpensive and too sumptuous, burdened with consideration for people, incompatible with the development of the market, commerce, and production, and, all in all, at the time was anti-economic. (*G* 53–54)

"Outmoded morality" and "economy of the gift . . . too dependent on chance"—there is reason to be surprised: Mauss suddenly goes back to situating gift exchange within an evolutionist perspective, suspecting it of being overly archaic, devaluing it in contrast to commercial economy, and, in the end, expecting from it the injection of a little generosity into the world of profit. We cannot follow him on this path. Once again he seems unable to realize that ceremonial gift exchange and the economy belong to two entirely different realms. There is no such thing as a "gift-exchange economy," as we saw in Chapter 4. There can be, however, systems of production in which resources are dedicated in priority to the preservation of the public procedures of recognition constituted by gift exchanges, as Malinowski very accurately notes with respect to the *kula*; in this case the volume of sumptuary offerings has an effect on the rest of the economy. Other very different situations also exist in which gift-exchange practices interfere unduly with the laws of the marketplace. In these cases it is dangerous and even immoral to rely on personal bonds to conduct transactions that are subject to public rules of justice. From this point of view the development of the contractual system has made possible the objectivity and equity that become necessary from the moment the exchange of goods is the aim sought rather than the establishment of personal bonds through these goods.

When equitable exchanges of goods are involved, gift-exchange relationships must give way to commercial relationships. There is a precise converse to this requirement: commercial relationships are not capable of creating bonds between humans and cannot aim to do so. Let me go further: the contractual bond is not and must not be the social bond.[21] This is not a trivial observation but one of the most serious issues faced by modern societies, in which contractual relationships tend to prevail as the model of all public and private relationships. In these societies a constraining, neutral, and efficient form of sociality also develops, in which the scarcity of personal relationships is compensated by excessive courtesy, by a highly formal but salutary civility: expressions of courtesy may be one of the last remnants of ritual relationships of gift exchange. The general hypothesis can be made that it is in the interest of advanced industrial societies, in proportion to their increasing complexity, to reduce personal relationships to a minimum in order to make the system itself manageable, since the functional cost of these relationships is very high. It is clear that contracts and monetary transactions make this possible. Any intrusion of a personal nature is viewed, then, as a risk of corruption. Abstract professional relationships become the only legitimate ones. Personal relationships are transferred to private life or to religious, athletic, artistic, political, or charitable organizations or to other forms of chosen communities. The emotions associated with these groups can take on public expression in the form of a gushing sentimentality. This does not necessarily amount to a social bond. Often it is even a symptom of its absence.

.   .   .

Between Aristotle and Simmel runs the thread of a different tradition, more open-minded in its approach to the question of money. This tradition includes the philosophers (foremost among which are the Scholastics) who conduct a reflection on the exchange of goods as one of the major forms of relationships of justice in the city. It can be said that within this tradition theories of currency redeem the legitimacy of money. From this perspective an abundance of testimonies can be found in the authors who developed the new discipline called "political economy," starting in the seventeenth century (and even in the sixteenth with Bodin, although the term itself seems to have appeared with Boisguilbert in 1695). This type of approach was reinforced by Cantillon, Galliani, Melon, Quesnay, and many others, but, above all, by the prestigious Scottish and English tradition from James Steuart to Adam Smith. They all attempt to develop a functional analysis and generally show little concern for the moral suspicions that haunt philosophers. It is precisely because the latter are so difficult to convince that one must look through their works for evidence of a shift in opinion.

Let me note, however, that the conceptual backgrounds against which Aristotle and Simmel framed these questions were hardly comparable. Aristotle raised his questions within the framework of the Greek city, where the economy was primarily conceived of as the efficient management of available goods in the service of a higher purpose defined as "the common good." The world was understood as a global entity whose state of equilibrium had to be preserved in the same way that the *oikos* was a closed system whose advantages had to be well managed. The Greeks certainly knew how to invest and develop,[22] but the primary aim was to sustain and ensure the growth of one's patrimony while preserving the equilibrium. Their worldview was mostly static. What threatened this order was the boundless yearning—*pleonexia*—for profit, the dangerous movement of accumulation—the bad form of chrematistic—that undermined justice in the exchange. Simmel wrote after the industrial revolution, in the middle of the financial revolution, and more generally at a time when the capitalist model was spreading—long after Adam Smith and shortly after Marx. He was Weber's and Sombart's contemporary. The economy had become the major form of activity of Western societies and the key to political power. It had overturned the old orders and transformed the nature of civilizations. It could not be separated from the democratic movements that were prevailing throughout the world. The question of money had become that of the role played by currency in this process. Aristotle remains concerned with justice, of which currency, as operator of proportion, is at the same time an expression and a means. Simmel's primary concern is with liberty: money understood as monetary instrument has been a constant factor in the increase of individual autonomy and the key to individual emancipation from the old statutory dependences. Aristotle situates the regulating function of currency within the framework of an order of things that by hypothesis must remain stable. Simmel, according to the modern historical worldview, does so within the framework of a movement of technical transformation and expansion to which no end can be assigned. Yet both are able to analyze the positive powers of the monetary instrument while keeping a distinction between these powers and the questions of the moral and immoral uses of money.

From this we must draw the conclusion that, in the city characterized by the differentiation of tasks and competences and the diversity of productions and needs, a useful exchange exists that belongs to the order of justice. In this exchange money plays the role of an instrument of equitable evaluation guaranteed by sovereign authority.[23] Money allows transactions to be objective and fluid and ensures the partners' autonomy. This order of justice is what subordinates *koinōnia* to *polis*, placing the association of interests in the service of the city. It is not a space for gift exchange, which belongs to a different realm whose purpose is not the exchange of goods but recognition. Before finally returning to the latter, we still have to assess the extent of the transformations that have affected the commercial realm.

Legitimate Figures of Commercial Exchange

By presenting in *Nicomachean Ethics* an analysis of currency that is simultaneously functional, political, and ethical, Aristotle makes obvious the necessity of currency in the exchanges between citizens and presents it as an indispensable instrument of distributive justice. He certainly does not fail to condemn profit (in the *Politics*, when analyzing the bad form of chrematistics) and to express concern about the risks to which merchants expose the city. It still remains that, in contrast to Plato's irrevocable judgment, his novel approach marks a first turning point in philosophy's relationship to money. Even when Aristotle states that between knowledge and money there is no common measure, he is primarily making a technical observation applicable to anything that is not divisible and does not lend itself to measurement in quantitative terms. This is why he recommends that the teaching of the masters of philosophy be compensated through gifts. In fact, this problem has been convincingly solved by medieval theologians: payment does not represent the purchase of knowledge but the teacher's compensation for his work. For this to be conceivable requires at least three conditions. First, knowledge must be viewed as acquired competence rather than as heavenly favor (on this point the Middle Ages seem to have been more modern than has often been claimed). Second, labor must be viewed not as servile in nature but as the normal activity of human beings.[1] Finally, the exchange ensured by currency must be viewed as a guarantee of liberty, as well as of justice. It must be recognized that something has permanently changed since Socrates' proclamation before the Athenian court, in which he pointed to his poverty as proof that he was telling the truth.

This transformation had already begun with the movement initiated by the Sophists, but recognizing it requires taking off Plato's eyeglasses in order to consider their thought and practices in a new way. This reconsideration has been accomplished by researchers during the past one hundred years, starting with an effort to reconstitute the available corpus, which was particularly incomplete and fragmented.[2] A different reversal contributed independently to dismissing the old suspicion: the legitimization of the figure of the merchant—a phenomenon inseparable from the whole of Western economic history. We will examine just one exemplary element: the praise of trade in the age of the Enlightenment, mainly as presented in Montesquieu. No less remarkable is the way in which, during the same period, writers and philosophers (Diderot, Kant, and Fichte) rallied to gain recognition for the rights of authors, in order to guarantee the income due from their publications and to put an end to the unauthorized reproduction of their works. Simmel was right: this involved new stakes in terms of liberty. The same liberty associated with the power provided by paying is also ensured in the psychoanalytical relationship. This is an ironic situation, since of all the relationships of training or therapy invented by modernity, psychoanalysis is certainly the closest to the relationship that used to bond the ancient *sophoi* to their disciples or the shamans to their patients—such is the relationship of transference, which for Freud constitutes the core of psychoanalytical therapy. This is a complex and fragile relationship in which the neutrality guaranteed by money plays a decisive role in the resolution of the conflict.

These are merely four cases of exemplary figures among many others that could have been chosen, but they should be sufficient to lead us to the following questions: are we witnessing the final triumph of the contractual relationship? Is our time the age of the wage-earning thinker? Of the rule of the marketplace? Of the collapse of the gift-exchange relationship?

Rehabilitating the Sophists

In our intellectual memory the Sophists have remained associated with the image of a pseudophilosophy, especially because of the attacks lodged by Plato (as we saw in Chapter 1) and by the entire tradition that relied on the judgments of the founder of the Academy. The first successful attempt at their rehabilitation was primarily due to a recognition of the modern character of the issues they raised or imposed in Greek cities, starting in the fifth century BCE and the Sophists' invention of the transmission of knowledge as a strictly professional activity. This invention presupposed an unprecedented dissociation of teaching from the initiatory relationship and from transmission through statutory belonging. To understand this transformation amounts to understanding the Sophists' demand for remuneration. It will also enable us to realize that an entire mode of relationship to goods—*khrēmata*—is at stake in their choice to be remunerated specialists.

Aretē: *The Acquiring of Excellence*

The first achievement with which the Sophists should be credited is undoubtedly their promotion of a new conception of education and culture by imposing qualifications based on knowledge rather than on aristocratic distinction. According to Werner Wilhelm Jaeger, "in the history of the human mind, the sophists are a phenomenon quite [as] necessary as Socrates or Plato; in fact, without them, Socrates and Plato could never have existed."[3] Jaeger's assessment is shared by most of those who have taken an interest in the Sophistic movement in the past few decades. According to the most ancient tradition, Greek culture was founded on a certain conception of *aretē*, a virtue or quality that would be better translated by the Italian word *virtù* and that is generally designated today by the term *excellence*. For noblemen it included courage, pride, a sense of honor, and generosity. These types of values associated with a warrior caste are not specific to Greece; they are observed in many traditional cultures.[4] The Sophists implicitly challenged this aristocratic and ultimately elitist model. They meant to impose the idea that what now prevailed was not gallantry in combat or the mastery of athletic practices but useful knowledge and know-how. This change of perspective clearly amounted to dispossessing the aristocratic class of its status as a model to be followed by the rest of society, and it entailed a devaluing of the type of competence passed on by this class. Ways of being, lifestyles, and privileged relationships to rulers, in short all the qualities that seemed to naturally belong to the "well-born" (*eugeneis*), were no longer viewed as capable of guaranteeing access to power. What mattered most was knowing how to speak and persuade: eloquence and the art of argument. While this mastery was acquired by the heirs of the aristocratic establishment in part through their social environment, it was now also becoming available to others in schools of rhetoric or philosophy. What now prevailed was knowledge. In this new hierarchy of values the dominant element was the art of discourse. The recognition of the importance of oratory skill in public action was not a new phenomenon—it was already frequently found in Homer. What was new was the fact that discourse was now an *art* that could be learned independent of any passing on by the group itself. The art of discourse could be learned from those who had identified its forms and its effects—in other words from experts (let us recall that "expert" was the first meaning of the term *sophist*) for whom language was an object of theoretical analysis and technical mastery.

But in this new conception of education the sophistic revolution involved an even more decisive element: the very idea that everything—including *aretē*—could be taught. In a way, the Sophists were proclaiming the principle of a generalized *educability*. This amounted to saying that the incomparable ability for judgment in public affairs that the aristocracy had always claimed for itself could be learned just like mathematics or, in an even more trivial manner, like the know-how possessed by musicians or weavers. In fact, this amounted to saying that the meaning of *aretē* itself had changed. This shift seemed unacceptable to the defenders of the tradition. For them *aretē* could only be transmitted through example, through continuous training, a sort of contamination from the elders to the young (as in *sunousia*, in which adults took charge of adolescents). For them the only authentic mode of transmission of *aretē* was practice. Pindar, who was a staunch supporter of this tradition, wrote, "What nature gives us is in every way best, but many have tried to win renown by taking lessons in prowess [*aretai*]" (*Oly.* 9.100).

Confronting the privilege of transmission "by inheritance," Protagoras advocated methodical learning. He resorted to an irrefutable argument. Let us suppose the city could only survive by teaching everyone the art of the flute; all would then learn it and would play with various levels of skill, but nothing would guarantee that the sons of flutists would play better than others (Plato *Pro.* 327b). In fact, beyond the logical power of the argument, it already expressed the conviction shared by the intellectual public that *aretē* was not primarily a moral disposition but an art that could be learned.

What this shift revealed was the undeniable intellectualization of Greek elites. This evolution, comparable to what can be observed in many

other societies and civilizations, is associated with the appearance of writing and of forms of accounting or of purely theoretical knowledge (such as
geometry, arithmetic, astronomy, and physics). It led to the emergence of
a group of experts, as had been the case very early on in Babylon, China,
India, and Egypt. From the moment writing devices emerge, a transformation occurs that tends to shift power away from pure force and to transfer it
to knowledge. Intelligence technologies prevail over physical means of domination. The emergence of the Sophists in Greece was the symptom of this
transformation. But in the Greek case the importance they took on—after
several generations of *sophoi*—was probably associated with two major phenomena. The first resulted from the more democratic character of alphabet-
ical writing—because it is easy to learn and to memorize, it makes possible
a faster accumulation and a broader circulation of knowledge.[5] The second
was due to the quasi absence of a sacerdotal caste (this function did exist
but in a very limited form). This intellectualization meant the end of the
Homeric and, therefore, of the heroic world and began the time of speech-
makers but also of scholars, men of letters, and men of the book.[6]

    This is the cultural and political background on which the novel
character of the Sophists' intellectual activity can be understood. As for
the theoretical question of the nature of *aretē* and the possibility for it to
be taught, it is extremely complex.[7] Most of our information comes from
Plato's dialogues and the statements within attributed to various Sophists. His views are certainly subtle, but they are also biased. On the point
we are considering, *Protagoras* and *Meno* are particularly important. Of
Socrates' various debates with these Sophists, several incontrovertible elements emerge regarding his agreements and disagreements with them.
First, it is clear that Socrates recognizes that education plays a crucial role
just as the Sophists recognize this—so much so that for Plato the responsibility to educate is inseparable from philosophical activity and from the
definition of politics. Second, like the Sophists (but for different reasons),
Socrates identifies *aretē* with knowledge—and, conversely, evil with ignorance. On this point he expresses his solidarity with Protagoras: "I expect
you know that most men don't believe us. They maintain that there are
many who recognize the best but are unwilling to act on it" (*Pro.* 352d).

    Their disagreement becomes apparent, however, when the goal is
to understand the source of *aretē*. For the Sophists *aretē* is the fruit of
education itself, which means that it cannot be passed on like a natu-

ral character (the example of the untalented son of the flutist provides an illustration of this thesis). Moreover, natural dispositions (Protagoras gives the examples of respect—*aidōs*—and justice—*dikē*—which Zeus gave humans to form societies) are nothing without an education that reinforces them and allows them to become realized. In *Meno* Socrates answers with the example of a young slave who, with the proper guidance provided by the questions he is asked, finds on his own the solution to the problem of geometry he must solve. For Socrates there is a source of *aretē* that is not and cannot be the effect of any techniques of learning, hence his method as midwife to the soul—described in *Theaetetus*—which consists of revealing to his interlocutor the knowledge or *aretē* that he already carries inside him. If this is indeed true, then it is a profound mistake to claim to teach what does not have to be learned but only needs to be liberated and made visible. The Sophists' error is then coupled with an imposture: they claim to teach to others what they already know and to sell to them what they already own. *Aretē* is innate, and it is given to all. The task of the wise man is to contribute to delivering it in those who possess it, or rather who contain it.

In addition to this major disagreement on the origin of *aretē*, there is another regarding its definition. When something must be defined, Socrates always dismisses answers provided in the form of lists of cases or circumstantial attributes of the thing in question. He demands to be told not what any particular *aretē* is but what *aretē* is in and of itself, since a particular thing (such as a particular circle) can only be known if the thing in question (the circle) is already known in general. The Sophists put up a constant resistance to this position in the form of pragmatic pluralism. If *aretē* is excellence, then it has to be excellence in something. There is no such thing as excellence in general but only relative to a given object or function, such as the excellence of the architect, strategist, or orator. Excellence in general would amount to excellence in nothing. Aristotle very accurately grasps what is at stake in this pluralism when he writes, explicitly referring to Plato: "For those who say generally that excellence consists in a good disposition of the soul, or in doing rightly, or the like, only deceive themselves. Far better than such definitions is the mode of speaking of those who, like Gorgias, enumerate the excellences" (*Pol.* 1260a25). This remains a fundamental philosophical debate on the question of the status of definitions and thus on the thought of the multiple. In many respects the sophistic positions are close to what could today be called transcendental pluralism.

Areas of Competence and the Right to Compensation

Because these *aretai* are diverse and specific, they have to be acquired separately. This is important with respect to the question of whether *aretē* can be taught and, as a consequence, whether teaching it should be remunerated. On one side is Socrates, who presents knowledge and *aretē* as innate dispositions—gifts from the deity—that cannot be subjected to profitable exchange. On the other side is the modern view of the Sophists, for whom talents—excellence—are acquired through education and training. In a city whose survival depends on the complementarity of tasks, this process entails the existence of professionals who must exchange their work for compensation proportional to their competence, just like the practitioners of any other trade.

By moving away from cosmology and by refocusing the questions on man (as Socrates does), the Sophists are developing a philosophy that has been rightly described as *pragmatic*. In this they are true to the original meaning of their name and are giving a new style to thought. Rather than a method (which is what Plato is seeking), they put forth *procedures*. Everything can be learned. Everything can be transmitted. But this is because language itself is an instrument, made up of different parts, articulations, forms, and mechanisms. What could appear as intangible reality is now understood as a mechanism whose cogs can be identified, whose construction can be mastered, and whose effects can be directed. Everything can be learned because there is no field of knowledge that cannot be described in terms of techniques and procedures. The Sophists proclaim the existence of determinisms in what appeared to be the realm of enigma or of purely natural talents associated with inspiration, such as poetry or eloquence. Eloquence and the art of persuasion can be acquired. Every type of mastery is based on a type of know-how.

This also explains the novel character of their relation to money. No explicit writings by the Sophists on this topic have survived, but it is very likely that the Sophists had a doctrine on this point. We can surmise what the premises of this doctrine might have been. Money, in the sense of currency, constitutes (or presupposes) a convention. It is a sign and a measurement of the relative value of goods, which makes it possible to govern exchanges within the city in an equitable manner. These are technical and hardly debatable aspects of the nature of currency. Plato himself recognizes them (in his *Laws*), even though he immediately denounces the danger involved in monetary circulation. It is even more plausible that the sophistic tradition is the source of the definition of money that Aristotle gives in *Nicomachean Ethics*. In Plato's writings, the very manner in which Protagoras and Hippias discuss their income without any self-consciousness testifies to the fact that they do not view the question of money as problematic.

It remains that neither Plato nor any of those who criticize the Sophists state how the latter use their income. None of the Sophists are blamed for living in luxury or in a morally scandalous manner. If they had done so, it is easy to imagine how the authors of comedies would have immediately taken advantage of it. Isocrates, who criticizes them elsewhere, notes: "None of those known as sophists will be found to have ever accumulated much money, but some lived in poor, others in moderate circumstances."[8] This suggests that they are beyond reproach, except for the fact that they charge for the transmission of knowledge. In the view of Plato and others this is reason enough for very deep suspicion, whereas the payment of honoraria is perfectly accepted in the case of poets who declaim in public, musicians, dancers, and artists in general, but also grammar teachers, athletic coaches, other educators, and, of course, physicians.[9] The Sophists claim to belong to this category of experts, though they are experts in nothing, and, above all, they claim to cover a field that belongs to philosophers. This, Plato cannot accept.

In the end what makes the Sophists daring is not only the fact that through their very practice they bring to light—or at least presuppose—the functional status of money (just as they do with respect to language) but also the fact that they place the activity of teaching at the same level as any other professional activity. What this means in their view is not that knowledge can be sold but that expertise must be compensated. A remarkable convergence emerges between the set of transformations that the Sophists bring to various forms of thought (theoretical, political, and moral) and the new attitude they display toward money. This set of transformations can be summed up with one phrase: *the technical shift*. What this means is that with the Sophists philosophy, politics, and morality become domains of competences and forms of know-how that can be acquired just like any other. The Sophists thus operate a surprising break with the old beliefs. It should be noted, however, that this breakthrough concerns only intellectual elites. It is associated with an attitude marked by firm agnosticism or even atheism. In this it cannot yet satisfy a widespread demand.[10] The rationalism of the Sophists remains that of a privileged intellectual circle.

This is why their relationship to money was not always understood. For it to be commonly understood would take the advent of a society in which access to knowledge is offered to the masses. Only with our modernity can the relation between money and knowledge take on real meaning. No one today challenges the necessary compensation of competence. From this point of view the Sophists anticipated an evolution that has since prevailed as legitimate. It would be worthwhile to trace the history of the crises that mark this evolution, such as the thirteenth-century conflict that pitted secular teachers who charged for their courses against members of the mendicant orders who taught free of charge at the university of Paris and elsewhere.[11] It would be useful to identify the time when the compensation of men of knowledge shifted from the classical form of *honoraria* to the common form of *wages*. The following conviction emerges: what is remunerated is not the nature of the thing taught or transmitted but the *work* provided in teaching. The Sophists can finally be exonerated: they never sold their knowledge. They asked to be compensated for the services they provided, just like any other competent person. Not only is Plato's criticism no longer understood, but Aristotle's theorem—which claims the impossibility of equivalence between knowledge and money and leads to resorting to gift-giving relationships—now appears as one of the forms of personal dependence analyzed by Simmel and from which wage earning has liberated us.

At the same time as this transformation was occurring, the figure of the merchant—which had been so insistently projected onto the figure of the Sophist—was itself undergoing a profound transformation.

Legitimizing the Merchant: Montesquieu's "Sweet Commerce"

Whereas the figure of the Sophist was not fully rehabilitated until recently, the rehabilitation of the merchant occurred much earlier. When the aim is to demonstrate the considerable change in the attitude of men of letters toward commerce and merchants that occurred during the first decades of the eighteenth century, Montesquieu's testimony is always called upon. In book 20 of his *The Spirit of the Laws,* as early as the first chapter, he gives the following praise, which has remained famous ever since: "Commerce cures destructive prejudices, and it is an almost general truth that everywhere there are gentle mores, there is commerce, and that everywhere there is commerce, there are gentle mores."[12] Actually, Montesquieu was not alone in developing this favorable analysis. The fact that the reasonable character of his position appeared as self-evident in the age of the Enlightenment was probably due to a slow but undeniable transformation that had occurred since the "urban revolution" of the twelfth and thirteenth centuries. This renewal of European cities had been inseparable from a general resumption of commercial exchanges, first around the Mediterranean and in northern Italy and later spreading to the great axes of circulation (the Rhone and the Rhine) and to the richest farming, mining, manufacturing, and urban areas of western Europe.

Braudel analyzes this intense movement of commercial exchange in which the earliest capitalism was formed.[13] The new merchant fortunes also constituted new political powers. In some cases, such as that of the Függers in Nüremberg or the Medici and Strozzi in Florence, great merchants and bankers determined the fate of princes or became princes themselves. A different world was already emerging, even though the desirable values in terms of manners, tastes, titles, and prestige were still defined by the old aristocratic models. As far back as the seventeenth century many works praise commerce and merchants, in England, of course, but also in France (such as Jacques Savary's classic, *Le parfait négociant,* published in 1675).

Montesquieu's praise of trade, therefore, takes its place within an already rich heritage. While his views on this question seem overly optimistic today, they are not naive. His basic economic thesis is a general one that was developed by every theoretician of exchanges at the time: commerce stimulates activity and increases collective wealth, and if an end is put to commerce, then every other form of wealth production is ruined. In Montesquieu's view the clearest example is the economic collapse caused by the discontinuation of commercial exchanges in the Roman Empire following the "barbarian invasions." This economic thesis is complemented by a cultural one: "The effect of commerce is wealth; the consequence of wealth, luxury; that of luxury, the perfection of the arts."[14] This makes possible a different interpretation of the history of civilizations. "National genius" is no longer deemed sufficient to explain technical or artistic achievements. One must understand how the material wealth of nations constitutes the initial condition of their success at the highest level. What is the engine of this movement? According to Montesquieu it is commerce. Furthermore, commerce is the instrument par excellence of a specifically civil bond between human beings, both internationally and locally. This is why Montesquieu assigns to this activity a role that would seem incomprehensible to Plato or even to Aristotle—and which is later rejected by Rousseau.

Montesquieu gives primary consideration to the realm of international relations. He views commerce between states as one of the main factors of international harmony: "The natural effect of commerce is to lead to peace. Two nations that trade with each other become reciprocally dependent; if one has an interest in buying, the other has an interest in selling; and all unions are founded on mutual needs" (*SL* 338). He later adds that "the history of commerce is that of communication among peoples" (*SL* 357). Thus war means that this communication either has stopped or has not taken place. Commerce is in some way the form par excellence of international civility. True, this is not a recent practice, but it does represent a new view, since positive relationships between communities or nations were traditionally considered to depend on gestures of recognition based on respect, gift exchanges, matrimonial alliances, and affinities in language or way of life. To consider that commerce is the initiator of this international civility clearly amounts to shifting the source of the bond between alien groups. This presupposes that relationships of mutual profit are capable of generating reciprocal attachments. This is the question that concerns us from the standpoint of the difference between gift-exchange relationships and commercial relationships. As we will see, Montesquieu has an accurate sense of this question, unlike most of his commentators.

This view of commerce as civilizing factor is, in fact, shared by many Enlightenment authors, such as Melon, Cantillon, and Condillac. Montesquieu's originality is that he modulates this thesis based on his theory of the three forms of government and the distinction he makes between them at the beginning of his book: republican, monarchic, and despotic. From the outset he dismisses despotic government as unfit for commercial relationships, clarifying immediately that there is an essential association between commerce and institutions respectful of public liberties (*SL* 340–41). But the two forms of government in which laws and common faith in institutions prevail do not promote the same type of commerce. This difference has important consequences. What prevails in monarchic government is "luxury commerce," whose aim is primarily to provide the goods that serve the nation in "its arrogance, its delights, and its fancies" (*SL* 340). This does not prevent commerce in useful things, but it subordinates it to this ruinously expensive priority. "The government of many," on the contrary, practices "economic commerce," whose primary aim is utility, which does its utmost to find the products to be exchanged at the best price and is "founded only on the practice of gaining little and even of gaining less than any other nation and of being compensated only by gaining continually" (*SL* 340). A nation of this kind, austere and efficient, cannot make luxury a priority. This is the only way to set in motion a cumulative spiral: "one commerce leads to another, the small to the middling, the middling to the great, and he who earlier desired to gain little arrives at a position where he has no less of a desire to gain a great deal" (*SL* 340). Montesquieu accurately senses the logic that Weber describes a century and a half later by calling this austerity "asceticism in the world" and this virtuous spiral "the spirit of capitalism." For Montesquieu this form of commerce is closely associated with the type of institutions that characterize free nations, as, in his view, England and Holland are.

This constitutes the first part of Montesquieu's analysis of commerce as an instrument of peace. Peace is all the more guaranteed when it involves relations among nations that practice "economic commerce" rather than "luxury commerce." Montesquieu has full confidence in the considerable power of commercial civility between nations. He does not speak, however, of a mutual attachment between partners; what he claims is that "if one has an interest in buying, the other has an interest in selling." Peace is the effect of well-understood self-interest. But what about the reciprocal bond within each society? At first it would seem that the same logic is at play: "Happily, men are in a situation such that, though their passions inspire in them the thought of being wicked, they nevertheless have an interest in not being so" (*SL* 389–90). This famous judgment sums up perfectly the entire movement of substitution of interests to passions that characterizes the reflection of philosophers and economists since the seventeenth century (and which Albert Hirschman so clearly brings to light).[15] In this view the interplay of unpredictable and incompatible passions is counteracted by the calculus of constant and complementary interests. Montesquieu appears to endorse the kind of discourse developed by so many thinkers of his century. Yet—and most commentators have failed to note this—as early as the beginning of book 20 of *The Spirit of the Laws*, which includes these so frequently quoted remarks on the "sweetness" of mores originating from commerce and the peace resulting for nations, he adds: "But, if the spirit of commerce unites nations, it does not unite individuals in the same way. We see that in countries where one is affected only by the spirit of commerce, there is traffic in all human activities and all moral virtues; the smallest things, those required by humanity, are done or given for money" (*SL* 338–39). It cannot be more clearly stated that the commercial relationship has destroyed the gift-giving relationship, whose purpose was to establish a warm and strong bond. A cold, or at least indifferent, calculus now prevails: "The spirit of commerce produces in men a certain feeling for exact justice, opposed on the one hand to banditry and on the other to those moral virtues that make it so that one does not always discuss one's own interests alone and that one can neglect them for those of others" (*SL* 339). Doing so amounts to introducing a little of the spirit of gift-giving into commercial exchange (in French this happens to be called a gesture *par dessus le marché*).[16] This generosity has been lost in nations where commerce is extensive, Montesquieu explains. He adds, "Hospitality, so rare among commercial countries, is notable among bandit peoples" (*SL* 339).

As great as Montesquieu's admiration for England and Holland may be, as great as his conviction that commerce between nations is an instrument of peace and even a powerful means of civilizing mores may be, he is still aware that this form of civility governed by self-interest remains external to human sensitivity. Thus, in the very passages where he grants to commerce this legitimization so long denied by philosophers, Montesquieu remarkably identifies the lack of social bond that characterizes commercial civility. He understands that the only kind of relationship capable of generating this bond is reciprocal generosity. This is the second element of his reflection, which commentators have generally failed to notice. In the end Montesquieu's most interesting lesson—one that contradicts an entire philosophical tradition—is that these two forms of civility are not mutually exclusive. But is it enough to assign one of these forms to external relationships and the other to internal relationships? Beyond self-interested exchanges, relationships between nations also—or above all—entail expressions of respect and public gestures of recognition and friendship. Conversely, we must accept the fact that relationships of justice (or contractual relationships) are indispensable to social life (this is clearly shown by Aristotle's definition of currency), while remaining aware that this "exact justice" is not sufficient to make a community possible.

In spite of this reservation it is clear that, for Montesquieu, as for most Enlightenment thinkers, the page on which the ancient malediction against commerce and money was written had now been turned. Moralists were still denouncing avarice and greed, and no one would have dreamed of contradicting them because these were exclusive *passions*, detrimental to society. Entirely different was the case of the pursuit of *self-interests*, which contributed to the well-being of all through their complementary effects. More profoundly still, self-interests captured dangerous passions and directed them toward the "innocent" activities associated with the increasing of wealth. It would only take one more step for the concept of "the invisible hand" to emerge: the spontaneous complementarity of individual self-interests alone would produce an equilibrium that would ensure the general order of society and the well-being of all.

The celebration of political passions still belonged to a heroic world whose values were combat and challenge, honor and glory. Their conflicts constituted the stage on which power was played out. But as early as the seventeenth century, Hirschman explains, this world was in the process of collapsing. The new model of self-interests was inseparable from the expansion of the economic sphere. Furthermore, it is clear that its logic was prevailing over the political sphere. Philosophers were increasingly experiencing the necessity to theorize the articulation between these two realms. They were encountering this necessity in the very activity by which they made their thought *publicly* known and from which they drew part (and sometimes the whole) of their *income*: the publication of their works. This development makes it possible, once again, to assess the extent of the break that had developed from the old traditions.

Compensating the Author

When Plato denounced the venality of the Sophists, his target was their activity as teachers, not what would today be called the means of dissemination—such as writing. The communication of knowledge still remained largely performed by oral means. This is how knowledge was passed on from one generation to the next.[17] Written documents were rare and costly objects. They would remain so for almost two thousand years. The dissemination of doctrines and knowledge was accomplished through schools of thought, organized groups, and, from the twelfth century onward in the West, the creation of universities.

Printed Books: The Emergence of a Marketplace

The advent of the printing press at the end of the fifteenth century transformed the status of knowledge. The stakes of knowledge were no longer restricted to conflicts between schools and trends; they also involved a marketplace. This was not a sudden discovery but something that happened gradually. The manufacturing of books was costly, and, just like today, publishers (then called *librarians*) had to sell their publications or to make up for the low sales of some books by the high sales of others. Neither writers nor scholars were prepared for this—less so than anyone else. With the advent of techniques of reproduction and dissemination, the quasi-statutory inability of writers to consider the relation between discourse and marketplace would throw them into a crisis of such breadth that the problem is still far from being resolved today.

At first it was as if writers, philosophers, and scholars had viewed the emergence of the printed document as a mere extension of the manuscript—a mere instrument of reproduction, if a more efficient one. When the *Great Book of the World* metaphor developed during the Renaissance, the stimulant for it may have been the multiplication of the printed book, but the philosophical model remained that of the handwritten book: the *Great Book of the World* was the single copy in which the author—whether God or Nature—directly wrote on the "pages" offered to readers.

Just as—according to Plato—writing added an arbitrary and external expression to speech, clerics since the fifteenth century similarly have viewed printing as merely adding broader propagation to writing. Philosophers, for instance, were well aware that this physical circulation was important for the recognition of their thought and the breadth and quality of the resulting public debate. But for them this dissemination remained a secondary phenomenon. In their view "librarians" remained artisans who composed copies of their writings for a certain number of current or future readers, just like tailors could make hundreds of copies of a uniform for a regiment. In their view there was no such thing as a marketplace for books because they did not even conceive that books, in which their writings were published, might be consumer goods.[18] Books were useful goods and certainly necessary to buy but in the same way that furniture, jewels, or paintings were bought. In traditional homes private libraries often remained separate and solemn places, comparable to chapels.[19]

The question of the book is central when considering the recognition of the value of the work. Explicitly recognized as a commercial object, the book gives rise to a formidable problem that is not raised by visual artworks (paintings, statues, jewelry, or furniture). In the latter case no matter how difficult it may be to determine the price of a painting, for example, it remains that a kind of consensus exists between what is measurable and what is incommensurable. This consensus is based at the same time on the artist's notoriety, on the traditions established within the profession (which are often precise), and on the role played by the symbolic compensations granted (public honors, gifts in kind, invitations, and statutory privileges).[20] Under these circumstances the work of art presents a kind of identity that is relatively easy to circumscribe: it coincides with the object. It cannot be reduced to the object, but it would disappear without it. The work of art is unique. It exists only within the boundaries of this physical reality, regardless of the value that the artist's *poiēsis* may have given to the material (Kant explicitly notes this difference, as we will see).

The case of books (including musical scores) is entirely different. Already, in its manuscript form and with reproduction by craft, the work conveyed by the book does not coincide with the object, of which there may be many copies (in the same way that a musical work can be performed any number of times). Even in its ancient form (rolls, tables, or loose sheets), the book already raises the question of the difference between physical medium—the book as object—and the work as such—the text written by the author. It is clear that this physical existence does not seem capable of playing a part in defining the value of the work—even though physical existence is essential, since without a sufficient number of copies the work risks disappearing. Until the invention of printing and regardless of the extent of an author's fame, books did not represent the possibility of profitable trade, so slow and costly was the process by which they were made. This explains the tendency to view books as rare and therefore precious objects, even if in principle this status had no relation to their content. Manuscripts were supposed to share the status of visual artworks. Yet everyone knew that this materialization was not what determined the value of a book as a work of discourse. The status of the manuscript was thus still ambiguously situated somewhere between that of the object and that of the text. These limitations meant that, unlike painters and sculptors, writers and scholars could not rely on the production of the object to ensure income and even less to gain wealth. For medieval theologians and philosophers what was assessed was less their work as written object than their activity as masters, teachers, or leaders of a school. This situation was not fundamentally different from that of the masters of the classical era. The activity of transmitting knowledge literally remained a *praxis*, an expression of the individual who spoke and whose discourse could not be evaluated like a thing, even when it was printed and compared to a work of art.

Aristotle's claim still applied: between knowledge and money there was no common measure. This was ultimately why the relationship between masters and students had to be based on the gift/countergift model. The book as *manuscript* had not fundamentally transformed the conditions of evaluating the production of knowledge. The applied criterion of evaluation remained that of speech—oral communication within small communities. But when the book became a *printed* object, it gave rise for the first time to a new kind of problem with respect to its assessment as a work and as a source of income for its author. This problem was due to the fact that the mechanical reproduction of the text turned it into a commodity. What was remunerated was no longer the author's activity but the book as object of which a large number of copies could be sold. This shift profoundly disrupted the traditional situation of the author. The difference between text and printed object was exacerbated. The more copies of a book that were made, the more the writing was likely to survive and be known, but the less the book had value as object (since the destruction of some of these copies involved little risk). At the same time, authors discovered that the production of large numbers of copies of their books could contribute to their income as much as or more than the compensation they received for teaching. They discovered the mediation of the marketplace. Yet, as we will see, the ancient reflexes and the old traditions still endured as if they had had a life of their own.

The existence of a marketplace entailed circuits of distribution, an identified customer base, author notoriety, and evaluation of the costs involved in book manufacturing. Notoriety could justify after the fact the number of copies published and reduce production costs. But this was not necessarily the case. Corneille's fame did not secure a large circulation for his works during his lifetime or after his death. Conversely, some works that were mediocre from a literary standpoint received considerable success. There is no doubt that the laws of the marketplace are different from those that determine the intrinsic value of the works. In the context of these transformations and questionings and almost three centuries after the invention of the printing press, writers and scholars began to raise in earnest the issues of their relationships with their publishers and of their rights as authors.

Dealing with these issues required an agreement on a definition of the legal status of books and, as a consequence, on the rights of their authors, which led to formulations that have remained genuine philosophical propositions.

Diderot, Kant, and the Value of Books

When Kant took a stand on the question of authors' rights, the debate had already been going on for at least two decades. The first writer who took a position in philosophical terms was Diderot in his *Lettre sur le commerce de la librairie*. He did so within the context of a creeping crisis involving an increase in forgeries, which ruined legitimate publishers and deprived authors of the income deriving from their work, but no legal protection existed yet. To justify the rights of authors over their writings, it was necessary to establish a clear relationship of ownership of the former over the latter. Diderot does so in the following terms:

What good could belong to a man if a work of his mind, unique fruit of his education, studies, efforts, time, research, and observations, if his most beautiful hours, the most beautiful moments of his life, his own thoughts, the emotions of his heart, the most precious part of his being, the part that does not perish but makes him immortal, did not belong to him? How can man, his very substance and soul, be compared to a field, a tree, or a vine equally given to all by nature in the beginning and only appropriated by individuals through cultivation, the first legitimate means of ownership? Who, more than the author, has the right to use his own thing by giving or selling it?—the owner's right takes precedence over the buyer's right. . . . Let me say it again, the author is the master of his work or no one in society is the master of his own good.[21]

The tone of his argument is impassioned, but his intention seems clear: what an author produces is the emanation of his or her very being and belongs to the author exclusively. This is the foundation of the author's rights over his or her writings; however, this apparent clarity conceals—or represses—highly complex problems. We must reexamine Diderot's text in order to bring to light its presuppositions—supported by an effective metaphorical foundation—and to assess its limitations and contradictions.

Diderot's first aim is to establish that a "work of the mind" is by nature the property of its author. It is not a good that has been acquired from the outside world but an emanation of the person from which it comes. It cannot even be distinguished from the person of the author: everything about him contributed to the work, from the training he underwent to the most intense and beautiful inner states he experienced—so much so that the work coincides with his very being. This "work" is therefore no ordinary property but property par excellence. It is even the essence of the self. What the author produced in his work is his own self—hence Diderot's comparison with a field cultivated by a farmer. As far back as one can remember, cultivation has been recognized as the foundation of the appropriation of the land (this is commonplace in Roman law, for instance). If an activity such as that of the farmer, which is applied to something external, is sufficient to found an unquestionable right of appropriation, then how could the author's right over his or her work be denied? As for the publisher's right, it is no more than a corollary of the author's right. It is merely a transferred right.

This argument seems entirely self-evident, yet it is strange if examined. It involves serious philosophical difficulties, as well as rather fuzzy legal implications. First, Diderot's definition of the work as emanating from the subject lumps together every aspect of life and merges the agent's activities (studies and research), his emotional states, and his productions. By doing so Diderot erases the old distinction between *praxis* and *poiēsis*. As a result the boundary between the author and the product becomes blurred. How could the author alienate something that is presented as inseparable from his very being? Apparent is Diderot's lack of a coherent theory of the producer and of the product or of a reflection on the mediation between the two. This is why this merged identity leads him to a legal position that is just as uncertain. And yet an old distinction, familiar to every jurist, exists between "personal law" (which involves persons and is the foundation of moral law) and "real law" (which involves *res*, the thing). This distinction would have been very useful to Diderot because it would have enabled him to establish a distinction between intellectual property and publishing rights; that is, between what is inalienable and what can be sold. This is why his statement, "the owner's right takes precedence over the buyer's right," does not solve anything. It amounts to claiming that the author can sell as a mere thing—and therefore alienate—what has just been described as an inestimable good, as the very substance of his being, as his soul, and which can therefore never be sold. He can sell what he wrote because nothing belongs to him to a fuller extent. What is it that is put up for sale, then? Is it the author's right over his writing or only the manuscript itself? Diderot fails to make this distinction. In fact, according to him the author is selling the one along with the other. He can do so because the writing belongs to him. We can surmise the serious contradiction to which this line of reasoning can lead: condoning the principle by which what is inalienable can be alienated. Diderot does not appear to be aware of this. But he draws the consequence of his argument with great consistency by proclaiming his admiration for the English system, in which books seem to have the same status as other commodities. Why? "Because in that country no difference is recognized between the purchase of a field or of a house and the purchase of a manuscript—and indeed there is none."[22] This conclusion is the inevitable consequence of the premise of his argument. Diderot is somehow juxtaposing a metaphysics of the author that situates the latter in a quasi-mystical higher realm with a realism of the marketplace that views without any qualms the sale of the products of the mind.

To be consistent with his own purpose, Diderot should have looked beyond mere property rights. And yet, despite his questionable formulations, everyone understood the meaning of his struggle in defense of the author and his or her rights with regard to publishers ("librarians"), as well as to pirating. The primary purpose of the author's absolute right over his or her work, which Diderot meant to demonstrate, was to guarantee that only the author's publisher—to whom this right had been transferred—would be legally authorized to publish his or her writings. In the eighteenth century, pirated publication was emerging as a serious problem. To counter it, a royal decree had instituted the "privilege" system, by which exclusive printing rights were granted to the legitimate publisher. Diderot proclaimed that the author was the only source of this legitimacy, which should guarantee his or her right to be paid. This is what he needed to demonstrate.

It was important, however, to give this demonstration a sturdier formulation by providing a rigorous clarification of the concepts of author, book, publisher, and reader. This is what Kant attempts to do in several concise writings. The most important ones are a short 1785 writing titled "On the Wrongfulness of Unauthorized Publication of Books" and the text titled "What Is a Book?" in the *Doctrine of Right* section of *The Metaphysics of Morals*, written in 1797. This short text belongs to the first part of the work, dedicated to "Private Right." The reason that leads Kant to declare his opinion on this topic is the same as Diderot's: to denounce pirating. Kant's definition of the book provides the starting point: "A book is a writing (it does not matter, here, whether it is written in hand or set in type, whether it has few or many pages), which represents a discourse that someone delivers to the public by visible linguistic signs. One who *speaks* to the public in his own name is called the *author* (*auctor*). One who, through a writing, discourses publicly in another's (the author's) name is a *publisher*."[23]

In this definition the two modes of existence of the book—as physical object and as element in the realm of ideas—are simultaneously distinguished from each other and interlocked with each other. From the outset Kant acknowledges that the book is, first of all, a manufactured object—whether by manual or mechanical means—and as such is identically reproduced in an indeterminate number of copies. But by immediately adding that these written signs constitute a discourse (*Rede*) addressed by the author to his or her readers, Kant underlines the fact that the book is not an object like any other. In the classical terms of Roman law—terms to which Kant constantly refers in his *Doctrine of Right*—the book, just like any other physical object, seems to have the status of a thing and therefore falls under the purview of "real law." As such, a book can be sold, and its buyer can use it as he or she wishes: read it, take care of it, loan it, resell it, or even destroy it. There is, indeed, an empirical level at which the book is in no way different from any other object of use and exchange.

What changes everything in the case of the book is the fact that the author cannot be separated from the work. He or she remains present in the printed words. This argument makes it possible to establish why the buyer of a copy of a book cannot reproduce it without causing substantial harm to its author and to its publisher. Kant's 1785 text shows this convincingly. The harm caused goes beyond financial harm alone. Without dismissing the latter, Kant puts forth a more fundamental reflection on the illegitimacy of piracy that articulates an entire set of concepts involving author, publisher, and readership—the only concepts that could determine the question of the right to publish a book and to make it available in the marketplace.

First, what is the status of the *author*? Kant defines the author as someone who has "property in his thought."[24] This means that, of all the phenomena pertaining to a subject, his thought is what is most exclusively his. The written discourse that expresses these thoughts thus remains inherent to the author's being. This initial belonging is constitutive and cannot be erased. This statement appears to be a reiteration of Diderot's formulations. But Diderot's main concern is the status of the work. He says nothing about the status of the author. Kant—and this constitutes the novelty and the power of his position—defines the author as the owner of his thoughts. This is what founds his *responsibility* over his writings as they are addressed to the public "in his own name." In this case, the term *own* applies to the author's ethical relationship to his addressee, not to some ineffable state of proximity to oneself. According to Kant, this "own" is the author's reason making itself public. This constitutes the privileged relationship between author and reader.

Second, what is the status of the *public*? Kant's choice of this term is significant. What it designates is not the indistinct masses of those who bought a book or of readers in general but all of those who, by judging the work presented to them—whether book, artwork, or political speech—make *a public use of their reason* (this use has been defined in *What Is Enlightenment?*). This is the "enlightened" public, the only public worthy of the name. Moreover, between the author and his public a specific relationship is initiated. The author only exists as author relative to a public. This is why the public has a right: the right that the book remain available. This involves the specific responsibility of the publisher.

The *publisher* is explicitly defined by Kant as the "representative" of the author: "there are grounds for regarding publication not as dealing with a commodity *in one's own name*, but as *carrying on an affair in the name* of another, namely the author."[25] This mandate does not merely have a commercial nature. It has to do with the very fact that the author addresses the public. In other words the publisher as representative also addresses the public on behalf of the author. The connection between publisher and author is therefore not only a relationship of real right over the ownership and sale of copies of the book—which belong to the realm of the alienable—but also a relationship of personal right over the intellectual property of the book—which belongs to the realm of the inalienable. It is because the publisher was assigned this mandate that he has the exclusive right to address the public through the author's book. This is also why piracy is illegitimate in two distinct ways: as theft—from the standpoint of real right—and as usurpation—from the standpoint of personal right.

We can now return to Kant's definition of the *book* with a better understanding of its dual status as commodity and as intellectual object. Kant deserves credit for preserving this duality, as an expert in copyright law rightly states: "He was the first in the history of thought who understood that a distinction must be kept between *discourse* ('a non-physical good') and its *physical* medium ('the thing'). He was the first to sense the existence of an original bond uniting an author to his discourse."[26] The power of Kant's argument lies in his demonstration that the commercial alienation of the book—a mere object produced, sold, and handled—in no way undermines the author's right of intellectual property, that is, the ownership that he retains over his thoughts and is publicly expressed in the book as discourse (*Rede*). How can this discourse be made available in the marketplace? Precisely through the mediation of the publisher, whose connection to the author is at the same time a relationship of personal law—since he is mandated by contract to represent the author—and a relationship of real law—since he contractually guarantees to the author income from the sales of the copies of the book. It is therefore the inalienable character of intellectual rights that guarantees the author's financial income, since without this character piracy would be legitimate and the author would receive no income from the sales. This involves a paradox: what guarantees the physical realm is the pure realm of ideas. And yet between these two levels there is no dichotomy but a dual articulation. Kant illuminates the connection that develops between marketplace and public space. It is because the book as object is disseminated in the marketplace thanks to the publisher that the discourse it contains can be known and that the public use of reason that is inherent to reason itself becomes possible between author and reader.

Kant's propositions have consequences with respect to the questions Plato raised regarding payment for the Sophists' teaching. Authors—even if they are as free of self-interest as the professor of philosophy from Königsberg—can and even must claim for themselves the income derived from the sale of their books, because the books represent labor that must be compensated. This labor can be represented by money, as Kant explains in the previous segment, "What Is Money?"[27] By the same logic, teachers can and must demand wages for their activities. This is, indeed, the order of justice in exchanges defined in *Nicomachean Ethics*, except that this order now governs every form of the transmission of knowledge. This shift in philosophical reflection on the legitimacy of the income derived from knowledge is made possible and even necessary by the emergence of printing—that is, by the fact (emphasized by Kant) that the book is at the same time *opus* (work) and *opera* (activity), at the same time *poiēsis* and *praxis* (which Diderot had not realized), whereas the master's words remain enveloped in his own presence and in the very act of speech. It took the separation accomplished by writing for the separation that had always been implicitly present in speech to become apparent.

Unexpectedly, this relation to live speech and the elaboration of a contract of separation implied by the objective character of payment also characterize psychoanalytical therapy.

Paying the Therapist: Freud's Argument on Money and Transference

The psychoanalytical approach to money is a complex one, often stimulating but often disappointing as well. It is stimulating in the way it questions money's symbolic relationship to the anal impulse and the yearning for appropriation. It is disappointing in its attempt to interpret the symbolism of money with a lack of rigor in its use of anthropological data.[28] In addition to these questions involving the symbolic status of money in general, psychoanalysis faces a different question that is specific to its own practice: the compensation of the therapist. Let us consider these two aspects in turn.

What is striking when we read psychoanalytical studies on the question of money as it has been elaborated by Freud, taken up by his immediate disciples (Geza Roheim and Sándor Ferenczi), and subjected to endless comment since is the surprising and constant confusion they show between the realm of gift exchange and the realm of commercial exchange, between the precious thing offered and the money accumulated or exchanged. Most of the examples cited, whether individual behaviors or social practices—such as ethnological or historical data or directly observed phenomena—pertain to relationships of gift exchange, but they are interpreted in terms of monetary exchange, self-interested calculus, profitable accumulation, or even—and this constitutes the most problematic kind of misunderstanding—in terms of "primitive capitalism."

In addition to these difficulties (associated at the beginning of the twentieth century with the fact that anthropological research itself was a new field at the time), there is another that is specific to the psychoanalytical approach as such in that it is meant to account for social practices based on hypotheses concerning individual psychogenesis. In the case of money psychoanalysis attempts to explain behaviors relative to objects, goods, and monetary signs; based on structures or impulses associated with the psychic formation of the subject—such as the different stages established by Freud.

Nevertheless, to challenge, at least to some extent, the psychoanalytical interpretation of money does not equal disqualifying psychoanalysis in general or even rejecting all of its hypotheses on this point. On the contrary, it is possible to take up many of its approaches and to reexamine them in the light of a pertinent analysis of either relationships of gift exchange or relationships of profitable exchange. This effort at establishing a distinction should even make it possible to give a new extension to many Freudian hypotheses concerning the anal impulse, the relationship to others, phenomena of generosity and retention, and the eroticization of the relationship to money.

Besides the clinical problem of the interpretation of money and of the emotions associated with it, psychoanalytical practice itself raises a specific issue: the *payment of the therapy*. On this point we must acknowledge Freud's remarkable insight and the lucidity of his directives regarding the symbolic role this payment plays in the transference relationship. It is perhaps above all on this point (in spite of the many slips due to the lack of rigor shown by some psychoanalysts) that the psychoanalytical interpretation of money demonstrates perhaps its greatest originality and fertility. This still requires, however, that its presuppositions be clarified in a more exhaustive way than has been the case until now, by precisely establishing the articulation between gift-exchange relationship and commercial relationship in the interaction between analyst and patient.

The psychoanalytic therapy as established by Freud is only possible thanks to a pact between analyst and patient, the conditions of which are explicitly stated. The rules agreed on by both parties are of two kinds. Some concern the very definition of the therapy—such as the fundamental rule presented to the patient and by which "everything must be said" (*alles sagen*), or the precise rules the analyst imposes on him- or herself and by which he or she must listen and abstain from intervening (at least up to a point). These rules obviously involve theoretical positions regarding the nature of the unconscious and the function of speech in the therapy. But there are also a certain number of rules with a more empirical character— even though they also involve more general presuppositions. They determine the intervals between the sessions (usually less than a week), their specific timing (day and time of day), and finally their price. This is the point that will concern me here.

In "Further Recommendations in the Technique of Psychoanalysis" Freud indicates what seems important to him in this financial relationship. He puts forth indications of a theoretical kind, as well as more practical ones, which nevertheless have clinical consequences. He notes that the analyst must approach financial questions with the utmost frankness. It is interesting that Freud compares this frankness to the frankness he demands from the patient regarding his or her *libido*. The two types of repression involved are reciprocal counterparts. The psychoanalyst, he writes, "may expect that money questions will be treated by cultured people in the same manner as sexual matters, with the same inconsistency, prudishness and hypocrisy."[29] These remarks confirm earlier analyses on the anal origin of our unconscious representations of money and of our behavior with respect to it.[30] The pact offered to the patient, therefore, amounts to having him or her take responsibility for this structure and to confronting him or her with this repressed element.

This is the background on which the modalities of payment are determined. The first of these modalities, directly inspired by this consideration, concerns the preclusion of bargaining. The analyst must clearly state the demands; the patient must know what to expect. How can the amount of the payment be set? This requires a criterion, some kind of reference. For Freud it is the honoraria received by surgeons, since the—very high—

level of professional competence required is comparable in both cases (this reference to surgery is recurrent in Freud's writing when his purpose is to provide a metaphor for the *operation* performed by the analyst).[31] Then comes a recommendation concerning the regularity of the payment: it can be either a monthly settlement or a payment after each session (the reason given is that debt should not be allowed to accumulate, but a deeper reason can be surmised). Freud then recommends payment in cash rather than by check, as if he deemed it advisable to call on the most traditional imaginary representations.[32] An additional clause specifies that since the patient is assigned a precise time personally reserved for him or her, payment is due even if the patient does not show up; Freud considers that this is the best way to counter the resistance that often discourages patients from attending the sessions.

These are the main dispositions recommended by Freud with respect to the question of payment. There is no doubt that they involve a contractual relationship unequivocally situated within the realm of commercial relationships, even though at no time does he mention profit or encourage excessive gains. It can be said that this is a commercial relationship in the sense defined by *Nicomachean Ethics* and the entire tradition of the fair price. From this point of view Freud remains within the framework of what used to be called "justice in exchanges." The psychoanalyst proposes a therapy in exchange for a reasonable compensation, as does any physician who exercises his art conscientiously. Psychoanalysis deserves additional credit for being able to treat an ill that no other discipline was capable of identifying until then. Freud insists, therefore, that the psychoanalytical activity is to be situated within the framework of other treatments and that it deserves the same type of professional consideration and compensation.

Yet the fact that Freud feels the need to state and explain this point with such emphasis suggests that he senses a difficulty that is not only due to the novel character of the therapy but comes from its very particular form as much as from its object. In both cases nonphysical elements are involved. The therapy is essentially conducted through language. As for the ill to be treated, it is not only psychic but also unidentified at the beginning—it will only be identified by the therapy itself. It is thus not surprising that formulating a precise evaluation of the treatment is difficult. In this case, just as much as in the case of philosophy, Aristotle's observation is relevant: "Between knowledge and money there is no common measure." But the paradox is even greater since in the case of psychoanalysis the possessor of knowledge—unlike the teacher—exercises his or her art by remaining silent, and the patient is the only one who speaks. To claim that Freud has the genius to sell the patient his or her own words would be a very weak witticism, since what these words constitute is not knowledge but a material made available for listening and thus presented to the competence of the therapist. This certainly involves the exercise of an art. But it is true that this art in its entirety operates within a pure arrangement of relationships. It is because of the invisible—purely psychic—character of the illness and of its treatment—which operates entirely through language—that with respect to clinical questions Freud is so insistent on using clear terms of comparisons (such as surgery). These comparisons help to indicate a level of competence and to justify the fee charged. One could conclude that all of this seems reasonable and leave it at that. But in doing so, one would miss the most important element in these clauses on the payment for therapy: its relationship with the *transference relationship*, which constitutes the central mechanism of the analytical treatment. Freud, however, does not explicitly theorize the connection between payment and transference. At most, he alludes to it in suggestive terms. We must reexamine this question, since it is probably the most decisive point of articulation between the efficacy of the therapy and the necessity of payment.

Within the analytical relationship, Freud calls transference the process by which the person of the analyst becomes the object of a—positive or negative—emotional shift on the part of the patient. This shift appears as the recurrence of a situation experienced in early childhood—such as trauma, conflict, or attachment—in which the analyst is now perceived as the substitute for the parental figures. According to Freud the stage of the therapy in which this process develops is extremely important. The analyst must handle its elements with the utmost care and the keenest attention, since the continuation of the therapy depends on it. Freud notes several remarkable aspects of this process, which becomes manifest at the moment when the most repressed elements reach the level of consciousness. Transference constitutes the sign of a progress in the therapy but also the expression of greatest resistance. The analyst is invested with a symbolic role, which he or she can use to actively influence the evolution of the elements of the conflict. But at the same time, by embodying the figures associated with the process of repression, the analyst provides the unconscious of the patient with an alibi for reinforcing this repression; hence the extreme ambivalence of the emotions experienced—whether tenderness or aggressiveness—which can be expressed by attitudes of rejection toward the analyst and even by a decision to end the therapy.

This exceptional function of transference also makes it possible for us to better understand the original status of the payment, thus clarifying a requirement Freud always states in categorical terms: the treatment should never be free of charge. Freud first gives empirical reasons for this imperative: the time required by a free therapy would be excessive, and, since time is money, the loss of earnings would be too significant.[33] In fact, Freud admits to having practiced free treatments. From this practice he draws the following conclusion:

The advantages which I sought in this way were not forthcoming. Treatment free of charge enormously increases many neurotic resistances, such as the temptations of the transference-relationship for young women, or the opposition to the obligatory gratitude in young men arising from the father-complex, which is one of the most troublesome obstacles to the treatment. The absence of the corrective influence in payment of the professional fee is felt as a serious handicap; *the whole relationship recedes into an unreal world*; and the patient is deprived of a useful incentive to exert himself to bring the cure to an end.[34]

This writing can be related to a remark found in an earlier lecture published in the same collection, about a fellow doctor who practiced a kind of amateur psychoanalysis: "His expectation must be therefore that the patient will offer him his secrets as a present, as it were, or perhaps he looks for salvation in some sort of confession or confidence."[35] Freud explains that this is something psychoanalysis should not accept. It involves a kind of rigged gift-exchange relationship in which the patient's secrets are exchanged for the analyst's benevolent understanding. Every gift-exchange relationship is indeed a challenge, a call for a reply. The patient forces the therapist to display benevolence toward his illness. By doing so, the patient saves him- or herself the effort required by anamnesis and reinforces his or her resistance. In the same way, therapy free of charge increases this resistance. Freud provides different reasons for this, depending on whether the patient is a young man or a young woman (assuming that the analyst is a man). A young woman will be tempted to view herself as the object of a favor and therefore as the target of a kind of seduction attempt. A young man will be tempted to view the therapist as a revival of the father figure, the "sovereign" who bestows his benevolence and turns his subordinate into a debtor. This is at least how these writings by Freud can be interpreted, since he does not develop his reflection on this topic any further, though he does provide us with the elements required to do so.

Payment for the therapy does more than provide a practical guarantee against these reactions. It constitutes the symbolic operation that precludes them from the outset. The reflection we have conducted on gift-giving and the commercial relationship makes it possible to consider the various aspects of the question of payment for the therapy in a different way. First, payment prevents the development of a purely personal relationship between psychoanalyst and patient. Although a relationship of trust is indispensable, it does not turn into an intimate relationship or a relationship of actual friendship as would be presupposed by the gift-exchange relationship. In this situation it is important that distance be preserved and objectivity created. What is at stake is not courtesy, gratitude, or benevolence but the treatment of an "illness" in which the psychoanalyst has no involvement. He or she must remain in the position of an arbiter. This is a relationship of justice, not of love. This may also explain why, in physical space, the psychoanalyst is placed behind the patient (a requirement for which Freud provides little clarification): the psychoanalyst must listen intently but must do so outside of the patient's gaze. Instead of bringing the partners face-to-face in a constant exchange of signs, this placement institutes an asymmetrical relationship between the patient's speech, which is made available for evaluation (and for transference), and the therapist who analyzes it.

Above all, payment prevents the psychoanalytical relationship from turning into a debt relationship. By paying, the patient secures a service. He or she is not forbidden from expressing gratitude—since gratitude always rewards a service, even one that is paid for, as expressed by the practice of tipping—but at least this gratitude comes as a supplement rather than as the reply for a favor. It is essential for the feeling of guilt that is already so prevalent in the patient's unconscious not to be compounded by a debt toward the psychoanalyst. Paying from the start liberates the patient from this dependence and ensures the necessary symbolic autonomy. At the same time, it avoids placing the analyst in the position of a benefactor-creditor, preventing an artificial debt from concealing a more essential obligation that is at the core of the phenomenon of repression. What is at stake, in addition to this question of freedom—which Freud does not explicitly discuss (and the best general statement of which can be found in Simmel's work)[36]—is also the socialization of the relationship of transference that is ensured by this payment. Without it "the whole relationship recedes into an unreal world."[37] Let me add that the amount paid represents labor already performed (by the patient), as well as labor being performed (by the psychoanalyst). In more general terms it embodies the implicit contract based on which every form of money operates as credit that always remains available within the institutional system in which the exchange takes place. By ensuring the conditions of objectivity of the transference relationship, payment integrates the therapy into a process of socialization.

Thus, within the psychoanalytical situation, and with respect to the psychoanalyst's remuneration, the gift-exchange relationship is viewed as dangerous, and only a payment following the contractual model appears capable of preserving the patient's autonomy. This requirement calls for discussion.

This situation is obviously the complete opposite of the relationship between philosopher and students prescribed by Plato and of which Socrates—who rejected every form of payment—constituted the exemplary figure. Yet it is known that, like other masters of wisdom, Socrates received gifts for his sustenance from those who came to listen to him. Far from generating a relationship of debt and therefore of dependence, this gift-giving relationship provided symbolic compensation for the priceless character of the teaching. In contrast, the payment required by the Sophists generated a situation of dependence, but the dependent party was the master who, unlike Socrates, was no longer able to choose those who deserved to be taught but had to accept as students all those who could pay for lessons. We must therefore ask why what was highly valued in the Socratic relationship between master and disciple is no longer desirable in the psychoanalytical relationship. Is it enough to say that the former was a relationship of knowledge whereas the latter is a therapeutic relationship? Not necessarily, since the latter involves the person of the therapist much more than does the former and thus seems better suited to the gift-exchange relationship.

Although this position could be supported, it would probably be futile to compare these two situations outside of their contexts—all the more so because what was at stake in the Socratic relationship was not merely teaching but also an attempt at conversion. It can therefore be accepted that Freud's recommendations are situated within the framework of a market society and refer to regulations that govern all professional activities. This is unquestionable, yet it does not account for the fact that the logic involved is not based on profit. What is needed is not to explain the importance of the patient's payment for the therapist's business—as in a purely economic approach—but to understand why paying for the therapy is preferable for the patient's own sake. What is involved here is a symbolic advantage, precisely the one defined by Simmel: to ensure the autonomy of the individual, whose payment liberates him or her from every form of personal dependence. In other words, the gift-exchange relationship is no longer relevant at the institutional level. The patient does not seek the therapist's assistance to create a bond of friendship but to be cured. This is why payment constitutes the appropriate relationship. But if the therapist happens to be a friend of the patient (which is generally not advisable) nothing prevents the therapist from establishing a gift-exchange relationship with the patient on the occasion of a celebration and outside the therapy. The order of justice must not be confused with the order of gift exchange—or with its Christianized forms, such as charity or *agapē*. It is better for the patient to pay than to receive false gratification and for the employer to provide fair wages than to give gifts to his employees. If such gifts are given, they can be accepted—but only as marks of esteem—and they can generate a more intense communal bond, provided that they are not meant to cover up a lack of equity in wages. In political societies the order of justice defines the elementary conditions of social life. The order of gift exchange is no longer indispensable as constitutive of the functioning of the institutional systems. *Yet without the gift-exchange relationship the community does not come into being.* As Pascal demonstrates, it is important not to confuse different orders, but as Leibniz shows, it is just as important to realize them all, or to make sure that they will complement each other.

.   .   .

This reexamination of a few figures of fair exchange mediated by money shows that the commercial relationship is not a priori the polar opposite of the gift-exchange relationship. The two are not situated at the same level. One is not the negation of the other, but there are circumstances in which one must prevail and the other give way. Their stakes are heterogeneous and yet constantly connected. When the purpose is to compensate work, compensation must be achieved in abidance with the agreement that has been conducted. When the aim is to express esteem or to reinforce a relationship, the appropriate means is gift exchange. There is a contractual economy, but it cannot be claimed that there is a gift-exchange economy. In the city, which is characterized by the distribution of occupations, what ensures the dignity and autonomy of each individual is fairly compensated labor. The wages paid are a right, not a favor. They involve an objective relationship, not an emotional bond. They are governed by norms of justice, not by the generosity of employers. This applies to every form of labor and to every recognized exercise of a competence. The Sophists were thus the first to claim the necessity to compensate teaching just like any other professional activity.[38] The activity of the merchant is now fully recognized, and his figure has ceased to be viewed as dishonorable, especially since the Middle Ages. There is more to this recognition: it is now accepted that commercial exchange generates a type of bond that—although it is not and must not be a personal one—may be capable of defining an original space of tolerance and civility (this was the profound conviction of Enlightenment thinkers). As for the writer, as Kant rigorously demonstrates, he or she must claim his or her rights as author and obtain fair compensation for the results of his or her labor publicly presented and made available in the marketplace. In an entirely different field the psychotherapist is obligated to preserve the objective character of the analyst-analysand relationship through the payment provided for the therapy in order to preclude any interference between the level of therapy and that of private bonds. Other figures could be added to this list of exemplary cases.

Finally, let me note that this evolution has not only been a recognition of the objective character of payment but also, inseparable from it, a shift from the concept of *honorarium* to that of *salary*, especially with respect to professionals. When a service is to be "honored," money is no more than an analogical expression of what is owed for that which remains priceless; a debt remains due. For centuries this was how teachers, scholars, physicians, lawyers, and artists were compensated. Although the term *honorarium* remains in use today, this use is purely formal. In fact, even though a margin of individual and agonistic evaluation remains in the activities in which market value is determined by notoriety (as in the case of artists and of all public figures), every form of compensation now has a contractual nature. Max Weber would have called this a shift toward greater rationality. Following Aristotle, it could be viewed as a shift toward justice in exchanges. But this would presuppose that his assertion—"Between knowledge and money there is no common measure"—has become obsolete and that his solution—to leave it to the gift-exchange relationship—is no longer relevant. Are we witnessing the extinction of this relationship? Or do we face, instead, the need to reexamine the concept of free obligation in very different terms?

Whatever the case may be, we must ask whether the initial animosity between money and philosophy can—and even should—be sustained. Is it still possible to situate oneself within the Platonic heritage of suspicion toward money without ignoring economic facts, in the way some people ignore the knowledge gained by physics or biology? It is clear that certain philosophical critiques of money do no more than reiterate the schemas of an imaginary representation based purely on the reading of classical texts. This is inconsequential. Yet should we claim that a page has been turned, that the old prohibition has been lifted, and that it must now be possible without any qualms to subject knowledge, competence, and intellectual labor to the standards of the marketplace, in the same way as other useful goods are subject to trade? The wages, research funds, and publishing profits received by teachers, researchers, and writers (whether the amounts involved are modest or considerable) testify to the fact that the mode of compensation of knowledge and talent is recognized as being inseparable from equity. Yet suspicion remains regarding a final triumph of the marketplace in this realm. Something refuses to give way that has nothing to do with a rejection of modernity.

We will finally have to confront this enigma once again and to understand why, beyond historical or cultural conditions, something priceless remains. We must examine what realities are still expressed and will perhaps never cease to be expressed by the necessity of pricelessness. This is the question Mallarmé asked about literature: "What good is it to traffic in what, perhaps, shouldn't be sold, especially when it doesn't sell?"[39] Does this mean that it should be given? But what is it that thinkers and writers give? Is it the intangible reality of the work? Does it amount to giving what has already been received and which calls for carrying on the gift and passing down *kharis*? This question arises once again: what is it that must be given and cannot be sold? And why?

Return/Exits

Return

As we come to the end of this book, let us look back and measure the distance we have traveled. It is a surprising journey perhaps, guided at first by the following questions: Are there such things as physical or non-physical goods that belong to the realm of the priceless? Are there goods that cannot be subject to any form of commercial valuation? Is there a relationship between money and truth—or rather the discipline for which truth is the fundamental issue? One clear signal for us was Socrates' statement reminding his judges that his teaching comes free of charge and that his poverty is the best witness to his truthfulness. The complete rejection of profit—for Socrates this is the price to be paid for speaking truthfully. It is also one of the main reasons for his profound opposition to the Sophists. We have seen how consistent and virulent Plato's criticism of them is. Surprisingly, he gives no real justification for this virulence, except for likening the Sophists to the despised figure of the merchant, who can sell without knowing the nature of his wares. For Plato this is the deceptive realm of the Sophist, mercenary of knowledge and peddler of things of the mind.

Aristotle provides two arguments that are more specific and, above all, decisive: (1) the very nature of knowledge makes it incompatible with monetary valuation because knowledge cannot be technically subject to quantifiable measurement; and (2) since masters of philosophy cannot be compensated with payment, the only remaining possibility is to honor them with appropriate offerings, as is done with parents or the gods.

The second statement constituted a turning point in our inquiry. By calling for gift-exchange relationships to compensate for the limitations of commercial exchange, Aristotle summons a symbolic substratum of considerable significance. When the price owed is impossible to determine, how is it that the gesture of offering a present can take the place of payment? Perhaps we sense that this is the right solution. Even so, its originality and complexity need to be fully understood: what does the gesture of giving, as simple as it is mysterious, presuppose among human beings? In the same way, why should the deities be honored with sacrifices? And what do we mean by "deities"? What situation or experience led to applying this designation to invisible beings? What do we owe them? Could there be an initial debt? Or a state of receptivity or passivity that would make every form of happiness, luck, knowledge, or power the result of a favor granted by a divine addresser? And how do we know that we are the addressees of this favor?

The requirement to take these questions seriously led us to the anthropological inquiry outlined above. It became clear that the initial problem—to reexamine the relationship between philosophy and the question of the priceless—cannot be divorced from the more global investigation into the ways in which different traditions have defined preciousness and usefulness as values—and as polar opposites. Our inquiry also asked what is appropriate for gift exchange and what is required for everyday subsistence. More fundamentally, it became a reflection on the mode of being of the human species insofar as it consists of entirely unique individuals who, while they claim autonomy, must nevertheless live together and form societies.

Our investigation produced the rather surprising findings noted earlier. Even if gift-exchange relationships are defined as the opposite of commercial relationships, their function is not to disallow the latter or, even less, to be their substitute. This is what we learned from ceremonial gift exchange—the foremost procedure by which humans, whether groups or individuals, *recognize one another* through a gesture of challenge, offering, and alliance. The purpose of ceremonial gift exchange is not to transmit goods as a quantum of wealth or to transfer property but to honor a partner; to assert oneself in the order of esteem, glory, and honor; to confirm one another according to the requirements of dignity, fidelity, rank, and sometimes allegiance; and, above all, to express reciprocal attachment. The primary value of those offerings is symbolic: on behalf of the giver, whether group or individual, they are a pledge of oneself—or even of the *self* as such. This is an essential point because the entire issue turns on this commitment, the risk taken, the challenge presented by an alliance—that is, the folly of binding *oneself* through reciprocal *offerings*. Therein lies the incalculable value of the thing given.

It is clear that gift-exchange relationships can be conceived neither in terms of commercial exchanges nor as an alternative to such exchanges. How can we then understand Aristotle's proposal—which may be no more than recognition of the general practice of his time—regarding the compensation to be provided to the master of philosophy? The answer is obvious: what is honored in the master's knowledge is something of which he is only the carrier or the mediator. To the gift that has been received, another gift must reply. But who gave the first gift? Aristotle does not say. He does not need to: everyone knows that it originates from a divine source. The relationship between master and student is not a mode of ceremonial gift exchange but a form of gift-giving that involves the invisible. What is given is not physical. It is a favor that calls for gratitude and of which material gifts are mere tokens. The generous gesture that honors the master of wisdom aims beyond him and into the realm of grace—where the splendor of what is given is excessive and sometimes crushing.

This realm already emerges in the status of the things that cannot be exchanged—precious things, *sacra,* kept in the community because they came from ancestors or deities. It does not define the enigma of ceremonial gift exchange but rather its limits, its fading away, the turning point toward the verticality of unilateral gift-giving. This unilateral character intensifies with the emergence of a debt that is no longer the equal reply to a ceremonial gift but becomes the obligation to reply to an excessive gift. There is also the requirement to compensate for excessive power over what has been received, as in pastoral and agricultural societies. A multiplicity of testimonies has convinced us that these observations account for the emergence of the phenomenon of sacrifice.

The relationships in question connect humans to one another and to deities through the mediation of goods with symbolic status. Those relationships matter more than the goods involved. In this context the function of gift exchange and of sacrifice is neither strictly economic nor antieconomic. These practices characterize societies in which the reciprocal bond and the relationship with the gods are primary, and subsistence activities are subordinated to these priorities. This was the case in all traditional societies. The crises of gift-exchange relationships and of the relationships with the deities have threatened or eroded this tradition. This shift has brought about on the one hand the internalization of gift-giving relationships and on the other the autonomy of commercial relationships and productive activities. One more step, and the power to give becomes reserved for God alone, while productive work and profitable exchanges are all that is left to humans. One step further leads us into a world that only relates to itself; into the radical finitude of the sphere of production and exchange; and, within or beyond this sphere, into the experience of a given without a giver. The gift from no one brings us back to thought centered on being. Such would be in a nutshell an account of the symbolic mutations in which we recognize the birth of our modernity, the announcement of its endless becoming, and the requirement to start over once again.

Exit 1
Priceless Goods and the Risk of Corruption

Let us take one more look back: what would it mean today for an emulator of Socrates to point to his own poverty as proof of the truthfulness of his discourse? Not much, unless he had to defend himself against a charge of financial corruption. Neither the quality of a master nor that of his knowledge is measured today by the extent of his destitution or the level of his compensation. We must therefore recognize that the wager presented at the beginning of our inquiry, in which the phrase "the price of truth" was understood in its literal sense, no longer holds. We can no longer understand it in the same sense as did the contemporaries of the Pre-Socratics, who blamed Simonides of Ceos for selling his poetry and putting *Alētheia* on auction. In the same way, we would no longer think of accusing the Sophists of venality, nor would we expect philosophers, scholars, or writers to give up their legitimate earnings, whether modest or considerable. The problem can no longer be presented in these terms. In this sense the question of the price of truth has been solved. We no longer identify the labor done by scholars or artists, which needs to be rewarded according to the requirements of justice, with the content of their research, the statement of their discourse, or the quality of their artworks. At this level money intervenes in terms of value in the marketplace, not of truth value of the object.

This is why the phrase "the price of truth" is correctly understood today in a purely metaphoric sense—as the effort required by a confession (telling the truth), the difficulties involved in an investigation (establishing the facts), or the symbolic cost incurred by an error (accepting the consequences).

The philosophical problem involved in the payment provided to masters, as demanded by the Sophists, cannot be defined as a moral crisis. Even in his most direct attacks against the Sophists, Plato confined himself to mocking remarks meant to delegitimize them, but he did not blame them for behaving dishonorably. After all, other professionals of speech—declaimers of poetry, actors, rhetors, and lawyers—were paid for their services. The Sophists' right to compensation was questioned because in Plato's view their discourse came too close to the domain of philosophy. Their discourse mimicked philosophical discourse in a threatening way, but the true character of the former was visible despite its concealment: by asking for money the Sophists acknowledged de facto that they were not philosophers. Those, however, who attended the lessons of Gorgias, Protagoras, Prodicos, Hippias, and others did not share this concern, even when they paid large sums of money to receive the Sophists' instruction. Today we would be inclined to agree with them. This is not new. Remarkably, Kant insists on including the cost of the transmission of knowledge in his general definition of money as the expression of price.[1] We have seen how Kant also most rigorously defends the legitimate income that an author should receive from his publications. This right, which has become very complex, now also covers scientific inventions and all sorts of artistic products.

The criteria governing what may or may not be the object of a commercial transaction seem to have changed over the course of our history, just as they vary from one culture to another. This could lead us to believe that the extension of commercial valuation to all possible goods would do no more than reflect the predictable evolution of criteria of judgment. This brings us back to the questions raised at the beginning of this book regarding the possibility of the "priceless," in short the existence of goods (objects, activities, social positions, or statuses) that can under no circumstance be bought or sold.

Michael Walzer confronts these questions in a chapter of his now classic book *Spheres of Justice*, where he develops a problematic according to which every society can be considered a "distributive community."[2] What does it distribute? A variety of social goods related to politics, the economy, education, health, security, religion, leisure, family, and so forth. Each set of goods forms a type of *sphere of justice*, that is, a specific autonomous set of distribution of those goods with its own criteria for organization, relationships, and equity (these criteria vary depending on whether they apply to a political party, a bank, a military camp, an athletic club, a religious group, or a school). Harmonious relations among these spheres depend primarily on the degree of respect granted by each to the autonomy of the others. When respect is not granted, a crisis ensues and conflicts arise that Walzer explains with the help of two concepts. The first consists of what he calls the problem of *predominance*: one sphere tends to impose its valuation criteria and rules of distribution over one or more of the other spheres. It could be said that this involves external control, when, for example, political power dictates its imperatives to a religious institution or vice versa. But at a deeper level the encroachment of one sphere on another can occur through what Walzer calls *conversion* structures: one sphere's model of rules infiltrates another or is adopted by another, as when the political becomes religious, the familial becomes military, or culture is reduced to leisure.

In this encroachment process, with its double trigger, one sphere, probably the most active, has not been mentioned: the commercial sphere. According to Walzer that sphere tends to be contiguous to all the others (although he does not explain how), and, most important, it functions through an instrument—money—that has for a long time been identified and denounced—by Marx for example—as "the universal procurer." In Walzer's view money is much more than this. Its function—to express the commercial value of goods, their *price*—seems to give it the power to translate *all* other values and to assign a price to them. In this boundless claim resides the risk of corruption. Corruption amounts to the conversion of "nonsellable" goods into commercial ones. It remains to be determined what "nonsellable" goods are. Walzer only calls on "shared values" and presents a list—an exhaustive one, he hopes—of the goods that can under no circumstances be obtained with money, such as personal freedom (one cannot purchase another person or sell oneself as a slave); political power (votes or public functions cannot be bought); and criminal justice (judges must not be bribed). One cannot buy freedom of the press, of religion, of speech, the right of assembly, citizenship, marriage partners, administrative offices, public honors, and other similar goods. This list of prohibitions constitutes an outer boundary that cannot be crossed. Within this boundary, other exchanges can be conducted peacefully. This is the space of the legitimate marketplace insofar as it ultimately remains subject to the imperatives of distributive justice.[3]

Walzer's approach to the problem of money and corruption is original, but it leaves several essential questions unanswered. Walzer notes that the commercial sphere has become predominant over and contiguous to all others, but he does not explain why. Perhaps he assumes that the answer is so obvious that it does not need to be stated: the expansion of the economic sphere as a whole, resulting from the development of capitalism. It may be unnecessary to recount a now-familiar history, but it is important to show that the economic sphere is unlike any other and cannot be placed at the same level as the spheres of security, education, health, or leisure. The economic sphere did not become predominant because it was able to prevail over the religious or military spheres, for instance. There is a specific reason for its importance: it involves the very condition of existence of any society—the means of its subsistence. Plato and Aristotle were already convinced that it constitutes the community of interests—*koinōnia*—without which the political sphere—*polis*—simply would not be possible. In classical societies the order of production and exchange remained subjected to the priorities of the political order. In traditional societies all subsistence activities and their surpluses are directed toward reinforcing reciprocal bonds (through gifts, festivals, and in some cases sacrifices). The aim is to increase the giver's prestige or to honor deities rather than to develop economic power. Those activities nevertheless involve the material condition for the existence of the group. Before anything else can be accomplished, the means of subsistence must be ensured, even if some are immediately converted into symbolic goods. This is therefore a determining condition—even though it does not presuppose any form of determinism.

There is a fundamental reason for the fact that in a certain type of society the economic sphere becomes autonomous and tends to predominate, as it does with capitalistic development. The exponential growth of production and exchange activities tends to respond to new developments such as demographic growth, new forms of knowledge, new technologies, and urbanization or to satisfy new objectives, such as furthering development or creating new representations or conditions of power—hence the growing hegemony of the commercial sphere and its interaction with all others. There are transactions at every level because every domain involves a rational activity of investment, cost-benefit analysis, and calculation of expenditures for development. For comparison's sake, let us examine the now-familiar example of Trobriand society described by Malinowski. The entire activity of production there is directed toward ceremonial exchanges that, indeed, constitute the dominant sphere.[4] In the Greek or Roman city social pressure obligated the wealthiest citizens to offer celebrations, commission monuments, or fund military expeditions. The political sphere, with all the values associated with public life, tended to capture all the others. In traditional Tibetan society this same function was reserved to the monastic institution.

But from the moment production and its growth have been constituted as autonomous and primary goals, as instruments and signs of power, then everything enters the economic circuit and tends to be subjected to financial assessment. All activities are seen in terms of cost. Everything has a price—including public celebrations, whether political, artistic, athletic, or religious. The economic sphere predominates because power itself depends on the means provided by the economy. But the reason why it only predominates to such a degree is that it involves what has always defined societies' means of subsistence and of material growth. It is within this framework, and as one aspect of the hegemony of the economy, that the commercial sphere contaminates all others. On the one hand, the moderns are no more mercenary than were the ancients. On the other hand, the potential—and the temptation—now exist to seek commercial equivalence for all sorts of goods because the market has become coextensive with society as a whole, with all its activities, statuses, and projects. This is the precise locus of the ethical question: why is it that, in spite of all we have seen, certain "goods" cannot—and must under no circumstances—be evaluated in commercial terms? To answer as Walzer does by pointing to a consensus on values only moves the problem further back, because the source of this consensus still remains to be identified. We must reexamine this question.

Walzer's second concept, the "structure of conversion," remains to be clarified. In this respect, also, the instrument of this operation—money—has a specificity that requires further analysis. To be sure, its power to express the price of all circulating goods risks being extended to all other possible goods. This temptation exists because the monetary instrument has incomparable plasticity. But before coming to this point, let us consider as an example the type of conversion required by political power. In order to be translated into the terms of the religious sphere, this power must gain access to leaders of the ecclesiastic institution or ensure that its priorities in terms of legitimization are disseminated by that institution. The same line of reasoning can be applied to military power aiming to be translated into the terms of the political sphere, and so on. All these modalities of action involve either procedures of direct intervention among the relevant agents or processes of transfer of models or values. The latter—processes—have a deeper effect and are thus more sought after. In general, both types of procedures are combined. Money happens to unite them both into one single, fast, and carefully focused operation. It uses its predominance by providing the material means needed (or, more directly, by buying influence). It works through conversion when it has already set a price for what is desired and ensured that this valuation will become a reference and determine choices, even when this occurs prior to or without any direct intervention. The ease with which this can occur results from the fact that, as general equivalence, money is an empty medium—or, more precisely, it is an entirely virtual medium.

This is true from two different standpoints. From the standpoint of the thing to be acquired, money can express any value, no matter how excessive. It only needs to set a price, provided that the price is accepted or even merely discussed. From the standpoint of the subject, money can capture any desire or passion and express it, since it provides access to all sorts of as-yet-indeterminate objects. Money is thus a substitute on both sides and can translate in both directions, from any object to any subject and vice versa. This makes both for its absolute indifference and for the disruptive power denounced by Marx, a power that is inseparable from the fluidity and flexibility ascribed to it by Simmel. Because, of all conversion structures, it is the fastest, the most efficient, and the most indifferent to agents—and therefore the most complete—it is also the most powerful means of influence and corruption. To be capable of corrupting, however, it must be the object of desire—and even of insatiable desire, as has always been claimed.[5] Such is indeed the danger of money according to Aristotle. *Why is it possible to accumulate money not only beyond any need but also beyond any ascribable limit?* Because money is an abstraction capable of representing every kind of possibility (goods, actions, interventions, investments, products, pleasures, relationships, and influences), it remains completely indeterminate and thus absolutely nimble—the key to a virtual world that cannot be saturated. All other needs and desires have limits imposed by satisfaction. The accumulation of money, in contrast, can continue without ever encountering such limits. In other words, *it is exempt from the law of decreasing marginal utility* (this is the limit or "margin" where a good is no longer sought because the demand has been satisfied in the act of consumption).[6] Money is the only good that escapes this law. This absence of limits—*apeira pleonexia*—fascinates Aristotle and remains for him incomprehensible and monstrous.

This is the risk inherent in money. It is not new. It is the correlative of money's power as a sign of value and as an instrument of valuation, exchange, reserve, and investment. What is new is the prodigious growth of the commercial sphere and the financial operations developed by the stock market system. No longer one sphere of activity among others, it is an entire cosmos. This is why money is not present only in limited interventions but everywhere. Walzer rightly notes that its power has become social and cultural. It buys membership in industrial societies inasmuch as legitimacy within those societies only accrues to those who have ongoing access to a certain amount of material goods—housing, communication, transportation, and leisure—in short, everything that depends on the marketplace. Without this access one is excluded both at a functional and at a symbolic level. To extend Walzer's argument, we can observe that social legitimacy or acceptance by the group is a nonphysical good accessible in our societies through physical goods obtainable by money. Is it possible to recognize this process without denouncing it? Or would such denunciation merely be the result of a misunderstanding?

Simmel views the possibility of monetary equivalence of goods and productive activities as one of the main sources of emancipation from ancient dependencies. In traditional societies the goods that bring acceptance by the group are not associated with purchasing power but with other qualities, such as generosity in gift-giving, courage in battle, skill in hunting, eagerness to help, and place in the social hierarchy. The facts that acceptance can be gained today by acquiring industrially produced consumer goods and that this acquisition is secured by wealth derived from wages or productive investment are in no way signs of corruption. Rather, they represent the opportunity for *homo laborans* to receive the fruits of his or her most mundane activities. Hannah Arendt insists that it is important for every activity to receive public recognition.[7] In societies dominated by warrior, clerical, or intellectual elites, craftsmen received scant recognition and merchants far less. Elites are now economic in nature, and in turn the producer-consumer demands advancement. But is this just a question of access to goods?

The concept of "spheres of justice" also gives rise to a different question. To define each sphere—as Walzer does—as an ensemble, each containing its own type of social *goods,* is significant. Not only does it suggest reducing the different spheres to the same level, which, as we have seen, decreases their explanatory power, but it situates them in a strange position of externality. Here we reach the limits of purely pluralistic theories. By thinking in terms of available goods, such theories tend to eliminate the question of the historical geneses of those goods: how were they acquired? From what transformations do they result? Furthermore, such theories tend to ignore the question of the axiological status of those goods, that is, of their order of priority and their foundation. It is thus legitimate to speak of *freedoms* of speech, of assembly, of circulation of goods and people, but the question remains of *freedom* as constitutive of the human being—not as a good but as something that coincides with his or her very being.

The language of "goods" manifests a kind of functionalist view. True, it does not describe mere goods meant to be used like other commodities, but it does speak in terms of opportunities that it is important to seize and to keep accessible. No matter what ethical requirements may be proclaimed within such a context, they remain recommendations to be prudent, civil, and socially tolerant. They cannot account for the imperative from which they arise and which they implicitly approve without stating it.

Confronted with this limit, should we, like Aristotle, conclude that only gift-exchange relationships are capable of meeting this imperative? Is any deduction possible at this point, or should we acknowledge that only a categorical imperative can allow us to move beyond the boundaries of finitude?

Exit 2
The Requirement for Recognition and Dignity

Among the modalities of distribution of social goods, Walzer considers the case of gift-giving. He presents two examples, beginning with a brief and relevant presentation of the *kula* exchange in the Trobiand Islands as described by Malinowski. We are now familiar with this example. The second example involves inheritance, specifically the legal rules in the Napoleonic code that guarantee equal shares to heirs of the same rank and, above all, ensure that all possessions will remain within the family. These rules prevent the deceased's will from favoring nonrelatives without evidence of a specific bond. Walzer notes that in both cases gift-giving does not follow the normal rules governing commodities but amounts to transferring property to others outside market norms and without the mediation of money.

This is one way of considering things; however, Walzer's parallel between the two examples is problematic because it presupposes that the category of gift-giving can be applied in the same manner to both. The case of inheritance only involves a donation given according to strict legal rules that do not aim at establishing a bond between the donor—who will be dead when his or her will is implemented—and the heirs, whereas the Trobriand *kula* exchange *has absolutely nothing to do with the transfer of property*. For readers of Malinowski, Mauss, or the present volume, such a definition of the act of giving cannot be accepted. The purpose of the *kula*—as of all ceremonial gift exchange—is not to give a good or to enrich a partner but to recognize the other through the good offered. Precious objects are given in order to express respect and thereby make the giver worthy of respect. What are, in fact, exchanged are generosity, glory, and honor. As we have seen, what is given in ceremonial gift exchange is *oneself* through the mediation of a good that constitutes a substitute and a pledge. The aim is always to create or preserve an intense social life between partners, through a multiple interwoven network of personal relationships. An obsessive focus on the things exchanged, as if they were goods separable from those who give them, always amounts to a radical misunderstanding of ceremonial gift exchange. To interpret the destruction of the victim as the essence of sacrifice, amounts to a similar misunderstanding. Furthermore, the realm of gift exchange does not encompass only the offer of goods with symbolic status. It always involves a set of courtesies and rituals. Those may be quite solemn, with proclamations or announcements using musical instruments, or they may be more modest, but they always entail respectful manners set by convention. Because gift exchange is first and foremost a way of recognizing one another, it always takes place in a dual situation, in which two individual partners or two groups face each other.

This demand for and offer of *reciprocal recognition*—which, once again, has nothing to do with the Hegelian struggle for recognition—is highly complex. It always plays on challenge, seduction, request, provocation, and the possibility of conflict, but it also always presupposes generosity, noble gestures, and unconditional outreach to the other. Above all, it remains governed by the triple obligation to give, to receive, and to reciprocate the gift. This is a paradoxical obligation, not only because it is at the same time free and required but also because for the partners it constitutes the reciprocal recognition of their freedom. The giver recognizes the other's freedom by honoring him, but he also claims his own freedom through his offer of munificent gifts, which amounts to a challenge for the other to do the same. This agonistic relation is first and foremost an equal one. When it loses this equal character, it does so under conditions that it does not generate but that are imposed on it. As we saw, it is the entire kinship system, beginning with matrimonial alliances, that makes the gift-exchange relationship a total social phenomenon and establishes it through time. It institutes the social bond both at the institutional and at the individual level.

In political societies this is no longer the case. *The public recognition of each person is ensured by the law*, before which all the members of the citizen community are equal. This status and dignity carry all sorts of rights. They also carry obligations, which are public and collective. Those rights and obligations can, indeed, be called "social goods," but this arrangement is not capable of guaranteeing or protecting the bond that connects each member of the community to another or to the entire community. Neither civil membership nor economic interdependence calls on us to recognize the other *as a person*. This limitation is constitutive of political societies and of the market system. The resulting emptiness can be filled by the collective offer of love from a god embracing a people or a community in the god's exclusive favor or by a charismatic leader inciting the ardent believers in his cause to relinquish their own self and to merge. The need for recognition can also strengthen the bonds within local communities, giving rise to what Weber calls "the religious ethic of fraternity." In those types of associations some forms of gift exchange endure, which may simply consist of services, mutual help, and emotional support. Beyond political institutions and commercial relationships those exchanges provide recognition of the priceless dignity of each human being, making up to some extent for the lack of specific recognition that plagues modernity.

Could this be the form that gift exchange takes in our societies? There would thus be a kind of distribution of responsibilities between the order of the law and of the marketplace, on the one hand, and interpersonal gift exchange, on the other. This would amount to the classic distinction between society and community. And yet one question remains that lies outside the sociology of relationships. What of the other—beyond nations and local groups, beyond these associations of every kind in which recognition is guaranteed from the outset? What of those who cannot claim any kind of membership familiar to us? Within the space of our daily life what of the strangers, the newcomers? How can we recognize other human beings outside of all community based on sharing and without any greeting procedures? Some answers can certainly be provided through the observation of Erving Goffman's studies, conducted with great competence, of unexpected encounters.[8] It should be noted that traditional cultures considered these difficulties and confronted them through all sorts of measures meant to protect strangers passing through, such as, in Greece, the figure Zeus Xenios took to test human hospitality.[9] Rome had laws intended to protect "peregrines," and the Koran makes hospitality a sacred duty. We should also take into account the efforts made by the Stoics— and taken up again between the end of the Middle Ages and the Enlightenment—to formulate a natural law capable of establishing a "personal right" based on reason, in other words a universal law governing the crossing of national boundaries or the interstices between them. This requirement becomes all the more urgent throughout modern societies as they become ever more cosmopolitan and individualistic. Yet beyond the support provided by local forms of civility or by universally accepted rules of behavior, the question remains as to the unconditional foundations— those that would be valid at any time and in any place—of the requirement to respect the stranger we meet or the unknown in the familiar event of every encounter.

Beyond ecological and cultural conditions, each of us must face this radical question: *Who is the other?* Levinas addresses this question and confronts it in the most exacting manner in *Totality and Infinity*. He elaborates his reflection on the encounter with the other through a very complex problematic in which the ethical requirement emerges as infinite, disrupting the closed order of totality characteristic of fundamental ontology. Who is the other whom we encounter? Our alter ego? No, Levinas explains. To claim that the other is merely another I would amount to understanding him or her based on ourselves, in other words to constructing the other based on our own subjectivity. This would point to the inadequacy of the phenomenological approach, which situates the other within the very structure of the subject as "being-for-the-other." "The alterity of the Other does not depend on any quality that would distinguish him from me, for a distinction of this nature would precisely imply that community of genus already nullifies alterity."[10] The other is not entailed as a possibility contained within an originally dual structure. This would mean that we, too, proceed from the other. We do not, and he does not proceed from us. The other always happens. He is pure event. He always comes from elsewhere, unexpectedly, unpredictably, not in any accidental sense but by definition. "The absolutely new is the Other" (*TI* 219). With respect to me the other is always radically other, and he thus manifests the infinite. He cannot be deducted from any ontological situation.

How can any relationship with the other be possible, then? It can be so precisely because it *happens*, and it happens only because the other's otherness is not already given in the sameness of our subjectivity. According to Levinas, what makes otherness happen as an encounter is the presence of the human face. "The face is present in its refusal to be contained. In this sense it cannot be comprehended, that is encompassed" (*TI* 194). It resists totality and manifests infinity. "The idea of infinity, the infinitely more contained in the less, is concretely produced in the form of a relation with the face. And the idea of infinity alone maintains the exteriority of the other with respect to the same, despite this relation" (*TI* 196). The face of the other expresses his irreducible otherness; it "rends the sensible" (*TI* 198). By doing so, it shows that the other is not us. He is free, and he resists our grasp. This resistance is constitutive of the other: "Resistance that is not resistance—the ethical resistance" (*TI* 199). This otherness does not originate from freedom. The reverse is true: "It is therefore not freedom that accounts for the transcendence of the Other, but the transcendence of the Other that accounts for freedom—a transcendence of the Other with regard to me which, being infinite, does not have the same significance as my transcendence with regard to him" (*TI* 225). The freedom we recognize in ourselves is not freedom to govern ourselves but freedom to answer the injunction carried by the face of the other. The ethical obligation that arises from the encounter with the other, the unconditional obligation to which the infinity of his face testifies, does not amount to a formal obligation but to an obligation to give—or to give ourselves. Our obligation to the other originates from his very presence. The ethical requirement proceeds from the other in the sense that it obligates us to recognize him unconditionally.

Could this be what Aristotle means by *philia*? Or the unilateral gift-giving discussed by Seneca? Is it a call to give for the sake of giving? The moral type of gift-giving that emerges when ceremonial gift exchange fades away amounts to generosity, kindness, and compassion. It ensures the preservation of the social bond in political societies. The ethical relationship that Levinas discusses, however, is not moral gift-giving. The ethical gesture is not benevolence directed at the other but the act of recognizing him in his absolute otherness. It is an absolute—and entirely fragile—injunction.

Are we closer to ceremonial gift exchange, this risky gesture of recognition of the other and expectation of his reply? To think so would also be to misunderstand Levinas. Ceremonial gift exchange is a social procedure of recognition. It is part of a complex system of rituals, which is why its representations and symbolisms are always local and associated with particular environments, conditions of material life, and forms of kinship. Thus its effectiveness remains local and cannot be exported. For example, the Dogon universe—in a key of water—could not communicate with the Greek world, which was in a key of fire. Paul understood this: the rituals of his community of origin cannot be imposed elsewhere. The message of his faith must do without them and go beyond them.

Is Levinas's question the question of the *universal*—in other words, of the recognition of every human being anywhere and in any circumstance? International law and human rights attempt to provide an institutional answer to this question, but the recognition of the other in his otherness—the imperative of absolute recognition—does not originate from positive law. The answer is found in the very event of the encounter. It happens in the recognition of the human face, in which it finds its starting point and its prescription. Without this initial, implicit, and constantly reaffirmed recognition, the gestures—of gift-giving, sharing, and respect—that confirm it and that reinvent communities at a local level would be impossible. The human face lies beyond the distinction between universal and singular. It is always a particular face—differentiated by age, gender, and ethnic characteristics—in a particular situation. As such it is always unique. It cannot be separated from the words the mouth utters, from the gaze that opens the eyes, or from the hand that gives—or hits. The entire body comes into view from the starting point of the human face, yet the human face is not circumscribed by any meaning, symbolism, image, or function. To say that it "rends the sensible" is to say that it immediately confronts us with the unconditional obligation to give ourselves. Singularities are given meaning by this affirmation that nothing precedes or makes possible, an affirmation present in any human face and that starts with the human face. What it brings is freedom, along with the law.

This is what we must grasp in ceremonial gift exchange itself. We must understand it in terms of its openness, its possibility, and its outer limit at the core of the most specific symbolism, as what accounts for the blending of challenge and anguish, of expectation and pride, of respect and violence, inherent in every encounter and expressed by the goods that are given and entrusted to what the partners are not: things and time. These goods are given and abandoned: ventured into the unknown space of the other.

This is the risk that commercial relationships cancel—for valid and respectable reasons. Commercial relationships do not require that the partners recognize each other but that they agree to exchange the goods necessary for ordinary living. It would be intolerable if every exchange of goods were understood as a request for recognition, but life would be un-livable if no exchange were understood as such a request. There is a legiti-mate realm of useful exchange, governed by relationships of equity in the community. Yet the distinction that has always been drawn between gift-giving relationships and commercial relationships rests on an accurate intuition: the former involves what is "priceless" or, rather, what is incom-mensurable. As we have seen, this transcendence does not characterize the thing given but only what the thing symbolizes: granted recognition, re-ciprocated honor, and shared respect. Beyond ceremonial procedures and locally constituted communities, no other justification exists for those re-quirements than the call to which the enigma of the human face testifies: its absolute dignity.

Let us then call priceless or inalienable those goods that cannot be subjected to commercial relationships without undermining and some-times destroying human dignity. This dignity is the ultimate reason why we must absolutely reject every act of corruption, humiliation, or exploitation. More ominously, any active negation of this dignity leads to a world in which the very possibility of recognition is annihilated, and nothing remains that could symbolize or mediate it. This is one way we can understand the account of the unspeakable experience of the extermination camp as presented by Primo Levi: "The personages in these pages are not men. Their humanity is buried, or they themselves have buried it, under an offence received or inflicted upon someone else."[11] Standing on the other side—although no symmetry can be claimed to exist between the two—the victims are as dehumanized as their torturers. Is it possible to escape destitution in this space of absolute contempt? For Levi the answer has a name and a face, those of a silent man, Lorenzo, of whom he writes:

However little sense there may be in trying to specify why I, rather than thousands of others, managed to survive the test, I believe that it was really due to Lorenzo that I am alive today; and not so much for his material aid, as for his having constantly reminded me by his presence, by his natural and plain manner of being good, that there still existed a just world outside our own, something and someone still pure and whole, not corrupt, not savage, extraneous to hatred and terror; something difficult to define, a remote possibility of good, but for which it was worth surviving.[12]

Outside of those circumstances to which nothing else can be compared, the threat that this just world may be forgotten looms in every attitude and every situation in which contempt, arrogance, or indifference deny not only benevolence but also simple human dignity. It is possible for a world to be entirely proper, quiet, protected, enclosed within its own comfort yet entirely despicable. Any group that aspires to constitute a community perceives this dignity as a promise, as something already given when, in the dreariness of subsistence activity, a space of encounter opens up in which we recognize each other as being infinitely different from this activity, different from the figure imposed on us by social destiny, a space where we meet to experience together *the honor of existing*. This is how Carson McCullers describes a small southern town at the time of the Great Depression: "The town itself is dreary; not much is there except the cotton mill, the two-room houses where the workers live, a few peach trees, a church with colored windows, and a miserable main street only a hundred yards long. On Saturdays the tenants from the near-by farms come in for a day of trade and talk. Otherwise the town is lonesome, sad, and like a place that is far off and estranged from all other places in the world."[13]

In this town, as anywhere else, there are destinies and intrigues, love and pain. A woman comes to town, energetic and sparing of words: Miss Amelia. She opens a café, and then something happens. At night, when every light has been turned off and the houses are cold, only this light remains along with the warmth of the café where, whether or not they go there, townsfolk know that others will be there and that at every moment the promise of an encounter remains open. It is a place where those who have the least in common can meet, have a drink, talk, and enjoy each other's company:

Miss Amelia had made red curtains for the windows, and from a salesman who passed through the town she bought a great bunch of paper roses that looked very real.

But it was not only the warmth, the decorations and the brightness that made the café what it was. There was a deeper reason why the café was so precious to this town. And this deeper reason had to do with a certain pride that had not hitherto been known in these parts. To understand this part the cheapness of human life must be kept in mind. There were always plenty of people clustered around a mill—but it was seldom that every family had enough meal, garments and fat back to go the rounds. Life could become one long dim scramble just to get the things needed to keep alive. And the confusing thing is this: All useful things have a price, and are bought only with money, as that is the way the world is run. You know without having to reason about it the price of a bale of cotton, or a quart of molasses. But no value has been put on human life; it is given to us free and taken without being paid for. What is it worth? If you look around, at times the value may seem to be little or nothing at all. Often after you have sweated and tried and things are not better for you, there comes a feeling deep down that you are not worth much.

But the new pride that the café brought to this town had an effect on almost everyone, even the children. . . . On such occasions they behave themselves decently and are proud. The people in the town were likewise proud when sitting at the tables in the café. They washed before coming to Miss Amelia's, and scraped their feet very politely on the threshold as they entered the café. There, for a few hours at least, the deep bitter knowing that you are not worth much in this world could be laid low."[14]

In this space of simple encounter and recreation, a sort of agora for ordinary folk, the threads of a frayed social fabric are rewoven. At the same time, a sense of honor and almost ceremonial civility is reborn, along with the pleasure of being together, and the certainty that the dignity that is experienced is the recognition we grant each other. This is life itself: it is given, and it remains priceless.

REFERENCE MATTER

Notes

OVERTURES

1. The beginning of *Phaedo* gives us this information.

2. Xenophon also emphasizes Socrates' radical lack of self-interest:

Nor did he make his companions lovers of wealth. For he rid them of the other desires, on the one hand; and on the other, he did not demand wealth (*khrēmata*) from those who desired him.

He held that, in refraining from this, he was attending to his freedom. And he called those who take pay for their association enslavers of themselves, because of its being necessary that they converse with those from whom they took their pay.

He marveled if someone professing to teach virtue would demand money and not hold it the greatest gain to have acquired a good friend, but would be afraid that one who had become a gentleman (noble and good) would not show the greatest gratitude toward one who had done him the greatest good deeds. (Xenophon *Memorabilia* 1.2.5–7)

3. See Vernant, *Myth and Thought Among the Greeks*; and Finley, *The Ancient Economy*.

4. The long debate opposing Socrates to Protagoras and Prodicus concerning a poem by Simonides shows that Plato considered him the direct ancestor of the family of Sophists (see Plato *Pro.* 339a–46e).

5. Detienne, *The Masters of Truth in Archaic Greece*, 106–7.

6. See Dodds, *The Greeks and the Irrational.*

7. In *Kapital* Marx derides the capitalist impulse, where "everything becomes saleable and buyable. The circulation becomes the great social retort into which everything is thrown, to come out again as a gold-crystal. Not even are the bones of saints, and still less are more delicate *res sacrosanctae extra commercium hominum* able to withstand this alchemy" (108). Péguy is even more incensed: "Money is everything and dominates everything in the modern world" (*Notre jeunesse*, 631). And earlier in the same text: "In this modern world entirely directed toward money and under the pressure of money, this pressure contaminates the Christian world itself and forces it to sacrifice its faith and mores for the sake of preserving economic and social stability" (604).

8. Shakespeare, *Timon of Athens*, 4.3.28–44.

9. Marx, *Early Writings*, 193.

10. Mandrin (1725–55) was a famous—and popular—outlaw and smuggler, active in the southeast of France. He was captured and executed by the king's forces. Saccard is the main character in Emile Zola's novel *Money*. A ruthless speculator, he causes the bankruptcy of his own bank and ruins his customers in a stock exchange crash.

11. See Smith, *The Wealth of Nations*, book 2, chap. 3; subsequent references are cited parenthetically in the text.

12. See Arendt, *The Human Condition*.

PART I. MERCENARY FIGURES

1. "Science is a gift from God; this is why it cannot be sold."

2. Diderot, "Réfutation suivie de l'ouvrage d'Helvétius intitulé *L'homme*," 568. This "refutation" is part of Diderot's posthumous publications. Unless otherwise noted, all translations are my own.—JLM"

3. Rousseau, *Confessions*, 34–35.

4. Ibid., 393.

CHAPTER I. PLATO AND THE SOPHISTS' MONEY

1. See the *Republic* 492ff; Cassin, *Le plaisir de parler*; and Canto, "Politique de la réfutation."

2. See Arendt, *The Human Condition*, esp. chap. 2.

3. *Epideixis* (usually translated as "exhibition") was a presentation that gave a kind of sample of the teaching offered. It was most often after hearing this *epideixeis* that young men registered to attend the Sophists' lessons. See Guthrie, *The Sophists*.

4. See, e.g., Untersteiner, *The Sophists*; Sprague, *The Older Sophists*; Jaeger, *Paideia*; Guthrie, *The Sophists*; Kerferd, *The Sophists and Their Legacy*; Romeyer-Dherbey, *Les Sophistes*; Cassin, *Le plaisir de parler*; Cassin, *Positions de la sophistique*; Romilly, *The Great Sophists in Periclean Athens*; and Cassin, *L'effet sophistique*.

5. See Guthrie, *The Sophists*, chap. 1; and Kerferd, *The Sophistic Movement*, chap. 4.

6. Guthrie, *The Sophists*, 29. "Practical instruction and moral advice constituted the main function of the poet" (ibid.).

7. Ibid., 30.

8. See, e.g., *Meno*: "The technical name for it is 'diagonal'" (85b).

9. See Lloyd, *Magic, Reason, and Experience*.

10. Marrou, *A History of Education in Antiquity*, 78. The term *aretē* is usually translated as "virtue," but "excellence" would seem more accurate.

11. See Detienne, *The Masters of Truth in Archaic Greece*.

12. "Rhetors, lawyers, artists, who would once have disgraced themselves by selling their talent, no longer had any scruples about selling their wares for the highest possible price. Everything was for sale, everything had a price, and wealth was the standard of social worth" (Glotz, *La cité grecque*, 365); see also Forbes, "Teachers' Payments in Ancient Greece."

13. "It seems that an incredible amount of money was received by every Sophist, but especially Protagoras, Hippias, and Prodicus for educating Callias the Younger, son of Hipponicus; they were precisely the ones that Plato's *Protagoras* showed gathered in the house of young Callias at the time when he had just inherited his father's fortune" (Capizzi, "Les Sophistes à Athènes," 176). What were the precise prices charged? It is known that Protagoras charged one hundred minae (i.e., ten thousand drachmas) for his course (Diogenes Laertius, *Lives of Eminent Philosophers*, 2:9.52.465). Prodicus had set a price of fifty drachmas for his series of lessons in grammar but only charged one drachma for a summary of the lesson (Plato *Cratylus* 384b), as Kerferd notes in *The Sophistic Movement* (24–27). See also Blank, "Socrates vs. Sophists on Payment for Teaching." This very factual approach remains one of the few available on this question. These were the currency units: one talent was worth sixty minae; one mina was worth one hundred drachmas; one drachma was worth six obols. It is estimated that one drachma represented the average daily income of a craftsman (i.e., about seventy-four U.S. dollars in 1978 or one hundred dollars in 2000, according to Kerferd). The ten thousand drachmas charged by Protagoras were for several years of training. The cost for Isocrates' entire training came to one thousand drachmas. If we accept Kerferd's figures, these amounts seem enormous. Kerferd obviously confuses buying power with income level. His estimate should be divided by five or even more.

14. Isocrates, "Against the Sophists," 3–4.

15. Ibid., 4–5.

16. See Dixaut, "Isocrate contre des sophistes sans sophistique."

17. As in *Meno* 90bff. (but this concession soon turns out to be ironic).

18. See Wolff, "Le chasseur chassé."

19. Protagoras himself claims that the Sophist operates in disguise (according to Plato): "I claim that the sophistic art is ancient, but that those who had a hand in it among the ancients were afraid of the opprobrium attaching to it, and disguised and concealed themselves" (*Pro.* 316d–e); this is followed by a list of masks taken up by ancient Sophists.

20. This process of division is obviously excessive. Plato even establishes a distinction within the art of striking between upward and downward strokes. According to some critics, by finally coming up with a scholarly name for angling (*aspalieutikē*), Plato has his character explicitly display his "pedantry." The satiric intent is unquestionable but seems to have been missed by many commentators.

21. It is quite clear that this list is parodic, while being very precise from the

chosen point of view. Plato's vocabulary, deliberately priggish, aims to point out the ridicule of sophistry's neologisms in the very process of defining the Sophist.

22. See Kerferd, *The Sophistic Movement*, 59–67.

23. Ibid.

24. Plato *Hippias Minor* 368b.

25. As early as the beginning of his plea, after summarizing the accusation against him, he adds, "You have seen it for yourselves in a comedy by Aristophanes—a certain Socrates being carried round on the stage, talking about walking on air and babbling a great deal of other nonsense, of which I understand neither much nor little" (Plato *Apo.* 19c).

26. In Athens *sunousia* was the practice by which the young formed a bond with adults in order to receive their education from them.

27. See Plato *Timaeus* 19e: "I am aware that the Sophists have plenty of brave words and fair conceits, but I am afraid that being only wanderers from one city to another, and having never had habitations of their own, they may fail in their conceptions of philosophers and statesmen and may not know what they do and say in time of war, when they are fighting or holding parley with their enemies."

28. In *Crito* the "Laws" admiringly address Socrates: "You would not have stayed home in it to a degree surpassing all other Athenians, unless it pleased you in surpassing degree. You never left to go on a festival, except once to the Isthmian games. You never went anywhere else except on military service. You never journeyed abroad as other men do, nor had you any desire to gain knowledge of other cities and their laws—we and this our City sufficed for you" (Plato *Crito* 52b–c). Diogenes Laertius briefly summarizes: "Unlike most philosophers, he had no need to travel, except when required to go on an expedition" (*Lives of Eminent Philosophers*, 1:2.27.153).

29. This is a recurrent criticism, also found in *Cratylus*, when Socrates advises Hermogenes that in order to take lessons from the Sophists, he should "pay them well and show gratitude besides" (391b).

30. For the value of currency see note 13 above.

31. In reference to the example given by Socrates, Xenophon writes, "The Sophists hunt rich young men, while the philosophers are available and amiable to everyone [*pasi koinoi kai philoi*]; they neither value nor despise men's fortunes [*tukhas*]" (*On Hunting* 13.9.87).

32. See, e.g., Blank, "Socrates vs. Sophists on Payment for Teaching."

33. A leading study on this question is Pringsheim, *The Greek Law of Sale*; Gernet's account, "Le droit de la vente et la notion du contrat en Grèce," is no less important.

34. This claim is made by Protagoras in *Protagoras* (328b) and confirmed by Aristotle in *Nicomachean Ethics* (9.1.1164a).

35. On *sunousia* see note 26 above.

36. The adjective *anthrōpinous* designated humans and had connotations of both finiteness (limited and ignorant being) and a specific realm (as opposed to the divine and animal realms).

37. Translators have chosen the term *knowledgeable*, since this indeed involves the breadth of knowledge, Socrates being contrasted with the Sophists, who claimed expertise; anyway, the term *sophos* connotes at the same time knowledge, know-how, and wisdom.

38. "Parmenides profits from a certain advantage. For him the philosopher is someone entirely set apart and especially chosen" (Gernet, *The Anthropology of Ancient Greece*, 355).

CHAPTER 2. THE FIGURE OF THE MERCHANT IN WESTERN TRADITION

1. See Vernant, *Myth and Thought Among the Greeks*, 235–301.

2. See Vidal-Naquet, *The Black Hunter*, 224–45.

3. See Finley, *The Ancient Economy*, 58ff.

4. The latter part of this statement might be rendered literally as "makes the city distrustful and unfriendly toward itself" (*autēn te pros autēn ten polin apiston kai aphilon poiei*).

5. Plato's contrast between good and bad *mimēsis* would require in-depth discussion that would not be relevant to this study.

6. See Rougé, "Marine et démocratie," 145.

7. One of the Seven Wise Men's best-known apothegms stated, "The land is safe; the sea is not" (cited in Dumont, *La philosophie antique*, 12). This suspicion is constantly found in Homer; see, e.g., Hartog, "Ulysse et ses marins"; see also Pépin, "Le symbolisme de la mer chez Platon et dans le néoplatonisme." Pierre Vidal-Naquet noted that for Plato Athens viewed its destiny as tied to the land; it originated from Gaia and Hephaistos; the marine world was that of Atlantis, which originated from Poseidon. See Vidal-Naquet, *The Black Hunter*, 268ff.

8. Quoted in Finley, *The Ancient Economy*, 42.

9. "The merchant cannot be pleasing to God" (cited in Weber, *General Economic History*, 357).

10. Weber, *Economy and Society*, 1:584.

11. Finley, *The World of Odysseus*, 67–68.

12. Hartog, "Ulysse et ses marins," 37 (see the *Odyssey* 14.230–34). See also Scheid-Tissinier, *Les usages du don chez Homère*, chap. 3, esp. 72.

13. Finley, *The Ancient Economy*, 144.

14. Gernet, *The Anthropology of Ancient Greece*, 318 (translation modified).

15. Cicero *De officiis* 1.150–51.

16. See Finley, *The Ancient Economy*, chap. 4.

17. Benveniste, *Indo-European Language and Society*, 113.

18. Ibid., 114.

19. Ibid., 114–15.

20. Ibid., 118.

21. Dumont, *Homo hierarchicus*, 165.

22. See Le Goff, *Marchands et banquiers du Moyen Age*.

23. See Duby, *The Three Orders*.

24. Baechler, *The Origins of Capitalism*, 70.

25. See Le Goff, *Marchands et banquiers du Moyen Age*; Le Goff, *Time, Work, and Culture in the Middle Ages*; and Le Goff, *Medieval Civilization*.

26. See Gurevich, "The Merchant": "The merchant's social prestige was fairly modest. The wealthy man aroused envy and ill-will, and people entertained serious doubts about his honesty and consciousness. In general, the merchant remained a 'pariah' in early medieval society. . . . The theologians were fond of repeating that 'the merchant's profession is not pleasing to God'" (246, translation modified).

27. Bad merchants existed, of course; their deeds were told in countless tales of abuse and dishonor. See, e.g., Le Goff, *Marchands et banquiers du Moyen Age*, chap. 3.

28. Quoted in Le Goff, *Time, Work, and Culture in the Middle Ages*, 65.

29. Quoted in ibid.

30. Vernant, *Myth and Thought Among the Greeks*, 235–301.

31. Le Goff, *Time, Work, and Culture in the Middle Ages*, 67.

32. I will discuss this further in Chapter 8.

33. Weber, *Economy and Society*, 1:584–85.

34. See Chapter 7 below; see also my article "L'éthique catholique et l'esprit du non-capitalisme."

35. See Austin and Vidal-Naquet, *Economic and Social History of Ancient Greece*.

36. See Serres, *The Parasite*.

37. See Chapter 4 below.

38. Arendt, *The Human Condition*.

CHAPTER 3. THE SCANDAL OF PROFIT AND THE PROHIBITION ON
APPROPRIATING TIME

1. The logical order might seem to be to begin an analysis of Aristotelian concepts about currency with his detailed presentation of it in *Nicomachean Ethics* because it was probably written before his *Politics* and above all because Aristotle presents his general definitions of currency there. I will return to this question, however, in Chapter 9, where I examine the positive view of money.

2. Aristotle *Pol.* 1.1.1252a: "Every community is established with a view to some good."

3. "While making has an end other than itself, action cannot; for good action itself is its end" (*NE* 6.5.1140b).

4. *Metaphysics* 9.6.1048bff.

5. Ibid., 6.1048b.

6. On this concept see Aubenque's in-depth study *La prudence chez Aristote*.

7. Finley, *The Ancient Economy*, 35–36.

8. See *Pol.* 1.1253ff; and *Rhetoric* 1.1361a.

9. Finley, "Aristotle and Economic Analysis," 42.

10. Franklin, "Advice to a Young Tradesman, Written by an Old One."

11. This reservation applies to Romeyer-Dherbey's otherwise excellent presentation of Aristotle's economic thought in *Aristote: Les choses mêmes*.

12. See Finley, *The Ancient Economy*, esp. 113–22.

13. According to *Nicomachean Ethics* (5.8). See the presentation in the first section of Chapter 9 below.

14. Aristophanes, *Wealth*, 277–78.

15. This category has been defined as follows: "The metics were free men, both Greek and non-Greek, domiciled in Athens or in Attica, some in a more or less permanent way, others for a more limited period of time" (Austin and Vidal-Naquet, *Economic and Social History of Ancient Greece*, 99).

16. See, e.g., Deuteronomy 23:19–20: "You shall not charge interest on loans to another Israelite, interest on money, interest on provisions, interest on anything that is lent. On loans to a foreigner you may charge interest, but on loans to another Israelite you may not charge interest." In the New Testament Jesus admonishes his disciples to "lend, expecting nothing in return" (Luke 6:35); he also says, "Give to everyone who begs from you, and do not refuse anyone who wants to borrow from you" (Matthew 5:42).

17. See Nelson, *The Idea of Usury*, 3–28. The question of simony could be revisited here but would require a lengthy digression.

18. Basileus the Great, "Homélie 2 sur le Psaume 14," 98.

19. Ibid., 99.

20. Gregory of Nysse, "Sermon sur les usuriers," 162.

21. Quoted in Le Goff, *Your Money or Your Life*, 28–29.

22. See Noonan, *The Scholastic Analysis of Usury*. To situate this question within economic history as a whole, see Braudel, *Civilization and Capitalism*, 2:559–65.

23. Cited in Le Goff, *Time, Work, and Culture in the Middle Ages*, 29.

24. Cited in Le Goff, *Your Money or Your Life*, 40, 39.

25. Cited in Le Goff, *Time, Work, and Culture in the Middle Ages*, 290; and in Noonan, *The Scholastic Analysis of Usury*, 43–44.

26. This was still Balzac's view: "Like Time, the bank devours its own children" (*Nucingen and Co.: Bankers*, 245).

27. See Gurevich, "The Merchant."

28. We will return to this in Chapter 7, when discussing Max Weber and Ernst Troeltsch's arguments.

29. Gustave Flaubert to George Sand, Dec. 4, 1872, in Flaubert, *Flaubert-Sand*, 294.

PART II. THE WORLD OF GIFT-GIVING

1. Seneca *De beneficiis* [*On Benefits*] 1.8.27.

2. Xenophon *Œconomicus* 2.8; Diogenes Laertius, *Lives of Eminent Philosophers*, 1:2.24–25.

3. Plato *Apology* 19 (my emphasis). On *sunousia* see Chapter 1, note 26.

4. Aristotle *Eudemian Ethics* 7.10.1243b21–22; subsequent references are cited parenthetically in the text.

5. Aristotle *Nicomachean Ethics* 5.5.1133b19–20; subsequent references are cited parenthetically in the text.

6. See, e.g., *Nicomachean Ethics* 4.5.1122b20–21. This attitude was so self-evident that in *Topics* Aristotle presents it as the epitome of common sense: "People who are puzzled to know whether one ought to honour the gods and love one's parents or not need punishment, while those who are puzzled to know whether snow is white or not need perception" (*Topics* 1.11.105a5–7).

7. Flaubert, *Flaubert-Sand*, 294.

CHAPTER 4. THE ENIGMA OF CEREMONIAL GIFT EXCHANGE

1. We must remember that the phrase *kinship system* does not designate the modern family but the organization of the group as configured by relationships of alliance, filiation, and consanguinity. There is a considerable anthropological literature on this topic (see Bonte, "Parenté").

2. On this concept see note 49 below.

3. Weber, *General Economic History*, 197.

4. Ibid., 238.

5. Mauss, *The Gift*, 4.

6. Polanyi, *The Great Transformation*, 50.

7. Ibid.

8. See Boas, *Contributions to the Ethnology of the Kwakiutl*.

9. Boas thus writes, "The economic system of the Indians from British Columbia is largely based on credit, just as much as the system of civilized peoples. . . . To contract debts on the one side, and to pay debts on the other, that constitutes *potlatch*. . . . Those who receive presents on the occasion of this celebration receive them as loans that they use in their current enterprises, but after an interval of a few years they must repay them with interest to the giver or his heir" (Boas, *12th Report on the North Western Tribes of Canada*, 54–55).

10. Malinowski, *Argonauts of the Western Pacific*, 84–85.

11. See Gregory, *Gifts and Commodities*.

12. The same could be said of F. Perroux's theory, which interprets gift-exchange economy as an alternative to the logic of capitalism or to state-controlled economy; he calls everything that was neither trade nor administrative constraint a gift. This would be an acceptable convention if he was not referring to an obvi-

ous misinterpretation of Mauss (156ff) (see Perroux, *Économie et société*). Another notable case of misinterpretation is found in George F. Gilder's *Wealth and Poverty*. Gilder claims that from the outset capitalism itself has had a function of generous contribution that is the source of subsequent productive activity; according to him capitalism is led to constantly renewing its free supply in order to boost itself. This view deserves discussion, but to present it as fact supported by Mauss, as Gilder does, shows an entirely distorted reading of *The Gift*. Comparing capitalistic supply to *potlatch* constitutes a fraudulent analogy.

13. This confusion is so widespread that in most social anthropology textbooks or treatises the question of ceremonial gift exchange is dealt with in the chapter on exchanges in general and as an interesting form of the circulation of goods, whereas it belongs to the field of institutional forms of authority and assignment of status.

14. In this case *utility* should be understood in its ordinary sense rather than in the sense it has in neoclassical theory.

15. On the specificity of the gift-exchange phenomenon see the rich collection of studies and debates presented by Alain Caillé in *Revue du MAUSS*: "Donner, recevoir et rendre"; "Le don perdu et retrouvé"; "Ce que donner veut dire"; "L'obligation de donner." See also Godbout and Caillé, *The World of the Gift*; and Caillé, *Anthropologie du don*.

16. "The terms that we have used—present and gift—are not themselves entirely exact. We shall, however, find no others" (Mauss, *The Gift*, 72–73).

17. Irwin Goldman rightly notes, "Kwakiutl have no sense of charity: for them, a genuine donor can give only to a genuine recipient" (Goldman, *The Mouth of Heaven*, 104).

18. On Mauss see Karsenti, *Mauss*; Karsenti, *L'homme total*; Fournier, *Marcel Mauss*; Tarot, *De Durkheim à Mauss*.

19. Mauss, *The Gift*, 26–27.

20. Ibid., 37. These pages by Mauss are the source that most inspires Georges Bataille in *The Accursed Share*. Recent research has made it possible to reassess this "mad *potlatch*." It is now known that this highly exacerbated form emerged fairly late—in the last decades of the nineteenth century—when demographic collapse had considerably reduced the number of prestigious positions available. At the same time, greatly increased trade with white colonists had created significant sources of income and therefore significant means of expense; in addition, the prohibition of warfare between tribes imposed by the Canadian government contributed in transferring rivalry to *potlatch* alone. See Barnett, "The Nature of the Potlatch"; and Codere, *Fighting with Property*; see also Mauzée's clarification in "Boas, les Kwakiutl et le potlatch."

21. Mauss, *The Gift*, 3.

22. "After having of necessity divided things up too much, and abstracted from them, the sociologists must strive to reconstitute the whole. By doing so they

will discover rewarding facts. . . . All these study or should observe, the behavior of total beings, not divided according to their faculties. . . . The principle and the aim of sociology is to perceive the whole group and its behavior in its entirety" (ibid., 80–81).

23. See ibid. 3, 79–80; subsequent references are cited parenthetically in the text.

24. This angle of approach is already apparent in a short 1923 writing titled "L'obligation de rendre les présents." Its complete statement in *The Gift* (some of the qualifiers of which seem questionable today) is as follows: "What rule of legality and self-interest, in societies of a backward or archaic type, compels the gift that has been received to be obligatorily reciprocated? What power resides in the object given that causes its recipient to pay it back?" (*G* 3).

25. See Lévi-Strauss, *Introduction to the Work of Marcel Mauss*, 45ff. Vincent Descombes strongly objects to this analysis; see his "Les essais sur le don."

26. It is hard to understand how this misinterpretation could have been made and could still be made by the most competent authors without assuming on their part a hasty reading of Mauss's writing. The stakes are significant: to presuppose that the same object must return from C to A amounts to making the good as such the crux of the question and misses the logic of the gift, which is not the good exchanged but the recognition granted and the bond created; worse, the movement of gifts ends up being viewed as a kind of zero-sum circular movement, in other words a quaint "archaic" custom.

27. Quoted in Mauss, *The Gift*, 11. Mauss's translation of *taonga* and *utu*, based on Best's English translation, no longer seems acceptable to contemporary researchers. The terms *precious object* and *reciprocation* should be used rather than *particular object* and *repayment*. Based on a more recent English translation of the Maori text, Maurice Godelier provides a satisfactory French version of it. See Godelier, *The Enigma of the Gift*, 50. This translation makes it even clearer that it is not the same *taonga* that moves from C to A. Therefore Godelier should not speak of a "return of the object to the original donor" (55).

28. Hence the essential presence of a third partner, whom Mauss wrongly finds superfluous (see *The Gift*, 11; according to Mauss, Ranaipiri's narrative "present[s] only one obscure feature: the intervention of a third person."); Dominique Casajus is well aware of this problem; see his "L'énigme de la troisième personne."

29. See Sahlins, *Stone Age Economics*.

30. Alain Caillé rightly speaks of a *gift paradigm* in his "Ni holisme ni individualisme méthodologique."

31. Goldman, *The Mouth of Heaven*, 124.

32. All of these questions will be discussed in Chapter 6.

33. It is therefore on purpose that the title of this chapter and the subtitle of this section are adapted from the title of Maurice Godelier's book, *The Enigma of the Gift*; this enigma does not seem situated at the same point; see below, "*Sacra*: Goods That Cannot Be Exchanged."

34. Strathern writes: "When they saw Taylor's white skin, they thought he must be one of the pale-skinned cannibals who figure in Hagen folktales, 'but then he gave us shell valuables in return for pigs, and we decided he was a human'" (*The Rope of Moka*, xii).

35. See Goodall, *The Chimpanzees of Gombe*; Waal, *Peacemaking Among Primates*; McGrew, Marchant, and Nishida, *Great Ape Societies*; Premack, "Why Animals Have neither Culture nor History"; McGrew, *Chimpanzee Material Culture*; Russon, Bard, and Parker, *Reaching into Thought*; Waal, *Tree of Origin*.

36. Malinowski, *Argonauts of the Western Pacific*, 95n.

37. "More generally, symbols are the materials with which linguistic conventions, social pacts, and tokens of mutual recognition pacts among free beings are constituted. Symbols are constituent elements of a language, in which those elements are considered relative to one another as forming a system of communication or of alliance, a law of reciprocity among subjects" (Ortigues, *Le discours et le symbole*, 61). This aspect is fundamental but it does not constitute the issue of symbolism in its entirety. More generally, a symbolism is an arrangement of sensible elements with differential values whose purpose is not meaning but performance. This definition applies to algebraic systems as well as to healing rituals, dances with masks, and forms of courtesy. Symbolism belongs to the order of value rather than to the order of meaning, to the mode of operation rather than to the mode of representation. On this issue, see Sperber's seminal *Rethinking Symbolism*.

38. This is the sense in which we can understand Lévi-Strauss's argument that it is not enough to determine a social origin of symbolism but that the symbolic origin of society itself must be understood. See "Introduction à l'œuvre de Marcel Mauss," in Lévi-Strauss, *Introduction to the Work of Marcel Mauss*, xxii.

39. I cannot endorse the views of Craig Stanford on this particular point, despite my interest in his excellent analysis "The Ape's Gift."

40. "In short, this represents an intermingling. Souls are mixed with things; things with souls. Lives are mingled together, and this is how, among persons and things so intermingled, each emerges from their own sphere and mixes together. This is precisely what contracts and exchange are" (*G* 20).

41. In *Les formes de l'histoire* Lefort writes that "every offering is to some degree agonistic" (28); but his turning the "savage" into a modern subject that "in giving breaks off the bond that unites him to the thing," and his claim that "through an identical gesture—giving—men confirm that they are not things" (27), are unconvincing. Along with many other authors, Lefort only understands the thing given as a potentially appropriable and consumable good, yet it is no such thing; it is the symbol and, above all, substitute of the giver, pledge of his own being. Far from cutting off the bond with "the thing," the gesture of giving expects that the thing given will express, testify to, and guarantee the bond between humans.

42. It is therefore not advisable to attempt to find an intersection between Mauss and Hegel, even through Kojève, as Bruno Karsenti proposes to do. In Hegelian

terms the struggle between opponents is frontal and begins without mediation, which is why it is deadly; death is only avoided by a posteriori introduction of the missing mediation, after one side has capitulated. This is an odd mediation since it resides in the very person of the vanquished as being spared—"servus." In ceremonial gift exchange the object is offered from the outset as pledge and substitute mediatizing the relationships between partners; conflict breaks out only if the gift is rejected or does not take place. As for *potlatch*, even in its most agonistic form it is not armed struggle but struggle through gifts, which is to say a duel through goods that "symbolize" the protagonists. The Hegelian model presupposes that the spirit of ceremonial gift exchange has disappeared. It defines the confrontational relationship between modern individuals. When the mediation provided by the thing given is no longer there, dialectics generates a third party. Certain approaches, such as Honneth's in *The Struggle for Recognition*, show the lack of an ethology of the encounter within the framework of the anthropology of gift exchange.

43. Alain Caillé identifies this essential motif in "Don et symbolisme" (143–44); he rightly emphasizes the difference between play and role.

44. See Huizinga, *Homo ludens*. Huizinga explicitly refers to Mauss and Kwakiutl practices (see 78–83).

45. Mauss, *The Gift*, 112n139. The notion of rhythm also developed by Mauss is very useful in order to understand the very source of the ludic pulsion. "Man is a rhythmic animal," he writes in his *Manual of Ethnography* (67).

46. Hamayon, "Pourquoi les jeux plaisent aux esprits," 80. See also Benveniste, *Indo-European Language and Society*: "Gambling is a truly religious act: the gods gamble" (143).

47. See "Agropastoral Societies and Sacrifice," in Chapter 5 below.

48. See note 37 above.

49. This confusion has been illustrated by a great diversity of authors. For instance, in *Des dons et des dieux* Alain Testart attempts to understand the specific obligation of gift exchange in reference to contractual relationships and not moral obligation; he then finds that the obligation to give is confused because it is consistent with neither of the two models. It involves an entirely different type of constraint: challenge and reply. In a very different direction Jacques Derrida (in *Given Time*) and Jean-Luc Marion (in *Being Given*) bring up the idea of pure giving as an objection to Mauss; there is beauty in this demand but also extreme misunderstanding, since it amounts to analyzing ceremonial gift exchange (which must generate public reciprocal recognition) by the standard of ethical giving (which can attain the nobility of abnegation through the self-effacement of the giver). The latter, which is celebrated by Seneca and calls for the concept of grace, has no more than a nominal relationship with reciprocal sumptuary offering (as we will see in Chapter 7).

50. In *Les institutions du sens* Vincent Descombes underscores the fact that from the outset the gift-exchange relationship has a triadic structure; in this he

appeals to Peirce against Russel (who keeps to empirical dyadic transfers): giving is always giving something to someone; this relationship is inherent to all so-called trivalent verbs, such as to grant, provide, procure, lavish, award, etc.); according to Peirce this triadic relationship presupposes a norm of exchange. From the start, and by definition, the relationship between the partners and the thing given—the mediating element—is ruled by a law; thus, as Descombes insightfully notes, the gift-giving relationship is not the transfer of a good from one partner to the other but a relationship between the partners through the mediation of the good. I must add that ceremonial gift exchange cannot be reduced to giving something to someone, which would instead define the contractual relationship—let us note that to sell is also a trivalent verb; the gesture of gift-giving consists of *giving one-self* to someone through the mediation of something. There are therefore two different types of triadic relationships.

51. The most interesting case Mauss notes is the Maoris' identification of the maternal nephew with precious *taonga* goods (see *G* 9).

52. See Hénaff, *Claude Lévi-Strauss and the Making of Structural Anthropology*, chaps. 2 and 3.

53. Lévi-Strauss, *The Elementary Structures of Kinship*, 51.

54. Ibid., 481.

55. A good example is provided by Paula Rubel and Abraham Rosman in *Your Own Pigs You May Not Eat*.

56. Godbout and Caillé, *The World of the Gift*, 10.

57. Gernet, *The Anthropology of Ancient Greece*, 79.

58. See Finley, *The World of Odysseus*, 99–100.

59. Ibid., 104–5.

60. Ibid., 107.

61. In Benveniste, *Indo-European Language and Society*, 71.

62. Ibid., 77.

63. Ibid., 71.

64. See Lévi-Strauss, "On Marriage Between Close Kin."

65. See Weiner, *Inalienable Possessions*.

66. The concept of *alienable good* has a legal origin and concerns selling and buying. Calling goods involved in the circuit of gift exchange alienable raises a serious problem; this is precisely what Gregory does in *Gifts and Commodities*. It must therefore be acknowledged that Weiner's use of this concept is purely analogical, which is acceptable with this reservation.

67. Godelier, *The Enigma of the Gift*, 72.

68. Ibid.

69. Ibid., 71.

70. This will be discussed in Chapter 5.

71. This phrase is already found in Mauss, and it has often been used as if it were self-evident. It has been more recently consecrated in David Cheal's book,

The Gift Economy; Mary Douglas takes it up again in her foreword to the 1990 Routledge translation of *The Gift*.

72. See Caillé, "Le don de paroles."

CHAPTER 5. THE AGE OF SACRIFICE

1. Bataille, *Theory of Religion*, 48–49.

2. Ibid. This serious reservation about Bataille's theory of sacrifice is not intended to question his notion of what he calls the "accursed share." Provocative sumptuary spending no doubt belongs to defiant ceremonial gift exchange, which makes it important to identify the *beneficiary*. Bataille does this when he analyzes *potlatch*, following Mauss; however, extravagant and completely gratuitous spending points rather to the intransitive destruction associated with modern individualism. Sade's work is probably the most obvious and radical evidence for this.

3. For more about this uncertain terminology, see 178 ff. below.

4. Benveniste, *Indo-European Language and Society*, 452.

5. Hubert and Mauss, "Introduction à l'analyse de quelques phénomènes religieux," 21.

6. See Rogerson, "Sacrifice in the Old Testament"; and Leenhardt, "La valeur du sacrifice dans le judaïsme d'autrefois et d'aujourd'hui."

7. Chantraine, *Dictionnaire étymologique de la langue grecque*, s.v. "sacrifice."

8. Benveniste, *Indo-European Language and Society*, 481–88.

9. See Detienne and Vernant, *The Cuisine of Sacrifice Among the Greeks*.

10. For a more detailed account see "The Orphic Dionysos and Roasted Boiled Meat," in Detienne, *Dionysos Slain*, 68–94.

11. Detienne, "Culinary Practices and the Spirit of Sacrifice," 7–8.

12. See Hubert and Mauss, *Sacrifice*.

13. Detienne, "Culinary Practices and the Spirit of Sacrifice," 20.

14. "A phenomenon does not need to be expressed verbally in order to exist. What one language says in one word, others say it in several. It is even totally unnecessary for them to express it" (Mauss, *Oeuvres*, 1:21).

15. Heusch, *Sacrifice in Africa*, 5.

16. See Evans-Pritchard, *Nuer Religion*. The Nuer are a population of herders from southern Sudan.

17. Heusch, *Sacrifice in Africa*, 12.

18. See, e.g., Leroi-Gourhan, *La religion de la préhistoire*.

19. The notion of hunter-gatherers, well known among anthropologists and prehistorians, is not as simple and homogeneous as one might think given its broad use; differences depending on regions and eras are important. Nevertheless, a certain number of fundamental characteristics legitimize the use of the term. The major works on this are Lee and DeVore, *Man the Hunter*; Service, *The*

Hunters; Bicchieri, *Hunters and Gatherers Today*; Lee, *The !Kung San*; and Testart, *Les chasseurs-cueilleurs, ou l'origine des inégalités*.

20. Testart, *Des dons et des dieux*, 29.

21. Chatwin, *The Songlines*, 70.

22. Hamayon, *La chasse à l'âme*, 333. Hamayon's research deals primarily with the Buriatian tribes of the Lake Baikal region of central Siberia.

23. Ibid.

24. Ibid., 374.

25. Goldman writes the following about the Kwakiutl: "Animals, for instance, give a power that is inherent in their own nature: beavers give their industriousness, grizzly bears their fierceness. Animals offer themselves as a comprehensive gift; they give their flesh, their form, their specific natures" (*The Mouth of Heaven*, 198). During the winter festivals this exchange is taken to extremes: abandonment of names, lineage, to the complete permutation of human attributes into those of animal-spirits: "In the winter they are organized in animal society, and, of course, as varieties of supernatural beings. No one then is, strictly speaking, a human being, and no one accordingly belongs to a lineage. . . . They live under a new spiritual jurisdiction. . . . The house becomes a spirit residence, the people become simulated spirits, and the great supernatural spirits come to live among them as among their own kind" (ibid., 104).

26. Bowers, *Mandan Social and Ceremonial Organization*.

27. Boas, *Ethnology of the Kwakiutl*, 1319.

28. Stevenson, *The Zuñi Indians*, 441.

29. This is in spite of the tendency of American ethnographers at the beginning of the twentieth century to call "sacrifice" any type of offering to the spirits.

30. Testart, *Des dons et des dieux*, 75.

31. See Duverger, *La fleur létale*.

32. Pierre Clastres's analyses on the reasons for war in Amazonian tribes are useful here. See *Archeology of Violence*, chaps. 11 and 12. On Amazonian societies see Lizot, *Tales of the Yanomami*; Descola, *The Spears of Twilight*; Clastres, *Chronicle of the Guayaki Indians*; and Dumont, *Under the Rainbow*.

33. Roberte Hamayon, *La chasse à l'âme*, 674.

34. Dournes, *Les populations montagnardes du Sud-Indochinois*; Dournes, *Pötao*; Leach, *Political Systems of Highland Burma*; Condiminas, *We Have Eaten the Forest*.

35. Hamayon, *La chasse à l'âme*, 737.

36. Ibid.

37. Ibid.

38. Biardeau, "Le sacrifice dans l'orthodoxie brahmanique," 19.

39. Dournes, *Les populations montagnardes du Sud-Indochinois*, 215n2.

40. "With a few very specialised exceptions a sacrificial animal is always a domestic animal which is the property of the 'giver' of the sacrifice, that is, of the

individual who expects to benefit most from the performance of the ritual" (Leach, "The Nature of War," 352). "Only domestic animals are sacrificed, never wild animals" (Testart, *Des dons et des dieux*, 73). The exceptions to this rule are particularly interesting. They are always animals with an intermediate status (identified with humans), such as the tortoise among the Zuñi, the hornbill among the Zulu, the pangolin among the Lele, and the bear among the Ainu: before the animal is sacrificed, it is captured and "changed into a human." This framework legitimates the use of the concept of a "sacrificial hunt," different from the various forms of ritual hunt that do not constitute sacrifices (see Heusch, *Sacrifice in Africa*, chaps. 2 and 3). Testart observes that "one sacrifices only one's dependents" (*Les dons et les dieux*, 74). The reason is not so much that they are weaker, as Testart claims, but that by their status they are part of their owner's very being. The Greek *oikos* and the Roman *familia* included cattle and other domestic animals as part of the body of the *oikonomikos* or of the *paterfamilias*.

41. It cannot be objected that hunter-gatherers had domestic animals that could be sacrificed: humans themselves. It is the change with respect to life that matters, and from then on the relationships between humans change. This only occurs with the domestication of plants and animals.

42. The phrase "pastoralists and agriculturalists" is convenient and common but not precise. The domestication of plants and animals was a slow and very complex process. Depending on material conditions (soil, climate, vegetation, and elevation) certain populations privileged cultivation of grains and pulses, others the raising of cows, sheep, pigs, or goats. This produced either very contrasting types of civilizations (pastoral or agricultural) or mixed types (agropastoral). In addition, earlier practices, especially hunting, remained active. We cannot examine all the different distinctions here. The two categories (hunter-gatherers, and pastoralists and agriculturalists) are poles rather than completely distinct sets. Nevertheless, although rare, pure forms do exist.

There is a vast literature on this subject, so I will cite here only a few representative works: Sauer, *The Domestication of Animals and Foodstuffs*; Hafez, *The Behaviour of Domestic Animals*; Ucko and Dimbleby, *The Domestication and Exploitation of Plants and Animals*; Ingold, *Hunters, Pastoralists and Rangers*; Zohary and Hopf, *Domestication of Plants in the Old World*; Helmer, *La domestication des animaux par les hommes préhistoriques*; Anderson, *Prehistory of Agriculture*; Ellen and Fukui, *Redefining Nature*; Cauvin, *The Birth of the Gods and the Origins of Agriculture*.

43. According to Roberte Hamayon this is an essential aspect of the difference between hunting and farming in Siberia: "Hunting, which does not allow for the accumulation of animals nor their controlled reproduction, is 'inextensible'; livestock farming opens the possibility of multiplying them and 'to make them become many'" (*La chasse à l'âme*, 325).

44. Marcel Detienne comments: "The city wages war on wild animals but sacrifices and consumes only domestic animals. The Greeks divide the animal world

in two: the animals that are hunted for the harm that they can cause, and those that are protected because of the services that men have come to expect from them" ("Culinary Practices and the Spirit of Sacrifice," 8). See also Schnapp, *Le chasseur et la cité*, esp. chap. 1, "Le chasseur entre bestialité et humanité."

45. Such a definitive statement cannot be made about most African agropastoral civilizations where warlike hunting primarily involves big cats and must be distinguished from domestic hunting for edible animals. In Dogon, Bambara, and Bantu mythologies, for instance, the bestiary of the savage world is very rich. The break between humans and wild animals is not as pronounced as in the Greek world. This could be associated with the scarcity of cities until the nineteenth century.

46. Hesiod, *The Works and Days*, lines 109–20.

47. See Detienne, *Dionysos Slain*, esp. chap. 4.

48. *Sacrifice: Its Nature and Function* was originally published in *L'année sociologique* 2 (1899): 29–138.

49. Hubert and Mauss, *Sacrifice*, 14.

50. Ibid., 10 (Hubert and Mauss's italics).

51. See Herrenschmidt, *Les meilleurs dieux sont hindous*, 124–43.

52. On *daksina* see Malamoud, "Terminer le sacrifice."

53. Herrenschmidt, *Les meilleurs dieux sont hindous*, 124.

54. See also Chapter 4, note 50 above.

55. Hubert and Mauss, *Sacrifice*, 11.

56. Ibid., 12.

57. Similarly, for the mountain people of Southeast Asia the buffalo is privileged. In other cases several types of animals "are appropriate for sacrifice" (goats, sheep, chickens), depending on the ceremony. Dogs are a special case (see Heusch, *Sacrifice in Africa*, 174–83). Besides the choice of the animal species, other criteria are important, such as sex, health, age, and color.

58. "How does it come about that 'sacrifice' although it properly means 'to make sacred' (cf. *sacrificium*) actually means 'to put to death'?" (Benveniste, *Indo-European Language and Society*, 452).

59. See Cartry, "Le suaire du chef."

60. This is indeed a *cult*, since referring to ancestors in a noncult mode is an entirely different phenomenon.

61. For the African case see Izard, "Engrammes du pouvoir."

62. See Bourdillon and Fortes, *Sacrifice*, 13.

63. Hubert and Mauss, *Sacrifice*, 2.

64. Mauss, *The Gift*, 167.

65. Herrenschmidt, *Les meilleurs dieux sont hindous*, 127.

66. Malinowski, *Argonauts of the Western Pacific*, 95; see also above, Chapter 4, 132. For a more detailed discussion see Smith, "Aspects of the Organization of Rites."

67. "Part of the original essence of sacrifice is the fundamental idea present in

both Roman and Veda religions, that sacrifice is intended to satisfy the gods' hunger and strengthen them. . . . Prayers to Roman gods often contain the expressions 'receive growth, extra strength'" (Moussy, *Gratia et sa famille*, 38). "The gods get their immortality from sacrifice. . . . Sacrifice is above all food for the gods" (Biardeau, "Le sacrifice dans l'orthodoxie brahmanique," 23).

68. See Duverger, *La fleur létale*. More than feeding the god, the question here is to ensure that the universe will not perish for want of the energy provided by human sacrifices.

69. Lévi-Strauss understands how this progressive mediation between humans and divinities is effected in sacrificial procedures, but he does not go further; see Lévi-Strauss, *The Savage Mind*, 223–28.

70. Heusch, *Sacrifice in Africa*, 12–13; Cartry, "Le suaire du chef," 146.

71. On this point see Ortigues, *Le discours et le symbole*; and Sperber, *Rethinking Symbolism*.

72. It is clear that explanations of sacrifice as a manifestation of destructive exuberance (Georges Bataille) or as a release mechanism expiating mimetic violence (René Girard) are incompatible with this analysis.

73. See Vidal-Naquet, *The Black Hunter*, esp. 15–38.

74. Ibid., 25.

75. See Detienne, "Culinary Practices and the Spirit of Sacrifice," 3.

76. See Vernant, "At Man's Table."

77. Ibid., 27.

78. Ibid., 35–36.

79. In many other cultures the preferred sacrificial animal is only eaten for the ritual. This does not mean that the function of the ritual is to make it edible but that the animal is the symbol of the herder's power, of what has been taken from the gods and must be at the same time returned to and shared with them.

80. Vernant, "At Man's Table," 38.

81. See, e.g., Lévi, *La doctrine du sacrifice dans les Brâhmanas*; Renou, *The Civilization of Ancient India*; Biardeau and Malamoud, *Le sacrifice dans l'Inde ancienne*; Malamoud, *Cooking the World*; Herrenschmidt, *Les meilleurs dieux sont hindous*.

82. Biardeau, "Le sacrifice dans l'orthodoxie brahmanique," 15.

83. Ibid., 16.

84. Ibid., 21.

85. Lévi, *La doctrine du sacrifice dans les Brâhmanas*, 18.

86. Malamoud, *Cooking the World*, 122.

87. Biardeau, "Le sacrifice dans l'orthodoxie brahmanique," 25.

88. Cited in Malamoud, *Cooking the World*, 45.

89. Ibid., 74–91.

90. This approach has been proposed by René Girard. There are many reasons why I do not find it convincing. The main one is that sacrifice is an act that

presupposes an addresser and an addressee. It is, above all, an irreversible offering to an invisible beneficiary whose response must be obtained, hence the immolation. As in ceremonial gift-giving, something of one's own must be offered—hence the choice of a domestic animal. The fact that the immolated being is called a victim does not mean that every victim is a sacrificed being. Lynchings, executions, or massacres are not sacrifices but victimization procedures; Girard convincingly analyzes their functioning as what he calls "mimetic rivalry." To avoid harmful conceptual errors, the two processes should not be confused. The confusion may have its source in the Christian heritage and arises from the fact—too rarely mentioned—that Jesus, like Socrates, was not "sacrificed" but executed as a troublemaker by a political power. This is truly an example of a "scapegoat." The sacrifice of Christ only occurred in a posteriori readings in evangelical preaching.

CHAPTER 6. THE LOGIC OF DEBT

1. Plato *Phaedo* 118a (translation modified).
2. Nietzsche, *On the Genealogy of Morals*, 70.
3. Ibid., 71.
4. In Malamoud, *Lien de vie, nœud mortel*, 195. See also Pigeot, "Note sur le vocabulaire du 'devoir' et de la 'dette' et sur l'expression de l'obligation en japonais": "Contrary to what occurs in French, the Japanese counterparts of the words designating 'duty' and 'debt' and the verbal idea of 'owing' are not related" (163); and Alleton, "Les expressions de la dette et du devoir en chinois": "In Chinese there is a clear distinction between the expression of debt and that of moral duty" (169).
5. Benveniste, *Indo-European Language and Society*, 145–58. Louis Gernet also notes that the debt-obligation moral genealogy cannot be generalized: "In the Greek language, one would look in vain for the dualism that the terminology of Germanic law and even, to a certain point, that of Roman law allowed" (Gernet, *The Anthropology of Ancient Greece*, 147).
6. See Chapter 3 above.
7. Mauss mentions this in *The Gift*: "Germanic civilization was itself a long time without markets. It remained an essentially feudal and peasant society, and the notions and even the terms 'buying price' and 'selling price' seem to be of recent origin" (60). This is an old heritage: according to Tacitus, "[the Germans] were not acquainted with loans on interest" (quoted in Benveniste, *Indo-European Language and Society*, 156).
8. The third part of Chapter 8 will present a more theoretical approach to the problem raised by these semantic intercrossings.
9. See Clastres, "L'économie primitive."
10. For instance, in the highly complex system of gift exchange still observed

in Japan, it is understood that a gift should be reciprocated neither too soon, since it is considered elegant to remain for some time obligated to the giver, nor through an overly valuable gift, which would amount to reversing the relationship and therefore erasing the debt and ending the interplay of gift exchange. See Jane Cobbi, "L'obligation du cadeau au Japon."

11. We saw earlier (Chapter 5) that this is the situation of hunter-gatherers from the Americas (see Boas regarding the coast of the Pacific Northwest). It is also found among Siberian hunter-gatherers (see Hamayon, *La chasse à l'âme*).

12. See Leach, *Political Systems of Highland Burma*; and Condominas, *We Have Eaten the Forest*.

13. This logic tends to become perverse: a *kuang* with many debtors can afford to anticipate returns and to keep sacrificing on credit: "Because of his renown, which brings him many 'givers,' a *kuang dööng* (great *kuang*) always owes 'debts of meat.' In order to be able to immolate more buffalos with pomp and generosity, which will increase their prestige in proportion, great *kuang* often do not even wait until they have entirely paid back their purchases in order to make new ones. . . . In other words, they practice a true debt strategy" (Condominas, "De la monnaie multiple," 108).

14. See Lévi, *La doctrine du sacrifice dans les Brâhmanas*; Biardeau and Malamoud, *Le sacrifice dans l'Inde ancienne*; Herrenschmidt, *Les meilleurs dieux sont hindous*; Renou, *Etudes védiques et paninénnes*.

15. Malamoud, *Cooking the World*, 93, 95. The following pages are to a large extent a presentation of Malamoud's analysis; subsequent citations of *Cooking the World* will be referenced parenthetically in the text.

16. Verdier, *La vengeance*, 1:14.

17. Ibid., 21.

18. Ibid., 24.

19. Ibid., 25.

20. See Lemonnier, *Guerres et festins*, esp. 92ff. Regarding wars between rival groups from New Guinea, the author mentions various kinds of restrictions or forms of suspension; for instance, the enemy may be warned of an impending raid; those who are to be killed may be selected; women may be allowed to move around unimpeded and to collect arrows; fighting may be interrupted because of rain; the two sides may decide on an alliance in order to hunt game that happens to pass by.

21. This equivalence between vindicatory obligations and obligations relative to matrimonial alliance is such that the two logics involved are interchangeable. Philippe Descola notes the following about the Jivaro of Amazonia:

It may be found surprising that the Achuar [a Jivaro group] equate the abduction of a woman with the death of a man and insist in both cases on compensation in the form of a rifle. But the fact is that reparation for infractions of the marriage code obeys the principle of a return to parity through payment of an indemnity. The principle involved is in every respect identical to that which governs vengeance for a murder. Deprived of a person who should by rights fall to him or over whom he exercises guardianship, a creditor considers himself authorized to compensate himself for his loss by eliminating the person who is responsible for it and who, on that account, owes him a life. . . . An exchange of goods, an exchange of women and an exchange of lives all belong to the same field of meanings and are designated by identical terms. (Descola, *The Spears of Twilight*, 250–51)

22. Verdier, *La vengeance*, 1:28.

23. These are societies that do not form a state but are nevertheless governed by an assembly that deliberates and makes decisions without reference to clan authority, for instance the Gamo from Ethiopia, which we will soon discuss.

24. It does not seem appropriate, therefore, to assume along with René Girard that sacrifice intervenes as a way to end the "uncontrolled violence" unleashed by cycles of vengeance (see Chapter 5, note 90). In fact these processes emerge in societies where sacrifice has lost its function of regulation of the cosmic and social order. To say that violence is "out of control" amounts precisely to saying that it is no longer coded as it can be within the framework of vindicatory justice.

25. See Godelier, *The Making of Great Men*.

26. This is precisely what we saw in Chapter 4 regarding the reversal of the Latin term *hostis*. See Chapter 4, "Strangers and the Gift of Oneself." At first *hostis* designated an ally from a different clan; but when the city emerged, if this clan belonged to a different city, *hostis* then became a stranger and potential enemy.

27. This hybrid status of vengeance is clearly apparent in the sequences of the settlings of scores between military leaders at the beginning of imperial Rome. See Thomas, "Se venger au forum."

28. These remarks are based on Jacques Bureau's "Une société sans vengeance."

29. Ibid., 223.

30. Evans-Pritchard, *The Nuer*, 26.

31. Ibid., 150ff.

32. See, in particular, Detienne, *The Masters of Truth in Archaic Greece*, esp. chap. 5, "The Process of Secularization," 89–106.

33. Verdier, *La vengeance*, 1:18–20.

34. Ibid., 18.

35. Ibid., 19.

36. Used by Verdier in the writing discussed, it is already found in Mauss. It is also the topic of François Rospabé's book *La dette de vie*.

37. Simplicius, cited in Seligman, *The Apeiron of Anaximander*, 19–20.

38. See, e.g., Heidegger, "Anaximander's Saying." What makes Heidegger's commentary disappointing is his arbitrary variations on etymology, as well as his obvious ignorance of the cultural context, as shown by this claim, which is meant to be critical: "But the saying says nothing of payment, penalty, or damages. Nor does it say that something is punishable or must be avenged (according to the opinion of those who equate vengeance with justice)" (268). Heidegger is right to reject the modern moral interpretation, but he does not see the logic of ceremonial

debt. Michel Serres situates this fragment in an original manner within the whole of Greek speculation on the unlimited—*apeiron* (see Serres, "Anaximander").

39. Lloyd, *Early Greek Science*, 20.

40. Ibid., 21ff.

41. See Gernet, *The Anthropology of Ancient Greece*, 143ff.

42. Chantraine, *Dictionnaire étymologique de la langue grecque*, s.v. "tino"; Scheid-Tissinier, *Les usages du don chez Homère*, 183ff: "In the *Odyssey* the same term is used by the giver entitled to receive a counter-gift and the injured party demanding compensation for what it has lost, the common element being the incurring of a debt" (189). It would be more accurate to say that the giver generates a debt.

43. Gregory Vlastos writes, "In Anaximander's famous fragment, the hot and the dry, encroaching upon the cold and wet in the summer, must 'pay' for their 'injustice' by suffering in return the like fate in the winter, when the cold and wet make converse aggression upon the erstwhile aggressors, completing one retaliatory cycle, to start another in endless succession" (*Socrates, Ironist and Moral Philosopher*, 182). This interpretation begins well and ends badly: it correctly perceives the reciprocal interplay of the elements but understands it in terms of modern vengeance when, instead, what is at stake is ceremonial debt.

44. Vernant, "The Lame Tyrant," 213.

45. Aristotle extends *philia* to animals (*NE* 1155a18). Euripides writes in praise of equality, giving as an example the good manners shown by day and night: "Equality set up men's weights and measures, gave them their numbers. And night's sightless eye equal[ly] divides with day the circling year. While neither, yielding place, resents the other" (*The Phoenician Women*, v. 541–45).

46. On the status of the character of Panurge and the narrative organization of *The Third Book* in general see Oumelbanine Zhiri's penetrating analysis, *L'extase et ses paradoxes*.

47. Rabelais, *The Third Book*, 264; subsequent references are cited parenthetically in the text.

48. See Guillaume d'Auxerre's statement, cited in Chapter 3 at note 25 above: "Augustine says that every creature is obliged to give of itself; the sun is obliged to give of itself in order to shine; in the same way, the earth is obliged to give all it can produce, as is the water."

49. But the state does not take charge of the victims' suffering, as Aristotle understands when he explains (in *Rhetoric* 2.1378a30–32) that anyone subjected to "undeserved contempt" has the right to demand that his honor (*timè*) be restored. Legitimate anger foreshadows a desire for vengeance, which, however, can only be achieved within the framework of public law, as required by the city. Aristotle still provides this essential definition: "Revenge and punishment, however, are different: punishment is for the sake of the person punished [the culprit], revenge for that of the avenger [the victim], so that he may be satisfied" (*Rhetoric* 1.10.1369b12–13). See Hénaff, "Dette de sang et exigence de justice."

50. See Bloch, *Feudal Society*; Kantorowicz, *The King's Two Bodies*; and Strayer, *On the Medieval Origins of the Modern State.*

51. This is an important aspect of the collection edited by Michel Aglietta and André Orléan, *La monnaie souveraine.* We will return to this in Chapters 8 and 9.

52. The United States, where this system of compensation is the most developed, is also the last Western country where the death penalty remains in the law and is enforced in the strictest way. It may be hypothesized that maintaining the death penalty somehow provides the last sanctuary for symbolic debt. Those sentenced to death are in a way required to testify by their death to the priceless character of life, the price of which is otherwise continually defined and bargained for in the marketplace.

CHAPTER 7. THE PARADOXES OF GRACE

1. Moussy, *Gratia et sa famille*, 411ff.

2. Ibid., 412.

3. See Benveniste, *Indo-European Language and Society*, chap. 17.

4. See Moussy, 250ff.

5. Ibid., 410.

6. Remarkably, this is precisely what Roberte Hamayon observes in an entirely different world, that of the Buriat from Siberia. Not only does Hamayon underline the fact that the shift from hunting culture to herding culture was associated with a shift from gift exchange—connected to alliance—to the practice of sacrifice offered to the ancestors—in which filiation prevails—(see Chapter 5 above), but she also observes that this entailed a shift from the idea of *luck* to that of *grace*:

> For the Buriat, grace—*xeseg*—manifests itself in the form of happiness and wealth, through the *portion* of meat received; it can also be contained in a latent or virtual manner within stones or an object that "came down" from the sky. . . . Things so-called *xesegten*, "endowed with grace" must not be relinquished at any cost. . . . For all these reasons the "grace" requested by the herder from his ancestors can be viewed as heir and homologous to the "luck" gained by the hunter from the spirit of the forest (or rather from his daughter). The two are obtained in different ways: seduction on the part of the hunter . . . ; appeal on the part of the herder. . . . They also manifest different values: luck is won by the beneficiary (who can even force it), whereas grace is granted to him. (*La chasse à l'âme*, 629–30)

7. See Scheid-Tissinier, *Les usages du don chez Homère*, 32ff; Chantraine, *Dictionnaire étymologique de la langue grecque*, s.v. "Charis."

8. Scheid-Tissinier, *Les usages du don chez Homère*, 32.

9. Ibid., 33.

10. This is the title of a book by C. Meier, *Politik und Anmut.*

11. Detienne, *The Masters of Truth in Archaic Greece*, chap. 4.

12. This was true of every form of debate, such as the one reported by Plato between Socrates, Protagoras, and Prodicus; in order to prevent the exchange of

arguments from becoming hostile, Prodicus makes the following suggestion: "Let your conversation be a discussion, not a dispute. A discussion is carried among friends with goodwill, but a dispute is between rivals and enemies. In this way our meeting [will have *the greatest beauty*] (*kallistē sunousia*)" (*Pro.* 337b).

13. Arendt, *Between Past and Future*, 218.

14. Finley, *Early Greece*, 145; Finley also notes, "Such sculpture, like the temple, symbolized the triumph of the community, a demonstration of its growing strength and self-consciousness" (145).

15. "The origin of the city lies, I think, in the fact that we are not, any of us, self-sufficient; we have all sorts of needs (*khreia*). . . . With this variety of wants they may collect a number of partners and allies into one place of habitation, and to this joint habitation (*koinōnia*) we give the name 'city' (*polis*)" (Plato *Republic* 369b–c).

16. The story is told by Protagoras, but he is not its author; it comes from a well-known mythical narrative. By having the Sophist tell it, Plato means to force him to accept that, regarding virtue and especially its political form, the essential element is given rather than acquired through education, as claimed by the Sophists.

17. See Lemaire, *Le monde de la Bible*; Bottéro, *Religion in Ancient Mesopotamia*; and Bottéro, *The Birth of God*.

18. The transcription I have chosen to use here, "Yahweh," is conventional but not used in scholarly literature; it has the advantage of being familiar to readers even though it is disputed among experts.

19. See Caquot, "La religion d'Israël."

20. Ibid., 382.

21. Ibid., 385.

22. On this point see Paul Ricoeur's fine analyses in *Memory, History, Forgetting*, esp. 478–86.

23. See, e.g., Vidal, "Les gestes du don"; and Goux, "Don et altérité chez Sénèque."

24. On this point see Paul Veyne's seminal work, *Bread and Circuses*.

25. See Chapter 3 above.

26. This is Jean-Joseph Goux's argument (see Goux, "Don et altérité chez Sénèque," 122).

27. Veyne, *Bread and Circuses*, 10. Veyne adds: "The free-born rich who made up the various orders of nobility—senators, *equites*, decurions—were naturally required to give more than others. This was not only because they had the means to do so but because their quality as men who were completely human imposed on them a duty to be responsive to all human ideals" (7).

28. Ibid., 5–6.

29. See Champeaux, *La religion romaine*, esp. chap. 6.

30. Tarot, "Repères pour une histoire de la naissance de la grâce," 109.

31. There is an immense literature on Paul's doctrine. See, e.g., Bornkamm, *Paul, Paulus*; Tresmontant, *Saint Paul et le mystère du Christ*; Breton, *Saint Paul*; see also Alain Badiou's philosophical approach, *Saint Paul: The Foundation of Universalism*. Assessing the decisive way in which Paul transformed the notion of *kharis* would require a more extended study (his transformation of this notion became the foundation for everything the Christian heritage elaborated with regard to the issue of grace) but this would be a work of exegis and theology.

32. Weber explicitly specifies his predecessors and audience: Lujo Brentano, Werner Sombart, Ernst Troeltsch, and Georg Simmel, not to mention lesser critics. Between the first (1904–5) and the second (1920) edition of the text, Weber's debate with these various authors became more specific as he responded to their new publications.

33. Fernand Braudel is the most prestigious author of this regrettable misinterpretation. He writes, "For Max Weber, capitalism, in the modern sense of the word, was no more and no less than a creation of Protestantism, or more precisely of Puritanism" (*La dynamique du capitalisme*, 69). His remarks on Weber in *Civilization and Capitalism* (2:580–81) are more nuanced.

34. Weber, *The Protestant Ethic and the Spirit of Capitalism*, 35 (my emphasis); subsequent references are cited parenthetically in the text. For those who would still wish for an immediate causal explanation, Weber adds, "the fact that certain important forms of capitalistic business organization are known to be considerably older than the Reformation is a sufficient refutation of such a claim" (91). Tawney's criticisms (1926), and above all those of Robertson, are largely the result of a misunderstanding. Claude Lefort remains ambiguous about this debate in *Les formes de l'histoire* (see 112–26).

35. Weber also cautions against the opposite excess: "On the other hand, however, we have no intention whatever of maintaining such a foolish and doctrinaire thesis as that the spirit of capitalism (in the provisional sense of the term explained above) could only have arisen as the result of certain effects of the Reformation, or even that capitalism as an economic system is a creation of the Reformation" (*PE* 91).

36. Ernst Troeltsch was a Protestant theologian and sociologist close to Weber and the author of important works, including *Protestantism and Progress*, from which I have quoted here (142–43, 173).

37. "Nevertheless, we provisionally use the expression spirit of (modern) capitalism to describe that attitude that seeks profit rationally and systematically" (*PE* 64).

38. See Le Goff, *Time, Work, and Culture in the Middle Ages*.

39. Weber does not confuse the novelty of the notion with the novelty of its importance. Indeed, the acknowledged significance of one's occupation as the earthly task of the Christian already had an important presence in medieval theology—especially in preaching—from the thirteenth century on. A good example is provided by the sermons of the Franciscan Berthold de Ratisbone, who preached in southern German towns in the thirteenth century. See Gurevich, "The Merchant."

Weber knows this preacher's texts, which he mentions in *The Protestant Ethic and the Spirit of Capitalism* (208). In the same way, Troeltsch writes, "The doctrine of the 'calling' (*Beruf*), as a doctrine of the systematic contribution of every worker to the *de lege naturae* appointed purpose of Society, had already long been a doctrine of Catholicism" (Troeltsch, *Protestantism and Progress*, 129).

40. The important question of Augustine's doctrine and heritage needs to be reexamined. This task is beyond the framework of this volume—and the competence of its author. Augustine's essential writings are *De gratia et libero arbitrio*; *De corruptione et gratia*; and *De predestinatione*.

41. (Parsons translated it as, "The elimination of magic from the world"; however, the phrase "disenchantment of the world" has become commonplace in English and is therefore used here.—Trans.) Weber observes that this disenchantment already affected ancient Judaism to a significant extent. In his view this explains the exceptional character of the Hebraic tradition—its modernity ahead of its time, its universalizing vocation, and its aptitude for success in the field of business. See Weber, *Ancient Judaism*.

42. Troeltsch, "Calvinism and Lutheranism." Louis Dumont's analyses of Calvin's positions confirm this; see Dumont, *Essays on Individualism*, 42–49.

43. See also 108 and 224n30: "The active energies of the elect, liberated by the doctrine of predestination, thus flowed into the struggle to rationalize the world." Weber explores this perspective more fully in other writings, such as *Sociology of Religion*.

44. In "Calvinism and Lutheranism" Troeltsch recalls Calvin's project to establish a kind of "sacred community."

45. Weber adds: "The traditional American objection to performing personal service is probably connected, besides the other important causes resulting from democratic feelings, at least indirectly to that tradition" (*PE* 224n30).

46. Troeltsch, *Protestantism and Progress*, 165–66. Troeltsch adds: "[Protestantism] never elevated artistic feeling into the principle of a philosophy of life, of metaphysics or ethics. . . . That was why it repelled the Renaissance. That is why, also, modern art everywhere proves the end of Protestant asceticism: it is absolutely opposed to it in principle" (168–69).

47. The most important writing on this issue is an essay written in 1915, rewritten in 1920, entitled "Religious Rejections of the World and Their Directions."

48. Ibid., 329.

49. Baudelaire, *The Parisian Prowler*, 21.

50. Why doesn't Weber dwell on the description and analysis of the world of—ritual and moral—gift exchange, even though he glimpses several aspects of it? There are several reasons. The first is that the issue did not really exist at the time as a sociological or anthropological *problem*. To be sure, there already was literature—such as Boas's and Thurnwald's—that precisely documented ceremonies of reciprocal gift exchange. Malinowski's *Argonauts of the Western Pacific* was

not published until 1922, however, two years after Weber's death, and Mauss's *The Gift* was not published until 1924. Even if Weber had lived longer, there is no reason to believe that he would have found this question more relevant from a theoretical point of view. In his research Weber shows very little interest in so-called primitive societies. References to them are scarce in his texts. Given his usual methodological flair, he may have thought that the literature available in this field was still weak and often poorly supported. In any case he restricts his analysis to the great civilizations and the religions associated with them, fields in which scholarship—and especially German scholarship—provided first-rate knowledge.

51. Weber explains that through its regularity, discipline, and rigor monastic life, this "asceticism outside of the world," constituted a remarkable attempt to develop a rational organization of life and a mastery of sensitivity; according to him the Reformation took this "rational asceticism" out of the monastery and placed it in the service of active life in the world.

52. Weber, "A Final Rebuttal to Rachfahl's Critique of the 'Spirit of Capitalism,'" 307.

53. This investigation could have been initiated by scholars coming from the Roman tradition. But Catholic theologians and intellectuals have generally limited themselves to challenging Weber's or Troeltsch's analyses, not in order to claim for themselves the modernity that these analyses deny them (how could they have dared to do so when "modernism" was the object of a strict indictment on the part of the Vatican), but to reaffirm the incommensurable character of faith in relation to the physical world, which is to say, in this case, to economic reality. The most influential attempt is that of Werner Sombart in *The Quintessence of Capitalism* (1913). Sombart sets out to show that scholastic thought constituted the theoretical framework for rationalizing economic life and that the condemnation of usury was, in fact, the prohibition of profit for profit's sake and promoted lending for productive investment. Finally, he shows how, in his treatise on the family, the great Florentine humanist Alberti had in the fifteenth century already defined the entire range of bourgeois virtues, the embodiment of which Weber finds in the Calvinist Puritans. In contrast, Sombart shows that from the outset the Reformers denounced usury and excessive wealth and that every Puritan sect was constantly led by this anticapitalist spirit. In short, Sombart reverses Weber's "theses" on every point. Weber replies to these objections by noting that the presence here and there of rationality in the management of goods, of an inclination to acquire wealth, or of a rigorous discipline of life, does not amount to the existence of the *capitalist spirit*.

54. Page numbers indicated parenthetically in the text are from the French translation, *La grâce du don: Anthropologie catholique de l'économie moderne.*

55. See, e.g., Nelson, *The Idea of Usury*; Le Goff, *Marchands et banquiers du Moyen Age*; and Le Goff, *Your Money or Your Life.*

56. Hence the emergence of the concept of *antidora*. For anyone familiar with classical Greek vocabulary this term seems odd. *Antidosis* (gift in return or exchange), a term used by Aristotle, is more expected. Clavero pretended not to know this and only referred to sixteenth-century Spanish treatises that used the Latin term *antidoron* or its later feminine form *antidora*; the dominant concept was that of a moral and statutory obligation rather than a legal one.

57. Domingo de Soto, cited in Clavero, *La grâce du don*, 55.

58. See Luc Boltanski's discussion in his *L'amour et la justice comme compétences*.

59. See Aristotle *Politics* I.1252a–1254.

60. I have attempted to briefly present this hypothesis in my article "L'éthique catholique et l'esprit du non-capitalisme."

61. The main statements of the Jansenist movement and the way Pascal takes them up should be reexamined from this perspective; this problematic is absent from Kolakowski's work *God Owes Us Nothing*.

CHAPTER 8. CEREMONIAL MONEY AND COMMERCIAL MONEY

1. This type of distinction is proposed by George Dalton in *Traditional Tribal and Peasant Economies*, 1–35. Dalton places on one side "primitive precious goods," which he calls *valuables*, and on the other "primitive monetary objects," defined as divisible objects (metal pieces, stones, and cowries), which he presents as a still awkward prefiguration of modern currency. This is more or less Max Weber's perception as well: "Never and nowhere could a man buy a wife for shells, but only for cattle, while in small transactions the shells were accepted because they were available in small denominations" (Weber, *General Economic History*, 237). If he were writing today, Weber would certainly grant that (1) the gifts associated with matrimonial alliance do not constitute purchase of the bride; (2) cattle are not found everywhere; and (3) in Melanesian societies, for example, already very accurately described at the beginning of the twentieth century by Thurnwald, pearls and seashells are a central element of the gifts offered by the husband's group.

2. Mauss, "Origines de la notion de monnaie," 106–12; subsequent references are cited parenthetically in the text

3. This is clearly apparent in some remarks made by audience members and in the discussion that follows Mauss's presentation; see Mauss, *Oeuvres*, 2:114–20.

4. In many passages from *The Gift* Mauss emphasizes this purely symbolic and ritual functioning of traditional currencies such as Fidji's *kere-kere*, Trobriand's *tambua*, and New Guinea's *tau-tau* (*G* 31, passim).

5. For instance, he frequently calls "trade" the great movement of *kula* in the Trobriand ("busy intertribal trade" [*G* 21]; "*Kula* trade is of a noble kind" [*G* 22]). The circulation of gifts in general would thus be "the market as it exist-

ed before the institution of traders and before their main invention—money proper" (*G* 4).

6. Mauss notes later that "the value of the copper objects among the Tlingit varies according to their height and is counted in numbers of slaves" (*G* 133n243).

7. See de Coppet, "La monnaie."

8. Ibid., 18.

9. Ibid., 21.

10. This has been discussed above in Chapter 6, regarding debt and vindicatory justice.

11. De Coppet, "La monnaie," 23–24.

12. This should have led de Coppet to a critical questioning of the problematic use of the term *currency*; this questioning is still absent from a more recent and detailed version of ceremonial exchanges in Are'are society; see de Coppet, "Une monnaie pour une communauté mélanésienne comparée à la nôtre pour l'individu des sociétés européennes."

13. This problematic will be discussed in the third section of this chapter.

14. In Rospabé, *La dette de vie*, 13–14. Caillé should have specified "symbolic debt," since the kind of debt Caillé discusses is never a financial debt.

15. Ibid., 10.

16. Mauss writes this in *The Gift*: "What is incorrectly called marriage by purchase" (32); Lévi-Strauss is quite categorical and precise on this point in *The Elementary Structures of Kinship* (see chaps. 10 and 16). This has since been the position of contemporary anthropology as a whole, with few exceptions.

17. Furthermore, in traditional societies, when this "payment" is made with modern money, it is still not a purchase. Modern money is used for symbolic exchange and as an equivalent to precious goods (cattle, jewelry, fabrics, ornaments, etc). This substitution does have long-term consequences, since it introduces increasing ambiguity and a dangerous cultural confusion between gift-exchange relationships and commercial relationships. On this point see the extensive literature provided by David Akin and Joel Robbins in *Money and Modernity*.

18. On proto-currency see Michel Servet, *Nomismata*. The same suspicion applies to the otherwise remarkable contributions collected in *La monnaie souveraine*, to the extent that they are based on the hypothesis of a genealogical connection between ceremonial currency and modern currency. That collection, however, raises a crucial issue: the specific form of social bond associated with modern currency is inseparable from the political institution.

19. "Trade created money rather than money trade," observes Pierre Vilar (*A History of Gold and Money*, 27). We must go beyond this obvious observation, however. A distinction must be established between the emergence of measuring units (which can be goods specifically chosen for this purpose, such as metal, grain, or other objects) and that of minted currency, whose origin is political and linked to the control exercised by sovereign power.

20. This was the case in ancient Greece; see Picard, "Les origines du monnayage en Grèce"; Will, "De l'aspect éthique de l'origine grecque de la monnaie"; and Will, "Réflexions et hypothèses sur l'origine du monnayage."

21. Malinowski, *Argonauts of the Western Pacific*, 99–100; subsequent references are cited parenthetically in the text.

22. Godelier, *The Enigma of the Gift*, 138–40.

23. Ibid., 140.

24. On Melanesian cultures see the extensive literature presented in Akin and Robbins, *Money and Modernity*. On Africa see Servet, "Démonétisation et remonétarisation en Afrique occidentale et équatoriale."

25. This attitude has run across our entire history. Natalie Z. Davis gives a good example of it regarding sixteenth-century French society (but also applicable to the medieval era) in *The Gift in Sixteenth-Century France*: "What is interesting about the sixteenth century is this sensitivity to the relation between gift and sale, this concern about the border between them. Rather than imagining a zero-sum game between gifts and commercial markets, or even a historical tug of war, we might better conceive of enduring interactions between gift-systems and sale-systems" (44). This assessment is undoubtedly true of every European country at the time and can be verified in every culture in which significant commercial exchanges have developed. Although Davis shows the extent to which gift-giving relationships and commercial relationships are intermingled, she observes that in the final analysis they remain distinct from each other. This is expressed by an extensive iconography on the two types of gesture. "The sale mode and the gift mode coexisted and interacted in sixteenth-century France, distinguished from each other by roles in which they cast donor and recipient or buyer and seller and by certain features of the transaction. Each had its own etiquette, language and body posture for presentation" (56).

CHAPTER 9. MONEY: EQUIVALENCE, JUSTICE, AND LIBERTY

1. Over a number of years Jean-Joseph Goux conducted a coherent reflection on the symbolic status of money as a form; see his *Symbolic Economies*; *Les iconoclastes*; *The Coiners of Language*; *Frivolité de la valeur*. The reflection presented here, starting from the question of ceremonial gift exchange, is situated in a different perspective.

2. See Gauthier and Jolif, *Éthique à Nicomaque*, 369ff. In his analysis of currency in Aristotle (see Polanyi, Arensberg, and Pearson, *Trade and Market in the Early Empires*), Polanyi does not deal with this question. Neither does Romeyer-Dherbey in his excellent chapter on money in Aristotle in *Les choses mêmes*.

3. On this question the authoritative work remains Armand Delatte's *Essai sur la politique pythagoricienne*.

4. See Euclid *Elements* 6.15: "If two triangles have their sides proportional, the

triangles will be equiangular and will have those angles equal which the corresponding sides subtend."

5. See Chantraine, *Dictionnaire étymologique de la langue grecque*, s.v. "Pascho."

6. See Chapter 5 above, "The Logic of Debt."

7. "Revenge and punishment are different things. Punishment is inflicted for the sake of the person punished, revenge for that of the punisher, to satisfy his feelings" (*Rhetoric* 1.10.1369b).

8. "The origin of a city lies, I think, in the fact that we are not, any of us, self-sufficient; we have all sorts of needs. . . . With this variety of wants (*chreia*) they may collect a number of partners and allies into one place of habitation, and to this joint habitation we give the name 'city' (*polis*)" (*Republic* 2.369b–c).

9. As we saw in Chapter 2, this framework of civic exchange did not imply the absence of professional trade and of a large-scale marketplace. See Bresson, *La cité marchande*, 108–30.

10. Trade in the classical age should not be viewed as overly archaic; see ibid., 263–308.

11. See Finley, *The Ancient Economy*; and Polanyi, Arensberg, and Pearson, *Trade and Market in the Early Empires*.

12. Serres, *Genesis*, 32, 39; see also Serres, *The Parasite*, 161–64.

13. This aspect, which seems essential to me, has been given little consideration in two otherwise excellent collections of studies on Simmel's sociological and economic work: Grenier et al., *À propos de "Philosophie de l'argent" de Georg Simmel*; and Baldner and Gillard, *Simmel et les normes sociales*.

14. Simmel, *The Philosophy of Money*, 292; subsequent references are cited parenthetically in the text.

15. These are only general characteristics; they vary to a considerable extent depending on the period and on the legal traditions of societies practicing slavery.

16. See Simmel, *The Philosophy of Money*, 342.

17. See Cuq, *Manuel des institutions juridiques des Romains*, 486ff.

18. Mauss, *The Gift*, 112n139. The concept of rhythm also developed by Mauss is very helpful to our understanding of the source of the ludic impulse. "Man is a rhythmic animal," he writes in *Manual of Ethnography* (67).

19. Although contracts of association, so-called society contracts, can involve several persons.

20. This gives rise to two paradoxical cases: the marriage contract—which Kant defines in strictly neutral terms of civil convention in *The Metaphysics of Morals*—and the contract of love submission, as in Sacher-Masoch, of which Deleuze analyzes the aporetic character (this aporia is that of a game, however, not that of the law).

21. It goes without saying that these claims do not apply to the theories of the contract as founding pact found in authors such as Grotius and Rousseau. The latter involve a model of representation of civil society as originating from a con-

vention assumed to have constituted a break with an earlier state of nature. This would involve a different and considerable debate.

22. See Bresson, *La cité marchande.*

23. On this point see Aglietta and Orléan, *La monnaie souveraine.*

CHAPTER 10. LEGITIMATE FIGURES OF COMMERCIAL EXCHANGE

1. See Le Goff, *Time, Work, and Culture in the Middle Ages.*

2. See Chapter 1, note 4 above.

3. Jaeger, *Paideia,* 1:291.

4. I should even say "in all traditional cultures," since these attitudes (which involve challenge, generosity, and prestige) are associated with the reciprocal requirement institutionalized by ceremonial gift exchange. My restriction concerns only the concept of a warrior class and is thus only applicable to certain types of societies with highly differentiated statuses.

5. See Havelock, *Origins of Western Literacy.*

6. See Goody, *The Logic of Writing and the Organization of Society.*

7. For an insightful discussion of the complexities of this issue see chap. 11 of Kerferd's *The Sophistic Movement.*

8. *Antidosis* 15 (cited in Kerferd, *The Sophistic Movement,* 26).

9. "It is clear," says Kerferd, "that to many it was the mere fact that they took fees, not the size of the fees, which was objectionable" (*The Sophistic Movement,* 25). Kerferd also mentions that the poet Pindar was paid ten thousand drachmas for his ode on the victory over the Persians (ibid., 25).

10. See Müller, "Sophistique et démocratie," 179.

11. See Le Goff, *Intellectuals in the Middle Ages,* 97–103. Le Goff explains that in the secular view masters of monastic obedience "were not true academics. They created disloyal competition at the university; they won over students and inspired many to enter a monastic vocation; living off alms, they asked for no money from students as payment for their lectures, and they did not feel bound by the material demands of university life. . . . They were not scientific workers, because they were not living off their teaching" (98).

12. Montesquieu, *The Spirit of the Laws,* 338.

13. See Braudel, *Civilization and Capitalism,* vol. 2, *The Wheels of Commerce.*

14. Montesquieu, *The Spirit of the Laws,* 357; subsequent references are cited parenthetically in the text.

15. See Hirschman, *The Passions and the Interests.*

16. *Par-dessus le marché* is a French idiom that means "to top it all"; its literal meaning is "above and beyond the marketplace."—Trans.

17. See Marrou, *A History of Education in Antiquity.*

18. See Davis, "Beyond the Market"; and Davis, *The Gift in Sixteenth-Century France,* 45. The crisis affecting the rights of authors was already patent at the time.

19. See Febvre and Martin, *The Coming of the Book*; Eisenstein, *The Printing Revolution in Early Modern Europe*; and Chartier, *Culture écrite et société*.

20. On painting in the Renaissance see Baxandall, *Painting and Experience in Fifteenth-Century Italy*.

21. Diderot, *Lettre sur le commerce de la librairie*, 30.

22. Ibid.

23. Kant, "What Is a Book?" 437.

24. Kant, "On the Wrongfulness of Unauthorized Publication of Books," 29.

25. Ibid. (Kant's emphasis).

26. Edelman, *Le droit d'auteur*, 39.

27. Kant, "What Is Money?" 434–36.

28. Geza Roheim's work, which is regarded as seminal on this topic, provides a rich collection of misinterpretations of the ethnographic facts it reports; the same can be said of William H. Desmonde; see the literature collected by Ernest Borneman, *The Psychoanalysis of Money*.

29. Freud, "Further Recommendations in the Technique of Psychoanalysis," 144.

30. See Freud, "Character and Anal Erotism."

31. "It is well known that the value of the treatment is not enhanced in the patient's eyes if a very low fee is asked. . . . But the psychoanalyst may put himself in the position of surgeons, who are both honest and expensive because they deal in measures which can be of aid" ("Further Recommendations in the Technique of Psychoanalysis," 144). Freud then presents this interesting calculus: "If one contrasts a computation of the never-ceasing costs of nursing homes and medical treatment with the increase of capacity to live well and earn well after a successful analytic treatment, one may say that the patient has made a good bargain. Nothing in life is so expensive as illness—and foolishness" (146).

32. But the reasons for Freud's attitude after 1918 (i.e., during the hyperinflation era) were practical. He even demanded payment in dollars to offset what had become daily devaluation.

33. Freud, "Further Recommendations in the Technique of Psychoanalysis," 144–45.

34. Ibid., 145 (my emphasis).

35. Freud, "On Psychotherapy," 68.

36. We should recall Simmel's central statement: "In the process of differentiation between the person and his achievement, money supports the independence of the person" (Simmel, *The Philosophy of Money*, 342).

37. Freud, "Further Recommendations in the Technique of Psychoanalysis," 145. According to Charles Malamoud this relationship to the real world is also involved in an entirely different question, the payment (*daksina*) due to the Brahman, which is an integral part of the sacrifice. It is neither mere wages nor a kind of gift. It constitutes the articulation between the sacrificial world and the everyday

world, and it prevents the former from being completely separated from the latter. At the same time it proclaims the sacrificer's autonomy relative to the performer of the sacrifice and even to the deities. See Malamoud, "Terminer le sacrifice." Malamoud himself observes that in this respect there is an interesting homology between the autonomy of the Indian sacrificer and the autonomy of the analyst according to Freud.

38. This does not mean that the income gained by the professionals of knowledge and the means by which it is gained—salaries or profitable publications—is now beyond all suspicion. From this standpoint a sociological and political analysis of these forms of income has yet to be conducted, although Jean-Claude Milner presents an incisive approach to the issue in his monograph *Le salaire de l'idéal*.

39. Mallarmé, *Divagations*, 225.

RETURN/EXITS

1. See Kant, "What Is Money?" 436.

2. "The idea of distributive justice has as much to do with being and doing as with having, as much to do with protection as with consumption, as much to do with identity and status as with land, capital, or personal possessions" (Walzer, *Spheres of Justice*, 3; see esp. chap. 4).

3. On this issue see Ricoeur, *The Just*, 76–93.

4. "By ranging the Kula as the primary and chief activity, and the rest as secondary ones, I mean that this precedence is implied in the institutions themselves." Even if ordinary trade takes place during the circuit, "the Kula is in all respects the main aim: the dates are fixed, the preliminaries settled, the expeditions arranged, the social organization determined, not with regard to trade, but with regard to Kula" (Malinowski, *Argonauts of the Western Pacific*, 101).

5. See Aristophanes *Plutus* 189.

6. This law was stated in the middle of the nineteenth century by Jean-Baptiste Say and restated at the beginning of the twentieth by Léon Walras. This economic trend, called neoclassical or marginalist, is part of the larger utilitarian trend.

7. See Arendt, *The Human Condition*, chaps. 3 and 4.

8. See Goffman, *The Presentation of Self in Everyday Life*; and *Interaction Ritual*.

9. "Strangers, beggars, all are sent by Zeus" (*Odyssey* 14.57–58).

10. Levinas, *Totality and Infinity*, 194; subsequent references are cited parenthetically in the text.

11. Levi, *Survival in Auschwitz*, 121.

12. Ibid.

13. McCullers, *The Ballad of the Sad Café*, 1.

14. Ibid., 40–41.

Bibliography

Aeschylus. *The Eumenides.* In *The Oresteian Trilogy,* translated by Philip Vellacott, 147–82. London: Penguin, 1956.

Aglietta, Michel, and Andre Orléan, eds. *La monnaie souveraine.* Paris: Odile Jacob, 1998.

Akin, David, and Joel Robbins, eds. *Money and Modernity: State and Local Currencies in Melanesia.* Pittsburgh: University of Pittsburgh Press, 1999.

Allen, R. E., trans. *The Dialogues of Plato.* 4 vols. New Haven, CT: Yale University Press, 1984–97.

Alleton, Viviane. "Les expressions de la dette et du devoir en chinois." In Malamoud, *Lien de vie, nœud mortel,* 169–86.

Anderson, Patricia C., ed. *Prehistory of Agriculture: New Experimental and Ethnographic Approaches.* Los Angeles: UCLA Institute of Archaeology, 1999.

Arendt, Hannah. *Between Past and Future.* 1954. New York: Viking, 1968.

——.. *The Human Condition.* Chicago: University of Chicago Press, 1958.

Aristophanes. *The Clouds.* Oxford: Clarendon Press, 1968.

——. *Wealth.* In *The Birds and Other Plays.* Translated by David Barrett. London: Penguin, 1978.

Aristotle. *Eudemian Ethics.* In Barnes, *The Complete works of Aristotle,* 2:1922–81.

——. *Metaphysics.* In Barnes, *The Complete Works of Aristotle,* 2:1552–728.

——. *Nicomachean Ethics.* In Barnes, *The Complete Works of Aristotle,* 2:1729–867.

——. *Physics.* In Barnes, *The Complete Works of Aristotle,* 1:315–446.

——. *Politics.* In Barnes, *The Complete Works of Aristotle,* 2:1986–2129.

——. *Rhetoric.* In Barnes, *The Complete Works of Aristotle,* 2:2152–269.

——. *Sophistical Refutations.* In Barnes, *The Complete Works of Aristotle,* 1:278–314.

——. *Topics.* In Barnes, *The Complete Works of Aristotle,* 1:167–277.

Aubenque, Pierre. *La prudence chez Aristote.* Paris: Presses universitaires de France, 1963.

Austin, M. M., and Pierre Vidal-Naquet. *Economic and Social History of Ancient Greece.* Translated by M. M. Austin. London: B. T. Batsford, 1977.

Badiou, Alain. *Saint Paul: The Foundation of Universalism.* Stanford: Stanford University Press, 2003.

Baechler, Jean. *The Origins of Capitalism.* Translated by Barry Cooper. Oxford: Blackwell, 1975.

Baldner, Jean-Marie, and Lucien Gillard. *Simmel et les normes sociales.* Paris: L'Harmattan, 1996.

Balzac, Honoré de. *Nucingen and Co.: Bankers.* In *La comédie humaine.* Vol. 19, 223–331. Boston: Hardy Pratt, 1899.

———. *Père Goriot.* 1834. Translated by Burton Raffel. New York: Norton, 1998.

Barnes, Jonathan, ed. *The Complete Works of Aristotle: The Revised Oxford Translation.* 2 vols. Princeton, NJ: Princeton University Press, 1984.

Barnett, H. G. "The Nature of the Potlatch." *American Anthropologist* 40:3 (1938): 349–58.

Basileus the Great. "Homélie 2 sur le Psaume 14." In Hamman, *Riches et pauvres dans l'Église ancienne,* 93–102.

Bataille, Georges. *The Accursed Share: An Essay on General Economy.* 1949. Translated by Robert Hurley. New York: Zone Books, 1988–91.

———. *Theory of Religion.* 1974. New York: Zone Books, 1992.

Baudelaire, Charles. *My Heart Laid Bare.* In *Intimate Journals,* translated by Christopher Isherwood, 24–61. London: Methuen & Co., 1949 [original publication in French: 1887].

———. *The Parisian Prowler.* 1862. Athens: University of Georgia Press, 1989.

———. "The Respectable Drama and Novel." 1851. In *Baudelaire as a Literary Critic.* Translated and edited by Lois Boe Hyslop and Francis E. Hyslop Jr. University Park: Pennsylvania State University Press, 1964.

Baxandall, Michael. *Painting and Experience in Fifteenth-Century Italy: A Primer in the Social History of Pictorial Style.* Oxford: Oxford University Press, 1972.

Benveniste, Emile. *Indo-European Language and Society.* Translated by Elizabeth Palmer. London: Faber, 1973.

Biardeau, Madeleine. "Le sacrifice dans l'orthodoxie brahmanique." In Biardeau and Malamoud, *Le sacrifice dans l'Inde ancienne,* 14–57.

Biardeau, Madeleine, and Charles Malamoud. *Le sacrifice dans l'Inde ancienne.* Louvain: Peeters, 1996.

Bicchieri, M. C., ed. *Hunters and Gatherers Today: A Socioeconomic Study of Eleven Such Cultures in the Twentieth Century.* New-York: Holt, 1972.

Blank, D. L. "Socrates vs. Sophists on Payment for Teaching." *Classical Studies* 4, no. 1 (April 1985): 1–49.

Bloch, Marc. *Feudal Society.* Chicago: University of Chicago Press, 1961.

Bloch, Maurice. *Prey into Hunter.* Cambridge, UK: Cambridge University Press, 2004.

Boas, Franz. *Contributions to the Ethnology of the Kwakiutl.* 1895–1913. New York: AMS Press, 1969.

———. *Ethnology of the Kwakiutl.* In *Thirty-fifth Annual Report of the Bureau of American Ethnology to the Secretary of the Smithsonian Institution, 1913–1914.* Pt. 2. Washington: Government Printing Office, 1921.

———. *The Religion of the Kwakiutl Indians.* New York: Columbia University Press, 1930.

Boltanski, Luc. *L'amour et la justice comme compétences.* Paris: Métailié, 1990.

Bonte, Pierre. "Parenté." In *Dictionnaire de l'ethnologie et de l'anthropologie,* edited by Pierre Bonte and Michel Izard, 548–58. Paris: Presses universitaires de France, 1991.

Borneman, Ernest. *The Psychoanalysis of Money.* New York: Urizen Books, 1976.

Bornkamm, Gunther. *Paul, Paulus.* New York: Harper and Row, 1971.

Bottéro, Jean. *The Birth of God.* University Park: Pennsylvania State University Press, 2000.

———. *Religion in Ancient Mesopotamia.* Chicago: University of Chicago Press, 2001.

Bourdieu, Pierre. *Outline of a Theory of Practice.* Cambridge, UK: Cambridge University Press, 1977.

Bourdillon, M. F. C., and Meyer Fortes, eds. *Sacrifice.* London: Academic Press, 1980.

Bowers, Alfred W. *Mandan Social and Ceremonial Organization.* Chicago: University of Chicago Press, 1950.

Braudel, Fernand. *Civilization and Capitalism, 15th–18th Century.* Vol. 2, *The Wheels of Commerce.* Translated by Siân Reynolds. New York: Harper and Row, 1982.

———. *La dynamique du capitalisme.* Paris: Artaud, 1985.

Bresson, Alain. *La cité marchande.* Bordeaux: Ausonius, Scripta Antiqua, 2000.

Breton, Stanislas. *Saint Paul.* Presses universitaires de France, 1988.

Bureau, Jacques. "Une société sans vengeance: Le cas des Gamo d'Ethiopie." In Verdier, *La vengeance,* 1:213–24.

Caillé, Alain. *Anthropologie du don.* Louvain: Desclée de Brouwer, 2000.

———, ed. "Ce que donner veut dire: Don et intérêt." Special issue. *Revue du MAUSS,* no. 1 (1993).

———. "Don et symbolisme." *Revue du MAUSS,* no. 12 (1998): 122–47.

———. *Don, intérêt et désintéressement.* Paris: Découverte, 1992.

————. "Le don de paroles: Ce que dire veut donner." In Caillé, "Ce que donner veut dire," 194–217.

————. "Ni holisme ni individualisme méthodologique." *Revue du MAUSS*, no. 8 (1996): 9–58.

Canto, Monique. "Politique de la réfutation. Entre chien et loup: Le philosophe et le sophiste." In Cassin, *Positions de la sophistique*, 27–51.

Capizzi, A. "Les Sophistes à Athènes." In Cassin, *Positions de la sophistique*, 167–77.

Caquot, André. "La religion d'Israel." In Puech, Henri-Charles, *Histoire des religions*, 1:380–461. Paris: Gallimard, 1999.

Cartry, Michel. "Le suaire du chef." In *Sous le masque de l'animal*, edited by Michel Cartry, 131–213. Paris: Presses universitaires de France, 1987.

Casajus, Dominique. "L'énigme de la troisième personne." In *Différences, valeurs, hiérarchie: Textes offerts à Louis Dumont*, edited by J. C. Galey, 65–77. Paris: EHESS, 1982.

Cassin, Barbara, ed. *L'effet sophistique*. Paris: Gallimard, 1997.

————, ed. *Le plaisir de parler*. Paris: Minuit, 1986.

————, ed. *Positions de la sophistique: Colloque de Cerisy*. Paris: Vrin, 1986.

Cauvin, Jacques. *The Birth of the Gods and the Origins of Agriculture*. Cambridge, UK: Cambridge University Press, 2000.

Champeaux, Jacqueline. *La religion romaine*. Paris: Le Livre de Poche, 1998.

Chantraine, Pierre. *Dictionnaire étymologique de la langue grecque*. Paris: Klincksieck, 1970.

Chartier, Roger. *Culture écrite et société: L'ordre des livres, XIVe–XVIIe siècle*. Paris: Albin Michel, 1996.

Chatwin, Bruce. *The Songlines*. London: Jonathan Cape, 1987.

Cheal, David. *The Gift Economy*. New York: Routledge, 1988.

Cicero, Marcus Tullius. *De officiis*. Translated by Walter Miller. Cambridge, MA: Harvard University Press, 1961.

Clastres, Pierre. *Archeology of Violence*. Translated by Jeanine Herman. New York: Semiotext(e), 1994.

————. *Chronicle of the Guayaki Indians*. 1972. Cambridge, MA: MIT Press, 1998.

————. "L'économie primitive." In *Recherches d'anthropologie politique*, 127–45. Paris: Seuil, 1980.

Clavero, Bartolomé. *La grâce du don: Anthropologie catholique de l'économie moderne*. Translated by Jean-Frédéric Schaub. Paris: Albin Michel, 1996. Originally published as *Antidora: Antropología católica de la economía moderna*. Milano: Giuffrè Editore, 1991.

Cobbi, Jane. "L'obligation du cadeau au Japon." In Malamoud, *Lien de vie, nœud mortel,* 113–21.

Codere, Helen. *Fighting with Property: A Study of Kwakiutl Potlatching and Warfare, 1792–1930.* New York: J. J. Augustin, 1950.

Condominas, Georges. "De la monnaie multiple" [On Multiple Currency]. *Communication,* no. 50 (1989): 95–119.

———. *We Have Eaten the Forest: The Story of a Montagnard Village in the Central Highlands of Vietnam.* New York: Hill and Wang, 1977.

Cuq, Edouard. *Manuel des institutions juridiques des Romains.* Paris: Plon, 1917.

Dalton, George. *Traditional, Tribal, and Peasant Economies: An Introductory Survey of Economic Anthropology.* Reading, MA: Addison-Wesley, 1971.

Davis, Natalie Z. "Beyond the Market: Books as Gifts in Sixteenth-Century France." *Transactions of the Royal Historical Society,* 5th ser., 33 (1983): 69–98.

———. *The Gift in Sixteenth-Century France.* Madison: University of Wisconsin Press, 2000.

Davy, Georges. *La foi jurée: Étude sociologique du problème du contrat, la formation du lien contractuel.* Paris: Félix Alcan, 1922. Reprint, New York: Arno Press, 1975.

de Coppet, Daniel. "La monnaie: Présence des morts et mesure du temps," *L'homme* 10, no. 1 (1970): 17–39.

———. "Une monnaie pour une communauté mélanésienne comparée à la nôtre pour l'individu des sociétés européennes." In Aglietta and Orléan, *La monnaie souveraine,* 159–211.

Delatte, Armand. *Essai sur la politique pythagoricienne.* Paris: Champion, 1922.

Derrida, Jacques. *Given Time.* Chicago: University of Chicago Press, 1992.

Descola, Philippe. *The Spears of Twilight.* London: HarperCollins, 1996.

Descombes, Vincent. "Les essais sur le don." In *Les institutions du sens,* 237–308. Paris: Minuit, 1996.

Detienne, Marcel. "Culinary Practices and the Spirit of Sacrifice." In Detienne and Vernant, *The Cuisine of Sacrifice Among the Greeks,* 1–20.

———. *Dionysos Slain.* Baltimore: Johns Hopkins University Press, 1979.

———. *The Masters of Truth in Archaic Greece.* New York: Zone Books, 1996.

Detienne, Marcel, and Jean-Pierre Vernant. *The Cuisine of Sacrifice Among the Greeks.* Translated by Paula Wissing. Chicago: University of Chicago Press, 1989.

Diderot, Denis. *Lettre sur le commerce de la librairie.* 1763. In *Œuvres complètes,* edited by J. Assézat & M. Tourneux, 18:11–12. 20 vols. Paris: Garnier Frères, 1876.

———. "Réfutation suivie de l'ouvrage d'Helvétius intitulé *L'homme.*" In *Œuvres philosophiques,* 563–622. Paris: Garnier Frères, 1964.

Diogenes Laertius. *Lives of Eminent Philosophers.* 2 vols. Cambridge, MA: Harvard University Press, 1980.

Dixaut, Monique. "Isocrate contre des sophistes sans sophistique." In Cassin, *Le plaisir de parler,* 63–85.

Dodds, Eric Robertson. *The Greeks and the Irrational.* Berkeley: University of California Press, 1951.

Douglas, Mary. "No Free Gift." Foreword to *The Gift,* by Marcel Mauss, vii–xviii. New York: Routledge, 1990.

Dournes, Jacques [Dam Bo]. *Les populations montagnardes du Sud-Indochinois.* Saigon: France-Asie, 1950.

———. *Pötao: Une théorie du pouvoir chez les Indochinois Jörai.* Paris: Flammarion, 1977.

Duby, Georges. *The Three Orders: Feudal Society Imagined.* Translated by Arthur Goldhammer. Chicago: University of Chicago Press, 1982.

Dumont, Jean-Paul. *La philosophie antique.* Paris: Presses universitaires de France, 1995.

———. *Les écoles présocratiques.* Paris: Gallimard, 1994.

———. *Les Sophistes: Fragments et témoignages.* Paris: Presses universitaires de France, 1969.

———. *Under the Rainbow: Nature and Supernature among the Panare Indians.* Austin: University of Texas Press, 1976.

Dumont, Louis. *Essays on Individualism.* Chicago: University of Chicago Press, 1986.

———. *Homo hierarchicus.* Translated by Mark Sainsbury. Chicago: University of Chicago Press, 1980.

Duverger, Christian. *La fleur létale: Économie du sacrifice aztèque.* Paris: Seuil, 1979.

Edelman, B. *Le droit d'auteur.* Paris: Presses universitaires de France, 1993.

Eisenstein, Elizabeth E. *The Printing Revolution in Early Modern Europe.* Cambridge, UK: Cambridge University Press, 1983.

Ellen, Roy F., and Katsuyoshi Fukui. *Redefining Nature: Ecology, Culture, and Domestication.* Oxford: Berg, 1996.

Euripides. *The Phoenician Women.* Chicago: University of Chicago Press, 1958.

Evans-Pritchard, Edward E. *The Nuer.* Oxford: Oxford University Press, 1940.

———. *Nuer Religion.* Oxford: Clarendon, 1956.

Febvre, Lucien, and Henri-Jean Martin. *The Coming of the Book: The Impact of Printing, 1450–1800.* 1958. London: Verso, 1990.

Finley, Moses I. *The Ancient Economy.* Berkeley: University of California Press, 1973.

———. *The Ancient Greeks: An Introduction to Their Life and Thought.* New York: Viking, 1964.

———. "Aristotle and Economic Analysis." In *Studies in Ancient Society*, edited by Moses I. Finley, 26–52. London: Routledge & Kegan Paul, 1974.

———. *Early Greece.* New York: Norton, 1970.

———. *The World of Odysseus.* London: Chatto and Windus, 1956.

Flaubert, Gustave. *Flaubert-Sand: The Correspondence.* Translated by Francis Steegmuller and Barbara Bray. New York: Knopf, 1993.

Forbes, Clarence A. "Teachers' Payments in Ancient Greece." *University of Nebraska Studies* 2 (1942).

Fournier, Marcel. *Marcel Mauss: A Biography.* Princeton, NJ: Princeton University Press, 2006.

Franklin, Benjamin. "Advice to a Young Tradesman, Written by an Old One" [July 21, 1748]. In *Papers of Benjamin Franklin*, edited by L. Laboree, 3:306. New Haven, CT: Yale University Press, 1961.

Freud, Sigmund. "Character and Anal Erotism." 1908. In *The Standard Edition of the Complete Psychological Works of Sigmund Freud*, Vol. 9, edited by James Strachey. London: Hogarth, 1908.

———. "Further Recommendations in the Technique of Psychoanalysis." 1913. In *Therapy and Technique: Collected Papers*, edited by Philip Reiff, 135–56. New York: Macmillan, 1963.

———. "On Psychotherapy." 1904. In *Therapy and Technique: Collected Papers*, edited by Philip Reiff, 89–95. New York: Macmillan, 1963.

Frontisi-Ducroux, Françoise. *Dédale: Les mythes de l'artisan dans la Grèce ancienne.* Paris: Maspero, 1975.

Gauthier, René Antoine, and Jean Yves Jolif. *Ethique à Nicomaque: Introduction, traduction et commentaire.* Louvain: Publications universitaires de Louvain, 1970.

Gernet, Louis. *The Anthropology of Ancient Greece.* Baltimore: Johns Hopkins University Press, 1981.

———. "Le droit de la vente et la notion du contrat en Grèce." In *Droit et société dans la Grèce ancienne.* Paris: Sirey, 1955.

Gilder, George F. *Wealth and Poverty.* New York: Basic Books, 1981.

Glotz, Gustave. *La cité grecque.* Paris: La renaissance du livre, 1928.

Godbout, Jacques, with Alain Caillé. *The World of the Gift.* Montreal: McGill-Queen's University Press, 1998.

Godelier, Maurice. *The Enigma of the Gift.* Chicago: University of Chicago Press, 1999.

———. *The Making of Great Men.* Cambridge, UK: Cambridge University Press, 1986.

Goffman, Erving. *Interaction Ritual: Essays in Face-to-Face Behavior.* Garden City, NY: Anchor, 1967.

———. *The Presentation of Self in Everyday Life.* Garden City, NY: Doubleday, 1959.

Goldman, Irving. *The Mouth of Heaven: An Introduction to Kwakiutl Religious Thought.* New York: J. Wiley, 1975.

Goodall, Jane. *The Chimpanzees of Gombe: Patterns of Behavior.* Cambridge, MA: Harvard University Press, 1986.

Goody, Jack. *The Logic of Writing and the Organization of Society.* Cambridge, UK: Cambridge University Press, 1986.

Goux, Jean-Joseph. *The Coiners of Language.* Norman: University of Oklahoma Press, 1994.

———. "Don et altérité chez Sénèque." *Revue du MAUSS*, no. 8 (1996): 114–31.

———. *Frivolité de la valeur.* Paris: Blusson, 2000.

———. *Les iconoclastes.* Paris: Seuil, 1978.

———. *Symbolic Economies.* Ithaca, NY: Cornell University Press, 1990.

Gregor, Mary J., ed. *Practical Philosophy.* Cambridge, UK: Cambridge University Press, 1996.

Gregory, C. A. *Gifts and Commodities.* London: Academic Press, 1982.

Gregory of Nysse. "Sermon sur les usuriers." In Hamman, *Riches et pauvres dans l'Église ancienne,* 160–69.

Grenier, Jean-Yves, et al. *À propos de "Philosophie de l'argent" de Georg Simmel.* Paris: L'Harmattan, 1993.

Gurevich, Aron. "The Merchant." In *Medieval Callings*, edited by Jacques Le Goff, 242–83. Chicago: University of Chicago Press, 1990.

Guthrie, W. K. C. *The Sophists.* London: Cambridge University Press, 1971.

Hadot, Pierre. *Qu'est-ce que la philosophie antique?* Paris: Gallimard, 1995.

Hafez, Elsayed S. E. *The Behaviour of Domestic Animals.* Philadelphia: Lee and Fabriger, 1968.

Hamayon, Roberte. *La chasse à l'âme.* Nanterre: Société d'ethnologie, 1990.

———. "Pourquoi les 'jeux' plaisent aux esprits et déplaisent à Dieu." In Thinès and Heusch, *Rites et ritualisation,* 65–100.

Hamilton, Edith, and Huntington Cairns, eds. *The Collected Dialogues of Plato, Including the Letters.* Princeton, NJ: Princeton University Press, 1978.

Hamman, Adalbert-G., comp. and trans. *Riches et pauvres dans l'Église ancienne.* Paris: Desclée de Brouwer, 1982.

Hartog, F. "Ulysse et ses marins." In Mossé, *La Grèce ancienne,* 29–42.

Havelock, Eric A. *Origins of Western Literacy.* Toronto: Ontario Institute for Studies in Education, 1976.

Heidegger, Martin. "Anaximander's Saying." 1946. In *Off the Beaten Track*, edited and translated by Julian Young and Kenneth Haynes, 242–81. Cambridge, UK: Cambridge University Press, 2002.

Helmer, Daniel. *La domestication des animaux par les hommes préhistoriques.* Paris: Masson, 1992.

Hénaff, Marcel. *Claude Lévi-Strauss and the Making of Structural Anthropology.* Minneapolis: University of Minnesota Press, 1998.

———. "Dette de sang et exigence de justice." In *Comprendre pour agir: Violences, victimes et vengeances*, edited by Paul Dumouchel, 31–64. Paris: Presses de l'Université de Laval et Harmattan, 2000.

———. "L'éthique catholique et l'esprit du non-capitalisme." *Revue du MAUSS*, no. 15 (2000): 35–66.

Herrenschmidt, Olivier. *Les meilleurs dieux sont hindous.* Lausanne: L'âge d'homme, 1989.

Hesiod. *The Works and Days.* Translated by Richmond Lattimore. Ann Arbor: University of Michigan Press, 1959.

Heusch, Luc de. *Sacrifice in Africa: A Structuralist Approach.* Bloomington: Indiana University Press, 1985.

Hindle, R. A. and J. Rawson. "Rituals: Signals and Meanings." In Thinès and Heusch, *Rites et ritualisation.*

Hirschman, Albert O. *The Passions and the Interests: Political Arguments for Capitalism Before Its Triumph.* 1977. Princeton, NJ: Princeton University Press, 1997.

Honneth, Axel. *The Struggle for Recognition: The Moral Grammar of Social Conflicts.* Cambridge, MA: Polity Press, 1995.

Hubert, Henri, and Marcel Mauss. "Introduction à l'analyse de quelques phénomènes religieux." 1906. In Mauss, *Oeuvres*, 1:3–88. Paris: Minuit, 1968.

Hubert, Henri, and Marcel Mauss. *Sacrifice: Its Nature and Function.* 1899. Chicago: University of Chicago Press, 1964.

Huizinga, Johan. *Homo ludens: A Study of the Play Element in Culture.* London: Temple Smith, 1970.

Ingold, T. *Hunters, Pastoralists and Rangers.* Cambridge, UK: Cambridge University Press, 1980.

Isocrates. "Against the Sophists." In *Isocrates I*, translated by David C. Mirhady and Yun Lee Too, 61–66. Austin: University of Texas Press, 2000.

Iteanu, André. *La ronde des échanges: De la circulation aux valeurs chez les Orokaiva.* Cambridge, UK: Cambridge University Press, 1983.

Izard, Michel. "Engrammes du pouvoir: Autochtonie et ancestralité." In *Le temps de la réflexion*, 4:299–323. Paris: Gallimard, 1983.

Jaeger, Werner. *Paideia: The Ideals of Greek Culture*, 1:291. 3 vols.. New York: Oxford University Press, 1962.

Kant, Immanuel. *The Metaphysics of Morals*. 1797. In Gregor, *Practical Philosophy*, 353–603.

———. "On the Wrongfulness of Unauthorized Publication of Books." 1785. In Gregor, *Practical Philosophy*, 23–35.

———. "What Is a Book?" In Gregor, *Practical Philosophy*, 437–39.

———. *What Is Enlightenment?* In *Foundations of the Metaphysics of Morals*. Chicago: University of Chicago Press, 1949.

———. "What Is Money?" In Gregor, *Practical Philosophy*, 434–36.

Kantorowicz, Ernst. *The King's Two Bodies*. Princeton, NJ: Princeton University Press, 1957.

Karsenti, Bruno. *L'homme total: Sociologie, anthropologie et philosophie chez Marcel Mauss*. Paris: Presses universitaires de France, 1997.

———. *Mauss: Le fait social total*. Paris: Presses universitaires de France, 1994.

Kerferd, George B. *The Sophistic Movement*. Cambridge, UK: Cambridge University Press, 1981.

———, ed. *The Sophists and Their Legacy*. Wiesbaden: Steiner, 1981.

Kolakowski, Leszek. *God Owes Us Nothing: A Brief Remark on Pascal's Religion and on the Spirit of Jansenism*. Chicago: University of Chicago Press, 1995.

Kummer, Hans. "Le comportement social des singes." In *La recherche en éthologie*, 249–62. Paris: Seuil, 1979.

———. *Social Organization of Hamadryas Baboons*. Chicago: University of Chicago Press, 1968.

Leach, Edmund. "The Nature of War." In *The Essential Edmund Leach*. Vol. 1, *Anthropology and Society*, edited by Stephen Hugh-Jones and James Laidlaw, 343–57. New Haven, CT: Yale University Press, 2000.

———. *Political Systems of Highland Burma*. Boston: Beacon Press, 1964.

Leakey, Richard E. *Origins: What New Discoveries Reveal About the Emergence of Our Species and Its Possible Future*. New York: Dutton, 1982.

———. *The Origins of Humankind*. New York, Basic Books, 1994.

Lee, Richard B. *The !Kung San*. Cambridge, UK: Cambridge University Press, 1979.

Lee, Richard B., and Irven DeVore, eds. *Man the Hunter*. Chicago: Aldine, 1968.

Leenhardt, Pierre. "La valeur du sacrifice dans le judaïsme d'autrefois et d'aujourd'hui." In *Le sacrifice dans les religions*, edited by Marcel Neusch, 61–84. Paris: Beauchesne, 1994.

Lefort, Claude. *Les formes de l'histoire*. Paris: Gallimard, 1978.

Le Goff, Jacques. *Intellectuals in the Middle Ages*. 1962. Oxford: Blackwell, 1993.

———. *Marchands et banquiers du Moyen Age*. Paris: Presses universitaires de France, 1956.

———. *Medieval Civilization*. Translated by Julia Barrow. 1964. Oxford: Blackwell, 1988.

———. *Time, Work, and Culture in the Middle Ages*. Translated by Arthur Goldhammer. Chicago: University of Chicago Press, 1980.

———. *Your Money or Your Life: Economy and Religion in the Middle Ages*. New York: Zone Books, 1988.

Lemaire, André. *Le monde de la Bible*. Paris: Gallimard, 1998.

Lemonnier, Pierre. *Guerres et festins*. Paris: Maison des sciences de l'homme, 1990.

Leroi-Gourhan, André. *La religion de la préhistoire*. Paris: Presses universitaires de France, 1966.

Levi, Primo. *Survival in Auschwitz*. Translated by Stuart Woolf. 1956. New York: Simon & Schuster, 1985.

Lévi, Sylvain. *La doctrine du sacrifice dans les Brâhmanas*. 1898. Paris: Presses universitaires de France, 1966.

Levinas, Emmanuel. *Totality and Infinity: An Essay on Exteriority*. Translated by Alphonso Lingis. Pittsburgh: Duquesne University Press, 1969.

Lévi-Strauss, Claude. *The Elementary Structures of Kinship*. Boston: Beacon, 1969.

———. *Introduction to a Science of Mythology*. New York: Harper, 1969–81.

———. *Introduction to the Work of Marcel Mauss*. 1950. London: Routledge and Kegan Paul, 1987.

———. "On Marriage Between Close Kin." In *The View from Afar*, chap. 6. New York: Basic Books, 1985.

———. *The Savage Mind*. Chicago: University of Chicago Press, 1966.

Lizot, Jacques. *Tales of the Yanomami*. 1976. Cambridge, UK: Cambridge University Press, 1991.

Lloyd, Geoffrey E. R. *Early Greek Science: Thales to Aristotle*. New York: Norton, 1970.

———. *Magic, Reason, and Experience: Studies in the Origin and Development of Greek Science*. Cambridge, UK: Cambridge University Press, 1979.

Lorenz, Konrad. *On Aggression*. New York: Harcourt, Brace, and World, 1966.

Malamoud, Charles. *Cooking the World: Ritual and Thought in Ancient India*. Translated by David White. Delhi: Oxford University Press, 1996.

———, ed. *Lien de vie, nœud mortel*. Paris: EHESS, 1988.

———. "Terminer le sacrifice: Remarques sur les honoraires rituels dans le brahmanisme." In Biardeau and Malamoud, *Le sacrifice dans l'Inde ancienne*, 155–204.

Malinowski, Bronislaw. *Argonauts of the Western Pacific*. New York: Dutton, 1922.

Mallarmé, Stéphane. *Divagations*. Translated by Barbara Johnson. Cambridge, MA: Harvard University Press, 2007.

Marion, Jean-Luc. *Being Given: Toward a Phenomenology of Givenness*. Stanford: Stanford University Press, 2002.

Marrou, Henri-Irénée. *A History of Education in Antiquity*. 1947. New York: New American Library, 1956.

Marx, Karl. *Early Writings*. Edited by T. B. Bottomore. London: C. A. Watts, 1962.

———. *Kapital*. London: George Allen and Unwin, 1943.

Mauss, Marcel. *The Gift: Forms and Functions of Exchange in Archaic Societies*. 1924. Translated by W. D. Halls. London: Routledge, 1990.

———. *Manual of Ethnography*. New York: Durkheim Press/Berghahn Books, 2007.

———. "A Note of Principle Concerning the Use of the Notion of Money." In *The Gift*, 100–102.

———. "L'obligation de rendre les présents." 1923. In *Oeuvres*, 3:44–45.

———. *Oeuvres*. 3 vols. Paris: Minuit, 1968–69.

———. "Origines de la notion de monnaie." 1914. In *Oeuvres*, 2:106–12.

Mauzée, Marie. "Boas, les Kwakiutl et le potlatch: Éléments pour une réévaluation." *L'homme* 26, no. 4 (1986).

McCullers, Carson. *The Ballad of the Sad Café*. In *Collected Short Stories, and the Novel: "The Ballad of the Sad Café."* Cambridge, MA: Riverside Press, 1955.

McGrew, William C. *Chimpanzee Material Culture: Implications for Human Evolution*. Cambridge, UK: Cambridge University Press, 1992.

McGrew, William C., Linda F. Marchant, and Toshisada Nishida, eds. *Great Ape Societies*. Cambridge, UK: Cambridge University Press, 1990.

Meier, Christian. *Politik und Anmut*. Berlin: Siedler, 1985; French trans. *La politique et la grâce: Anthropologie politique de la beauté grecque*. Translated by Paul Veyne. Paris: Seuil, 1987.

Milner, Jean-Claude. *Le salaire de l'idéal: La théorie des classes et de la culture au XXe siècle*. Paris: Seuil, 1997.

Montesquieu, Charles de. *The Spirit of the Laws*. 1748. Cambridge, UK: Cambridge University Press, 1989.

Mossé, Claude, ed. *La Grèce ancienne*. Paris: Seuil, 1986.

Moussy, Claude. *Gratia et sa famille*. Paris: Presses universitaires de France, 1966.

Müller, Reimar. "Sophistique et démocratie." In Cassin, *Positions de la sophistique*, 179–93.

Musil, Robert. *The Man Without Qualities*. 1930. New York: Knopf, 1995.

Nelson, Benjamin N. *The Idea of Usury: From Tribal Brotherhood to Universal Otherhood.* Princeton, NJ: Princeton University Press, 1949.

Nietzsche, Friedrich. *On the Genealogy of Morals.* Translated by Douglas Smith. Oxford: Oxford University Press, 1996.

Noonan, John T., Jr. *The Scholastic Analysis of Usury.* Cambridge, MA: Harvard University Press, 1957.

Ortigues, Edmond. *Le discours et le symbole.* Paris: Aubier, 1962.

Parry, Jonathan, and Maurice Bloch, eds. *Money and the Morality of Exchange.* Cambridge, UK: Cambridge University Press, 1989.

Péguy, Charles. *Notre jeunesse.* In *Oeuvres en prose, 1898–1908.* Paris: Gallimard, Pléiade, 1959.

Pépin, J. "Le symbolisme de la mer chez Platon et dans le néoplatonisme." Congrès de l'Association Guillaume Budé. Tours et Poitiers, 1953.

Perroux, François. *Économie et société: Contrainte, échange, don.* Paris: Presses universitaires de France, 1963.

Picard, Olivier. "Les origines du monnayage en Grèce." In Mossé, *La Grèce ancienne,* 157–71.

Pigeot, Jacqueline. "Note sur le vocabulaire du 'devoir' et de la 'dette' et sur l'expression de l'obligation en japonais." In Malamoud, *Lien de vie, nœud mortel,* 163–67.

Pindar. *The Complete Odes.* Translated by Anthony Verity. Oxford: Oxford University Press, 2007.

Plato. *Apology.* In Allen, *The Dialogues of Plato,* 1:79-104.

Plato. *Apology.* Translated by Hugh Tredennick. In Hamilton and Cairns, *The Collected Dialogues of Plato,* 3–26.

———. *Cratylus.* Translated by Benjamin Jowett. In Hamilton and Cairns, *The Collected Dialogues of Plato,* 421–74.

———. *Crito.* In Allen, *The Dialogues of Plato,* 1:117–29.

———. *Crito.* Translated by Hugh Tredennick. In Hamilton and Cairns, *The Collected Dialogues of Plato,* 27–39.

———. *Hippias Major.* Translated by Robin Waterfield. In *Plato: Early Socratic Dialogues,* edited by Trevor J. Saunders, 217–65. London: Penguin, 1987.

———. *Hippias Minor.* In *Ion; Hippias Minor; Laches; Protagoras,* 31–45. Translated by R. E. Allen. New Haven, CT: Yale University Press, 1996.

———. *Laws.* Translated by Benjamin Jowett. Amherst: Prometheus Books, 2000.

———. *Meno.* Translated by W. K. C. Guthrie. In Hamilton and Cairns, *The Collected Dialogues of Plato,* 353–84.

———. *Phaedo.* Translated by Hugh Tredennick. In Hamilton and Cairns, *The Collected Dialogues of Plato,* 40–98.

———. *Protagoras.* In *Ion; Hippias Minor; Laches; Protagoras,* translated by R. E. Allen, 3:169–223. New Haven, CT: Yale University Press, 1996.

———. *Symposium.* In Allen, *The Dialogues of Plato,* Vol. 2.

———. *Theaetetus; Sophist.* Cambridge, MA: Harvard University Press, 1977.

———. *Timaeus.* Translated by Benjamin Jowett. In Hamilton and Cairns, *The Collected Dialogues of Plato,* 1151–211.

Polanyi, Karl. *The Great Transformation.* 1944. Boston: Beacon, 1957.

Polanyi, Karl, Conrad Arensberg, and Harry Pearson, eds. *Trade and Market in the Early Empires: Economies in History and Theory.* Glencoe, IL: Free Press, 1957.

Premack, David. "Why Animals Have neither Culture nor History." In *Companion Encyclopedia of Anthropology,* edited by Tim Ingold, 350–65. London: Routledge, 1994.

Pringsheim, Fritz. *The Greek Law of Sale.* Weimar: Bohlaus, 1950.

Rabelais, François. *The Third Book of the Heroic Deeds and Sayings of the Good Pantagruel.* In *The Complete Works of François Rabelais.* Translated by Donald M. Frame. Berkeley: University of California Press, 1991.

Renou, Louis. *The Civilization of Ancient India.* Calcutta: Susil Gupta, 1954.

———. *Etudes védiques et paninénnes.* Paris: Boccard, 1960.

Richman, Michelle. *Reading Georges Bataille: Beyond the Gift.* Baltimore: Johns Hopkins University Press, 1982.

Ricoeur, Paul. *The Course of Recognition.* Cambridge, MA: Harvard University Press, 2005.

———. *The Just.* Chicago: University of Chicago Press, 2000.

———. *Memory, History, Forgetting.* Chicago: University of Chicago Press, 2004.

Robertson, Hector Menteith. *Aspects of the Rise of Economic Individualism.* Cambridge, UK: Cambridge University Press, 1933.

Rogerson, J. W. "Sacrifice in the Old Testament: Problems of Method and Approach." In Bourdillon and Fortes, *Sacrifice,* 45–59.

Romeyer-Dherbey, Gilbert. *Aristote: Les choses mêmes.* Lausanne: L'âge d'homme, 1985.

———. *Les choses mêmes: La pensée du réel chez Aristote.* Lausanne: L'âge d'homme, 1983.

———. *Les Sophistes.* Paris: Presses universitaires de France, 1985.

Romilly, Jacqueline de. *The Great Sophists in Periclean Athens.* Oxford: Clarendon, 1982.

Rospabé, François. *La dette de vie: Aux origines de la monnaie.* Paris: Découverte, 1995.

Rougé, Jean. "Les galériens d'Athènes: Marine et démocratie." In Mossé, *La Grèce ancienne*, 145-56.

Rousseau, Jean-Jacques. *Confessions*. Translated by Angela Scholar. Oxford: Oxford University Press, 2000.

Rubel, Paula, and Abraham Rosman. *Your Own Pigs You May Not Eat: A Comparative Study of New Guinea Societies*. Chicago: University of Chicago Press, 1978.

Rudhardt, Jean, and Olivier Reverdin, eds. *Le sacrifice dans l'antiquité*. Vandoeuves-Genève: Fondation Hardt, 1981.

Russon, Anne E., Kim A. Bard, and Susan Taylor Parker, eds. *Reaching into Thought: The Minds of the Great Apes*. Cambridge, UK: Cambridge University Press, 1996.

Sahlins, Marshall. *Stone Age Economics*. Chicago: Aldine Atherton, 1972.

Sauer, C. O. *The Domestication of Animals and Foodstuffs*. Cambridge, MA: MIT Press, 1952.

Scheid-Tissinier, Evelyne. *Les usages du don chez Homère*. Nancy: Presses universitaires de Nancy, 1994.

Schnapp, Alain. *Le chasseur et la cité*. Paris: Albin Michel, 1997.

Seligman, Paul. *The Apeiron of Anaximander: A Study in the Origin and Function of Metaphysical Ideas*. London: Athlone Press, 1962.

Seneca. *Ad Lucilium epistolae morales*. 3:CXV.318-31. Translated by Richard M. Gunmere. Cambridge, MA: Harvard University Press, 1957.

———. *De beneficiis* [*On Benefits*]. Vol. 3 of *Moral Essays*. Translated by John Basore. Cambridge, MA: Harvard University Press, 1980.

———. *On the Happy Life* [*De vita beata*]. In *Seneca: Dialogues and Essays*, translated by John Davie, 85–111. Oxford: Oxford University Press, 2007.

Serres, Michel. "Anaximander." In *Origins of Geometry*. Manchester: Clinamen, 2001.

———. *Genesis*. Translated by Geneviève James and James Nielson. Ann Arbor: University of Michigan Press, 1995.

———. *The Parasite*. Translated by Lawrence Schehr. Baltimore: Johns Hopkins University Press, 1986.

Servet, Michel. "Démonétisation et remonétarisation en Afrique occidentale et équatoriale." In Aglietta and Orléan, *La monnaie souveraine*, 289–324.

———. *Nomismata: État et origines de la monnaie*. Lyon: Presses universitaires de Lyon, 1984.

Service, Elman R. *The Hunters*. Englewood Cliffs, NJ: Prentice-Hall, 1966.

Shakespeare, William. *Timon of Athens*. Cambridge, MA: Harvard University Press, 1965.

Simmel, Georg. *The Philosophy of Money*. London: Routledge, 1990. Originally published as *Philosophie des Geldes* (Leipzig: Duncker and Humblot, 1900).

Smith, Adam. *An Inquiry into the Nature and Causes of the Wealth of Nations.* 1776. Oxford: Clarendon, 1976.

Smith, Pierre. "Aspects of the Organization of Rites." In *Between Belief and Transgression: Structuralist Essays in Religion, History, and Myth,* edited by Michel Izard and Pierre Smith, 103–28. Chicago: University of Chicago Press, 1982.

Sombart, Werner. *The Quintessence of Capitalism: A Study of the History and Psychology of the Modern Business Man.* Translated and edited by M. Epstein. New York: Fertig, 1967. Originally published as *Der Bourgeois: Zur Geistesgeschichte des modernen Wirtschaftmenschen* (München: Duncker und Humblot, 1913).

Sophocles. *Antigone.* In *The Three Theban Plays.* Translated by Robert Fagles, 55–128. New York: Penguin, 1984.

Sperber, Dan. *Rethinking Symbolism.* Cambridge, UK: Cambridge University Press, 1975.

Sprague, Rosamond K., ed. *The Older Sophists.* Columbia: University of South Carolina Press, 1972.

Stanford, Craig. "The Ape's Gift: Meat-Eating, Meat-Sharing, and Human Evolution." In Waal, *Tree of Origin,* 95–117.

Starobinski, Jean. *Largesse.* Chicago: University of Chicago Press, 1997.

Stevenson, Matilda C. *The Zuñi Indians.* In *Twenty-third Annual Report of the Bureau of American Ethnology.* Washington: Government Printing Office, 1905.

Strathern, Andrew. *The Rope of Moka: Big-Men and Ceremonial Exchange in Mount Hagen, New Guinea.* Cambridge, UK: Cambridge University Press, 1971.

Strathern, Marilyn. *The Gender of the Gift: Problems with Women and Problems with Society in Melanesia.* Berkeley: University of California Press, 1988.

Strayer, Joseph. *On the Medieval Origins of the Modern State.* Princeton, NJ: Princeton University Press, 1976.

Tarot, Camille. *De Durkheim à Mauss: L'invention du symbolique.* Paris: Découverte, 1998.

———. "Repères pour une histoire de la naissance de la grâce." *Revue du MAUSS,* no. 1 (1993): 90–114.

Tawney, R. H. *Religion and the Rise of Capitalism.* New York: Harcourt, Brace, 1926.

Testart, Alain. *Des dons et des dieux: Anthropologie religieuse et sociologie comparative.* Paris: Armand Colin, 1993.

———. *Les chasseurs-cueilleurs, ou l'origine des inégalités.* Paris: Maison des sciences de l'homme, 1982.

Thinès, Georges, and Luc de Heusch. *Rites et ritualisation.* Paris: Vrin, 1995.

Thomas, Yan. "Se venger au forum." In Verdier, *La vengeance,* 3:65–100.

Thurnwald, Richard. *Bánaro Society: Social Organization and Kinship of a Tribe in the Interior of New Guinea.* New York: Kraus Reprint Corp., 1964 [1916].

Tresmontant, Claude. *Saint Paul et le mystère du Christ.* Paris: Seuil, 1956.

Tricaud, François. *L'accusation: Recherche sur les figures de l'agression éthique.* 1977. Genève: Dalloz, 2001.

Troeltsch, Ernst. "Calvinism and Lutheranism." 1909. In *Gesammelte Schriften*, 4:254–61. Reprint, Aalen, Germany: Scientia, 1966.

———. *Protestantism and Progress: A Historical Study of the Relation of Protestantism to the Modern World.* 1912. Boston: Beacon, 1958.

Ucko, P. J., and G. W. Dimbleby, eds. *The Domestication and Exploitation of Plants and Animals.* Chicago: Aldine-Atherton, 1969.

Untersteiner, Mario. *The Sophists.* Oxford: Blackwell, 1954.

Verdier, Raymond, ed. *La vengeance.* 4 vols. Paris: Cujas, 1980–86.

Vernant, Jean-Pierre. "At Man's Table: Hesiod's Foundation Myth of Sacrifice." In Detienne and Vernant, *The Cuisine of Sacrifice Among the Greeks*, 21–86.

———. "The Lame Tyrant: From Oedipus to Periander." In Vernant and Vidal-Naquet, *Myth and Tragedy in Ancient Greece*, 207–36.

———. *Myth and Thought Among the Greeks.* London: Routledge and Kegan Paul, 1983.

Vernant, Jean-Pierre, and Pierre Vidal-Naquet. *Myth and Tragedy in Ancient Greece.* Translated by Janet Lloyd. New York: Zone Books, 1988.

Veyne, Paul. *Bread and Circuses: Historical Sociology and Political Pluralism.* London: A. Lane, 1990.

Vidal, Denis. "Les gestes du don: A propos des trois Grâces." *Revue du MAUSS*, no. 1 (1993): 61–77.

Vidal-Naquet, Pierre. *The Black Hunter: Forms of Thought and Forms of Society in the Greek World.* Baltimore: Johns Hopkins University Press, 1986.

Vilar, Pierre. *A History of Gold and Money, 1450–1920.* London: Humanities Press, 1976.

Vlastos, Gregory. *Socrates, Ironist and Moral Philosopher.* Cambridge, UK: Cambridge University Press, 1991.

Waal, Frans B. M. de. *Chimpanzee Politics: Power and Sex Among Apes.* Baltimore: Johns Hopkins University Press, 1998.

———. *Peacemaking Among Primates.* Cambridge, MA: Harvard University Press, 1989.

———, ed. *Tree of Origin: What Primate Behavior Can Tell Us About Human Evolution.* Cambridge, MA: Harvard University Press, 2001.

Walzer, Michael. *Spheres of Justice: A Defense of Pluralism and Equality.* New York: Basic Books, 1983.

Weber, Max. *Ancient Judaism.* Glencoe, IL: Free Press, 1952.

———. *Economy and Society: An Outline of Interpretive Sociology.* Edited by Guenther Roth and Claus Wittich. 2 vols. Berkeley: University of California Press, 1978.

———. "A Final Rebuttal to Rachfahl's Critique of the 'Spirit of Capitalism.'" 1910. In *The Protestant Ethic and the "Spirit" of Capitalism and Other Writings*, edited and translated by Peter Baehr and Gordon C. Wells, 282–339. London: Penguin, 2002.

———. *General Economic History.* 1927. New Brunswick, NJ: Transaction Books, 1981.

———. *The Protestant Ethic and the Spirit of Capitalism.* 1905. Translated by Talcott Parsons. New York: Charles Scribner's Sons, 1958.

———. "Religious Rejections of the World and Their Directions." In *Essays in Sociology*, 323–59. New York: Oxford University Press, 1958.

———. *Sociology of Religion.* Boston: Beacon, 1963.

Weiner, Annette. *Inalienable Possessions: The Paradox of Keeping-While-Giving.* Berkeley: University of California Press, 1992.

Will, Edouard. "De l'aspect éthique de l'origine grecque de la monnaie." *Revue historique* 212 (1954): 209–31.

———. "Réflexions et hypothèses sur l'origine du monnayage." *Revue de numismatique* 17 (1955): 5–23.

Wolff, Francis. "Le chasseur chassé." In *Études sur "Le Sophiste" de Platon*, edited by Pierre Aubenque, 17–52. Naples: Bibliopolis, 1991.

Xenophon. *Memorabilia.* Translated by Amy Bonnette. Ithaca, NY: Cornell University Press, 1994.

———. *Œconomicus.* Translated by Sarah B. Pomeroy. Oxford: Clarendon Press, 1994.

———. *On Hunting [Kynēgetikos].* Warminster, UK: Aris and Phillips, 1999.

Zhiri, Oumelbanine. *L'extase et ses paradoxes: Essai sur la structure narrative du Tiers Livre.* Paris: Champion, 1999.

Zohary, D., and M. Hopf. *Domestication of Plants in the Old World.* Oxford: Oxford University Press, 1988.

Index of Names

Subject Index

Cultural Memory | *in the Present*

Samira Haj, *Reconfiguring Islamic Tradition: Reform, Rationality, and Modernity*

Diane Perpich, *The Ethics of Emmanuel Levinas*

Marcel Detienne, *Comparing the Incomparable*

François Delaporte, *Anatomy of the Passions*

René Girard, *Mimesis and Theory: Essays on Literature and Criticism, 1959-2005*

Richard Baxstrom, *Houses in Motion: The Experience of Place and the Problem of Belief in Urban Malaysia*

Jennifer L. Culbert, *Dead Certainty: The Death Penalty and the Problem of Judgment*

Samantha Frost, *Lessons from a Materialist Thinker: Hobbesian Reflections on Ethics and Politics*

Regina Mara Schwartz, *Sacramental Poetics at the Dawn of Secularism: When God Left the World*

Gil Anidjar, *Semites: Race, Religion, Literature*

Ranjana Khanna, *Algeria Cuts: Women and Representation, 1830 to the Present*

Esther Peeren, *Intersubjectivities and Popular Culture: Bakhtin and Beyond*

Eyal Peretz, *Becoming Visionary: Brian De Palma's Cinematic Education of the Senses*

Diana Sorensen, *A Turbulent Decade Remembered: Scenes from the Latin American Sixties*

Hubert Damisch, *A Childhood Memory by Piero della Francesca*

José van Dijck, *Mediated Memories in the Digital Age*

Dana Hollander, *Exemplarity and Chosenness: Rosenzweig and Derrida on the Nation of Philosophy*

Asja Szafraniec, *Beckett, Derrida, and the Event of Literature*

Sara Guyer, *Romanticism After Auschwitz*

Alison Ross, *The Aesthetic Paths of Philosophy: Presentation in Kant, Heidegger, Lacoue-Labarthe, and Nancy*

Gerhard Richter, *Thought-Images: Frankfurt School Writers' Reflections from Damaged Life*

Bella Brodzki, *Can These Bones Live? Translation, Survival, and Cultural Memory*

Rodolphe Gasché, *The Honor of Thinking: Critique, Theory, Philosophy*

Brigitte Peucker, *The Material Image: Art and the Real in Film*

Natalie Melas, *All the Difference in the World: Postcoloniality and the Ends of Comparison*

Jonathan Culler, *The Literary in Theory*

Michael G. Levine, *The Belated Witness: Literature, Testimony, and the Question of Holocaust Survival*

Jennifer A. Jordan, *Structures of Memory: Understanding German Change in Berlin and Beyond*

Christoph Menke, *Reflections of Equality*

Marlène Zarader, *The Unthought Debt: Heidegger and the Hebraic Heritage*

Jan Assmann, *Religion and Cultural Memory: Ten Studies*

David Scott and Charles Hirschkind, *Powers of the Secular Modern: Talal Asad and His Interlocutors*

Gyanendra Pandey, *Routine Violence: Nations, Fragments, Histories*

James Siegel, *Naming the Witch*

J. M. Bernstein, *Against Voluptuous Bodies: Late Modernism and the Meaning of Painting*

Theodore W. Jennings, Jr., *Reading Derrida / Thinking Paul: On Justice*

Richard Rorty and Eduardo Mendieta, *Take Care of Freedom and Truth Will Take Care of Itself: Interviews with Richard Rorty*

Jacques Derrida, *Paper Machine*

Renaud Barbaras, *Desire and Distance: Introduction to a Phenomenology of Perception*

Jill Bennett, *Empathic Vision: Affect, Trauma, and Contemporary Art*

Ban Wang, *Illuminations from the Past: Trauma, Memory, and History in Modern China*

James Phillips, *Heidegger's Volk: Between National Socialism and Poetry*

Frank Ankersmit, *Sublime Historical Experience*

István Rév, *Retroactive Justice: Prehistory of Post-Communism*

Paola Marrati, *Genesis and Trace: Derrida Reading Husserl and Heidegger*

Krzysztof Ziarek, *The Force of Art*

Marie-José Mondzain, *Image, Icon, Economy: The Byzantine Origins of the Contemporary Imaginary*

Cecilia Sjöholm, *The Antigone Complex: Ethics and the Invention of Feminine Desire*

Jacques Derrida and Elisabeth Roudinesco, *For What Tomorrow . . . : A Dialogue*

Elisabeth Weber, *Questioning Judaism: Interviews by Elisabeth Weber*

Jacques Derrida and Catherine Malabou, *Counterpath: Traveling with Jacques Derrida*

Martin Seel, *Aesthetics of Appearing*

Nanette Salomon, *Shifting Priorities: Gender and Genre in Seventeenth-Century Dutch Painting*

Jacob Taubes, *The Political Theology of Paul*

Jean-Luc Marion, *The Crossing of the Visible*

Eric Michaud, *The Cult of Art in Nazi Germany*

Anne Freadman, *The Machinery of Talk: Charles Peirce and the Sign Hypothesis*

Stanley Cavell, *Emerson's Transcendental Etudes*

Stuart McLean, *The Event and Its Terrors: Ireland, Famine, Modernity*

Beate Rössler, ed., *Privacies: Philosophical Evaluations*

Bernard Faure, *Double Exposure: Cutting Across Buddhist and Western Discourses*

Alessia Ricciardi, *The Ends of Mourning: Psychoanalysis, Literature, Film*

Alain Badiou, *Saint Paul: The Foundation of Universalism*

Gil Anidjar, *The Jew, the Arab: A History of the Enemy*

Jonathan Culler and Kevin Lamb, eds., *Just Being Difficult? Academic Writing in the Public Arena*

Jean-Luc Nancy, *A Finite Thinking*, edited by Simon Sparks

Theodor W. Adorno, *Can One Live after Auschwitz? A Philosophical Reader*, edited by Rolf Tiedemann

Patricia Pisters, *The Matrix of Visual Culture: Working with Deleuze in Film Theory*

Andreas Huyssen, *Present Pasts: Urban Palimpsests and the Politics of Memory*

Talal Asad, *Formations of the Secular: Christianity, Islam, Modernity*

Dorothea von Mücke, *The Rise of the Fantastic Tale*

Marc Redfield, *The Politics of Aesthetics: Nationalism, Gender, Romanticism*

Emmanuel Levinas, *On Escape*

Dan Zahavi, *Husserl's Phenomenology*

Rodolphe Gasché, *The Idea of Form: Rethinking Kant's Aesthetics*

Michael Naas, *Taking on the Tradition: Jacques Derrida and the Legacies of Deconstruction*

Herlinde Pauer-Studer, ed., *Constructions of Practical Reason: Interviews on Moral and Political Philosophy*

Jean-Luc Marion, *Being Given That: Toward a Phenomenology of Givenness*

Theodor W. Adorno and Max Horkheimer, *Dialectic of Enlightenment*

Ian Balfour, *The Rhetoric of Romantic Prophecy*

Martin Stokhof, *World and Life as One: Ethics and Ontology in Wittgenstein's Early Thought*

Gianni Vattimo, *Nietzsche: An Introduction*

Jacques Derrida, *Negotiations: Interventions and Interviews, 1971-1998*, ed. Elizabeth Rottenberg

Brett Levinson, *The Ends of Literature: The Latin American "Boom" in the Neoliberal Marketplace*

Timothy J. Reiss, *Against Autonomy: Cultural Instruments, Mutualities, and the Fictive Imagination*

Hent de Vries and Samuel Weber, eds., *Religion and Media*

Niklas Luhmann, *Theories of Distinction: Re-Describing the Descriptions of Modernity*, ed. and introd. William Rasch

Johannes Fabian, *Anthropology with an Attitude: Critical Essays*

Michel Henry, *I Am the Truth: Toward a Philosophy of Christianity*

Gil Anidjar, *"Our Place in Al-Andalus": Kabbalah, Philosophy, Literature in Arab-Jewish Letters*

Hélène Cixous and Jacques Derrida, *Veils*

F. R. Ankersmit, *Historical Representation*

F. R. Ankersmit, *Political Representation*

Elissa Marder, *Dead Time: Temporal Disorders in the Wake of Modernity (Baudelaire and Flaubert)*

Reinhart Koselleck, *The Practice of Conceptual History: Timing History, Spacing Concepts*

Niklas Luhmann, *The Reality of the Mass Media*

Hubert Damisch, *A Theory of /Cloud/: Toward a History of Painting*

Jean-Luc Nancy, *The Speculative Remark: (One of Hegel's bon mots)*

Jean-François Lyotard, *Soundproof Room: Malraux's Anti-Aesthetics*

Jan Patočka, *Plato and Europe*

Hubert Damisch, *Skyline: The Narcissistic City*

Isabel Hoving, *In Praise of New Travelers: Reading Caribbean Migrant Women Writers*

Richard Rand, ed., *Futures: Of Jacques Derrida*

William Rasch, *Niklas Luhmann's Modernity: The Paradoxes of Differentiation*

Jacques Derrida and Anne Dufourmantelle, *Of Hospitality*

Jean-François Lyotard, *The Confession of Augustine*

Kaja Silverman, *World Spectators*

Samuel Weber, *Institution and Interpretation: Expanded Edition*

Jeffrey S. Librett, *The Rhetoric of Cultural Dialogue: Jews and Germans in the Epoch of Emancipation*

Ulrich Baer, *Remnants of Song: Trauma and the Experience of Modernity in Charles Baudelaire and Paul Celan*

Samuel C. Wheeler III, *Deconstruction as Analytic Philosophy*

David S. Ferris, *Silent Urns: Romanticism, Hellenism, Modernity*

Rodolphe Gasché, *Of Minimal Things: Studies on the Notion of Relation*

Sarah Winter, *Freud and the Institution of Psychoanalytic Knowledge*

Samuel Weber, *The Legend of Freud: Expanded Edition*

Aris Fioretos, ed., *The Solid Letter: Readings of Friedrich Hölderlin*

J. Hillis Miller / Manuel Asensi, *Black Holes / J. Hillis Miller; or, Boustrophedonic Reading*

Miryam Sas, *Fault Lines: Cultural Memory and Japanese Surrealism*

Peter Schwenger, *Fantasm and Fiction: On Textual Envisioning*

Didier Maleuvre, *Museum Memories: History, Technology, Art*

Jacques Derrida, *Monolingualism of the Other; or, The Prosthesis of Origin*

Andrew Baruch Wachtel, *Making a Nation, Breaking a Nation: Literature and Cultural Politics in Yugoslavia*

Niklas Luhmann, *Love as Passion: The Codification of Intimacy*

Mieke Bal, ed., *The Practice of Cultural Analysis: Exposing Interdisciplinary Interpretation*

Jacques Derrida and Gianni Vattimo, eds., *Religion*